DIVORCE AND REMARRIAGE

DIVORCE
AND REMARRIAGE

by
Theodore Mackin, S.J.

PAULIST PRESS
New York/Ramsey

Acknowledgments

In this volume passages are quoted from the following titles with the permission of their publishers: from *The Jerome Biblical Commentary,* copyright © 1968, with the permission of Prentice-Hall Publishing Company; from *Medieval Handbooks of Penance,* Records of Civilization, Sources and Studies no. 29, by John T. McNeill and Helena M. Gamer, copyright © 1938 by Columbia University Press; from *Luther's Works,* Volume 21, copyright © 1956, used by permission of Concordia Publishing House; from *Luther's Works,* Volume 36, copyright © 1959, with the permission of Fortress Press; from *Luther's Works,* Volume 46, copyright © 1967, with the permission of Fortress Press; from *The Book of Concord,* The Confessions of the Evangelical Church, edited by Theodore C. Tappert et al, copyright © 1958, with the permission of Fortress Press, from *The Classics of International Law,* Volume 2, edited by James Scott Brown, copyright © 1964 by Oceana Publishers; from *Marriage Studies,* Volume 2, edited by Thomas P. Doyle, O.P., copyright © 1982 by The Canon Law Society of America; from *The Jurist,* Volume 34, copyright © 1974, with the permission of The Canon Law Society of America.

The passages from the Old Testament quoted in this volume are taken from *The New American Bible,* copyright © 1970, by The Confraternity of Christian Doctrine, and are used with the permission of the copyright owner (all rights reserved).

The translation in English of the canons on marriage in the revised Code of Canon Law of the Catholic Church are taken from *The Code of Canon Law in English Translation,* copyright © 1983, with the permission of the William B. Eerdmans Publishing Company.

Library of Congress
Catalog Card Number: 83-61998

ISBN: 0-8091-2585-4

Published by Paulist Press
545 Island Road, Ramsey, N.J. 07446

Printed and bound in the
United States of America

Contents

tion, 100. The Principles Grounding Justinian's Divorce Legislation, 101. Non-Divorce Dissolutions, 102. Dissolution by Repudiation for Cause, 104. Justinian's Final Legislation, 106. The Reasons for Justinian's Permissive Legislation, 107. Notes to Chapter 5, 109.

to my mother, Theresa

FOREWORD

This volume examines, from its beginning to the present, the Roman Catholic doctrine and discipline concerning divorce and remarriage. It is an inquiry into a history.

To inquire here and examine accurately one must distinguish and even separate two issues that are interwoven in this history. The first is the Catholic authorities' claim that the doctrine interprets Christ's mind in the matter, both his own expression of his mind in the New Testament Gospels and St. Paul's expression of it in his First Letter to the Corinthians. The other issue is the Catholic authorities' effort to establish marriage as indissoluble, as invulnerable to the human will to dissolve it. The evidence suggests that the authorities have engaged in this effort as either a finer, more exact interpretation of Christ's will or as a kind of opportune reinforcing of it.

The reader will find soon enough that in the course of examining this history I have come to doubt the Catholic authorities' success in this twin enterprise. What has crippled it, I think, has been their insistence on two dubious strategies in trying to establish marriage's indissolubility. The first has been that of trying to establish it by writing it into a prescriptive definition of marriage, by simply declaring that marriage—taken in the abstract—is a non-voidable contract, and then using the definition as a juridical device for blocking the possibility of dissolution.

The second dubious strategy has been that of trying to find in the New Testament teaching the warrant for this later-twelfth-century declaration of marriage's indissolubility. The authorities' successive locating and relocating of marriage's last rampart against dissolution, the not-to-be-crossed line of indissolubility, suggest that their effort has enjoyed an arguable success. This is especially evident in face of the authorities' own insistence that the papal "power of the keys" can dissolve all marriages lying beyond that line, outside that rampart—even those which they themselves call naturally indissoluble.

I am aware that to pass that judgment publicly at this moment in the history of marriage may be most ill-advised. Marriage in Western society just now needs all the friends it can find. A huge cultural tide is running

1

toward its trivialization. However adroitly or unadroitly the Catholic authorities have designed their strategy for holding spouses in their marriages, they have done this with a near passionate concern to save marriages, to protect children and wives, to keep a society and its values from being torn apart from within. I share their concern. So let me declare where I stand in the matter.

I regard a marriage as the most precious of all human relationships. I agree with the Yahwist author of the Garden parable in Genesis 2 where he states the priorities of commitment for a married man: "For this reason a man shall leave [even] his father and mother and cleave to his wife; and the two become one body."

I suspect that in whatever degree happiness can be found in this life it can be found at its most inclusive and intense in the sexually expressed and lasting intimacy that a marriage is. Therefore I consider any true divorce—by true divorce I mean the sickening and dying of this intimacy, the shattering of the man's and woman's oneness— as one of the two or three most grievous tragedies available to human beings. I also think that when divorce becomes epidemic in a society, when it becomes trivially available in it, that society is destroying itself.

Before beginning this examination I must make three distinctions in the meanings of words and in the realities they designate.

Just above I took note of divorce that is truly the dissolution of a marriage. This hints that I think not every civil decree of divorce is the dissolution of a marriage. I do think this. I am convinced that a portion of such decrees whose size is impossible to verify dissolves not marriages but only legitimized sexual partnerships. Between such partnerships and marriages there is a difference. I accept the descriptive definition of a marriage that the Catholic bishops offered in the Second Vatican Council (in their Pastoral Constitution on the Church in the Modern World): "a man's and a woman's intimate sharing of marital life and love"—a covenant in which by an irrevocable consent they make a gift of their persons to one another. I suggest that a considerable portion of the marriages in Western society are less than this covenant, less than this total and intimate sharing. Consequently when such partnerships crumble and vanish, the problem they constitute is not the problem of divorce. They make up one sector of a vaster problem, which is the trivialization of persons and of their need and desire for lasting intimacy.

The second distinction divides the two terms "divorce" and "dissolution." These are not always used as synonyms, either in Western civil law or in Catholic marriage law.

There have been many ways of dissolving marriages in the long history of the human race. Divorce has frequently designated but one of these ways, usually an effective exercise of judicial authority in a society. Other methods of dissolution have been dismissal of one spouse by the other (usually the wife by the husband); both spouses' common withdrawal of the will to be married to one another; the reduction of one of the spouses to slave status, or a spouse's being taken into permanent captivity or incarceration; the entry of one or both spouses into a religious order and their pronouncing of its vows. Because of this I have chosen in this volume to ordinarily use the terms "divorce" and "to divorce" because this examination is mainly of the possibility of exercising judicial authority to end a marriage.

The third and last distinction is one that touches the reality itself of a marriage. For centuries the vocabulary of the jurists has included the complex term "the bond of marriage." While it may have been launched somewhere as a metaphor to describe how spouses are joined, the term has not remained such. Many Catholic jurists insist on a distinction between two realities that is implicit in the term. One of these realities, they maintain, is marriage taken as the relationship of a man and a woman rooted in their wills, emotions and conduct. The other is marriage taken as a legal category—marriage the bond. They do not identify this bond with the contract when they call a marriage a contract; they use the contract to define the relationship. Rather they think of the bond as a juridical category.

Pope Paul VI said, in February 1976, that what a man and woman really do in marrying—rather, what is done to a man and woman when they marry—is that they are "inserted" into this category, which is objectively "there," apart from their wills and emotions, and is invulnerable to them. He insisted that this legal category, this bond, is the heart of a marriage, a marriage in its essence, and it is invulnerable to the spouses' will to dissolve it because it is by nature indestructible.

The reader may take for granted that this statement will come under scrutiny in due time within this volume.

I wish to express my thanks to the following persons for their helping me to prepare this volume: To Dr. Stefan Kuttner, Director of the Medieval Institute of Canon Law at Boalt Hall in the University of California at Berkeley, and to his staff, for making the Institute's valuable Robbins Collection available to me and helping me with my research in it; to Rev. Pieter Huizing, S.J., rector of Canisiuscollege, Nijmegen, for his help in interpreting the current revision of the Catholic marriage law; to Rev. Urbano Navarette, S.J., rector of the Gregorian University, Rome, and consultor to the Pontifical Commission for the Revision of Canon Law, for the same help; to Rev. Thomas Green, professor of Canon Law in the Catholic University of America, for providing me with copies of the draft of this revision; to Rev. William Rewak, S.J., president of Santa Clara University, for generously subsidizing the work of research that has gone into this volume; to Rev. Robert Dailey, S.J., professor in the Jesuit School of Theology at Berkeley, for his critical reading of the first draft of this volume; to Patricia Roca, doctoral student in the same school, for reading this draft and criticizing its prose for intelligibility; to Ethel Johnston, secretary of the Department of Religious Studies at Santa Clara University, for typing the final draft of the manuscript; to Theresa Fowler for proofreading this draft—a maternal favor done now for the second time.

1. INTRODUCTION

Let me begin this examination of the Catholic doctrine and discipline of divorce and remarriage by constructing, as a paradigm, a fiction which replicates life in a way not unfamiliar to ministers of religion and to others who counsel in marriage. The central figure in the fiction is a woman fifty-two years old. Two years earlier she was abandoned by her husband after twenty-nine years of marriage. Both had been baptized in infancy in the Catholic Church. Therefore their marriage is presumed in Catholic law to be a sacrament, since there is only one criterion in this law for determining the sacramentality of a marriage, and this is the baptism of both spouses. That the marriage is also consummated as a sacrament is concluded from the evidence of four children born of the marriage. All these are now adults living independently of their parents.

The husband has made clear that he has no intention of resuming married life with this woman. Two months after leaving her he began civil divorce proceedings, which she did not contest. And when the final decree of divorce was handed down, he attempted a second and civil marriage.

She and another man, a widower also a Catholic, are strongly attracted to one another. They have experienced a beginning happiness as friends and companions. They have come to love one another and wish to marry.

Our question concerning them asks whether, according to the Catholic doctrine and discipline of divorce and remarriage, they may do so.

The answer is that they may not. They are morally obligated not to attempt marriage with one another. If they were to attempt it knowing of this obligation and flouting it freely, they would be deemed to sin seriously, and would continue in this sinful state if they were to live as though married to one another.

Why this negative obligation? Whence the sinful act and sinful state? To these questions the answer is that the husband's decree of civil divorce was simply ineffective in dissolving his marriage with this woman. Their marriage continues in existence. Being still his wife she would commit adultery if she were to live as though married to the man whom she now loves.

There is also this refinement in the answer to the question, that she

5

may not attempt the second marriage because this marriage is an impossibility. It would be immoral for her to pretend to do the impossible. The reason for this impossibility is that the Catholic marriage law defines marriage in such a way as to make polygamy impossible. It is the union of one man and one woman. Thus not only is a person forbidden plural simultaneous spouses, but having more than one simultaneously is impossible.

But this question asking why the woman in the paradigm cannot marry a second time is consequent on a prior question: How is it that despite being abandoned by her husband, and despite his completing the civil divorce and going through a second and civil marriage ceremony, she is still married to him and will be until one of them dies?

In the public mind this question may seem to have a simple answer: "The Catholic Church forbids divorce." But in reality the answer is far more complicated than that. It is not even accurate to begin with. It is an exceedingly complex mixture of "She could remarry if . . ." and "However she cannot because . . ." The complexity has taken literally nineteen centuries to reach its present state. The intent of this volume is to examine this complexity, to trace its history, to explain what it is all about.

Let me get to the task by first laying out, with as deliberate a simplification as possible, what the complex answer says.

The Catholic Church's teachers, its bishops with the Pope at their head, say that marriage is an indissoluble relationship. The clearest and most exact assertion of this indissolubility is found in the Catholic law on marriage. This is in Book IV of the newly revised Code of Canon Law, Part I, "The Sacraments," Title 7, "Marriage." There Canon 1056 says "The essential properties of marriage are unity and indissolubility; in Christian marriage they acquire a distinctive firmness by reason of the sacrament."[1]

Note that in the syntax of this canon the object of predication of the two traits, unity and indissolubility, is not the real-life relationships of men and women anywhere and everywhere in the world. And it is certainly not only the marriages of those who live in the Judeo-Christian tradition. The object of this predication is rather a kind of concrete universal. The canon says that marriage anywhere, at any time, whether past or future, prescinding from any culturally developed differences, demands of its nature abstractly considered that it be unitary and indissoluble. Or—to say the same in a different way—the canon affirms that if a heterosexual relationship is to be a marriage, it must, among all its traits, have these two. And since in real life the traits cannot have been realized indefectibly until the death of at least one of the spouses (no matter how veteran the union, one of the spouses can always *try* to dissolve or polygamize it), the union is truly a marriage only if from its beginning both spouses intend that it be unitary and undissolved until it ends with the death of one of them.[2]

But what does Canon 1056 really mean in implying that the indissolubility is one of the traits of marriage belonging to its essence regardless of particular time and place? Does it mean that once a man and woman are husband and wife they cannot *not* be such to one another for any cause short of death? Does it mean that this indissolubility simply defies the effort of any human agency to destroy it—in the same sense that once a woman has borne a male child, as long as they live no human agency can make them to be not mother and son? Or does it mean that while the marital union is fundamentally vulnerable to obliteration (some agency *could* divorce it), it is unconditionally forbidden that anyone try to do this?

The last of these suggested answers is closer than the former two to what Catholic teaching means by the essential indissolubility of marriage. As we shall see, Catholic authorities have recorded a long history of divorcing two kinds or qualities of marriages. One of these is already hinted at in Canon 1056; these are marriages that are not sacraments because both the spouses are unbaptized, or because only one of them is baptized. The other kind is the marriage that is unconsummated, whether it be a sacrament or not.[3]

Reading backward from this practice of dissolving marriages into the theory justifying it, one must infer the obvious, that despite defining marriage the natural institution as indissoluble, the Catholic Church's legislators really do not believe it to be so.

Consequently we must ask again what Canon 1056 means by the adjective in saying that marriage has indissolubility as an "essential" property. And glancing at the clause in the canon following that one, what does it mean by saying that the sacramentality of the marriage of two Christians gives unique, special firmness to this indissolubility if the latter is not real but only apparent? A kind of defining strange to the non-specialist as well as to the philosopher and theologian is at work here. Is its intent not to describe reality, but to prescribe the qualities of legal categories? If the latter, for what reason and for how long has Catholic law thought of marriage as a legal category?

To search out the answers to these and to kindred questions is the intent of this volume. It should be evident by now that the current Catholic doctrine and discipline concerning the possibility of divorce and remarriage are complicated to a degree that even most Catholics hardly suspect. This doctrine and discipline are the product of nineteen centuries of inference from two main sources. These are the New Testament instructions about divorce and remarriage, and the anthropological interpretations adopted by the Church from two legal traditions, Roman custom systematized in the Justinian code, and the complex of Lombard, Frankish and Germanic custom that the Romanized Church encountered on expanding into central Europe.

Outline of the Catholic Teaching on Divorce and Remarriage

The current point of arrival in Catholic teaching after centuries of use of the sources named just above is, in outline, what follows here.

First, no merely human authority is capable of dissolving any kind or quality of marriage, not even the non-sacramental marriages of non-Christians. The Catholic Church does not accept as valid any dissolution decreed by any civil court in any circumstances. It denies that any such court has the authority sufficient to effect the dissolution. The reason for this denial the Church finds in Jesus' words, "Therefore, what God has joined man must not separate" (Mark 10:9 and Matthew 19:6). It sees in these words not only a prohibition but a declaration of impossibility.

But the Church does claim authority in itself, given to it by God in Christ, to dissolve certain kinds or qualities of marriages. This authority it claims to have been given only to the bishop of Rome, the Pope, as a facet of "the power of the keys" conferred by Jesus on Peter and his successors for all of history, as recorded in the Synoptic narrative in Matthew 16:19: "I will give you the keys of the kingdom of heaven. What you bind on earth will be bound in heaven, and what you loose on earth will be loosed in heaven." (The same power of binding and loosing given to an indefinite number of disciples according to Matthew 18:18 is not interpreted to have conferred this same power to dissolve marriages on any of these disciples other than Peter, nor on their successors.)

But this power to dissolve limits its own competence. It is effective for terminating a marriage that is not consummated (but it is effective even if the marriage is a sacrament), or for terminating a marriage that is not a sacrament (even if it is consummated). The acknowledged limit on this power to dissolve is that it is not effective in terminating a marriage that is a sacrament and that is consummated as a sacrament. In effect Catholic teaching says that only this last quality of marriage is unexceptionably indissoluble.

Before listing the subspecies of non-sacramental marriages about which the Church claims competence to dissolve, it will help to explain a second form in which Catholic tradition says that marriages can be dissolved. This is the use of the Pauline privilege.[4]

This use is grounded biblically in an interpretation of Paul's First Letter to the Corinthians, chapter 7, verse 15. The passage is part of his instruction to the Christian community of that Greek city in reply to questions it had put to him by letter. He begins his replies in verse 1: "Now, as for the matters you wrote about . . .." After instructing the unmarried, widows included, he turns in verse 10 to the married.

> 10. To the married I proclaim (although it is not I but the Lord) that a wife must not separate from her husband. 11. But if she does separate, she must either remain unmarried or return to her husband. And the husband must not dismiss his wife.

It is part of the interpretation leading to the conception of the Pauline privilege that with these words Paul specifies what must be done where the troubled marriage is of two Christians, and that in the verses that follow he instructs concerning conduct where the marriage is religiously mixed, that is, where it is of a Christian spouse and a non-Christian.

> 12. To the rest my counsel (not the Lord's) is that if any brother has a wife who is not a believer but who is willing to live in peace with him, he is not to dismiss her. 13. And if a wife has a husband not a believer, but who is willing to live in peace with her, she is not to dismiss him.

After assuring the Christian spouses (in verse 14) that, far from being made unholy by their marriages with unbelieving spouses, their spouses are made holy by marriage with them, Paul turns to counseling those Christians whose unbelieving spouses will not live with them in peace. And it is in this verse 15 that the traditional ground for the Pauline privilege is found.

> But if the unbelieving spouse departs, let him depart. In such cases the believing husband or wife is not to play the slave. Rather, God has called you in peace.

The key to the theory of the privilege is found in the interpretation of the last two clauses of this verse. Paul is taken to mean not only that the Christian husband or wife is not obligated to continue cohabitation with the unbelieving spouse, but that he or she is no longer bound in and by the marriage, and is free to marry again. This interpretation is reinforced by the contrasting instructions wherein Paul insists (in verse 11) that if the two spouses who separate are both Christians, they must either remain single or be reconciled, but where (in verse 15) the separation is of a non-Christian from a Christian spouse, he omits this insistence.

Neither the theory of the privilege nor its use as an instrument for dissolving non-sacramental marriages dates from the early Christian centuries. Pope Clement III, who died in 1191, was the first to grant the use of the privilege in approximately the way it is understood in current Catholic law.[5]

The conditions for the use of the Pauline privilege and the steps involved in its use are the following:

> Both parties to the first and dissoluble marriage are unbaptized.
> Later (how much later makes no difference) one of the parties receives Christian baptism. This may be in any Christian denomination, although if in a denomination not Catholic, the use of the Pauline privilege would not come into question unless one of the parties to this first marriage sought later to marry a Roman Catholic.
> Following the baptism the unbaptized party "departs" from

the marriage. This may take the form of physical departure, including civil divorce; or it may consist of the unbaptized party's refusal to live in married peace with the baptized.

If the latter seeks the use of the Pauline privilege, Catholic authorities will inquire into the causes of the departure. If they find that the baptized party became the cause after having been baptized, the use of the privilege is not granted. This inquiry (in canonical terms, the interpellation) asks also about the will of the unbaptized and departed spouse to seek reconciliation and to reconstitute the married life in peace, and about his or her desire to receive baptism. If he or she is willing to seek reconciliation and to live in peace, the use of the privilege is not granted. The Catholic authorities can dispense from these interpellations if making them is impossible or if it is otherwise evident that the unbaptized party is the cause of the departure and has no intention for reconciliation.

If the unbaptized and departed spouse's replies to the interpellations are negative, the baptized party is free to enter a second marriage. Under the 1917 Code of Canon Law where the use of this Pauline privilege was granted, the second marriage had to be with a Roman Catholic, although at times papal authority extended the effectiveness of this privilege so that the newly baptized party could take a baptized non-Catholic or even an unbaptized person as second spouse. In the newly revised Code, Canon 1147 states that for serious reasons the bishop under whose authority the new Catholic lives (his or her local ordinary) can authorize him or her to take a baptized non-Catholic or an unbaptized person as second spouse.

The first marriage is dissolved at the moment the second marriage vows are pronounced, and by the pronouncing of them. Thus not any ecclesiastical authority, but the second pair of spouses themselves are the agents who dissolve the first marriage.

The use of the Pauline privilege is also called an exercise of the Privilege of the Faith. This has two meanings. The first is that once a person has become a Christian he or she acquires the prerogative to live life's most valuable relationships in a Christian way, and therefore to live a Christian marriage. The second meaning of the privilege is that all substantial but practically insoluble doubts about the first and non-sacramental marriage—about the validity of that marriage, the identity of the spouses, the continuing existence of the marriage—are resolved in favor of the second and sacramental marriage.

To touch on the first of these meanings, as the theory undergirding the Catholic marriage law is currently proposed, a Christian marriage must be a sacramental marriage, and cannot be otherwise. And this requires that both spouses be baptized. Within this interpretation it is difficult to understand how a use of the Pauline privilege where the newly baptized person is allowed to form a second and non-sacramental marriage with an unbaptized person is an exercise of the Privilege of the Faith at least in its first sense. This use of the Pauline privilege is conceded in Canon 1147 of the marriage law.

Dissolution by Solemn Vows of Religious Life

An agency of dissolution that throve for centuries in Catholic law and custom was dissolution by one or both parties' entering monastic life (or more accurately, religious life) and pronouncing there the vows of the religious order. The express naming and enabling of this agency has been removed from the revised Catholic marriage law. But the possibility that Catholic men and women may enter religious life and pronounce its vows despite having been married is retained in the law in a way that I shall explain in a moment.

From as early as the fifth century Catholic authorities acknowledged that the vows taken in monastic life could dissolve a marriage. In later centuries these came to be the vows taken in consecrated religious life generally. But the marriage that these vows could dissolve could not have been consummated. The reasoning here was that once a sacramental marriage is consummated—but not until then—it gains absolute indissolubility. And according to this ancient discipline it was the pronouncing of the vows, not a dissolution or dispensation coming from an ecclesiastical authority, that dissolved the unconsummated marriage.

As this agency of dissolution was formulated in Canon 1119 of the 1917 Code of Canon Law, the vows must have been of valid religious profession in an authentic religious order. Religious profession consists of a person's pronouncing the three solemn vows of poverty, chastity and obedience. The vow of chastity has two solemn effects, one of which is to constitute an invalidating impediment against the person's subsequently marrying. The other, now no longer mentioned in the marriage law, was that of dissolving the person's marriage if this was not consummated.

But the possibility of a married person's securing a dissolution of his or her marriage and then entering religious life remains in Canon 1142 of the revised law. This states that an unconsummated marriage, whether of two baptized persons or of one baptized and an unbaptized person, can be dissolved by papal authority for a just cause. The formulation in Canon 1142 is the following:

> A non-consummated marriage between baptized persons or between a baptized party and an unbaptized party can be dissolved by the Roman Pontiff for a just reason, at the request of both parties or of either of them, even if the other is unwilling.

The change in the formulation of the law, and the removal of solemn religious vows from among the agencies dissolving a marriage, is evident if one contrasts this canon with Canon 1119 of the now superseded Code of 1917.

> An unconsummated marriage of baptized persons, or of one baptized and one unbaptized person, is dissolved either by the agency itself [*ipso iure*] of the pronouncing of solemn religious vows, or by a dispensation granted for a good cause by the Apostolic See, whether both parties or either party requests this, and [in the latter case] even if the other party opposes the dissolution.

The Dissolution of Non-Consummated Marriage by Papal Dispensation

The two canons quoted just above declare clearly the power and authority of the Pope to dissolve marriages that are not consummated. Note that where old Canon 1119 named this power and authority as that of the Holy See (*Sedes Apostolica*), new Canon 1142 states that this power and authority belong to the Pope (*Pontifex Romanus*). The distinction is more than merely verbal. Since the authority of the Holy See can be delegated and exercised as delegated, to make clear that the power and authority to dissolve unconsummated marriages is possessed and exercised only by the Pope it was necessary to word the canon so as to make this reservation exact.

Like the institution and use of the Pauline privilege, this dissolving of unconsummated marriages began well along in Catholic history. Although Alexander II (1159–1181) was the first Pope to decide in favor of dissolution in this circumstance, the practice did not gain currency until the fifteenth century under Martin V and Eugene IV.

Here the immediate agency of dissolution is the Pope's act of dispensing. What he is said to dispense from is one of the effects of the natural contractual consent of the spouses, namely the bond that is otherwise indissoluble. This is not dispensation in the strict sense of the term, since it is not directly a relaxation of the law of nature which is said to make the marriage indissoluble. Rather it dispenses from an effect of the human act of consenting in marriage.

The possibility of the Popes' dissolving marriages by this dispensation is said to be grounded in two areas. One we have already seen, their possession of "the power of the keys" to bind and to loose. The other is that a marriage is formed in two steps, and does not gain its absolute indissolubility until the second of them has been completed. The first step is the exchange of marital consent, and this produces the *matrimonium ratum,* the (merely) contracted marriage, which is not yet invulnerable to dissolution by the power of the keys. The second step is the consummation of the marriage by the first act of intercourse after the exchange of consent, which produces appropriately the *matrimonium consummatum.*

But not even consummation by itself makes a marriage finally invulnerable to dissolution by papal power of the keys. This absolute indissolubility comes only when a marriage is a sacrament and has been consummated as a sacrament. The reasoning here is theological. The cause of a marriage's indissolubility is not, despite Canon 1056's saying so, its natural, inherent property of indissolubility. Rather this cause is the fact that the marriage of two Christians is an image, a sacrament of the union of Christ and the Church; and because the latter union is imperishable, so must its image on earth be imperishable (not, however, beyond the death of at least one of the spouses). But until the spouses have had their first complete intercourse after forming their sacramental marriage the latter's imaging of the imperishable Christ-Church relationship is not complete. Thus the causation effecting the imperishability of the earthly image has not worked its effect completely. (Not so coincidentally the consummation of the marital contract and the completion of the sacred imaging are said to be accomplished in one and the same act.)

Dissolution of Non-Sacramental Marriage by Papal Dispensation

Because, as I said above, the acknowledged cause of marriages' absolute indissolubility, where they have this quality, is their being Christian sacraments and consummated as such, it follows that marriages not sacraments or not consummated as such remain vulnerable to the papal power of the keys to dissolve them. This power has in fact been used since the first quarter of the present century to dissolve such marriages.

The use of this power has a more remote historical beginning, which I shall mention now but detail in a later chapter. This beginning was in the apostolic constitutions of three sixteenth-century Popes, Paul III, Pius V and Gregory XIII. On June 1, 1537 Paul III issued the constitution *Altitudo,* which instructed missionaries in Africa and the Indies how to proceed with polygamous males who wished to receive baptism, who thus had to reduce their marital condition to monogamy, and this with their first and therefore only true wife, but who could not recall which among their wives was in fact the first. Paul ruled that in this case a man could keep whichever of his wives he preferred, could marry her by present expression of marital consent—but only after his first and now anonymous marriage had been dissolved by papal dispensation. (If the wife he chose happened, apart from anyone's knowing it, to be the woman he had first married, he did the thing unique in Catholic marriage annals of marrying the same woman twice.) The possibility of the Pope's dissolving the first marriage lay in its not being a sacrament because neither party to it was baptized at the time it was formed.

Pius V's constitution of August 2, 1571, *Romani pontifices,* ruled for a husband in almost the same situation. Before baptism he had been married polygamously, but was obliged to dismiss all his wives but one if he were to receive baptism. This constitution ruled that he was allowed to keep as his one wife whichever woman was willing to accept baptism along with him, even if he knew that she was not his first and true wife. His marriage to the latter was dissolved by the papal dispensation. This constitution did not instruct the husband about his conduct in the event more than one of his wives wished to be baptized along with him. But presumably Paul III's constitution already provided that he could take as his wife the woman among those seeking baptism whom he preferred.

Gregory XIII's constitution *Populis* of January 25, 1585 envisions a circumstance produced quite commonly by the raiding of native populations in Africa and their exportation into slavery. Spouses married while unbaptized were separated permanently, and one or the other would, after being baptized in the New World or the Indies, seek to marry a second time. This constitution permitted the newly baptized party to remarry following the dissolution of the first marriage by papal dispensation. It especially authorized ecclesiastical authorities in the territory of the newly baptized person to dispense him or her from the obligation of inquiring about the will of the first spouse when this inquiry was impossible or at least severely difficult.

But the most unique feature of Gregory's constitution ruled that the second marriage was to be considered valid even if it were later found out that the other spouse too had been baptized before the papal dissolution of the first marriage, with the consequence that that first marriage had thereby become a sacrament. In this case the papal dispensation was able to dissolve the marriage not because it was non-sacramental, but because, though it had become a sacrament without the knowledge of either spouse (!), it had never been consummated as a sacrament.

Modern Papal Dissolution of Non-Sacramental Marriage

The modern use of this papal power to dissolve marriages that are not sacraments dates from 1924. On November 6 of that year at the request of the bishop of Helena, Montana Pope Pius XI granted the dissolution of a marriage under the following conditions and in the following way. The wife was a baptized Christian, an Episcopalian; the husband was unbaptized. Thus the marriage was not a sacrament (whether it was consummated or not was irrelevant).

The husband secured a civil divorce and the Episcopalian wife attempted a second marriage, thus verifying departure from the marriage as this is understood in Catholic law. The husband subsequently asked for baptism in the Catholic Church and sought to marry a Catholic woman. Pius XI granted a dissolution of his first and non-sacramental marriage. This he did in order to free the man to enter a sacramental marriage—to make use of "the favor of the faith." It is possible that the husband could have been baptized after the civil divorce but before the papal dissolution of his first marriage, although in fact he was not. At the moment of his baptism that marriage would have become a sacrament. Nevertheless it could still have been dissolved provided he had not subsequently consummated it as a sacrament.[7]

This dissolution can be granted as well if it is the Christian non-Catholic party in the first marriage who subsequently becomes a Roman Catholic and wishes to enter a second and sacramental marriage.

A second, similar, but slightly different kind and condition of marriage was dissolved by Pope Pius XII on July 18, 1947. In this case the baptized party was a Roman Catholic man, married to an unbaptized woman with a dispensation from the impediment barring this kind of marriage in Catholic law. The marriage disintegrated and the wife secured a civil divorce. Later, wishing to become a Catholic and to enter a sacramental marriage with another Catholic, she sought and obtained a dissolution of her first and non-sacramental marriage. The Catholic husband in the first marriage could have done the same provided he could prove that he had not been the cause of the marriage's disintegration.[8]

In 1959 this dissolution of marriage by papal authority reached its fullest extent when it was applied for this first time to the following case. A first marriage was non-sacramental because contracted by an unbaptized man and a baptized Protestant woman. These spouses secured a civil divorce; thus there was departure from the marriage as this is understood in Catholic law. The husband, wishing subsequently to marry a Catholic woman, petitioned and was granted a dissolution of his first marriage even though he did not request baptism in the Catholic Church and had no intention of doing so. What is extraordinary in the case is that according to Catholic tradition the dissolution of the first marriage has ordinarily been effected only so that the person favored by the dissolution may enter a second marriage that is a sacrament. But in this case, because the man did not accept baptism, the second marriage was not a sacrament. The dissolution was thus not warranted by "the favor of the faith" in the sense of opening the way to a new and sacramental marriage.[9]

More dissolutions lacking this facet of "the favor of the faith" were granted during the following decade. But the practice was ended in the early 1970's—or was apparently ended then. On December 6, 1973 the Church's Congregation for the Doctrine of the Faith published a set of instructions for the use of this dissolution of a non-sacramental marriage that clearly allowed for the subsequent marriage's not being a sacrament.[10]

Such in outline is the current Roman Catholic teaching and discipline concerning the possibility and the permissibility of divorce and of remarriage after divorce. The very complexity of the teaching betrays that it is the product of a history, and suggests too that it is the latest point of arrival in an undulating history that may not yet have reached its end. Insofar as it can be said to have had a distinctly Christian beginning this history began with Christ's words spoken of marriage as he knew it among his own people in his day—but perhaps too of every marriage anywhere and at all times: "Therefore, what God has joined man must not separate." That the apparently absolute intent of this statement has been attenuated by the authorities in the community Jesus founded is obvious. How they have attenuated it and why they have done so are the thematic questions in the examination making up the chapters that follow.

NOTES

1. On January 25, 1959, Pope John XXIII announced that the Catholic Church would revise its entire Code of Canon Law. The work of revising began early in 1966. The revised Code was promulgated on January 25, 1983, and became effective on November 27 of that year.

As the work of revising progressed the numbering of the canons in the Code was changed several times. They are numbered in this volume according to the officially promulgated edition of the Code.

In the 1917 Code this canon is numbered 1013; the specification of unity and indissolubility as the two traits essential to marriage is in its paragraph 2. But the wording of this paragraph and that of new Canon 1056 are synonymous, although the latter canon inverts the sequence of the last two phrases.

The last clause in the canon clearly implies that the indissolubility of marriages that are not Christian sacraments is somewhat less than impervious to dissolution. This qualified indissolubility is sometimes irreverently called "dissoluble indissolubility."

2. Appropriate at this point is an example illustrating the complex consequences of thinking about marriage in this abstractly defining way. Since the assertion of unitariness is about marriage anywhere, anytime, what is to be said of the polygamous unions of the Hebrew patriarchs and kings remembered in the Old Testament? Was Abraham, for one, married to both Sarah and Hagar? Or only to Sarah because marriage is by nature unitary? Or to neither because he plainly married with the understanding that he could take plural wives, an intention against one of the essential traits of marriage and having (according to Catholic marriage law) an invalidating effect even on non-Catholic marriages?

The conventional explanation meant to resolve this difficulty is that it is not a primary but only a secondary precept of the natural law that a marriage be monogamous. Consequently God, the designer of marriage, can for the greater good dispense a person from the obligation to not marry polygamously. Because of this explanation may one say that while in the Code of Canon Law there is only one definition of marriage, in the mind of God there are two?

3. It may help to explain at this point the difference between dissolution of a marriage and annulment. The latter is a declaration that the union in question, purportedly a marriage, has in fact never been a marriage. In the Church the Ordinary authority in a diocese can make this declaration. A dissolution, by contrast, is an effective action. It takes an acknowledged marriage and puts it out of existence. By an annulment the parties are declared to have been always single; by a dissolution they are made single once again. As noted already, only the Pope has this power to dissolve.

4. A full treatment of the use of this privilege is in the best English-language

study to date of the Catholic juridical discipline of marriage written for the non-specialist, *Christian Marriage*, by George H. Joyce (London, 1949), pp. 467–487.

5. In his *De Adulterinis Coniugiis* (On Adulterous Spouses), Book 1, chapters 19–22, St. Augustine interpreted the passage in a far less permissive way. He understood Paul to no more than allow the Christian spouse's dismissing the non-Christian either because of physical adultery or because of the "spiritual adultery" of paganism. He made no mention of this dismissal's freeing the Christian spouse to remarry. In fact he understood Paul to counsel the Christian and the pagan spouses' staying together if they could do so peacefully, because unilateral dismissal could easily offend and scandalize, and could drive the unbaptized spouse to adultery. This last concern betrays that Augustine did not think Paul meant that the non-Christian's willing departure ended his marriage with the Christian.

6. This dissolution of a non-consummated marriage by solemn religious profession is virtually unheard of today. But details of the history of this practice are not without interest. In the early centuries of the practice one of the spouses could enter a religious order and dissolve the marriage by pronouncing its vows even against the will of the other. In fact the practice was used in part as an escape route for children of families (usually noble families) where their marriages were arranged and were unwanted by them—not at all a rare phenomenon where the marriages of noble children were negotiated by procurators across miles of separation, where the vows were exchanged by proxies, and the man and woman (or more likely boy and girl) met for the first time perhaps months after becoming husband and wife.

Thomas Aquinas reported in the thirteenth century (in his *Commentarius In Libros Sententiarum Petri Lombardi*, Liber IV, Distinctio 27, Articulus 3, Quaestiuncula 3, ad 2m) the long-standing custom requiring the spouses to allow one another a two-month grace period before having to grant the marriage debt for the first time and thus consummate the marriage. The first of the three reasons he records justifying this practice was to allow the spouses time to decide on entry into a religious order and to take steps to do so if either decided for this. (The second reason was to allow time to prepare the nuptial celebration, which was customarily separate from the exchange of vows. The third reason was to keep the husband from regarding intercourse as too easy and banal a thing by obliging him to delay his gratification for the two months.)

7. This dissolution is reported in T. L. Bouscaren, *Canon Law Digest*, Vol. 1, pp. 552–554.

8. This case, known colloquially to canonists as The Fresno Case, is reported in T. L. Bouscaren, *op cit.*, Vol. 3, p. 485. A synonymous case is reported there on pp. 486–487, wherein the parties to the first marriage were an unbaptized woman and a Catholic man. This marriage, valid in Catholic law but not a sacrament, disintegrated, and the wife secured a civil divorce. She then sought Catholic baptism and wished to marry a Catholic man. She petitioned a dissolution of her first marriage, and this was granted by Pius XII on January 30, 1950. Three months later the husband in her first marriage was told by the Holy Office (the Vatican congregation) that he was free to enter a second marriage, again with an unbaptized woman.

9. This case is reported in *Canon Law Digest*, 1955–1959 Supplement, Canon 1127, page 5.

10. The following set of procedural norms accompanied the Congregation's instruction.

I. The person petitioning the dissolution may be baptized or not. In any case the following are the indispensably necessary conditions for granting the dissolution.

1) In the marriage to be dissolved one of the spouses must have remained unbaptized throughout the entire period of conjugal life together (that is, the marriage must have remained non-sacramental because this spouse was not baptized).

2) If the originally unbaptized party was subsequently baptized, the spouses must not have consummated the marriage that had thereby become sacramental.

3) The unbaptized person or the baptized non-Catholic whose earlier marriage is dissolved in this case in favor of the faith must leave the Catholic spouse in the new marriage free to profess his or her religion and to baptize and rear the children as Catholics.

II. The following conditions must be met in addition:

1) There must be no possibility, because of continued radical and incurable division, of restoring conjugal life in the first marriage.

2) There must be no danger of scandal from the grant of the dissolution.

3) The spouse petitioning the dissolution must be shown not to be the culpable cause of the failure of the first marriage; and the Catholic party with whom the new marriage is to be contracted must not have been the guilty cause of the separation in the first marriage.

4) The other spouse in the first marriage must be questioned, if possible, and not be reasonably opposed to the granting of the dissolution.

5) The spouse who seeks the dissolution must see to the religious education of any children from the first marriage.

6) Just and equitable provision must be made for the first spouse and any children from the marriage.

7) The Catholic party with whom the new marriage is to be contracted must live in accord with his or her baptismal promises and must be concerned for the welfare of the new family.

8) If the person seeking the dissolution is in the process of converting to the Catholic faith, there should be moral certainty that if the baptism cannot take place before the marriage, it will do so at least afterward.

III. The dissolution is more easily granted where there is serious doubt on other grounds of the validity of the first marriage.

IV. It is possible to dissolve the marriage between a Catholic and an unbaptized person which was entered with a dispensation from the impediment of disparity of cult (i.e., where the other party was unbaptized) on the following conditions:

1) Provided the conditions established in numbers II and III are verified.

2) If it is verified that the Catholic in that marriage, because of the availability of few Catholics where he or she lived, could not have married

otherwise than he or she did, but yet could not live according to the Catholic religion in that marriage.

V. The dissolution of a Catholic's legitimate marriage [i.e. with an unbaptized person] after a dispensation from the impediment of disparity of cult is not granted to the Catholic petitioner in order that he or she may enter a new marriage of the same kind, i.e. with another unbaptized person.

VI. The dissolution of a legitimate marriage which was contracted or validated after a dissolution of a previous legitimate marriage is not granted.

Paragraph II, 8 above verifies my statement at the end of this chapter that despite the stricter demands set by this instruction on remarriage after dissolution of a non-sacramental marriage, it is still permitted that the second marriage may be not a sacrament. For Paragraph II, 8 allows that the second marriage may take place *before* the baptism of the as yet unbaptized person, during his or her preparation for baptism. But after the wedding he or she could suffer a change of mind about being baptized. But the marriage would remain—and would remain non-sacramental.

This information is taken from *The Jurist,* Vol. 34 (1974) pp. 418–419.

2. THE JEWISH CONTEXT OF EARLY CHRISTIAN TEACHING

The instructions about divorce and remarriage in Chapter 7 of Paul's First Letter to the Corinthians and in the Synoptic Gospels are unintelligible unless one studies them in the context of their Jewish tradition. In his letter Paul takes care to distinguish between instruction that is exclusively his (probably from the beginning of the chapter through verse 9, then from verse 12 onward) and instruction he had received as a command from the Lord (verses 10–11). It is in these two verses that he came closest to saying what Jesus is reported in the Synoptics to have said about divorce and remarriage. And what he said there is conditioned severely by the Jewish tradition of his time. The two longer passages that quote him, Mark 10:1–12 and Matthew 19:3–12, are narratives recording his argument with a group of Pharisee teachers—presumably the same argument despite the two accounts' divergencies—about the Jewish law of divorce and remarriage. We could get "pure," context-free statements on the subject from Jesus only if we took his replies to the Pharisees out of his exchange with them. But in that case they would be unintelligible.

The first step in understanding the Jewish teaching on divorce and remarriage current in Jesus' time is to avoid anachronism. When spouses seek a divorce today in the Western world they ask the civil authority to dissolve their marriage. They take for granted that only this authority can be the agent of marriages' dissolution; they do not presume to exercise this agency themselves. A different way of dissolving marriages according to classic Roman law supposed that the spouses could themselves do this dissolving. They did so by withdrawing their wills to be married, their *affectio maritalis,* just as they had created their marriage by asserting and linking these wills.

From its beginning Jewish law sponsored a different way of dissolving marriages, and at least in Palestine this remained the only way as long as Israel survived as a nation. Only the husband could dissolve the marriage.

20

He did so by dismissing the wife, by "sending her away." The most that the wife could do, by an interpretation of the law developed under the Tannaitic rabbis, was to compel the husband to dismiss her. But even then he was the sole agent of the dissolution. He had a direct power over her and over the marriage that she did not have. As early as the Book of Deuteronomy (24:1) the Hebrew verb *shalle'ah* designated this act on the part of the husband. Presumably the Synoptic Gospel editors chose the Greek verb they did, *apolúein,* to designate this unilateral act of the husband. In every instance they use this transitive verb in the active voice; and in every instance they have the wife, not the marriage, as its direct object. The husband dissolves the marriage not directly, but indirectly by dismissing the wife. In 1 Corinthians 7:11 Paul uses a different verb, *aphiénai,* but it too is transitive and he uses it in the active voice to designate the husband's act. And it has not the marriage but the wife as its direct object. He forbids this act to the husband where both he and his wife are Christian, and he does so because he is relaying Jesus' command. (He also forbids a certain act to the wife where both spouses are Christian. To do this he uses the verb *choristhénai,* thereby suggesting a complication in understanding Jesus' teaching as he received and interpreted it, since the verb at least seems to introduce into this teaching divorce according to Roman law. We shall examine this complication in its place.)

The Legal Warrant for Dismissal

The dissolution of marriage in the fashion just identified comes under comment at several points in the Old Testament.[1] The principal passage, that which came to serve as the legal warrant for divorce, and for the specific form this took in Jewish life, is at the beginning of the Book of Deuteronomy's Chapter 24. The warrant is there only implicitly because the passage's intent is not to establish divorce but to block the legal indecency of a man's remarrying the woman he has once dismissed. The passage presumes the prior establishment of divorce, and divorce by unilateral dismissal of the wife.

> 1. When a man, after marrying a woman and having rela-
> tions with her, is later displeased with her because he finds in her
> something indecent, and therefore he writes out a bill of divorce
> and hands it to her, thus dismissing her from his house: 2. if on
> leaving his house she goes and becomes the wife of another man,
> 3. and the second husband, too, comes to dislike her and dismiss-
> es her from his house by handing her a written bill of divorce; or
> if this second man who has married her dies, 4. then her former
> husband, who dismissed her, may not again take her as his wife
> after she has become defiled. That would be an abomination
> before the Lord . . .

Especially for Christians, as for any students of the diverse Christian interpretations of the New Testament teaching on divorce and remarriage, interest in this passage must focus on verse 1. There the taken-for-granted ground for Jewish divorce is named. It is the "something indecent" in the wife, the *erwat dabar* according to the Hebrew of Deuteronomy. If the legal deficiency—or the delinquency, as some rabbis insisted—were found in the wife, this gave the husband the right to dismiss her. Inevitably disagreement about the meaning of *erwat dabar* would surface. The term's reference is most generic, literally "the uncleanness of a thing." And the disagreement would itself divide. It would turn not only on the specific reference of these terms (which kinds of deficiency and delinquency do they designate?); it would ask also whether the warrant to dismiss was limited to the referents of *erwat dabar*. Or were there others?

The first of these arguments echoes in the test to which the Pharisees put Jesus in Matthew's account of their confrontation with him (19:3–12). They presume the prior acceptance of Deuteronomy 24:1 as the warrant for divorce by unilateral dismissal, and they ask Jesus, "Is a man permitted to dismiss his wife for just any reason?" Two disagreeing interpretations of *erwat dabar* had in fact appeared in the generation before Jesus, one coming from Rabbi Hillel, the other from Rabbi Shammai. According to Matthew's account the Pharisees asked Jesus if he went along with Hillel's opinion that a husband could dismiss his wife for just about any reason (or did he agree with Shammai that only if serious sexual misconduct were proved against her could the husband do this). Of course the more fundamental dispute, threatening to preempt that one, was always possible. That Jesus probably insisted on raising this prior dispute seems evident in the testing to which the Pharisees put him in Mark's version of the confrontation (10:1–12): "Then some Pharisees came to him and asked him if a husband is permitted to dismiss his wife—asked him this to put him to the test." That is, did Jesus acknowledge that there were any grounds at all for a man's dismissing his wife? Did he teach about divorce according to Torah? On this point was he faithful to the law of Moses, or did he here too have a rebellious teaching of his own?

The Source of the Legal Warrant

But behind this legal warrant for divorce by unilateral dismissal lay the presumed anthropological reason establishing the possibility of the warrant. This reason is given in an old rabbinic interpretation of what is done in the act of marrying. It is not that a man and woman come together in the act of marrying, and certainly not that they come together from equally valent points of origin. Rather the man is understood to *take* a wife, while the woman is never said to take a husband. His taking her is an act of establishing his proprietorship over her. So what he took he could eventually get rid of if he chose.

This understanding of the act creating a marriage was thought to be reinforced by key passages in Torah. According to the Garden parable in Genesis 2 and 3, the story of the first man and woman, God formed the woman by taking a rib from the man's side after casting the latter into a deep sleep and building up flesh on the rib. He brought the product of this artistry, the woman, to Adam. The moment was then Adam's, and he filled it with a summary comment, with his evaluation of the creature God had formed from his flesh and had brought to him to heal his loneliness. Adam said of the woman,

> This one, at last, is bone of my bones
>   and flesh of my flesh.
> This one shall be called "woman" [ishshah],
>   for out of her man [ish] this one has been taken.

Thus, in taking Eve Adam took back what had first been taken from him. And two interpretations of his evaluation of the woman are possible, neither contradicting the other. In saying that the woman is bone of his bones and flesh of his flesh Adam took her as the sharer of every experience in his life, from those wherein he was strongest ("bone of my bones") across the entire range of experiences to those in which he was weakest ("and flesh of my flesh"). He took her as his intimate companion in everything.[2]

The second interpretation has it that with these words Adam the husband asserted his superior position in the union and his legal rights pertaining to this superiority.[3] His claim that in being given to him as his wife the woman was given to him as his property is, again, justified by the fact that she had first been taken from him, from his own body. Thus for a man to marry was not so much to enter into a state, to form a union—although it was both of these.[4] It was for him first and principally to acquire a new possession. (This provides the meaning of adultery under old Jewish law. It was not infidelity, the reneging on a promise, the violating of a holy union. If the adultery was the wife's, she violated rather her husband's property right over her. As for the husband's adultery, an asymmetry had to enter the explanation. Since his wife had no property right over him, he could commit adultery only by having intercourse with another man's wife—by violating his property right. If his intercourse were with an unmarried girl, he violated her father's property right. This was not adultery, although as a violation it had its punishment. The Deuteronomic Code [22:28–29] prescribed that he must pay the father an indemnity of fifty silver shekels. He must marry the girl, must take her as his second wife—and suffer the domestic turmoil this would probably bring on him; and he could never divorce her.)

That in taking Eve as his wife Adam regained his own possession and established his proprietary right over her is, according to this interpretation, corroborated by the Yahwist author's editorial comment in Genesis 2:24 that follows immediately on Adam's evaluation: "That is why a man leaves his father and mother and clings to his wife, and the two of them become one body."

Interpretation of the Deuteronomic Divorce Text

I have already pointed out that in Jesus' generation two schools of rabbis, those of Hillel and of Shammai, debated the meaning of the term *erwat dabar* in Deuteronomy 24:1. This "uncleanness of a thing" perpetrated by a wife, this shameful conduct of hers—to what specifically did it refer? This was the focus of the rabbis' disagreement. But about a different point in this law they found no disagreement; and this we must explain first. When a husband decided to dismiss a wife, he had first to write out the writ of dismissal, the bill of divorce. In sequence the marriage was not dissolved until the husband had both written the bill and had sent the wife out of his home. This put a brake on his acting in anger and consequently dissolving his marriage with a haste he might later regret. The fact too that the law most severely forbade his remarrying a wife once divorced (recall that this is the formal intent of the legislation in Deuteronomy 24:1) helped to hold him back from a precipitous decision.

The writ of dismissal was called in Hebrew *sefer keritut,* and in the Greek of the Septuagint translation of Torah, *biblíon apostasíou.* The formulation of the writ was not fixed by law, at least not by Jesus' time. It may have commonly been phrased "She is not my wife nor I her husband," for this is Hosea's declaration by which he assured his children that he had dismissed their faithless mother (Hosea 2:4). According to some rabbis a wife could write her own writ of dismissal, but its validity depended on its bearing her husband's signature. The most fundamental purpose of the writ was to serve as her proof that she was single again and thus free to remarry. The wife once dismissed and thus no longer a wife ordinarily returned to her father's house, taking with her the dowry that she had brought to the marriage to provide against widowhood or divorce. If she had borne children these remained with the husband. As an exception to this she could take a nursing infant with her; but if this was a male child she had to return him to the husband by his sixth birthday. She was free to remarry, but not to a priest (according to Leviticus 21:7). But her chances for a second marriage may have been hurt severely by the fact of her dismissal, especially if the husband had proved some serious failure on her part. If this failure was her inability to produce a child (and the sterility was ordinarily presumed to be hers), her chance for remarriage was nil.

The dispute in Jesus' time about the reference of *erwat dabar* had begun with the great rabbis Hillel and Shammai themselves a generation earlier. Hillel the Elder was regarded as a sage (a *zugot*) and the greatest of Israel's interpreters of the Law during the period of the second temple, which spanned from about 200 B.C. until the destruction of Israel at the end of the bar-Kochba revolt against Rome in 135 A.D. Though born in

Babylon, he passed his years as interpreter–teacher, from c. 20 B.C. to 20 A.D. in Jerusalem. Shammai, a native Palestinian, began his teaching a decade earlier. Hillel was known for his gentleness and for his liberality in interpreting the reference of *erwat dabar* (and ironically therefore for the severity of consequences for Jewish women because of this liberal interpretation). Shammai was the severe teacher, a conservative interpreter of this reference (and therefore the benign friend of Jewish wives constantly vulnerable to dismissal).

In the twentieth century we know of Hillel's and Shammai's interpretations of the causes warranting a wife's dismissal only in the traditions preserved in their respective schools. For this reason it is probably impossible to sift out of the traditions that which comes from the masters and that which comes from their disciples and their successors.[5]

That the scholars and teachers of the law would construe these causes discordantly was inevitable for a reason we have already seen. The causes were drawn from Deuteronomy 24, from one verse therein, and even from one part of a phrase—*erwat dabar*. But the terms taken by themselves had only the most generic signification. And in the context of their use they had a most imprecise reference. This was, again, variously "something shameful," "the indecency of a thing," "a shameful thing." This bound the scholars to ask whether, if she were to be the subject of *erwat dabar,* the wife must commit a moral fault; or whether, moral fault aside, some non-moral deficiency in her could make her its subject.

The terms are used in Deuteronomy 23:5, and show there how varied their range of reference could be: "Since the Lord, your God, journeys along with your camp to defend you . . . your camp must be holy; otherwise if he sees *anything indecent* in your midst, he will leave your company" (italics added). The verses preceding this one suggest the kind of indecency the author had in mind here. Verses 11 and 12 prescribe that after a nocturnal emission a man must bathe ritually. The emission was not regarded as a moral fault, but by it a man incurred ritual uncleanness, as did a woman by reason of her menstrual discharge (Leviticus 15:19–24). Verses 13–15 command the burying of human excrement. Failure to do so was an indecent thing, although not clearly a moral fault. Thus, along with the signification of conduct morally reprehensible, *erwat dabar* could refer to anything physically repulsive or even displeasing. The two significations became the greater part of the substance of disagreement between the schools of Hillel and of Shammai.

Shammai and his disciples, both in his own and in succeeding generations, interpreted Deuteronomy 24:1 narrowly. For them *erwat dabar* indicated as grounds for a husband's dismissing his wife only some moral fault in her, specifically some fault in her sexual conduct, and some serious fault there. Her adultery was the most obvious of such faults, but not the only one.[6]

Tractate Gittin (9:10), witnessing to a rabbinic instruction of probably the second century, says of the Beth Shammai, "The school of Shammai has said: the husband must dismiss his wife only when he has found in her a matter of shame (i.e., something shameful); for Deuteronomy 24:1 means 'because he has found in her a shameful thing.' "[7]

But Hillel and his school interpreted the reference of *erwat dabar* broadly. Certainly to their minds it referred to serious sexual delinquency in the wife. But apparently drawing on the terms' reference in Deuteronomy to situations and conducts not morally delinquent, this school insisted that they referred to other conduct and conditions in the wife than moral delinquency. Tractate Gittin reports this too in its chapter 9: ". . . the school of Hillel [interprets *erwat dabar*] broadly to refer to anything at all that is indecent, not only to sins of unchastity."[8] But having insisted on this, the Hillelites were faced with the problem of finding a criterion for the non-moral "indecencies" in a wife that justified her husband's dismissing her. To find this they appear to have returned to the text of Deuteronomy 24:1 itself. There they read that the subjective motive for a husband's dismissing his wife (on finding *erwat dabar* in her, whatever its nature) is that he is displeased with her: "When a man, after marrying a woman and having relations with her, is later displeased with her because . . ." This suggested to the Hillelites that the criterion of indecency in a wife could be her husband's displeasure with her.[9]

Would this mean that the displeasure warranting his dismissing her must in its turn be warranted by some de facto indecency in the wife? Hillelite opinion divided on this question as well. One side insisted that there must be some objective deficiency in the wife, although it could be as trivial as her having fairly regularly served poorly prepared meals. Rabbi Akiba (c. 135 A.D.) took a contrary view, which must have been as concessive to the husband as theory could get. He urged that even a quasi-objective deficiency in the wife could warrant her dismissal—for example, the fact that her husband has found a woman more desirable to him than she. In this case the wife's *erwat dabar* became her lesser desirability. What Akiba did was to dissect Deuteronomy 24:1 and to find in the distinct words and phrases distinct grounds for dismissal. Thus, reading in reverse order, the husband may find an indecency, or shamefulness, in the wife. He may also find simply "something" in her. Finally he may find her simply displeasing, lacking in favor or comeliness, at least by comparison with another more comely and pleasing woman.[10]

Specific Grounds for Dismissal

But on the cautious hither side of such permissiveness other Hillelite interpreters sought to name truly objective deficiencies in the wife that might warrant her dismissal. Naming these deficiencies and thereby fixing the specific grounds for dismissal became a main work of this school. (Although the dispute between the Hillelites and the school of Shammai still throve in the first generation of the Christian era, eventually the Hillelite interpretation won out.)[11]

Because the list of deficiencies is recorded in the teachings of rabbis of all the generations from Hillel and Shammai down to the end of the Tannaim (c. 200 A.D.), we have no way of knowing the exact content of the list during the first two generations of the Christian era, the span of about sixty years during which the Gospel was formed. But the grounds must have been already numerous and varied enough at least by 70–80, by the time the Matthean editor compiled his version of the Gospel. For he has the Pharisees test Jesus with the question, "Is a man permitted to dismiss his wife for just any reason?" And if he records the question as it was in fact asked (although it is more likely that Mark's version of it is the more accurate), then the list was numerous and varied even at the time of Jesus' ministry.

What follow here are some of the faults, or mere deficiencies, that the rabbis deemed justification for dismissing a wife. (Taken for granted, although not listed, are such objectively serious delinquencies as adultery and abortion, the latter whether successful or merely attempted.)

Rabbi Akiba (c. 135 A.D.), as we have already noted, allowed that a wife's poorly prepared meals could justify her dismissal.

Chapter 9:50 of tractate Gittin identified as unchaste conduct warranting dismissal the wife's going outdoors with head uncovered and hair in disarray, or with arms bare, or with garments torn. The same tractate (in paragraph 89) cites Rabbi Meir (c. 150) naming as sufficient ground the wife's eating or drinking in public, or her nursing her child in public, her spinning cloth in public, or her bathing with men.[12]

The conduct of a wife that violated a command either of Moses or of later Jewish law justified her dismissal according to Tractate Kettubot 7:6 (reported in the Targums of Onkelos and Jerusch on Deuteronomy 24:1). And the violations of the law needed not have been in the domains of sexuality or marriage. A wife who served her husband ritually unclean food, or who failed to sleep apart from him during her menstrual days, or failed to dispose of old leaven during Passover, or who took vows but failed to keep them—in all these she violated a Mosaic command. She violated Jewish law if she went outdoors with head uncovered or spun cloth in public. Rabbi Abba Scha'ul (c. 150) considered as such a violation the wife's discourteous and scolding treatment of her husband's parents in his presence. Rabbi Tarphon (c. 100) considered a violation of the law a wife's discussing intimate matters with her husband at such a pitch and volume that neighbors could overhear her.[13]

Conduct which, without actually violating law or command, nevertheless brought her husband into disrepute justified a wife's dismissal. The fact itself that she gained the reputation of a "bad wife" brought this disrepute, for she at least failed to bring honor to him. Certainly an habitually cranky and scolding wife, or a lazy wife, or one who refused to perform the tasks proper to a wife brought dishonor on her husband and justified his dismissing her.[14]

Finally the failure of the wife to meet the conditions or assumptions on which the marriage was contracted justified her dismissal. Tractate Kettubot 7:7 prescribed that if a man bethrothed to himself a woman whom he presumed to be bound by no vows, the betrothal was taken as invalid if he subsequently found that she was in fact bound by vows. And if the betrothal was completed in marital cohabitation, but only then did he find out about the vows, he could dismiss the wife. So too if he married her on the supposition that she had no physical defects. The parallel passage in Kettubot 7:8 takes as a concealed vow justifying dismissal the wife's refusal to eat meat, or to drink wine, or to wear attractive clothing. A commentary in the Tosephta had it that any physical defect making a man unfit for the priesthood, if found in a woman, made her unfit to be a wife. In addition such physical defects in a wife as bad breath or body odor made her likewise unfit.[15]

Protection for the Wife

What we have examined thus far suggests a record of unrelieved selfishness on the part of Jewish husbands and a defense of this selfishness by unfair customary law written by males for male prerogatives. While it is true that the rabbis never relaxed their protection of what they considered the husband's rights in marriage, many were nevertheless sensitive to unfair treatment of wives and to the cruelty the law could work on them. They sought accordingly to write into Jewish law some protection for them.

In sequence the first restriction put on male caprice in dismissing wives came in the century before the Christian era with Rabbi Simon ben Shotach's making of the *kettubah* into an enforceable document (according to Tractate Kettubot 84b). This was to make it a binding financial settlement. Such settlements had been in Jewish marriage arrangements from biblical times. They were agreements entered ordinarily by the two sets of parents concerning the nature and quantity of the dowry that the bride's father was to provide her, and of the *mohar,* the sum that the groom was to deposit with the bride's father. The *kettubah* especially recorded the groom's financial obligation to the bride both during the marriage and in the event of his dismissing her. It was signed by witnesses who acted in her behalf. And it provided for her sustenance not only in the event of dismissal but in the event of her husband's death as well. Thus both the *kettubah* and the *mohar* served as a kind of bond that under specified conditions had to be restored to the one who had posted it.

But there were also conditions under which the husband did not have to restore the dowry to the wife on his dismissing her. Flagrant delinquency on her part, of the kind that caught public attention and gave scandal, exempted him from restoring it. And predictably this exemption and the conditions and conduct warranting it brought on the kind of argument among the lawyers that so readily ended in disadvantage for the wives. Tractate Kettubot 7:6 specified that a woman who violated Jewish law forfeited her right to the return of the dowry on being dismissed. It also specified some kinds of the violations that earned this forfeiture: such, for example, as her going outdoors with head uncovered, her spinning cloth in the street, her conversing indiscriminately with men not related to her by blood or marriage, her cursing her husband's children in his presence, her persistence in talking in her house in a voice loud enough to be overheard by the neighbors.[16]

A second protection for the wife, according to Tractate Jebamoth 14:1, was this: that an insane husband could not dismiss his wife, because his writing and conveying the *get pitturin,* the writ of dismissal, had to be a conscious act. Nor could a husband dismiss an insane wife, since, deprived of his protection, she would be vulnerable to mistreatment.

But the most thorough attempt at righting the scales of justice came in later rabbinic laws extending to wives a counter-ploy against husbands with whom they were unhappy. They could compel them to grant the *get pitturin* that would dissolve the marriage and free them to seek a second and happier marriage. The rabbis of the Talmudic period both established the legal means whereby a wife could compel her husband to give her the writ, and listed the grounds on which a wife could demand to be dismissed. The ordinary means were for the court of the elders to bring pressure upon the husband until he called witnesses, wrote out the *get,* and conveyed it to the wife in the presence of witnesses.

Again quite predictably the rabbis differed about the grounds on which a wife could compel her husband to do this. Tractate Kettubot 77a specified as such a ground the husband's unwillingness or even inability to support his wife properly. The same tractate (13:5) named as a ground the husband's refusal to consummate the marriage. Kettubot 5:6 said that if a man vowed not to have intercourse with his wife, the school of Shammai allowed him two weeks to change his mind and consummate the marriage; the school of Hillel allowed him one week. If at the end of the permitted period he did not withdraw his vow and consummate, the law compelled him to free her by dismissal. Correlatively a woman could free herself by vowing not to consummate. The husband had the right to annul this vow. But if she persisted in her refusal, he could dismiss her, though at the cost to her of his keeping the dowry.

Still in the domain of her husband's conduct, the law acknowledged the wife's right to demand dismissal if he demanded against her will that she migrate from her homeland with him, if he tried to force her to take vows which she regarded as unworthy or impossible, if he continued in an occupation which made married life unbearable for her, even if before the marriage she had agreed to this occupation, if he transgressed the law of Moses with her or tried to force her to transgress it, or if he were habitually quarrelsome or cruel.[17]

Outside the domain of conduct but in that of involuntary deficiency on the husband's part, rabbinic law granted the wife the right to demand dismissal if the husband were impotent or became so, if after ten years of childless marriage the husband was proved to be the sterile partner, if he contracted a contagious and dangerous disease, or if he developed a loathsome disease or physical defect that aroused revulsion in her.

In all this the same law established the counter-measure designed to protect the husband, that the wife must get the writ of dismissal from him ultimately by his free choice, no matter the legal pressure she brought to compel him to give it. Thus the writ was invalid if the effective reason for his giving it were coercion, or if he were coerced to give it while of unsound mind.

Among other points of the law's concern for divorce developed by the rabbis was this, that marriages religiously and ethnically mixed because contracted with a Gentile could be dissolved automatically by either husband or wife. The writ of divorce was required only where both spouses were Jewish.

Even a Jewish couple could divorce by mutual consent, without need for a court of the elders to establish responsibility for the breakdown of the marriage, as in other and later legal systems. But even in cases of divorce by mutual consent the formality of dissolution was the dismissal of the wife. And for this the writ was required.

If while still underage (which in Jewish law meant younger than twelve years) a girl was forced into betrothal or marriage by her mother or brothers after her father's death, she could make a renunciation of the marriage or the betrothal that automatically ended either. She had a right to this renunciation even in defiance of her father if she had already been once dismissed from a marriage.

Finally, only by the late rabbinic enactment known as the *Herem de Rabboni Gershon* in c. 968–1026 A.D. did it become prohibited for a Jewish husband to dismiss his wife against her will.[18]

The Religious Warrant for Dismissal

When a modern student seeks to account for the principal causes of this legal tradition so weighted against equal justice for women, it is not enough to look only to the ancient and universal assumption among the Semitic peoples that legally, at least, women were equivalently children. There was a source of the uneven justice that was anthropological and religious. I refer here not to the Semitic myths of the gods that featured mortal enmity and fighting to the death between male and female deities. (The struggle between Apsu and Ti'amat in the *Enuma elish* is for us only the best known example of this divine fury between the sexes that must have been a projected image of something that men and women felt toward one another on earth—perhaps as warrior and hunter males struggled to take emotional dominance away from archetypal matriarchs of the old agricultural societies of the Fertile Crescent.) In the Hebrew Scriptures themselves—despite their profound rejection of the heterosexual polytheism of the old Semitic myths—male-female conflict runs as a recurring theme. However consciously Israel's poets and prophets rejected the mythic supposition that earthly and human existence began in a mortal duel of male and female deities, at least unconsciously the same supposition infiltrated their explanation of the origin of misery in the human race. They sought to explain this origin poetically as the consequence of prideful disobedience, deceit and cowardice within the first husband-wife relationship. And since in the explanation—which is the parable of the first man and woman in the Garden of Eden (in Genesis 2 and 3)—the woman is blamed for the first prideful disobedience, but the man mainly for cowardice, she was to be blameworthy forever in her daughters, in the women and wives of all history. Their lot was to be forever vulnerable to punishment for the misery that their mother Eve had brought into the human race and therefore upon their sons and husbands.

I take it as established by responsible scholarship that the narrative of the first couple in the Garden of Eden is not a factual record but an etiological parable. That is, it is a parable that seeks to account for causal origins—in this case for the causal origin of misery in the history of mankind, including the misery that is sin. It is part of the genius of the Hebrew poet-prophet (and to my mind compelling evidence of his interpretation's divine inspiration) that he broke from the powerful etiological assumption that had dominated the minds of his Semitic predecessors. This assumption was that the misery afflicting human beings from the beginning of their history has been mainly the work of capricious gods and goddesses who had formed men and women in the first place as pawns in their own deadly games. The Hebrew said no to this gigantic silliness. He put the blame where he saw that it belonged, in men and women themselves, in their pride and foolishness. Call him the first existential moralist; he cut through inauthenticity and cowardice, and accepted responsibility for what the human condition had become. "We have brought our misery upon ourselves," he insisted. And he devised the parable to suggest how this had been done.

A painstaking exegesis of the parable is not in order here. It will be enough to make the points that follow. The interpretation is my own.

When the tempter (portrayed in the parable as the serpent) came to destroy the first couple's relationship with Yahweh God—and thence the relationship with him of all future generations—he had to lure the man into sinful rebellion. For a Hebrew assumption dictating the etiology of the parable is that inherited moral ruin comes down through the paternal line—and necessarily so, since only the father has the moral-legal status giving his sins destructive power over his children and his children's children.

The tempter knew his victim well, where to find his fatal weakness. About this weakness the parable had earlier delivered a clear hint, one all the more revealing because it had come from Yahweh himself: "It is not good for the man to be alone." His weakness was his need for the woman. Indeed she had been given him in consideration of this need. Again Yahweh had declared this need clearly enough: "I will make a suitable partner for him." And Adam had agreed about her suitability; from the bottom of his heart he had agreed: "This one, at last, is bone of my bones and flesh of my flesh." So the tempter's strategy was virtually hand-delivered to him: to get the man, first get his woman; then he will be easy.

As the parable's narrative unfolded, the tempter did not in fact, as a kind of second effort, have to get the man at all. The woman herself supplied the tactic for that part of his strategy: "The woman saw the tree was good for food, pleasing to the eyes, and desirable for giving wisdom. So she took some of the fruit and ate it; and she also gave some to her husband, who was with her, and he ate it."

This is how the Yahwist, the male poet-prophet, interpreted the beginning of human misery. It came in a disaster at the tender heart of the first man's life. The woman given to him because he needed her, his mate as dear to him as his own life, opted for prideful disobedience to Yahweh God. And knowing his weakness, his fatal need for her and his fear of life without her, she tempted him. He fell so easily—not, like her, out of prideful disobedience, but because he could not say no to her.

Such was Adam's explanation when later Yahweh came in anger to demand an accounting for the ruin of his creation, a ruin betrayed in the man's and woman's sudden guilt at their nakedness: "Who told you that you were naked?" Yahweh demanded. "You have eaten, then, of the tree of which I had forbidden you to eat?" Adam's excuse was to echo in the male psyche for the rest of time: "The woman whom you put here with me—she gave me fruit from the tree, and so I ate it."

Yahweh punished both the man and the woman, and through them their descendants. Now the earth itself would be their enemy. As long as they lived in obedience they lived in a garden of delights. They had to do no more than tend it. But now because of their disobedience they were driven from the garden, out onto a harsh and alien land. The man especially would have to live in misery as he struggled to wrest a living from it.

> Cursed be the ground because of you!
> In toil shall you eat its yield
>   all the days of your life. . . .
> By the sweat of your face
>   shall you get bread to eat,
> Until you return to the ground
>   from which you were taken.

The woman's punishment struck at her body, and precisely where she was most vulnerable as a woman.

> I will intensify the pangs of your childbearing;
> in pain shall you bring forth children.

But the punishment struck also at her soul. And there it took the form of fitting retribution for what she had done to her husband and through him to all his children for all time. Now her need for him, her sexual need, would take over her life. And where, at the crucial moment in the garden, his need for her had brought him low, now her need for him would keep her his servant-child forever.

> Yet your urge shall be for your husband,
> and he shall be your master.

Jewish husbands, and all others who read the book of Genesis as divinely inspired, could not fail to notice that this punishment was God's will, that the husband should be master to his wife. (In Hebrew he is to be her *Ba'al*, which is her "lord." And as late as Jesus' time the proper address of wife to husband in Israel was "my lord.") Thus the etiological parable of the woman's rebellion in the garden, surely the product in part of a poetic projection of the male experience in marriage, turned about and became a model for the right order in marriage: the husband, despite his weakness, expected to be lord and master, mentor to his wife, her enfranchised punisher; the wife, proved in her insubordination, expected to be submissive, and forever deserving of punishment.

From there it was an easy step to the conclusion that divorce by dismissal of the wife from his home is one among fitting punishments a husband may levy upon a wife, a daughter of Eve, who had in some way continued her ancient mother's faithlessness. Just as easy was the conclusion that she who deserved punishment should in no way be able to execute this punishment of dismissal from the home and the marriage.

Wives as Faithless According to the Prophetic Tradition

Jewish men who read and pondered certain passages in the prophetic writings may have found in them oblique confirmation of this inherited supposition that wives need watching and easily merit punishing. I refer to those passages which are extended metaphors portraying Israel as a wife faithless to her husband, Yahweh God. Because they are metaphors these passages have as their intent not to offer a commentary on the conduct of wives. It is rather to mirror vividly the religious inconstancy of the people Israel, their repeated apostasy from the pure worship of the God of their fathers and their going over to the gods of their pagan neighbors. But the husbands who read these passages came under a temptation of their own, which was to ignore their metaphoric reference and to concentrate instead on the scenario itself of the metaphor.

The Metaphor in the Book of Prophecy of Hosea

The earliest such passage begins the Book of the prophet Hosea (who was active in Israel, the northern of the two kingdoms, toward the end of the reign of Jeroboam II, c. 750 B.C.). This was one of the brief periods of tiny Israel's relative affluence and power, periods during which her people dallied with the cults of her pagan neighbors, a dalliance indicted by Hosea, Jeremiah and Ezekiel as adultery.

In Hosea the metaphor is so elaborate as to be a living parable. If one reads the passage as an historical account, Hosea was commanded by Yahweh to take as his wife the prostitute Gomer. The divine intent here was a dual one. It was first that Gomer's faithlessness, her running to pagan lovers, would dramatize metaphorically Israel's faithlessness in going to the pagan gods and their cults on the silly persuasion that it was from them that her affluence and power had come. But secondly and principally Yahweh intended that Hosea's response to this faithlessness was to make clear to the Israelites something about himself and the quality of his love, and something about the tragedy that came upon Israel again and again. This dual meaning unfolded in the following way.

To begin with, Hosea's (Yahweh's) taking Gomer (Israel) as his wife was an act of compassion, since she was already a prostitute.

She bore Hosea three children and returned to her harlotry. Hosea's first words were to their children:

> Protest against your mother, protest!
> for she is not my wife,
> and I am not her husband (2:4).

Although this declaration may have been later adopted as the formula of dismissal in the Jewish divorce action, it is here a cry of sorrowful anger, not Hosea's repudiation of Gomer and the death of their marriage. For he goes on immediately to set forth the strategy of his punishment for the faithlessness. It is anything but repudiation; and it is the heart of the metaphoric meaning. It makes clear something about Yahweh's love, and something about the recurring tragedy in Israel's history. Hosea (Yahweh) will punish Gomer (Israel) by disgracing her before her lovers.

> . . . I will strip her naked,
> leaving her as on the day of her birth;
> I will make her like the desert,
> reducing her to an arid land . . . (2:5).

> So now I will lay bare her shame
> before the eyes of her lovers,
> and no one can deliver her out of my hand.
> I will bring an end to all her joy . . . (2:12–13).

But the intent in this punishment was not to destroy. Hosea (Yahweh) had no desire to abandon his wife forever. The punishment was designed to bring her to her senses and then bring her back to him. Having been stripped of all things and driven into the desert, and, because of this, abandoned by her false lovers, she was to recognize who had been her first lover and her faithful lover—and she would return to him.

> While she decked herself out with her rings and jewels,
>> and, in going after her lovers
>> forgot me, says the Lord . . . (2:15).
> Therefore I will hedge in her way with thorns
>> and erect a wall against her,
>> so that she cannot find her paths (2:8).
> If she runs after her lovers,
>> she shall not overtake them;
>> if she looks for them she shall not find them.
> Then shall she say,
> "I will go back to my first husband,
>> for it was better with me than now" (2:9).
> So I will allure her;
>> I will lead her into the desert
>> and speak to her heart (2:16).
> From there I will give her the vineyards she had,
>> and the valley of Achor as a door of hope.
> She shall respond then as in the days of her youth . . . (2:17).[19]

Reading this part of Hosea Jewish husbands of later generations could take one or both of two disparate impressions from it. They could also draw from the metaphoric parable two sets of partly interlocking norms for conduct toward their wives.

The first impression could be that here is a model for the love of a husband whose wife has in fact been unfaithful. Despite the infidelity, even despite its recurrence, his own love was never to fail. He was always to take back his faithless wife. The reason for his doing so was that Yahweh has committed himself to take Israel back unfailingly. And underlying this was the deeper reason, namely that husbands were to make their own Yahweh's reason for his unfailing love: he means for his marriage to Israel to be perpetual, imperishable.

> I will espouse you to me forever;
>> I will espouse you in right and in justice,
>> in love and in mercy;
> I will espouse you in fidelity,
>> and you shall know the Lord (2:21–22).

Jewish husbands could take as well a different impression from their reading of the parable, and could do so especially if they ignored its didactic intent. The impression was multifaceted and began with this, that when a man takes a woman to wife, he does her a favor. She is weak and inclined to faithlessness. So his marrying her may be a move to protect her. Especially because he has thus graced her with a protecting marriage, he has the prerogative of punishing her if she does prove unfaithful, and even the duty of punishing her if he reads Hosea's marital vocation into his own marriage.

If he does the latter he has also the prerogative and the duty to take back and to love unfailingly the wife who repents after her infidelity. But stuck into the side of the mind of a husband pondering such heroic compassion was his awareness of what another part of the Scriptures, the law of Moses, allowed him to do to an unfaithful wife, allowed him in both the Deuteronomic code (Deuteronomy 22:22) and in the Levitical holiness code (Leviticus 20:10). He could have her killed, along with her accomplice. Even if by Jesus' time the capital sentence was an empty one, voided by gentling custom and the Roman occupation government's preempting of all capital punishment, the severity of the traditional punishment verified the severity of the offense. And in any case the presumption that the husband could take from the parable was that wives are the weak ones. They need watching; they deserve the punishing.

The Metaphor in Jeremiah

Jeremiah taught and counseled in the surviving southern kingdom, Judah, during the last generation before its destruction in 587 B.C. by the Babylonian general, Nebuchadnezzar.

The theme of his prophetic utterance was substantially the same as that of Hosea a century and a half earlier in the northern kingdom before its destruction at the hands of the Assyrians. Following the religious and social reform under King Josiah, and the latter's death at Megiddo in 609, the people of Judah returned to their old involvement in the cults of their pagan neighbors. As Hosea had done, Jeremiah likened this to the fall into infidelity of a once loving and faithful wife.

> I remember the devotion of your youth,
>   how you loved me as a bride,
> Following me in the desert,
>   in a land unsown (2:12).

The people's participation in the cults Jeremiah condemned with exactly the metaphor Hosea had used: it was a flagrant promiscuity.

> On every hill, under every green tree
>   you gave yourself to harlotry (2:10).

But what of the unfailingness of Yahweh's love for Judah, his faithless bride? Did Jeremiah believe, with Hosea, that not even the depth and persistence of the bride's infidelity could kill this love?

> If a man sends away his wife,
>   and, after leaving him,
>   she marries another man,
> Does her first husband come back to her?
>   Would not the land be wholly defiled?
> But you have sinned with many lovers,
>   and yet you would return to me! says the Lord.
> Lift up your eyes to the heights and see,
>   where have men not lain with you?
> By the wayside you have waited for them
>   like an Arab in the desert.
> You defiled the land
>   by your wicked harlotry.
> Therefore the showers were withheld,
>   the spring rain failed.
> But because you have a harlot's brow
>   you refused to blush (3:1–3).

And the bride, Judah, is made to ask:

> Even now do you not call me, my father,
>   you who are the bridegroom of my youth?
> Will he keep his wrath forever,
>   will he hold his grudge to the end? (3:4–5).

Though partly like his response in Hosea's utterance, Yahweh's here shows a striking difference. It is to Israel, Judah's sister in the north, his earlier bride, that he will give his forgiveness (3:11–17). When forgiveness goes to Judah, the husband-wife metaphor is abandoned. Literally and prosaically they are the people of Judah who will join with those of Israel to seek forgiveness, and find it (3:18).

The Metaphor in Ezekiel

By far the most elaborate version of this metaphor makes up the sixteenth chapter of the Book of Ezekiel. There it is crafted in such detail that it is an integral story, even a novelette. The plot is substantially identical with its versions in Hosea and Jeremiah, but shows refinement in certain details.

Israel is the abject, abandoned girl-child, found and taken as his own by the king (Yahweh) once she has grown to the age of marriage.

> Again I passed you by and saw that you were now old
> enough for love. I spread the corner of my cloak over you to
> cover your nakedness; I swore an oath to you and entered into a
> covenant with you; you became mine, says the Lord God (16:8).

But Israel the bride, luxuriating in her beauty and her new wealth,
prostitutes herself to every new lover (every pagan nation and its cult) who
comes near her.

> But you were captivated by your own beauty, you used your
> renown to make yourself a harlot, and you lavished your harlotry
> on every passer-by, whose own you became (16:16).

Because of this obscene infidelity Israel's husband will punish her and
will do so by gathering her lovers together and disgracing her before
them—and they will finish the punishment.

> I will now gather together all your lovers whom you tried to
> please, whether you loved them or loved them not; I will gather
> them against you from all sides and expose you naked for them
> to see. I will inflict on you the sentence of adulteress and
> murderess. . . . I will hand you over to them. . . . They shall lead
> an assembly against you to stone you and hack you with swords
> (16:37–40).

But in the end her husband will have compassion and forgive Israel.
He will do this because he has made a covenant of love with her, and,
unlike her, he is faithful to his covenant.

> I will deal with you according to what you have done, you
> who despised your oath, breaking a covenant. Yet I will remem-
> ber the covenant I made with you when you were a girl, and I
> shall set up an everlasting covenant with you. Then you shall
> remember your conduct and be ashamed. . . . For I will reestab-
> lish my covenant with you, that you may know that I am the
> Lord, that you may remember and be covered with confusion,
> and that you may be utterly silenced for shame when I pardon
> you for all you have done, says the Lord (16:59–63).

Again, Jewish husbands reading and meditating on these three prophets could fasten their attention on any one or more of the several facets of
their metaphor. Like Paul they could note that the relationship of husband
and wife is, in its most excellent form portrayed in Ezekiel's denouement, a
covenant, one in which both husband and wife swear themselves to faithful
love. They could notice too that it is the husband who takes the initiative
in forming the covenant and does so out of compassion for a woman

abjectly his inferior. Moreover, in forming the covenant the husband gives everything and stands to gain little, while the wife gains everything and has to give nothing more than her faithful love.

The husbands could also ponder that in every version of the metaphor it is the wife who is weak, fickle, and the faithless one, and that she uses the very gifts given her by the husband who has rescued her to attract many lovers and prostitute herself to them. They could see clearly that the husband punished her in all justice.

Finally they could be brought up short by the denouement offered in each version of the metaphor except Jeremiah: after she is punished the wife is forgiven and taken back, and the marriage is begun anew. They could set this in its stark contrast with the Deuteronomic law that forbade a husband's taking back a wife he had once dismissed. From this conflict they could draw one of multiple conclusions: that it is the Lord's will that husbands be finally forgiving, even to overriding the law and taking back a wife once dismissed; or that taking back a faithless and punished wife is the divine will provided the punishment has not gone as far as dismissal; or that the law is the clearer expression of the Lord's will, and faithless wives, who according to this law could pay with their lives, must be punished by dismissal.

But whichever conclusion they chose to draw, it would be easy for the Jewish husbands to begin with the assumption that the ancient prophets had suggested clearly: that wives are more likely the destroyers of marriages, and guardian-punisher is one of the vocations within the vocation of husband.

NOTES

1. Taking the major passages in the sequence in which they appear in Torah, they are the following:

Leviticus 21:7 (in the Code of Legal Holiness): "A priest shall not marry a woman who has been a prostitute or has lost her honor, nor a woman who has been divorced by her husband; for the priest is sacred to his God."

Substantially the same is said in positive command in Leviticus 21:14, and as part of the same Code: "The priest shall marry a virgin. Not a widow or a woman who has been divorced or a woman who has lost her honor as a prostitute, but a virgin, taken from his own people, shall he marry; otherwise he will have base offspring among his people. I, the Lord, have made him sacred."

This disability of the divorced woman is mitigated slightly at a later point in the Levitical Holiness Code (22:13) where this lists the persons who may and also who may not eat the food offered at sacrificial banquets: "But if a priest's daughter is widowed or divorced, and having no children, returns to her father's house, she may then eat her father's food as in her youth. No layman, however, may eat of it."

The Deuteronomic Code sets two causes voiding a husband's right to dismiss his wife. Deuteronomy 22:14 prescribes that a husband falsely accusing his wife of being not a virgin at the time of the wedding suffers, among other penalties, perpetual loss of the right to dismiss her. Deuteronomy 22:29 prescribes that a man taking the virginity of an unmarried and unbetrothed girl must pay her father fifty silver shekels, must marry her, and can never divorce her.

2. This interpretation is proposed by Walter Brueggemann in his essay, "Of the Same Flesh and Bone," in *The Catholic Biblical Quarterly*, 32.4 (1970), pp. 532–542.

3. Abraham R. Bloch offers this interpetation in *The Biblical and Historical Background of Jewish Customs and Ceremonies*, N.Y., 1980, pp. 23–24.

The interpretation deserves serious criticism and has got it increasingly from modern scholars. One of the most available and most intelligent of these is offered by Phyllis Trible in her volume *God and the Rhetoric of Sexuality* (Philadelphia, 1978). She points to evidence that in the Garden parable the product of God's work of forming mankind (*hā'ādām*) was not one human being but two. Certainly the choice of nouns there does not indicate a first and single male. The noun to designate such, *ish*, was available but was not used until later in the parable, in verse 23. Moreover the noun designating the product of God's work, *hā'ādām*, is translated literally as "the earth creature." Hence Trible's double conclusion. Not only was the first human being not a male from whose maleness the female was taken. But an alternative rabbinic interpretation, that the first human being was an androgyne, and that the forming of the woman was God's separating the two sexes out from the original androgynous one, is not supported by the Genesis text.

4. Bloch adds another facet of interpretation. He reports (pp. 24–25) that the phrase "take a wife" could, in its historical context, mean either the physical transfer of a wife to her husband's home, or the performing of the rite of marriage. He insists that in context the phrase has the latter meaning. Evidence from elsewhere in Torah suggests this. According to Genesis 24:6–7 Isaac *brought* Rebecca into the tent of Sarah, his mother, and this was the physical transfer. But then he *took her* (this is the marriage rite) and she *became his wife* (this is the consummation of the marriage). Bloch holds that this meaning—that the taking of a wife refers to the wedding—is supported by the absence, in Torah, of the verb "to take" from any instance of marriage that did not involve a wedding ceremony. This is verified in the marriages of Abraham with Hagar (Genesis 16:2) and of Jacob with Bilhah and Zilpah, the handmaids of Rachel (Genesis 30:4 and 9).

5. A brief sketch of the generations of interpreters of the Jewish law may help in understanding the development of these traditions as well as the difficulty of separating, in the traditions, the teaching of masters from disciples and successors.

The epoch in which the rabbis—non-priestly, non-ecclesiastical layman scholar-lawyers—became the acknowledged interpreters of the law for Israel began at about 200 B.C. These scholars, from the beginning until the generation of Hillel and Shammai, were called the *zekenim rishonim*, "the former elders." (The Pharisees came to be recognized as a distinct religious group within Israel from about 150 B.C. Some but not all of them were rabbis, teachers of the law.)

Beginning with Hillel and Shammai the rabbis were called the *Tannaim*, a name that is valid until c. 200 A.D., after which the title *Amoraim* became current. Rabbinic interpretation and teaching of course continued past 200 B.C., and indeed down through the centuries. But the golden age of the rabbis ended at about the close of the third century of the Christian era.

The pupils and successors of Hillel and Shammai, men therefore who may have been among the Pharisees with whom Jesus disputed, included respectively

Rabbi ben He He and Rabbi Jonathan ben Uzziel, and Rabbis Dostai, Eleazar ben Hananiah, Joezer ha-Birah, Johanan ben ha-Horanit, and Bava ben Buta in the school of Shammai. Gamaliel I, the teacher of Paul and therefore also a contemporary of Jesus, stood independently of the schools of Hillel and Shammai.

Along with the titles of teachers-interpreters in the different espochs go the titles of the collections of their interpretations. While the Talmudic period is said to have begun with the ascendancy of the rabbis about 200 B.C. (and to have lasted until 500 A.D.), "Talmud" as a title—"the teaching of the law"—refers to two collections that were in formation from c. 170 A.D. until the end of the Tannaite period indicated just above. There was the Jerusalem Talmud, which was, in its formation, the fruit of the discussions and elaborations of Rabbi Juda ha-Nassi, who taught from 170 to 220 A.D. in Judea. The Babylonian Talmud, as its name indicates, was formed by the discussions and elaborations of rabbis in the sizable Jewish colony that had grown up in the Tigris-Euphrates valley during the exile that began with the Babylonians' exportation to their homeland of Jewish captives starting in 597 B.C.

The largest portion of Talmudic material was the Mishna, which means literally "repetition of the law." Its sources were, in turn, the interpretations and other sayings of the Tannaite teachers (the first of whom, in Israel, were Hillel and Shammai). It was codified by Rabbi Judah the Prince in the second and third centuries A.D. Other Talmudic material consisted of the *baraithoth,* sayings coming down from earlier teachers but not included in the Mishna. The *baraithoth* were gathered into the *Tosephta* ("the addition") or into the *Ghemora* ("the complement"). The Mishna and the Ghemora together, without the Tosephta, constitute the Talmud.

The teachings on marriage and divorce come under the Order Nashim in both Talmuds and are distributed among three tractates. The tractate *Kettubot* deals with marriage contracts, tractate *Kiddushin* with marriage itself. Tractate *Gittin* contains the interpretation of the law on divorce and remarriage. It is the ninth and last chapter of this tractate *Gittin* (in the Jerusalem *Talmud*) that contains parts of formulae of bills of divorce. It concludes with a dispute between the school of Hillel and that of Shammai about the grounds on which a man could dismiss his wife.

It is upstream through the generations of this Mishnaic material that a student must work to find out the terms of this debate in Jesus' generation—as the student finds also that it is upstream through generations of Gospel material that he or she must work to find out Jesus' reaction to and comment on the debate in his generation.

6. The Septuagint Greek translation of the verse seems to support the Shammai interpretation, since it renders the key clause *hóti hêuren en autê áschēmon prâgma*—"because he has found in her a shameful deed" (*prâgma*). The noun signifies primarily a personal act.

7. Quoted in Hermann Strack u. Paul Billerbeck, *Kommentar Zum Neuen Testament aus Talmud und Midrasch.* Fünfte Unveränderte Auflag, München, 1969. Erster (Doppel-) Band: Das Evangelium nach Matthäus, s. 315. The authors' commentary adds, "Thus the school of Shammai interprets *erwat dabar* narrowly to refer to a shameful thing, that is, a sin of unchastity."

8. *Ibid.*

9. *Ibid.*, pp. 314–315.

10. Strack and Billerbeck say (*ibid.*) that what Akiba did was to construe the

causal clause "because he has found something shameful in her" as conditional. Thus the passage yielded to him the following: "If she, first, finds no favor in his eyes; secondly, if he finds something shameful in her; thirdly, if he finds anything else in her."

11. Thus E.P. Cohen in *Everyman's Talmud,* N.Y., 1932, p.167. Cohen cites the opinion of Josephus in the latter's *Antiquities of the Jews,* IV, 8, 23: "He who desires to be divorced from his wife for any cause whatever (and many such causes happen among men), let him in writing give assurance that he will never cohabit with her any more." Here Josephus clearly identifies one of the purposes of the writ of dismissal, that of a kind of quit-claim given by the husband, a verification of the woman's freedom from her erstwhile husband's proprietary right over her.

12. In Strack and Billerbeck, *loc. cit.,* p. 315.

13. *Ibid.,* p. 316.

14. *Ibid.*

15. *Ibid.,* pp. 316–317.

16. Cf. Cohen, *op. cit.,* p. 168. Anyone who has lived in a Mediterranean city, town or village is aware that peasant wives seem hardly ever to talk in a voice that can't be heard by the neighbors.

17. For details in this regard see Cohen, *op. cit.,* p.169, and Strack and Billerbeck, *op. cit.,* pp. 23–24.

18. On this point, see *The Principles of Jewish Law: The Hebraic Law of Jerusalem,* edited by Menachem Elon. *Encyclopedia Judaica,* Jerusalem, 1975, col. 367.

19. Modern editors have rearranged the sequence of verses here, judging this a correction of the traditional text needed in order to recapture a coherent development of the speaker's plan.

20. It is of course a commonplace in the Catholic theology of marriage that the source of the imperishability of Christian marriages is this imperishability of Yahweh's marriage with Israel, and the claim (purportedly borrowed from Ephesians 5) that Christian marriages are to image, and reenact, this divine imperishability.

3. DIVORCE AND REMARRIAGE IN THE SYNOPTIC GOSPELS

Jesus' own instruction on divorce and remarriage has come down to us in the two traditions that we inspected briefly in Chapter One. What is taught in one of these traditions is conditioned thoroughly by the Palestinian Jewish doctrine and discipline of divorce that we have just examined. This is the Synoptic tradition, found in Luke 16:18 (obviously the most succinct version of it), in Mark 10:2–12, and in Matthew in two places—within the anthology of Jesus' instruction titled the Sermon on the Mount (5:31–32) and in a longer narrative passage (19:3–12). The teaching in the other tradition seems to be slightly if at all conditioned by the Jewish teaching. This is the Pauline tradition found in 1 Corinthians 7. It was the first of the traditions to be put in the written form that we now possess, although it is not clearly sprung from the earliest Christian version of Jesus' own instruction.

I call these passages traditions in the following sense. Paul says of the most salient part of his instruction that "it is the Lord's" (1 Corinthians 7:10). His way of getting it from Jesus, whom he had never met during the latter's ministry, was most probably not through private revelation. Nor does he seem to mean by his authenticating phrase that this small and particular part of his instruction differs from the rest of it in that it is inspired by the Spirit of the Lord while the rest is not. He would hardly have admitted about such critical instruction that it was his private concoction. What he most probably means is that he had learned Jesus' instruction in one of the early Christian communities, along with its warrant as part of that community's collective memory of the Lord's teaching. Consequently as a point of instruction it was already in vigor in at least one community before Paul ever heard of it. If we may trust the sketchy biography (in Acts 9 and 11) and autobiography (in Galatians 1) of Paul's earliest Christian years, this was most probably a community in Syria.

The same is true, with modifications, of the Synoptic versions. Two of the three Synoptic authors, Luke and the Matthean editor, had never listened personally to Jesus. Mark may have done so personally and immediately. But if he was John Mark, the companion of Paul and Barnabas first mentioned in Acts 12:25 rather than the young man who fled naked into the night after Jesus' arrest in the garden of olives (Mark 14:51–52), then he was more likely from Antioch in Syria, and would never have heard Jesus personally. If this Mark the editor of the Gospel was later the companion and amanuensis of Peter that tradition claims he was, he would most probably have got his knowledge of Jesus' instruction at second hand from Peter's instruction.

In any case what these three Synoptic author-editors give to us are Jesus' words on divorce and remarriage already filtered through the catechetical instruction of different first-generation Christian communities. The significant differences in their several versions of the words are therefore as much ascribable to these early catecheses as they are to the differing editorial intents of the editors themselves. This is enough of a hint for now of the difficulty we in the twentieth century encounter in trying to recover exactly what Jesus said. For it takes no more than a cursory reading of these versions to espy their disagreements in conveying what each implies is a faithful account of Jesus' instruction.

The following are the versions of Jesus' instruction. Luke (16:18) records him as saying,

> Everyone who dismisses his own wife and marries another commits adultery; and anyone who marries a woman who has been dismissed by her husband commits adultery.[1]

Mark's version (10:1–12) is far more detailed and is significantly different. One point of the difference is that here Jesus' instruction is set in a narrative of confrontation and dispute with some Pharisees.

> 1. And leaving there he came to the district of Judea beyond the Jordan. Again crowds gathered around him, and again, as was his custom, he taught them. 2. Some Pharisees came up and asked him, "Is a husband permitted to dismiss his wife?" They asked him this in order to put him to the test. 3. In reply he said, "What did Moses command you?" 4. They answered, "Moses permitted a man to write a writ of dismissal and to send her away." 5. But Jesus told them, "Because of your hardness of heart he wrote that command for you. 6. But from the beginning of creation 'Male and female he made them.' 7. 'For this reason a man shall leave his father and his mother and shall cleave to his wife; 8. and the two shall become one body.' So that they are no longer two, but one body. 9. Therefore what God has joined man must not separate."
> 10. Back again in the house the disciples asked him about this. 11. He said to them, "Whoever dismisses his wife and

marries another commits adultery against her. 12. And if she dismisses her husband and marries another, she commits adultery."

Matthew's first and shorter version from the Sermon on the Mount (5:31–32) is the following:

> 31. It was also said, "Whoever dismisses his wife must give her a writ of dismissal." 32. But I say to you, whoever dismisses his wife, except in the case of her *pornéia*,[2] makes her to commit adultery; and whoever marries a woman who has been dismissed, he commits adultery.

Matthew's longer passage, like Mark's, is set in the narrative of confrontation with representatives of the Pharisees (19:3–12). That it reports with crucial variations what is purportedly the same conversation tells again of the difficulty I have just mentioned in the preceding note.

> 3. Some Pharisees came up to him, and to test him said to him, "Is a man permitted to dismiss his wife for just any reason?" 4. He said in reply, "Don't you know that he who created them in the beginning 'made them male and female'?" 5. And he said, " 'For this reason a man will leave his father and his mother and will cling to his wife, and the two shall become one body.' 6. So they are no longer two, but one body. Therefore what God has joined man must not separate." 7. They said to him, "Why then did Moses command 'to give the writ of dismissal and so dismiss her'?" 8. He said to them, "Because of your hardness of heart Moses permitted you to dismiss your wives. But in the beginning it was not so. 9. I say to you that whoever dismisses his wife, except for her *pornéia,* and marries another commits adultery." 10. His disciples said to him, "If this is the way it is with a man and wife, it is better not to marry." 11. He said, "Not everyone can accept this teaching, but only those to whom it is given. 12. Some there are who are eunuchs from their mother's womb; some have been made so by men; and some have made themselves so for the kingdom of God. Let him accept this teaching who can."

Whether Paul hews to the heart of the Synoptic tradition and how far beyond it he goes because he was addressing a partly non-Jewish and wholly non-Palestinian audience may emerge in this passage from his First Letter to the Corinthians (Chapter 7).

> 1. Now, as for what you wrote, "Is it good for a man that he not touch a woman?" 2. because of the danger of impurity let

each man have his own wife, and each woman her own husband.
3. Let the husband render his debt to his wife, and likewise she
hers to her husband. 4. A wife has not authority over her own
body, but her husband has it; just as a husband has not authority
over his own body, but his wife has it. 5. Do not deny one
another, except by agreement and only for a time, lest Satan put
you to the test because of your lack of self-control. 6. I say this
as a matter of suggestion, not as an obligation. 7. What I wish is
that all should be as I am; but each has from God his own gift,
one person one gift, another another.

8. I say to the unmarried and to the widows, it is good that
they remain as I am. 9. But if they cannot contain themselves,
let them marry, for it is better to marry than to burn. 10. To the
married I proclaim—it is not I who do so, but the Lord—that a
wife is not to be separated from her husband. 11. And if she is in
fact separated, she is either to remain unmarried or is to be
reconciled to her husband. And a husband is not to dismiss his
wife.

12. To the rest I say (and here it is I, not the Lord), if a
brother has a wife who is a non-believer, and she agrees to live
with him in peace, he is not to dismiss her. 13. And if a wife has
a husband who is a non-believer, and he agrees to live with her in
peace, she is not to dismiss the husband. 14. For the non-
believing husband is sanctified in the wife, and the non-believing
wife is sanctified in the husband. If this were not so, your
children would be unclean—whereas they are holy. 15. But if
the non-believing spouse separates, let him separate. The brother
or the sister is not to play the slave in such matters, for God has
called us in peace. 16. For how do you know, wife, if you will
save your husband? Or how do you know, husband, if you will
save your wife?

The evident intent of the Synoptic authors was to convey to their
readers Jesus' mind concerning divorce and remarriage. Because of this, as
I have already suggested, our effort at understanding Jesus' own intent
runs upon immediate difficulty. For the Synoptics' intent became active
from thirty-five to forty-five years after Jesus had spoken his mind (modern scholarship assigns approximately 65 A.D. as the date of composition
of Mark's Gospel, and at least another decade as that of Luke and
Matthew, while Jesus' death is reckoned with reasonable accuracy at 30
A.D.). They sought to direct Jesus' words helpfully to audiences exclusively Christian although converted from either Judaism or paganism in
varying proportions from audience to audience. But Jesus had spoken his
mind to an audience made up exclusively of his own Palestinian Jewish
people. He had also shaped his words to function as a criticism of Jewish
conduct contemporary with himself, and at least apparently to resolve a

Jewish dispute still going on in his generation after having begun a generation earlier with the rabbis Hillel and Shammai.

We have our uncertain record of what Jesus said about divorce and remarriage because his disciples listened to and remembered this with varying fidelity and subsequently passed down through different first- and second-generation Christian communities the content of this remembering. That the Christians of those generations believed Jesus intended his words also for them was a product of their interpretation of his intent, as our conviction that he meant them also for us in the twentieth century is a product of our interpretation of it. The precise normative hold of Jesus' words to his Palestinian Jewish hearers on our marital conduct in the twentieth century is also a matter of our own interpretation. And this interpretation, even when coming from the Catholic *magisterium,* has been anything but unchangingly univocal, as I have already suggested and will show later in voluminous detail.

Jesus' Instruction in Luke 16:18

Jesus' instruction on divorce and remarriage is found in its simplest form obviously in the passage in the Gospel according to Luke: "Everyone who dismisses his own wife and marries another commits adultery; and anyone who marries a woman who has been dismissed by her husband commits adultery."

Some New Testament scholars insist that this version of the instruction is the closest among the Synoptics to Jesus' own words. Their main reason for saying this is that Luke has not put his version into the narrative setting of Jesus' confrontation and dispute with the Pharisees that Mark and Matthew use, a setting they consider conventional and artificial. Luke, by contrast, includes it simply as a free-floating parenetic utterance of Jesus, one of his words of moral instruction making up an artificially gathered anthology of Jesus' instructions in this part of his Gospel—the great journey of instruction that begins with 9:51 where Jesus sets out for Jerusalem and his death.[3]

This interpretation has its merits but is not compelling. Its strength depends on the accuracy of applying at this point a principle of New Testament exegesis, the principle that in the Gospel passages' process of formation across the thirty-five to forty-five years from Jesus to the evangelical editors, statements which were at first passed along in clusters free of real-life context were later set fictively in narrative contexts in order to make them more easily rememberable and to give them existential clout. This may be the accurate judgment about some passages, but it is at least not self-evidently true about most, including Jesus' instruction on divorce and remarriage. It is not unreasonable to think that Luke may have done the reverse, that he found Jesus' instruction in a real-life Palestinian narrative setting, but extracted it from the latter because it meant little to his Gentile audience in Asia Minor or elsewhere.

At any rate, according to Luke Jesus' audience for this instruction is made up of his followers alone, for he has introduced the entire artificially gathered instruction with the formulary, context-setting line, "Another time he said to his disciples . . ." Nothing about this context suggests that Jesus' instruction disturbed a considerable group of his fellow Jews. As we shall see, both Mark and Matthew report emphatically otherwise on this point.

Luke's version of Jesus' instruction is singular also in what it does not have him do. It does not record his ordering that spouses, whether his followers or others, not divorce. He does not, as do Mark (10:9) and Matthew (19:6), quote Jesus' terse prohibition, "Therefore what God has joined man must not separate." He does not have Jesus forbid divorced spouses to remarry, nor have him say that it is impossible for them to remarry because their attempt at divorce is ineffective. Luke has Jesus only state the consequences of a man's engaging in two kinds of conduct: if he dismisses his wife (the Jewish manner of divorce) and marries (or tries to marry) another woman, he commits adultery; if he marries (or tries to marry) a woman who has been dismissed, he commits adultery. What is more, the entire final clause of this version of Jesus' words—". . . and anyone who marries a woman who has been dismissed by her husband commits adultery"—may be an addition to Jesus' own words in the form of a logical extension of the first clause in the instruction, "Everyone who dismisses his own wife and marries another commits adultery . . ." The final clause is found also in Matthew 5:32, which suggests that it is from the Q-source that both Luke and Matthew use for their parenetic passages. But it is missing from both Mark and Paul.

Finally, Luke has Jesus say nothing about the conduct of women, a silence that is curious, since he compiled his Gospel for an audience familiar with and ruled by the Roman law that allowed a wife to either dissolve her marriage in agreement with her husband, or to end the marriage by "repudiating" her husband, not for an audience ruled by the Jewish law that allowed only the divorce of a husband's dismissing his wife. To instruct Christians living under Roman law he even uses the verb *apolúein* employed by the Synoptic tradition to designate this unilateral dismissal of the wife under Jewish law.

Jesus' Instruction in Mark 10:1–12[4]

Mark's version of the Synoptic tradition is set in a seemingly real-life context of dispute between Jesus and a group of Pharisees. Whether this is factual reporting or a useful fiction we have no way of knowing for sure.[5] The dispute itself about divorce is preceded by an introduction of the persons involved in it, Jesus and the Pharisees. Earlier, while in the house at Capernaum (9:33),[6] Jesus had instructed the Twelve concerning children and little ones, treatment of whom he regarded as treatment of himself. But now he left Capernaum in Galilee and traveled eighty miles southward into the territory of Judea and across the Jordan. Once again the crowds come to him and move about with him. And once again, as is his custom, he teaches them. For Jesus is a rabbi—one who teaches. We must understand this characterization of him against the background of the numerous other texts in which Mark presents Jesus to us as an extraordinary Jewish rabbi. Both friends and enemy call him "Rabbi"—Teacher.[7] He teaches in the synagogue (1:2 and 6:2) and in the temple (11:17, 12:35 and 14:49), and he teaches as he moves about (6:7).

And this is the point on which the Pharisees in this narrative come to test him—to find out whether he is an authentic teacher, whether he teaches according to the law of Moses. As in 8:11f and 12:13f—the instances immediately preceding and following this one in which the Pharisees approach him, and the only other passages in which Mark uses the expression "in order to test him" of human agents—here Mark presents the Pharisees as Jesus' adversaries coming with the hidden agendum of catching him in his words. Perhaps they have heard through others that in the matter of Jewish husbands' dismissing their wives Jesus takes a stand disagreeing with the law. So they confront him in order to find out about this disagreement first-hand.[8] And they are confident that when they do, they can show that he contradicts Moses. Once they do this, they can discredit him in the eyes of the people, who have already accepted him as a teacher who, unlike the Pharisees, "teaches new things—and with power and authority" (1:27). But Jesus will show them that the contrary is true, that Moses' command about a man's dismissing his wife clashes with what God has demanded from the beginning of creation about the relationship of man and wife.

In this Marcan version of the Synoptic tradition Jesus' words have first a double and heterogeneous audience, then afterward a single and homogeneous one. That is, Mark has Jesus first make his point in the dispute with the Pharisees, while his disciples listen. Later, when he is alone with the latter, and probably at their troubled request, he makes his instruction more exact: "Back in the house again the disciples began to question him about this. He told them . . ." (10:10–11). Thus, as far as Jesus' own intent is concerned—that is, his intent apart from the range of relevance in his words themselves—Mark has it aimed first at the Pharisees and through them at the Jewish people generally. He then, in the second conversation, has Jesus direct his intent at his disciples (and through them also at the Jewish people?). And because Mark is repeating Jesus' words thirty-five years after they were first spoken, he judges them applicable to the Christian community for which he compiled his Gospel, the community in Rome. If we did not otherwise know the intended readers of his Gospel, we could guess that they were not Palestinian Jews living under the law of Moses, but a community outside Palestine, of mixed Jewish and Gentile ethnic stocks, and living under Roman law while uncertain as to how firmly they were bound by the law of Moses contained in the Sacred Scriptures they accepted as their own. For Mark has Jesus, in verse 12, forbid a wife's dismissing her husband—a proscription meaningless for a Palestinian Jewish audience, since the law of Moses had no provision for a wife's doing this, nor did rabbinic jurisprudence at this time. (So it is obvious that Mark, along with Luke—and with Matthew and with Paul in 1 Corinthians 7, as we shall see—felt free to revise Jesus' words and interpolate in them. Verse 12 contains merely the most obvious of Mark's interpolations.)

The Pharisees begin their challenge with the abrupt question in verse 2: "Is a husband permitted to dismiss his wife?" (The infinitive in Mark's Greek is *apolúein,* as in Luke's.[9] It designates simply and accurately the Jewish divorce procedure of Jesus' time.)

In verse 3 Jesus answers the Pharisees in a fashion just as blunt as their own, but by putting a question to them: "What did Moses command you?" The supposition in his choice of verb here must have irritated the Pharisees because it challenged a supposition of their own. Their reaction to this challenge appears in their reply to Jesus' question in verse 4. They correct him, for they insist that Moses did not *command* them but ". . . Moses *permitted* a man to write a writ of dismissal and to dismiss her."

But Jesus comes back at them insistently (in verse 5): "Because of your hardness of heart he wrote that *command* for you." Jesus' religious logic here, though so familiar to the Jews of his own time and earlier, is strange to the Western religious mind. In Jesus' eyes the legal warrant for a man's getting rid of his wife is a command set down by Moses which obligates Jewish husbands to disobey God's law—but obligates them only because of their already fixed hardness of heart. This is a prophetic interpretation proportioned to one kind of significant moment in the history of the people Israel. They had again and again been faithless to the Lord's commands. One of the consequences of this faithlessness was that he had given them "laws that were not good"—not so much as a punishment as to bring them to realize that he is still their Lord. This is Ezekiel's thought in his book of prophecy (20:25) where he speaks in the words of Yahweh who is recalling to the people their history of disobedience: "I gave them laws that were not good, commands they could not bear . . . so that they might realize that I am Yahweh." This faithlessness was at its worst when Moses, on coming down from Sinai with the tablets of the law, found the people adoring the golden calf. Jesus' implication here is that the accepted practice of getting rid of unwanted wives is a continuation of this same spirit of faithlessness, and *because* of it the people were given "a law that was not good." Their hardness of heart drew upon them Moses' command to dismiss their wives. Were they not thus stubborn they would have received neither command nor permission.

The Pharisees challenged Jesus' teaching on its fidelity to the law of Moses, and reductively on its fidelity to God's will. Jesus does not end his counter-challenge by pointing out to them that they have mistaken Moses' command for his concession to their stubbornness, and by pointing out too that the command not only does not come from God, but that it is Moses' command to go on and disobey God's will in a way that their forefathers had already stubbornly decided to do.

Jesus goes beyond this. He pushes his counter-challenge back beyond Moses to God's will itself. In verse 6 he points out to them what they should have known by quoting words from the Book of Genesis that they should not have misunderstood. From the creation poem (Genesis 1:27b) he reminds them: "But from the beginning of creation 'male and female he made them' . . . ." "From the beginning" suggests to the Pharisees that their interpretation of the husband-wife relationship is not what God had originally intended, that their interpretation is an innovation, and an innovation that contravenes God's will for marriage.

". . . male and female he made them": it is God's design that there are the two complementary sexes; therefore marriage is his design and his will has the rightful claim on its conduct.[10]

Once Jesus took the argument back to the Genesis passages his hearers may well have scanned in memory all that these verses had to say about the first man-woman relationship as God had designed it. The motive for his bringing the woman into existence was drawn from the man's need: "The Lord God said, 'It is not good for the man to be alone' " (2:18a). The man had been put in a garden of delights, to keep it and rule over its denizens. But still his life was incomplete, even unhappy. Therefore the Lord God's decision: "I will make a suitable partner for him" (2:18a). (The "helpmate for him" found in so many English translations conveys the meaning poorly, for the Hebrew noun designates literally "someone alongside him," "someone suited to him." The being that the Lord God provides for the man's need that is loneliness is much more his partner than his helper.)

When, according to this parable, the forming of all the other animals had failed to produce the suitable partner, the Lord God "cast a deep sleep on the man, and while he was asleep he took out one of his ribs and closed up its place with flesh. The Lord God then built up into a woman the rib that he had taken from the man" (2:21–22). So it was a being of his own kind that God gave to him because it was not good for him to be alone. But this being was also strikingly different from him, and the difference was sexual. She was a woman.

The man's welcome to her, his verdict on his new partner, was rich in meaning: "This one at last is bone of my bones and flesh of my flesh" (2:23). To understand these words as no more than the man's acknowledgment that the woman is of the same material stuff as himself, or even that she was taken from his own flesh and bone, is to catch the words' least meaning. "Flesh and bone" make up a word-pair appearing more than once in the Old Testament. "Flesh" by itself can mean not only one component of the body, but in a certain context it means bodily and even human frailty. It means "flesh-weakness." Bone can have the meaning of strength and power—"bone-strength." But when combined the two terms signify more than just two realities in juxtaposition. Together they create a new meaning, and a meaning that goes beyond physical power and weakness. Flesh-weakness and bone-strength are antitheses in combination, and the antitheses include not only the two extremes but all degrees between them. They include the full range of a person's character traits, from his weakest to his strongest.

Thus when the man said of the woman that she is "bone of my bones and flesh of my flesh," he meant that she was to share his strength and his weakness and all that lay between them. She was to be his partner in every contingency of life. Theirs was to be a companionship not to be sundered by changing circumstances. It was to be one of constancy, of abiding loyalty.[11]

We can measure the strength of Jesus' argument—both its strength and its weakness—in quoting from Genesis the words "male and female he made them" if we attend to the distinction between two kinds of directives about conduct commonly employed in the Jewish sacred writings. One is the *halakha,* an apodictic law or command that says exactly what must be done or must not be done. The Legal Holiness Code in Leviticus 17—26 contains much halakhic material. The other kind of directive is the *haggadha,* an example of right conduct held out as an ideal, a goal to be striven for. The story of Job's patience under trial is an extended *haggadha.*

Given one shaping or another of a person's moral consciousness, one or the other of these kinds of directives would grip and hold his conduct more effectively. The Pharisees with whom Jesus argues here are teachers of the law. They have been bred to what is specifically legislated or commanded. Consequently they would accept Jesus' quoting God's decision to make the first human beings one man and one woman, one husband and one wife, as only a *haggadha*—a primitive and ideal pairing, but no more than that. They would never see in it the binding force of an unambiguous divine command, such as is obvious in the creation poem (1:28): "Be fertile and multiply; fill the earth and subdue it." (In obedience to this command they readily dismissed wives who were infertile, or with whom they could not "subdue the earth.")[12] The phrase would have no binding force for them unless Jesus extended its meaning to link it with a *halakha.* This Jesus does, and he does it by reaching again into that part of Torah that the Pharisees had overlooked, the Garden parable in Genesis 2.

He quotes, "For this reason a man shall leave father and mother and shall cleave to his wife; and the two shall become one body" (2:24). This is the *halakha,* the law and command following from the divine plan. It is reasonable to presume that Jesus shares the intention of the parable's author at this point. This is to make clear the intimacy and the totality of the first sexual relationship—the model of marriage set by God. The two verbs in the command belong to the language of covenant. They say first that a man shall "abandon" his father and mother (the Hebrew verb is *asav*). He does so in order to enter a new covenant, this one with the woman who is his wife. He joins her; he cleaves to her (the verb is *davaq*, also a covenantal term).

Jesus thus points out to the Pharisees what they had apparently forgotten. To be husband and wife a man and woman enter and live a covenantal commitment to one another. And it is a most precious commitment, more precious than even a man's attachment to and love of his father and mother. For it warrants his "abandoning" them.

In this command Jesus includes the last words of the Yahwist author's comment in the parable: ". . . and the two of them become one body." The reference here is not primarily to sexual union, although this is implied and intended. "Body" here designates a person's nature in its mortality and frailty. By extension it designates also a person's human identity. So in repeating this, the Yahwist's final comment on the man-woman union, Jesus reminds the Pharisees that according to God's will a man is so joined in marriage to his wife that they become as one person in the law and before the people. With this Jesus implies two things at least. If a man would not think of ruining the less precious relationship with his parents, how then could he think of ruining the more precious relationship with his wife? And if in marrying a man becomes "one body" with his wife, one person in the law and before the people, how could he get rid of his own person? (Paul later voices a kindred thought in Ephesians 5:28–29 when telling the Christian husbands of that community how they ought to love their wives: "In the same way husbands must love their wives as they love their own bodies; for a man to love his wife is for him to love himself. A man never hates his own body, but he feeds it and looks after it . . .")

In verse 9 Jesus ends the argument with the Pharisees by adding his own *halakha*. It is a most unambiguous and emphatic command: "Therefore what God has joined man must not separate." The verbs in the Greek New Testament text carry a powerful weight of meaning ". . . what God has *joined*" is conveyed by *synzeugnúein*, ". . . must not *separate*" by *chorízein*. Here in the active voice these two transitive verbs denote quite simply what is said in the English translation: "to join" and "to separate." Their use gains power by their close affinity to the meaning, in the cultural vocabulary Mark uses, that they gain when they are used in the middle voice: *synzeugnýsthai* then means "to marry"; *chorízethai* means "to separate" from a husband or wife. (Here too is an instance in which the Hebrew verbs took their derivation from the Greek. For "join together" the rabbis of the period used *ziwwegh* or *zawweg*, taken from the Greek *zeugnúein*. While the verbs may mean "join together" in any way, they were also used of God's joining together a husband and wife.[13] And the form *izdawwagh* means "to marry.") What Jesus tells the Pharisees then is equivalently "What God has married into one, man must not divorce." In other words, it is not the husband who is the lord of the marriage, but

God. It is God's authority that has joined him to his wife. Therefore no man, not even the husband, has the authority to separate them, and any pretense at doing so is an attempted arrogation of God's authority. Therefore too it is not the husband's will that keeps him and his wife together, but God's will. The husband stands always under God's judgment in his treatment of his wife.

The Later Conversation with the Disciples, Mark 10:10–12

The dispute with the Pharisees has its sequel and conclusion in a later conversation between Jesus and his disciples alone (verses 10–12): "Back again in the house the disciples asked him about this . . ." Apparently those of the disciples who had overheard his exchange with the Pharisees suspected that what he had said to them had consequences for them. These they would want to know in detail.

It is possible that this second conversation is the useful fiction that some interpreters say Mark uses. For Mark had a special task as a teacher in the Christian community of the second generation for which he compiled his Gospel. Where Jesus' instruction and command had been for an exclusively Jewish audience living under a law that allowed only divorce by the husband's dismissing his wife, Mark's audience (at least the Gentile portion of it) lived under Roman law that allowed the wife too to "repudiate" her husband, as it also allowed both spouses to simply dissolve their marriage by abandoning it, by withdrawing their wills to be married to one another.

If this second conversation is a fiction,[14] what Mark does in it is to have Jesus, with the help of his disciples' questioning, instruct Mark's own Roman audience in detail about the practical consequences for them of his having laid down the law to the Pharisees. One of these consequences is a kind of unintended by-product of Jesus' command. That is, Jesus first explains (in verse 11) that whoever dismisses his wife and marries another commits adultery against the wife. (The verb in the first clause here is the same that had been used in the Greek version of the first conversation, the argument with the Pharisees. It is *apolúein,* the verb chosen almost two centuries earlier by the Septuagint translaters of Torah to designate a husband's dismissing his wife.) With this Mark has Jesus change the definition of adultery for his Jewish followers. Until then a man, married or not, committed adultery only if he had intercourse with another man's wife or another's betrothed. And if a man thus committed adultery, it was an offense not against his own wife but against the other husband or fiancé. His adultery was not infidelity to his own wife but a violation of the other man's exclusive right to his wife's or his fiancée's sexual acts—a trespass on his property. (If the husband's intercourse outside his marriage was with a woman unmarried or unbetrothed, this was not adultery. But a wife's intercourse with any man other than her husband, married or not, was adultery—a violation of her husband's exclusive right to her sexual acts.) But now according to Jesus a husband's dismissing his wife and marrying another woman is adultery against his wife, infidelity to her, a violation of their covenantal relationship.[15]

Jesus' concluding words, in verse 12, are almost certainly Mark's interpolation. He has Jesus say, "And if she dismisses her husband and marries another, she commits adultery." The verb in the conditional clause, *apolúein*, is identical with the verb referring in verse 11 to the husband's conduct—the unilateral dismissing of the spouse. Such an instruction to Jews whose law, at least in Jesus' time, never conceived of a wife's dismissing her husband is unrealistic. But it is not at all unrealistic in the socio-historical setting, the Christian community in Rome, for which tradition says Mark compiled his Gospel.

One may construe the Roman law of divorce in two distinct but closely related ways. In addition to the dissolution of marriage by the bilateral withdrawal of the spouses' wills to be married to one another, one may say that the law allowed either spouse to end the marriage by "repudiating" the other. Or one may say that while neither could dismiss the other, either could end the marriage by unilaterally withdrawing from it. (We shall examine this law more closely in the next chapter. And in that chapter we shall see how Paul's instruction to the Corinthian Christians on divorce reckons with the difference between Jewish and Roman divorce law.)

Mark's choice of *apolúein* to designate the kind of divorce Jesus forbids to both husbands and wives suggests that if he is adapting Jesus' instruction to Christians living under Roman law, he is construing this law to allow either spouse to dismiss the other. In any case Mark seems to have felt free to write these lines for Jesus to speak, confident that he knew what he would have said had he addressed the situation of his followers living under Roman law.

But all this still leaves a residual question, an important one. If Mark has Jesus forbid the ending of marriage by dismissal of the spouse (or the ending of it by unilateral abandonment of the spouse), does he also have Jesus forbid the other dissolution that Roman law allowed, the bilateral withdrawal of the will to be married to one another? It is strange that Mark seems not to have attended to this in a purported instruction of Jesus that he invented precisely in order to apply his teaching to the marriages of Christians living under Roman law. Or did Mark think this form of dissolution sufficiently proscribed by Jesus' command closing the first conversation, "What God has joined man must not separate"? And did he think this because he trusted that his use of the verb used conventionally in Roman law to designate this dissolution, *chorízein,* would take care of the matter? It is not unreasonable for us to share the Roman Christians' curiosity, and perhaps perplexity, on this point now nineteen centuries later.[16]

Jesus' Instruction in Matthew 5:31–32

As I have already pointed out, the Gospel according to Matthew has two versions of Jesus' instruction on divorce and remarriage, the first and shorter version a more or less independent logion within the Sermon on the Mount (5:31–32), the second and longer a narrative, as in Mark, of Jesus' confrontation with a group of Pharisees (19:1–12).

In its setting the Sermon version is the fifth in a series of logia of Jesus. Like it these are brief, complete as independent units of catechetical instruction, meant to convey the core of Jesus' moral teaching on discrete points of conduct. We are familiar with the series: "You are the salt of the earth . . ." (5:13–16); "Do not think that I have come to abolish the law or the prophets . . ." (5:17–20): "You have heard that it was said to our ancestors, 'You shall not kill . . .' But I say to you . . ." (5:21–26); "You have heard that it was said, 'You shall not commit adultery . . .' But I say to you . . ." (5:27–30). The last two take the form of the "Not only that, but even more . . ." antithesis that Jesus sets between the tradition his hearers have learned and the new morality that he teaches them.

Matthew's shorter version of Jesus' instruction on divorce and marriage takes the latter form:

> 31. It was also said, "Whoever dismisses his wife must give her a writ of dismissal." 32. But I say to you, whoever dismisses his wife, except in the case of her *pornéia,* makes her to commit adultery; and whoever marries a woman who has been dismissed, he commits adultery.

The passage is similar enough to Luke's to suggest with reason that both were taken from a single source. Since they are too dissimilar from Mark in their agreed similarity, it is most unlikely that either borrowed from him. It is far more likely that both borrowed from the Q-source. In both content and style their passages are Q-source material. Yet their significant similarities are only two: both use the verb *apolúein* to designate the kind of divorce that Jesus says leads to adultery. And they have perfectly synonymous final clauses: ". . . and whoever marries a woman who has been dismissed, he commits adultery."

Their differences within such brevity, and despite their sharing the same ruling intent, are striking. Luke does not have Jesus recall that the law of Moses obliges a husband dismissing his wife to give her the writ of dismissal. His Gentile audience, being unfamiliar with this point of law and the practice, would be confused by its mention. Where Luke has Jesus say the adulterous consequence of a man's dismissing his wife is that he commits adultery if he remarries, Matthew has Jesus name the adulterous consequence that by dismissing his wife the husband makes *her* an adulteress.[17] Therefore, reading both versions strictly, Luke does not have Jesus say that there is anything wrong in a man's merely dismissing his wife, whereas Matthew does. Finally, Matthew has Jesus include the exceptive phrase, "except in the case of her *pornéia,*" whereas Luke does not.

Finally it is to be noted that the two passages picture Jesus speaking to homogeneous, if not identical, audiences. In Luke the audience is those of Jesus' disciples who walk with him on the journey from Galilee to Jerusalem. In Matthew it is those of his disciples who go out with him to the mountainside in Galilee and listen to his instruction. In either case the identifying of the audience is artificial. This identity is significant only in the audience's role in each instance as representative of all those for whom Luke and Matthew thought Jesus intended his teaching on divorce and remarriage.

The Version in Matthew 19:1–12

The grand outline of Matthew's narrative version of Jesus' instruction is similar to that of Mark's version. The similarity is most probably an effect of Matthew's having borrowed the narrative from Mark. Thus in Matthew as in Mark a group of Pharisees come to Jesus to put him to the test; he responds by putting them to the test. They appeal against him to Moses; he corrects their interpretation of Moses and goes back beyond Moses to what God had established in the beginning. He ends the dispute with his own terse statement. In a second conversation alone with his disciples he explains his statement in more exact detail.

But within this similarity there are significant differences. In consideration of his own readers, to meet their needs and answer their questions, Matthew takes liberties with his borrowed material. To begin with, the point on which the Pharisees put Jesus to the test is not, as in Mark, his authenticity as a teacher, nor his fidelity to the law of Moses in the matter of divorce and remarriage. According to Matthew they come to force him, if possible, to commit himself to one side or other of a dispute current among the rabbis, and to a lesser degree among the people. Apparently they hope that whichever side he chooses, Jesus will alienate and lose the adherents of the other. This dispute we examined in the preceding chapter. It was going on between the disciples of two great rabbis of the generation preceding Jesus' own, Hillel and Shammai. We recall that the two had disagreed on and debated the meaning of a crucial term in Deuteronomy 24:1, the passage in Torah that served as source and principle for Jewish divorce legislation:

> 1. When a man, after marrying a woman and having relations with her, is later displeased with her because he finds in her something indecent, and therefore he writes out a bill of divorce and hands it to her, thus dismissing her from his house . . .

Hillel and Shammai had disagreed first of all on the referent of the term "something indecent" (*erwat dabar* in Torah; *pornéia* in the Greek of the Septuagint translation of Torah and of the Synoptic passages we are examining). They disagreed also over the conjunction or the disjunction of the husband's subjective displeasure with the wife's objective *erwat dabar*. For the former's displeasure to warrant his dismissing the wife need it be warranted in turn by the indecency in the wife? Or could his displeasure justify the dismissal apart from any warrant by the indecency?

Shammai had been restrictive in his interpretation and, by comparison, benign to the wife. The husband's displeasure must be warranted by *erwat dabar* in the wife, and this term referred only to proved adultery on her part, or some conduct equivalently delinquent. Hillel had been concessive and, by comparison, hard on the wife. He had insisted that the husband's displeasure is separable from any objective indecency in the wife, and that this indecency could include numerous kinds of conduct, from her adultery to her unsatisfactory meals.

Matthew's formulation (in verse 3) of the Pharisees' opening question to Jesus shows the thrust of their testing: "Is a man permitted to dismiss his wife for just any reason?" This formulation may have been inspired by their already acquired awareness that on other points Jesus relaxed the rigorous demands of the law where he saw a need to do so. Now they would turn this liberality to his disadvantage; they would see if he were willing to accept the consequences of adopting publicly one side of a widespread debate. They also ground their question to him in a blind assumption that Jesus' reply will challenge. They assume that the burning question about divorce asks which are the legally admissible grounds for husbands' dismissing their wives. At least apparently Jesus will point out to them that the question burns on quite other grounds—may husbands dismiss their wives at all?

A second notable difference in the two narratives is this, that where Mark had Jesus reply immediately "What did Moses command you?" to the Pharisees' opening question, and only later direct their attention to what God had established in the beginning, Matthew has him reply to their opening question by going back immediately to what God had established in the beginning. That is, Matthew has Jesus take the question away from Deuteronomy, from Hillel and Shammai, and relocate it at the beginning of Genesis where God's initial will about husbands and wives had been revealed:

> 4. He said in reply, "Don't you know that he who created them in the beginning 'made them male and female'? 5. And he said, 'For this reason a man will leave his father and his mother and will cling to his wife, and the two shall become one body.' 6. So they are no longer two, but one body. Therefore what God has joined man must not separate."

All that this primitive divine constitution for husband and wife had meant in Mark is meant here too: God is the Creator of the complementary sexes and therefore the Creator of marriage; indeed the very creating of the two distinct sexes was so that they might unite as one. Any marriage goes on under God's authority, not men's. His marriage is a relationship more precious to a man than his filial tie to his father and mother—which he would never think of rejecting. By marrying he becomes one person with his wife before the people and in the law, so how could he think of dismissing his own person?

What all this leads to morally and legally Jesus gathers into his own terse command: "Therefore what God has joined man must not separate." No man may think that he can undo God's work. In fine, if we combine what Matthew records of Jesus' instruction with what is in Mark, we find Jesus virtually redefining marriage for his hearers. For them it is a relationship mainly for the happiness and convenience of the husband, and can be manipulated for his one-sided advantage. Jesus denies this and insists instead that it is a union designed by God for the happiness of women as well as of men.

Matthew's reversal of sequence from that in Mark's narrative continues. Now after Jesus has appealed to a higher authority, and has interpreted it to them, the Pharisees riposte by citing Moses (verse 7): "They said to him, 'Why then did Moses command to give the writ of dismissal and so dismiss her'?" In Mark's version the Pharisees said that Moses permitted them to dismiss their wives; here Matthew has them say, in defense of their conduct, that they are obeying Moses' *command,* implying virtuous obedience on their part. Then, as in Mark, here too Jesus corrects their choice of verb, but in doing so reverses the choice of verbs recorded by Mark: no, they do not have the excuse of Moses' command. Rather (verse 8) "He said to them, 'Because of your hardness of heart Moses *permitted* you to dismiss your wives.' " And he reminds them again of the authority greater than Moses: "But in the beginning it was not so."

Finally (in verse 9) Jesus brings his instruction to its most exact focus. Speaking on his own authority he says flatly, "I say to you that whoever dismisses his wife, except for her *pornéia,* and marries another commits adultery."

As Matthew records the conversation with the Pharisees, this statement of Jesus ends it.[18] But within this closing statement is the exceptive clause, the discovery of whose meaning has been so notoriously difficult down through the centuries since it first appeared in the Gospel tradition. However for the purpose of good tactical handling, our first question asks not about the meaning of the clause, but about its authenticity. Neither Mark nor Luke has it or any camouflaged form of it. So did Jesus utter the phrase but they and Paul omitted it for whatever reason? Or did Jesus not utter it, but Matthew invented it and interpolated it in Jesus' discourse for his own reason? Scholarly finding now tends strongly to the conclusion that the latter is the genesis of the phrase.[19] Then, assuming the accuracy of this finding, one must wonder about Matthew's motive for inventing the phrase for Jesus to speak.

The most reasonable explanation of this motive I have come upon is grounded in the ethnic-religious makeup of the Christian community for which Matthew compiled his Gospel. From overwhelming evidence internal to the document this community must have had extensive knowledge of the Jewish Scriptures, of Jewish social and religious customs, of the traditions of the fathers, of rabbinic teaching and Jewish law. Its problems, questions and preoccupations were most characteristically Jewish. In short, the great majority of this community must have consisted of converts to Christian discipleship who had remained Jewish in every sense I have suggested above. Therefore their concerns about divorce and remarriage were Jewish, and some of these concerns were not shared by the communities for whom Mark, Luke and Paul wrote. (This concurs with a tradition about the Matthean Gospel that it was compiled for a mainly Jewish, second-generation Christian community in Syria, possibly in Antioch itself.)

Being Jewish-Christian this community would know of and have lived by, and perhaps be still living by, the divorce legislation of Deuteronomy. It would probably have alive within itself the disagreement over the referent of the *erwat dabar* of the Deuteronomic passage, and would even have inherited in some strength the Hillel-Shammai debate. The members of this community would have asked Matthew, the rememberer and sharer of Jesus' teaching, what the Lord had had to say, if anything, about the disagreement. If Matthew did not in fact know whether Jesus had said anything on the subject, he nevertheless would feel free to include in his Gospel what he thought Jesus would have said. Or perhaps he had learned some other authoritative persons' opinion on what Jesus would have said. But in any case he represents his opinion as Jesus' own judgment.

In any case also, his opinion of Jesus' judgment is a clear attenuation of what appears Jesus' own unexceptionable command, "Therefore what God has joined man must not separate." In historical sequence his attenuation was not the first (Paul's attenuation had preceded his by a decade, as we shall see), nor was it to be the last. But where Paul's justification for attenuating was the departure (by civil divorce according to Roman law?) of an unbelieving spouse, Matthew's was a woman's coming to her marriage with the moral-legal disability of "something indecent," or her incurring this indecency in the course of her marriage.

The Meaning of Matthew's Exceptive Clause

What then is more probably the meaning of this exceptive clause, quoted above, of the *pornéia* whose presence in the wife Matthew has Jesus admit justifies her husband's dismissing her, and keeps him from sending her into adultery if he does so (5:32), and from committing adultery if he remarries after doing so (19:9), and from committing adultery if he marries a woman who has been dismissed because of it (5:32)?[20]

One interpretation says that *pornéia* in both of the exceptive clauses designates a legal disability in the woman denoted in rabbinic vocabulary by the *erwat dabar* of Deuteronomy 24:1. Rabbinic teaching, following Torah, recognized multiple kinds of legal disability or uncleanness for marriage: sexual impotence, Gentile parentage, infertility, consanguinity or affinity within a forbidden degree, slave status of the girl's father at the time of the wedding. The Book of Leviticus, chapter 18, is the source in Torah of legal judgments on these cases. In the New Testament there are different examples in 1 Corinthians 5 and in the Acts of the Apostles 15:20–29. The vocabulary of Catholic marriage law would call these disabilities invalidating impediments or conditions. In rabbinic interpretation they were not causes of the invalidity of the union, but were grounds for the legitimate dissolving of it.

Jews coming into the Christian community brought this rabbinic tradition with them. They would want to know if it still held, and would want to know this from the words of Jesus. An interpretation within this interpretation says that the first converts wanting to know this were Jesus' own disciples, and that they put the question to Jesus himself. Obviously this interpretation supposes that the Matthean author did not invent the exceptive phrase, but that Mark and Luke omitted it because their readers were Jewish converts only in the minority, whereas Matthew kept it because his readers were almost all Jewish converts to Christian discipleship.

The interpretation continues that after rejecting both Hillel's and Shammai's grounds for dismissing a wife validly married, Jesus acknowledges the rabbinic tradition in favor of dissolving unions that were in fact not marriages, that were invalid because of one or more of the "impediments" mentioned above.

The interpretation has this weakness, that immediately after Jesus' statement including the exceptive clause in Matthew 19, his disciples react in alarm by retorting, "If this is the way it is with a man and wife it is better not to marry." The reaction is unrealistically anxious if Jesus has accepted the tradition of the rabbis about dismissing a wife for any of the many kinds of disabilities this tradition recognized. It allowed a husband stuck with an unwanted wife sufficient escape routes from her. He need not have felt as trapped as the disciples seem to have felt. This inconsistency in the narrative suggests that the exceptive clause does not refer to invalid unions or validly dissoluble unions, but to something found rarely in a wife. Or the inconsistency suggests that the conversation as we read it synthesizes statements made at various times and in various places by Jesus, his disciples and the Pharisees. If the latter is true, then in the passage we have Matthew's quite free interpretation, not a record of Jesus' teachings.

Van Tilborg suggests an interpretation of the exceptive clause that favors its exclusively Matthean authorship and also accounts more reasonably for the alarmed reaction of the disciples even if one takes this reaction as no more than a part of the fictional narrative setting invented by

Matthew.[21] Van Tilborg says that the clause is more understandable if we interpret it in the light of Matthew 1:18–19. There Joseph is said to contemplate dismissing Mary because he has found her pregnant even before they come together in marriage. In Jesus' time a girl who was not a virgin when coming to her first marriage could no longer be stoned to death as Torah provided (Deuteronomy 22:20–21). Yet it was the custom, when the bride was neither a widow nor a divorced woman, for the marriage to take place on the fourth day of the week, so that if the husband found her not a virgin, he could accuse her before the court, which held session only on the fifth day.

According to this interpretation the exceptive clause would mean that a man who dismisses his wife and marries another commits adultery except in the case where he has found a first wife not a virgin. In this case he has the right to dismiss her and to remarry. This would be the understanding in the mainly Jewish Christian community for which the Matthean editor compiled his Gospel, a community familiar with the story of Joseph and Mary. And this would account as well for the reaction of Jesus' male hearers in the narrative. Since Jewish girls ordinarily married at twelve or thirteen years, after a childhood guarded carefully by their parents, coming to marriage without their virginity was a rare enough occurrence. The escape routes for unhappy husbands would be proportionately rare.

If this interpretation of the exceptive phrase is the accurate one, it suggests even more strongly that the phrase did not originate with Jesus. For while it has exegetical strength as an interpretation of *Matthew's* meaning, it is religiously and morally weak as an interpretation of Jesus' mind. According to it Matthew asks his readers to believe that in Jesus' mind the new husband's acceptable reaction to his bride's coming to their marriage not a virgin is to get rid of her by formal divorce. This is wholly inconsistent with Jesus' instructions concerning forgiveness—concerning forgiveness in place of the law's imperatives and permissions. It is also inconsistent with Jesus' insistence elsewhere that among his followers men and women be treated with an equal morality.

Yet a third interpretation says that *pornéia* designates an incestuous union that may and must be ended. A subvariant of this interpretation is proposed by Joseph Fitzmyer in his essay I have already cited. His case is the following.[22] The Damascus document, an Essene text first discovered at the end of the last century, contains a passage (in CD 2:14—6:1) consisting of an exhortation to Palestinian Jews not members of the Essene community. Using the device of God's speaking in the first person it criticizes the moral conduct of these Jews. One of the kinds of conduct criticized is their unchastity, their *zenut*. And two examples of this are singled out: the taking of two wives during a lifetime, whether by polygamy or by divorce and remarriage (which contravenes Torah in Genesis 1:27 and 7:9), and the practice of taking nieces and nephews in marriage (against Torah in Leviticus 18:13). Thus the Essenes who produced the

Damascus document linked polygamy, divorce and incestuous marriage under the one condemnation as *zenut*. Fitzmyer's tentative conclusion is that designating *pornéia* as the one cause justifying a Jewish husband's dismissing his wife and remarrying points to such an incestuous marriage as was condemned in the Essene document. (Whether such a union was valid, or whether it was valid but illicit, is not explained in any of the interpretations I have come upon. If the latter is supposed, then Matthew concedes to human authority, in this case to the husband's, the competence to dissolve true marriages.)

This interpretation, like the others outlined here, must remain tentative despite its obvious strength. Its accuracy depends on an historical fact that will be difficult to verify. It is most probable that the exceptive clause is a second-generation addition to the Synoptic tradition made by the Matthean editor himself. The best evidence sees him as a non-Palestinian Jew working outside Palestine to instruct a Christian-Jewish community. How likely would he have known of a Palestinian document whose circulation was relatively limited?

Let us suppose too that the Jews-become-Christians of Matthew's non-Palestinian community did accept the marriages that the Damascus document deemed incestuous. This interpretation must suppose that Matthew had an initial animus against such unions to motivate him to use the Essene condemnation against them in the first place. And, finally, there is no other evidence that the Christian communities of the first and second generations forbade to Jewish converts marriages that their customs allowed them. It is true that Roman law generally forbade the marriages of first cousins. But it is to be proved that Roman law on this matter obliged Jewish converts to Christianity, or that it obliged them in Syria, where the Matthean Gospel was most probably compiled.

A fourth interpretation has it that Jesus goes along with Deuteronomy 24:1 and with rabbinic tradition in allowing a man to dismiss a wife who has committed adultery. Thus far this interpretation has Jesus agree with Rabbi Shammai. But it has him differ from Shammai in saying that the husband may not remarry after the dismissal, and that if he should attempt to do so, he would commit adultery. In this case the separation would not be a true dissolution, since a man once again single after dismissing his wife would commit adultery only if he sought to marry a woman who had been dismissed invalidly. The interpretation accounts reasonably for the disciples' alarm following Jesus' statement.

But the same weakness appears in this interpretation that was found in the second: it asks the reader to accept that Jesus recommends, or at least allows, that the appropriate conduct for a man finding his wife in adultery is to dismiss her out of hand. Even if one should find this acceptable in the face of Jesus' repeated instruction on forbearance and forgiveness, it fails to explain his silence in this passage on the prerogative or the obligation of wives whose husbands have been found in adultery. Beneath and behind all these interpretations is the clear evidence of Jesus' insistence on fairness, on equal responsibility for husbands and wives. That there is nothing from him in this passage about the conduct of a wife with an adulterous husband would argue again that the exceptive clause comes not from Jesus but from Matthew himself.

What of the interpretation that has gained the widest acceptance, not only in numbers but in its acceptance for centuries, that *pornéia* designates the wife's adultery justifying her husband's dismissing her and remarrying? This is the interpretation that was adopted by the Christian Roman rulers at least until the crumbling of the empire in the West. It is the interpretation that was taken by the rulers of the surviving Eastern Catholic empire, and remains the official interpretation of the Eastern Catholic churches to this day. It is also the interpretation accepted in the majority of the Protestant churches.

The following points of evidence are against admitting that at least in Jesus' mind *pornéia* would designate the wife's adultery as the misconduct establishing the one justification for her husband's dismissing her and remarrying.

First, the tone and the sequence of Matthew's version of the dispute with the Pharisees has Jesus refusing to take sides with the followers of either Hillel or Shammai, and refusing even to grant that a choice between the two rabbis' interpretations of Deuteronomy is a significant issue. But if the one exceptional justifying ground were the wife's adultery, Jesus would be presented inconsistently as siding with Shammai.

If the clause is Matthew's interpolation made in order to answer a question put to him by his second-generation Christian audience, and if *pornéia* in *his* mind designates the wife's adultery, then his interpretation has forced an inconsistency into Jesus' thought. It is also an obvious attenuation of what he had Jesus say in verse 6: "Therefore what God has joined man must not separate."

Evidence against even Matthew's intending *pornéia* to designate the wife's adultery is found in this, that in the vocabulary of his Gospel he has both a noun for "adultery" and a verb for "commit adultery." They are *moichéia* and *moichéuein*. The verb is there in the principal clause of 19:9 to designate what a husband does who remarries after dismissing his wife (except in the event of her *pornéia*). He uses the same verb in conveying Jesus' teaching about adultery in 5:27–30 and in his instruction on divorce and remarriage in 5:31–32. Presumably he would have used the same noun or the same verb in the exceptive phrase in 19:9 if he had intended, or had understood that Jesus had intended, that it is the wife's adultery that justifies her husband's dismissing her and remarrying. The only escape from this presumption is that Matthew chose *pornéia* as a catch-all designation of the wife's sexual misconduct in marriage, including her adultery. But if this were the case, then the disciples' consternation at having only a rarely found escape route from an unwanted marriage is poorly accounted for.

It is worth noting again a third time that dismissal and final abandonment as the conduct of a husband against his adulterous wife are inconsistent with the forgiveness that Jesus made such a general and persistent demand on the conduct of his followers. The one-sidedness of granting this prerogative only to the husband against the adulterous wife is doubly inconsistent with the Jesus we meet elsewhere in the Gospel.

A sixth and, for our purposes, a final interpretation draws on Jesus' response to the disciples' shocked reaction in verse 10: "If this is the way it is with a man and wife, it is better not to marry." This reaction and response, and Jesus' counter-response, make up Matthew's version of the second and later conversation alone with the disciples that in the Markan version is set off more clearly. But like Mark's version of the second conversation it is devised in order to offer Jesus (or just as likely Matthew himself) a chance to explain a point that would be wasted on the hostile Pharisees but is most necessary for those intending to be Jesus' followers.

Jesus acknowledges and in a way agrees with his disciples' consternation. His instruction indeed put a severe demand on husbands, a demand too severe for many. For he says (verse 11), "Not everyone can accept this teaching . . ." If not everyone, then who can? The answer in turn to this suggests just how severe the demand is. No one can accept it on his own strength, ". . . but only those to whom it is given." Whatever the substance of the demand, it is one that a man can meet only with help given him by God, only with God's enabling grace.

What this humanly insupportable demand is will be intelligibile if we can find out the meaning of the term "eunuch" in the Jewish tradition in which Jesus lived, especially the meaning as a rabbi would understand and intend it. For one of the effects of Jesus' demand is to make of the husband a eunuch, and, in the circumstances envisioned by Jesus, a eunuch for the Kingdom of God, for the way of life inaugurated by Jesus in obedience to his Father.

In this statement it is little likely that we have Jesus' demand on men who have remained unmarried for the sake of the Kingdom. This is not what "eunuch" means in context, for the context is not a discussion of lifelong celibacy, nor is the disciples' anxiety about such a celibacy. They are anxious about what Jesus says they must accept after a marriage has failed in some way. In fact the word "eunuch" in the rabbinic vocabulary of Jesus' time simply did not refer to a man's being married or not. It referred more properly to his inability to have children, and it did not distinguish carefully between his infertility and his wife's. It referred in fact to a man who has been unable to produce children. (In the rabbinic texts the question about the eunuch was not whether he could marry, but, for example in Jebamoth 8:4, 5, 6, whether the wife of a eunuch must accept the stipulation of the Levirate law when he dies—that is, whether she must bear children to her deceased eunuch husband by sexual liaison with his brother, and whether a eunuch himself comes under the stipulation of this law if his married brother dies childless. And never in the rabbinic tradition does "eunuch" refer to a man who is unable to have sexual intercourse.)[23]

We may infer reasonably, then, that whatever *pornéia* means in the exceptive clause allowing a man to dismiss his wife and remarry, it does not include sterility in the wife making *him* a eunuch. If the phrase comes from Jesus himself, in it he informs his followers obliquely that if they would be of his Father's kingdom, they must be willing to be "eunuchs." In effect they must not dismiss their wives because of their inability to give them children, and take another and fertile woman to wife. They must remain with their wives and thus remain childless.[24] For a Jewish husband to hear this, he to whom children were so precious because so substantial to the very meaning of his life, was to take shock indeed. It may really be better for him never to marry with the hope of having sons and daughters, than to do so and then be condemned to having this hope forever frustrated.

If this interpretation is correct, it does not tell us what *pornéia* means. But by an excluding logic it tells us that a most grievous deficiency in a wife, her inability to bear children to her husband, is for Christ's followers not a cause justifying husbands' dismissing such wives. It seems likely too that in this contrived second conversation Matthew has done some conflating. He has used the occasion to bring Jesus' instruction on the treatment of sterile wives from elsewhere in his teaching ministry and here make it share the seriousness of his instruction on divorce and remarriage generally.

In the end, I think, we simply cannot know exactly the meaning of the exceptive clause in these Matthean passages. We can, however, come to the solidly probable conclusion that the phrase is not Jesus' but a device within Matthew's attempt to interpret Jesus' mind. Whatever his success in interpreting it accurately, he did take up the task—to interpret and adapt—that no one who chooses to live by Jesus' words can escape.

NOTES

1. These translations of the New Testament passages are my own from the critical text of *The Greek New Testament,* edited by Kurt Aland, Matthew Black, Bruce M. Metzger and Allen Wikgren, London, 1966. I am especially concerned that the nuances of meaning born of the Palestinian Jewish context of the Synoptic versions be reflected in the translations. For example, using the generic verb "to divorce" (as almost all English-language editions do) to name the way marriages were dissolved in that context is misleading. It fails to capture what the Greek verb of the original text, *apolúein,* denotes, namely the husband's unilateral dismissing of the wife.

2. I have kept this key word in Matthew's Greek just because its meaning for twentieth-century readers is so vague. The several translations of it—for example, "her unchastity," "her uncleanness," "her fornication," even "her adultery"—are

all dubious. To use any of them to the exclusion of the others is therefore misleading. Our uncertainty concerning the meaning Jesus intended for his own words, *erwat dabar,* added to the uncertainty about the meaning the Matthean editor intended in translating Jesus' words by the Greek noun *pornéia,* exemplifies how difficult it is for us to recover exactly what Jesus said—and exactly what he said not only according to the Matthean version but in the Markan and Lucan as well, since neither of these includes the exceptive phrase that Matthew does.

3. This characteristic of the instruction suggests strongly that Luke drew it from the Q-source, the collection of catechetical instruction (whether a written collection or only verbal is still debated) that circulated in the second-generation Christian communities. The existence of this source is held in reasonable hypothesis as part of the explanation of the Synoptic authors' source material. Mark is thought to have drawn only minimally from it, more amply from local traditions available to him, but (according to one theory) mainly from Peter's preaching and teaching. Luke and Matthew are thought to have taken the sequence of their Gospels and much of their narrative material from Mark and from local traditions available to each, but the bulk of their catechetical instruction from the Q-source. Typical Q-source material is what we read in the Sermon on the Mount. (The "Q" is an abbreviation of the German noun "die Quelle," which designates literally "the source.")

4. For this examination of the Markan and Matthean versions of Jesus' instruction I have drawn heavily from J. H. A. van Tilborg's essay, translated in German as "Exegetische Bemerkungen zu den wichtigsten Ehetexten aus dem Neuen Testament," in *Für Eine Neue Kirchliche Eheordnung: Ein Alternatifentwurf,* edited by P. J. M. Huizing, Düsseldorf, 1975 (published originally in Dutch as "Exegetische notities bij de belangrijkste huwelijksteksten uit het Nieuwe Testament," in *Alternateif Kerkelijk Huwelijksrecht,* Antwerp, 1974.

5. Bultmann, for example, thought the debate format a reflection of a later conflict, perhaps in the second Christian generation, between the authorities in one or more Christian communities and rabbinic teachers.

6. The later dubious role of this house in Mark's narrative tells against the latter's factual accuracy. As we shall see, the narrative contains two conversations: Jesus' dispute with the Pharisees and his subsequent explanation to his disciples of what he had said to the Pharisees. The second of these conversations is prefaced by the phrase, "Back in the house . . ." (10:10). If Mark here has in mind the house in Capernaum he had mentioned in 9:33, he supposes that Jesus' explanation had to be delayed the four or five days needed to return the eighty miles northward from Judea to Capernaum. But this narrative problem is voided by the fact that, according to Mark's sequence of events, Jesus did not return to Capernaum at all, but went from the site of this confrontation in Trans-Jordan directly to Jerusalem, where he was arrested, tried and executed. Thus, if the narrative setting of Jesus' instruction on divorce and remarriage is Mark's fiction, he has fitted it into his Gospel carelessly.

7. His disciples in 4:39, 9:38, 10:35, 13:1 and 14:14; the people in 5:35 and 9:17; the rich young man in 10:17–20; the Pharisees and Herodians in 12:14; the Sadducees in 12:19; and the scribes in 12:32.

8. In his essay, "The Matthean Divorce Texts and Some New Palestinian Evidence" (in *Theological Studies* [Vol. 37.2, 1976] pp. 197–226) Joseph Fitzmyer suggests that the point on which the Pharisees test Jesus is whether he adheres to Torah in countenancing dismissal of the wife, or whether he sides with the teaching

of the Qumran Essenes of Judea that forbids divorce to the ideal king, to his prince, and by a fortiori conclusion, to the people. (The text disclosing this Qumranite teaching, and one of the referents of Fr. Fitzmyer's title, is the Temple Scroll, from Qumran Cave XI.)

9. This is also the verb that Matthew uses in the Infancy Narrative of his Gospel (1:19) to designate Joseph's decision to dismiss Mary on finding her pregnant. The verb was used by a few Hellenistic writers to designate the divorce they knew (thus Dionysius of Halicarnassus, a Greek historian of the generation before Jesus, in his *Roman Antiquities,* 2.25.7; and Diodorus Siculus in his *Histori-cal Books,* 12.18,1–2). Where the verb appears in biblical passages composed or translated in Greek, it has one or other of two significations: "to set free, to release, to pardon, to forgive debts"; and "to dismiss, to send away." It is used for divorce by dismissal in 1 Esdras 9:36, in the Septuagint translation of Deuteronomy 24:1, and of course in the Synoptic tradition that we are examining. (See W. F. Arndt and F. W. Gingrich, *A Greek-English Lexicon of the New Testament and Other Early Christian Literature,* Cambridge and Chicago, 1957, pp. 95–96.) As we shall see, Paul also uses the verb *aphiénai* in 1 Corinthians 7 along with *chorízein* to designate divorce. The kinds of divorce to which these two verbs refer must be found from both the literary and the socio-historical context of his letter.

10. David Daube, in his *The New Testament and Rabbinic Judaism* (New York, 1973), pp. 72ff, argues that this verse presupposes and contains the rabbinic tradition that the first human being was androgynous, and created so by God. The evidence adduced for this was that the Hebrew text of Genesis 1:26–27 wavers between the singular and the plural when speaking of the first man and woman: "God created man in his image, in the divine image he created him; male and female he made them." The rabbis' conclusion from this was that only of an androgynous human being could one speak in both the singular and the plural after naming both genders. The tradition came too from the effort to reconcile two passages in Genesis: ". . . male and female he made them" (1:27); and the Garden parable's information that God formed the first woman from the flesh of the first man (2:18ff). If the woman was taken from the man, he must have first contained womanness in himself. This male-femaleness of the first human being echoes the myth of the androgyne proposed in Plato's *Symposium* (189C ff), and is perhaps drawn from the rabbis' acquaintance with this dialogue. The tradition implies that the intimate, even ontological oneness of the man and the woman is God's intent, the ideal he proposes, the goal he urges, the very meaning of marriage. Divorce, then, frustrates God's intent, blocks the realizing of the ideal and the attaining of the goal.

11. Walter Brueggemann has developed this meaning in his essay "Of the Same Flesh and Bone," in *The Catholic Biblical Quarterly,* Vol. 32.4 (1970), pp. 532–542.

12. The nature and the uses of the *halakha* and the *haggadha* are explained in Daube, *op. cit.,* pp. 72–79.

13. Daube, *op. cit.,* p. 368.

14. Fiction or not, this is not the only passage in his Gospel in which Mark reports such a sequel conversation. He does so in 4:10–34 (the sequel-explanation of Jesus' first parables), in 7:17 (the same kind of explanation of Jesus' earlier instructions about things clean and unclean), and in 9:28–33 (his explanation to his disciples of their inability to exorcise effectively the demoniac child).

15. Some interpreters question the authenticity of the words "against her" in

Jesus' statement. They suggest that Mark interpolated it, for neither Luke nor Matthew has it in his version of the same logion. If this second conversation is a fiction, of course, the question of authenticity arises only on the assumption that for the fiction Mark borrowed words that Jesus had actually spoken.

16. Van Tilborg (*op. cit.,* p. 14) suggests another troubling consequence of the crossover of Jesus' instruction from Jewish law to Roman. Since Jewish law, from which Jesus did not exempt his followers, allowed a husband multiple wives, the husband (according to Jesus' instruction read literally and strictly) did not commit adultery against his first wife, was not unfaithful to her, by taking a second wife provided he did not dismiss the first. But this law allowed the wife no such latitude; it did not make polyandry available to her.

But Roman law allowed not even polygyny. So Christian husbands living under Roman law would commit adultery if, even while keeping a first wife, they were to attempt marriage with a second.

That Jesus would leave an opening for this inequality and unfairness in his instruction (unfairness not to the Roman husbands but to the Palestinian Christian wives!) is inconsistent with his obvious attempt to end such institutionalized injustice. So one is left wondering how possible it was for Mark to pass on Jesus' instruction at all authentically. Perhaps he thought he resolved the inconsistency very simply by recording Jesus' citation of Torah, "And the *two* [not three or more] shall become one body."

17. The point of fact latent in Matthew's version of the adulterous consequence may be elusive to the twentieth-century student. Why would a husband's dismissing his wife make her an adulteress? The seemingly most obvious answer may be found in the options available to a dismissed Jewish wife in Jesus' time. None of them was attractive. She could become someone's servant (and therefore equivalently a slave). She could return to her father's house, or to a brother's house if her father were dead, and live there in awkward semi-widowhood. Or she could become a prostitute (and commit the adultery Jesus warns against?). If this is what Matthew has Jesus mean, then he has him say also that this sad consequence to the wife of her husband's dismissing her is cancelled if he dismisses her because of her *pornéia,* whatever this sexual misconduct may be. Not that her husband does not similarly drive her into the *conduct* of a prostitute, but because her *pornéia* during the marriage somehow keeps his dismissing her from turning her into a prostitute despite her descending into the conduct of one. In short, she had already become one.

This interpretation is a strained one. But it has been advanced as an element of the explanation of the wife's *pornéia* during marriage, that it designates her adultery. Perhaps the more accurate modern conjecture is a far simpler one: Jesus acknowledges what actually goes on among his people, that in many or even most cases dismissed wives remarry, and do so because it is the least painful option available to them. But he considers their second marriages adulterous; and the husbands who dismiss these wives are substantial cooperators in their subsequent adultery.

Or the simplest explanation of all may be that the clause ". . . he makes her to commit adultery" is not Jesus' to begin with, but Matthew's interpolation. Of the four Synoptic versions of Jesus' instruction, only Matthew 5:31 has it. Not even his own narrative version in Chapter 19 has it.

18. This last logion is identical, as far as it goes, with the version of it in the Sermon on the Mount. But it omits the second and balancing clause found in the

Sermon instruction: ". . . and whoever marries a woman who has been dismissed, he commits adultery."

19. The two most telling reasons for concluding that Matthew invented and added the phrase are, first, that it is missing from both Mark and Luke, and Paul takes no notice of the exception proposed in it. Second, there is Matthew's practice of making his own additions to Jesus' sayings. He adds two extra petitions to the Lord's Prayer in 6:10b, 13b (compare Luke 11:2–4). He adds to the Beatitudes in 5:3a, 6a (compare Luke 6:20b–21). He expands Peter's confession of Christ's messiahship and adds Christ's reply to Peter, in 16:16–19 (compare Mark 8:29). Compare also Matthew 13:12b with Mark 4:25 and Luke 8:18; Matthew 25:29 with Luke 14:26.

20. The word *pornéia* appears, of course, elsewhere in the New Testament. In 1 Corinthians 5:1 it designates incest; in 1 Corinthians 6:13 prostitution or going to a prostitute; in 2 Corinthians, Colossians 3:5 and Ephesians 5:3 lustful conduct generally. In Acts 15:20, 29 it refers apparently to marriage and intercourse with close kin, perhaps within degrees of kindred named in Leviticus 18. Matthew himself uses the term elsewhere only in 15:19, where he names it along with other evil acts such as murder and adultery. Obviously it is a term used with generic reference to any kind of delinquent sexual conduct involving a partner.

21. *Op. cit.,* pp. 17–18.

22. *Loc. cit.,* pp. 213–223.

23. Strack and Billerbeck (in *Deutsches Wörterbuch Zur Neutestamentlichen Wissenschaft Aus Talmud Und Midrasch,* I, 806) cite from the Talmud that a eunuch is like an infertile woman: as she is made infertile by God's hand, so too is he. The misfortune of being a eunuch was precisely this unfruitfulness in marriage.

24. As he does in Mark's version of the encounter with the Pharisees, so here too Jesus challenges the Jewish law seriously. For to teach that a husband must stay with a childless and sterile wife, that he must not dismiss her even after ten years, is in the view of the same Jebamoth (6:6) to oppose the law itself.

4. DIVORCE AND REMARRIAGE IN THE PAULINE TRADITION

What Paul wrote in his First Letter to the Corinthians, Chapter 7, is not a comprehensive teaching about marriage. (This passage was quoted in full in the previous chapter.) If he ever offered such, it has not come down to us. What the passage is in substance is his answers to particular questions put to him in a letter coming from the Christians of Corinth. His letter in answer to them is 1 Corinthians; he wrote it from Ephesus probably in the spring of 57 A.D. Paul himself had founded this Christian community at Corinth, drawing its recruits mainly although not exclusively from the city's synagogue community. Thus his intended readers were a mix of Jews and Gentiles. And the complication brought by this mixture is evident in Paul's instruction where his choice of words suggests his referring to divorce now according to Jewish law, now according to Roman law.

Because of his concern, as an apostle, to teach an over-arching, comprehensive Gospel, Paul's instructions ordinarily took him far beyond local and particular concerns. But this never kept him from writing for a particular situation where he thought this was needed. In so many instances he said and wrote what he did because of questions or problems put to him by particular communities in their particular situations. Sometimes he was able to expand his reply to them beyond the local concern. But sometimes too his way of answering kept him from developing his thought in such a way as to give all the data their fair chance. This is especially true for the concept of marriage that emerges here in his instruction to the Corinthian Christians. As I said just above, it is not comprehensive. It is not his theology of marriage, not even in part. (We must wait until Ephesians 5 for the first elements of that.) It is his ethical judgment on certain attitudes toward marriage thriving among the Corinthian Christians.

Paul's attitude toward marriage must have been conditioned by his own way of life. It was highly mobile. He traveled constantly, was intensely active, working all day, often teaching during the night—preoc-

71

cupied, worried, depressed, exalted, passionately involved with groups of people, loved, hated, in many ways a driven man. He deemed his own way of life incompatible with married life as he knew it in his own culture. In it marriage was not usually entered for reasons of love, since more often than not it was arranged by parents, and in any case was entered for the sake of family and children. Therefore marriage did not ordinarily engage men and women in their most serious desire, at the depth of passion that energized such a life as Paul's. For him, to marry was to let oneself be trapped on the surface and quotidian level of life.

His attitude was conditioned also by a sense of crisis in and for the Christian communities. He saw persecution in their near future, as it had already fallen upon him personally. With most other Christians of his time he expected the early return of the risen Christ and the end of history. Given these suppositions it was consistent for him to advise against such inconsistent conduct as marrying and bringing children into a world that was soon to end. Marriage's one obvious utility was to provide a sinless outlet for sexual urgency for those who could not contain themselves.

In the same vein he reasoned that the present age, the inherited and conventional condition of the human race, had passed away. The Kingdom, the end time, had already arrived; the followers of Jesus had already entered it. But marriage is an institution belonging to the present age. Those who have entered the Kingdom ought to give up things belonging to this age, and give them up for the Kingdom in order to be fully in and of it. This he recommended to the unmarried; he was too much the realist to command it.

1 Corinthians 7:11–24, 39–40

In the sequenced structure of the letter Paul begins his instruction about marriage just after completing in Chapter 6 a clear and emphatic instruction about fornication, about the Corinthian men's going to the city's prostitutes. The motive to which he appealed there against their going to the prostitutes is more nearly an element of a theology of marriage than one finds in his instruction on marriage itself: their bodies are not their own; these belong to the Lord (although a few verses later he will tell both the husbands and the wives of this community that their bodies belong rather to one another than to themselves). More than belonging to the Lord, their bodies are even temples of the Holy Spirit. And Paul tightened the logical noose: a man who has intercourse with a prostitute becomes one body with her, and thus defiles the temple of the Holy Spirit. (The thought, with logic reversed, may resurface in Chapter 7 where he assures Christian spouses married to non-Christians that, far from being defiled by intercourse in such a marriage, they sanctify their spouses thereby.)

It is at this point that he takes up the Corinthians' questions (verse la): "Now, as for what you wrote . . ."

There is nothing in the wording of verse 1b itself to tell us whether it is Paul's own statement or a question he cites from the Corinthians' letter to him. If it is his own statement—"1a. Now, as for what you wrote, 1b. it is good for a man that he not touch a woman"—what follows in this passage is a loose and quite detached sequel to this first point of advice. Here he would begin by proposing an ascetical ideal not only of celibacy but of chastity—advice not only not to marry, but to avoid sexual exchange whether married or not. For the Greek of his statement *gýnaikos mē háptesthai* does not mean "do not touch a woman," but "have no sexual relations with a woman."

But this fits ill, as I have suggested, with his advice that follows immediately. So it is more likely that in verse 1b he is citing the Corinthians' own question back to them in order to answer it. They had heard of an ascetic ideal, possibly from persons of Gnostic tendency in their own community, and had asked about it: "Is it good for a man that he not touch a woman?"

To the question as asked Paul's answer in verses 2 and 3 is negative: no, it is not good. But his reason for so answering is not optimistic: because of *pornéia*—because of temptation to sexual immorality of an unspecified kind, which can come upon women as well as men—let each man have his own wife and each woman her own husband. (And here we recognize the scriptural origin of the later Patristic notion of marriage the vocation of the weak, marriage the *remedium* for concupiscence, the excusable outlet for sexual urgency.)

What follows in verses 4 to 8 are probably not answers to distinct questions but advice that Paul gives on the occasion of, and in order to amplify, his reply to the first question the Corinthians did ask. The advice touches the sexual conduct of husbands and wives. Indirectly but clearly Paul asserts the mutuality and the equality of their status and their rights.

> 4. A wife has not authority over her own body, but her husband has it; just as a husband has not authority over his own body, but his wife has it. 5. Do not deny one another, except by agreement and only for a time in order to be free for prayer; then return again to one another lest Satan put you to the test because of your lack of self-control.

That sexual relations may be the paying of a debt is an idea that has rabbinic orgins. But the idea of equality in sexual rights and obligations is more Stoic than Jewish. The obligation to honor the spouse's right is exactly that—an obligation, not a matter of choice. The reason it is an obligation, to protect one another from being tested beyond strength, makes clear that not only the obligation is shared equally by husband and wife, but so too is a deep and serious dependency. The assertion cf such equality of wife with husband is found nowhere else in the Bible.

Paul gives no reason for his thinking that spouses will be freer for prayer if they abstain from sexual intercourse. He may be passing on to his Corinthian readers a discovery he had made about himself in his own marriage. Or it may be part of the undeniable Stoic inheritance in his education. The thought would be later used richly by the Fathers and its valence universalized: if a man seeks an entire life of prayer, then he must live an entire life without sexual intercourse.

When Paul counsels the spouses to resume normal sexual activity after the short time given to prayer, and gives as his reason that protracted abstinence may test them beyond their moral strength, we have once again the implicit evaluation of married sexuality as a safeguard from sin. We are also a small step closer to the Patristic opinion that, along with the conceiving of a child, serving as such a safeguard is one of the two only excuses for intercourse.

In verse 6 Paul sets a limit on the binding force of what he has just said: It is not a command but a point of advice, his own advice. This is a distinction he makes more than once in the passage. And he makes it again immediately in slightly different words: "What I wish is that all should be as I am." He is at the time without a wife, leading a life of sexual abstinence. As a Pharisaic Jew he had almost certainly been married, but it is clear that throughout his ministry he lived a celibate life (he made the point clear in Chapter 9 of this same letter, verses 5 and 15, that unlike the other apostles he traveled without a "sister"—a word in the early Church designating a Christian wife). We have no way of knowing if, by the time he began his ministry, he was a widower, had divorced his wife according to Jewish law, or had been divorced according to Roman law. But that he had experienced married life personally would, in his mind, lend validation to that advice to the married he acknowledged as his own and not the Lord's.

He adds in verse 7 a thought that is fundamental to this understanding of the vocations available to a Christian: whichever vocation a Christian chooses, it is a gift from God, a *chárisma* from him. Does Paul hint in this that a Christian trying to live either the married or the celibate life as though it were not such a gift takes unwise risks, or that a Christian could decide unwisely about which gift he or she had received? The point is the everlastingly difficult one about a person's knowing God's will for him. Paul's optimism about knowing, or at least living, this providence emerges in verses 17–24 where he counsels the Corinthian Christians to continue living the form of life that had been theirs before their conversion.

From this point in the letter Paul sets about advising, one after the other, four categories of persons in the Corinth community about marriage and therefore about their sexual situation: the widowed, married couples both of whom are Christian, married couples where only one is Christian, and those not yet married. It is on the second and third of these categories of persons that our interest will mainly fasten. We may assume reasonably that the Corinthian Christians had asked about marriage for each of these kinds of persons, or had at least asked questions opening the way for Paul's detailed instruction about them.

His advice to the widowed is consistent with what he had said just before:

> 8. I say to the unmarried and to the widows, it is good that
> they remain as I am. 9. But if they cannot contain themselves,
> let them marry, for it is better to marry than to burn.

Here again Paul reinforces the notion-to-come of marriage as the lesser of two gifts, the default vocation of the weak. One must grant that he here advises those who have already been married and have been deprived abruptly of the sexual pleasure of marriage. But their being widowed he sees as a freeing from the excessive concern for the affairs of the world that he points out later in verses 32–35. He does not say why it is better to be married than to burn with passion, but it is consistent to infer that he here has in mind the same reason he had offered the married for their not abstaining sexually for more than a short time—lest they be tested (by Satan?) beyond their strength. (The case for Paul's being himself a widower is strengthened by his advice here to the Corinthian widowed that they remain as he himself is.)

When Paul turns to counsel spouses both of whom are Christian he makes simply clear first that now his counsel is rather a command, and, second, that the command comes not from himself but from Christ.

> 10. To the married I proclaim—it is not I who do so, but
> the Lord—that a wife is not to be separated from her husband.
> 11. And if she is in fact separated, she is either to remain
> unmarried or is to be reconciled to her husband. And a husband
> is not to dismiss his wife.

Much can be said by way of laying bare the meaning of this command that has been so salient in the Roman Catholic teaching about divorce and remarriage. Let us begin with the more obvious matters, with the questions about the instruction-command whose answers lie easier at hand.

First there is the reason for Paul's including this point of instruction. Very probably the Corinthians' letter to which he has already begun his response on one major point (and perhaps two) had included a question about this most grievous matter of dissolving marriages. Both laws that the Corinthian Christians knew of, the rabbinic and the Roman, sanctioned divorce. Perhaps some of them had made use of one or the other of these laws since becoming Christians. Or perhaps without having done so they were curious about the mind of Christ concerning a custom so deeply rooted in the histories of all the ancient peoples.

We must recall the differing modes of divorce available to spouses under the two systems of law. The rabbinic allowed only one kind of divorce, as we have seen; this was the husband's dismissal of his wife. The wife could take action only indirectly by compelling her husband to dismiss her. Yet even this was a development of rabbinic law that had not clearly entered Jewish life as early as Paul's First Letter to the Corinthian Christians.

The Roman law sanctioned divorce in three ways. One had long since fallen into disuse, since it was possible only where a man married by coempting the authority that a girl's father or guardian had had over her (in marrying he assumed their *manus* over her, and this he gained by a kind of legal conveyance). A marriage formed and maintained in this way the husband could dissolve by dismissing the wife. But since marriage in this form had all but disappeared from Roman society by Paul's time, divorce in this mode had likewise disappeared.

The second mode of divorce was repudiation, and Roman law made it available to both husband and wife. Either could repudiate the other, could get rid of him or her, provided the other had given some cause for the repudiation recognized by the law.

Finally there was the dissolution *communi consensu,* by common consent. No cause needed be given for this; neither spouse took action against the other. Both agreed on equal terms to end the marriage. They did this by withdrawing the *affectio maritalis,* their wills to be married.

(It is more accurate because more inclusive to say that Roman law determined that a marriage could be ended in any of seven distinct ways. These included the dissolutions described just above, the penal deportation of one of the spouses into exile, the condemnation of one or both of them to slavery—the effective ending of the marriage since slaves were denied *connubium,* the right to be married—separation by detention in captivity, and prolonged absence of either spouse for whatever reason.)

While Paul assures the Corinthian Christians that he is passing on to them Christ's own command in the matter, true to his editorial style he does not purport to quote Christ's own words—to pass on a *logion* stored in the active catechetical instruction of the early Christian communities. It is for the student to determine, if possible, with which of the Synoptic *logia* on this subject Paul's instruction "from the Lord" is more nearly synonymous. It appears closer to the instruction in Mark 10 than to that in Matthew 19. This judgment is strengthened by the fact that this First Letter of Paul to the Corinthians is earlier in composition than any of the Gospels. On the supposition that the history of Gospel composition was a developmental one, the earlier the composition the more likely its instruction was not subjected to developmental interpretation by being applied to the resolving of later and regional difficulties among Christians.

To get finally to the part of the instruction that yields far more stubbornly to interpretation, against which mode of dissolution practiced by or at least known to the Corinthian Christians does Paul direct Christ's command? Is it against a kind of mitigated dissolution, the wife's separating from her husband while yet remaining married to him in her mind and in the mind of the the community—a separation motivated by ascetic fervor to live a celibate and more perfect life? This is hinted at, though weakly, by Paul's use of the verb *chōrízein* in directing Christ's command first of all at the wife. This signifies "to separate."[1] But in this passage the verb is in the passive voice of its aorist infinitive—*me chōristhénai*. The command therefore is that the wife is not to be separated. It does not forbid her to take some action; what seems forbidden rather is that some action be taken against her. What is more, the use of this verb in a command laid only upon the wife would suggest that only wives were separating—if such were the interpretation. But paired with this verb is another, *aphiénai,* designating what the husband is commanded not to do. It conveys perfectly the husband's act of dissolving his marriage by dismissing his wife—the dismissal sanctioned by rabbinic law, or the repudiation by Roman law. Coupled with *aphiénai, chōristhénai* points clearly to what is done to a wife when she is dismissed or repudiated; she is separated.

Let us then try the hypothesis that Paul here applies a command of Christ that he intends should rule, or perhaps even correct, conduct that the Corinthian Christians were carrying on in the context of rabbinic law. We recall again that this law allowed only one kind of dissolution, the husband's dismissing his wife, and that the only action the wife could take to end the marriage was to try to compel her husband to dismiss her.

In this context, as I have just suggested, the verb *aphiénai* designating the act that Christ's command forbids the husband is fitted perfectly to translate the dismissal of the wife allowed the husband by rabbinic law. What then may *chōristhénai* designate as the conduct forbidden the wife? Either, as I have suggested too, that as the correlate to and effect of the husband's dismissing action she is not to be dismissed (and the passive verb supports this), or, less likely, *chōristhénai* designates an attempt by the wife to compel her husband to dismiss her. I say this is less likely because the sense here would be "She is not to get herself dismissed," an action which would be conveyed poorly by a verb in the passive voice.

Let us take the other hypothesis that is reasonable here, that Paul applies the command of Christ to the dissolving of marriage according to Roman law. We recall that this is evidently what Mark does in his recording that Christ forbade not only the husband's dismissing his wife, but that she dismiss her husband—an action impossible for the wife under rabbinic law but available to her under Roman law.

If we suppose that this is the context to which Paul directs Christ's command, his choice of the verb *aphiénai* to designate the action forbidden the husband is apt. He must not repudiate his wife. But the choice of *chōristhénai* to designate what was forbidden the wife fits poorly in this context. In a roundabout way only it may say what the husband must not do to the wife by forbidding that which must not happen to her. She must not be separated.

But if Paul has this Roman law of dissolution in mind, he ought, like
Mark, to forbid the wife as well to repudiate her husband, and, for the sake
of consistency, to use the verb *aphiénai* about her too, as Mark had used
apolúein to designate the action forbidden the wife as well as the husband.
Or does Paul's failure to do this reflect his effort to be more faithful to the
words of Christ as he has learned them? It is virtually certain that Christ
did not forbid Jewish wives to dismiss their husbands, since according to
rabbinic law they were powerless to do so in any case. Thus, since Paul
knew of no such command from Christ touching the conduct of wives, he
does not, like Mark, presume to interpret Christ's mind regarding wives'
repudiating their husbands under Roman law by inventing and interpolat-
ing a command from him not to do so.

The upshot of this is, I think, that Paul supposes a context for his
recalling Christ's command, a context that is rabbinic law. But this has its
own unsatisfactory feature. For the Christians to whom he relays this
command are citizens of the Roman empire and residents in one of its
major cities. It is generally agreed that a significant portion of this
community was Jewish-Christian, but enough of it was Gentile for Paul
to have had to reckon with the Gentile Christians' understanding of
divorce as they had this from Roman law.

Another feature that must strike the careful reader here is the at least
apparent incompleteness of Paul's instruction in verse 11. In a prohibiting
command he specifies what must not be done in the event a dissolution of
marriage is attempted. But the prohibition applies only to the wife. He says
of her, "And if she is in fact separated, she is either to remain unmarried
or is to be reconciled with her husband." He says nothing about the
husband, who must surely be an object of equal concern for an apostle
instructing Christians about conduct ruled by the Lord's command. And it
is not a rigorous reading of the text to simply assume that because Paul
sets these limiting alternatives for the wife he intends them also for the
husband.

But even more striking is the meaning that seems to emerge from
Paul's selection of terms where he spells out the alternatives available to a
separated wife. With this I hint at a theoretical issue of serious concern to
later bishops, canonists, theologians and beleaguered Christian spouses
that is left unresolved in this passage.

To get at the issue note first that this instruction, which Paul says
comes from the Lord, touches only those marriages in which both spouses
are Christian. He is to instruct later, in verses 12–16, about marriages in
which one spouse is Christian and the other is not. And to probe the issue
more finely, Paul seems here to convey Christ's unambiguous command
that where both spouses are Christian, the marriage is not to be dissolved
by dismissal, although it is Paul who restricts the command's reference to
marriages both of whose partners are Christian, where Christ had meant it
for any and all spouses. But it is not clear that he understands Christ to say
that for two Christian spouses, dissolving their marriage is not only

forbidden but also impossible. The same said more succinctly and in the language of later Catholic law: we do not have here Christ's mind on the radical indissolubility of the marriage of Christian spouses.

This distinction is not over-fine. It is common enough in both ethics and law to find conduct, of which a person is otherwise capable, forbidden to that person. Thus the Catholic Church's law of clerical celibacy forbids marriage to men it acknowledges to be capable of marrying—and has traditionally acknowledged by subsequently dispensing some of them from this law while holding nevertheless that they remain priests for all their lives. On the other hand there are kinds of conduct of which certain persons are incapable—as Catholic marriage law says, by implication in the way it defines marriage, that the conduct essential to marriage cannot be executed homosexually, and that therefore a homosexual marriage is impossible.

Whoever says that Paul here records Christ's teaching that to dissolve a marriage where both spouses are Christian is not only forbidden but impossible, he draws his own inference from Paul's statement of this teaching. But what is clear is that Paul has both attenuated Christ's command as we know it from Mark, and that he has expanded it within the attentuation. The former he has done by limiting the unqualified "What God has joined man must not separate" to marriages wherein both spouses are Christian. The expansion he has effected by adding an implicit reason for the application of the command to Christian spouses (and to them alone): the fact that both are believing Christians. (Here is the biblical source of the traditional Catholic teaching that the marriage of two Chrisitans, once consummated, is radically indissoluble, that it *cannot* be dissolved by any authority on earth—but that *only* such a marriage is radically indissoluble.)

It follows therefore that when Paul adds that a woman who has been separated from her husband by divorce (and by the divorce that is unilateral dismissal according to Jewish law) must either remain unmarried or be reconciled with him, we do not know if he commands this because he holds that despite the dismissal the woman is still married to her husband—and for this reason *cannot* marry another. His choice of a key adjective suggests that he thinks her effectively divorced, that the dismissal has put her marriage out of existence. He says, "And if she is in fact separated, she is either to remain *ágamos* . . ." In his vocabulary in this letter *ágamos* designates someone unmarried for whatever reason. He uses it in verse 8 to designate those who are unmarried by reason of widowhood. He uses it again in verses 32 and 34 to designate the unmarried who are better able than the married to attend to the things of the Lord.

Thus a rigorous reading of the text argues that Paul did not, in conveying the teaching of Christ, think the dissolution of the marriage of two Christians is impossible, however unexceptionably he thought it forbidden. But if he does think divorce possible for two Christians, he does not explain why, after the effective though forbidden divorce, the woman must not marry again. We also do not know why he does not lay the same prohibition on the erstwhile husband who had divorced her by dismissal in the first place. We do know that the other alternative he offers the divorced woman—to return to, and presumably remarry, her erstwhile husband—was a violation of Jewish law as written in Deuteronomy 24:1–4.

"The Pauline Privilege": 1 Corinthians 7:12–16

Paul then moves on to the case of a husband-wife relationship that must have been common in the early communities: one spouse becomes Christian after some years in the marriage, the other does not.

Nineteen centuries later we comprehend only faintly the early Christians' sense of the transformation, of the newness of everything "made new in Christ": of the passing of all things from the condition of the present age to that of the Kingdom. The new Christian converts of the first generations could not have helped but ask about their "old" marriages whether these survived this summary transformation. And from the details of Paul's reply to the question we can infer that the Christian spouses had a specific worry: Did the continued cohabitation with their still pagan spouses keep them from holiness? Did it make them unclean? And if it did, ought they not for the sake of holiness end such marriages?

Paul begins his reply by indicating the particular group to whom he addresses it, and by pointing out as well that his reply contains his own advice, not a command from Christ: "12. To the rest I say (and here it is I, not the Lord) . . ." This makes doubly clear that the married couples to whom he has just relayed the command of the Lord (in verses 10 and 11) are Christian on both sides, because here, in addressing "the rest," he is clearly also addressing married couples—but couples one of whom is not Christian.

He has two kinds of advice for these couples, the kinds distinguished according to the attitude and conduct of the non-Christian spouse. The first sets at rest the naive Christian fear that marriage to a non-Christian is an obstacle to holiness, perhaps that sexual intercourse with a pagan spouse subjects the Christian to the uncleanness of this world:

> . . . if a brother has a wife who is a non-believer, and she agrees to live with him in peace, he is not to dismiss her. 13. And if a wife has a husband who is a non-believer and he agrees to live with her in peace, she is not to dismiss the husband.

Here Paul clearly thinks and writes within the categories of Roman law. That is, he counsels Christian wives not to divorce their pagan husbands by dismissing, or repudiating, them, an act impossible under Jewish law. The Greek verb he uses in counseling the wives here not to dismiss their pagan husbands is the same he uses in counseling the husbands: *aphiénai*. In offering this counsel does he implicitly accept that even a Christian spouse could otherwise effectively end a religiously mixed marriage by divorcing it in this way under Roman law?

The Corinthian spouses' worry about being held back from holiness Paul neutralizes by reversing their implied logic with a typical rabbinic logic of his own (in verse 14). The children of these marriages are holy, and this can have come only from holy parents. Therefore instead of the Christian spouses' having been made unholy by life with the non-Christian, the latter have been made holy by life with the Christian. He does not explain the nature of this holiness of the non-Christian spouses. But his thinking here is a significant advance in the religious understanding of his society. In the Jewish community the family came under the sanctifying Mosaic covenant by reason of the husband-father. Paul here takes for granted that the Christian wife-mother too can have this sanctifying influence on her pagan husband. And the line of influence is the reverse of what rabbinic law contemporary with Paul thought it to be. That is, far from uncleanness contaminating the clean, as the rabbis taught, Paul insists that the clean makes holy the unclean.

His second kind of advice envisions a Christian married to a non-Christian who will not live together in peace—indeed who will not live together at all. His advice to the Christian spouse is not to try to hold the marriage together, not to labor at reconciliation, but to let the other go: "But if the non-believing spouse separates, let him separate" (verse 15). The verb Paul here uses for "separate" is *chōrízein,* the verb he had used in verses 10 and 11 to relay Christ's command to Christian wives having Christian husbands—that they were either not to be dismissed, or were not to try to get themselves dismissed. But where in verses 10 and 11 he had used the verb in its passive voice, here he uses it in the middle voice (*chōrízetai*). This designates a self-contained action, something that the agent does not do to someone else but simply does.

Which of the traditional divorce actions known to him is Paul here counseling? Since he makes no distinction between non-Christian husband and non-Christian wife, he must be assuming Roman law. This being the case, he is not counseling the Christian spouse to repudiate the non-Christian, nor vice versa. He knows well that the verb for this repudiation is *aphiénai*. Indeed the verb *chōrízetai* (middle voice) points clearly at dissolution *communi consensu,* the dissolution of the marriage by common consent sanctioned by Roman law.

What Paul advises in effect is that if the Christian spouse finds that the non-Christian withdraws his or her will to be married, then the Christian is to do the same. He acknowledges that the non-Christian may and even must take the initiative in this withdrawal of wills; he accepts that this initiative can change the married condition of the Christian, and even that it should change it. He admits the non-Christian's decision as a factor in his own interpretation of Christ's will in the matter.

At this point we come upon the question whose answer carries such a weight of meaning: Does the kind of separation that Paul counsels here constitute an effective divorce, an act that ends the marriage, so that the parties, the Christian as well as the non-Christian, become single and can marry again? Posing the same question from a different approach, does Paul who had surely heard of Jesus' epigrammatic final word in his dispute with the Pharisees—"Therefore what God has joined man must not separate"—interpret this word to not bind the marriages of Christians with non-Christians?

Beginning in the twelfth century, as we have seen, the Popes have answered this question in the affirmative; they have accepted this attenuation of Jesus' command. And they have appealed to Paul's advice to the Christian Corinthians as the warrant for accepting this attenuation.

Such sources for an answer as we have are found within the same verse 15, in the clauses that follow immediately. In them Paul obviously offers as the reason for his advice that the Christian spouse let the unwilling pagan spouse go, that "the brother or the sister is not to play the slave in such matters, for God has called us in peace." The coupled nouns, brother and sister, are conventional to designate adult male and female members of the Christian community. The verb *douléuein*—here in the subjunctive of negative command (*ou dedóulōtai*)—signifies "to be a slave," or "to play the slave."

To which form or forms of slavery does Paul here insist that the Christian spouse is not bound? To cohabitation only, so that the enslavement ends when cohabitation ends, although the marriage itself continues undissolved despite its ending? Or does he mean that not only cohabitation but the marriage itself is the enslavement to which the Christian spouse (and the non-Christian too, of course) is no longer bound?

Before trying to answer these last questions two helpful reflections are in order. First, whichever the kind of separation Paul counsels and allows, in his mind its possibility is grounded in the lack of Christian belief, and the conduct attendant on this lack, in one of the spouses. (Reading this logic in reverse order, it follows that the reason blocking such a separation is the fact of Christian belief in both spouses.) Correlatively the ground for *using* this possibility Paul sees to be the refusal of the non-believing spouse to continue the marriage—not merely the lack of peace in it. The initiative, as I have said, is in the hands of the non-Christian spouse; his or her decision to depart is what frees the Christian from some kind of marital slavery.

Second, the kind of separation of the spouses that would leave them still husband and wife—the "separation from bed and board" familiar in Catholic marriage law—was unknown to either Jewish or Roman law, as I have mentioned earlier. Presumably had Paul counseled this novel kind of separation, he would have had to explain both its nature and his reason for insisting it was the only kind of separation possible, or at least the only kind permissible. And he has not here repeated his command (in verse 11) to two believing spouses who separate, that if the wife does separate and will not reconcile, then she must remain unmarried. Paul would have been bound in conscience to repeat this command if he thought that in this second case too remarriage was either impossible or forbidden, or both.

"For God has called us in peace." It is not easy to determine what this statement means precisely as Paul's justification for the Christian spouse's letting the non-Christian depart and complete the divorce action. He does not say exactly that the Christian spouse is not held to the marriage because he or she is called to peace. He does not say that the failure of peace in the relationship causes the end of the marriage or is justification for divorcing it. What he says exactly is that because the Christian has been called by God in peace, he or she is not to try to prevent the divorce initiated by the non-Christian spouse. The reason is clear enough by implication: to try to force the non-Christian spouse to stay within the marriage would destroy the peace in which God calls a person to the Christian life, and apparently the peace in that life to which God calls him or her. Is this because marriage is for a Christian a call to God's peace? Or because all Christians are called to peace, but no unpeaceful marriage ought to be allowed in the way of this call's realization?

Asked yet another way, what does Paul think is the justification for his introducing this exception to the general obedience to Jesus' command, "Therefore what God has joined man must not separate"? It is not that one of the spouses is unbaptized, for Paul counsels Christian spouses to keep and cherish their spouses when these are unbaptized but live in peace with them. It is not by itself that the non-Christian spouse has left and completed the divorce action. It is that the attempt at reconciliation would destroy the peace between persons that is the needed condition for living a Christian life. In short, it is the compelling need for this peace that, in Paul's mind, justifies the Christian's accepting the dissolution of his or her marriage—that justifies his or her suffering this exception to the obedience to Jesus' command.

The twin rhetorical questions in verse 16—"For how do you know, wife, if you will save your husband? Or how do you know, husband, if you will save your wife?"—are almost an afterthought, intended to strengthen Paul's case for the Christian spouse's letting the non-Christian end the marriage. Here Paul may speak from accumulated experience: there is little likelihood that marital peace is regained where the departure and divorce are opposed and further cohabitation is coerced. If he includes a more extended meaning—that there is no guarantee that the Christian spouse could be an effective agent for the non-Christian's salvation (even after the latter's conversion?)—he contradicts in some degree what he had said in verse 14 about the non-Christian spouse's being made holy by the Christian.

Afterthought and Reversal in Paul's Instruction?

But the two passages we have just examined do not contain the last things that Paul had to say about the permanence and impermanence of marriage. At the end of 1 Corinthians 7 he offers what seems a summation in epigrammatic form.

> 39. A woman is bound for as long as her husband lives. But if her husband dies, she is free to marry whomever she wills, so long as this be in the Lord.

This Paul says with full awareness that he has earlier in the letter declared that if a Christian wife separates from her husband she must either be reconciled with her husband or remain *ágamos*—unmarried— and that he has instructed that unwilling pagan spouses be allowed to leave the marriage lest the Christian be trapped in a kind of slavery. What he says in verse 39 must take some degree of its meaning from these two earlier instructions. In the face, then, of these two instructions, what does Paul mean by saying with general reference that a wife, presumably any wife, is bound in such a way that she may marry again only after her husband's death? Or does Paul intend that verse 39 clarify something left unclear in the two earlier instructions, namely that the two departures they envision do not end the marriage? (If this is the clarification, the Catholic practice of the Pauline privilege has ignored it.)

This brief declaration in verse 39 must have been in Paul's mind at the time as one item in an inventory of epigrams, since he repeats it in Romans 7:1–3 in slightly expanded form and in a different context. (He wrote 1 Corinthians most probably in the early spring of the year 57, Romans in the winter of 57–58).

The context of the remark in Romans 7 is Paul's explanation that a Jewish Christian is freed from the binding force of the law of Moses once he has become a follower of Christ—has, to put it metaphorically, died to his former life. The explanation employs an analogy: a man is bound by the law only as long as he is alive, but is freed from it at death, just as a wife is bound to her husband as long as he lives, but is freed from this bond at his death.

> 1. Or don't you know, brethren (I speak to those who understand the law), that the law rules a man for only as long as he lives? 2. For a married woman is bound by the law to her husband while he lives. But if he dies, she is freed from the rule of her husband. 3. And if she marries while her husband still lives, she will bear the name of adulteress.

The analogy is not symmetric. Where the man in the first facet of it is freed from the law when he himself dies, the wife in the second facet is said to be freed from her husband not when she dies, but when he does. And whereas in the first facet the man is said to be bound by the law, in the second the wife is said to be bound to her husband by the law.

In what way do the two uses of this epigram qualify one another's meanings? In Romans Paul seems to reason on Jewish premises, since it was not true that under Roman law a wife was bound to her husband's authority as long as he lived. Nor was it even true that a man was bound to Roman law as long as he lived, since he could be punished by reduction to slavery and thus put outside the law.

If the passage in Romans presumes Jewish law, Paul uses the marital facet of his analogy presuming that a wife is bound to her husband as long as he lives. This was true in Jewish law only if she abandoned him, not if he dismissed her. If this assumption in Romans 7 rules also in the epigram's use in 1 Corinthians 7, then even there Paul asserts a wife's being bound to her husband only in the event she has abandoned the marriage, has separated from it. But if this is the accurate interpretation, why did Paul there designate a woman separated from but still married to her husband as *ágamos,* as unmarried? The use of this adjective to designate a woman separated but still married would have been a simple neologism of law on Paul's part. He would have owed his perplexed readers an explanation—an explanation of which there is not a hint in 1 Corinthians.

I suspect it is futile to try to ferret out Paul's carefully reasoned meaning from these distinctly written passages. I suspect this because I first suspect that these passages do not contain any careful reasoning. At their writing Paul had not resolved the issue of marital permanence versus marriage's dissolution in his own mind. Like other difficult realities of a moral-religious kind, that was still in gestation in his thinking. What the reader finds in these passages is, I suspect, the report from one stage of this unfinished gestation.

Reflections on the New Testament Divorce Passages

It is clear that the teaching on divorce and remarriage that the Church has inherited from the first two generations of its history during which its Gospel was produced is an inventory of instructions of which all but three are presented as coming from Jesus himself. But among those said to come from him there is only minor verbal synonymity. Therefore it is to date impossible for us to recover accurately all that Jesus said about divorce and remarriage.

Yet the diverging accounts of his instruction are all elements of the Gospel; their divergency itself is an element of it. It seems reasonable to see the causes of this divergency in the differing needs of the several Christian communities that accepted and passed on the original instructions of Jesus. A few of these communities, perhaps in the persons of Mark and of the Matthean compiler, considered themselves justified in adding to (or perhaps subtracting from) Jesus' own words to provide for their own needs. This tells us something of the self-awareness of these communities, specifically that they believed themselves to be guided by the Holy Spirit to remember and understand what Jesus had taught, and guided also to apply his teaching by developing it. Although they would not have described it in this way, they thought of the Gospel as a divine message in process, in the process of unfolding and applying itself in the day-to-day needs of their lives. They saw no reason to freeze the process permanently in their own generation.

Because every element of the instruction on divorce and remarriage is part of the Gospel (and this includes the instruction in 1 Corinthians, even that part coming from Paul himself), it would falsify our reading of this Gospel if we were to single out one element, play it off against the others and make it over-ride them. Any justifying criterion for doing this would have to be found outside the Gospel. And we could use this criterion for only one purpose. This would be to support the judgment that one or other part of the instruction is more helpful to our particular needs, but certainly not that it is in some abstract way more true than the others.

Every element of the instruction was in its origin contextual. It was an answer to a question posed by a particular Jewish-Christian or Hellenistic-Christian community, or offered as the resolution of a conflict, or the satisfaction of a serious curiosity, in one of these communities. In short, each element's reference was at its origin particular. Christians of later generations do not read the Gospel intelligently if they simply assume that solely because a point of instruction has been taken into the Gospel it has thereby gained universal reference, and that if it is a point of instruction about conduct, it binds that kind of conduct in every Christian of every generation. For example, from the fact that Paul instructed the wives of Ephesus to defer to their husbands it does not follow that Christian wives of every century and every nation thereafter are held to defer to their husbands. The expansion of reference from the particular to the universal is a move that must be justified. Yet some of Jesus' parenetic statements are unarguably universal—although these are not easily identified. (I think that in the matter of divorce his final word to the Pharisees—"Therefore what God has joined man must not separate"—is such a statement. So too on a much grander scale is his own most personal command recorded in John 15:12: "This is my command, that you love one another as I have loved you." I think this binds any man or woman of any time or place who would be his disciple.)

Points of Gospel instruction limited in their original reference can later be made to bind all Christians. This extending and applying are one of the offices of a Church teaching under the guidance and the empowering of God's Spirit. For example, under this guidance and empowering the Church can forbid Christian spouses to abandon one another because

Jesus forbade Jewish husbands to abandon their wives. Presumably it would do so for the good of the spouses, of their children and of the larger societies they comprise. But a reference it can expand it can also contract—again, if need be, for the good of the spouses, of their children and of the societies in which they live.

When anyone expands the reference of contextually offered Gospel instruction he or she must cross historical-cultural lines carefully. For example, one must not read later and accrued word-meanings back into Gospel statements. I have already suggested one instance in which such vigilance is needed. When Jesus is presented as telling Jewish husbands (in both Mark 10:11 and Matthew 19:9) that they commit adultery if they dismiss their wives and marry another woman, he did not contradict their law in its limited understanding of the perimeters of adultery. That is, he did not tell such husbands that they committed adultery if and because they took a second wife, in order, for example, to have children by the latter on finding that they could have none by the former. He told them that they committed adultery if they dismissed their first wife and married a second wife—apparently even if they did this in order to have children by the second wife because the first could give them none. This is the divorcing that Jesus condemned and forbade.

And when he sealed the condemnation with the command, "Therefore what God has joined man must not separate," the kind of separation he had in mind may have been this imperious dismissal. Paul, in allowing the kind of divorce he did, and the Matthean author too, if he allowed a kind of divorce in his exceptive clause, seem to have understood Jesus' command in this qualified way. Whether Jesus forbade other kinds of divorce, such as the mutually accepted dissolution, whether he thought a marriage could die, could pass out of existence, from neglect and abuse— his answers to these we cannot find in his command itself. We must infer them from the earlier clauses in his argument with the Pharisees.

What Is Conclusive in Jesus' Instruction

Despite my seeming pessimism about finding out with certainty what Jesus taught about divorce and remarriage, I am convinced that we can with reasonable accuracy discern his teaching in some of its parts. The following, I think, are among the most evident and serious of these parts.

In his dispute with the Pharisees Jesus appealed to the creation poem of Genesis 1 and to the garden parable of Genesis 2 and 3. Therefore he subscribed to the truth of their religious anthropology concerning marriage. That is, he affirmed that the two complementary sexes are God's design, and that as a consequence their coming together in sexual union is his intent. This union, however men and women form it and name it, is the most valuable of all possible unions of persons. It is meant to be so inclusive and complete that the man and woman go before their people as one person.

Jesus' underlying intent in saying what he did about divorce and remarriage was fixed primarily on a serious abuse among his own people. This was the cruelty brought upon women by the accepted practice of husbands' divorcing them by unilateral dismissal. He meant to condemn this practice among his people and to forbid it among his followers.

As a corollary to this fundamental demand for fairness and for marriage grounded in lasting care, Jesus also redefined adultery for his people and for his followers among them. He expanded the meaning of adultery from the narrow violation by another man of a husband's exclusive sexual right over his wife, to include the violation of the marriage's "one flesh" relationship by either spouse. The new definition of adultery is intelligible now only within the demand for marital fidelity.

To return to a point made above, since no man can end his marriage by dismissing his wife, a husband who tries to remarry after dismissing his wife commits adultery. And a man, married or not, who tries to marry a woman who has been dismissed, commits adultery. By inference, the woman who cooperates knowingly and willingly in either of such attempts at remarriage also commits adultery.

Does Jesus' instruction contain an assertion of the radical indissolubility of any and all marriages? It is necessary to say again what this uniquely Roman Catholic term means. Stated most simply, radical indissolubility means that the only way a marriage once created can end is by the death of one of the spouses, that it is a relationship that is imperishable as long as both spouses live. A Catholic who understands marriage to be this kind of relationship, if asked *how* it came to be of this kind, would answer predictably that at the dawn of creation God made it such—as evidenced in Jesus' command, "Therefore what God has joined man must not separate."

This suggests the alternate interpretation of Jesus' instruction vis-à-vis marriage's indissolubility. It is that such is God's will for the permanence of any marriage that any attempt by men and women to end it, under whatever circumstances and for whatever motive, is a contradiction of his will. This interpretation says that Jesus' instruction did not touch the question of marriage's inherent indissolubility, that is, whether it is at all possible for human beings to end a marriage short of death. It left this question open. But his instruction so unexceptionably forbade anyone's trying to end a marriage that, whether it is possible for one to do so or not, the attempt is inescapably disobedient and therefore sinful.

I find no evidence in Jesus' instruction that argues for or against the first of these interpretations of indissolubility. It is significant for our consideration that this question about marriage's indissolubility, taken in abstraction from marriage experienced both benignly and abusively by his people, was not asked by either the teachers of his people or by the people themselves.

Jesus' instruction came closer to indissolubility in the second sense, the unexceptionability of his Father's will that no human being be permitted to dissolve a marriage. Yet here too the evidence is inconclusive. It is corollary to Jesus' ignoring the issue of the *inherent* indissolubility of marriage that we cannot find with certainty that he taught that any human will is powerless to dissolve a marriage as well as being forbidden to do so. Apparently Paul as well as the Matthean author thought that he did not teach this. Thinking this, they introduced their exceptions to his command, "Therefore what God has joined man must not separate." We shall see, in the following chapters, in what ways the Roman Catholic authorities have down through the centuries introduced their own exceptions to the same command.

NOTE

1. David Daube suggests (*op. cit.*, p. 364) that Paul's instruction at this point may suppose divorce and remarriage according to the Roman law rather than the Jewish. In the Latin of this law, he points out, the verbs used to designate a husband's repudiating his wife are *expellere, dimittere, exigere.* These are well translated into Greek by the verb Paul uses, *aphiénai.* But to designate a wife's repudiating her husband Roman law used the verbs, *abire* and *discedere*—to leave, to depart. Two reasons accounted for this heterogeneous choice of verbs to designate identical divorce actions. First, because the residence was usually owned by the husband, the wife, even when dissolving the marriage by repudiating her husband, had to "depart" from the home and, in an imprecise and popular sense, from the marriage. Second, because of the severe social disadvantages coming upon wives who repudiated their husbands, the former were slow to use their legal right to repudiate. Thus custom found the majority of divorced marriages dissolved by the husbands' repudiating the wives, in which case the latter would have literally to depart the home and the marriage. In either case, whether the wives repudiated or were repudiated, the verb *chōrízein* that Paul uses translates sufficiently the Latin *abire* and *discedere* if these are understood as designating what the wives must do on being repudiated. Thus Paul's forbidding the Christian wives to depart (in verse 11) is the correlate to his forbidding their husbands to repudiate them.

5. DIVORCE AND REMARRIAGE IN THE ROMAN EMPIRE

According to the Acts of the Apostles communities of Christians were formed outside Palestine early in the first Christian generation. It is accurate enough to date Paul's conversion in 36 or 37 A.D., and this took place, according to Acts 9, as he approached the city of Damascus in southern Syria, intent on searching through the synagogues there, arresting any followers of the Christian way, and hauling them back to Jerusalem for punishment. This itself does not point clearly to the formation of distinct Christian communities, but it does suggest how these communities came to be formed. They began with the conversion of synagogue Jews to the following of Christ, and subsequently expanded as the entire synagogue population followed in conversion, or as the converted fraction broke away and formed an independent community. It was inevitable too that as long as the multiplying of the communities was done in this way, marriages in them would be regulated within the purview of Jewish law.

But within those same years new communities were formed in another way. Acts 11 points out one of the effects of the persecution of the Jerusalem Christians by the Jewish authorities following the preaching and the execution of the deacon Stephen. A number of these Christians fled Jerusalem and formed new communities not only elsewhere in Palestine but in other cities along the Mediterranean coast. Principal among these was Antioch, the capital of the province of Syria, and third city in the empire after Rome and Alexandria. There the Christians made converts not only among the Jews but especially among "the Greeks," non-Jewish citizens, freedmen and slaves of the empire. And here, as in other cities where the majority of the new Christians were Gentiles, marriages were regulated within the purview of Roman law. Yet we must keep in mind what we came upon in the Gospel according to Mark as well as in Paul's First Letter to the Corinthians, that in the Christian communities whose population was part Jewish, part Gentile, this regulation must have been dual and indecisive, both rabbinic and Roman.

The intent of this chapter is not to examine how the appointed teachers of the Christian communities reacted to this change of purview for the regulation of marriages, nor how they worked at resolving the ambiguity in this regulation where the communities consisted of both Jewish and Gentile converts. This intent is rather to examine the Roman law itself of divorce and remarriage, to trace its history through three stages: through the law already in effect at the time the Christian communities sprang up in the empire during the reigns of Tiberius, Gaius (Caligula) and Claudius I; the modification of this law (minimal, as we shall see) through the years of the empire until the start of its Christianization under Constantine in the first third of the fourth century; finally its modification under the Christian emperors, and especially at the hands of the two great codifiers of Roman law, Theodosius II toward the middle of the fifth century, and Justinian just under a century later.[1]

Divorce and Remarriage in the Early Empire

By the time the governance of Rome became that of an empire under Augustus in 27 B.C. its law acknowledged the following ways in which a marriage could end: by the death of one or both spouses, or by certain events, accidental or intentional, that were held to destroy the marriage—thus the prolonged absence of a spouse, reduction of a spouse to slave status as the punishment for crime, captivity that separated the spouses, military enlistment on the part of the husband (a provision of the law enacted by Augustus himself), and deportation in punishment for certain crimes.

Then there was dissolution effected by one or both spouses on his or her initiative, and this was of three kinds. First was the repudiation of a wife by a husband who had married her by taking her in transfer from the authority (*manus*) of her father or her tutor into his own (a form of marriage virtually extinct by the beginning of the empire). This form of divorce most nearly approximated the husband's unilateral right to dismiss his wife established in rabbinic law. The philosophy of marriage arguing for the husband's right to thus repudiate his wife held that when a woman was married by passing from the *manus* of her father to that of her husband, she never escaped the status of a daughter. And since a father could repudiate his daughter, so too could a husband repudiate the woman who was by legal equivalence his daughter. But in no case could a daughter repudiate her father.[2]

But because marriage by transfer of *manus* had vanished, this form of repudiation had also vanished. It had been established probably as early as the Law of the Twelve Tables during the fifth century B.C.; the earliest recorded instance of its use dated from the fourth century.

With spouses commonly joined, by the beginning of the empire, in the free marriage, in the *matrimonium liberum* available to a woman provided she had emancipated herself from the authority of parent or tutor, two other forms of dissolution were available to the initiative of either spouse. The first of these was dissolution *communi consensu,* by common consent. It was accomplished *bona gratia,* with no allegation of marital fault acknowledged by the law and consequently no punishment prescribed by the law for such fault. The spouses needed only withdraw their *affectus maritalis,* their will to be married, and to demonstrate in a recordable way the fact of this withdrawal.

The other form of dissolution of the free marriage was, like the earliest established by the Law of the Twelve Tables, a repudiation, a dismissal of one spouse by the other. But now in the empire it was available to both spouses. It was a contentious action in which one spouse accused the other of a fault specified by the law as a ground for the repudiation. A study of the Roman divorce law from beginning to end shows a quantitatively dominant concern with the establishing, modifying and refining of these grounds, and with the punitive consequences of a successful repudiation. It is important to note that unlike litigious divorce in the modern West, the dissolution under Roman law was accomplished not by a judicial decree of a civil authority, but by the one spouse's act of dismissing the other.

I have mentioned just above that Roman legislators and jurists busied themselves much with the establishing, modifying and refining of the grounds on which one spouse could dissolve the marriage by repudiation. Two most obvious grounds were one alleged frequently by both spouses, and one that could be alleged only by the wife. The former was adultery, the latter *lenocinium,* the husband's forcing his wife into prostitution. What the other grounds for repudiation were at the time the Christian communities began to spring up in the empire, say in the reign of Claudius, cannot be found in Roman documents of that generation. One must read later documents, the collections of decrees from prior centuries made by later jurists, and these jurists' commentaries on the earlier decrees.

Without trying to locate the establishment of this or that ground on the calendar of Roman history, and with no pretense at an exhaustive inventory, we find that the accepted grounds for repudiation included, along with the adultery and *lenocinium* already mentioned, these crimes or faults: murder, sorcery, treason, plotting against the spouse's life, brigandage or the harboring of brigands, violation of sepulchres, perjury, drunkenness.

Faults on the wife's part warranting her husband's dismissing her, but not her dismissing him if found in him as well, included her striking him, her attending theatres, gladiatorial games or circuses without his permission, and her dining or bathing with other men without his knowledge or permission.

As in Jewish law, both rabbinic and pre-rabbinic, the Roman law understood adultery asymmetrically. The husband committed adultery only if he had intercourse with another man's wife, but a wife committed adultery if she had intercourse with any man other than her husband. Apparently, however, his bringing an unmarried women into the home he shared with his wife and having intercourse with the woman there constituted a ground for his wife's dismissing him.

And to judge from the contemporary satirical comment on the ease and frequency with which marriages were dissolved, spouses must have commonly coerced or cajoled one another into the most available divorce of all, the dissolution *communi consensu.*

At what point in the history of the empire dissolution of marriages reached epidemic proportions is difficult to say. But as early as Augustus himself this first of the emperors tried to introduce an element of seriousness into the divorce by repudiation by demanding certain observable steps whereby authorities could verify that the repudiation had in fact taken place. This he did in his *Lex Iulia et Papia Poppaea.* Until that time the repudiation had been accomplished simply by the pronouncing of a formula such as *Tuas res tibi habeto,* equivalently "Take your things and go," or, more succinctly, *Agito*—"Get out." Augustus' decree mandating the verifiable steps[3] had an additional braking effect in that a husband seeking to prosecute a wife he had accused of adultery could do so only *after* he had made the written declaration of repudiation which named this ground for it.

Even so divorce continued so commonly and so frequently that Rome's social commentators satirized the practice savagely. The most pointed of them are well known to Christian apologists, who have quoted them again and again as pagan witness against pagan immorality. In his *De Beneficiis* the Stoic teacher Seneca portrayed what he deemed a common phenomenon among Roman matrons. While arguing in his Book 3 that the great number of beneficiaries who were shamelessly ungrateful to their benefactors should not be made public lest ingratitude be taken by the people as a common and therefore acceptable attitude, he pointed out how, in parallel fashion, the shameless exhibition of infidelity and divorce by certain highborn Roman women had as its consequence a casual and widespread imitation of their conduct:

> We really ought not let it be known how great the number of the ungrateful is, for the sheer multitude of those who offend in this way takes away any shame over it. . . . Thus is there any woman at all who is now embarrassed at being divorced after certain highborn and illustrious women have come to reckon their age not by the number of consuls but by the number of husbands they have had—these women who leave home in order to marry, but marry in order to divorce? They shrank from this scandal as long as it was rare. But now that no news report is

without its divorce case, they have learned to imitate what at one time they only heard about.[4]

A generation later another Spaniard come to Rome, Martial, the master of the epigram, commented sarcastically to his friend Faustinus on the paradigmatic conduct of a certain Telesilla:

> Since the day the Julian law was reenacted for the people, Faustinus, and Chastity got her orders to take lodging in our homes, we now count thirty days more or less—and Telesilla is just marrying her tenth husband. A woman who marries that often doesn't really marry. By law she is an adulteress. For myself, I am less offended by straightforward prostitution.[5]

Half a generation later Juvenal, another but non-epigrammatic satirist, offered his reflections on wifely infidelity and divorce among the Romans. In his notorious Satire VI—from beginning to end of its seven hundred lines an anti-feminist diatribe whose theme is "Why marry as long as there is still time to hang yourself?"—he singled out the frivolous motives for which men marry and the equally frivolous reasons for which they dismiss their wives.

> And why is Censennia, on her husband's witness, the perfect wife? Because she brought him a million sesterces—and that is the price for his calling her chaste. He has not withered under Venus' darts nor ever been burned by her torch. It was the dowry that set him afire, the dowry that shot those arrows. . . .
> And why does Sartorius burn with love for Bibula? If you can dig your way to the truth, it is the face he loves, not the woman. But let just three wrinkles appear, or let her aging skin begin to sag; let her teeth lose their luster or her eyes their gleam, then will his steward relay to her the command, "Pack your bags and get out. You've become a bore. You blow your nose too much. Get out—and be quick about it. There's another wife coming who doesn't have the sniffles."[6]

What accelerated this epidemic spouse-changing, which in its severest form was found only among the rich, were the decline of ancient family traditions, the search by childless couples for second and fertile spouses, the fragility of marriages contracted for political strategy or for financial gain, and of course the utterly permissive law. As easy divorce grew more frequent it created its own climate of toleration and approval, as we have just seen Seneca point out. Divorce came to be considered the normal thing, the thing to be done and talked about. The French historian M. Humbert cites as a revealing statistic that among twenty-five thousand tomb inscriptions from the Roman world, there are only twenty-eight containing the praise of a *univira,* a woman who had but one husband.[7]

Imperial Legislation for Divorce and Remarriage

When we ask what those in the empire who made and promulgated the law were doing to regulate divorce during those years, we must attend to the work of two classes of persons (and we shall see that they were doing precious little). The first were the emperors, the supreme legislators in their own right. The second were the jurists, specifically a few great jurists of the classical period in Roman law, whose interpretations were used as authoritative sources and even as law. These were Gaius, Julius Paulus, Aemilius Papinianus, Ulpianus and Modestinus. The one among these who had the most lasting effect on later Roman law was probably Ulpianus (d. 228). From his commentaries *Ad Sabinum* and *Ad Edictam,* from his elementary handbooks the *Institutiones* and the *Definitiones,* and from his written opinions in the *Disputationes, Opiniones* and *Responsa* fully one-third of Justinian's *Digesta* of the sixth century drew its material. In the fifth century the emperor Valentinian II named these five men as the jurists whose opinions were to be followed in deciding cases.[8]

To scan sequentially the little that these men—both the emperors and the jurists—did about the regulation of divorce covers a brief span, since those of them who said or did anything were clustered tightly enough on the calendar.

The emperor Hadrian (117–138) enacted in his *Liber Secundus de Adulteribus* that a man who at the end of his travels brought home with him another man's wife and compelled her to divorce him by repudiation was to be banished into exile for three years.[9] Hadrian said nothing, however, to indicate that the attempt at divorce was ineffective, or that the man could not marry the woman on his return from exile.

Julius Paulus, in his thirty-fifth book *Ad Edictam,* specified the quality of intent needed to effect a divorce. He insisted that this must be the intent to separate the parties permanently. Consequently whatever was said or done in the heat of anger to separate the spouses was not valid until the passing of time manifested the fixed intent to separate. Consequently too if a man gave his wife notice of repudiation in a moment of anger, but she returned to him soon after and he accepted her, it was to be concluded that he had not truly dismissed her.[10]

The same Julius Paulus determined that no divorce by repudiation was to be taken as ratified unless the sending of the note of repudiation could be attested to by seven adult Roman citizens in addition to the freedman sent by the husband as a messenger to convey the note.[11]

Modestinus ruled in his first book of *Regulae* that a freedwoman who had married her patron could not dissolve the marriage by departure from it against her husband's will unless she had been manumitted by her father-in-law—in which case she could depart without her husband's permission and over his objections.[12] Apparently this was a qualification put on the earlier *Lex Iulia de Maritandis Ordinibus* which had forbidden a freedwoman married to her patron to divorce him. But Ulpianus pointed out that this law, rather than depriving her of the capacity to do so, simply ruled that if she divorced in this way she had no claim for the restoration of her dowry and no capacity to remarry without her patron's consent.[13]

In Book 13 of his *Digesta* Ulpianus asked whether an insane wife could both divorce her husband by repudiating him and be divorced by him. He answered that she could be repudiated because she was legally in the same condition as one who receives no notice (*in ignorantis loco*), and the law had long accepted by custom that the note of repudiation, though required to be sent, need not be received in order to be effective. Ulpianus denied, however, that either an insane wife or her curator could repudiate the former's husband, but admitted that her father could do this for her.[14]

Such are the minuscule items of legislation and jurisprudence regulating divorce in the Roman empire during the nearly three centuries from the beginning of Claudius' reign until Constantine made the first move to restrain the universal caprice. It was most likely out of his at least remote sympathy for the Christian ideal of marital stability that he made this move, although he never personally took Christian instruction as a catechumen, and accepted baptism only on his deathbed.

Changing Divorce Legislation in the Christianized Empire

Now we shall see in considerably finer detail what the gradual Christianizing of the empire did to change the Roman attitude toward and law controlling divorce and remarriage. And since the gradualness of the Christianizing helps account for the surprisingly gradual and even snail-pace approach of the law to the Gospel teaching, it will be helpful to trace the major steps in the empire's slowly becoming a Christian state.

Valerian mounted the next-to-last imperial attempt to destroy Christianity by persecution in 257–261. When his successor, Gallienus, recognized the futility of such attempts, he promulgated an edict of toleration that suspended Nero's proscription of the Christian religion. But after forty years of peace the emperors Diocletian in the eastern empire and Maximian in the west brought down upon the Christians the last and cruelest of the persecutions. It lasted in both sectors of the empire from 302 until 305, until the two emperors abdicated and their successors, Constantius and Constantine, halted it in the west. It continued in the east under Galerius and Maximian until 308. In that year Galerius capitulated and issued another edict of toleration, while Maximian gave in a year later.

Constantine became master of the western empire with his victory over Maxentius in 312 at the Milvian bridge on the outskirts of Rome. In consort with Licinius, now emperor in the east, he issued the Edict of Milan in 313, which granted full freedom to all religions in both sectors of the empire. But the cult of the imperial gods remained the established religion of the empire.

Historians estimate that at this time no more than ten percent of the empire's population professed Christianity, and even this portion was concentrated in the cities. The ancient religion of the imperial gods was to remain rooted for decades in two disparate sections of the populations—in the peasant farming folk, especially those in the provinces, and in the second level of government made up of the old patrician families, the senators and the prefects.

They were Constantine's sons who began the gradual suppression of the imperial religion. Constantius I in 356 forbade idolatry and ordered the closing of the pagan temples, although in Rome and elsewhere in the west these enactments were not enforced and the traditional cult remained the de facto religion of the empire.

During his brief reign from 361 to 363 Julian mounted a reaction against the gradual Christianization and undertook to purify and reorganize the imperial religion. But his death in battle ended the brief effort.

For fifteen years after Julian's death imperial authority treated both the traditional cult and Christianity impartially. But Gratian (375–383) finally ended the "establishment" of the former in the western empire by renouncing the title *Pontifex maximus* and taking away the imperial subsidy from the priestly colleges and the vestal virgins.

By his Edict of Thessalonica on February 28, 380 Theodosius I in effect established Christianity as the state religion in the eastern empire. In 391 he forbade pagan ceremonies in Rome as well as in the east; and in the following year he issued a universal edict forbidding all pagan sacrifices, whether public or private, including devotions to the household deities.

On August 5, 395 Arcadius and Honorius decreed the strict application of the Theodosian edict forbidding pagan sacrifice, and added to the proscription the traditional funeral banquets and the pouring of libations before meals. The temple priests and other temple servants were stripped of their remaining privileges in 396. And in 408 entry into court service was forbidden to all who were not Christian.

But since the Christian emperors never mounted a systematic persecution of the pagans in their population, decades were to pass before the old cults disappeared entirely. As late as April 9, 423 Theodosius II issued an imperial constitution finally ordering the destruction of the remaining pagan temples and shrines. And in the meantime the diversions so dear to the pagan Roman population (and to many Christians) were being closed down. In 399 the emperors Honorius and Arcadius suppressed the gladiatorial games. And in 392 and 425 imperial ordinances interdicted theatrical performances and athletic contests on Sundays.

A rough estimate of the empire's population of about one hundred million at the end of the fourth century divides it almost equally between pagans and Christians, although the proportion of Christians was much higher in the east than in the west.

The Christian Emperors' Reform of the Divorce Law

Although it is not quite accurate to call Constantine a Christian emperor, he did begin the legislation which, continuing across two centuries until Justinian, was intended to put some restraint on the frivolity of divorce under Roman law.

In his Code of the fifth century Theodosius II reports that Constantine had decreed the following changes. A wife could no longer cite as grounds for dismissing her husband his drunkenness, his gambling or his womanizing. Only homicide on his part, his preparation of poisons (to be used in sorcery—or perhaps for abortion) and his violation of sepulchres were to justify her dismissing him.[15] The sanction for her dismissing him for any other cause was not the nullity of her attempt at divorce but the punitive measure of her being deported into exile, along with the loss of her dowry as well as the nuptial gifts.

Constantine put a restraint in turn on the causes justifying a husband's dismissing his wife. Henceforth he was permitted by law to dismiss her only for her adultery, for her preparing of poisons, or for procuring. If he dismissed her for other causes, he was to return her dowry to her. He was also forbidden to marry again, although the penalty for his remarrying was not the nullity of this attempt, but license to his first wife to take in its entirety the dowry brought by the second wife.[16]

In the matter of dissolution by the prolonged absence of one of the spouses Constantine ruled that a woman who had for four years no word from her husband in military service could remarry with impunity provided she had first inquired without success with the competent military commander and had informed him of her intent to remarry. This was a mitigation of Octavian Augustus' legislation at the beginning of the first century that active enlistment not only deprived a man of the *connubium,* the right to be married, but also annulled or suspended the legal effects of his marriage contracted validly before his enlistment.

In 421 Theodosius himself and Constantius in the eastern empire, and Honorius in the west, decreed the following regarding divorce by dismissal and the grounds for it. If a woman repudiated her husband but failed to prove against him one of the legally acknowledged causes for repudiation, she was to lose the dowry and the nuptial gifts; she was to be deported into exile; she could not remarry, nor could she return to the husband whom she had dismissed.

If she could prove slight faults (*leves culpae*) against him, she lost the dowry and nuptial gifts and the right to remarry, but was not sent into exile. If, after dismissing her husband for slight faults, she committed adultery (by attempting to remarry?), he could institute dismissal proceedings against her, and after succeeding in these could then prosecute her for adultery. The legislation apparently meant to interpret her repudiation as invalid if attempted on grounds of only slight faults in the husband, since only thus could her subsequent attempt at remarriage be deemed adultery.

But if the wife could prove against her husband serious delinquency according to the law, she could dismiss him, she retained dowry and nuptial gifts, and she could remarry, but only after an interval of five years. This legislation stated explicitly that the five-year delay was intended to verify that the wife had dismissed her husband out of execration of his sins rather than out of desire for another man.[17]

How little concern this Christian imperial legislation had for the equal protection of women emerges as we look at the conditions set for the husband's licit and valid repudiation of his wife.

If a husband could prove serious delinquency against his wife, he could dismiss her, keep both the dowry and the nuptial gifts, and remarry immediately.

If he alleged serious delinquency on her part but could not prove it, could however prove slight delinquency, he could dismiss her and recover the nuptial gifts from her while having to leave to her the dowry. And he could remarry after an interval of two years.

Finally, if the husband could prove no cause for dismissal against the wife at all, but dismissed her nonetheless, he forfeited to her both the dowry and the nuptial gifts and was forbidden to remarry. But that this decree did not doubt the effectiveness of his divorce action in ending the marriage is evident in this, that the wife might remarry after a year's delay (a delay traditional for the woman in order to avoid uncertainty about paternity in the event she were pregnant at the time of the dismissal).[18]

Seventeen years later, in 438, Theodosius made the most serious attempt by a Christian emperor within the two centuries following Constantine's legitimizing of the Christian religion, to bring Roman marriage and divorce legislation into even remote correspondence with the Gospel.[19] More will be said later about the forces delaying the development of the legislation we now acknowledge as traditionally Catholic. But for the fifth century itself we have no way of knowing how faithfully even as permissive a law as the Theodosian Code was observed. It was a time of political turmoil and of the breakdown of social and juridical institutions. What seems clear is that from the time the two constitutions, Constantine's of 331 and Honorius' of 421, were included in the Theodosian Code, they conflicted with and remained unacceptable to popular custom, even in a population moving gradually toward a Christian majority. So strong was the resistance to the new divorce legislation that in 439, a year after introducing his Code, Theodosius felt compelled to put his reform effort in reverse, declaring that it was too difficult to go beyond the demands of the ancient laws. In his Novel 12 he abolished all the Code's restrictive norms on divorce by dismissal, as well as the penalties for their violation; he decreed that dismissal should again be ruled by the ancient laws and the jurisprudence of the classical epoch (i.e., of the second and third centuries).

Eleven years later, in a constitution promulgated in 449, Theodosius, and now Valentinian with him, sought to recoup the relative failure of the attempt at marital reform in his Code of 438. They forbade dismissal without a just cause, at the same time establishing a long list of such causes, whether crimes or other acts they deemed damaging to the stability of marriage.

In this new constitution husband and wife were treated with less inequality. Thus the husband's adultery was for the first time taken as a cause justifying the wife's dismissing him, as her adultery had always justified his dismissing her. Constantine's legislation calling for the exiling of the dismissed adulterous wife was abrogated. The penalties imposed for dismissing a spouse for reasons other than those established by law were made the loss of the dowry and of the nuptial gifts. In addition to adultery dismissal of either spouse was justified if he or she were found guilty of poisoning, of treason, of forgery, of violation of sepulchres, of theft from a church, of kidnaping, of harboring brigands, and of plotting the murder of the spouse. Faults exclusive to the wife justifying the husband's dismissing her were her staying away from home for the entire night, her attending games or theatres he had forbidden her, and her striking him. Faults exclusive to the husband justifying the wife's dismissing him were his participation in brigandage or cattle-rustling, his beating her, and his having intercourse within their home with lewd women. The last-named conduct was not deemed adultery by the law unless the other women were married, but not even then if they were of inferior social rank.

A wife who dismissed her husband for just cause was obliged to wait a year before remarrying. But if she had dismissed her husband for any cause not acknowledged by the law, she had to wait five years, under threat of losing both dowry and nuptial gifts. No period of waiting was imposed on a husband who dismissed his wife for just cause; but if for a cause not acknowledged by the law, he suffered the same forfeiture and was forbidden to remarry within two years.[20]

What of the other form of divorce, not repudiation of one spouse by the other on the allegation and proof of some delinquency, but the simple non-contentious dissolution *communi consensu,* the mutual withdrawal of *affectus maritalis?* Did the Christian emperors up to and including Justinian, a century later than Theodosius II, put any restriction on this?

Justinian's Legislation

Flavius Petrus Sabbatius Justinianus, a Latin-speaking Macedonian born in 483 and educated in Constantinople, came to the throne of the Byzantine empire in 527 at the age of forty-four. Shortly thereafter he set up a commission supervised by the jurist Tribonius which was to examine the constitutions in effect at the time and to draw from them a new and re-vised Constitution. This work was completed in two years and the new Constitution, comprising ten books, was promulgated in 529. All earlier legislation not included in it was repealed automatically.

A year later, in December 530, Justinian formed a second commission to go through the writings of the Roman jurists until his time—Paulus, Modestinus, Ulpianus *et al.*—and to complete a digest-simplifcation of their jurisprudence. This commission completed its work in three years, and on December 16, 533 Justinian published it as the *Pandecta* in fifty books containing 9,123 articles taken from thirty-nine jurists. In its Latin version the *Pandecta* is called the *Digesta* (in English simply The Digest). As he had done with his Constitution in 529, so here with the publication of The Digest Justinian ruled that all earlier law drawn from the treatises of the jurists (the *ius vetus*) was repealed.

In the meantime Justinian's jurist-specialist Tribonius had decided that the extant *Institutiones* of the third-century jurist, Gaius, were obsolete and needed replacing. Accordingly just before the publication of The Digest, he published on his own initiative the revision titled *Institutiones Iustinianae.*

At the same time and under the same mandate the commission Justinian had established in 528 was at work on a new codification, a code of Roman law, meant to replace the *Codex* Theodosius had promulgated in 438. This was completed and promulgated in 534 with the force of law as the *Codex Repetitae Praelectionis.* It was arranged in twelve books, containing 4,652 constitutions, the earliest dating from Hadrian (117–138), the latest from Justinian himself. This is the Code of Roman law that has come down to the modern world.

But Justinian's work as a legislator hardly ended in 534 with the publication of The Code. From then until 565 he issued numerous ordinances which bear the name *novellae* (in English *novels*). The largest collection of these contains 168 *novellae,* some of them by Justinian's successors, Justin II and Tiberius I. The *Versio Vulgata* contains 134 of the *novellae* in Latin, the edition first known in the Middle Ages and the version used most extensively by the medieval jurists.[21]

Because so much of Justinian's earlier legislation is repeated in the later—for example a year after his accession he specified in what way the husband's impotence becomes grounds for the wife's dissolving the marriage, but repeated this after 534 in Novel 22—it is more convenient to examine this legislation topically than sequentially. I will do so under three headings: the principles grounding his divorce legislation, the termination by causes other than divorce, and termination by divorce.

The Principles Grounding Justinian's Divorce Legislation

In Novel 22, Chapter 3, he reiterated what had been declared three centuries earlier about the immediate cause that creates a marriage, but changed one significant substantive. Where the classical jurists had said that it is the consent of the parties that creates a marriage, here Justinian said: "It is the mutual will to be married that creates a marriage" (*Nuptias itaque affectus alternus facit;* in Greek, *gámon mèn oun diathésis amóibaia poiêî*).[22]

In the same novel Justinian declared in principle the possibility and the right of persons to remarry after the dissolution of a marriage. And to warrant this he enunciated an even more fundamental principle, one that seems to contradict flatly Christ's *logion* in the Synoptic Gospels: "Once persons have come together in marriage, whether this is done by simple expression of wills or also with the offering of dowry and nuptial gifts, this is by all means effective even after a [prior] dissolution, whether done with penalty or without it; for in the affairs of men whatever is bound can be loosed."[23]

In the chapter immediately following Justinian sets out the ways in which a marriage can be dissolved even while both parties live: "During the lifetime of both contracting parties marriages are dissolved, some by the consent of both parties according to an arrangement acceptable to both [about which nothing is said here]; others for a kind of legitimate cause that is called *bona gratia* [without accusation or penalty]; others apart from any cause; and yet others for a legitimate cause."[24]

The category of dissolution that is last-named here—dissolution for a legitimate cause (*cum causa rationabili*)—seems to designate the contentious dissolution wherein one spouse dismisses the other with the note of *repudium,* on the ground of some delinquency acknowledged by the law. We shall see presently that Justinian inventoried such grounds generously and in detail.

Non-Divorce Dissolutions

In the same Novel 22, Chapter 5 Justinian reaffirms what had been accepted as an agency capable of dissolving marriage from the time of Augustine and even before the turn of the fifth century. He grants to either spouse the right to dissolve the marriage unilaterally and to depart from it provided this is done in order to take up a life of vowed celibacy and chastity. He distinguishes this from the case in which one spouse may be sentenced to a life of celibacy in a monastery because of some delinquency in the marriage.[25] Church authorities would later set as a condition of this dissolution that the marriage be not consummated. Justinian does not.

In Chapter 6 of this same novel he further qualifies the law he had earlier enacted (in his Code, Book 5, Chapter 17, 10) concerning a husband's impotence as a ground for his wife's dissolving the marriage. Where his earlier legislation had said that a wife may dissolve the marriage by a note of repudiation beginning from two years after the marriage was first contracted, Justinian here extends this delay to three years. He gives as his reason for this extension that some men recover their potency only *after* two years in the marriage. Here, as in the earlier legislation, a husband can be dismissed against his will, and the note of repudiation can be sent either by the wife herself or by her father.[26]

In Chapter 7 he takes up the tradition of dissolution by reason of one spouse's being taken away into captivity, as happened in the wars so frequent on the empire's frontiers and during the barbarian raids into Italy. Here he uses language indicating that the tradition according to which captivity of one spouse terminates a marriage has survived to his time on the rationalization that a captive falls legally to the status of a slave; and a slave lacks *connubium,* the right to be married.

Justinian rules here in two directions. Despite the captivity, as long as the spouse held captive is known to be alive, the marriage remains. And if the other and free spouse attempts a second marriage nonetheless? He rules that this spouse may in fact remarry, but must forfeit the dowry and nuptial gifts (forfeit them to whom, he does not say). In this case the second marriage apparently functions as a dissolution, albeit an unjustified one. Otherwise the remarrying spouse must be punished, at least in the woman's case, for adultery.

But Justinian rules also that as long as the captive spouse is not known with certainty to be dead, the other must wait five years before remarrying. He or she may then do so without penalty despite having no further information about the spouse held in captivity. In any case, no *repudium* is required.

What if the spouse presumed dead after five years should later return? The now dissolved marriage, Justinian rules, does not revive spontaneously. Since according to the law it has passed out of existence at the end of five years, if it is to be renewed, new marital consent must do this.[27]

In Chapters 8 and 9 Justinian modifies the long-standing law prescribing that the person against whom a criminal judgment of deportation has been passed ceases to be married because the deportation renders him civilly dead. Even before Justinian's time Christian emperors had mitigated this consequence of penal deportation. Justinian's Constitution reports (in Book 5, Chapter 17) that Emperor Alexander Severus had ruled (in 229) that the sentence of deportation does not automatically dissolve the marriage, although the crime that it punished might itself occasion a legitimate repudiation.

Here in Novel 22 Justinian rules that where the condemned is a citizen, the deportation has no effect on his marriage because, as he explains, no citizen is to be reduced to slave status by punishment.[28] But in the next chapter (9) he qualifies this qualification, enacting that if the deported convict is a freedman or woman, or the child of such, this punishment does end his or her marriage because it does for them have the effect of reduction to slavery and hence loss of *connubium.*[29] In Chapter 13 he returns to the subject and there rules simply, "Deportatio . . . non solvit matrimonium," noting that his predecessor Constantine had already made this determination in a particular case, and that he himself had done the same.[30]

Two hundred years earlier Constantine had enacted that if a husband left home for military action, and within a space of four years had not communicated with his wife, had given no indication of his *affectus* (his will to be married) in her regard, the wife could enter a second marriage without penalty provided she first notified her husband's military commander and he had acknowledged this notification. Justinian records this in Chapter 14 of this Novel 22, but goes on immediately to modify the Constantinian legislation. He rules that the wife must wait out ten years of silence on her husband's part before she may remarry with impunity. And to do this she must also have tried to contact him by letter or by messenger; he himself must have either expressly rejected their marriage or have continued in his silence; and she must have informed his commander of her intention to take another husband.[31]

But a few years later Justinian wrote this part of the law even more severely in Novel 117, Chapter 11, ruling that the wife of such a husband becomes free to remarry only on proof of his death. And she must wait a year before remarrying after the rumor of her husband's death has been confirmed under oath by witnesses testifying before the military authorities. If she remarried without having taken the precaution specified here, she and her new consort were liable to punishment for adultery.[32]

Dissolution by Repudiation for Cause

In Chapter 15 of this Novel 22 Justinian turns finally to the inventory of causes, or grounds, which legitimize the spouses' dissolving their marriage by repudiation. He separates into paragraphs 1 and 2 respectively the causes justifying the wife's repudiating the husband, and vice versa. He points out that he is no more than repeating the causes legitimized a century earlier by Theodosius the Younger. But in Chapter 16 he adds three causes to those legitimizing a husband's repudiating his wife.

In paragraph 1 he enacts (again) that a wife may repudiate her husband if she can prove one or more of the following delinquencies against him: murder, treason, perjury, the preparing of poisons, violation of sepulchres, theft from churches or shrines, brigandage or the harboring of brigands, cattle-rustling, kidnaping, attempting the murder of the wife or plotting it, intercourse with other women in the home he shares with the wife, and adultery (distinct from the last-named in that this designates his intercourse with another man's wife). If she could prove any of these against him, she could end the marriage by repudiating him and could keep her entire dowry as well as the nuptial gifts.

About male adultery among the Romans, a husband's intercourse outside the marriage was traditionally not considered adultery unless this were with another man's wife, but not even then if she were of low social status. According to the *Lex Iulia de Adulteris* no man could be prosecuted solely because, though married, he had intercourse with a woman other than his wife. But he could at least be liable to full punishment if he had intercourse with a woman who was married, or if he committed rape. But even in these cases it was not his wife who could prosecute him, even after repudiating him. The jurisprudential reason here was that no woman could act as an accuser in public proceedings except in cases of murder of a parent, a husband, a child or a patron, or for the forgery, concealment or defacing of certain wills.[33] Theodosius' legislation made no change in this tradition. But Justinian, as we shall see, apparently did grant to the wife the right to punitive action in the event of her husband's adultery.

The grounds legitimizing in turn a husband's repudiating his wife were, as enacted by Theodosius, the following delinquencies: murder, the preparing of poisons, violation of sepulchres, sacrilege, brigandage or the harboring of brigands, plotting against the husband's life, attending, without the husband's knowledge or without his permission, parties not arranged specifically for her, staying away overnight without just cause against the husband's will, attending games in the circuses or theatrical plays against his will, striking him, and of course her adultery.[34]

In Chapter 16 Justinian added three causes to those inherited from Theodosius: the wife's procuring her own abortion, her bathing with other men, and her discussing potential marriage with another man.

If a husband could prove any of these causes against his wife, he could dissolve their marriage by repudiating her, and he could keep all the dowry as well as the nuptial gifts.

One must take care not to impose on this legislation anachronistically a legal qualification belonging to a later age. In both the Theodosian and the Justinian legislation the function of these causes was limited to legitimizing the repudiation of one spouse by the other. They were not set as causes needed to make the repudiation valid. That is, the legislation of both emperors did not intend to make impossible the dissolving of a marriage by repudiation. But what it did was to try to restrain hasty and frivolously motivated dissolution by setting severe penalties for repudiating without legally acknowledged cause. Thus if a wife repudiated her husband without proving one of these causes against him, she lost the dowry and the nuptial gifts. She lost *connubium* for five years—and thus could not remarry for five years. (Even if she dismissed her husband for legitimate cause, Novel 22, Chapter 16 ruled that she must wait one year before remarrying lest there be doubt about the paternity of any child she might be carrying unborn at the time of the dismissal.) If the husband repudiated his wife without proving one of the legitimizing causes against her, he lost dowry and nuptial gifts, and was forbidden to remarry within two years. These penalties were set by Justinian, and his setting them implied that either spouse had the capacity to dissolve the marriage at will, since they were intended as punishments for an act completed effectively but against the law.

In his later legislation, in Novel 117, Justinian amended these inventories of causes by abbreviating them. Thus a wife could dismiss her husband if she could prove any of five delinquencies against him: if he plotted treason or failed to delate others whom he knew to be plotting it; if he plotted against her life or failed to inform her of others' plotting against it, or failed to vindicate her against the plotters; if he tried to put her out for prostitution (the crime of *lenocinium*); if he accused her of adultery but could not prove it; if he had intercourse with other women in his own home or went frequently to other women at a house in his own city.

In turn a husband could dismiss his wife if he could prove any of the following against her: her failure to disclose to him any treasonous plotting she had come to know of; her plotting against his life or failure to inform him of others' doing so; her adultery; her bathing with other men against his will; her staying outside the home overnight against his will, unless with her parents; her attending, without his knowledge or without his consent, the theatres, circuses or athletic contests. If he repudiated her without cause and thus drove her out of his house, he could not use her overnight absence against her as a legitimizing cause.

Justinian's Final Legislation

Still later, in Novel 134, Chapters 10 and 11, Justinian rounded off his legislation that regulated the substance of divorce and remarriage. In Chapter 10 he specified quite exact penalties for adultery by either spouse. It is said to have been prompted by the unsatisfactory effects of the legislation we have just seen.

He enacted that the penalties for adultery that Theodosius had legislated be inflicted not only on the adulterer but on any who had cooperated in the crime. But he added a compassionate clause providing that if an adulterous male were married, he could keep the dowry and the nuptial gifts. But the rest of his assets were to be distributed to his descendants and ascendants through the third degree, if he had any; but if he did not, they were to go into the public treasury.[35]

In the same chapter he laid a special penalty on the wife convicted of adultery. Along with the statutory penalties she was to be imprisoned in a monastery. If her husband wished within two years to take her back, he could do so without penalty. If he had married again in the meantime, this was to be no obstacle to his freeing and taking back the incarcerated first wife. He was to dismiss the second wife. But if he let the two years pass, or if he died before they did so, the adulterous wife was to have her head shaven; she was to assume monastic garb, and was to remain in the monastery for the rest of her life. As for her estate, two-thirds of it was to go to her descendants, the other one-third of it to the monastery. If she had only ascendants, her estate was to be divided between them and the monastery.

In Chapter 11 of this Novel 134 Justinian made his last and most innovative modification of the imperial law on divorce.

First he enacted that henceforth no spouse was to be dismissed except for one of the causes stated in the law (i.e., in Novel 117). Perhaps more importantly still, he ruled that in the future no marriage was to be dissolved by mutual consent. He set as the penalty for any man's or woman's dissolving a marriage for any other cause than those now left in the law, that his or her estate be distributed to their descendants, and that the culprit, whether man or woman, be confined to a monastery for the rest of his or her life. He added the escape clause that if a spouse who had dissolved a marriage illegally wished to rejoin the other before being sent to the monastery, this was to be permitted.

Be it noted that nowhere in this chapter does Justinian rule that an illegal attempt at dissolution is ineffective. It is only forbidden. Nor does he say that in principle a second marriage attempted after an illegal dissolution is null and void. His legislation sought rather to block this attempt by threatening monastic incarceration, and by leaving as the only escape from the incarceration a return to the once dissolved first marriage.

The Reasons for Justinian's Permissive Legislation

If we may take Theodosius I's Edict of Thessalonica in 380 as the act which established Christianity as the religion of the Roman empire, we ought to ask at least briefly how the divorce legislation of Justinian, a Christian emperor a century and a half later, could agree so little with the New Testament teaching on the same subject. One could hardly doubt that if both Ulpianus, the classical Roman jurist, and Augustine, the Catholic bishop, could have examined Novels 22, 117 and 134, the former would have found them familiar and mainly acceptable as instruments for regulating divorce and remarriage, while Augustine would have been outraged. But Ulpianus was the pagan, while Augustine was Justinian's brother Christian.

Let me suggest the following reasons for the slight influence of the New Testament on Justinian's divorce legislation, and for that matter on the younger Theodosius' legislation of a century earlier. (And whatever the degree of influence of any of these reasons taken singly, certainly each was reinforced by its interlocking with all the others.)

Probably underlying all other reasons was Justinian's character. He was, along with Constantine but far more than he, the quintessential Byzantine caesaro-papist. He considered himself head of the Church at least in the east, the appointer of bishops, the protector and mentor of Popes, the guardian of orthodoxy, supervisor of forms of worship, and of course supreme and unassailable legislator.

At the same time, whether he acknowledged the fact or not, he was presiding at the demise of the old empire as it was simultaneously torn internally by feuding factions and attacked from without by powerful barbarian peoples. His desperate work of holding the empire together became in part an exercise in pragmatic compromise. He must have been convinced he could take no stand on principle, even had he been inclined to do so, that would alienate any needed ally or stir up more dissent within the empire. Consequently his legislation embodied, at its best, what he thought possible and necessary, not what he thought demanded of him by any authority he may have acknowledged outside and above himself.

In this regard both Theodosius and Justinian had to reckon with the pre-Christian tradition of divorce whose roots were centuries-old in the empire's population. There was first of all a considerable portion of the population that remained pagan. Even when the old imperial religion was disestablished and Christianity put in its place, even though the pagan priesthood was abolished and the pagan ritual interdicted and its temples and shrines torn down, no persecution of the pagan population as such was ever mounted by the Christian emperors. It was never a crime to be a pagan, as it had been for the two hundred and twenty years from Domitian to Constantine to be a Christian. So the pagans' dearly cherished right to dissolve unwanted marriages was a powerful tradition with which Justinian had to reckon in formulating his legislation.

Then there was the huge portion of the Christian population that had become Christian just because the imperial persecutions had ended and just because Christianity had gained the ascendancy and was becoming the religion of the future. Political expediency that had once urged at least superficial devotion to the imperial cult now urged a shift of devotion to the Christian, and with superficiality still unchallenged. Where conversion involved little more than a change of political allegiance but only minimally a change of heart, it was not to be expected that the cherished legal right to dissolve an unwanted marriage would be easily given up. Even if Justinian had stood in principle for the abolition of this right, he almost certainly felt himself in no position to challenge the right radically. The most that he did, as we have seen in his Novels 117 and 134, was to put some restraint on the ease with which dissolutions could be executed.

And there is clear enough evidence that Justinian did not stand in principle against this right, although he saw the right rooted not so much in the empire's citizens as in his authority. We have seen that in Chapter 3 of Novel 22 he enunciated what he apparently regarded as a philosophical principle legitimizing the legislation that flowed from it: "Once persons have come together in marriage . . . this is by all means effective even after a [prior] dissolution. . . . For in the affairs of men whatever is bound can be loosed." This declaration from a Christian ruler who began his Code by invoking the name of the Lord Jesus Christ,[36] and who cannot have been ignorant of the latter's "Therefore what God has joined man must not separate," suggests how little his governing conscience felt itself ruled by Christian norms.

Perhaps Justinian did what so many other Christians did: he took to be just as authentic as any of the Gospel texts on divorce and remarriage the exceptive clause in Matthew 5:32 and 19:9—"But I say to you, whoever dismisses his wife, except in the case of her *pornéia,* and marries another, commits adultery." And trusting in the authenticity of the phrase he worked a logical excursus from it as follows: Jesus never meant that there are no causes warranting a man's dismissing his wife. Her unchastity he himself says is such a cause; and there are other delinquencies in marriage as grievous as unchastity, and some of them worse. Therefore by the rule of equivalence there must be other causes warranting dismissal.

And if this dismissal is available to husbands, then by the same law of equivalence and in virtue of fairness, it ought also to be available to wives. It remains only to determine authoritatively what these other causes are. And it goes without saying that this determining is to be done by him whose office it is to mediate God's law to the people in the civil law—the emperor.

Justinian was not brought up short by any contradictory legislation or judicial declaration coming from the Christian bishops. For the simple fact is that there was not, in the early Christian population, any sense of separate jurisdictions. In its juridical dimension the Church was the empire and the empire was the Church—at least in the minds of such men as Theodosius and Justinian. There were no separate Church courts. And when the empire crumbled to the point where courts were left vacant for want of appointment by the emperors, bishops came to preside in many of them.

The ground from which the Fathers and the Popes challenged the imperial divorce legislation was biblical and doctrinal, as we shall see in the following chapter. And we shall see in a still later chapter that it was not until an emperor came into power who willed that a rigorous Gospel interpretation shape divorce legislation that this legislation came near to reflecting the Gospel. This emperor was Charlemagne, two and a half centuries down history's road from Justinian.

NOTES

1. The following are the sources I have used for this examination: the *Codex Theodosianus,* edited by Paul Krueger, Berlin, 1923–1925; the *Corpus Iuris Civilis,* Vol. 1, containing Justinian's *Institutiones* edited by Paul Krueger, and the *Digesta,* edited by Theodor Mommsen; Vol. 3 containing Justinian's *Novellae,* edited by Rudolf Schoell and Wilhelm Kroll, Berlin, 1954. A useful digest of the history of Roman marriage law is Percy F. Corbett's *The Roman Law of Marriage,* Oxford, 1969 (a reprint of the 1930 edition).

2. The legal form of this repudiation where a husband had gained *manus* over his wife by the fictive purchase of it from her father called *coemptio* was *remancipatio.* That is, the wife was excluded from the new family in which she had become a legal daughter. This exclusion had the effect of ending her marriage.

3. Examples of these steps, which could be and were used in varying combinations, were simple separation of the spouses for a reasonable time, restoration of the dowry, a written declaration, and a second marriage itself.

4. Translated from the Latin in *Seneca, The Moral Essays,* Volume 3, Loeb Classical Library, Cambridge, 1935, pp. 154–156.

In the rest of the passage Seneca turns the point of his attack against the Roman wives' infidelity: "Is there any shame at all about adultery now that it has come to such a pass that the only use to which women put their husbands is to tantalize their lovers? Chastity is taken as no more than evidence of homeliness. Where will you find a woman so unattractive, so miserable that she cannot find at least a couple of lovers—and have to divide her time equally between them? And the day is not long enough for her to take care of all of them, but she must be carried in her litter to one and then spend the night with another. That woman is naive and out of touch with the times who doesn't realize that having no more than one lover is now called marriage."

Lucius Annaeus Seneca was born in Cordoba in 4 B.C., came to Rome a young man, learned the Stoic way of life and became tutor to Nero. He died in 65 A.D.

5. Translated from the Latin of Martial, *Epigrams,* Loeb Classical Library, London, 1930, p. 360.

The "Julian law" to which Martial refers may well have been the *Lex Iulia* noted above, or perhaps the *Lex Iulia de Adulteris,* enacted also by Augustus, which prescribed a compulsory form in which the *repudium* was to be drawn up and delivered to a spouse who was being dismissed. It could be either oral or written, but its delivery was to be verified by seven witnesses. Its purpose too was to verify that the repudiation had taken place.

Marcus Valerius Martialis came to Rome in 64 A.D. at the age of twenty-four. He lived and wrote there—and entertained Rome's cynical society—for thirty-four years. He was wrong, of course, in judging Telesilla an adulteress according to the law. There was no more in Roman law that forbade her quick turnover of husbands than forbids it in American civil codes.

6. Translated from the Latin of *Juvenal and Perseus,* The Loeb Classical Library, London, 1930, pp. 92 and 94. Juvenal wrote his satires in his later years, during the reigns of Domitian, Nerva and Trajan. He was born in 60 and died c. 128.

7. In *Le Mariage a Rome: Etude d'histoire juridique et sociale,* Milan, 1972, p. 112.

8. Students of Roman law commonly divide its history among the following four epochs: the mid-republican period, from 450 to 150 B.C. (the Law of the Twelve Tables was passed in 451–450); the later republican period, to c. 45 B.C.; the early empire and classical period, which is itself divided into an early sub-period from Hadrian's accession in 17 A.D. to the end of Commodus' reign in 192, and a later sub-period from Commodus'⁷ reign in 192 to the end of Alexander Severus' reign in 238; and the post-classical period, the epoch of the great emperor-legislators, Theodosius II and Justinian the most prolific among them. All five of the jurists canonized by Valentinian flourished during the classical period.

The Romans distinguished two parts in their law, the Law of Nations, that portion of their legislation that they applied to foreigners as well as to themselves (the *Ius Gentium*) and the Civil Law (the *Ius Civile*), that part which they applied to themselves only.

9. This is recorded in Justinian's *Digesta,* Book 24, Part 2, Paragraph 8, *De Divortio et Repudio,* in *Corpus Iuris Civilis,* p. 356.

10. *Ibid.,* par. 3, p. 355.

11. *Ibid.,* par. 9, p. 356.

12. *Ibid.,* par. 10, p. 356.

13. *Digesta,* Book 24, ch. 2, par. 11 and Book 23, ch. 2, par. 45 (quoted in Corbett, *op. cit.,* p. 239.)

14. In Justinian's *Digesta, loc. cit.,* par. 4, p. 355.

15. This is in *Theodosiani Libri XVI cum Constitutionibus Sirimondianis et Leges Novellae ad Theodosium Pertinentes . . .* ediderunt Theodorus Mommsen . . . Paulus M. Meyer, Voluminis I, Pars Posterior, Berolini, 1905, pp. 155–156.

Theodosius' record of his own and his predecessors' divorce legislation is in Book III, chapter 16. An English translation of this legislation is in *The Theodosian Code and Novels and the Sirmondian Constitutions* . . . by Clyde Pharr, Princeton, 1953.

16. *Theodosiani,* etc., *loc. cit.,* Liber III, cap. 16, 1, p. 156.

17. *Ibid.,* cap. 16, 2, pp. 156–157.

18. *Ibid.*

19. Born in Constantinople, Theodosius became emperor of the east in 408 at the age of seven years, and ruled until his death in 450. In 436 or 437 he set up a commission to codify the mass of imperial legislation that had accumulated since the reign of Constantine. He promulgated his Code in 438, and gave it the force of law on January 1, 439. One of its provisions was that no constitution published from the time of Constantine's accession was to be valid unless included in this *Codex Theodosianus.*

20. This Theodosian legislation subsequent to the promulgation of his *Codex* is outlined in Corbett, *op. cit.,* pp. 244–245, where he quotes from Justinian's record of it in his own *Codex,* Book 5, Chapter 17, 8.

21. All of Justinian's legislation is gathered into the *Corpus Iuris Civilis* and published most recently as *Corpus Iuris Civilis,* Editio Sexta, edited in three volumes by Paul Krueger, Theodor Mommsen and Wilhelm Kroll, Berlin, 1954. The *Codex* is in Volume 2, the *Novellae* in Volume 3.

22. *Corpus Iuris Civilis;* Vol. 3, p. 149.

23. *Ibid.* The Latin text is "Cum enim semel convenerint seu puro nuptiali affectu sive etiam oblatione dotis et propter nuptias donationis, oportet causam omnino sequi etiam solutionem aut innoxiam aut cum poena, quoniam horum quae in hominibus subsequuntur, quidquid legatur solubile est."

24. *Ibid.,* pp. 149–150. The Greek verb for "dissolved" (*distrahuntur* in the Latin) is *dialúontai,* a replication of the *lúontai* used in the Synoptic Gospels to designate the dissolving of a marriage by dismissal under rabbinic law.

25. *Ibid.,* p. 150.

26. *Ibid.*

27. *Ibid.,* p. 151.

28. *Ibid.,* pp. 151–152.

29. *Ibid.,* p. 152.

30. *Ibid.,* p. 154.

31. *Ibid.*

32. *Op. cit.,* p. 561.

33. Corbett, *op. cit.,* pp. 141–142.

34. *Corpus Iuris Civilis, loc. cit.,* pp. 155–156.

35. *Op. cit.,* p. 685.

36. *Op. cit.,* Vol. 2, p. 4.

6. CHRISTIAN TEACHING AND DISCIPLINE UNTIL THE FOURTH CENTURY

When one moves from an inspection of the New Testament passages into a study of the subsequent Christian conduct and teaching concerning divorce and remarriage, it is important to get clear of some misconceptions and to avoid the falsifying method of study that would result from them.

One such misconception is that by the close of the apostolic age at the end of the first century the Christians were aware that they had two volumes of Sacred Scriptures, so to speak, the Old Testament and the New Testament; that since both were divinely inspired, but the inspired words on divorce and remarriage in the New Testament came from Jesus, his words simply corrected those of the Old Testament where the two disagreed about divorce and remarriage; and that therefore the Christian teachers' fairly simple task was to mine the Gospels for Jesus' instructions and apply them to the ruling of Christian marital conduct.

Even a casual student of the first three generations of the early Church knows that when the Christians of that epoch thought of the divinely inspired Scriptures, they thought of what we now call the Old Testament. The realization that writings produced by members of their own communities also belonged among these Scriptures, that these writings had equal value as teaching sources along with the Hebrew writings, came to life only gradually. To be sure, the writings that were eventually gathered into the collection that is now the New Testament appeared in steady sequence beginning with Paul's two letters to the Thessalonians in the early 50's. Though all these writings, with the exception of Paul's letters to the Romans and to the Ephesians, were written for a local community or even a person, gradually they were circulated among other communities and began to be grouped homogeneously. There was probably a collection of some of Paul's letters by the end of the first century, for there are references to some of them in Clement of Rome (96 A.D.) and in Ignatius of Antioch (110 A.D.). And 2 Peter 3:16, which dates probably from about 125, indicates a collection of Paul's letters about which its audience knows, and about which it says that they are of the same value and authority as "the other Scriptures."

But how early was there a New Testament in approximately the sense in which we understand the name?

> Although in the 2nd cent. the Pauline epistles came into acceptance, just when did this acceptance mean that the Christian writings were being put on a par with the Jewish Scriptures? When did the concept of a NT emerge? In *2 Pt. 3:16* (c. 100–125?) we find writings of Paul put on a par with "the other Scriptures," but we are not certain that this indicates a total equality with the OT. By the mid-second century Justin (*Apol.* 1:67) witnesses to the fact that the Gospels and the writings of the apostles were being read in conjunction with the OT at Christian liturgical services. About the same time *2 Clem. 4* cites Isaiah then Mt. as "another Scripture." Probably, however, it was Marcion with his rejection of the OT in favor of a truncated collection of 10 Pauline epistles and Lk who brought to the fore by way of opposition the belief that the Christian writings form a unity with the OT.[1]

What we must infer from this is that when the Christians, say, from 50 to 200, looked through their own received teachings to find God's mind concerning divorce and remarriage, they did not find and use a New Testament opposed to and correcting an errant Old Testament. What they found were the remembered words of Jesus forbidding an unjust treatment of Jewish wives. But it was a treatment that had been tolerated and even legislated by Moses, and presumably tolerated and legislated with God's approval. (And this was not the worst of the uncertainties with which the Christian teachers had to deal.)

What is more, the relevant words of Jesus were kept alive by memory first through oral teaching in quite separate Christian communities, or at most in separate districts. Thus these districts produced their own traditions of Jesus' instruction on divorce and remarriage (of them we know only the Synoptic tradition, divided among the Lukan, the Markan and the Matthean; and the Pauline, which the Apostle hints that he had learned from an earlier tradition).

And we have already seen that among these traditions there was no unanimity. Each was plainly an adaptation and interpretation of Jesus' own teaching. The Matthean tradition had him allowing a husband's dismissal of his wife for her *pornéia,* but Luke, Mark and Paul mentioned nothing of this. Paul reported that Jesus forbade a husband's dismissing his wife apparently for any cause, but implied clearly that if the husband did this the wife was no longer married (and must not remarry). Paul also extemporized his own resolution of a problem probably common in the mixed Jewish-pagan Christian communities: he advised that a Christian spouse could let an unwilling pagan spouse "depart." Matthew, Mark and Luke did not hint at such a resolution of a common Christian problem, even though they must have been familiar with it in the communities for which they compiled their versions of the Gospel.

But though both Matthew and Paul evidently expanded and interpreted the teaching of Jesus (as did Mark in the way we have seen), neither of them touched the question bred by their interpretation: Do the dismissal for *pornéia* and the departure of the unwilling pagan spouse free all the erstwhile spouses to marry again? This question the Fathers of succeeding generations could not avoid. And they would have to answer it by themselves, adapting and interpreting the words of Jesus as they had got them in the already adapted and interpreted traditions of Paul and the Synoptics. What combination of forces—unanimity of regional teachings, prestige of this or that Father, application of ecclesiastical authority—would eventually produce a single fixed and universal doctrine? How soon would this be done? And when done, would it be another interpretation of Jesus' teaching, and, if so, how faithful to his original teaching (presuming any bishops or councils were confident they could recapture this)? The modern student may be surprised to find that the first one thousand years of Christian history would go by before unanimity would be established even in the Western, Latin sector of the Church—not to mention that the disagreement between the Latin West on the one hand and the Orthodox East on the other would become permanent.

Jesus' words remembered as uncertainly as this hardly promised to be an effective weapon against the mentality and the practice of divorce so epidemic in the Roman empire.

Divorce and Remarriage Among the Early Christians

It does not force the facts of the case to say that the early history of Christian attitude and conduct regarding divorce and remarriage is divisible into three stages. Without assigning exact dates to the transitions from one stage to the next we can say that the first included the early decades, the first generation and part of the second, during which the Christian communities were populated mostly by converts from the synagogue communities of the diaspora and by slaves. Because Roman citizens were a minority in these communities, the communities' questions and problems about divorce and remarriage were not the usual ones reflected in the imperial legislation we reviewed in the preceding chapter. Since, for example, the law denied to slaves the *connubium* permitting marriage but allowed them only the legitimate concubinage of *contubernium,* the heads of the Christian communities faced two questions unfamiliar in the larger Roman society, and one question that was all too familiar in it. The first two asked whether the Christians ought to obey the law forbidding the marriages of citizens with slaves (in many instances the answer was no), and whether *contubernium* was marriage of the kind referred to in their instructions by Jesus and the apostles (here the answer seems to have been an unequivocal yes).

The familar question grew in turn out of the second of these. *Contubernium* had no rights before the law. Any slave's master could block his or her forming even this relationship. He could also end it by killing one of the partners, by selling one of them, or by simply forbidding its continuation. It was common practice also that the male members of a Roman household exploit the female slaves sexually; and markedly less common but not unheard of that a wealthy and independent matron exploit the male slaves for the same purpose. There must have been serious problems of fidelity and perseverance in monogamy in the lives of slaves secretly become Christian.

The first stage of this history passed into the second when citizens of the empire began to join the Christian communities in significant numbers. As they did they brought with them the questions about fidelity, divorce and remarriage proper to men and women living in an environment and under the law common to citizens. It is significant that most of those who became Christians were already married when they did so. And they had married in the Roman way with all the Roman suppositions about fidelity, divorce and remarriage. Moreover, as we saw in an earlier chapter, citizens who married as Christians did not experience a form and a process of marrying different from that of other citizens. For at least the first three centuries of Christian history this form and process were still non-ecclesiastical, family-supervised and family-executed. Christian citizens did not think they were doing a fundamentally different thing in marrying than did other citizens when they married. This had consequences at the other end of a marriage, for when it became imperative to decide whether a marriage should go on, or who the spouses really were, who would do this deciding? Would the parties themselves do this, as was done without hesitation in ten thousand instances among their fellow citizens? Or would the authorities in the Christian communities intervene to decide?

A significant feature of Christian life for at least the first three centuries of its history was that religious conversion was not necessarily a respecter of marriages. A husband alone might become a Christian, and in a few rare instances bring into the particular community the problem of using his *manu potestas,* his marital authority over his wife, to compel her to conversion as well. Or a wife alone might be converted. And if she belonged to one of the patrician families in which this by now rare *manu potestas* still survived, then this authority of her husband was put to the challenge by her conversion. But even in the *matrimonium liberum* of the overwhelming majority of Roman marriages, in the free-choice relationships in which both men and women married when and whom they wished, there was bound to be serious trouble where one spouse became Christian and the other did not. It is easy to agree with those historians of early Christianity who have searched among the causes of the imperial persecutions and have suggested that converted wives and their threat to ancient marital mores helped as much as any cause to bring the public temper to the flash-point. How frequently marriages were in effect destroyed by the Christian conversion of one of the spouses is not measured accurately by the single notice in the canonical Scriptures where Paul takes up the issue in 1 Corinthians 7:12–16.

Consensual divorce, the easy dissolution by mutual consent of the spouses, hardly caused the Christians any anguish of indecision for at least the first three centuries. This is evident *a posteriori* in the absence of any concern about it in those records we have from the early communities. *A priori* it is unthinkable that such divorce could have become a problem during these centuries in face of Jesus' words in the Synoptic tradition on the origin and value of marriage in his Father's will, and in face of the flat forbidding of divorce in the Pauline and Markan versions—the two that were best known outside Palestine. Faithful monogamy was a most seriously urged ideal and a most seriously imposed obligation. And the seriousness with which the ideal and the obligation were accepted through and past the fifth century we shall see presently in some representative statements.

The problems, the questions and the consequent indecision arose because of what the Christians shared with their non-Christian families, friends and neighbors of those early years: weak and sometimes wanton human nature, and tragedy striking their marriages in the form of banishment into exile, enslavement, captivity, or a soldier-husband's disappearance in battle. Where the weak or the wanton committed adultery, repentance followed by severe penance was thought to repair the delinquency insofar as this was an offense against God and the community. But what of personal offense to the spouse? While Roman law *commanding* divorce by dismissal of the adulterous spouse might seem needlessly severe after repentance and in face of the willingness to do penance, the older Roman tradition *allowing* dismissal seemed reasonable. But did Jesus' instruction forbid dismissal even for this reason of adultery? If it did not, was remarriage after such dissolution possible, at least for the innocent spouse? If it did forbid dissolution even after adultery, did it also forbid separation of the spouse from bed and board? What of the clause appearing twice in Matthew's version of Jesus' instruction, wherein the latter seemed to make an exception, to allow dissolution by dismissal among his own people and apparently also among his followers when *pornéia* was found in the wife? And if any misconduct in marriage came within the compass of *pornéia,* did not adultery?

The second stage in this history of the Christian attitude and conduct regarding divorce and remarriage passed into the third when Christianity became the established religion of the empire, when citizens moved over en masse into the Christian population for social and political gain, and Christians slowly became the numerical majority. To understand what happened at this juncture we must note again the demographic and therefore legal peculiarity in the empire that served to complicate the question of divorce and remarriage once the Christians became the majority. Those in the population bound (and privileged) by marriage legislation were the citizens. In a proportion that is difficult if not impossible to measure after so many centuries, those who became Christians in the early generations of both the Church and the empire were in great part non-citizens. Consequently from before the middle of the first century until near the end of the fourth, when Christianity became the established religion and citizens began seeking baptism in droves, a tradition regarding divorce and remarriage had grown up in the Christian communities separate from and antithetical to the legally established Roman tradition.

But when the Christian emperors, beginning with Constantine, began the long, inching and painful diminishing of divorce, the subjects of their legislation of diminution were in the majority citizens still lodged in the tradition of divorce, many of whom never became Christian and never intended to. At the same time those Christians born into Christian families, as well as those recently converted, found available within Christian discipline by this time a normative system of divorce and remarriage that, as we have seen and shall see again, made demands tempered far below the severity of the New Testament teaching in Mark or even in Paul. And it would be unrealistic to suppose that the born-into-family Christians, as well as the converts, did not, in the spirit of Christian mitigation, take advantage also of the mitigated demands of the imperial legislation. After all the Church had no legal system of its own. It had moral discipline. It otherwise lived by Roman law and urged obedience to it. Roman citizens were juridically conscious men and women. The separation of moral right and wrong from acceptance of the legally permissible did not come easily to them. Consequently learning a new morality of divorce and remarriage while living under a law and in a tradition so permissive about such practices also did not come easily to them.

One may suppose that at the same time the former group, that sector of the population that rejected the newly established religion, reacted vigorously against the attempts to diminish the easy availability of divorce. During the two centuries from the establishing of Christianity until Justinian's attempt at a substantial revision of the divorce law, the Christian proportion of the population increased and the non-Christian proportionally decreased. What the percentages were by the year 536 we have no way of knowing accurately. Nevertheless the modern Catholic has reason to be surprised at the leniency of the reform legislation we saw in the preceding chapter, legislation decreed by a Christian emperor for a population Christian in its majority, already two hundred years after theirs had become the one enfranchised religion. The same modern Catholic must be surprised too that the laws intended to rule Christians in their divorcing and remarrying were legislated by civil rulers in Constantinople, not by religious rulers in Rome. This is because it is first difficult to understand in the twentieth century the place of the Christian emperor in the Church—at least the place that he arrogated to himself. He was an officer of the

Church, a summoner and a president of ecumenical councils. He was accepted as one of the mediators of God's will for the Christian people. Consequently there was a real if not conclusive opinion that the divorce legislation of Theodosius II and Justinian was an expression of the will of God. Moreover, was this legislation not, in its many parts, a legitimate inference from the Matthean exceptive clause? Were not the causes for dismissal set down by this legislation explications of what was implicit in the *pornéia* of that clause?

The exegetical and historical survey making up the preceding chapters has already gathered in enough evidence to warn the reader away from any assumption that the early Christian communities presented a single, exact, unambiguous and unchanging teaching about divorce and remarriage. These qualities were lacking in the New Testament instruction itself. The subsequent effort to apply this instruction to the legally anomalous and violently interrupted marriages of the outlaw Christian communities produced no early clarity. And what was gained by the fifth century was muddied by the attitude and conduct of the citizens who became Christians out of expediency.

Like the Christian acquisition of the doctrine of the Trinity of persons in God, the Christian doctrine and discipline for divorce and remarriage were a gradual and discontinuous appropriation. These developed unevenly in different local communities, unevenly from one epoch to another, from one region to another, or even within one and the same community. In the absence of a Christian legislation that would take form only much later with the convoking of the first local synods and then the general councils, what assumed the value of law were the customs of the local communities. But of these customs, diverse as they were, we have no direct and explicit evidence; we have it only indirectly and implicitly in the writings of Christian authors of those centuries in those communities. From these writings and from the conduct that the writings suppose, we can reconstruct in some measure the attitudes, the conduct and the norms of the communities.

The Christian Ideal of Monogamy

But beginning with at least the second century we find the most explicit evidence from many communities of an effort converging in one project. This project was to show that marriage at least in principle is to be absolutely monogamous. By monogamy here I mean not only that a Christian is to have but one spouse at a time, but in all the span of his or her life only one spouse. In its extreme form the monogamous ideal urged a faithful widowhood against remarriage even after the death of a spouse.

Historical accuracy demands our acknowledging as one of the sources of this monogamous ideal the teaching of pagan ascetics and philosophers, especially of such Stoic masters as Seneca and Marcus Aurelius. The Christian apologetes of the early centuries returned constantly to the point that the personal and community conduct of Christians showed a human dignity missing in the accepted morals of the empire. The Stoics taught and lived lives of the same dignity, and the Christians were not hesitant in comparing themselves favorably with the Stoics. Nevertheless the essence of the doctrine of Christian monogamy came from the Gospel. When the early Church, through the mouths of its bishops and preachers and in the conduct of its members, proposed the ideal of monogamy, it did so as the realization of the Creator's original design for men and women, and as the will of Jesus contesting the too easy repudiation of wives among his own people. This much the ordinary citizen of the empire could understand with reasonable effort.

But the Christians proposed their ideal of monogamy also as an element in the mystery of redemption, of the new creation that Jesus as Christ meant to bring about. The love union of husband and wife was to be taken up into this realization and made a manifestation and a reenactment of Christ's love for his Church. As such the union could not be other than faithful and perpetual. This the ordinary citizen of the empire could understand only with great difficulty or not at all. Nevertheless this insistence on permanent and faithful marriage as a mirror of the union of Christ and his Church, this assertion of monogamy as a characteristic of Christians, runs as a motif through most of the Christian writings on the subject.

In the following pages I shall either quote or cite statements of early Christian writers urging faithful monogamy on their people. We must take care, again, to read these statements in their historical contexts and according to the intent of their authors. The latter said what they did about divorce and remarriage not with the understanding that they were reasserting formally appropriated Church doctrine, that is, the bishops' unanimous, carefully phrased, definitive declarations on disputed points. For while it is true that many of these writers were themselves bishops and were teaching as appointed pastors of their people, their primary intention was to pass on Jesus' instruction and commands—either the substance of them, or explicitations of what they thought implicit in them, or conclusions they drew from them, or interpretations they ventured in light of them. That these writers were anything but unanimous in their explicitations, conclusions and interpretations is both obvious and inevitable, since the traditions of Jesus' words come down to them were anything but unanimous and certain, as we have already seen.

I do not think it unfair to the early Fathers if we look in their teachings for answers to questions they did not ask. Nor in doing so do we predetermine what we eventually find there. Even before we approach the Fathers' writings these questions have historical legitimacy because of the uncertain answers that came from the New Testament teaching and because of the forms of dissolution common under Roman law. The Fathers had to deal with those uncertain answers and reckon with those forms of dissolution. And I believe we can set these questions as guides for the search while acknowledging in advance what has already been made clear about this early patristic teaching, namely the universality of the ideal of faithful monogamy in the marriages of Christians.

Question 1: May spouses dismiss one another—according to either the model of rabbinic law, or to that of Roman law, or perhaps according to both?

Question 2: May spouses end their marriage by the dissolution *communi consensu*—by common consent?

Question 3: Even if they may dismiss one another for any reason or reasons, do they commit adultery if they subsequently attempt remarriage? In the event of such permitted dismissal does the innocent party, the one who justifiably dismisses, commit adultery if he or she subsequently attempts remarriage? Does the guilty party, the one justifiably dismissed, commit adultery if he or she makes the same attempt?

Question 4: If one or the other party, the guilty or the innocent, commits adultery by subsequently attempting remarriage, *why* does this attempt entail adultery?

Question 5: If this or that Father thought one or more kinds of marriage to be indissoluble—to be invulnerable to dissolution by any cause short of death—what did he think the cause of this indissolubility? God's will manifested in the teaching of Jesus? The nature itself of marriage, its intrinsic indissolubility? Something special about the marriages of Christians? If this, what is the something special?

Henri Crouzel suggests in his recent study *L'eglise Primitive Face Au Divorce*[2] that the witness coming down to us from the Christian teachers of the two centuries before the advent of Constantine and the gradual Christianization of the empire has special value for two reasons. The first is that these teachers were closer to the age of the apostles themselves, "closer to the sources," as it were. The second is that these two centuries were the epoch of the imperial persecutions of the Christian communities. To be a Christian then could cost heavily, even the price of one's life. Therefore becoming a Christian demanded a severe and clean break with pagan morals, including the pagan morals of divorce and remarriage. But in the decades and centuries after Constantine, when Christianity had become the established religion and there was political advantage in embracing it, the urge to compromise the Christian teaching with pagan law and custom became powerful. Therefore Crouzel's conclusion: the Christian teaching of the later epoch was infiltrated here and there by this compromise.

That calendar proximity to the apostolic sources in fact aided fidelity of recollection and transmission is the more likely state of the evidence, and may be presumed, provided one keeps in mind that the sources themselves were clearly not in agreement about what Jesus had taught.

But one should at the same time not assume two other facts as self-evident. One is that the Christian teaching on divorce and remarriage after Constantine, during the fourth and fifth centuries, at any point in fact contained compromise with pagan law and morals. A presumption on this point could mask the possibility that what is called compromise were heterogeneous, but not necessarily heterodox, conclusions about the possibility of divorce and remarriage drawn from ambiguously witnessing apostolic sources.

The second presumption of fact to be avoided is this, that the pre-Constantinian teaching, even if free of compromise with pagan morality and law, was free also of all para-Christian thinking about the excellence of marriage—free of an attitude that may have conditioned Christian conclusions about remarriage under any condition, even that of widow-hood after the death of a first spouse. We shall see that the African Christian writer of the third century, Tertullian, was bitterly opposed to remarriage even in widowhood. Why he took this attitude and how widely it was shared, even in less bitter fashion, are factors significant for under-standing the Christian attitude toward remarriage after divorce itself.

In an essay of this length it is not possible, nor for that matter is it ad-visable, to do an exhaustive study of each of the ante-Nicene Fathers' statements on divorce and remarriage. I am not here attempting a patristic theology on the subject. I hope rather to offer sufficient exemplary witness of the teaching and discipline in vigor in various Christian communities of the time.[3]

Ignatius of Antioch

The earliest surviving statement coming down to us from outside the canonical Scriptures that suggests the marriage of Christians ought to be faithful and lasting is in Ignatius of Antioch's letter to his fellow bishop, Polycarp of Smyrna. (The letter is one of seven that Ignatius wrote to various church communities during the first decade of the second century, as he was being taken in bonds from Antioch to Rome, and to martyrdom in the latter city. The letter to Polycarp he wrote during his stop in Troas.)

Like the canonical letters of Paul, James, Jude and the author of the Petrine letters, Ignatius' are a mixture of instruction on points of religious belief and of exhortation to holiness, with the first of these often contained implicitly in the latter. The brief passage in Ignatius' letter to Polycarp in which he exhorts the married echoes the content and style of the latter, hortatory parts of Paul's letters to the Romans, the Galatians, the Colos-sians and the Ephesians. In fact Ignatius appears to have had Paul's instruction to the married Christians of Ephesus clearly in mind when he wrote to Polycarp. The relationship he uses as a norm for the holiness of married love is the same that Paul uses in Ephesians 5:25.

Tell my sisters [the Christian wives in Polycarp's church at Smyrna] to love the Lord and to be content with their spouses in flesh and in spirit. Likewise to my brothers proclaim in the name of Jesus Christ that they are to love their spouses as the Lord loves the Church. . . . For those who marry and are taken in marriage, it is right that they do so with the approval of the bishop, so that they may marry according to God's will and not out of lust. Let everything be done for the glory of God.[4]

The exhortation is explicit; the doctrine about marriage is implicit and must wait for later Christian teachers to draw it out: since Christian husbands ought to love their wives as Christ loves the Church, and because Christ's love for the Church is unfailing, so too should the Christian husband's love be unfailing. (On the other hand it is not clear that a comparable unfailingness is implied in Ignatius' urging the Christian wives to love the Lord and be satisfied with their husbands.)

Justin Martyr

Thirty-five to forty-five years later, between 148 and 161, Justin addressed his First Apology to the emperor Antoninus Pius. His purpose in writing it was to defend the Christians against the accusations of moral dissoluteness that were common at the time, and to do this by explaining the strictness and indeed the nobility of their moral conduct. In Chapter 15 he wrote of the Christian practice of temperance (or chastity). After citing Jesus' words, in Matthew 5:28, on lustful gazing, and his words in 5:29 on avoiding scandal, he quoted his instruction on divorce and remarriage in 5:32b and in 19:12, pointing out that Christians marrying a second time sin in doing so.

> Just as those who enter a second marriage, justifying this by human law, are sinners before our Master, so also are they sinners who look at a woman to lust after her.[5]

It is in this passage that we find for the first time in Christian literature the Greek term *digamía* (a second marriage).

It is used as the converse of *monogamía*. *Digamía* designates not the condition of a person having two spouses simultaneously. Roman law, unlike the Hebraic, did not allow polygamy in this sense. It referred generally to a person, man or woman, who has had two successive spouses, with the first relationship having been dissolved either by divorce or by the death of the first spouse. It is significant for understanding the Christian attitude toward remarriage that even a man or woman remarrying in widowhood was said to be *dígamos*. And some Christian teachers, as we shall see in a moment, passed moral judgment—severely negative moral judgment—on *digamía* entered even from widowhood. This judgment hints at a reason for condemning any and all second marriages, a reason that the early Christian teachers may have found already implied in Paul's (and Ignatius') using Christ's love for the Church as model and norm for husbandly love among Christians. Since Christ's love is faithful despite death and beyond it, so too ought that of Christian spouses be just as invulnerable to the sundering effect of death.

But to return to Justin's use of the term, by *digamía* he meant marriage after dissolution according to Roman law, or perhaps (because he cites Jesus' words in the Matthean tradition) after the husband's dismissing his wife. Of such *digamía* he says that it is a sinful state. The question whether as a state it is also impossible of realization because of the first marriage, he does not ask. Nor does he ask the companion question whether in this case the first marriage survives, i.e., whether two simultaneous marriages are possible.

The Shepherd of Hermas

The Shepherd of Hermas was composed in the second century, probably by 150 or 160 by a Christian author who remains anonymous to us. In form it is Hermas' fictional vision of, and dialogue with, his angel shepherd. The central theme of the work appears in the latter's instruction to Hermas: it is by the spirit and practice of penance that the Christian comes to a holy life. The influence of this work in the Western Church in its century was immense.

The Shepherd is divided structurally into a series of "visions," of similitudes (or parables) and of precepts. Precept IV is a conversation between Hermas and his shepherd, the latter here presented as the Angel of Penitence.[6] Hermas asks about the conduct demanded of a Christian husband if he finds that his wife, also Christian, is committing adultery. Does this husband sin if he continues to live with her? The angel's reply is that he is to dismiss her. (Here Migne, PG, has the text only in Latin. The verb "to dismiss" is *dimittere.*) And he is to remain by himself (*per se maneat*). But—and this is the matter of main concern for us—the angel adds that if the husband remarries after dismissing his wife, he too commits adultery.

Here the author seems to have the angel remind Hermas of Christ's teaching recorded in the Synoptic tradition, specifically in Mark 10:11 and Luke 16:18: "Everyone who dismisses his wife and marries another commits adultery (against her)." However, though this adulterous consequence of the innocent husband's remarrying may be the focus of our concern, it is not the author's. For he has Hermas put his next question to the angel: What if, after being dismissed, the wife repents and wishes to return to her husband? Is he to take her back? The answer is yes, but with a qualification. If the husband does not take back the dismissed but now repentant wife, he sins seriously. But he is to take her back only once because—and this is the author's focus of concern—for the Christian only one repentance is possible.

It is at this point that the author's explanation (through the angel) begins to confuse the issue for the student of the early Christian teaching. Until this point it has seemed clear enough that the reason forbidding a Christian husband's remarrying even after dismissing an adulterous wife is that, as the angel says, he commits adultery if he does so. But the angel himself does not leave the matter at that. He says rather that the husband must not remarry precisely because his wife may repent and wish to return to him. He must keep the way open for her.

The angel then complicates the matter further by instructing Hermas about a Christian spouse's obligation in case of a metaphorical kind of "adultery": What if a Christian spouse lapses into the adultery of paganism? The answer is that here too if he or she refuses to repent, dismissal is obligatory lest the religiously faithful spouse participate in the apostate's sin. But here too the faithful spouse must not remarry after dismissing the other. And the reason the angel gives for forbidding this is not that the remarriage would be literal adultery on the faithful spouse's part. It is rather the same as the reason given just above: the way must be kept open for the repentance and the return of the spouse who has lapsed. Is this, then, what the author thinks is immoral about remarriage after justly dismissing an adulterous or apostate spouse, that it denies to the latter the possibility of repentant return? It is hard to find a decisive answer where the author himself is indecisive.

Athenagoras

We come again upon the severe judgments against *digamía,* a second marriage in any circumstance, in Athenagoras' Supplication for the Christians. This Athenian philosopher become Christian addressed his Supplication to the emperors Marcus Aurelius Antoninus and Lucius Commodus between 176 and 178. His motive in doing so was the same as Justin's in his Apology, to vindicate the moral probity of the Christians against the common slanders on their conduct. He extolled and urged monogamy in marriage so seriously as to oppose remarriage even after the death of a spouse—even to the point of calling such remarriage disguised, or respectable, adultery. About divorce and subsequent remarriage he was just as clear as Justin, but more specific and forceful in calling the latter not only sin but adultery.

> In fact our lives are ruled not by the delivering of discourses but by the witness and the teaching of our conduct. We either remain as we were born or we stay within a single marriage. In fact a second marriage is an adultery, that is only speciously worthy of honor. He who dismisses his wife and marries another, says our Scripture, commits adultery. It forbids us to repudiate a wife whose virginity had been ended or to take another woman. He who deprives himself of his first wife, even if she be dead, is a

disguised adulterer because he transgresses the hand of God, for
in the beginning God created but one man and woman.[7]

At the end of this passage we find a ground for the accusation of
adultery that will complicate even further the Christian theology of marital indissolubility. There was a hint in Ignatius that the reason for the
unfailingness of a Christian marriage is to be found in the unfailingness of
Christ's love for the Church. But here in a condemnation of remarriage
even in widowhood, so severe as to call it disguised adultery, Athenagoras
offers a different reason. He says that such a second marriage is a
repudiation of the first wife even though she has died. But why is it a
repudiation? And why is the second marriage an adultery?

Athenagoras' answer here reaches into the Old Testament parable of
creation in Genesis 1, and it must therefore touch not only Christian but
all Jewish and even pagan spouses. In the beginning God fashioned the
first marriage. Its partners were but one man and one woman. Because of
this primeval monogamy, Athenagoras seems to say, no man or woman
can ever have more than one spouse without committing adultery.

If this is indeed what Athenagoras intends, his severity is astounding.
He goes far beyond Paul and his tradition. In 1 Corinthians 7:8–9 the
latter had no more than urged widows to remain unmarried, while granting realistically that remarriage is the better thing for those who find
continence in widowhood too difficult. If we accept Athenagoras' statement literally as a verdict of adultery on remarriage in widowhood, then
we must see in him an early example of the anti-sexual rigorism that was
to overtake some of the Fathers, most notably Tatian, a near-contemporary of Athenagoras, and Tertullian a century later. But if an Encratite
rigorist, for example, why did Athenagoras not look askance also at first
marriages? There is no evidence that he did so. But one may suspect that
he took to a logical extreme the command of universal monogamy he
thought implied in the proto-typical monogamy of the first marriage as
this is portrayed in Genesis.

Plainly he saw a normative force in the structure of what he thought
to be history's first marriage, a normative force that most later teachers in
the Church were to find rather in the structure of Christ's metaphorical
marriage with the Church. For them the latter was to be the "great
sacrament" obligating Christian spouses to unfailingness—although only
during the span of their years together on earth. Athenagoras seems to
have found this sacrament in the marriage of the first man and woman.

Theophilus of Antioch

In 181 or 182 Bishop Theophilus of Antioch in Syria wrote his
apology, The Three Books to Autolycus, to a pagan and perhaps even a
fictive friend. Like Justin he sought to refute the charges of immorality

brought against the Christians; and in claiming for them a standard of morality higher than that of the pagans he quoted Matthew 5:32. But he reversed the sequence of its clauses so as to eliminate any ambiguity: "(32b) Whoever marries a woman who has been dismissed, he commits adultery: and (32a) whoever dismisses his wife, except in the case of her *pornéia,* makes her to commit adultery."[8] Later (Book 3, no. 15)[9] he said of the Christians that among their most prized virtues they observe *monogamía.* As we have seen, in the Greek language of his time the noun implied rejection of sequential bigamy.

Since, in quoting Matthew 5:32, he had also quoted the passage's exceptive clause exactly, did Theophilus consider that the husband who remarries after dismissing a wife guilty of adultery himself remains innocent of adultery? Or does he commit adultery of his own by remarrying after this dismissal? One could with reason say this in reply: since a man who marries a woman dismissed by her husband commits adultery in doing so, this must be because she is still married to the first man. Consequently the first man is still married to his dismissed wife; thus for him to attempt remarriage while she is still alive would entail the adultery of simultaneous *digamía.*

But this answer remains tentative and weak in Theophilus' mind, and for two reasons. First, he himself does not work out this answer. In fact he does not even ask the question that would inspire it. Secondly, when one restores the clauses of Matthew 5:32 to their original sequence, it may be that the exceptive clause has its excepting effect not only for a husband who dismisses an adulterous wife, but also for the man who marries her. That is, a man commits adultery if he marries a dismissed woman, except in the case where she has been dismissed for adultery.

The Alexandrian Teaching: Clement

The earliest Christian teaching about marriage that could be called a theology was done in the catechetical school at Alexandria. Through the second and third centuries the two most active teachers in the school were Clement (c. 150–215) and Origen (c. 185–254). Unlike Justin, Athenagoras and Theophilus, they wrote not to defend the Christians against pagan slanders, but to defend marriage itself against the persistent attacks of Christians infected with the Gnostic contempt for the flesh, for sexuality· and for marriage.[10]

In his defense Clement produced some of the most exquisite statements on marriage that have come down from Christian antiquity. He insisted that marriage is for the perfection of the persons and the mutual fulfillment of the spouses (in The Pedagogue, Book 1, Chapter 4); that marriage gives itself to collaboration with God in the work of creation by transmitting life (The Pedagogue, Book 2, Chapter 10, 83); that it is a holy state of life (Stromata, Book 3, Chapter 12), so much so that a person who succeeds in living in the love of God amid the worries of family life surpasses one who lives the life of virginity (Stromata, Book 7, Chapter 12, 70). The marital union is a union according to the will of God, but it cannot be other than a single union of one man and one woman.

Clement gets at the question of divorce and remarriage only in the twenty-third and last chapter of Book 2 of his Stromata. He begins there with what seems a simple repetition of the New Testament instruction.

> The Scriptures counsel us to marry and command us never to depart from this union. They state this in a most clear law: "You shall not dismiss a wife except by reason of her *pornéia.*" Moreover they consider it adultery where one remarries as long as either of the divorced spouses is still alive.[11]

Clement takes *pornéia* here to designate adultery on the wife's part. Then after a long clause suggesting how she may avoid any suspicion of this, he continues:

> A man who takes a wife who has been dismissed commits adultery, says the Scripture. For if one dismisses his wife, he commits adultery against her; that is to say, he forces her to become the object of adultery. And not only he who dismissed her becomes the cause of her sin, but also he who takes her, for he puts her in the situation of sin. If he did not take her, she would return to her husband.

In these two passages Clement does not help greatly in clarifying the Scripture's teaching on divorce and remarriage. For one thing, he does not quote the Gospel instruction but only paraphrases Christ's words in the Synoptic tradition.

In the last clause of the first passage above he chooses a participle that in its context creates ambiguity. What I have translated as "*divorced* spouses" (which others may translate as "*separated* spouses") is in its Greek original *kechōrisménon.* The reader may recognize here the root of the verb used commonly in the Greek of the time—*chorízein*—to designate dissolution of marriage in a general sense. If Clement means that dismissal of an adulterous wife no more than separates the spouses while leaving them still married, his choice of the participle is careless. But if he thinks that the dismissal truly dissolves the marriage, his choice is accurate but leaves us without an explanation for his thinking that the wife's subsequent remarriage is adultery.

Again, Clement points out that according to the Scriptures nothing other than a wife's adultery warrants her dismissal from a marriage. He says at first clearly that adultery is the consequence of either spouse's remarrying as long as both are still alive. But does he imply that there is an exception to this consequence if the dismissal is punishment for the wife's adultery? He is not clear on this point.

If his second paragraph quoted above is an attempt to clear up this point, it does not succeed. Here he explains how the two men involved both participate in the inevitable adultery. The husband who dismisses his wife does so by compelling her to become the object of adultery, not—at least in this passage—by his remarrying after dismissing his wife. The second man, he who presumes to take the dismissed woman as his wife, participates in adultery not (if we take Clement literally) by his marrying her but by his putting her in a situation of sin. And Clement adds (as his explanation of this sinfulness?) that if the second man did not try to take her as his wife, she would return to her husband.

At the other extreme one can surely not interpret Clement to say that the Gospel teaching permits remarriage by either spouse after the wife's dismissal for adultery. But at best he does little to make clear the meaning of the adultery that is committed in such remarriage, nor does he make clear whose is the sin and how it is committed.

The meaning of the New Testament teaching is even less clear from Clement's riposte, in Book 3 of the Stromata, Chapter 6, to the Gnostic rigorists who contemn marriage because it engages the spouses in impurity. He argues against them that the union of the two spouses in one flesh is God's plan and will. And to verify this he adds Jesus' interdiction against the dissolving of this union.

> What did the Lord reply to those who questioned him about the act of repudiation, asking if it is permitted to dismiss one's wife, since Moses permitted it? "Moses wrote that," Jesus said, "because of your hardness of heart. Have you not yourselves read that God said to the first man, whom he fashioned, 'The two of you shall be one flesh'?" Hence he who dismisses his wife, except in the case of her *pornéia,* makes her the object of adultery.[12]

Taking Clement's words here literally, we find him saying that the adultery in the case is the wife's because she is made an object of it, and by implication the husband's because he compels her to become such an object. But he does not participate in her adultery even in this way if he dismisses her because of her *pornéia.*

What of adultery by reason of remarriage, by either the dismissing husband or the dismissed wife? Clement takes up this question later in the same chapter, but only in the case of the husband who has dismissed a wife guilty of *pornéia.* There he seems to say that Christ forbade his remarrying, but strains the meaning of the last verses of Matthew 19 in doing so.

> After the Lord had passed judgment on the act of dismissal, certain of his hearers asked, "If this is the way it is between husband and wife, is it better for a man not to marry?" Jesus

replied, "Not everyone can accept this teaching, but only those to whom it is given."[13]

Clement perhaps sees Christ forbidding remarriage for the husband who has dismissed his wife guilty of *pornéia*. But is this because his remarriage would be itself an adultery? Clement seems to imply that it would be when he explains that if athletes can live continent lives, so too can Christian men once their wives are dismissed. But is this the reason that Clement demands continence of them, that a second sexual union after dismissing a wife would be adultery? Probably. But from elsewhere in the Stromata doubt that this is the reason, or is at least the only reason, creeps in. For Clement did take up elsewhere the question of the permissibility of remarriage in widowhood. In Book 1 he suggests a hierarchy of values of the different states of life.

> We consider blessed the celibacy of those to whom God has given this gift. We admire *monogamía,* and the chastity of a single marriage, insisting that each spouse should share the pains and bear the burdens of the other, for fear lest one who imagines himself to stand should fall. As for a second marriage, if someone burns, says the Apostle, let him marry.[14]

Thus, unlike some of his Christian predecessors and contemporaries, Clement does not condemn remarriage in widowhood, but he regards it as only a remedy for concupiscence.

Then in Book 3 (Chapter 12) he explains the reason for his preference for remaining unmarried after the death of a spouse.

> And if the Apostle allows one a second marriage as a concession to the fire of passion and failure of self-mastery, one does not sin against a precept, for such marriage is not forbidden by the law. But such a person does not attain in all its vigor the perfection of conduct sought for by the Gospel. For he who remains free attains a heavenly glory—he who preserves the union that death has dissolved and who obeys willingly the divine plan that brings him without division into the worship of the Lord.[15]

Here at the end there is a hint, although only a hint, that the imperishability of the marital love union is grounded only in the Christian's bond with Christ. This bond can overcome even the dissolving of marriage that is death's otherwise natural effect on it. Is it illogical to argue in reverse from this conclusion, that for Clement nothing else but this bond makes a marriage imperishable, that even if dismissal under human law does not dissolve it, other created causes can do so? If so, then

here in the middle of the third century we have the seeds of later Catholic
theological development.

Origen

The unclarity and indecisiveness of this early Christian interpretation
of the New Testament teaching about divorce and remarriage are little
remedied by the treatment of this teaching at the hands of Origen,
Clement's successor at the catechetical school in Alexandria. Origen offered this interpretation in his Commentary on the Gospel According to
Matthew.[16]

Because the first books of this commentary are lost (what has survived begins with Matthew 13:36), Origen's interpretation of Matthew
5:31–32 is lost with them. But he works through an extended interpretation of Matthew 19:3–12 in Book 14, Chapter 16 through Book 15,
Chapter 5. (Because the chapters in Book 15 have to do with those men
who have become eunuchs for the Kingdom of God, we may confine
ourselves to the last nine chapters of Book 14.)[17]

He begins with an exegesis of Jesus' reply to the Pharisees who came
to put him to the test. Jesus denied that a man could dismiss his wife for
just any cause, cited the passage in Genesis telling of God's making "one
flesh" of the first man and woman, and added his own verdict: "What God
has joined, no man must separate." Therefore the conclusion to that point:
if a man tries to dismiss his wife, he tries to undo what God has done.

In Chapter 17 Origen ventures into a metaphor that verges on
allegory and perhaps becomes the latter. Noting that Paul implied that
"two in one flesh" is to be said of the marriage of Christ and the Church,
Origen points out that this is not Christ's first marriage. That had been
with the synagogue (a metonym for the people of Israel). But as a bride the
synagogue had proved faithless, had even willed her spouse's death, and
had thus abandoned him (rather than that he had repudiated her).

In Chapters 18–20 Origen interprets the Pharisees' objection to Christ
that Moses permitted the repudiation of wives in whom *pornéia* is found.
This prompts a further allegorical excursus on Christ and the Synagogue.
He did indeed give to her the writ of dismissal, but only after she had
abandoned him. And he did later take another spouse. But Christ can and
will take Israel back despite Deuteronomy's forbidding this, since he is the
maker of the Law and therefore above the Law. And he will do this in the
fullness of time, when all nations will be gathered in to salvation.

Does this allegory assume that Origen holds that it is possible and
even permitted to a husband to dismiss his wife for her *pornéia* and then to
remarry? Cereti contends that the entire passage would be unintelligible if
Origen did not assume this, since the dynamics of allegory begin with a
fact that is observable in the visible domain, then seek to interpret this fact
as a sign of an invisible, higher reality.[18] Crouzel denies not that the

passage works with this assumption, but that it leads to the conclusion that dismissal and remarriage are permitted.[19]

Thus far nothing is conclusive for us in Origen's exegesis of this Matthean text beyond what is obvious, that Christ has forbidden a man to dismiss his wife and marry another. But beginning with Chapter 22 Origen takes up a question that he himself calls severe and difficult. Perhaps to our surprise the question does not ask why a man may not remarry after dismissing an adulterous wife, but why St. Paul insists (in 1 Timothy 3:1–3, 12 and in Titus 1:5–6) that those in high ministry in the Church be men "of one wife," and why he insists too (in 1 Timothy 5:9) that if a woman is to be included among the widows in the Church, she must have had but one husband.

To answer his question Origen turns to another allegory. This time it is that men who marry a second time are a visible symbol of a soul that has sinned and repented. But such a soul is not worthy of high ministry in the Church.

Cereti finds hidden in this question and its allegorical answer an assumption that he regards as crucial evidence concerning divorce and remarriage in the churches that Origen knew of.[20] He reasons that if Church ministry was denied to men who had had two wives, then there must have been such men in these churches. But to be "a man of one wife" at that time meant not only a man whose marriage excluded simultaneous polygamy, not only a man who refused to remarry in widowhood, but also one who had not remarried after dismissing his wife. Thus if there were "men of two wives" in those churches, there is evidence here of men who had remarried after dismissal (and thus disqualified themselves from ministry). Cereti adds that Origen's context itself supports this conclusion, since this context is a commentary on Matthew 19, which deals with remarriage after dismissal but not with remarriage in widowhood.

From the beginning of Chapter 23 to the end of Book 14 Origen treats of dismissal and remarriage according to the new law. And it is in Chapter 23 that he provides us with the historical evidence that is most helpful.[21] For it is here that he examines Jesus' reply to the Pharisees who protested that they taught dismissal of wives because Moses allowed this in the law. Jesus' reply was that Moses allowed this because of their hardness of heart. Origen goes on to point out not only in the Old Testament were some permissive laws given because of human weakness and hardness of heart, even though according to the noblest part of the law "it was not so in the beginning." But such concessions to human weakness are found also in the new law. When enumerating these he comments on a case (or perhaps on some cases) apparently familiar in his time.[22] Because it (or they) are the pivot of the evidence here, it is worth quoting Origen verbatim.

Already, apart from the Scriptures [or contrary to them] certain heads of the Church have permitted a certain woman to be married while her husband is still alive. They have done this apart from [or contrary to] the Scriptures in which we read, "The wife is bound to her husband as long as he lives," and "If she gives herself to another man while her husband is still alive, she is legally an adulteress." However they have not acted altogether unreasonably. This accommodation is allowed in lieu of even worse ones, even though apart from [or contrary to] that which was written and handed down from the beginning.[23]

What to say of this, Origen's note about an event familiar in his time? That he knew of it, but disapproved of it, and denied that the woman's first marriage was dissolved, leaving her free to remarry? Or that he disapproved of it (as he obviously did) but conceded that the woman's marriage was dissolved and that she had truly remarried?

The evidence of his own judgment is inconclusive. On the other hand he says in so many words that the bishops allowed the woman (or women) in question to marry while her husband (or their husbands) still lived. The verb he uses is conventional for "to be married"—*gaméisthai*. On the other hand he says at the end of the following chapter (24), "Even though a woman seems to marry a second man, she is an adulteress if her husband is still alive. So also does a man commit adultery and is not a husband even though he seems to marry a woman who had been dismissed. This our Savior has shown us."[24]

But whatever Origen's own judgment on the case, Cereti points out what is most significant about this passage.

How does Origen judge this conduct? Does he condemn it outright as contrary to Scripture (a traditional interpretation which enjoys a measure of plausibility)? Or does he rather judge it with a certain sympathy, as an example of a concession which, although not found in Scripture, is not however entirely unreasonable; which can be helpful in avoiding greater evil; and which can be seen as analogous to other concessions in the Scriptures— and as such is consistent with God's way of acting in the history of salvation? This question and these answers are at bottom irrelevant to our concern here. What is to the point is that Origen witnesses to the fact that such a practice went on, and that to condemn such a practice he appealed only to texts from St. Paul that refer to strictures on wives.

But if one keeps in mind the situation of women in the Church in the society of Origen's time, it is absolutely unthinkable that bishops in the Church would have ever thought of conceding to women something that was not as a matter of practice conceded to men. It was more likely this, that some bishops bothered by the flagrant injustice in the unequal treatment of men and women in similar circumstances, and wanting to promote a greater equality, sought to grant to women what was considered licit for men. The difficulty they found in the way of this was precisely the texts of St. Paul—1 Corinthians 7:39 and Romans 7:2–3—that Origen quotes in his commentary, texts which at that time were interpreted literally and applied only to women.[25]

Witnesses in the Churches of Africa and Rome

After Alexandria Carthage was the second most active and intelligent theological center among the communities of the second and third centuries. It was also one of the two churches in the Latin West (Rome was the other) from which we have significant evidence for their interpretation of the New Testament teaching concerning divorce and remarriage. From Minucius Felix, Novatian and Lactantius we have brief statements; from Tertullian, a contemporary of Origen and just as copious a writer as he, we have an extended examination of the subject.

Minucius Felix wrote the earliest of the Latin apologies in his dialogue, Octavius, probably sometime during the two decades, 174–197. The work takes its title from the name of the fictive Christian principal in the dialogue. The Christians had been accused of incestuous sexual conduct; in the conversation with his friend Caecilius, Octavius refutes the charge. In doing so he enunciates clearly and simply the Christian principle of faithful monogamy in marriage.

> But we, we carry our modesty not on our countenances but in our spirits. We willingly join ourselves to the bond of a single marriage. We either know but a single wife, out of the desire to procreate, or we know none at all. Our meals are not only modest but sober. We are not given to banquets and our feasts are not drinking bouts, but we temper our joy with sobriety. Our words are chaste, our bodies even more chaste, and the majority of us enjoy the perpetual virginity of an inviolate body, but do not glory in this. So far from us is the desire of incest that some of us blush even at a chaste union.[26]

A passage from his On the Good of Chastity *(De Bono Pudicitiae)*, written by the Roman priest Novatian shortly before the middle of the third century, repeats two points of Christian teaching that are by now familiar in this epoch.

> The laws concerning chastity, my brothers, are from antiquity. Why do I say from antiquity? Because they were given with men themselves. For the woman was made from her husband so that she might know no other man but him; and the woman was

given back to her husband so that once she had been taken from him and returned, she might need no other man.

The Scripture thus says that they shall be two in one flesh, so that which had been one might return to one, so that a separation without return might not give occasion for the introduction of another.

Hence the Apostle declares the husband to be the head of the wife so that he may praise chastity by the union of the two. For just as the head cannot be fitted to the members of another person, so the members cannot belong to the head of a stranger. The head belongs to its members and the members to it. Both are joined by a natural bond in a mutual accord for fear lest some discord arise which would destroy by separation the bond of divine covenant.

And he added, "He who loves his wife loves himself. For no one hates his own body, but nourishes it and cares for it, as Christ does the Church . . ."

Thus Christ rendered so great honor to chastity when he commanded that a wife not be dismissed except for her adultery . . .[27]

The passage is noteworthy only because in it Novatian turns to Paul's metaphor of the husband as head of the wife to argue for the indestructibility of the marital bond. But he does not take the metaphor as far as later theologians were to take it. He does not argue for this indestructibility by pointing to the metaphorical bond of marriage between Christ and the Church. He stays rather with the physical demands of an analogy built in the metaphor: just as it is unthinkable that a head could be separated from its natural body and joined to another, so is it equally unthinkable that a husband could be separated from his wife and joined to another. We shall see that even those of Novatian's colleagues who acknowledged this metaphor did not find in it the probative force that he does.

Tertullian

The priest theologian Tertullian (c. 155–220) is certainly the most representative witness of a strain of teaching in the Latin churches, at least until he moved over into Montanism and came to condemn any second marriage at all, even in widowhood, as fornication and finally as adultery. He was married. And from his Catholic period dates his essay in two books, To My Wife (*Ad Uxorem*). In these books as in a kind of spiritual testament, he passed on to his wife points of counsel that he wanted her to remember and act on after his death. The most important of these points he developed throughout the entire first book. He recommended that after his death she not remarry, because absolute monogamy is the Christian ideal, and that no excuse should weaken her resolve to remain unmarried, not weakness of the flesh, nor desire for earthly goods, nor even the desire for children. A second marriage would go against God's will, his will manifested in permitting the death of her husband. It would be an obstacle to her holiness, as Catholic belief indicates in refusing certain ecclesiastical dignities to men who remarry.

But since a second marriage, no matter how ill-advised, cannot be condemned absolutely, and because there are examples of Christians who remarried in widowhood, Tertullian wrote the second book to exhort his wife that if she really insisted on remarrying, she at least marry a Christian. Here he lingered on the harm that comes of a religiously mixed marriage, and pointed in contrast to the beauty of a union of two believers, who are united not only in the flesh but in the spirit as well.

At the very beginning of this Book Two Tertullian mentions divorce and remarriage almost in passing as he comments disapprovingly on some Christian women who, in remarrying, have taken pagan husbands.

> Recently, my dearest fellow servant in the Lord [this is to his wife], I set forth for you as well as I could what a holy woman whose marriage has ended ought to do. Now I turn to a second point of advice. It has to do with a human weakness about which the recent examples of some women give warning. They were offered, either by divorce or by their husbands' deaths, the opportunity to live lives of continence. But they not only rejected this opportunity for so great a good, but not even in remarrying did they remember right discipline that demanded they marry in the Lord.[28]

In the lines that follow immediately Tertullian scolds these women on two counts. The first is, as suggested in the quotation just above, that by remarrying they have passed up the chance for a life of virtuous continence. The second is that in remarrying they have taken pagan husbands. But—and this is the significance of the passage for our examination— nowhere does he scold those among these women because they have remarried after divorce. And divorce, along with widowhood, is obviously one of the two conditions he had in mind, since his word for it is *divortium*. What is more, in apparently permitting remarriage after divorce, he does not reserve this to men, as would urge a literal reading of the divorce passages in Matthew which contain the exceptive clause.

Later (in Paragraph 8) he comes back very briefly to the subject of divorce. Regarding Paul's instruction in 1 Corinthians 7 about the marriage of a Christian with a pagan, he asks why, if by trying to hold together such a marriage the Christian is made unclean, he is not allowed to divorce the pagan spouse as well as let him or her depart. His answer is that in the first place the Lord instructs here, through Paul, that such a marriage is rather not to be contracted than that it is to be dissolved, and that the Lord has forbidden divorce (*divortium*) except on the ground of unchastity (*stupri causa*).[29] At least at this writing Tertullian's mind on the subject seems clear enough: divorce is permitted to Christians (although only because of the unchastity of the spouse). Remarriage too after such divorce is permitted. And both the divorce and the remarriage are permitted to women as well as to men. But above all, Tertullian seriously urges continence as the Christian choice of those whose marriages have ended.

Among his works completed after he had become fully Montanist, his *Against Marcion* (*Adversus Marcionem*) contains the most significant comments on divorce and remarriage. By this time his mind was set rigorously against remarriage in any circumstance and for any cause. But about divorce itself he was inconclusive and apparently even self-contradictory.

In Book IV he is arguing with Marcion about the subject dearest to the latter's heart, that between the old law and the new law there is fundamental and irreconcilable disagreement, and arguing with him precisely in this passage on a particular area of disagreement, namely Christ's proscription of divorce where Moses permitted it. Tertullian's rejoinder is that Christ's disagreement with Moses on this point is not as thorough as Marcion thinks.

> 4. I say in fact that Christ has forbidden divorce only conditionally, when a man dismisses his wife in order to marry another [*si ideo quis dimittat uxorem ut aliam ducat*].[30] "He who has dismissed his wife," he says, "and has married another, has committed adultery, and he who has married a wife dismissed by her husband is likewise an adulterer"—that is, when she is dismissed precisely for the reason that does not allow dismissal, namely so that he may marry another [*ut alia ducatur*]. He who marries a wife dismissed illicitly is an adulterer since she has not been dismissed.
>
> 5. A marriage that has not been rightly dissolved [*non rite diremptum*] remains in existence. And to marry while it remains is adultery. Thus if Christ has forbidden one to dismiss a spouse under a certain condition, he has not forbidden it entirely. And that which he has not forbidden entirely, he has otherwise permitted, when the reason for his forbidding it ceases. Thus he does not teach in contradiction of Moses . . .
>
> 6. The rightness of divorce thus has Christ as its defender. And thus too he confirms Moses' teaching when the latter allows dismissal for the same cause that he does: where some unchaste deed [*negotium impudicum*] is found in the wife. For he says, in the Gospel of Matthew, "He who dismisses his wife, except by reason of her adultery, makes her an object of adultery." . . .
>
> 7. . . . Thus you see Christ continuing knowingly in the path of the Creator, both in permitting dismissal and in forbidding it. You see him concerned with marriage no matter where you turn,

for he denies the separation of the spouses in forbidding dismissal, as he protects marriage from defilement when he permits divorce because of adultery. So be ashamed that you do not unite those whom your Christ has united; and be ashamed too for separating spouses without justification by the cause that Christ approves.[31]

In the passage Tertullian clearly interprets Christ's teaching in the Matthean version of the Synoptic tradition to permit a husband's dismissing his wife on the one ground that she is an adulteress, but on no other. He does not say that Christ permits the wife to dismiss her husband on the same ground, although he certainly knew that Roman law permitted this. And by logical consequence, once the adulterous wife has been dismissed (about this he says that in this case the marriage is rightly *dissolved—rite diremptum*), he may remarry—provided (according to one interpretation) he has not dismissed even an adulterous wife so that he may remarry. If he attempts remarriage, or if any man attempts marriage, with a woman dismissed for any other reason than her adultery, this itself is adultery.

But in Book 5, although still working at refuting Marcion, Tertullian seems to change his mind about Christ's agreeing with Moses.

Now we must consider marriage, which Marcion forbids more resolutely than does the Apostle. For the Apostle, though he prefers the good that is continence, yet allows one to both contract marriage and to use it, and exhorts that one rather save a marriage than dissolve it. Christ clearly forbids divorce, while Moses permits it. And Marcion, when he forbids to his faithful any marital union ... and when he commands dismissal in preference to marriage—whose teaching does he follow, Moses' or Christ's? Yet the Apostle, when he orders a wife not to depart from her husband—and, if she has left him, to either remain unmarried or to be reconciled to him—he has allowed dismissal by not forbidding it in every case. And he has defended marriage by first forbidding that it be dissolved; and if it be dissolved, to be restored.[32]

If Tertullian is now indecisive about Christ's permitting divorce even by dismissal of an adulterous wife, he is clear enough that St. Paul acknowledges and allows divorce at least in that case where a wife has left her husband (or has been dismissed by him). He says simply that one of the alternatives Paul allows this wife is that she remain unmarried—*innupta*. His second way of saying what has happened to her marriage is that it has been disjoined, separated—*disiunctum*.

The question of remarriage surfaces again in Tertullian's later works written when he was fully Montanist. In his Exhortation on Chastity (*De Exhortatione Castitatis*) he expressly condemns remarriage under any circumstances.[33] He argues that absolute monogamy has its warrant in both man's creation and his redemption. In the former it is clear that in providing companionship for the first male, God provided him with only one woman although he could have provided more. As for the redemption, St. Paul himself interpreted the words of Genesis, "the two shall become one flesh," to designate Christ and the Church in their spiritual marriage. And in this union there is but one Christ and one Church. This union with one bride is Christ's *sacramentum* and hers. He adds that the monogamy Paul asked of the Church's ministers ought to be demanded of all Christians because all participate in the priesthood, and in case of necessity can fulfill the priestly office. It is here that he insists that second marriages are a form of fornication.

It is to be noted too that from the metaphor, in Ephesians 5, of Christ's marriage with the Church, he drew the conclusion that went logically far beyond what Augustine and the later theologians were to draw from it. By the normative force of this metaphor a Christian husband's and wife's union is indestructible, according to Tertullian, not only in this life but on into eternity. This passage written during his Montanist years is also the first upon which we come (since Paul) that calls the love-union of Christ and the Church their *sacramentum*. But he does not say this of the marriage of two Christian spouses.

Now fully Montanist, Tertullian pursued the theme of absolute monogamy in yet a third essay, On Monogamy (*De Monogamia*). In it he put his final and unqualified condemnation of remarriage: it is nothing but adultery.[34] Paul's counsel in 1 Corinthians 7:9 favoring remarriage as a preventative of sin he twists to refer only to those Christians who have been widowed before their conversion.[35] Throughout this essay he interprets the Synoptic instruction about remarriage after dismissal inflexibly: no matter the reason for the dismissal of the wife, if she remarries both she and her new partner are adulterers. If her husband who dismissed her attempts remarriage, he too is an adulterer.[36]

Summary

A number of things are evident about the Christian teaching and discipline concerning divorce and remarriage by the end of the third century. First and most inclusively, they set themselves against the permissiveness and promiscuity of Roman society. Fidelity to the teaching of Christ demanded of spouses a monogamy until death.

But the living out of this fidelity in the intricacies of life was not without its uncertainties. For example, severe judgment was passed on even the man who dismissed his wife for her adultery and then remarried, but the reason for the judgment was not at all points clear. It may have been because the remarriage blocked the unfaithful wife's chance at repentant return to her husband.

Everywhere Christian teachers and people took for granted that the exceptive phrase in the Matthean version of Christ's instruction came from Christ himself. But everywhere too there appeared uncertainty about the meaning and the application of this exception. There is partial evidence that some Christian authorities permitted remarriage after dismissal for adultery as the lesser of two evils.

During these two centuries there are the first traces of what was to become the theological reason for the invulnerability of Christian marriages to dissolution. From as early as Ignatius of Antioch at the beginning of the second century Christians saw in the love union of Christ and his Church a reason for holding Christian marriages invulnerable to dissolution.

NOTES

1. *Jerome Biblical Commentary,* "Canonicity," p. 530. The earliest ecclesiastical decisions seeking to establish a biblical canon were made by regional councils in North Africa. Three of them named a list of Old Testament and New Testament writings coinciding with the list that was to be accepted later by the universal Church. These were the Councils at Hippo in 393, the Third Council of Carthage in 397 and a later council there in 415. But for Catholics the canon of New Testament books was set definitively and finally only in the Council of Trent's decree of April 8, 1546, *De Canonicis Scripturis.*

2. Paris, 1970, no. 13 in the series, *Théologie Historique,* Etudes Publiées par les Professeurs de Théologie à l'Institut Catholique de Paris, p. 41.

3. Along with Crouzel's volume cited just above an excellent and more recent study of the same evidence has been done in Italian by Giovanni Cereti, *Divorzio, Nuove Nozze E Penitenza Nella Chiesa Primitiva* (Bologna, 1977). Cereti had been a pupil of Crouzel, and in his volume challenges the accuracy at crucial points of the former's reading of patristic evidence on divorce and remarriage (just as Crouzel had written his work in order to gainsay Victor Pospishil's hasty and hardly careful presentation, in 1967, of that evidence in his *Divorce and Remarriage: Toward a New Catholic Teaching.*

Studies in English on this subject, along with Pospishil's, are by Anthony J. Bevilacqua, "The History of the Indissolubility of Marriage," in The *Catholic Theological Society of America: Proceedings of The Twenty-Second Annual Convention,* 1967, pp. 253–307; and in George H. Joyce, *Christian Marriage,* London, 1948.

4. In PG, Vol. 5, Col. 724.

5. In PG, Vol. 6, Col. 350.

6. In PG, Vol. 2, Cols. 918–919.

7. Supplication for the Christians, Chapter 33, in PG, Vol. 6, Cols. 965–968.

8. Book 3, no. 13, in PG, Vol. 6, Col. 1139.

9. *Loc. cit.,* Col. 1141.

10. See my treatment of Clement's teaching on the goodness of marriage in my earlier volume, *Marriage in the Catholic Church: What Is Marriage?,* Chapter 4.

11. In PG, Vol. 8, Col. 1096.

12. In PG, Vol. 8, Cols. 1150–1151.

13. *Ibid.,* Col. 1154.

14. *Ibid.,* Col. 1103.

15. *Op. cit.,* Col. 1183.

16. This is in PG, Vol. 13, Cols. 829–1600.

17. *Op. cit.,* Cols. 1223–1252.

18. *Op. cit.,* p. 209.

19. *Op. cit.,* pp. 80–81 His reason for denying this is that in Chapter 21 Origen attempts another allegory that implicitly challenges this conclusion. In this allegory the human soul, existing before its incarnation at conception, is married to an angel. But because of some uncleanness the soul is dismissed by the angel (is incarnated), is "married to another man." Crouzel understands this soul to be signified on earth by the synagogue of which Origen had written in Chapter 17; and "the other man," to which she is later married, to be Christ. The consequence is, according to Crouzel, not that the synagogue-bride enters into a second marriage with a different man, but that she returns, after long dismissal, to her first spouse, Christ.

Whether Cereti is right or wrong, I cannot agree with Crouzel's interpretation, because he forces a dubious correlation of the two allegories.

20. *Op. cit.,* pp. 210–211.

21. In Chapter 24, the last of this book, Origen notes that a Jewish critic could point out that because of his exceptive clause recorded in Matthew 5:32 Jesus was no less permissive than was Moses in Deuteronomy 24:1. Origen replies that the cases are not equal. Moses allowed dismissal for whatever husbands regarded in their wives as "something unclean" that forfeits her pleasure in his eyes, while Christ allows dismissal only for the wife's *pornéia,* which Origen takes to be her adultery. (And it is perhaps evidence of Origen's own assumptions in all this that he says in so many words that because of this adultery Christ allows the marriage to be *dissolved.*) And the verb Origen chooses for this is the familiar *dialúein* (*op. cit.,* Col. 1248). Just a bit earlier too he had said (Col. 1247) that adultery is the only cause for which Christ allows a marriage to be dissolved (again *dialúein.*).

22. The species of human weakness, or hardness of heart, other than that exemplified in this case, that Origen sees treated permissively in the new law are found (1) in the situation of a spouse who, though wanting to practice continence temporarily, is constrained not to expose a weaker spouse to greater temptation than the latter can bear (1 Corinthians 7:5), and (2) the widows whom Paul advised (in 1 Corinthians 7:9) that they remarry if they cannot persevere in continence (*ibid.,* Col. 1246).

23. *Ibid.,* Col. 1246. I have offered two translations of the adverbial phrase, "apart from the Scriptures" or "contrary to the Scriptures," because it has the Greek preposition *para* with the accusative, which can take either meaning.

24. *Ibid.,* Col. 1250.

25. *Op cit.,* pp. 214–215.

26. Chapter 31, in PL, Vol. 3, Col. 337.

27. Chapters 5 and 6. In *Corpus Christianorum, Series Latina IV: Novatiani Opera,* Turnholt, 1972, p. 117.

28. In *Corpus Christianorum, Series Latina I: Tertulliani Opera, Pars 1,* Turnholt, 1954, pp. 381–382.

29. *Loc. cit.,* p. 386.

30. *Op. cit.,* p. 365. The second clause here is obviously a final clause. Commentators disagree on whether in Tertullian's mind the clause designates

subjective purpose or objective. If the former, Tertullian is saying that Christ forbids a man to dismiss his wife when he does so for the subjective motive that he wishes to marry another woman. If objective, he is saying that Christ forbids a man to dismiss his wife when the consequence of this is that he marries another. If the finality here is subjective, then Tertullian implies this consequence, that if a man dismisses his wife for adultery and *without* the motive of marrying another, Christ permits both the divorce and the remarriage. But if the finality is objective, then Tertullian means that the subsequent attempt at remarriage renders the prior divorce at least illicit, and the marriage illicit and perhaps null.

31. *Ibid.*

32. *Op. cit.,* p. 368, paragraphs 6 and 7.

33. Chapter 5, in *Corpus Christianorum, Series Latina II, Tertulliani Opera, Pars 2,* p. 1022.

34. Chapter 9, in *op. cit.,* p. 1241.

35. Chapter 10, in *op. cit.,* pp. 1242–1243.

36. He is most explicit on this point in Chapter 9, p. 1241. The African, Lactantius, contemporary of Constantine and tutor of his oldest son, Crispus, took note of the Christian marriage morals when writing his The Divine Instructions (*De Divinis Institutionibus*). The point he made bears on the moral demands that are laid equally on husbands and on wives:

"One ought not think, as the Roman public does, that only the wife is guilty of adultery when she remarries, but that a husband is innocent even if he takes several wives. With equal obligation the divine law has so united the two in a marriage that is a single body, that anyone who divides in two the union of this body is an adulterer. Moreover, lest anyone think himself authorized to put limits on the divine precepts, to do away with any calumny or chance of fraud these precepts add that he who marries a woman dismissed by her husband is an adulterer. That man is an adulterer who except in the case of her sin of adultery dismisses his wife in order to marry another. For God has not willed that the one body be disjoined and torn" (in PL, Vol. 6, Cols. 719–720).

7. CHRISTIAN TEACHING AND DISCIPLINE IN THE FOURTH CENTURY

It is not an arbitrary reading of history to see the fourth century as a time of transition and development in the Christian doctrine and discipline of divorce and remarriage. At the beginning of the century the imperial persecutions came to an end. Licinius published the Edict of Toleration. By the end of the century the ancient pagan cults of the gods had been proscribed and Christianity instead was the established religion of the empire. The Christian portion of the empire's population was on its way to being the majority, and citizens by the thousands accepted baptism for unheroic motives of political expediency, bringing with them their barely converted attitudes toward divorce and remarriage. Bishops and councils of bishops were compelled to take public action about the conduct flowing from these attitudes.

To this point, the passing of the third century into the fourth, the Christian teaching on divorce and remarriage had developed a solid center but indecisive edges. From the New Testament traditions, the Synoptic and the Pauline, the Christians knew that Jesus had made radical demands. Where applied successfully to real life these demands shut down the easy consensual divorce that Roman law allowed. They sought also to put an end to divorce by dismissal of the spouse—except (and here was the indecisive edge) where this was done to a spouse guilty of adultery. The evidence shows that virtually no one doubted that the Matthean exceptive clause came from Jesus himself. And since in Jesus' words there was a demand for an end to the unequal and unfair treatment of women, the Christian teachers could not avoid asking if this clause extended its prerogative to wives as well. Could they dismiss their husbands where these were guilty of adultery?

The decisions on these matters by the majority of the Christian teachers until the end of the third century were first yes, certainly husbands could dismiss their wives when these committed adultery. And to say this these teachers used the verbs that in the language of the time commonly designated the dissolution of a marriage. As to whether wives could also dismiss their husbands when these committed adultery, some teachers ignored the question; some said yes, some no. The same assortment of answers came back to the question about remarriage after this one licit dismissal—the second marriage of the innocent husband who had dismissed a guilty wife, or of an innocent wife who had dismissed a guilty husband; or the first marriage of an as yet unmarried man or woman sought as a spouse by an innocent man or woman who had earlier dismissed a guilty spouse.

About one remarriage—or attempt at remarriage—all agreed that it is adulterous. This is the attempt of a man to marry a wife who has been dismissed for some cause other than adultery, and therefore dismissed unjustly. As for the remarriage of a guilty and dismissed spouse, this awaited further reflection on the part of the teachers of the fourth and fifth centuries—and awaited especially the disciplinary action of the bishops of these and following centuries.

And always there was the plight, and the question, of the spouse abandoned unintentionally—because his or her mate had been sent into punitive exile or reduced to punitive slavery, or captured by raiding barbarians, or had disappeared in foreign military action. What of the spouse left behind? Was he or she, whose gift of the Spirit was obviously to be married, to be obligated to struggle in a life of continence for which just as obviously no gift had been given? Or was he or she to be allowed to find a second spouse? If so, under which conditions? But if not, why not?

Running through all this was the current of persuasion that the ideal in marriage for any Christian man or woman, the holiness to which all Christians are called, is absolute monogamy. As we have seen, this meant no second marriage at all, not even in widowhood. The source from which this ideal was drawn was an element in the narrative in Genesis that was taken as factual history. Of the first human beings God had formed one woman from the body of one man. He had bound them into a marital union exclusively theirs. He had made them two in one flesh, and Jesus had recalled this to his Pharisee interlocutors as proof against their discipline of divorce and remarriage. What is more, Paul had suggested that in the most perfect of marriages, that of Christ and his Church, there could be no more than one husband and one wife.

There was also a reason of asceticism that was alleged against remarriage in widowhood. It may have been drawn from the Stoic strain that ran through much of the ethical teaching contemporary with the birth of Christianity, an ethical teaching that the Christians were concerned to match and even surpass. There is only one motive justifying sexual intercourse, the Stoics insisted, the conceiving of children. Apart from this motive intercourse even within marriage is suspect, and the node of suspicion was that lust was at work.[1] Thus the argument against remarriage in widowhood: if a man or woman had had children in a first marriage, but once widowed was seeking a second marriage, the presumed motive for this was sexual pleasure. This logic was reinforced in the Christian mind by what Paul advised in 1 Corinthians 7:8–9. There he expressed his clear preference that widows remain unmarried. But the one reason he accepted as over-riding this preference was exactly the lust that the Stoics suspected, and the widow's or widower's inability to dominate it in a life of attempted continence. Thus along with the Stoic ethic, Paul left in the Christians' mind the persuasion that there is ordinarily only one motive for remarrying, and it is not one to boast of. It should not surprise us then to find some few Fathers condemning remarriage in widowhood outright, as Tertullian become Montanist did savagely, and to find more of them permitting it, after the example of Paul, but demanding a period of penance, before the second marriage, for the surrender to human weakness.[2]

When we examine the records available from the fourth century, we come upon two kinds of evidence. With one we are already familiar, the writings of the Fathers, the teachers of the Christian communities. The fourth century offers a treasure of these because it was the age of Basil of Caesarea, of John Chrysostom, of Gregory of Nyssa, Gregory of Nazianz, and Cyril of Jerusalem in the East, and, in the West, of Ambrose through the last third of the century, and of Jerome and Augustine at its end.

The second kind of evidence consists of the decrees published by the councils of bishops as they sought to regulate the conduct of their Christian people in the matter of divorce and remarriage. We shall be curious, in turn, about two kinds of evidence within these decrees. One consists of the conduct that the decrees either prescribed or proscribed—what the Christian people were obligated by ecclesiastical discipline to do or not do about divorcing and remarrying. The other consists of the doctrinal warrant offered for this disciplinary obligating—when and if it is offered. And a helpful frame of reference for the examination of these disciplinary decrees is the bishops' manner of dealing with the problem of remarriage after divorce executed according to the Roman law by which their people lived.

The Patristic Teaching in the Fourth Century

I said at the beginning of this examination of the patristic teaching that it would not be exhaustive. Accordingly what I intend to do with the Fathers of the fourth century is to sift through their teaching for interpretations which show an advance, a step beyond what had been said by the end of the third century. But as an exception to this, three of them deserve detailed attention, since Basil and John Chrysostom were the most effective and lasting creators of the marriage discipline in the East, while Ambrose, along with Jerome and Augustine, was the same in the West.

Once we have sifted through the teaching of these three great Fathers, and through that of their lesser contemporaries, we will have bridged to the beginning of the fifth century, to Jerome and Augustine themselves. And in them we will find the most evident and decisive advance in the Christian judgment on divorce and remarriage since Paul himself.

The first of the fourth-century Fathers deserving attention is the lesser Basil, bishop of Ancyra in Galatia from about 336; he marks the first notable, though still modest, advance in this century. His essay, On the True Integrity of Virginity, he dedicated to Letoios, bishop of Melitene.[3] In it he explained why a consecrated virgin cannot be freed from her commitment: Christ, the spouse to whom she is engaged, is immortal. To explain this mystical marriage and its demands Basil developed its analogy with marriage in real life. Therein lies the passages' value to us, namely Basil's interpretation of the demands for perpetuity of the marital relationship.

> Do you not understand that he who marries a wife who has been dismissed commits adultery? Even if she has been dismissed with just cause, the Scriptures say, her husband is still alive. Then why do you trouble a dismissed wife? Why do you not allow time, to her on the one side to correct the faults that were the reason for her dismissal; and on the other, time to him who dismissed her, so that in his mercy on her in her repentance, he may recover her who is a member of his own body? This you can do instead of preempting the moment of her correction and marrying the dismissed woman while her husband is still alive. Let her be, say the Scriptures. Or better still, let her return to her living spouse and be taken back by him as a spouse become even more beautiful. Or let her, as neither widow nor spouse, undergo chastisement for the sin that obliged her husband to dismiss her.
>
> But you, before even understanding the fault that has merited her dismissal, and wanting the right to live with her, in an absurd way you render her even more shameless in her sin. In continuing to commit adultery with her as with a stranger, and while her husband still lives, you absurdly stimulate her tendency to sin within her married life.[4]

The passage is a rich résumé of a biblically supported and demanding position regarding divorce and remarriage. The woman in this example has been dismissed for just cause; she has sinned against married life itself. And this hints that her sin was adultery. The man who dismissed her justly is called her still living husband, her living spouse. But even though he has dismissed her with just cause, she is still a member of his body. Thus the marital union of husband and wife that Paul had expressed in the head-body metaphor of Ephesians 5 still describes this woman's relationship with her husband. Basil does not say so expressly, but her relationship precisely as understood in virtue of this metaphor is the reason why she is still his wife despite being dismissed by him. Head and body cannot be separated; Christ and the Church cannot be separated. Consequently, Basil hints, neither can this man and woman be separated.

I say that Basil hints at this. He does not say it all explicitly. Although he uses Paul's metaphor, he draws from it only a modest portion of the conclusion that will be drawn later. He does not claim to see probative force in the analogy of the two marital relationships, the metaphorical (Christ and the Church) and the physical (this husband and his wife). His reasoning does not proceed "*Because* the relationship of Christ and the Church is indestructible . . ." but "*Just as* the relationship of Christ and the Church is indestructible, so too is that of the husband and wife."

Basil of Caesarea

The other and better-known Basil, the bishop of Pontus in Caesarea and one of the four great Cappadocians, shows across the sequence of his writings at least an apparent change in his judgment about the permissibility of remarriage after dismissal.

He composed his *Moralia* before 365, during his sojourn as an anchorite near Pontus. This work contains a number of briefly formulated precepts that he corroborates with texts from the Scriptures. Each precept constitutes a chapter, and several chapters are grouped in rules. Rule 73 treats of marriage; its first two chapters deal respectively with separation and remarriage.[5]

A husband must not separate from his wife nor a wife from her husband unless one of them is taken in the act of adultery, or is an obstacle to the other's entrance into the service of God. The texts cited in support of this rule are predictably Matthew 5:31–32 and not so predictably Luke 14:26: "If anyone comes to me and does not hate his father and his mother, his wife, his children, his brothers and his sisters, etc. . . ."

It is interesting that the verb Basil chooses to designate the prerogative allowed a spouse who catches the other out in adultery is not the *apolúein* or *aphiénai* that conventionally signifies dismissal (repudiation), but *chorízein,* the verb which signifies a spouse's voluntary departure from a marriage. It is interesting too that he allows this prerogative to one spouse who finds the other hindering his or her entrance into a more seriously dedicated form of religious life. This form must have included celibacy and chastity, since those are the features of such a life most directly hindered by marriage. Basil may also refer to the situation envisioned by Paul in 1 Corinthians 7:15, that of a Christian spouse whose peace in his or her practice of the Christian faith is torn up by an unbelieving spouse. If he does, there is this difference, that where Paul had advised that the Christian spouse let the other depart, here Basil advises that the former take the initiative, that he or she do the departing.

Chapter 2 of this Rule 73 answers the question coming necessarily from Chapter 1: What of remarriage after separation for these reasons? Here an asymmetry appears in Basil's instruction. In Chapter 1 he had advised concerning one spouse's "departure" from a marriage. But now his counsel is for spouses who have either dismissed or been dismissed. (Anyone who delves into the writings of these early Christian teachers soon grows familiar with these instances of small carelessness.)

> It is not permitted to him who has dismissed his spouse to marry another. Neither is it permitted to a woman who has been dismissed by her husband to marry another man.

Taken literally this chapter looks to cases quite different from those in Chapter 1. It also leaves us uninformed about the prerogative of remarriage for, to take but one case, a woman whose husband has left her in order to enter religious life. Basil brings it to light, raises curiosity about it, but neglects to pronounce on it. But soon enough Christian authorities will rule that this "abandoned" spouse may remarry.

The second literary genre in which Basil taught about divorce and remarriage was his canonical regulation as a bishop. This is preserved in three letters he addressed in 374 and 375 to Amphilochius, bishop of Iconium. (These are numbered by the editors as Letters 188, 199 and 217.)[6]

Amphilochius had asked Basil how he should decide in some particularly embarrassing cases of divorce and remarriage. Basil drew his answers from two sources, the Scriptures and the unwritten penitential customs of the church of Cappadocia. The latter were customs established not by Basil himself but by predecessors whom he called "the Fathers." At points he supplemented these customs by adding his judgment concerning cases they did not touch. And at points too he was mildly critical of them as not perfectly conformed to the Scriptures. But he respected them for their value as tradition.

These canons have been made a kind of primary source of the Eastern churches' marriage law. And the history of the development of this law shows a familiar dynamic. Basil's canons were at his time particular rulings in quite particular circumstances and conditioned by them. Then, abstracted from this historical context, they have at crucial points grown into universal law for the Christian East.

In his Canon 9 he makes the general case that Christ's strictures against abandoning a spouse, except in the case of adultery, be applied equally to men and to women.

> The Savior's reply, according to the logic of his thought, applies equally to men and to women: they are forbidden to abandon conjugal life except for adultery. But custom does not understand the matter thus. In regard to women we find exact instructions. The Apostle says thus: "A man who goes to a

prostitute is one body with her"; and Jeremiah, "If a wife gives
herself to another man, she shall not return to her husband, but
once defiled she shall remain defiled"; and again, "He who keeps
an adulterous wife is impious and stupid."

Custom commands a woman to keep her adulterous husband and a husband living in fornication. Consequently I do not
know if one can say if she is an adulteress. For the accusation in
this case bears upon the woman who has dismissed her husband,
no matter what her reason for abandoning her marriage. Even if
she has been beaten and could not bear this, she should have
been patient under it rather than separate from her spouse. Even
if she could not have borne up under the harm done to her, she
had no sufficient reason. If it was because her husband was living
in fornication, we have in church custom no directive pertaining
to this. There is no command that a wife separate from an
unbelieving husband, but that she have patience because the
outcome is uncertain. . . . Consequently she who abandons her
[unbelieving] husband is an adulteress if she goes to another. The
husband who is abandoned is excusable, and a woman who lives
with him is not condemned. But if the husband goes to another
woman after abandoning his wife, he also is an adulterer because
he makes his wife an adulteress. And she who lives with him is
an adulteress because she has brought to herself another woman's husband.[7]

Granted Basil is here reporting to Amphilochius the customs of the
Christian communities in Cappadocia rather than offering him his own
judgment. In any case he shows how diffuse could become the Christian
discipline drawn from the New Testament instruction—obviously here
from Matthew 5:32 and 19:9—three centuries after this was first put into
writing. What is evident is that in the churches that Basil represented
considerable sympathy was shown to a spouse who had been abandoned by
the other, be the former husband or wife. These churches refused to say
forthrightly that remarriage involved them in adultery. By logical consequence they were just as reluctant to call adulterous the men or women
whom they took as second spouses. The condemnation for adultery they
reserved for a spouse who abandoned the other and remarried (unless this
was a husband who dismissed an adulterous wife?), for a man who married
a woman who had been dismissed for whatever reason, for a woman who
married a man who had dismissed his wife unjustly, and for a woman who
dismissed her husband for any cause at all and then remarried.[8]

In Canon 35 Basil apparently offers his own judgment in the case of a
husband who has been abandoned by his wife.

About an abandoned husband, one must first examine the
reason for his being abandoned. If it appears that his wife left

him without cause, he merits being pardoned, she being punished. The pardon is accorded the husband so that he may be in communion with the Church.[9]

Since this canon presumes that the husband is without fault, it would seem that that for which he is pardonable is his taking a second wife after being abandoned by the first.

Two other canons, 46 and 77, offer further details of the demands made on those involved in a second marriage after one spouse has abandoned the other.

(Canon 46) A woman who has been espoused to a man without knowing that he has been temporarily abandoned by his wife, if she is subsequently dismissed at the return of the first wife, has committed fornication, but without knowing it. But there is no obligation to dismiss her from the marriage. It would be better if she stayed as she is.[10]

Canon 77 is Basil's explanation of a mitigated treatment accorded by local tradition to husbands who have abandoned their wives and then remarried.

He who abandons the wife to whom he is legally married and marries another, he is, according to the Lord's declaration, subject to the judgment of adultery. But our Fathers have ruled that such men should be for one year among those who weep [the first step in the process of penitential return to communion], for two years among those who hear, for three years among the prostrate, and during the seventh year with those who stand among the faithful—and thus render themselves worthy of the sacrament if they have done this penance with tears.[11]

This canon clearly has the intent of setting the conditions for return to communion of a Christian man who has remarried after dismissing his wife. Not listed among these conditions is that he take back his first wife or send away the second. By its silence the canon appears to accept the second marriage as *fait accompli.* And doing the penance is not a condition for continuing this second marriage, but for returning to communion.

Gregory of Nazianz

Gregory of Nazianz was bishop of Constantinople from 380 until his death a decade later. In his Sermon 37 on Matthew (paragraph 7) he pleaded with the men of his community to maintain a marital fidelity exactly equal to that which they demanded of their wives. In effect he demanded that if their wives' intercourse with another man be punishable as adultery, so should theirs with another woman. But it is one of

Gregory's reasons for demanding this equality that interests us. It is the farthest advance we have seen thus far in developing the valence implicit in Paul's marital metaphor of Christ and the Church. Gregory reasons in the following way:

> The two of them, say the Scriptures, shall be in one flesh. Then let this one flesh be accorded the one same honor. And it is by this example that Paul promulgates the law of chastity. How and in what way? "This is a great mystery; I refer to Christ and the Church." It is a beautiful thing for the wife to honor Christ through her husband; it is a beautiful thing also for the husband to not denigrate the Church through his wife. "Let the wife," says the Apostle, "honor her husband"—for this has to do with Christ. But the husband too, let him keep his wife in his care, for so does Christ with the Church.[12]

Gregory's insight here is a rich one. Not only does the love relationship of Christ and the Church serve as a normative example for the husband and wife in their treatment of one another. But in this treatment they affect Christ and the Church; they are avenues for one another's conduct—the wife for the husband's effect on the Church, the husband for the wife's address to Christ. Even if this application of the Pauline metaphor results in the dissimilar and unequal roles for the two spouses in the Christ-Church economy, Gregory has touched a rich vein. But he mines it very little for the conduct of Christian spouses regarding divorce and remarriage.

Evidence from three bishops in the churches of Asia Minor will help at this point to recall the context in which this discipline for divorce and remarriage first took form. But our keen modern concern for finding out the permissibility and indeed the possibility of true divorce and then remarriage was by no means the first concern of these Christian teachers in the fourth century. Two others preoccupied them. One we have already seen in passing—the concern to bring a fair and equal morality to rule the conduct of both men and women, and do this in part by ending the concession to male sexual need, a concession established in custom and even in law, that refused to see a husband's having lovers and even concubines as sinful so long as these were not other men's wives. The other concern, but one interlocked with the first, was to get Christian spouses to see their marriages not as liaisons become marriages sanctioned by Roman law, but as relationships of respect and caring love designed by God.

For one of these statements we go back to Gregory of Nazianz. As bishop of Constantinople he was asked to rule in the case of a citizen, Verian, who wished his daughter to dismiss a husband whom she loved. The method of dismissal was to be the writ of dismissal, the *biblíon apostasíou*. The girl was torn between respect for her father and love for her husband. In his Letter 144, addressed to Olympios, the civil governor in the case, Gregory announced flatly his attitude regarding dismissal: "[It] is simply contrary to our laws, even if the Romans judge the matter otherwise." He clearly sets Christian *law* in contradiction to the civil law of the time—although he could not have meant a Christian statutory system, which had not yet come into existence, but Christ's Gospel teaching.

In a second letter (no. 145), addressed to Verian himself, Gregory insisted that he had never been involved in a marital dismissal. He added that if Verian insisted on his daughter's giving the writ of dismissal, he must engage another intermediary, that his own duty as bishop was to seek the good of all parties as a Christian understood this.

What does not escape notice here is the residual indecision on Gregory's part. Though personally and as a Christian bishop adamantly opposed to dismissal of a spouse, he does not forbid a Christian father from going the route of Roman civil law if he insists on the dismissal. Nor does he say in a doctrinal way that this dismissal is ineffective, impossible. He simply washes his hands of the affair.

Another Gregory, bishop of Ancyra and the brother of Basil of Caesarea, recalled the divine origin of marriage in his canonical letter written to Letoios of Melitene. He used the letter to enunciate points of discipline for sexual-marital conduct. In Canon 4 he distinguished fornication from adultery while pointing out the immorality of both. He is pointing obviously at the attitude so common in his time that a husband does not sin if he goes outside his marriage sexually provided the woman he goes to is not married or engaged. He acknowledges the distinction that "certain Fathers," his predecessors, have made: adultery is sinful because it is injustice, the unjust invasion of what belongs to another man, but a husband's taking a concubine or lover is not to be called adultery. It is rather fornication.

A rare and even sublime view of marriage appears in Gregory's Life of Macrinus.[13] He tells there how his sister responded after the death of her fiancé, when her parents urged her to take as husband one of a number of men they had arranged for her.

> She replied that it was absurd and against the divine law for her to not be satisfied with the one marriage her father had arranged for her, but to be forced instead to look to other men. For it is the nature of marriage that a woman have but one husband, as she also experiences but one birth and one death. She insisted firmly that the man who had been her fiancé by the will of her parents was not dead but was living in God through his hope in the resurrection. He was not dead but was on a journey. It was therefore absurd to not keep faith with him while he was on this journey.

That this Christian attitude is irreconcilable with remarriage even in widowhood is obvious. But what especially catches the eye is the reason at the heart of the young widow's refusal to remarry. She had promised her fiancé that she would keep faith with him. Since he was not really dead, but they were no more than separated for a time, how could she not continue to keep faith with him? Is this the *sacramentum* of marriage understood as the promise, the pledge? Augustine will say in more than one place that it is this *sacramentum,* where it is present, that makes a marriage indestructible (although he will limit the indestructibility to life this side of death). And if it is the Christian belief that death does not end life which gives the *sacramentum* its holding power, we can see here the beginning of the theology that will later say it is the commitment of a husband and wife to one another in Christian faith that ultimately makes their marriage indestructible—but theirs only.

The Antiochian Fathers

Theodore of Mopsuestia was the most accomplished exegete of the School of Antioch, the friend and comrade in studies of John Chrysostom. He wrote a Commentary on Matthew,[14] and in one of his reflections on 5:31–32 he suggests a theological reason that will be developed later. It is a consideration that borrows from a Platonic view of reality. Writing of the situation of a woman who has been dismissed by her husband he grants that according to outward appearance (*katà phainómenon*) she may indeed be a stranger to her husband. But according to spiritual reality (*katā noóumenon*) she is still her husband's body, for once at the beginning God had joined her to her husband, had given her to him in order to form one flesh with him. And it is this spiritual reality that is the heart of the marriage. Consequently not even the husband who has dismissed her can remarry, since he is still married to her.

No very fine consideration of this reasoning is needed to verify how close it lies to that of Gregory of Nyssa that we saw just above. At least for Christians the heart of their marriage is a reality that is trans-empiric and lasting. It at least seems to be something other than their perishable *affectus maritalis,* their will to be married, something that is the product of this will. And this reality apparently lives in the domain of signification, since it points to a reality other than itself (in this case Christ's marriage with the Church), and draws its meaning and value from this other reality.[15]

John Chrysostom

John Chrysostom deserves detailed attention because along with Basil he was the most enduringly influential teacher in the Eastern Church.

He wrote his Treatise on Virginity in Antioch in 382.[16] In it he joined his fellow bishops' challenge to the sexual mores of his culture by insisting that spouses hold equal rights in marriage—that according to 1 Corinthians 7:3 the wife has a right to her husband's sexual conduct equal to his right over hers. But predictably he qualified this by admitting that although in the beginning God had designed this equality, because in the Garden Eve had led Adam into sin, wives are now subject to their husbands and owe obedience to them.

He goes on to warn wives that even if their marriages become a slavery for them, they ought to bear this. In any case they have only two options in a marriage they find unbearable. They may reform the husband, if this is possible. If it is not, they must, as he has already said, bear their living martyrdom patiently. But then he relents and acknowledges that Paul has given a kind of *post factum* permission to wives who have left their marriages. They are not obligated to return to their husbands, but neither can they remarry as long as the latter are still alive. And here John uses a metaphor in a normative way. Just as a consecrated virgin can never marry because her spouse lives eternally, so a wife cannot remarry while her husband still lives.

In this essay he does not address the question of the dismissal of an adulterous spouse and subsequent remarriage. He interprets Deuteronomy 24:1 in the same way that Theodore of Mopsuestia does: Moses allowed Jewish husbands to dismiss their wives lest they rid themselves of them by murder.

During the year 390 John gave a series of homilies in Antioch on the Gospel according to Matthew. In his Homily 17 we have his commentary on Matthew 5:31–32.[17] He follows the text in saying that a man who dismisses his wife exposes her to the sin of adultery, while a man who marries a dismissed wife commits adultery because she is still wife to the husband who dismissed her. So the dismissed wife must lead a celibate life for as long as her husband lives. As for the husband's dismissing his wife, this he may do if she has committed adultery lest he countenance this sin in his own home.

For reasons that are not evident John chooses here not to take up the challenge of the exceptive clause. He does not ask and answer the question whether the man who dismisses his wife for her adultery may remarry. As for the guilty wife's remarrying, his general prohibition against any dismissed wife's doing so seems to rule in her case.

He reaches Matthew 19:3–12 in his Homily 62.[18] Here he urges that the reason why marriages must not be dissolved is that in the beginning God created one man and one woman, and commanded that the one man and one woman be united to form one body. Hence Jesus' command: "What God has joined . . ." Moreover (and here John attempts another argument-by-metaphor) to try to dissolve a marriage is to act against nature, since husband and wife form one body, and it is against nature to cut and sever one's body.

John's judgment on this complex matter gains no clarity in his Homily 19 on 1 Corinthians 7:1–40 delivered in Antioch in 392.[19] Here he reaffirms what Paul had declared about the equality of a wife's sexual rights with her husband's. He continues that in the case of *pornéia* spouses *must* separate. And he asks why Paul demands this but permits a Christian spouse to remain with an unbelieving spouse. His answer is that only with a spouse who commits *pornéia* does the other become defiled. He clearly understands *pornéia* to refer to adultery; so he shares the opinion of his time holding dismissal in the case of adultery to be a moral obligation.

But in this homily John speaks expressly only of the husband's dismissing an adulterous wife. And here his rhetoric takes him far out beyond the shallows. He says that where a wife has committed *pornéia* her marriage is already dissolved, and the verb he uses in participial form here is conventional and clear in its meaning. It is the *dialúein* of the legal language of divorce.[20] And he caps this by saying that after his wife's fornication her husband is no longer a husband (*metà tēn pornéian ho anēr ouk éstin anēr*). If despite all this he still thinks that a dismissed wife is married to her husband as long as he lives, in this homily he has used most careless language to describe the destructive consequences of a wife's infidelity.

Back in Constantinople in 398 John delivered three homilies on marriage within a few days. The first of these, Homily 19,[21] is mainly an exegesis on 1 Corinthians 7:2–4. It opposes divine law to human law, demanding equal chastity in marriage of both husbands and wives, and branding as adulterers not only faithless wives but husbands who go to prostitutes, who seduce their female slaves, or take mistresses.

In the second homily, Homily 26, he returns to the severe contrast between what divine law commands and human law (in this case Roman law) permits.[22] He follows Paul in 1 Corinthians, saying in a general and unnuanced way that a dismissed wife must not take another husband as long as the husband who dismissed her still lives. Despite getting from him the writ of dismissal she is bound to him for the length of his life.

But may the husband remarry if the cause for his dismissing his wife is her adultery? Again at this crucial point John fails in clarity. For one thing, he is commenting on Paul, not on Matthew and his exceptive clause. About husbands he says the following:

> What shall we say [on the day of judgment] to him who will judge us when, after presenting and reading to us his law, he will say, "I have commanded that you not take to yourself a wife who has been dismissed, and have told you that such conduct is adultery. How have you dared to contract a forbidden marriage?" . . . Indeed he who has dismissed his wife except for one cause, which is her fornication, he who has married a dismissed wife while her husband still lives, are condemned equally with the dismissed wife.

John continues rhetorically that the folly in taking a dismissed woman as wife culminates in a man's eternal punishment for adultery. Similarly punished are those husbands who dismiss their wives without just cause, and those men who marry women dismissed for any cause, if they do so while the latters' husbands are still alive.

But what of the husband who, after dismissing his adulterous wife, takes to wife another woman who has not been dismissed, in her first marriage? Does he come under the same condemnation for adultery? John does not say so. Indeed he does not advert to the situation. And we are left to interpret his silence.

His third homily, Homily 29, adds nothing of consequence.[23] But he does exacerbate in his readers' minds their uncertainty about his meaning when he says that whereas civil law allows a husband to dismiss his wife for a plenteous repertory of faults in her, Paul demands that such a fault-ridden wife be kept—except when among these faults is her *pornéia*. Then she may and must be dismissed. Again, may her husband remarry provided this is not with a dismissed woman? Again John does not say.

But if he fails to be decisive about the possibility of a wronged husband's remarrying and therefore about the fundamental indissolubility of a Christian marriage, he writes intelligently and beautifully about the ideal of monogamous marriage. To a young widow grieving at the recent loss of her husband he insists that the communion in love with her husband that began in their marriage has not ended. For those who believe in the resurrection, married love is not defeated.

> Indeed the affection you bear him you can keep up as much now as you did in the past. Such is the power of love that it is not limited to persons present to us, to those near us or visible to us. But you long to see your husband face to face. And I know this is your most intense desire. So keep your bed untouched by other men, and take great care to lead a life like your husband's. Surely then you will go to rejoin him, not for five years (as you once did), not for twenty, nor for 100, nor 1000, or 2000, or 10,000 or 100 times 10,000. But you shall love him for ages endless and eternal. You will meet him again vested not in the bodily beauty he had when he left you, but in another beauty, another brightness more luminous than the rays of the sun.[24]

The Western Fathers

It should come as no surprise in the long view of history that this uncertain teaching among the Eastern Fathers about the permissibility of a husband's remarrying after dismissing an adulterous wife should have produced a canonical discipline permitting him to do just that—and eventually permitting an innocent wife as well to remarry after dismissing her adulterous husband.

But what of the teachers in the Christian West at the same time, in that sector of the Church that eventually produced the severer discipline denying the right to dissolve a marriage for adultery or for any other delinquency, and denying even the possibility of it? Were the sources of this severity already evident in what these Fathers wrote and said in the fourth century?

Bishop Hilary of Poitiers composed what was probably his first work, his Commentary on Matthew, near the middle of this century. He addressed the questions already so familiar in both East and West, and he showed the usual unwillingness to draw out the consequences of Matthew's exceptive clause for Christ's proscription of dismissal of a spouse.

> Seeking to bring fair treatment to all [Christ] prescribed especially that wives should remain in the peace of their homes. He added many things to the law [of Moses] and deducted nothing from it. And about this improvement one could hardly complain. For the law had granted the freedom to give the writ of dismissal, but now the Gospel faith not only expresses to the husband its desire for peace but puts the blame on him for his spouse if she is forced into adultery by marrying a second time, driven to this by his dismissing her. It prescribes no other reason for departing from the marriage except that which would defile the husband by the company of a wife who has made herself a prostitute.[25]

In the last line here Hilary interprets Paul's reference (in 1 Corinthians 6:15–16) to a man's going to a prostitute as applying to a husband's keeping a wife who has committed adultery. He may dismiss her; indeed he must do so lest he be defiled. His designation of what this dismissal effects is trenchant. The husband who does it departs from the marriage; he ceases to be married (*desinit a coniugio*).

But may the husband who thus obediently dismisses his faithless wife later remarry? Hilary does not say.

In Homily 4 of his first book of homilies, written c. 365, Bishop Zeno of Verona spoke of fornication and dismissal.

> Thus, since they [husband and wife] are a single flesh, a single mystery [*sacramentum*] of the divine creation, because the woman has been made from her husband and therefore, juridically speaking, they are of the same lineage, there is no doubt that whichever of the two deceives will receive a terrible punishment in eternity.[26]

Zeno's discourse here is about the demands of chastity and the perils of unchastity. It is not formally about marriage. Consequently he does not develop his thought that the union of a husband and wife is a *sacramentum* of the divine creation. He does not explain how it is that being made of the same flesh, husband and wife are such a sacrament, nor why he sees their oneness-in-flesh not in their coming together in marriage but in the origin of Eve from Adam's body. Evidently Zeno is not ready theologically to arrange the facets of the analogy as they will be later—to show how the love relationship of husband and wife, because of its analogy with the marital metaphor of Christ and his Church, makes of the relationship a mirror of the latter "marriage" and puts on the relationship the demand of the latter's indestructibility.

Ambrose of Milan

The influence of Ambrose on the later doctrine and discipline of divorce and remarriage in the West is second probably only to that of Augustine. But unlike Basil and John Chrysostom in the East it is not, with Ambrose, that he wrote or spoke so copiously on the subject. His influence is due rather to Augustine's having heard and read his words. It is due also to a distinction that, among his peers, he seems to have been the first to discover, a distinction about kinds of marriages. We shall come in a moment to this distinction which is contained in Book 8 of his Commentary on Luke.

But first, in Chapter 6, Paragraph 31 of his essay, On Virginity, he comments on Matthew's exceptive clause: "He [Jesus] reminded them that a marriage is not to be dissolved [*non solvendum*] except because of fornication."[27] By *fornicatio* Ambrose clearly means adultery by one of the spouses. And taking his choice of verbs at face value, one must understand him to say that even before the innocent spouse dismisses the adulterous, their marriage has been dissolved. If he means otherwise—that perhaps not the marriage itself but only cohabitation has been ended—his choice of the verb *solvere* to designate what happens is imprudent. Its common meaning in his society was "to end the marriage."

In Book 8, Paragraph 2, of his Commentary on Luke (*Expositio Evangelii secundum Lucam*) we find Ambrose's interpretation of 1 Corinthians 7:15 and the reason Paul offers for the Christian spouse's allowing the pagan to depart from the marriage.

> I must first, I think, speak of the law of marriage so as to treat afterward the prohibition of divorce. Certain persons think, in fact, that every marriage is of God, especially since it is written "What God has joined no man must separate." So then, if every marriage is of God, it is not permitted to dissolve any marriage. Why then has the Apostle said, "If the unbelieving spouse departs, let him depart"? His discernment here is admirable. He wanted no motive for divorce to remain available to

Christians, and has shown that not every marriage is of God. For it is not by God's authority that Christians marry pagans, since the law forbids this.[28]

As I suggested just above, Ambrose here makes a true innovation in the history of the Christian teaching on divorce. He takes the ancient logic—"No mere human authority can dissolve a marriage because marriages are joined by God's authority"—and makes a crucial qualification in it. *If* a marriage is indeed joined by God, no mere human authority can dissolve it. But not every marriage is so joined. For example, the marriage of a Christian with a pagan is not (saying this, Ambrose saves Paul's orthodoxy). Much less is the marriage of two pagans joined by God. Only the marriage of two Christians is.

The conclusion from this, which Ambrose clearly intends, is that those marriages not joined by God can be dissolved by human authority. (With this he also implies an interpretation of Paul's instruction that has been rejected by most Catholic scholars since his day. Where they have insisted that Paul meant only that the pagan spouse's departure effects a separation from bed and board, Ambrose understands it to be a true dissolution of the marriage. For this is the target of his logic, to show that because such a marriage is not joined by God it can be dissolved by human authority. And he mentions here no other dissolving act than the pagan spouse's departure.)

Ambrose seems unbothered by the fact that Jesus spoke his mind, "Therefore what God has joined man must not separate," to an exclusively Jewish audience. He is happy to interpret Jesus to have only his future Christian followers as the referents of his command.

He has more to say in this Book 8. He tells the Christian husbands among his readers, "Take care not to dismiss your wives, for this would be to deny that God is the author of your marriages" (Paragraph 4).[29] "You dismiss your spouses as if with full right, without regret; and you think this is permitted because human law does not forbid it. But the law of God forbids it. You obey men but reject God" (Paragraph 5).[30] Moses' prescription for divorce in Deuteronomy 24:1 is that of a Jew, not of a Christian; and he gave it because of the hardness of men's hearts. He permitted the dismissing of wives, but God did not command it. God's law from the beginning is "Thus a man will leave his father and his mother and will cleave to his wife, and the two will become one flesh." Ambrose hints at the theology of the sacrament when he adds that for a man to dismiss his wife is thus for him to tear away part of his own body (Paragraph 7).[31]

In Paragraph 8 Ambrose returns to the notion that the religiously mixed marriage of a Christian and a pagan is not of God and is therefore not ruled by the law of God.

This place shows those things that were written [in the law] not by God but because of human weakness. Hence the Apostle:

"To the married I proclaim—it is not I who do so, but the Lord—that a wife is not to be divorced from her husband." And later, "To the rest I say (and here it is I, not the Lord), if a brother has a wife who is a non-believer, and she leaves him . . ." Thus where there is an unequal marriage there is no law of God. And he [Paul] added, "But if the non-believing spouse departs let him depart." Thus at one and the same time the Apostle does two things: he denies that the law of God permits that any and every marriage be dissolved; and he does not give a command nor grant authority [to dissolve] to the spouse who leaves, but he excuses the fault of the one who is left.[32]

In Paragraph 9 he takes up again his notion of the uniqueness of the marriage of two Christians.

> . . . because Jesus had said that not even the least part of the law is to be abandoned, he added, "Anyone who dismisses his wife and marries another commits adultery." So the Apostle writes wisely when he says that this is a great *sacramentum* of Christ and the Church. Here therefore you will find a marriage that is undoubtedly joined by God, since Jesus himself said, "No one comes to me unless the Father who has sent me draws him." For the Father alone could join this marriage. Therefore Solomon said in a spiritual sense [*mystice*], "God shall prepare a wife for a man" (Proverbs 19:14). Christ is the husband; the Church is the wife—by her love [*caritate*] a wife and by her integrity a virgin.[33]

With this Ambrose as exegete lays out in discrete fashion what his pupil Augustine will in a few years as theologian seek to synthesize. The invulnerability of a marriage to dissolution lies in some way in its being a *sacramentum*. And by this Ambrose apparently means that the invulnerability mirrors the relationship of Christ and the Church. A marriage thus invulnerable is the kind (and the only kind) that is joined by God (or, with logic reversed, because only such a marriage is joined by God, it alone is invulnerable). It is joined thus because God draws the spouses into it; in it he gives the woman to the man. And to finish off the analogy, to correlate the two sides of it, each with its own internal relationship, he adds metaphorically that Christ is the husband and the Church is the wife.

In his treatise On Abraham (*De Abraham*), Book 1, Chapter 4, Paragraph 25, Ambrose comments to his catechumens on the place of Hagar in the patriarch's life.

> But I urge you, husbands, especially you who intend to receive the grace of the Lord, that you not unite yourselves to an adulterous body (for he who joins himself to a prostitute is one

with her), nor to give your wives this occasion for divorce [*nec dare hanc occasionem divortii mulieribus*]. Let no one flatter himself by using some pretext of the laws of men. Every fornication is adultery; and it is not permitted to a man to do that which is forbidden to a woman. The same chastity is demanded of a man as of a woman. Everything committed with her who is not the legitimate spouse is condemned as the crime of adultery. You have taken note then of what you must avoid lest you show yourselves unworthy of the sacrament.[34]

What does Ambrose mean by *sacramentum* at the end of this paragraph? It can mean the vow or commitment that his catechumens are about to make in their baptism. Or it can designate *sacramentum* as mystery, and refer again to their baptism under a different aspect, their participation in the death and resurrection of Christ. Or it can designate the commitment that they have made or will make in their marriages.

Since he has in mind his male catechumens he warns them against the common acceptance of husbandly infidelity, pointing out to them that to go to a prostitute while married is to commit adultery, and (most significantly for our study) that in so doing a Christian husband will give his wife grounds for divorcing him. The noun he uses at this point, as the parenthetical quotation shows above, is simply *divortium*. There is an historical difficulty here, that Roman law in Ambrose's time did not allow wives to dismiss their husbands for the latter's adultery. If Ambrose refers here to an action on the part of the wives that is authorized by the Church, he may be presuming that within Christian custom wives could take an initiative in dismissing their faithless husbands in virtue of the Synoptic exceptive clause.

In Chapter 7 of this same Book 1 Ambrose reflects on Abimelech and Sara.[35]

> Any union of a man or woman that is not celebrated by some sort of marriage is blameworthy. So learn then, you who are moving toward the grace of baptism as candidates for the faith, how severe is the discipline of continence. No one must know any other woman but his wife. The right to marry has been given to you lest you sin with another man's wife. You are bound to a wife; do not seek for a dissolution, for you are forbidden to take another wife as long as your first wife lives. For to seek another when you already have your own wife is the crime of adultery, all the more serious because you think to get for your sin the approbation of the law. Your fault would be more tolerable if your sin were hidden than if you were to invoke wantonly the law's approbation. You commit adultery not only by sinning with another man's wife, but in any relationship that does not have the nature of marriage.

Not only does Ambrose here put his male catechumens on guard against adultery, but he affirms with total clarity that a husband cannot contract a true second marriage while his spouse still lives. Thus a Christian cannot take advantage of the civil law that allows this. Trying to do so worsens his sin by giving him the appearance of legitimacy. And adultery for a husband consists not only in having sexual relations with another man's wife, as in the Jewish and Roman view of things, for any time a married man unites with a woman other than his wife, he commits adultery even though this second woman is not married.

Does Ambrose nevertheless allow that the Matthean exceptive clause qualifies this apparently absolute prohibition? He makes no mention of the clause at this point.

The Ambrosiaster

But until the sixteenth century the opinion about Ambrose common among Catholic theologians was that elsewhere in his writings he had spoken very clearly on the point—that he had allowed a husband to dismiss his wife, to dissolve his marriage, because of her adultery, and precisely in virtue of Matthew's exceptive clause. I say until the sixteenth century because until then a commentary on 1 Corinthians 7 that approved this dissolution was thought to be the work of Ambrose. But in that century scholars verified that it was the work of an exegete of the fifth century whose name is lost to posterity. Because the work was thought for so many centuries to be that of Ambrose, its author bears the pseudonym *Ambrosiaster*. The pertinent passage is the following.

> "To the married I proclaim (although it is not I but the Lord), that a wife must not separate from her husband. But even if she does separate, she must remain unmarried. . . ." Such is the Apostle's counsel. According to it if the wife leaves her husband because of his evil conduct she must remain unmarried, " . . . or return to her husband": if she cannot contain herself, he says, because she is unwilling to battle against the flesh, let her return to her husband. The woman is not permitted to remarry when she has left her husband because of his adultery or apostasy . . . because the inferior cannot live by the same law as the superior. But if the husband apostatizes or tries to use his wife perversely, she can neither marry another man nor return to her husband. "And a man must not dismiss his wife": but here is understood implicitly "except in case of her fornication." For this reason Paul does not add, as he does when instructing the wife, "If he leaves her, he must remain unmarried." For a husband is allowed to take a second wife when he has dismissed a sinful first wife. For the man is not to be held to the law in the same way as the wife. He is indeed the head of the wife.[36]

Whoever the Ambrosiaster was, he did not, like so many of the Fathers, skirt the exceptive clause when it came to explaining Christ's teaching concerning divorce and remarriage. He is quite clear that he thought husbands were ruled, even as Christians, by a different law from that which ruled the wife. And he just as clearly took the exceptive clause to mean that a Christian husband could dismiss an adulterous wife and remarry.

Note about his interpretation that there is no evidence that this is one side of a debate in his territory or his place, that he is trying to gainsay a contrary judgment. From internal evidence his is an expression of at least a tolerated opinion, one accepted as commonly as others about the permissibility of a husband's remarrying after dismissing an adulterous wife. It is significant that in commenting on Paul's instruction to the Corinthians the author borrows the Matthean exceptive clause in order to clarify what he thought unclear in Paul. To do this he had to see no contradiction between Paul and Matthew but only an incompleteness in the former. Nor did he seem to be contending with a fixed tradition shaped in the Church according to the Pauline teaching. It is significant too that he justifies the husband's privileged conduct by saying that he can use the *law* differently than the wife can. This hints at conduct at least tolerated in the Western Church wherein the author wrote, and perhaps even legitimized it. It is hardly surprising that this interpretation of Christ's words in Matthew, thought for twelve centuries to be that of one of the great Fathers of the Western Church, would work its effect for all those centuries.

Papal Declarations in the First Four Centuries

The earliest surviving statements coming from a Pope are those of Innocent I, who was bishop of Rome from 401 to 417. In a letter to Victricius of Rouen in 404 he responded to the latter's request for information about the discipline of the Roman Church concerning marriage.[37] Innocent included fourteen regulations in his reply, explaining that they were not new but had been taken from the teaching of the apostles and the Fathers. Yet the only ruling on the dissolution of marriages that he passed on to Victricius touched the conduct of wives. According to Rule 13 marriage is dissolved for a wife only by the death of her husband. (Even this stipulation is carried in a rule forbidding consecrated virgins who had married to be admitted to the penitential process before the death of their husbands.)

In 405 Innocent wrote to Exsuperius, bishop of Toulouse, to answer several questions on marriage.[38] In paragraph 6 of his letter he declared adulterous all married Christians who attempt remarriage while their spouses still live. Both husbands and wives are to be barred from communion. From the Gospel passages he quoted it is clear that Innocent in this instruction avoided the question of the exceptive clause touching the husband dismissing his wife for her adultery.

Of Innocent's declarations on divorce and remarriage scholars have given most attention to his letter addressed between 410 and 417 to Probus, a magistrate in the imperial government.[39] During the pillaging of Rome by the Goths under Alaric in 410, Ursa, a Christian wife, was captured and carried off. Her husband, Fortunius, making use of Roman law that considered a marriage dissolved when the spouse was taken captive, entered marriage with another woman, Restituta. But Ursa was later released; she returned to Rome, sought without success to reclaim her husband, then presented her case to Pope Innocent.

The latter made a special point of declaring his judicial competence over the appeal, then presented his decision: "Wherefore we decide, in accordance with the prescriptions of the Catholic faith, that this is the marriage which was established by divine grace in the first place; and that the marriage entered with the second woman can in no way be legitimate as long as the first wife still lives and has not been dismissed by divorce."[40]

The decision does not, of course, bear directly upon the status of a marriage purportedly dissolved by a husband dismissing an adulterous wife. But dismissal of the latter is clearly alluded to in the last clause here of Innocent's ruling. Does he mean by it that if Fortunius had dismissed Ursa, perhaps on the ground of her adultery, he would have been free to marry Restituta? Those who deny this say that in the clause Innocent intended to strengthen the case against Fortunius' attempt at a second marriage on the ground of Roman law, since the latter had alleged no grounds for lawful divorce even according to this law.

But this argument limps, because according to Roman law once a spouse was captured and stolen away and reduced to a condition equivalent to slavery, no divorce was needed. The marriage ended with the capture and removal of the spouse. On the other hand, if what Innocent does here is to assert the demands of divine law in derogation of civil law, he seems to say that even according to divine law Ursa's case could have been decided differently had Fortunius been able to divorce according to this law. The implication then is that this law does permit divorce by dismissal. As in so many cases, here too the exact meaning of the statement remains unclear.

NOTES

1. For a survey of this point of the Stoic sexual ethic see my earlier volume, *Marriage in the Catholic Church: What Is Marriage?*, Chapter 4.

2. Cereti treats this matter at length, *op. cit.*, Chapter 1, "La Predicazione della Monogamia nella Chiesa Primitiva," pp. 105ff.

3. In PG, Vol. 30, Cols. 669–810.

4. *Loc. cit.*, Col. 751.

5. In PG, Vol. 31, Cols 849–851.

6. In PG, Vol. 32, Cols. 663–684; 715–752; 793–810.

7. In PG, *loc. cit.,* Cols. 673–674.

8. In Canon 21 Basil reports a custom strange to the mind of a modern Western Christian. If a married man living with his wife has intercourse with another woman, even if this is done within his own home this is not reckoned adultery provided the other woman is unmarried. His sin is called rather fornication. He is not because of it obliged to separate from his wife. And his wife is obliged to continue living with him provided he puts the other woman out of his house. But he must do penance for this fornication. This may be a continuation of the ancient interpretation of adultery not as infidelity to one's own spouse, but a violation of another man's right to exclusive sexual access to his wife. (In PG, *loc. cit.,* Col. 722)

9. In PG, *loc. cit.,* Col. 727.

10. *Loc. cit.,* Col. 730.

11. *Loc. cit.,* Cols. 803–804.

12. In PG, Vol. 36, Cols. 290–291.

13. In PG, Vol. 46, Col. 946.

14. In Crouzel, *op. cit.,* pp. 171–172

15. But that Theodore himself did not comprehend the potential of his argument here seems evident in his later Commentary on the Prophet Malachi. Commenting on Chapter 2, verse 16 of the prophecy he said, " 'But if you [the husband] have come to hate her, dismiss her,' says the Lord God of Israel." Taking this literally as God's command Theodore must account for it reasonably. He tries to do so by appealing to the divine prudence in permitting the lesser sin in order to avoid the greater. Because of the hardness of husbands' hearts, as Jesus pointed out, God gave them this permission to dismiss their wives lest they do violence to them, even to the point of murder. Theodore was convinced that in offering this counsel through the mouth of Malachi, God made clear why Moses (in Deuteronomy 24:1) allowed Israel's husbands to dismiss their wives. In this passage he says nothing about the permissibility of either the husband's or the dismissed wife's subsequently remarrying.

16. In PG, Vol. 48, Cols. 533–596.

17. In PG, Vol. 57, Col. 259.

18. In PG, Vol. 58, Cols. 595–604.

19. In PG, Vol. 61, Cols. 151–160.

20. *Loc. cit.,* Cols. 155–156.

21. In PG, Vol. 51, Cols. 151–160.

22. *Op. cit.,* Cols. 218–219.

23. *Op. cit.,* Cols. 225–242.

24. Quoted in Cereti, *op. cit.,* pp. 124–125.

25. In PL, Vol. 9, Cols. 939–940.

26. In PL, Vol. 11, Col. 299.

27. In PL, Vol. 16, Col. 273.

28. In PL, Vol. 15, Col. 1765.

29. *Ibid.,* Col. 1766.

30. *Ibid.,* Col. 1767.

31. *Ibid.*

32. *Ibid.*

33. *Loc. cit.,* Cols. 1767–1768.

34. In PL, Vol. 14, Col. 431.

35. *Op. cit.,* Col. 442.

36. In *Corpus Scriptorum Ecclesiasticorum,* Vol. 81, *Ambrosiastri Qui Dicitur Commentarius in Epistulas Paulinas, Pars II, In Epistulas ad Corinthios,* Recensuit H.I. Vogels, Vindobonae, 1968, pp. 74–75.

37. In PL, Vol. 20, Cols. 478–479, Letter 2.

38. *Op. cit.,* Cols. 499–501, Letter 6.

39. *Op. Cit.,* Cols. 602–603, Letter 36.

40. *Ibid.* In Innocent's Latin this decisive part of his judgment is formulated as follows: "Quare, domine fili merito illustris, statuimus, fide catholica suffragante, illud esse conjugium, quod est primitus gratia divina fundatum; conventumque secundae mulieris, priore superstite, nec divortio ejecta, nullo pacto esse legitimum."

8. THE TREATMENT OF ADULTERY IN THE EARLY CHURCH

Modern Roman Catholics accustomed to unanimity in their bishops' statements on serious matters are probably surprised at the hesitation and partial disharmony among the bishops of the fourth century when speaking on divorce and remarriage. But the surprise dissipates when one takes account of certain conditions under which those bishops taught.

It is the nature of episcopal teaching that it seeks to preserve a tradition and apply it to current questions and problems. But a tradition needs time to take its form, and while it is forming it will pass through argument and disagreement. The third and fourth centuries were themselves the period during which a Catholic tradition on divorce and remarriage was under formation—during which two traditions in fact were taking form, the Eastern Catholic and the Western, with the pace of the former far outstripping that of the latter. So the student should take for granted that the fourth century would show a variety and a dialectic of opinions.

The raw material with which the bishops of these centuries worked to form their traditions was itself heterogeneous. This was the New Testament traditions, both the Synoptic and the Pauline. We have seen the discordances within the Synoptic tradition itself, and of it over against the Pauline. And of course there was the Matthean exceptive clause, about which no one seemed to doubt that it came from Jesus himself. Because of it any later attempt to assert the absolute impermissibility for Christians of divorce and then of remarriage after divorce had to be carefully qualified. The same qualification would be necessary *a fortiori* for whoever would also assert the impossibility in addition to the impermissibility of divorce and remarriage for Christians. We have seen how this caution showed itself in so many of the Fathers. They asserted the Gospel ideal of fidelity to and perseverance with one spouse but chose to say nothing about what was permitted one spouse who had dismissed another because of the latter's adultery. The student is never quite sure when coming upon this

166

apparent omission whether it really is a calculated ignoring of a thorny question, or whether the Fathers' earlier declaration of the Christian ideal of fidelity and perseverance includes and over-rides the exception contained in Matthew's clause.

The modern student must consider this too, that a religious tradition gains momentum when this religion's teachers all attend to what the others are saying, learn from one another, and come together to labor at a consensus in judgment of the question at hand. Catholics today who think and talk of "the Church" must understand how commonly the Christians of the fourth century thought and talked of "the churches." Not that they were unaware that as Christians they formed a single body of believers and worshipers. But the rudimentary communication systems of the time, the hazards of travel, and the social and political chaos of the fourth century worked to keep the Christian communities in relative isolation from one another. And it is not likely that the Fathers themselves, the men who were forming the Catholic traditions, heard or read one another from church to church. Basil and Chrysostom in the East were unaware of what Ambrose was saying in the West, and vice versa.

And one may say without grievance about so many of the statements we have from the Fathers that they are not carefully thought through. If we did not know this from the fact itself that the statements appear in homilies, it would be evident in the casual way in which they frequently quote the Scriptures. For at times they simply misquote them—not seriously, but at times reversing the order of clauses, or conflating discrete phrases into one, or substituting a preferred noun or verb for the original. This light touch is evident, finally, in their unwillingness or unconcern, or perhaps in some cases even their inability, to draw obvious conclusions from their own statements or from scriptural passages—to see what was implicit in what they quoted or said and then to wring the explicit conclusion out of it. The most transparent example of this that we have come upon thus far, I think, is the persistent disinclination to work out what is implicit in Paul's analogy in Ephesians 5—to try to say what follows for the marriage of two Christians if it is a mirroring on earth of the metaphoric marriage of Christ and the Church.

Given this historical-cultural context of the fourth-century patristic teaching, it is nevertheless true that the bishops of the period did meet at times in council, most often in regional councils but twice in ecumenical or general council. One may expect that from these meetings unequivocal consensus statements came forth. Did the bishops in any of these councils take up the question of divorce and remarriage and leave us their statements on it? They did, but not so much as determinations of a canonical or even doctrinal issue, as rulings on a moral issue. This moral issue was the one we have become familiar with by now in this study, that of adultery and how to discipline the Christian men and women who were guilty of it and came forward in the church to accuse themselves of it.

All the evidence shows that the Christians of these early centuries were much like ourselves. They knew and accepted the ideal and obligation of fidelity and unfailingness in their marriages. But while honoring them in word some failed them in conduct. We need not simply presume this as a consequence of the ordinary human weakness the early Christians shared with the rest of the race. The Acts of the Apostles tells us candidly of serious faults in the first communities: bitter disputes, personal alienations, schisms, heresy, deceit, egotism. The apostolic Fathers, Clement, Ignatius, and the author of the *Didache* wrote of bishops and priests beset by pride and avarice and ambition, of deacons who robbed funds meant for widows and orphans, of apostates, cowards and traitors under persecution, of class-conscious and elitist Christians. Almost all the early Christians were converted in adulthood, after having formed their moral habits in some solidity. It would be unrealistic to think that at their conversion they were transformed into saints in an instant. Despite the instruction, penance and scrutinies they underwent in preparation for baptism, some brought lifelong habits with them, and these included habitual ways of thinking and acting about marriage.

Apparently from the very beginning the Christian communities adopted a common means of dealing with serious sins within themselves. This means had two parts: first, exclusion from the life of the community (excommunication) in whole or in part, with the significant exclusion being from participation in the Eucharist; second, penance to be performed for a specified period as a sign of repentance leading to reacceptance in the life of the community. The earliest example of such excommunication is in 1 Corinthians 5:1-5 where Paul commands that the incestuous man be excommunicated so that he may repent. The frequency and the ordinariness with which excommunication and penance are mentioned in the early literature is an indirect witness to the commonness of serious delinquency in the Christians.

But the serious sin calling for penance about which we are concerned here was adultery and divorce followed by remarriage—the latter regarded by the early communities as a specific form of adultery. That neither of these kinds of conduct was rare in the communities is evident in the frequency with which they were condemned by councils and bishops and in the Christian writers' constant exhortation against them as forbidden by the divine law. It is at them that most of the patristic passages we have thus far examined aim their admonition and instruction.

We must make a careful distinction in the object of these bishops' and writers' concern, one that is also the concern of this study. They exhorted against and punished adultery in two senses. First there was the kind of infidelity, the cheating of a spouse that is a serious sin, but an infidelity at least intended to be intermittent and temporary, with no abandonment of the spouse in mind, nor any marriage with the partner in infidelity after the abandonment. Adultery in this sense was punishable under Roman law, little though the law controlled the conduct especially of husbands in this domain. And they were these husbands who, after Christianity became the state religion in 381, brought their sexual habits with them as they sought baptism in droves.

The other kind of conduct denominated adultery by the early Church was one that was in fact sanctioned by Roman law. This was remarriage after divorce—divorce whether by mutual consent or by unilateral dismissal. This too the converts had learned as a custom. And its hold on them, and their hold on it, was kept strong by the fact itself of its being sanctioned by law, even after this law had been revised by the Christian emperors.

To understand the Christian authorities' reaction to adultery in the second sense above we must recall a fact noted earlier about their sense of legal identity. During these early centuries, in fact throughout the first Christian millennium, these authorities claimed no duplicate jurisdiction over the marriages of Christian spouses—that is, they did not claim their own jurisdiction in addition to civil jurisdiction. They accepted the latter as the sole jurisdiction, expected the Christians to live under it and its laws, and—most significantly—held to no system of canonical validity or invalidity of marriages independent of that civil jurisdiction. They accepted marriages formed by Christians according to civil law. They required no particular *forma* of marriage as obligatory, no ceremony of marital consent, for at least the first seven centuries (and neither did they require a particular *forma* as necessary for validity of marriage for the first sixteen centuries). The Church's only obvious intervention in these marriages was to purge them of vestigial pagan elements (mainly the offering of sacrifice to the gods), and to introduce prayers into them, gradually adding priest or bishop as leader of the prayers and giver of the nuptial blessing.

When a Christian sought to end a marriage he or she went through the civil procedure for doing so, minimal as it was. (Divorce, whether by dismissal or by mutual consent, was not the effect of a judicial sentence, as it is in our day. What the law required was only that either divorce be completed in a way that was verifiable according to law.) Remarriage, whether deemed licit by the Church authorities or not, was effected by the same civil procedure. Where Church authorities deemed it illicit, along with the divorce that preceded it, their reaction was to oppose to this use of civil law by Christians the law of God governing marriage as revealed in Christ's teaching. They declared the Christian, because of the remarriage, a sinner by the sin of adultery. They excluded the adulterer from communion, which meant not only from the Eucharist but from all religious activity shared in the Christian community. Finally they imposed a penance and its observance as a condition for readmission to communion. About their demanding the dissolution of the second union and a return to the first, authoritative opinions were divided according to the causes and motives bringing about the dissolution and remarriage.

Whatever any particular Father may have personally thought about the matter, the Church had no ecclesiastical jurisprudence that held the first marriage to be still in existence despite the civil divorce and second marriage. This second marriage was considered adultery because it violated God's law and was an offense against the spouse, not because it was an ineffective attempt at marriage following an ineffective attempt at dissolution. For the concept of marriage as a natural bond impervious to dissolution did not yet exist in the Christian or in any other mind.

As we have seen, the Fathers opposed God's law to human law mainly at two points. They condemned the commonly accepted inequality of Roman-Hellenistic moral judgment which allowed a husband's intercourse with a single woman but condemned a wife's intercourse with a single man. They forbade such conduct to the husband as well, calling it the sin of adultery. And they opposed God's law to the civil law allowing divorce by dismissal and then remarriage. This combination made the Christian a sinner; the remarriage itself made him or her a sinner who was specifically an adulterer.

But what must surprise a modern Catholic is that when a Christian of these centuries violated marriage by divorcing and even remarrying, the Fathers before Jerome and Augustine at the beginning of the fifth century did not consider the adultery in this case a sin beyond forgiving, even when the sinner remained in the second marriage. This sin, like all others, could be brought under God's mercy and forgiveness. Nor did they insist that in every case, despite the civil divorce, the first marriage remained and the second was void. The conduct to which they obligated the civilly divorcing Christian spouse was not unanimously and unconditionally that he or she return to the first marriage. As explained above, this conduct was that the adulterer be barred from communion, seek forgiveness for the adultery, and do penance for it.

With this attitude and this discipline taught by so many in the Church it is readily understandable that the canons of the councils in these early centuries never declared divorce and remarriages of Christians void, or demanded that the new marriages be dissolved. The councils respected in substance the competence of civil law, but ordered that the divorcing and remarrying Christian undergo the penitential discipline already described.

As we look into the details of this surprising discipline we shall see again that the Christian reaction to divorce and remarriage remained indecisive and inconsistent at critical points. One of the most troubling inconsistencies was in some degree foreseeable. Christian husbands who dismissed their wives for the latters' adultery enjoyed the prerogative in virtually every Christian community of remarrying, and of doing so without being excluded even temporarily from communion or having to undergo penance. This privileged practice had emerged especially by the end of the second century. It was the fruit of a growing insistence, that grew close to unanimity, that the exceptive clause in the Matthean version of Jesus' instruction designated adultery or some other sexual conduct just as seriously delinquent. And of course in the clause, read literally, it is only the husband who may profit by the exception.

Evidence shows that indeed in some cases dismissal of adulterous wives was prescribed as obligatory for the husband, especially if he was a cleric. There were two sources for this prescription. First, the ambience of so many communities was Jewish, and these had the tradition that commanded the dismissal of an unfaithful wife. There was also the Roman law, the *Lex Iulia de Adulteris*, which obliged a husband to dismiss his wife within sixty days after first finding out about her infidelity. Christian authorities wanted to not seem less rigorous in their discipline ruling marital fidelity than, for example, the Stoic moralists. Finally the Christian sense, shared with rabbinic Judaism, that holiness should not be contaminated by association with sin made the dismissal seem a moral duty.

Hermas' voice in The Shepherd demanding that a husband who had dismissed his wife for her adultery remain unmarried because she might want to return to him was a lonely one. From this time, the mid-second century until Augustine, although Christian teachers exhorted husbands to take back their wives who repented after infidelity, none insisted that this was obligatory. Inevitably this left the opening for the question about such husbands' remarrying. The answer to it we know from the practice in the communities that appears to have been common and unrestricted from at least the end of the second century through the fourth in both the Eastern and Western Churches, and thence enshrined in permanent tradition in those of the Christian East. That is, a husband who had dismissed his wife for her adultery and had remarried was admitted to communion without having first to do penance. In other words, remarriage at least for the husband in such a case was deemed permissible by the Christian authorities. For the two centuries in question no canon of any council, no ecclesiastical writer, demanded excommunication of and penance by husbands who dismissed unfaithful wives and remarried, even though these penalties were exacted for other faults. The source of this permissiveness, since it graced only the cheated husband, must, as I have said already, surely have been the literal reading of the Matthean exceptive clause that excused only the husband from adultery if he remarried after dismissing his unfaithful spouse.

The one text during this epoch that clearly prescribes a kind of penance for the husband dismissing an unfaithful wife—in this case a penitentially-felt postponement—is number 23 of the canons attributed to Gregory the Illuminator, the apostle of Armenia (dating from perhaps 365).

> A husband is permitted to dismiss his wife by reason of her adultery, but he must abstain from the marriage bed a year after doing so.[1]

Reading the canon rigorously we find that the "penance" imposed is not for his remarrying, but for the husband's dismissing his unfaithful wife. And nothing in the canon forbids his remarrying after the year's delay.

A reasonably careful survey of the Christian writers on the subject of adultery, divorce and remarriage, beginning in the middle of the second century and continuing at least until Augustine, shows them applying the name "adulterer" to the following kinds of persons:

A husband who remarries after dismissing his wife without just cause.
A man who marries an abandoned or dismissed wife.
A wife who remarries after dismissing or abandoning her husband without just cause.
A woman who marries a man who has dismissed his wife without just cause.
A dismissed wife who remarries.
A woman who remarries after dismissing her adulterous husband.

The same writers never call the following persons adulterers:
A husband who remarries after dismissing an adulterous wife.
A husband who remarries after being abandoned by his wife.
A woman who marries a man in either of these two cases.

Disciplinary Canons from the Councils of Bishops

We have on record disciplinary canons concerning divorce and remarriage coming from four regional councils during the fourth century. The earliest of them was held in the autumn of 305 or 306 in Elvira, Spain. Nineteen bishops met there under the presidency of Hosius of Cordova. Among their canons they published three which were intended to regulate divorce and remarriage. All of them pertain to the conduct of women and to the discipline consequent on it.

> Canon 8: Likewise women who without cause abandon their husbands and remarry are not to receive communion even at the end.[2]

The canon envisions the conduct of a woman who either dismisses her husband or simply abandons him. It singles out one who does this without cause, thereby implying that dismissal or abandonment *with* cause may be an acknowledged possibility and may call for different treatment.

The consequence of a woman's abandoning her husband without cause is that she is to be denied communion (either the sacrament itself or participation in the entire life of the Christian community) for the rest of her life. The canon does not say that she is not married to her second partner. Neither does it legislate a punishment for the man who abandons or dismisses his wife without cause.

Canon 9 takes a step toward answering a question left over by Canon 8: May a woman remarry who has abandoned her husband *with* just cause?

> Canon 9: A Christian woman who abandons a Christian husband because of his adultery and wishes to remarry is forbidden to do so. If she remarries, she is not to receive communion until the husband she has abandoned has died, unless perhaps extreme illness demands it be given to her.[3]

The canon names the one cause for which a Christian woman could abandon her husband, even though he is himself Christian. This is his adultery. So it does not forbid her to do this. But what it does forbid her is to remarry as long as her husband is still alive, and it punishes her doing so by excluding her from communion (here understood as the receiving of the sacrament). But unlike the woman who abandons her husband without just cause and remarries, this woman even in her remarriage is not to be denied communion absolutely. In serious illness she may receive it; and leaving her second marriage is not named as a condition of her receiving communion in this extreme case. Is this because the bishops consider that despite the second marriage she is not living in adultery? But if they think she is not, why do they forbid her communion in good health as long as her first husband is still alive? They offer no elements for an answer to either question.

> Canon 10, Part 2: If a Christian woman marries a man who has dismissed his wife although the latter was innocent, and if the woman knew that the man was married and had left his wife without justification, she is not to receive communion even at the end of her life.[4]

The canon legislates—and strangely so—for the second wife of the Christian man who dismisses his first wife without just cause. It does not punish him but punishes the woman whom he presumes to take as his second wife. Not he, but she is to be denied communion for the rest of her life, and no exception to this is made in case of her serious illness.

But the canon's formulation prompts two questions and leaves them unanswered. Is there any penalty for a woman who marries a man who has dismissed his wife for just cause, because of her adultery? The bishops seem not to worry about this case despite the solid likelihood that they met it among their people. For if there were Christian women in southern Spain who accepted marriage with men who had earlier dismissed innocent wives, more probably there were women who accepted marriage with men who had dismissed guilty wives.

The second question is prompted by the canon's qualification, that a woman is to be punished only if she in fact knew the wife dismissed as her predecessor had been dismissed despite her innocence. What if she thought her guilty and that she had been dismissed because of that guilt? What if she thought her predecessor guilty at the time she, the second woman, accepted marriage with the husband, but found out later that she was innocent? Neither this nor any of the other canons address these questions.

To repeat an earlier reflection on this local legislation at the dawn of the fourth century, for some reason not explained it bears only upon the conduct of Christian wives, and because the legislation was thought necessary, the conduct it was meant to rule must have been sufficiently common. But husbands also who dismissed unfaithful wives must have remarried in the territories ruled by these bishops. This we may take for granted. Yet the bishops apparently saw no need to legislate for these husbands.

The Council of Arles

Eight or nine years later, in 314, a council of bishops met at Arles in France to instruct their people caught up in the Donatist controversy. In its Canon 10 (or 11) these bishops ruled as follows:

> As for young husbands who apprehend their wives in adultery—husbands who are young and who are forbidden to marry—we prescribe that in so far as possible they be advised not to take a second wife as long as their first wife, even though adulterous, is still alive.[5]

The canon has drawn copious scholarly commentary. The most necessary critical things to be said about it begin with the observation that the text as it has come down may be faulty in omitting the negative particle before "forbidden" in the second clause, and the conditional "if" from before "husbands" in the same clause, so that its correct reading would be ". . . if they are young husbands and are not forbidden to marry." The inconsistency of the clause, as we have it, with the counsel that follows argues that its condition is flawed and that it needs the suggested interpolations.

The canon is pastoral in its tone and in its intent. It states that young Christian husbands who have found their wives in adultery are (or perhaps are not) forbidden to remarry, presumably after dismissing these wives. The bishops' intent in the full canon was probably to synonymize the moral restrictions on the husbands here with the severe ones put on wives by the Spanish bishops at Elvira. The canon almost certainly attempts to restrict an earlier and more lenient discipline in the matter. But even as a restrictive effort its address to the young husbands is to *exhort* them to not remarry, and only insofar as exhortation is possible (or reasonable?). It says nothing about excommunication or penance as sanctions for their dismissing and remarrying. Finally, in view of the unusual hortatory character of a canon touching a serious disciplinary matter in a regional church, this was probably the indecisive product of disagreement and then of compromise among the bishops in the council.

But this permissiveness appears closed off in the version of the canon in the *Codex Lucensis,* which adds to those of Arles six more canons drawn from a later council held in the same city. The first of the additional six is listed as Canon 24 of the first council. It specifies a punishment for the husbands who remarry after dismissing their wives for adultery while these wives are still alive. They are to be excommunicated. Yet even this severe measure does not answer the question asking whether the second marriages are to be punished because they are attempted invalidly and are therefore adulterous, or simply because they are sinful though valid. (As I have already pointed out, it is in fact anachronistic to refer to marriages in the fourth century being considered invalid. This, along with its correlate "valid marriage," is a concept belonging to marriage law six or seven centuries in the future. Consequently the judgment on a second marriage in the third or fourth century that it is adultery is not *eo ipso* an oblique judgment of its invalidity. It is rather a judgment on the grave sin of the person who entered this union.)

Almost a century after Arles the bishops of western Africa met in the eleventh council of Carthage. The influence of St. Augustine, whose teaching on divorce and remarriage we shall inspect in detail in the following chapter, is evident in the council's Canon 8. This is a statement of the other side of the argument. It takes indirect note of the continuing conflict between the law of God proposed by the Church and the imperial law almost a century after Constantine's conversion. And it seeks to wipe out the distinction between the kinds of conduct approved or forbidden for husbands on one hand, and for wives on the other.

> We decree that according to the discipline of both the Gospel and the apostles, neither the husband dismissed by his wife nor the wife dismissed by her husband may remarry. But both must remain unmarried or be reconciled to their spouses. If they disobey this law, they must do penance. Application must be made for the promulgation of an imperial ban in the matter.[6]

But even in this canon the usual indecisiveness has its place. The punishment proportioned to the violation of divine and Church law on divorce and remarriage was by this time excommunication. But these bishops of Africa do not even hint at it here. And what seems more striking yet is that even with Augustine present they do not demand that those who have remarried leave their new spouses and return to their first marriages. They command only that these spouses do penance. The principal thrust of their decree seems to be an effort at equalizing the treatment of husbands and wives.

Canon 8 of the Council of Nicea

That this discipline of penance for Christian spouses who divorced and remarried was established commonly, if not universally, is evident in a roundabout way from the first of the Church's ecumenical councils, held at Nicea in 325. I say "roundabout" because what its Canon 8 dealt with formally and directly was not divorce but the reacceptance of the schismatic Novatian clergy into an active place in the Church and its ministry. This schism had an interesting history. Understanding Canon 8 calls for an outline of it.

Novatian was a member of the clergy of Rome, a priest, at the middle of the third century. He played an especially influential role in this clergy after Pope Fabian was killed in the persecution of Decius in 250, when, because of the difficulty of electing his successor during the persecution, these clergy governed the Roman community. During that year, before the election of Pope Cornelius in 251, the clergy of Rome sent a letter to Bishop Cyprian of Carthage warning him against a too-lenient treatment of those Christians (the *lapsi*) who had apostatized during the persecution. Cyprian attributed the letter to Novatian himself. It urged that apostates showing good will could be readmitted to communion after a long and severe penance, but that the ill could be readmitted immediately without penance. Within the year the Roman clergy wrote a second letter to Cyprian, again urging severity in readmitting the apostates. This letter too came almost certainly from Novatian.

Novatian's personal ambition complicated the next months and years seriously. He wanted the papacy dearly and worked to get it. In his bitter disappointment at Cornelius' election he gathered a group of sympathetic clergymen about himself, all of them moral rigorists, and had them elect him bishop of Rome. In reaction Pope Cornelius in 251 gathered at Rome a synod of sixty bishops, along with priests and laymen. The synod excommunicated Novatian and his followers. It also reaffirmed the availability to the Christian apostates of forgiveness and readmission after penance.

The errant point of discipline contributing to the reasons for Novatian's and his followers' excommunication was their insistence that the Church refuse readmission to communion to Christians who had committed certain sins "which lead to death." What Novatian wished to do about these sinners was to exhort them to repentance and penance, but leave them to God's mercy.

In his pastoral letter, On the Good of Chastity (*De Bono Pudicitiae*) IV, 5–7, Novatian himself named adultery as one of the grave sins that merit no forgiveness. And a Novatian catechism reported by Pacianus of Barcelona in his Letter III, *Against the Treatises of the Novatians,* written at the end of the fourth century, denied that the Church could forgive grave sins committed after baptism. If this and Jerome's report are accurate, they point to the doctrinal challenge within the rigorist discipline, the limitation put on the Church's power to absolve from sin.

Novatian was sixty-four years dead by the time the bishops convened at Nicea in 325. His rigorist sect, by now called the Cathari—"the pure ones"—had continued after him, but by the time of Nicea some of its adherents were themselves seeking readmission to the mother Church. The intent of the council's Canon 8 was to state the conditions under which the Novatian clerics, both bishops and priests, could be readmitted and restored to their ministry. The canon names what they must acknowledge about the Church's discipline of penance and forgiveness:

> As for those who call themselves "the Pure Ones," and who seek to enter the universal [catholic] and apostolic Church, it seems right to this great and holy council that once hands have been imposed on them [in forgiveness] they can remain in the clergy. But before all else they shall promise in writing to conform to the teaching of the universal and apostolic Church and to make it the rule of their conduct; and thus they shall communicate both with those who have married a second time and with those who failed under persecution, but for whom the time [of penance] has been completed and the moment of reconciliation has arrived. Thus they shall be held to follow in all things the teaching of the universal and apostolic Church.[7]

Obviously the canon presumes that the lasting, exact part of recusance by the Novatians was their refusal to share communion—Christian life generally and the Eucharist in particular—with those who had remarried after divorce, as also with those who had apostatized under persecution. In the Greek vocabulary of the canon the term translated "those who have married a second time" is *dígamoi,* literally "the twice-married." For the purpose of this inquiry it is crucial to know the referent of this term in the minds of the Nicean bishops. Before identifying this referent I note that the bishops themselves offer no explanation of their use of the term. Apparently they thought its referent to be common, well-known and universally accepted. Or to say the same thing in reverse, the referent they intended for it was already established when they included the term in their Canon 8.

The term *dígamoi* (and its close Latin equivalent *digami*) was current in the Christian writing of the late second and then the third century. It generally referred to persons living in a second marriage, whether men and women after being widowed, or those remarrying after dismissing a spouse without just cause, or men after dismissing an adulterous wife. The Christian writers made at least no verbal distinction in referring the term to these three categories of persons. Those Fathers whose attacks against *digamía* are known to us were opposed to second marriages without

distinction, as we have seen, and in their opposition they did not differenti-
ate the remarriage of widows from the remarriage of the divorced. In
either case the remarriage seemed to them a violation of Christian fidelity
to the indestructible marriage of Christ with his spouse the Church, of
which Christian marriage is meant to be a living image in the world. When
Hippolytus of Rome criticized Pope Callistus for accepting the *dígamoi*
into the ranks of the clergy, he referred to both remarried widowers and to
those who had remarried after divorce. A set of apostolic constitutions
coming from Syria at the time of Nicea prescribed in its Canon 17 that
dígamoi could not be clerics, and in its Canon 18 made clear that the term
referred equally to remarried widowers and to men married to divorced
women. At the same period a man marrying for the first time but taking a
widow as his wife was occasionally called a *dígamos*.

Some Catholic historians, as well as canonists, have contended that
Nicea's Canon 8 demanded this, that the Novatian clergy accept that the
Church can and must admit to communion after penance those *dígamoi*
who were such for having remarried in widowhood, and that those who
were such for having remarried after divorce were, on the contrary, to be
left in their excommunication unless and until they left their adulterous
second marriages.

This interpretation labors under a serious difficulty. It imposes a
restricted reference, and even a changed reference, on the term *dígamoi* as
it is used in the canon, one that the bishops of Nicea did not intend. They
meant it to designate those Christians whom the Novatians insisted could
not be readmitted to communion even after repentance. But the Novatians
never said that remarried widowers or widows were to be thus excluded,
neither of themselves nor in consort with the remarried after divorce. No
one before or after Nicea, not even the Novatians themselves, said that
Christians remarrying in their widowhood committed a sin unto death.
Not even Tertullian become a Montanist, who finally called any remarriage adultery, said that this adultery was such a sin. It is true that later
Novatians excluded remarried widows and widowers from communion.
But it is simply false to say that the Novatian teaching inspiring Nicea's
Canon 8 was that remarriage in widowhood is a grave sin that the Church
must not and even cannot forgive. So the penitents, whom the bishops of
Nicea named *dígamoi* and about whom they said that the Novatian clergy
must reaccept them to communion, can have been only the other Christian
married commonly called this name—those who had either remarried
after divorce or had married a divorced person.

That is the evidence which emerges from a philological examination
of the council's referent for the term *dígamoi* in its Canon 8. But the
question remains: Did all or at least most of the pastors of the Church in
fact absolve and readmit to communion Christians who were adulterers for
having dismissed their spouses and remarried—at least the husbands who
had done this, if not the wives?

The sin of adultery, even in the sense of infidelity within a lasting marriage, was at first rare in the Christian communities. Most Christians were baptized as adults, and the baptism was understood to forgive all sins committed earlier. Moreover a rigorous reform of life took place during the catechumenate after the first conversion and before baptism; a man or woman was not baptized unless successive scrutinies showed that the reform had been sincere and thorough.

Origen, in his Second Homily, names seven ways in which sins in the Christian community could be forgiven: by baptism, by public penance, by the suffering of martyrdom, by charitable (eleemosynary) giving, by forgiving the offenses of a brother or a sister (meaning those of a fellow Christian), by converting a brother or a sister from his or her sinful conduct, and by the abundance of charity covering a multitude of sins. There lingered some uncertainty whether grave sins, such as apostasy, murder and adultery, could be forgiven in these ways. Because of the uncertainty such sins were treated with discretionary diversity until a common penitential order emerged in the churches toward the end of the second century. These sins were submitted to the formal penance, the exomologesis, wherein the repentant apostate, murderer or adulterer asked the head of the community for forgiveness, and was assigned a period of severe penance. If this was sustained faithfully, at its end the sinner was absolved and readmitted to communion in the Eucharist. These features were common in the exomologesis: it was public, it was non-repeatable in the sense that a person could be forgiven and reconciled in this way after baptism only once in a lifetime, and it was understood that the forgiveness and reconciliation were effective through the bishop's power to bind and to loose.

What is clear from the records of the time is that until Tertullian began his migration toward Montanism at the end of the second and the beginning of the third century, no significant writer denied that any and all sins could be forgiven at least through formal penance. Hermas at the middle of the second century said expressly (in his Shepherd, Mandate IV), that the adulterous can be forgiven. In his essay On Modesty (2, 12–26), written after he had become a Montanist, Tertullian violently attacked a Catholic bishop's edict in favor of forgiving fornication and adultery—he insisted that the Church either cannot or must not forgive apostasy, murder and adultery. It seems evident from this that forgiving them was common enough in the churches to fire up his anger. In his *Philosophoumena* (IX, 12, 20–26) Hippolytus of Rome attacked Pope Callistus for forgiving grave sins generally. It is significant that for both Tertullian and Hippolytus the *dígamoi,* the twice-married, were among the adulterers. And The Teaching of the Twelve Apostles (II, 21–24), a document appearing in Syria between 210 and 220, expressly exhorted bishops to absolve murder, apostasy and adultery. Cyprian himself had begun his bishopric in Carthage as a rigorist. In his Three Books of Testimony Against the Jews (III, 28) he claimed that certain grave sins are unforgivable. But once the Novatian schism infiltrated his community, he took the position that all sins could be forgiven. In his Letter 55, written in 252, he named the adulterous as expressly among those capable of receiving forgiveness through penance.

It is clear enough, therefore, in the records of the years from the middle of the second century through the beginning of the fourth, that despite the bitter protest of such as Tertullian, Hippolytus and Novatian, adulterers were absolved and readmitted to communion along with repentant apostates and murderers. But there remains one more question about those repenting after adultery, and it is the crucial question. Were divorced and remarried Christians permitted to remain in the second marriage after penance, reconciliation and readmission to communion? Or were they obliged to relinquish the second relationship as an unexceptionable condition of reconciliation and readmission—and perhaps even to return to the original marriage?

By way of preparing for as exact an answer to the question as is possible, we must repeat some details of Roman cultural-legal history explained earlier. The modern Catholic is always tempted to take for granted that the repentant divorced and remarried Christians of the first three centuries and more were required to abandon the second relationship because it could not be a marriage and was therefore sinful, and that it could not be a marriage because the first marriage still existed despite the civil divorce and therefore impeded the second marriage. But this presumption is an anachronism. The Christians of these centuries had no concept of marriage as an ontological or even juridical bond underlying the surface existential relationship—a bond which survived even the irreversible destruction of the relationship itself. Marriage construed as such a bond was a legal invention awaiting the arrival of the canonists of the twelfth century. (Even when Augustine at the beginning of the fifth century insisted that a marriage survives its social destruction his acute mind could think of no better way to designate what survives than to call it *quiddam coniugale,* a certain marital something. And when he pinpointed exactly what keeps two Christians' marriage indestructible, he looked not to the marital bond itself but to the *sacramentum* coming to the marriage from the spouses' baptisms.) The early Christians, most of them born and bred in Roman-Hellenistic society, shared this society's cultural and legal understanding of marriage's nature—a man's and a woman's sharing in all of life, a sharing created by the *affectio maritalis* (the will to be married) and caused ongoingly by this *affectio,* so that when this is withdrawn, the marriage dissolves and disappears. Only gradually and across the span of centuries did the Church move toward the notion of marriage as the ontological-juridical bond that is formed and realized contractually.

From their Scriptures the Christians knew that God forbids destroying a marriage by divorce (although, as we have seen at length, they remained unsure whether this bound even the husband whose wife is an adulteress), and that to destroy the marriage is gravely sinful, at least if done without just cause. But they took for granted that what was forbidden could be done, that they *could* annihilate their marriages. Therefore what they understood to be sinful in the complex folds of such an event was the destroying of the first marriage and the taking of the second spouse. Whether the union with the new spouse was sinful depended on whether their disobedience to God's will still survived or whether they had sought forgiveness, done penance and been absolved from the past act of destroying their marriage and going to another man or woman. For the bishops to have insisted that a condition for forgiveness and readmission to communion of the divorced and remarried was that they abandon the second relationship because the surviving first marriage impeded it, they would have had to innovate and propagate a concept of marriage unsuspected by their people. There is no evidence that the bishops did this.

But did the bishops demand the abandoning of the second relationship as a punishment for the earlier sin, or because, for some reason internal to the second relationship itself, that relationship was sinful? Again there is no evidence that they demanded this once the sinful Christian had repented and done penance. Such concrete instances as we know of the treatment of remarriage provide clearer outlines of this discipline. These were instances in which bishops demanded that certain sexual relationships, some of them purportedly second marriages, be given up. Bishop Cyprian in his Epistle 4 commanded that those of his deacons living with consecrated virgins end such cohabitation. In its Canon 2 the Council of Neocaesarea in about 318 demanded that a widow married to her brother-in-law, apparently in consideration of the Jewish law of the levirate, separate from him as a condition of reconciliation. The best-known as well as the earliest instance of enforced separation is found, of course, in Paul's command to the man in the Corinthian community to end his incestuous cohabitation with his father's widow (of a second marriage). But probably to our modern surprise the opinion was widespread in the early Church that in Paul's Second Letter to the Corinthians (2:7–8) he both forgave the incestuous man after his excommunication and penance and permitted him to remain with the woman.

> . . . The punishment already imposed on the man in question
> is enough; and the best thing now is to give him your forgiveness
> and encouragement or he may break down from so much misery.
> So I am asking you to give some definite proof of your love for
> him. What I really wrote for, after all, was to test you and see if
> you are completely obedient.

About any obligation to take back the divorced wife, these same early bishops (for whom the Old Testament was as surely the revealed word of God as were the Gospels) accepted as normative Deuteronomy's instruction about wives dismissed for adultery. They were not to be taken back. This is evident in Origen's Commentary on Matthew (XIV:2), in Basil's Canon 9 (for Amphylochius), in Jerome's Letter to Amanda, and in Cyril

of Alexandria's essay On Adoration and Worship in Spirit and in Truth
(VIII). Only Augustine contradicted this discipline, citing, in his On
Adulterous Marriages (II, 6–10) the example of David's taking back the
errant Michol.

In the domain of civil law a constitution of the emperors Diocletian
and Maximian coming from the end of the third century forbade anyone's
being forced either to enter a marriage or to take back in reconciliation the
spouse from an earlier and dissolved marriage. This constitution remained
in force and unchanged throughout the history of the empire, and was
included by the Christian Justinian in his revision of the law in 536 (Code:
Book 5, Chapter 4, 14). The Christian emperors did take means to control
the citizens' divorcing and dismissing of spouses, but these means consisted of the threat of penalties such as the loss of dowry and of dotal gifts, deportation into exile, and forced claustration.

Regional Councils in the Christian East

This treatment of the divorced and remarried, whose acceptance the
bishops of Nicea made obligatory for the Novatian clergy seeking reacceptance and restoration to their ministry, continued as a substantial element
of the life of the Eastern Church. Other regional councils both before and
especially after Nicea, and the statements of later Eastern bishops, attest to
this. The Council of Neocaesarea in Cappadocia, held between 314 and
325, declared in its Canon 3:

> As for those who have married more than once, the period
> established [for their penance] is known, although their conduct
> and their fidelity may shorten this time.

And in its Canon 7:

> Priests are not to take part in the nuptial banquets of those
> marrying for the second time. For if the man who has remarried
> later asks to do penance, what will a priest say who has already
> consented to his marriage by taking part in the wedding feast?

Canon 20 of the Council of Ancyra, that met probably in 314, declared:

> If a man's wife was an adulteress, or if a man has committed
> adultery, he must spend seven years in his return to that which is
> perfect, proceeding through the stages that lead thereto.

That the adultery referred to here is not an episode of infidelity, but is
rather remarriage after divorce, is evident in that the Eastern churches (as
indicated in Basil's Canon 34) demanded of wives who committed adultery
secretly that they not do the established public penance. They were instead

to do a private and even secret penance, continuing life in the Christian community so that their husbands might not discover their infidelity. But in any case it was unheard of that a husband whose wife had committed either kind of adultery should be obliged to do penance. The first clause of the canon "If a man's wife was an adulteress . . ." can refer only to a man who has married a woman dismissed from her first marriage because of her adultery. Canon 87 of the Synod of Trullo offers a kind of authentic interpretation of Ancyra; it set a penance of seven years for men who had dismissed their wives and remarried, as also for those who had married a dismissed or abandoned wife.

The Council of Laodicea meeting between 343 and 380 decreed in its Canon 1:

> In conformity with ecclesiastical law we have decreed that communion must be given with forgiveness to those who entered legally and freely into a second marriage [without having contracted a clandestine marriage], but after an established period and once they have given themselves to prayer and fasting.

I have mentioned just above and earlier in this chapter the canons that have come from Basil, as bishop-metropolitan of Caesarea, to Bishop Amphylochius of Iconium, as replies to the latter's questions about disciplinary matters that had been brought to him. In them Basil appoints different penances to be performed by married Christians who have sinned in different ways. These canons, almost unknown during the century of their origin, came gradually to serve as the principal source of the canon law of the Eastern Church. That they have influenced this Church's discipline for divorce and remarriage is obvious. Canon 4 prescribes two years of public penance for *dígamoi* as a condition for their readmission to communion. In the canon itself it is not clear which kinds of persons are designated as *dígamoi*. They may be widowers who have remarried, except that Canon 41 seems to exclude remarried widowers from penance altogether. They may be men who have divorced and remarried. Canon 24 hints at this, and also at the possibility that they are remarried widowers, though in a confused way by prescribing that the penance for *dígamoi* is that which is sufficient for widowers. But Canon 77 specifies expressly that men who have divorced and remarried are to do seven years of penance before being readmitted to communion. And in this canon it is clear that persons quite distinct from remarried widows are meant.

Summary and Conclusions to This Point

Before going on to examine the minds of Jerome and Augustine on divorce and remarriage, let us turn back to the brief repertory of questions posed in Chapter Six as guides in the search through the Fathers of the first three and a half centuries. It is clear by now that what we have found to provide an answer to these questions is anything but satisfactory. But assembling such elements of the answers as we have is self-evidently helpful.

Question 1: May spouses dismiss one another—according to either the model of rabbinic law or to that of Roman law, or perhaps according to both?
Answer: For one cause only could one spouse dismiss the other, for the sin of adultery. This right was conceded to the husband by all the Fathers, and by some it was even thought obligatory for him. To the wife it was conceded by most. The warrant for the dismissal was universally the Matthean exceptive clause. The legal guide and procedure was the dismissal sanctioned by Roman law.

Question 2: May spouses end their marriage by the dissolution *communi consensu*—by common consent?
Answer: No, not in the sense understood in Roman law. If understood as the Christian spouse's acceding to the departure of a pagan spouse that dissolved the marriage, yes (following Paul in 1 Corinthians 7:15), in the few instances in which a Father reviewed such a case.

Question 3: If they may dismiss one another for any reason or reasons, do they commit adultery if they subsequently attempt remarriage? In the event of such permitted dismissal does the innocent party, the one who justifiably dismissed, commit adultery if he or she subsequently attempts remarriage? Does the guilty party commit adultery if he or she makes the same attempt?
Answers to the first and second questions here: Most of the Fathers skirted this question. A few acknowledged cautiously that a husband or wife dismissing a spouse could remarry without committing adultery, but only if the dismissal were justified by the adultery of the other spouse.
Answer to the third question: Yes.

Question 4: If one or the other party, the guilty or the innocent, commits adultery by subsequently attempting remarriage, *why* does this entail adultery?
Answer: The guilty party commits adultery because there is no word in either the Gospels or the epistles of the New Testament granting to an adulterous spouse the right to dismiss the other. The right to remarry, where acknowledged, seems to have been linked necessarily with the right to dismiss.

Question 5: If this or that Father thought one or more kinds of marriage to be indissoluble—to be invulnerable to dissolution by any cause short of death—what did he think the cause of this indissolubility?

Answer: Here a cautious qualification is needed. Indissoluble marriage as the non-voidable contract in the 1917 Code of Canon Law, marriage the indestructible juridical category, had not been conceived of at the end of the fourth century.

Some of the Fathers thought a marriage's invulnerability to dissolution comes from outside it, others from within it as well. Where from outside it, the cause of indissolubility is God's will, his authority overriding and voiding any human authority's pretense at dissolving. Thus Jesus' words, "Therefore what God has joined man must not separate."

One interpretation of this clause leaves unanswered the question asking if any human authority is otherwise capable of dissolving a marriage. It says only that God's will has blocked the exercise of this authority if it does in fact exist. Another interpretation has it that because it is God's authority that joins a man and woman in marriage, the latter simply transcends the dissolving power of human authority.

Where a marriage's indissolubility was thought to come from within it—of course designed by God as thus interiorly invulnerable—a variety of reasons were suggested for this. A husband and wife are two in one flesh, legally and morally a single person before the law. Thus they can no more be divided into two persons than a human body into two bodies.

A specification of this drawn from Paul's metaphor in Ephesians 5 said that husband and wife are related as head and body, and on the strength of the metaphor the head and the body cannot be separated and live.

Again, the marital relationship was said to be a *sacramentum* in one or both of two senses. Either it is a commitment, a promise that is of its nature non-voidable, so that the makers of the promise not only must not renege on it, but cannot. Or the marriage may be (also) a *sacramentum* in the sense of a *mystérion,* an earthly image of a transcendent and sacred reality. This reality was thought to be the "marriage" of Christ and the Church. And the indestructibility of the earthly marriage was said to derive from its being such a mystery—although none of the Christian literature of these centuries that I have read says expressly that a marriage is in fact indissoluble because it is an image of the indestructible Christ-Church relationship.

Closing the chapter we recall what Ambrose said in qualifying Christ's command, "Therefore what God has joined man must not separate." In his mind only the marriage of two Christians is joined by God in the way that Christ intended here. With this the way is open to the theological reasoning that only a marriage that is the earthly image of Christ's metaphoric marriage with his Church is joined by God in the way that Christ intended, and therefore only it is invulnerable to any human effort to dissolve it. And since in theology as elsewhere most answers themselves breed the next generation of questions, the way will soon be open to asking what makes the marriage of two Christians such an image.

NOTES

1. Cereti, *op. cit.,* p. 192.

2. "Item feminae, quae nulla praecedente causa reliquerint viros suos et alteris se copulaverint, nec in finem accipiunt communionem."

3. "Item femina fidelis, quae adulterum maritum reliquerit fidelem et alterum ducit, prohibeatur ne ducat; si duxerit non prius accipiat communionem nisi (is) quem reliquerit de saeculo exierit, nisi forsitan necessitas infirmitatis dare compulerit."

4. "Quod si fuerit fidelis quae ducitur ab eo qui uxorem inculpatam reliquerit, et cum scierit illum habere uxorem quam sine causa reliquit, placuit nec in finem dandam esse communionem."

An alternative reading of the last clause here has come down to us: ". . . at the end she is to be allowed communion" (". . . in fine huiusmodi dari communionem"). But scholars consider this the less likely of the two readings.

5. "De his qui coniuges suas in adulteris deprehenderunt, et idem sunt adulescentes fideles et prohibentur nubere, placuit ut, quantum possit, consilium eis detur ne alias uxores, viventibus etiam uxoribus suis licet adulteris, accipiant."

6. Cereti, *op. cit.,* p. 190.

7. Denzinger-Schönmetzer, *Enchiridion Symbolorum* . . ., 32nd edition, 1963, no. 127, p. 53.

9. JEROME AND AUGUSTINE

If at this point we may for a moment glance far into the future, we notice that by the end of the sixteenth century two doctrines of divorce and remarriage, and the two disciplines correlated to them, had grown to completion in the Catholic churches, one in the Orthodox East, the other in the Roman West. In the latter a marriage could be dissolved only by the highest ecclesiastical authority, only if it were not a Christian sacrament, or, if a sacrament, only if it were unconsummated. A marriage that is a Christian sacrament, and consummated as a sacrament, cannot be dissolved by any authority on earth. Consequently any attempt of persons to have civil authority dissolve any marriage is null. Consequently, also, any attempt at marriage following a so-called civil divorce is null, and any intercourse by the partners to this second union is adultery because at least one of them is already married.

In the Orthodox Catholic churches generally even a sacramental marriage of two Christians, consummated or not, can dissolve in its own failure. And the churches may take official action to acknowledge this dissolution. Both the persons who were once spouses in the now dissolved marriage may remarry as members of the church; but the second marriage, even if with a Christian, is not considered a sacrament.

In the preceding chapter we reviewed the teachings of most of the major Fathers that helped centuries earlier to produce these two positions. That of the Orthodox churches is ascribable principally to Basil of Caesarea and John Chrysostom (with considerable help from the imperial legislation of Theodosius II and Justinian). But we have not yet seen a patristic teaching in the West equivalently as far-reaching in its effect.

This chapter will examine the equivalent teaching in the West. It came from two men who knew one another as intellectual colleague-opponents and exchanged a long and politely rancorous correspondence over the interpretation of the Scriptures. These were Jerome and Augustine. They gave to the Western Church both the scriptural interpretation and the nascent theology to provide the doctrine fitted to the conservatism and even severity of the Gothic Catholic communities of Spain and North Africa in which the present Western discipline seems to have begun.

187

Jerome is probably more responsible for the scriptural interpretation, Augustine certainly for the theology. But Ambrose too must be acknowledged as one of the architects of the Western doctrine, since it was to him that Augustine listened during those few crucial years in Milan. It is hardly to be doubted that Augustine noticed the theme of the marital *sacramentum* in the archbishop's discourses and espied in it the heart of the Christian accounting for how the marriages of the baptized are invulnerable to the human will to dissolve.

Jerome

In Book 1 of his Commentary on Matthew Jerome takes up Jesus' instructions on divorce as these appear in sequence in this Gospel.[1] He begins therefore with 5:31–32 and comments briefly on these verses, which he quotes in this truncated form: "It was also said, 'Whoever dismisses his wife must give her a writ of dismissal.' But I say to you, whoever dismisses his wife, etc."

What Jerome says here includes an assumption about the history of Christ's instruction, which also accounts for the brevity of his commentary on these two verses. His assumption is that in the later passage (19:1–12) Christ will explain why Moses permitted Jewish husbands to give the writ of dismissal to their wives. Christ's explanation, according to Jerome, will be that Moses allowed this because of the Jewish husbands' hardheartedness. That is, Moses did not approve of dismissal, but wished to forestall the murder of the wives (*non discidium concedens sed auferens homicidium*). And Jerome concludes with what is apparently his own judgment on Moses' reason: It was much better to permit the sad breakup of the marriage (*lugubrem discordiam*) than to have blood shed because of hatred.[2]

Jerome does not provide the evidence for his thesis that Moses' motivation in permitting the dismissal of wives was to make way for the lesser of two evils—divorce in preference to murder (nor evidence that Jewish husbands so frequently murdered their wives that Moses deemed this permissive legislation necessary). Neither does he explain the sources for his interpretation of Christ's mind, that the latter himself thought Moses legislated the writ of dismissal in order to forestall this Jewish uxoricide.

In Book 3 of the commentary Jerome subjects Matthew 19:1–12 to a considerably more detailed examination.[3] He begins by setting the scene and explaining the motivation of the scribes and Pharisees in drawing Jesus into the dispute about Moses' legislation permitting the writ of dismissal. They sought to trap Christ in a dilemma. If he took one side, agreeing that a man may dismiss his wife for just any reason, and marry another (the Hillelite position, although Jerome does not identify it as such), Jesus would seem to approve of unchastity (an anachronism of interpretation on Jerome's part, since the Jews of Christ's time did not think divorce and remarriage even for slight reasons to involve unchastity). But if Christ denied that a man might dismiss his wife for just any reason, he would seem to teach sacrilegiously against Moses, and through Moses against God (a misinterpretation on Jerome's part, since if Christ had denied this Jewish divorce on many and frivolous grounds he would not have challenged the Mosaic law but only have sided with the school of Shammai against the Hillelites in the interpretation of the law). He explains that Christ so formulated his answer to the trapping question as to skirt the Mosaic enactment in Deuteronomy and take the issue back to natural law as well as to God's first command to husbands and wives. And he adds that in this command is found God's authentic will, not just his concession to the needs of sinful men, as in Moses' legislation in Deuteronomy.[4]

Jerome continues, explaining what Jesus meant by reminding the Pharisees that (as reported in Genesis) God has created man male and female. Jerome finds the key to Jesus' meaning in the fact that the nouns are in the singular number—man (*masculum*) and woman (*feminam*), not men (*masculos*) and women (*feminas*). He says that Christ understood this choice of singular number to mean that a second marriage, after divorce, is forbidden, that the first man and woman—and all men and women—are to confine themselves to one marriage only. Jerome does not extend this exegesis, however, to the question of remarriage in widowhood.[5]

When Jerome explains Christ's logion, "What God has joined no man must separate," he glances sideways at what Paul had written in 1 Corinthians 7:29 about a different form of separation in marriage. He begins by explaining that God did his joining when he made the first man and woman to be "one flesh." No man can dissolve this union; only God can—perhaps (*forsitan*). Then he begins the first of two equivocations on the word "separate." A husband separates what God has joined when, because of his desire for another woman, he dismisses his wife. (Jerome does not ask whether he separates what God has joined if he dismisses her for some other motive.) The second equivocation has it that it is God who separates—and separates what he himself has joined—when husbands and wives live together as though they were not such, and do this by mutual consent for the sake of God's service because "the time is short." Thus the implied inclusion of 1 Corinthians 7:29: "Brothers, this is what I mean: our time is growing short. Those who have wives should live as though they had none."[6]

In explaining Moses' permissive legislation allowing Jewish husbands to dismiss their wives Jerome repeats what he had said in his exegesis of Matthew 5:31–32, but adds one consideration: Moses did this to avoid the greater evil, namely Jewish husbands' murder of their wives, or their forcing them into prostitution because of their lust for wealthier, younger or prettier women. He adds a point in clarification: Christ did not say that

God permitted the lesser of these two evils, but Moses did. In any case, God could not contradict himself by subsequently permitting what he had earlier forbidden.[7]

The part of this commentary that was to be remembered and used by Christian scholars and teachers for centuries appears in Jerome's exegesis of verse 9: "I say to you that whoever dismisses his wife, except for her *pornéia,* and marries another commits adultery." The part I refer to contains Jerome's interpretation of Matthew's exceptive clause, his interpretation of the *pornéia* that Jesus allowed as the one cause that justified a man's dismissing his wife. It contains also Jerome's interpretation of the effect of this dismissal, the kind of relationship he thought consequent on the dismissal.

He begins by asserting something that may be a jab at the Roman divorce law still in effect in his time that permitted dissolution by the spouses' withdrawal of their *affectus maritalis.* He says that it is only her *fornicatio* (his translation of the Greek *pornéia*) that ends a wife's *affectus.* What is more, because she has by her *fornicatio* divided the "one flesh" into two, and by it has also separated herself from her husband, the husband is not to keep her lest he too come under condemnation. It is clear by now that in Jerome's own vocabulary *fornicatio* as the translation of *pornéia* designates nothing other than the wife's adultery. For he concludes this first part of his exegesis by adding, "Therefore wherever there is a *fornicatio* or even the suspicion of it, the wife may be readily dismissed." And he quotes here in support of his judgment Proverbs 18:22, "He who keeps an adulterous wife is irreligious and stupid."[8]

Then Jerome explains what he thinks the consequences of this justified dismissal for the possibility of the husband's marrying again later.

> But it could happen that a husband may falsely accuse his innocent wife, and because he desires a second marriage, impute crime to her. Therefore he is commanded to dismiss his first wife [where she has committed adultery] in such a way that as long as she lives he may not take a second.

His meaning is unclear. Does he intend to say that the kind of dismissal Christ allows here only *forbids* the husband's remarrying, and forbids it because wives are sometimes accused of adultery falsely? Does he thus think Christ forbade the husband's remarrying as a way of protecting falsely accused wives? Or does he think that Christ meant the dismissal for the wife's adultery to be not a true dissolution unless the accusation against her of adultery be true? He further muddies the meaning by adding this excursus:

> It is as if he [Christ?] were to say, "If it is not because of lust but because of crime that you dismiss your wife, why, after going

through the misery of that first marriage, do you risk the dangers of a second?"

Jerome continues with some fairly private logic that may also contain an anachronism on Jewish law. He says that because according to this law a wife could also give the writ of dismissal to her husband (which may have been true under rabbinic revision of the law by the time Jerome wrote this commentary in 398, but certainly was not in Jesus' time), Christ's words are to be taken as forbidding the wife too to remarry.[9]

What of the last clause of this facet of Christ's instruction, "And whoever marries a woman who has been dismissed, he commits adultery"? Does Jerome say, as centuries of Catholic interpreters have understood Christ's words, that the reason a man marrying a dismissed wife commits adultery is that she is still married to the husband who dismissed her? His curt comment is here no clearer than one or two earlier ones have been: "And because a prostitute and a wife who have once committed adultery fear no opprobrium, the second man is told that if he marries such a woman he commits the crime of adultery."[10]

But if Jerome was uncertain about Christ's mind concerning the possibility itself of a spouse's remarrying after dissolution, he was most clear and decisive in his own judgment on the matter. In 394, four years before writing his commentary on Matthew, he had written a letter to his priest friend, Amandus, in which he answered three questions that the latter had sent to him.[11] The last of these asked the following question: "Can a woman participate in the life of the Church without sin if she has left a husband who had committed adultery and sodomy, and if she has been forced into a second union?"

Jerome answers by citing chapter 7:3 of Paul's Letter to the Romans: "So if she, a married woman, gives herself to another man while her husband is still alive, she is legally an adulteress." He insists that with this Paul removes all excuses, that he defines most clearly that as long as a woman's husband still lives, if she marries another, she commits adultery. He adds that this is true even if she has left her first husband because of his crimes. He points out that Paul said this not on his own authority but on that of Christ expressed in Matthew 5:32. He fixes his reply finally on the point of Amandus' question, for the latter had asked about a wife virtually abandoned by her husband because of his crimes. Even so, Jerome reminds him, Christ said that one who marries a dismissed wife commits adultery.[12] And as a kind of capstone to his reply he observes that if the woman has in the meantime come to love the consort to her second union and yet wants to take communion, she should recall what Paul said in 1 Corinthians 10:21: "You cannot drink the cup of the Lord and the cup of demons. You cannot take your share at the table of the Lord and at the table of demons."

The upshot of all this must have been that Christians of later generations, reading Jerome's commentary on Matthew in light of his letter to Amandus, would readily conclude that he understood that the dismissal of an adulterous spouse permitted by Christ does not dissolve the marriage but simply separates the two while leaving them married until the death of one of them.

Jerome's Letter 77 to Oceanus on the Death of Fabiola

In the summer of 401 Jerome wrote a letter to his friend Oceanus in order to inform him accurately about the life and marital conduct of Fabiola, a Christian woman of the Roman aristocracy who had recently died.[13] The letter is in effect a funeral eulogy, a defense of Fabiola against certain unnamed detractors in the Christian community. Why Jerome thought she needed defending is evident in her dismissing her husband and remarrying. Why he thought she deserved defending appears in his account of her husband's vicious character, of her weakness in the face of her own passion, and of her poor instruction in the Gospel. The points Jerome makes in his letter are the following.

So far as Roman law itself is concerned, the husband's vicious life had given Fabiola full cause to end her marriage to him by dismissing him.

A Christian justification for her dismissing him he finds in a logical extension of Christ's teaching as presented in Matthew 19. If it is permitted a husband to dismiss his wife for her adultery (Jerome takes for granted that the passage's *pornéia* designates adultery), by equal justice a wife must be permitted to dismiss her husband for his adultery. Indeed Jerome finds scriptural evidence for the wife's *obligation* to separate herself from a promiscuous and adulterous husband. By the familiar logic of inversion and extension he applies to the wife's credit the aphorism of 1 Corinthians 6:16: "He who is joined to a prostitute becomes one body with her." And he makes the point that the law of Christ makes equal demands on husband and wife. Unlike Roman law it does not excuse a husband's going to prostitutes or debauching the female slaves of his household, while condemning him only for rape or for taking another man's wife.

As to the Christian accusation against her that after justifiably dismissing her husband Fabiola did not remain unmarried, Jerome does not deny that she did wrong in remarrying. But one must understand her reason for doing so. She was very young and vulnerable; she was a powerfully sensuous woman. Paul had said, "It is better to marry than to burn." Fabiola thought it better to enter even a dubious marriage than to try to live hypocritically a life of pseudo-chastity. Again Paul had said (in 1 Timothy 5:14–15) that he prefers for young widows that they marry and bear children so as to give the enemies of the Christian communities no cause to speak ill of them.

As for her decision to remarry, she simply did not understand the full meaning of the Gospel teaching which forbids a wife to remarry as long as her husband still lives. Because of her prudent concern for herself Fabiola had failed to escape one wound of the devil in her effort to escape several others. Jerome ends by recounting the full public penance that Fabiola did after the death of her second husband, and, after her readmission to communion, her life consecrated to the service of the sick and the poor.

For what sin does Jerome think Fabiola did penance? Certainly not for the sin of dismissing her husband. This he thought both permitted to her by the instruction of Christ in Matthew 19 and even commanded by Paul in 1 Corinthians 6. Then it was clearly for the sin of disobedience to the Lord's command, relayed by Paul (and extended logically by Jerome himself), that a wife who is dismissed or who leaves her husband is not to remarry. But the possibility of keenest interest to us is this: Does Jerome think that Fabiola did penance for having committed adultery by attempting a second marriage while her husband still lived, in addition to simply disobeying the command of the Lord via Paul? He does not say that this was the motive of her penance, even though he otherwise uses the occasion of this explanation to Oceanus to point out that, unlike the Romans, the Christians have a comprehension and a just estimate of what is adultery. They insist that a husband commits it even if he goes to a prostitute or if he copulates with one of his female slaves. Oceanus had written because of his perplexity about the honorable burial given a Christian woman who had sinned so openly and flagrantly. Since Jerome replied in order to explain and to excuse her conduct, this was the occasion for him to say exactly what needed excusing. On the evidence it appears that this was her disobedience to the command of the Lord—which Jerome admits she did not understand clearly. How significant is it that Jerome does not explain wherein her misunderstanding lay?

Jerome's *Adversus Jovinianum*

The last of Jerome's reflections on divorce and remarriage that we shall review is a passage in his essay Against Jovinian.[14] In the essay he takes Jovinian severely to task for the latter's demeaning of virginity. An obvious contribution to Jerome's scolding must be the words of Scripture that praise and prefer virginity; and the best-known of these words is in 1 Corinthians 7.

> 8. To those not married and to widows I have this to say: It would be well if they remain as they are. . . . 29. From now on those with wives should live as if they had none. . . . 32. I should like you to be free from all worries. The unmarried man is busy with the Lord's affairs, concerned with pleasing the Lord; 33. but the married man is busy with the world's demands and occupied with pleasing his wife. . . . 34. The virgin—indeed every unmarried woman—is concerned with the things of the Lord, in pursuit of holiness in body and in spirit. The married woman, on the other hand, has the cares of this world to absorb her.

Jerome goes through this chapter of the epistle, commenting on it verse by verse. But since his concern is elsewhere than on divorce and remarriage, he alludes only in passing to the verses in which Paul instructs on dismissal and departure from marriage. About verse 4—"A wife has not authority over her own body, but her husband has it, etc."—he says this:

> The entire question concerns those who are united in marriage, whether they are permitted to dismiss the spouse, that which the Lord forbids in the Gospel. . . . But he who has once taken a spouse may not abstain from her except by mutual agreement; nor may he give the writ of dismissal to a wife who has not sinned. And he must render to his spouse that which is her due.[15]

About verses 10 and 11, Paul's instruction relayed from the Lord, that Christian spouses must neither depart from their marriage nor be dismissed from it, Jerome observes only: "This passage does not touch the private controversy. In fact what it teaches, according to the mind of the Lord, is that a wife is not to be dismissed except for her *fornicatio;* and if she is dismissed, she must either be reconciled to her husband, or, if not, she cannot remarry as long as her husband is still alive."

Consistent with his habit of forced exegesis, Jerome inserts into this Pauline tradition of Christ's instruction the exception—dismissal only because of the wife's *pornéia*—found only in the Matthean version of it. He also rounds off Paul's thought in a way that the Apostle himself had not: ". . . she cannot remarry *as long as her husband is still alive*" (the final phrase here is not Paul's but Jerome's). He does not essay any explanation for Paul's commanding the wife to not remarry despite her being once again unmarried (*ágamos* according to Paul) as a consequence of her being dismissed.

Augustine

The essays in which Augustine worked out his thinking on divorce and remarriage were produced across a span of a quarter-century, from 394 until 419. To verify whether his thinking underwent development during this time it will help to record the calendar of his production. It is obvious that some of these essays were exclusively about marriage matters, while others touched marriage only as one of their lesser parts. This is true, for example, of the first on the calendar.

394:   The Sermon on the Mount (*De sermone Domini in monte*)
394:   Against Adimantus (*Contra Adimantum*)
396:   On 83 Diverse Questions (*De diversis quaestionibus 83*)
401:   On the Good of Marriage (*De bono coniugali*)

404–414: On the Literal Interpretation of Genesis (*De Genesi ad litteram*)
413: On Faith and Works (*De fide et operibus*)
418: On Marriage and Concupiscence (*De nuptiis et concupiscentia*)
419: On Adulterous Marriage (*De adulterinis coniugiis*)

De Sermone Domini in Monte[16]

Augustine begins his commentary on Christ's key words, in Matthew 5:31–32—"It was also said, 'Whoever dismisses his wife must give her a writ of dismissal.' But I say to you, whoever dismisses his wife, except in the case of her *pornéia,* makes her to commit adultery; and whoever marries a woman who has been dismissed, he commits adultery"—by offering a reason for Moses' commanding that a husband dismissing his wife give her this writ. This is to in turn give him pause. Knowing that with the writ she will be free to remarry, he may be slow in dismissing her.[17]

Augustine does not question the authenticity of the exceptive clause. He acknowledges Christ's allowing the wife's *pornéia* (which he translates *fornicatio*) as the one cause warranting her dismissal. But he immediately uses 1 Corinthians 7:10–11 as a principle of interpretation of this Synoptic *logion.* As Paul there relayed Christ's command that if a wife leaves her husband, she is either to remain unmarried or is to be reconciled to him, so here, if a husband dismisses his wife legitimately, he is either to be reconciled to her or to live a life of celibacy. He is not to take another wife. At this point Augustine does not make clear why this husband must not remarry, whether because he is still married to his first wife despite having dismissed her, or simply because Christ (with the help of Paul) has forbidden him to do so.

But what is the nature of the *fornicatio* that Christ allowed as the one cause justifying a wife's dismissal? (Augustine interrupts his attention to this question to note that equally the only cause justifying a wife's dismissing her husband is his *fornicatio,* thus making his own addition to and interpretation of Christ's instruction.) He argues to the conclusion that by *fornicatio* Christ meant a wife's religious infidelity. How does he get this conclusion? Again by using Paul's First Letter to the Corinthians as an exegetical instrument for interpreting Christ's instruction to his fellow Jews.

Augustine has Paul repeat Christ's instruction and get it to forbid wives to leave their husbands and husbands to dismiss their wives, but only where both are Christian. Where one spouse is a pagan Paul did not command the Christian spouse to not dismiss the pagan. From this last Augustine draws two conclusions. The first is that Paul must have permitted a Christian spouse to dismiss a pagan (which is a misinterpretation, since what Paul said at this point was that the Christian spouse was not to hinder the pagan spouse's leaving). The second conclusion was that since what warrants the Christian spouse's dismissing the pagan is the latter's paganism, then what Paul thought warranted this dismissal is the lack of Christian faith—and thus what Christ must have meant by the *fornicatio* warranting a Jewish husband's dismissing his wife was her lack of (Christian?) faith. As Augustine puts it:

> Therefore it is permitted to dismiss a pagan spouse, although it is better not to do so, but according to the command of the Lord it is not permitted to dismiss a spouse except for *fornicatio*. Thus *fornicatio* is the paganism itself.[18]

And he names, as examples of this infidelity, paganism, idolatry or any evil superstition.

He finishes off this convoluted logic by concluding that because Christ did not command but only permitted a husband to dismiss his wife guilty of fornication, he left the opening for Paul to advise that a Christian husband need not dismiss his infidel wife, but leave her the opportunity to become a Christian.[19]

What follows in Augustine's logic at this point could have been read with all sympathy by a magistrate of the Roman courts. If failure of religious faith (*infidelitas*) is *fornicatio*, and idolatry is *fornicatio*, and avarice is idolatry, then avarice too is *fornicatio*. Indeed any illicit desire is *fornicatio;* any conduct in which the soul uses the body evilly is such. Because of any such conduct a husband may without sin dismiss his wife or a wife her husband. And a man who dismisses his wife because she forced him into *fornicatio*, he too may use this permission of the Lord—to dismiss his wife "because of [her] *fornicatio.*"[20]

Augustine turns then to ask the meaning of Christ's instruction, "And he who marries a woman who has been dismissed, he commits adultery." What he asks is whether the woman in this case commits adultery along with the man.

To get his answer to this question about Matthew 5:32 he crosses immediately to Paul's instruction in 1 Corinthians 7 and urges that it makes a great deal of difference whether the woman has been dismissed or has herself dismissed her husband. If the latter is the case, her action was clearly adulterous because she must have dismissed her husband out of desire for another man. But if she has been dismissed by a husband with whom she desired to stay, it follows that the man who marries her commits adultery, though it is not certain that she does. But he adds immediately that it is difficult to understand how, if a man and a woman intend and desire equally to have intercourse, one of them could thereby commit adultery but the other not. What is in any case clear is that in marrying the second man the woman who had been dismissed causes him to commit adultery. This last is what Christ forbade. And this is why, whether dismissed by her husband or dismisser of her husband, she must either remain unmarried (*innupta*) or be reconciled with her husband.[21]

What especially catches the modern Catholic eye in this interpretation is Augustine's implication that the divorce by dismissal of the spouse—whether according to Jewish law or according to Roman—indeed dissolves a marriage, and even a marriage of two Christians. For if he thought that the dismissal did not dissolve the marriage, he would have said unambiguously that the dismissed wife's remarrying is adultery. But it is on this point that he declares his uncertainty. He is not sure she is to be accused of adultery.

Or does he say this because he has a much subtler definition of adultery? He seems to say that this woman may be saved from adultery because, though accepting the second marriage, she still desires her husband, while the man who marries her after her dismissal marries her despite this her desire, and thus commits adultery.

Does Augustine mean that adultery is more a matter of desire and intention than of conduct? He closes his exegesis-commentary on this Matthean passage by recording and musing on a story apropos of this understanding of adultery that has come to him from Antioch. The true-life event had occurred almost fifty years earlier, during the reign of Constantine.

Acendinus, both prefect and consul, was owed a gold talent by a certain debtor and threatened the latter with death if he did not repay it by a certain day. But the man was already in prison, so obviously he could not repay the debt.

A wealthy citizen of the city heard of the debt and the threat, and decided to exploit the situation. To the debtor's young and beautiful wife he made an offer. If she would be his for one night, he would give her a gold talent. The wife informed her husband of the offer and asked his permission to accept it. He approved and even commanded that she do so.

Augustine's question is this: Since, according to St. Paul in 1 Corinthians 7:4–5, the spouse's right to the body belongs not to him or herself but to the other spouse; because the wife in this case had asked her husband's permission to give her body to the wealthy man for one night; because the husband, exercising his right over her body, not only gave her this permission but commanded that she give herself to the rich man; and because she had intercourse with the latter not out of lust for him but out of love for her husband—did she not in her intercourse really give her body to her husband? Did she not thereby avoid adultery?

Augustine's answer to his own question is vague. He says that one may judge the woman as seems best to him, but must keep in mind that the story is not drawn from the words of Scripture (*de divinis auctoritatibus*). He admits that once one hears that the woman did what she did at her husband's command, human sensibility is not so offended as it would be if one were to hear of this kind of conduct apart from its real-life context. This strengthens one's suspicion that Augustine may well see the malice of adultery not in the deed itself but in the motive. For this woman's complex motive was to both save her husband's life, and in saving it to obey him.[22]

But there is one thing of which Augustine remains certain. There is no more than one cause justifying the dissolution of a marriage. This is *fornicatio,* understood as the religious infidelity he has defined in this chapter.[23]

Contra Adimantum

In 394 Augustine wrote this essay to refute Adimantus, a long-since-deceased disciple of Mani, who had written in a way that pitted New Testament texts against those in the Old Testament in order to show the inconsistencies and even contradictions from testament to testament.[24] Thus, for example, Adimantus set Luke 18:29–30 against Genesis 2:18–24. The former he interpreted to say that whoever would follow Christ must leave home, parents and family, including his wife, while the latter supposedly conveyed God's command that a man is to leave his father and mother and join permanently to his wife.

But Augustine found words of Christ in the Gospels that sustained the passage in Genesis. Matthew 19:9, with the help of 5:32 grafted into it, says it clearly: "But I say to you, whoever dismisses his wife, except in the case of her *fornicatio,* makes her to commit adultery; and if he marries another, he commits adultery."

Augustine distinguishes here two acts on the part of the husband. He dismisses his wife; and if he does this for any reason other than her adultery, he makes her to commit adultery. This adultery Augustine understands to be the wife's attempting a second marriage. But if it is for her adultery that the husband dismisses her, he is not morally responsible for the adultery of her second marriage, since she has already committed adultery.

The second act is the husband's remarrying after dismissing his wife. It is clear that if he does this after dismissing her for some reason other than her adultery, he himself commits adultery. But if the dismissal is for her adultery, does he himself commit adultery if he attempts remarriage? On this point Augustine is not decisive. He does not say expressly that in this case too the husband commits adultery.

But he finds in the New Testament a circumstance in which one spouse ought to leave the other. This is in Paul's instruction in 1 Corinthians 7:12–15, in which Augustine carelessly interprets Paul to say that if a pagan spouse will not tolerate the Christian life of the other spouse, the latter ought to leave the pagan (whereas what Paul himself said is that if the pagan will not live in peace with the Christian and wishes to abandon the marriage, the Christian should not stand in the way of this). Augustine develops his free interpretation of both passages in the following way.

> If then someone abandons the kingdom of God because he does not wish to leave a spouse who is unwilling to tolerate a Christian husband, he is accused by the Lord. In like manner, a

man who leaves his wife by giving her the writ of dismissal if this
is not justified by her *fornicatio* or by his seeking the kingdom of
God, he is equally blamed by the Lord. Thus these two Gospel
passages are not in contradiction, nor are the Gospel and the Old
Testament. For here in the Gospel the wife is joined to her
husband so that they may together merit to possess the kingdom
of God. Thus it is prescribed that he abandon his spouse if she
prevents her husband from attaining the kingdom.[25]

About the question that the Catholic Church was six centuries later to
answer affirmatively in what has come to be known as "the Pauline
privilege"—that is, after being abandoned by the pagan spouse who will
not tolerate the other's Christian life, may the latter remarry?—Paul says
nothing.

De Diversis Quaestionibus 83

About the year 396 Augustine drafted an *opusculum* consisting of his
reflections on and answers to a selection of questions. There is no unity
among these eighty-three questions; the work has simply the title, *De
diversis quaestionibus 83*. His glance at the issue of divorce and remarriage
is the final question.[26] In substance it is a partial exegesis of Matthew 5:32.
It proposes to explain the meaning of the *fornicatio* that Jesus supposedly
named as the one reason justifying a husband's dismissing his wife.
Augustine reasons to his answer in the following way.

If the Lord has accepted *fornicatio* as the only cause for
dismissing a spouse, but did not forbid the dismissing of a pagan
spouse, it follows that paganism is what is here designated
fornicatio.

That Jesus allowed only *fornicatio* as a justifying cause for dismissal is
evident in the Matthean passages as Augustine understood them. That he
did not forbid dismissing a pagan spouse Augustine purports to find in
Paul's permitting this dismissal. His logic here is that in recording what
the Lord has commanded Paul forbade a Christian spouse to dismiss a
Christian spouse, but in allowing a Christian spouse to dismiss a pagan
spouse Paul qualified this with "I say (not the Lord) . . ." Thus his
conclusion: since the Lord had not commanded that this not be done, he
must not have objected to its being done.

This is one interpretation of *fornicatio* in Matthew 5:32 that Augustine offers—a pagan spouse's paganism. He then tries a second interpretation. If one wishes to understand the term to mean fornication in the
common sense of a spouse's illicit intercourse apart from the marriage,
Christ's words can admit this interpretation. For he was referring to

Christian spouses when he said that *fornicatio* is the one cause justifying dismissal.

Ignoring the possibility that Christ may (even if these words are his and not Matthew's) have had both Christian and non-Christian couples in mind, Augustine reinforces this second interpretation by applying to it a logic whose elements he sees in 1 Corinthians 7:12–15. Since the sole cause for which one spouse may either dismiss or abandon the other still leaves him or her obligated to either seek reconciliation or remain unmarried, then one may conclude that the *fornicatio* Christ had in mind is adultery, because (again) where the *fornicatio* was one spouse's paganism, the Christian spouse was not obligated to be reconciled.

At the end of this tortured logic one ought to ask Augustine the following question. Since, where the *fornicatio* is one spouse's paganism, the Christian spouse is not obligated to reconcile (as the spouses must where both are Christian), is this Christian spouse also not obligated to remain unmarried (as he or she must where both spouses are Christian)? The later Catholic answer to this is that yes, the Christian spouse may remarry by use of the Pauline privilege. But Augustine himself does not ask the question.

De Bono Coniugali

Augustine's *De bono coniugali* of 401 was written as a reply to the Pelagian accusation against him that he sided with the Manichees in their condemnation of marriage as inherently evil because it involves men and women in carnal conduct.[27] One of Augustine's counter-arguments was that marriage cannot be inherently evil because the conduct native to it, sexual intercourse, produces children, an effect that is by nature good. He agreed with the Christian thinking current in his time that because of the fall of the first parents and the consequent unleashing of concupiscence in men and women, even the most devout married Christians almost always sin venially in their sexual intercourse. But the motive of producing the good effect, the child, excuses this slight sinfulness. This in fact is the *raison d'être* of sexual intercourse and of marriage, their goal—procreation. It gives meaning to them and it excuses lust in intercourse provided it is not excessive.

But having said this he had to face the obvious question. If a man and woman marry virtuously for this goal of marriage, explicitly to produce a child, but find that they cannot because of sterility, can they not dissolve this marriage so that at least the fertile partner (thought usually to be the husband) may marry again so as to produce children for the Kingdom of heaven? Far from being sinful, would not a dissolution of the first and sterile marriage and entry into the second marriage be acts of virtue?

With this Augustine has opened a new chapter in the history of Christian thinking on divorce and remarriage. It is not so much that he has closed on the question from a new angle, away from the traditional instruction in the New Testament. We have already seen, and shall see much more fully, that he makes himself accountable to this teaching. But he has suggested, although in different form, the qualification that Ambrose suggested: perhaps not every union thought to be a marriage is really such. Or the same qualification in yet different form: perhaps there are marriages whose interior holding power differs from that which people ordinarily recognize, so that this binds the spouses even when the natural reason for their staying together is voided. As we shall see presently, Augustine finds this extraordinary holding power in the *sacramentum* of marriage.

His first address to the question in *De bono coniugali* is in Chapter 7, and this is by the ordinary route.[28] He asks whether, as the Sacred Scriptures allow a husband to dismiss his wife for her adultery, he may remarry after the dismissal. (He presumes that the *pornéia* of the exceptive clause designates the wife's adultery.)

His first reply is that the Scriptures themselves make a tangled knot (*difficilem nodum*) of this question. He explains by pointing out that in 1 Corinthians 7:10–11 Paul says that according to the Lord's command a wife is not to depart from her husband, but that if she does so, she is either to remain unmarried or to be reconciled with him.

He reasons from this point: the wife must not depart (nor remain unmarried) except from a husband who has committed adultery, lest in departing from an innocent husband she cause him to commit adultery. And he concludes: "So I do not see how a husband can be allowed to remarry after dismissing his adulterous wife since a wife may not remarry after leaving an adulterous husband."[29] (Neither Christ nor Paul had said anything about a wife's leaving her husband because of his adultery.) Then Augustine subsumes this particular issue of remarriage after justified dismissal into his theology of the *sacramentum*.

> So strong is the marriage bond that not even for the sake of procreation can it be dissolved. The divine command forbids this. What then is the meaning of such firmness of the marital bond? It could not have such strength unless it served as a *sacramentum* of something greater, something that remains integral even in the face of men who desert it and of those who want to dissolve it.

> Thus even with divorce the marital covenant (*confoederatio*) is not dissolved, so that even though separated they, the spouses, remain married to one another, and both husband and wife commit adultery with the persons to whom they are joined after divorcing.

> But only in the City of God, in his Holy Mountain, is such the case with a wife.[30]

Three things catch and hold attention here. First, it is the *sacramentum* of a marriage that makes it invulnerable to the spouses' attempt to dissolve it. Second, as a consequence, even if they go through with the divorce action their marriage is not dissolved; they are still spouses to one another though living apart, and if they attempt remarriage, both commit adultery. And Augustine says this even about the divorce that is dismissal of an adulterous spouse. Third, the invulnerability of a marriage to dissolution because of its *sacramentum* is found only among the citizens of the City of God, who we know, from Augustine's rhetorical vocabulary elsewhere in the essay, are the baptized members of the Christian Church. And disconcertingly at the end he says that it applies in the case of the wife.[31]

The following observations about each point are in order. About point one, Augustine does not here say exactly what the *sacramentum* of a marriage is. But by reaching to the end of the passage we find that it is apparently an element only in the marriages of Christians.

On the second point, Augustine is perhaps for the first time in the Christian writing on the subject clear and decisive that, whatever the reason for it, the divorce action allowed by civil law leaves the spouses still married to one another, and that the apparent dissolution effected by the divorce is no more than the "separation from bed and board." Again joining this with what he says at the end of the passage, it would follow that a civil divorce action is ineffectual in this way only in the marriages of two Christians.

Finally, why this is true only of Christians Augustine does not explain at this point. But one may rightly suspect that the explanation is for the moment hidden in the meaning of the *sacramentum* that he adduces here. Why at the end he limits his explanation to "*talis est causa cum uxore*" is not clear. There is equal likelihood that he does not mean for the phrase to limit his logic's applicability to the wife, but that it is a rhetorical flourish echoing the apostles' stunned reaction to Jesus' instruction in Matthew 19, where they commented (in verse 10): "If this is the way it is with a man and wife, it is better not to marry." Augustine would have read the passage in Latin, and seen the first clause end with "*si talis est causa cum viro et uxore.*"

In Chapter 15 he asks and answers the question about the possibility of dissolution and remarriage for the man who has married expressly in order to procreate but finds that his wife is sterile.[32]

He realizes that he has lent considerable vitality to the question by his defense of marriage against its Manichee enemies. He has insisted that marriage is of its nature good, and that this goodness is found in three traits that are natural to it. These are the fidelity natural to marriage, offspring, and its *sacramentum*.

But what of the man who has married expressly in order to father offspring but finds that he has married a sterile wife? The very good which he has sought by marrying is impossible for him to attain. Why then should he not be permitted to dismiss his sterile wife and marry another who may be fertile?

As he begins his answer he deflects the question slightly by proposing to meet the objection on only Christian grounds and only as it touches Christians.

> Once a marriage has been entered in the City of God [again Augustine's figure for the Church]—where since even the first joining of two human beings spouses have a certain sacrament of marriage [*quoddam sacramentum nuptiarum gerunt*]—this marriage can be dissolved in no way except by the death of one of the spouses. For the bond of marriage [*vinculum nuptiarum*] remains even if the offspring should, because of obvious sterility, not be forthcoming. Thus though the spouses know they will never have children, they may not separate and remarry even for the sake of having children. If they were to do this, they would commit adultery with their second partners, being still married to one another.[33]

One must take care to note that Augustine does not here see the bond of marriage and the *sacramentum* to be one and the same reality. Nor does he explain the relationship between the two. What he does is to imply by his logic that the *sacramentum* has an effect on the bond, and that this effect is to make the bond indestructible. What the nature of this *sacramentum* may be he does not explain. Nor therefore does he explain in what way the *sacramentum* gives the marital bond this indestructibility. Finally, with a certain inconsistency he has limited his argument to the marriages of Christians, yet so far seems to call the *sacramentum* one of the traits of marriage taken generally that makes it good.

But in Chapter 18 he begins to explain what this *sacramentum* is and how it renders the marital bond indestructible.[34] The entry for this explanation he finds in the explanation, in turn, for insisting that the bishops in the Church be men of but one wife—either husbands in monogamous marriages or unmarried widowers. The demand for this is found in the fact that from many souls there is to be formed one City [of God] having one heart and one soul unto God.

> For this reason [*propterea*] the *sacramentum* of marriage of our time has so been brought back [*reductum est*] to one man and one wife that the pastors of the Church may not be ordained unless they be husbands of one wife (1 Timothy 3:2 and Titus 1:6).[35]

Augustine adds that this is understood more clearly by those who have insisted that a man who as either a pagan or a catechumen married a second time is not to be ordained. And this not because of any sin on his part but because of the *sacramentum,* for all sins are forgiven in baptism.

He tries another analogy in this effort to explain the *sacramentum.* Just as because of the *sacramentum* a woman who as a catechumen lost her virginity cannot after baptism be numbered among the consecrated virgins (even though her sin was forgiven by her baptism), so it does not seem absurd to say that a man who has married more than once, even though he has not sinned, has lost a certain rule or character of the *sacramentum* [*normam quamdam sacramenti amisisse*]. And this rule of the *sacramentum* is required not for the merit of a virtuous life but as something necessary for the seal [*signaculum*] of ordination.

But what exactly is this rule or character of the *sacramentum,* and why is it required for the seal of ordination? It is that the marital relationship of the bishop and his wife signifies the relationship of Christ to the unity of many peoples submissive to him as to one husband. We know by now that this analogy incorporating the metaphorical marriage of Christ and the Church is crucial to the Catholic theology of divorce and remarriage. Augustine's articulation of it therefore merits exact translation.

> And through this, just as the plural wives of the patriarchs signified our churches of the future, made up of many nations, that would be subject to the one spouse, Christ; so our bishops as the husbands of one wife signify the union of many nations in subjection to the one spouse, Christ.[36]

Augustine adds immediately that this union of nations subject to Christ will become perfect only in the next life. Therefore his full conclusion: the monogamous bishop is a sign of the perfect *future* union of all nations subject to the one spouse who is Christ.

> Therefore just as the *sacramentum* of several marriages in olden times signified the future multitude of all peoples on earth subjected to God, so the *sacramentum* of the monogamous marriages of our time signifies the future union of all of us subject to God in one heavenly city.[37]

Therefore too, Augustine continues (and this is the conclusion for which he has devised this analogy), it has never been permitted that a woman pass from one husband to another while the first is still alive, just as apostasy and passing to another religion is always evil. And he returns to the challenge we saw earlier: not even the desire for offspring justifies a woman's leaving a sterile husband in order to remarry: "For in our marriages the sanctity of the *sacramentum* is of more value than the fertility of the womb." (*In nostrarum quippe nuptiis plus valet sanctitas sacramenti quam fecunditas uteri.*)[38]

What exactly is Augustine's logic here? It is hardly likely that he is reasoning that unless the marriages of Christians be indissoluble their bishops will not be men of one wife and will therefore fail to be signs of the perfect union, in afterlife, of many nations subject to the one spouse who is Christ. Such causal links are nowhere in evidence in his reasoning.

Does any light come of his saying that both a woman wishing to be enrolled among the consecrated virgins must have her *sacramentum,* and a man wishing to be a bishop must have his *sacramentum?* Does he use the term here equivocally or analogously? What seems common to the two predications of the term is that in such case a relationship to God is asserted. Augustine makes clear that no sin or innocence of sin is involved in either relationship. What then is there in each relationship making it a *sacramentum?*

About the relationship of the woman he does not say. But about that of the bishop he seems to say that his relationship to God consists of this, that his marriage signifies the obedient relationship to Christ of many peoples joined in union. This function of signifying seems to be the *sacramentum* in the bishop's marriage. And at this point Augustine takes a kind of deontological step: a bishop's marriage should or *must* do this kind of signifying if he is to be a bishop.

But how does Augustine move logically from that deontological conclusion to the quasi-ontological conclusion that *therefore* it is impossible for the marriage of two Christians to end by dismissal or departure, that it is indestructible except by death? Unless one wishes to say that he takes a *saltus logicus* at this point, an unwarranted logical leap, one must settle for the interpretation that the demand on the bishop for monogamy in order to sustain his *sacramentum* has no causal relationship to the demand on *all* Christian marriages for indissolubility, but that this demand on the bishop is only an illustration of the assertion that since his *sacramentum* can put a demand on him, so the *sacramentum* of the unordained married can put a demand on their marriages.

To say the kindest thing about it, the path of Augustine's logic here is hardly laid out clearly. Only two things about the *sacramentum* of the marriages of Christians emerge clearly. First, it and it alone is the cause for the indissolubility of these marriages short of death. Second, the *sacramentum* of Christian marriages lies in their signifying the union of all Christians subject to God—subject not now but in the life after death.

Note that unlike the later theology of indissolubility that will be drawn from Augustine, he himself does not here say that the marriage of two Christians is a sacrament in that it is a sign of the relationship of Christ and the Church. He does not even say that this marriage is a sign of the relationship between all peoples and God now in the course of history. Rather, it is a sign of this relationship in its perfection that will come in the next life. And Augustine seems unworried that the fulcrum of his theological logic, the indestructible and eternal *signatum* that Christian marriage in this life must signify by remaining indestructible, does not yet exist. Not only is it not yet a holding constant to the human-relationship variable on earth, but it has not yet its own existence.

Two questions about Augustine's reasoning remain for now. First, how does he know that the marriage of two Christians has a *sacramentum* that is precisely the signifying function that he ascribes to it? Where did he find this out (that is, what is his verification for this premise in his argument)? He does not offer evidence for this. He who has a passage from the Scriptures to support so many countless theses has none at this moment—not even from Ephesians 5.

Second, and more to the point of his conclusion, why, granted that the marriage of two Christians is such a sign, *must* it be indissoluble? This is not to ask about a moral imperative binding two Christians in their marriage because it is a sign of an indestructible divine-human relationship. It is to ask rather the cause-effect relationship of two alleged facts— one fact the cause, the indestructibility of the divine-human relationship taken as true by revelation in the Scriptures; the other the effect, deduced as true because of the truth of the first fact. In short, how does Augustine move logically from the truth of the first of these facts via causality to the truth of the second? For reasons of his own he does not explain this. Nor does he anticipate the rejoinder to his reasoning that what it concludes to at most is that two Christian spouses are bound morally to try in their marriage to imitate, to reenact, the indestructibility of the love relationship of Christ and his Church.

Chapter 24 of *De bono coniugali* is the third from the essay's last.[39] It is the beginning of a peroration or résumé of his thesis that runs through all the chapters. Again Augustine names the three goods found in a marriage and making it itself by nature good. But now he makes an overdue precision. Two of these goods, offspring and fidelity, are found in every marriage. But the third, the *sacramentum,* is found only in the marriage of two Christians. However he here names these goods in a slightly different fashion. Instead of fidelity (*fides*) he says that this good is found *in fide caritatis,* in the fidelity of charity. Instead of offspring (*proles*) he says that this good is found *in causa generandi* (in the source of generation). These two goods are found among all peoples. But there is a third that is found only among the people of God, and this he does not name as the *sacramentum.* He says rather that this good is found *in sanctitate sacramenti,* in the holiness of the *sacramentum.*[40]

Of this last-named good he says, "Because of this holiness [not because of the *sacramentum* itself, if we read him literally] it is sinful for a woman departing, because dismissed by her husband, to marry another man while her husband is still alive." He adds immediately that not even for the sake of bearing children by a second marriage—the children who were the motive for marrying in the first place—is her marital bond dissolved except by the death of her husband.

But why is it that a failure of one of the causes creating a marriage is not a ground for its dissolution among Christians? Augustine does not ask this question explicitly, but he does imply it in the analogy that he offers immediately—another analogy whose key element is the *sacramentum*.

> Although that is the sole reason why the marriage took place, even if this for which the marriage took place does not come about, the marriage bond is not loosed except by the death of the spouse. Just as if an ordination of the clergy takes place in order to gather the people, even if the congregation does not gather, there yet remains in those ordained the *sacramentum* of orders. And if, because of any fault, someone is removed from clerical office, he retains the *sacramentum* of the Lord once it has been imposed . . .[41]

Again, by using the terms distinctly Augustine makes clear he thinks the marital bond, the *vinculum,* is distinct from the *sacramentum* of marriage in Christian spouses. He does not consider the marital bond in itself to be indestructible. Rather it is among Christians the *sacramentum* of their marriage that makes it so. Among them the *sacramentum* apparently comes to or is a quality of this bond.

And it seems clear enough that by *sacramentum* in this context Augustine refers not to the relationship of the spouses to one another, not to their relationship's character as an earthly image of the relationship of Christ and the Church, as the later theology of Christian indissolubility will understand the *sacramentum*. He thinks of this rather as each spouse's commitment to God, or perhaps their joint commitment to him. Whatever it is, it is something in the soul of each spouse having the same indestructibility as the *sacramentum* of orders in the soul of an ordained man.

Though implying clearly that the sanctity of the spouses' *sacramenta* is the cause of their marriage's indissolubility, he does not explain *how* this sanctity causes it. Certainly he does not claim that it does so because of a causal analogy with the *sacramentum* of orders. He implies this analogy only as an illustration in his argument: thus, if one *sacramentum* can cause indestructibility so too can another.

De Genesi ad Litteram

Augustine worked for thirteen years at his On the Literal Interpretation of Genesis, completing it in twelve books in 414.[42] In Book 9, Chapters 3 and 5, when commenting on God's motive, in Genesis 2, for creating the first woman, he argued that the only way in which the woman was truly a helpmate of the man was in her bearing children to him. In Chapter 7 he returned to the same thought but went beyond it to assert other goods for marriage, one of which is to confine sexual incontinence to venial sin by keeping it within marriage and motivated by the desire for procreation.

Here he used the occasion to recapitulate what he had asserted in his recently completed *De bono coniugali,* that the three goods in it making marriage itself good are fidelity, offspring and the *sacramentum.*

> By fidelity the spouses take care not to have intercourse with partners outside the marriage. By the good of offspring the spouses take care to accept children lovingly, nourish them kindly and educate them religiously. By the *sacramentum* they take care not to separate the marriage; and if dismissed, not to remarry even for the sake of children.[43]

The passage is almost an *obiter dictum* and calls for no comment other than a note of surprise that Augustine finds no cause for the permanence of a Christian marriage in the good that is fidelity.

De Fide et Operibus

In the second of his Retractations (paragraph 78) Augustine explains the origin of this essay, On Faith and Works, that he wrote in 413.[44] He had been asked about some Christian writings proposing the opinion that while it is certain that faith is necessary for salvation, a person can be saved without works. Consequently pagans who are living in an habitually sinful state and show no will to get out of it can be admitted to baptism. For the strength of the sacrament will by itself lead them to change their lives. And in any case, if they have faith and persevere in it, they will be saved even though they remain in the sinful state, since they will in the end be purified by the cleansing fire of which Paul writes in 1 Corinthians 3:11–15. But without baptism they will surely be lost eternally.

Augustine's answer to this opinion is significant for a study of his mind on the possibility of remarriage after divorce because in it he says so clearly what he thinks of this: a person attempting remarriage after dismissing a spouse lives in adultery.

He suggests that those who propose this discipline are moved to do so because they know that men and women who have dismissed their spouses and then remarried are not admitted to baptism; for Christ has made clear, he urges, that these second unions are not marriages but adulteries.

> Since they cannot deny that what Truth unambiguously calls adultery is in fact adultery, they plead that men and women be admitted to baptism who are so caught in this trap that unless they are accepted into baptism they will prefer to live and even to die with no sacrament at all rather than to be forced from the bond of adultery.[45]

Augustine's reply to the proposal, in the following six chapters, is a long and resounding "no." Those who have remarried after dismissing their spouses are living in the sin of adultery. To be baptized is "to put on the new man." But to do this is impossible unless the old man be put off first.[46]

In Chapter 7 he turns to a question that occurs to him as grounded in reality.[47] What if a woman until then unmarried takes another woman's husband without knowing that he is already married? Does she commit adultery? No, he answers. If she never comes to know of his existing marriage, she will never be an adulteress. But from the moment she does find this out, she begins to be one from the fact of her having intercourse with another woman's husband. Her case is parallel to that of a man who takes possession of some property without knowing that it belongs to another. As long as he is ignorant of that ownership, he is in good faith and does not sin. But the moment he comes to know of the ownership he is in bad faith and sins against justice if he continues to hold it.

> So when such immorality is corrected—that is, when adulterous unions are ended—this ought not to grieve us as though marriages were being divorced. For in the City of God, the Church, not only is the bond of marriage held to but also its *sacramentum;* so that Christians do not permit that one man give his wife over to another, as Cato was praised for doing among the Romans.

Augustine closes the question at this point. He has nothing more to say to those who propose the strange discipline of admitting to baptism men and women who continue to live in adulterous second unions. They do not claim that these people do not live in sin; they do claim that they do not live in adultery, for they want not to be openly contradicted by the teaching of the Lord in the Gospel.[48]

Tractatus 9 in Ioannem

Augustine wrote his one hundred and twenty-four essays on the Gospel of John in 416 or shortly thereafter. His commentary on Christ's miracle at the wedding feast in Cana of Galilee is in *Tractatus 9,* paragraph 2.[49] It contains modestly significant claims for the goodness of marriage against the Manichee despisers of it who were never out of his mind. It repeats also the patristic commonplace that Christ forbade a husband's dismissing his wife except for her *fornicatio;* and Augustine again makes clear that by this sin he understands the wife's adultery.

> The reason for the Lord's coming to the wedding feast on being invited was, aside from the mystical signification involved in doing so, that he wished to confirm that he is the creator of marriage. For in the future there were to be those about whom the Apostle said that they forbid marriage, claiming that it is evil and created by the devil; whereas in the Gospel the Lord, when

asked whether a man is permitted to dismiss his wife for just any reason, replied that this is forbidden except for her *fornicatio.* And you will recall that in this reply he said, "Therefore what God has joined man must not separate."

Those who are well instructed in the Catholic faith know that God created marriage, and that whereas the conjoining of the spouses is done by God, their divorcing is done by the devil. But in the event of a wife's *fornicatio* it is permitted to dismiss her because a woman who has not kept marital fidelity with her husband has from the beginning not willed to be a wife.[50]

Augustine takes for granted that the narrative of the miracle is historically factual. Many responsible modern New Testament interpreters do not. Granted Christ attended a wedding feast at Cana which only the Fourth Gospel records, the miracle narrative may well be a midrashic story, a quasi-parable designed by someone in the Johannine school to clarify exactly what John thought to be the symbolic and therefore real meaning of the physical event, to show the superiority of the new covenant of Christ over the old.

Augustine's formal intent in the passage is to be exegetical, specifically to explain why Christ came to the wedding feast. The first part of Christ's motivation as Augustine interpreted it served his long polemic against the Manichees mentioned above: Christ came to the wedding to show the goodness of marriage, even to confirm the belief that marriage is his creation. As added evidence for both points of belief Augustine reminds his readers that Christ said elsewhere, "What God has joined man must not separate."

He contributes to his standing argument against divorce and remarriage by first saying rhetorically that divorce is the invention of the devil, and then arguing that the reason a man is permitted to dismiss an unfaithful wife is that in violating marital fidelity she shows that she never willed to be his wife to begin with—surely the most facile of exegetical history's many interpretations of the Matthean exceptive clause, as well as a presumption of fact about every wife who has ever committed adultery.

Following this he advances a point that seems out of place given the purpose of his essay, but a point that was to be used by the medieval Scholastics in their logic demonstrating that Christian marriage is a sacrament. That is, a woman who vows virginity to God is involved in a marital situation or relationship. How is she? In that by her vowing she takes part in the marriage of the entire Church with the spouse who is Christ.

And not even women who vow their virginity to God are uninvolved with marriage (although by their vow they hold a higher level of honor and holiness in the Church). For along with the entire Church they participate in that marriage in which Christ is the spouse. So for this reason the Lord came to the wedding when invited, so that he might make marital chastity more firm and show the *sacramentum* [the hidden meaning] of marriage, for the groom, in that marriage was an image of the Lord; and to him it was said, "You have saved the good wine until last," that is, the Lord's Gospel.[51]

It is of more than passing significance that Augustine asserts the marital relationship of Christ and the Church as one element of an analogy clarifying not a point about the marriages of Christians but about vowed virginity in the Church. It is significant because this analogy will be used endlessly in centuries to follow as a kind of middle term in a demonstration of the impossibility of dissolving the marriage of two Christians. Thus, the marital relationship of Christ and the Church is indestructible, but the marriage of two Christians is an earthly image of that of Christ and the Church; therefore the earthly marriage too is indestructible.

But if in this theology the sense of the analogy were that intended by Augustine himself, it would not help to produce the traditional conclusion about the indestructibility of Christian marriage. For when Augustine clarifies the point he is making about marriage, he himself does not try to establish the husband-wife, Christ-Church analogy, and then draw the conclusion that because the Christ-Church relationship is indestructible so too is the husband-wife relationship. What he does say at this point is unhappily ambiguous, and one is not quite sure how to interpret this last, long statement that is a peroration. In it he seeks to summarize his answer to the implied question that opens the chapter, "Why did the Lord come to the wedding feast?" In the peroration he gives his two reasons: to strengthen marital fidelity [the case for it], and to manifest the *sacramentum* of marriage.

In Augustine's judgment Christ did the first of these by making his presence at the wedding testify to the goodness of marriage, to his authorship of it—leaving the implication that to claim its dissolubility by divorce is to deny this divine authorship. Does Augustine think in addition that he himself has strengthened the case for fidelity against divorce by linking the wife's marital commitment to the commitment of the woman vowing virginity—strengthened because the latter woman in turn is involved in the Church's marriage with Christ, a marriage that is indestructible?

I think this explanation is only improbably in Augustine's intent, because the reader would have to supply too many links in the logic of explanation—always a dubious way of ferreting out a writer's meaning. The largest of the missing links is this, that in order to demonstrate that the wife's relationship to her husband is indestructible *because* her relationship to him is both linked to and is of a kind with the relationship of the virgin vowed to Christ and thereby participating in the Church's marriage to Christ, Augustine must be made to imply that (1) the virgin's marital relationship is indestructible (2) *because* the Church's marriage relationship to Christ is indestructible. Perhaps Augustine meant to say this. But if he did, this is not clear in his own words. And besides, Catholic tradition has not held its people's vows of virginity and the relationship with Christ and the Church established by them to be indestructible, but only that this vow and the relationship must never be violated.

It is significant in the history of the Catholic theology of marriage that incautious theologians have looked to the second thing Christ intended to do in coming to the wedding feast—to manifest the *sacramentum* of marriage—and found Augustine saying that Christ not only made marriage a sacrament but made it so at Cana, and in making it a sacrament there, at least among his followers, he made it indissoluble. This is erroneous because it reads into Augustine's word *sacramentum* in this context later theology's meaning for the word. Here he has *sacramentum* designate marriage's inner and hidden meaning, and, in the particular case of the marriage at Cana, its private inner and hidden meaning.

Augustine claims that Christ's presence reveals this meaning in *this* marriage in the groom's functioning as a symbol of him. That is, in the groom's keeping the physically real wine of better quality until the last after the inferior wine has been drunk, he symbolizes Christ's keeping the superior metaphorical wine of the Gospel until the inferior metaphorical wine of the Old Testament has been exhausted.

Now even if we grant Augustine's accuracy in saying that the groom is a symbol of Christ, what he says the groom symbolizes is not (in union with his own bride) the indestructible union of Christ with his bride the Church, but Christ's coming to transform Old Testament prophecy (the inferior wine) into the New Testament Gospel (the new and superior wine). What does "Gospel" mean in this narrow context? Only Christ's words about marriage, so that the wedding feast's and the miracle's hidden meaning, according to Augustine, is a validation of Christ's teaching about marriage's indestructibility? Or does "Gospel" here mean the all-inclusive message of Christ? The answer to this is not explicit in Augustine's own words. But evidence points to the second of the two answers offered here, because in what follows in the succeeding chapter there is no further discussion of marriage, just as in the preceding chapter the issue was not marriage.

De Nuptiis et Concupiscentia

It is in his essay completed in two books in 418, On Marriage and Concupiscence,[52] that Augustine turns finally to a formal use of Paul's marriage metaphor in Ephesians 5 to demonstrate the indissolubility of Christian marriages.

> For not only fertility, whose fruit is the child, is urged on the
> Christian married, and not only chastity, whose bond is fidelity,

but also a certain *sacramentum* of their marriage is urged. Hence it is that the Apostle says, "Husbands, love your wives just as Christ loved the Church" (Ephesians 5:25).[53]

From only this much two questions surface immediately. Is Augustine here saying something about the invulnerability to divorce of all marriages, or only of those wherein the spouses are Christian? And how is the meaning of the *sacramentum* illumined by one's understanding of Christ's love for the Church?

In answer to the first question, it seems that Augustine means to say that the *sacramentum* as a cause of indissolubility is found only in the marriage of two Christians, although when, a few lines later, he supports his explanation with a citation from the Gospels, he uses Christ's words in Matthew 5:32 that were spoken to non-Christians. Here again, though not yet developed, is the source of the subsequent Catholic teaching that only a marriage of two Christians is finally invulnerable to divorce—is radically indissoluble, to use the vocabulary of this teaching.

To find how Augustine's understanding of the marital *sacramentum* is illumined by his understanding of Christ's love for the Church we must follow his reasoning through this passage.

Now the substance of this *sacramentum* is this, that the man and woman joined in marriage persevere inseparably as long as they live; nor may spouse be separated from spouse except for reason of fornication (Matthew 5:32). For this is what is maintained between the living Christ and the living Church, that they never for all eternity be separated by divorce. So well is this *sacramentum* kept in the City of God, in his holy mountain (Psalm 47:2), which is to say in the Church of Christ, among married Christians who are surely members of Christ, that even when women marry or are taken in marriage specifically in order to have children, it is never permitted to leave a sterile spouse in order to marry a fertile one. If one were to do this, he or she would be guilty of adultery (Matthew 19:8–9), not according to the law of this world, which permits without delict the giving of the writ of dismissal and the taking of another spouse, the conduct that the Lord is said to have permitted Moses to grant the Israelites because of their hardness of heart. So firmly does the bond of their marriage survive between the spouses that even when separated they are married rather to one another than to the new consort. For they would not be joined in adultery to the new unless they still remained spouses to one another. Then, once the husband with whom a woman has been joined in true marriage dies, she can make into a second true marriage what has been until then no more than adultery.[54]

Augustine says that the substance, the *res,* of the marital *sacramentum* is the husband's and wife's unfailing perseverance in marriage. Apparently he means that this *res* is a quality of the marital union unique to two Christians. He does not say what later theologians will say, that the union of two Christians has indissolubility as an *effect* of its being a sacrament, and is in turn a sacrament in that it is an earthly image of the indestructible union of Christ with the Church. According to Augustine the indestructibility is in the marriage first and of itself as an effect of the spouses' Christianity.

What then in the spouses' Christianity is the cause of their union's indestructibility? Apparently it is a bond of commitment to God that cannot be destroyed. For toward the end of this passage Augustine uses another analogy.

> . . . just as the soul of an apostate Christian, in a sense abandoning his marriage with Christ, even though he loses his faith, does not lose the *sacramentum* of faith that he received in baptism. Or if he has lost it by apostasy, he would get it back in returning. But he who apostatizes has it to intensify his punishment, not in order to merit his reward.[55]

What Augustine intends in the comparison is transparent. As the apostate's *sacramentum* of his "marriage," his faith commitment, to Christ cannot be destroyed even by his apostasy, neither can the spouses' sacramentum, their commitment, be destroyed by divorce.

It is not entirely clear, in this passage, whom Augustine intends the termini of this marital *sacramentum*-commitment to be. Are they the two spouses in their relationship to one another? Or the spouses singly to God? Or the two of them together to God? Because he compares the marital *sacramentum* to that of baptism, whose termini are the individual person and God, he appears to mean also that the termini of the marital *sacramentum* are not the spouses in their commitment to one another, but either or both in their commitment to God.

Just before the passage quoted immediately above Augustine uses a compound term that is interesting because of its crucial location in his logic, but irritating because its semantic content is so vague. He is explaining why it is that despite their divorce-separation and even their attempted remarriages, two Christian spouses remain married to one another until one of them dies.

> Thus for as long as they live there remains a certain conjugal something (*quiddam coniugale*) which neither separation nor union with another can move. But it remains to indict them for their crime, not as the bond of their covenant (*vinculum foederis*).[56]

It is this "certain conjugal something," he goes on to say, which remains in the soul of each divorced spouse, just as the baptismal *sacramentum* remains in the soul of the apostate Christian. If, however, this "certain conjugal something" is not itself the bond of their covenant with one another (the *vinculum foederis*), then what it seems to be is their commitment to God, but now a violated commitment. To say the least, this understanding of the marital *sacramentum* thus far is barely identifiable as the genetic ancestor of the marital sacrament that Catholic theologians will elaborate seven centuries later.

But Augustine has more to say about the *sacramentum* in this first book of *De nuptiis et concupiscentia.* This is in Chapter 21, and it seems to be the *locus classicus* in which Catholic theologians have found the first clear sketch, though brief, of the theology of indissolubility of marriage whose heart is the marriage metaphor of Christ and the Church. Despite its length I quote the passage in full in order to establish the above-mentioned sketch in its context.

If now in our time we could in some way interrogate these goods of marriage, asking them how the sin could have been propagated by them in little ones, the conduct of conceiving would reply, "I would be much happier in paradise had the sin not been committed. For to me belongs that divine blessing, 'Increase and multiply.' . . . For this good work dissimilar members of the dissimilar sexes have been designed. They existed before the sin but not as a cause for shame."

The fidelity of chastity would reply, "If there had been no sin, what could live safer in paradise than myself, where neither my own lust nor that of another would have tempted me?"

The *sacramentum* of marriage would reply, "Before the sin it was about me that these words were said in Paradise, 'A man will leave his father and his mother and shall cleave to his wife, and the two shall become one body' (Genesis 2:24)." "This is a great sacrament," says the Apostle, "in Christ and in the Church" (Ephesians 5:32). Therefore this which is great in Christ and in the Church is quite small in each and every husband and wife, but is the *sacramentum* of inseparable union.

Which of these could it be in a marriage from which the bond of sin could pass down to later generations? From none of them. And clearly the good of marriage is found fully in these three goods; and still in our day a marriage is good by virtue of these three goods.[57]

This is a juncture in Augustine's argument with the Pelagians who have accused him of siding with the Manichees in their condemnation of marriage as evil. He has adduced the three goods of marriage—offspring, fidelity and the *sacramentum*—to verify its inherent goodness. But he has also done a complicating thing: he has insisted that in virtually every marriage since the sin of the first parents of the race sexual intercourse has been sinful because of the activity of concupiscence in it. The concupiscence he sees as a sinfulness inherited from the sin of the first parents. Now he is seeking to account for the handing down of this sinfulness from generation to generation. He denies that anything natural to marriage, anything designed into it by God, causes this handing down. Here he exonerates one by one the goods whereby marriage itself is good.

To go analytically through Augustine's reflections here, he has, first, apparently forgotten that he once said that the *sacramentum* is found only in the marriages of Christians. For here he says that it was of the *sacramentum* that the words, distinctly pre-Christian in source and in reference, were spoken, "A man shall leave his father and his mother, and shall cleave to his wife, etc."

His interpretation here of Ephesians 5:32 is perhaps the source of centuries of subsequent misinterpretation of it. For he can be read in such a way as to have him make the husband-wife relationship the referent of Paul's "This is a great sacrament." But for Paul himself this referent is the Christ-Church relationship.

The last clause of the same paragraph may stand as the core, the very tiny core, of Augustine's theology of sacramental indissolubility. He gives the two correlated facets of his familiar analogy—the relationships that exist between Christ and the Church on the one side, and between the Christian husband and wife on the other. He asserts their homogeneity and their difference—the inequality of the similar relationships. The relationship is great between Christ and the Church, small between husband and wife.

Then in the most forthright direct predication he names what the *sacramentum* is in each relationship. It is the inseparable union. With this it seems that he has chosen the cultural meaning of *sacramentum* for this explanation, namely its meaning as vowed commitment. So it seems at least in this passage that the sacramentality, and therefore the indissolubility, of a (Christian) marriage lies not in its functioning as an earthly image of the indestructible Christ-Church relationship but rather in its being a relationship *like* that indestructible relationship.

This passage offers its own answer to the question of Augustine's method of theologizing here, the question about how he uses the metaphor of the Christ-Church marriage in explaining the human marital *sacramentum*.

Because he understands *sacramentum* here as the vowed commitment, he does not use the metaphor in the causative analogy that later generations of churchmen and theologians will use. That is, he does not, like them, say "*Because* the Christian spouses are members of a Church which is the bride of Christ in an indestructible union, and *because* their union is like that of Christ and his bride, their bond too is *made* indestructible by that union."

Perhaps instead he uses the metaphor as the determining element in a manifesting analogy in which the determined element is the relationship of the Christian spouses. Thus, "You will understand how unfailing the marriage of two Christian spouses in fact is (because of their marital *sacramentum*) by understanding the unfailingness of Christ's union with his Church."

Or perhaps, but less probably so, he uses the metaphor as a moral model, as though he were implying "This is how unfailing a marriage of two Christians *ought* to be, as unfailing as the love relationship of Christ and his Church."

De Adulterinis Coniugiis

In 419 Augustine addressed his essay in two books, On Adulterous Marriages, to Bishop Pollentius who had proposed to him his own interpretation of the Synoptic statements on divorce and remarriage, and of the kindred statement in 1 Corinthians 7. So this last of Augustine's treatises on the subject is his most direct and formal effort to set out a doctrine and discipline for it.[58]

Pollentius' proposal, in outline, was the following. If in a marriage there is no adultery, the spouses have these choices: to remain married; to separate on the initiative of only one of them if he or she considers the marriage intolerable, or otherwise wishes to live a life of continence; if they separate but find celibate life unacceptable, they must not seek new marriages but must return to one another. But if there is adultery, the innocent party may divorce unilaterally and may remarry.

Augustine's reply follows Pollentius' proposal in order. He points out in Chapters 1 and 2[59] that where in a marriage there is no adultery, not only may a spouse not remarry after departing from the marriage, but he or she is forbidden by the Lord's command (conveyed by Paul) to depart from the marriage at all. He adds that only one cause justifies one spouse's either dismissing the other or departing from the marriage, and this is the other spouse's adultery. He insists that this is clear in Christ's instruction in the Sermon on the Mount, and that it is to departure for this reason alone that Paul refers in 1 Corinthians 7 where he says of the wife, "But if she is in fact divorced . . ."

In Chapter 3 he finishes off the thought begun in that citation of 1 Corinthians 7.[60] If Paul, in relaying the Lord's command, allows that the wife may depart but adds that even she must remain unmarried, then it follows too from the Lord's command that not even her husband's adultery justifying her departure justifies also her remarrying. Augustine comes back in Chapter 6 to the same interpretation: where both spouses are Christian, if the husband commits adultery, his wife may leave him but may not remarry. But if her husband has been faithful, she may not leave him for any reason.[61]

In Chapter 8 he attempts an interpretation of the Matthean exceptive clause, but this time in its version and context found in Matthew 19.[62] He says that if Christ had allowed husbands, after dismissing their wives for adultery, to remarry *because* of this adultery, he would have destroyed the equal rights of men and women. For he did not in his exceptive clause allow women to dismiss their adulterous husbands. But we know, Augustine continues, that the rights of husbands and wives are equal because of what Paul says in 1 Corinthians 7:4: "A wife does not belong to herself but to her husband; equally a husband does not belong to himself but to his wife." As for the admitted unclarity in the exceptive clause, Augustine insists that it is resolved by Christ's clear and simple statements on the subject in Mark and in Luke. (Again Augustine engages in an easy exegesis, using Paul to clarify the meaning of Matthew, and Mark and Luke to resolve indecision in Matthew. There is almost certainly a doctrinal assumption underlying this, namely that the Holy Spirit is in any case the one principal author of all scriptural passages. Consequently what he says in one place through one human instrument may be used to clarify what he says somewhat obscurely elsewhere through another human instrument. What the human instruments understood and intended to say is not seriously important to this understanding of divine inspiration and authorship of the Scriptures.)

In this same Chapter 8 Augustine closes a loophole that Pollentius suggested, that a spouse's adultery is equivalently his or her death because it causes the death of the soul; therefore the innocent spouse, having the status of widowhood, is free to remarry.[63] To this Augustine replies that it was of a wife dismissed for adultery that Christ said that anyone who marries her commits adultery. Therefore she cannot be considered dead. He does not say where he found out that it was to a wife dismissed for adultery that Christ referred in this case, nor does he advert to the fact that the school of Hillel in Christ's time allowed the dismissing of wives for multiple reasons and that Jewish husbands readily guided their conduct by the teaching of this school.

In Book 2, Chapter 5, Augustine returns to his theology of indissolubility that equivalates the effect of the marital bond with the effect of the *sacramentum* of baptism.

> Even though a [Christian] person be excommunicated for some crime, the *sacramentum* of baptism remains in him, and will always remain, even though he never be reconciled with God. So too, even though a woman be dismissed for her infidelity, the bond [*vinculum*] of her marital covenant remains in her, and will always remain even though she never be reconciled with her husband. It will end only when her husband dies. But the

person excommunicated will never lose the *sacramentum* of baptism, even if he is never reconciled with God, because God never dies.[64]

Note that here in his analogy, as in *De bono coniugali* and *De nuptiis et concupiscentia,* Augustine does not make the two analogated relationships to be spouse-with-spouse and Christ-with-Church. So he does not in the analogy imply that the spouses are indissolubly bound because the bond of Christ and the Church is indestructible, and because their baptism makes the spouses' union an earthly image of the Christ-Church union. (The reader will surely by now recognize this as the theology of indissolubility worked out by later Catholic theologians.) There is no causal analogy here at all. That is, there is no *because* in Augustine's reasoning; there is only a *just as.* The marital bond has the effect of indissoluble binding of spouse to spouse *just as* the baptismal *sacramentum* has the effect of indissoluble binding of the Christian soul to God. Is this because the marital bond too is a *sacramentum?* At least in this passage Augustine does not say so.

And again there is the question of the termini of this marital bond that Augustine says is as indestructible (as long as both spouses live) as the baptismal *sacramentum.* Does he mean that these termini are the spouses one with another? Or each spouse singly with God? Or both together with him? As in the passage above from *De nuptiis et concupiscentia,* the point is not entirely clear. Because Augustine says the woman's bond remains until her husband dies, the two of them are apparently the termini bonded. But the baptismal bond is indestructible because it is of the Christian with God, who never dies—which raises the question asking *why* the marital bond should be indestructible during a lifetime, even though husbands die, *just as* the baptismal *sacramentum* is indestructible because God does not die. The causal link from the second of these propositions to the first, the *because,* is what Augustine never supplies. He ends his reasoning on the subject with an unverified assertion of similarity—indeed of similar ontological conditions of indestructibility of two different kinds of relationships.

It may be too that in the end, here in his last words on the subject, he returns close to a divine voluntarism about the indissolubility of a Christian marriage. He insists that despite the irreversible apostasy of a Christian man the *sacramentum* of the baptism in his soul, the terminus in him of his personal relationship with God, never perishes *because* God never dies. This is to say that God's will to hold the man in this relationship never lapses despite the man's will to destroy the relationship. God's will over-rides the destructive effort of the man's will. From this Augustine reasons that so too, despite the wife's equivalent apostasy from her husband, despite her will to destroy their marital bond, this bond survives. Why? Not for a reason of symmetry that a perfect analogy would demand, namely that her husband's over-riding will continues to hold the bond in

existence (as God continues to will the baptismal *sacramentum* in the soul
of the apostate), but apparently because God wills that the marital bond
remain—despite the absence of any reason or cause within the wills of the
spouses for its remaining. This seems to make the marital bond a bond of
the individual spouse to God's will, but a bond held to unilaterally, only by
God. Or does Augustine imply that where the marital bond is of two
Christians, it itself becomes one terminus of a bond with God, and that
because God wills this "vertical" bond with himself to be indestructible,
the "horizontal" bond between the spouses is, as an effect, also indestructible? Whether this is so—and if it is, why it is—Augustine does not explain.

Summary

Jerome's and especially Augustine's bequests to the Western Church
were immense and long-lasting. They are found, I think, mainly in two
forms. One is in the exegesis of the New Testament passages on divorce
and remarriage. This part of the bequest is the persuasion that the presumed words of Christ in the Matthean exceptive clause warranting a
husband's dismissing his adulterous wife warrant not a true dissolution of
their marriage but only a separation that leaves them still married to one
another. Jerome and Augustine interpreted Christ's instruction conveyed
by Paul in 1 Corinthians 7:10–11 in the same way: the Christian wife who
departs from her Christian husband does not thereby dissolve the marriage, but like the dismissed wife in the exceptive clause she is no more
than separated from him while still married to him as long as he lives.

Because of the boundless prestige that these two Fathers gained
among Western canonists and theologians once their works were copied by
the early medieval monks and circulated in the schools, this exegesis of the
New Testament passages was accepted among them virtually without
question. The "separation from bed and board" thus became lodged
securely in the Western theology and canonical discipline of marriage.
And since any student who took a second glance at the texts could notice
that Christ's words were addressed to non-Christians, he could conclude
quickly that invulnerability to divorce by human authority must be a
quality of all marriages, not only of those among Christians. This in turn
was virtually an invitation to find what it is in marriage the pre-Christian
"natural" institution that makes it thus invulnerable. The way was open to
reinventing marriage as a non-voidable contract, and the canonists of the
twelfth century took this way easily.

The other part of the bequest is nearly exclusively Augustine's. One
would call it his theology of the *sacramentum* of marriage except that he
never worked carefully enough to settle a consistent meaning for the key
terms, to forge a catena of reasoning and to verify his conclusions rigorously enough to form a true theology. What he did was, by the force of his
abundant and hurried rhetoric, to bring within reach of one another the
elements of such a theology. In doing so he provided for those satisfied

with reading him superficially an answer to the question that asks what it is in the marriage of two Christians that makes it radically indissoluble, invulnerable to the attempt of *any* human agency to dissolve it, not only to the attempt of civil authorities but to that of the highest ecclesiastical authority itself. He identified the cause of this invulnerability as the *sacramentum* of a Christian marriage. And though he sorted about indecisively among various meanings of the term, and never made up his mind about the components of the analogy of the earthly husband-wife relationship with the metaphorical Christ-Church marriage, he fixed in the Western Catholic mind the assumption that when a marriage of two Christians stands beyond all power and authority to dissolve it, it is there because of its *sacramentum*. It was for the theologians and, in a degree perhaps surprising to us today, for the canonists too of later centuries to explain more carefully the nature of this *sacramentum*.

NOTES

1. This is in *Corpus Christianorum, Series Latina,* Vol. 57, *S. Hieronymi Presbyteri Opera,* Turnholti, 1969; *Pars I, Opera Exegetica, 7: Commentariorum in Matthaeum Libri IV.*

2. *Op. cit.,* p. 32, lines 636–643.

3. *Op. cit.,* pp. 165–169, lines 710–820.

4. *Ibid.,* pp. 165–169, lines 710–724.

5. *Ibid.,* lines 725–730.

6. *Ibid.,* p. 166, lines 737–743.

7. *Ibid.,* lines 749–760.

8. *Loc. cit.,* p. 167, lines 761–769.

9. *Ibid.,* lines 775–777.

10. *Ibid.,* lines 777–780.

If I have more than hinted that Jerome's commentary on these texts of Matthew is unsatisfactory, I only echo his own appraisal of his work here. He dictated the entire commentary at the request of his friend Eusebius, who was about to leave Palestine for Rome and wanted to read it as refreshment for his soul during the sea voyage. Jerome completed the dictating in less than two weeks during March of 398. He warned Eusebius that he had dictated it so rapidly that when he, Eusebius, read it, he would think it rather something done by a stranger than by his friend Jerome. (In *op. cit., Praefatio,* p. V.)

11. In P.L., Vol. 22, Cols. 560–565.

12. *Loc. cit.,* Cols. 562–563.

13. The letter is in P.L., Vol. 22, Cols. 690–698.

14. *Adversus Jovinianum,* in P. L., Vol. 23, Book I in Cols. 211–282, Book II in Cols. 281–338.

15. *Loc. cit.,* Cols. 219–220.

16. In *Corpus Christianorum, Series Latina,* Vol. 35: *Aurelii Augustini Opera, Pars VII, 2: De Sermone Domini in Monte,* Turnholti, 1967. Augustine's commentary on Matthew 5:31–32 is on pp. 41–56, lines 893–1215.

17. *Loc. cit.,* lines 893–912.

18. *Loc. cit.,* lines 1081–1084.

Augustine's word for "pagan" is *infidelis*. But translating this as "unfaithful" would create ambiguity in this context.

19. *Ibid.,* lines 1085–1094.
20. *Ibid.,* lines 1107–1133.
21. *Ibid.,* lines 1134–1151.
22. *Ibid.,* lines 1169–1210.
23. *Ibid.,* lines 1211–1215.
24. In P. L., Vol. 42, Cols. 129–172.
25. *Op. cit.,* Col. 133.
26. In P.L., Vol. 40, Cols. 11–100.
27. In P.L., Vol. 40, Cols. 373–396.
28. *Loc. cit.,* Cols. 378–379.
29. *Ibid.*
30. *Ibid.*
31. "Nec tamen nisi in civitate Dei, in monte sancto eius (Psalm. 47:2) talis est causa cum uxore" (*ibid.*).
32. Cols. 385–386.
33. *Loc. cit.,* Col. 385.
34. *Loc. cit.,* Cols. 387–388.
35. *Ibid.*
36. *Ibid.,* Col. 388.
37. *Ibid.*
38. *Ibid.*
39. *Op. cit.,* Cols. 394–395.
40. *Ibid.,* Col. 394.

In this enumeration of the three goods of marriage Augustine supplies a New Testament passage in support of each of them. The good that is the *causa generandi* he finds in 1 Timothy 5:4: "I think it is best for the young widows to marry again and have children." The *fides castitatis* he supports with 1 Corinthians 7:4: "A wife has not authority over her own body, but her husband has it; just as a husband has not authority over his own body, but his wife has it." The *sanctitas sacramenti* he supports from the same place: "A wife is not to be divorced from her husband." One presumes that Augustine uses these passages as illustrations, not as sources of knowledge, since the first says nothing about the nature of marriage, the second is about marital rights, not about moral virtue, and the third contains no hint of *sacramentum,* but is more likely a conclusion Paul derived from his hearing of the same tradition that was soon to produce the Synoptic divorce texts.

41. *Ibid.*
42. *Liber Primus* of the Commentary is in P.L., Vol. 34, Cols. 245–598.
43. *Ibid.,* Col. 397.
44. In P.L., Vol. 40, Cols. 197–232.
45. *Loc. cit.,* Col. 197.
46. *Ibid.,* Col. 198.
47. *Loc. cit.,* Col. 203.
48. *Ibid.*
49. The essays are in P.L., Vol. 35, Cols. 1379–1976. *Tractatus 9* is in Cols. 1458–1459.
50. *Ibid.,* Col. 1458.
51. *Ibid.,* Col. 1459.
52. Book I is in P.L., Vol. 44, Cols. 413–437; Book II in Cols. 438–474.

53. *Op. cit.,* Book I, Chapter 10, Col. 420.
54. *Ibid.*
55. *Ibid.*
56. *Ibid.*
57. *Loc. cit.,* Col. 427.
58. It is in P.L., Vol. 40; Book I in Cols. 451–470, Book II in Cols. 471–486.
59. *Loc. cit.,* Cols. 451–453.
60. *Ibid.,* Col. 453.
61. *Ibid.,* Cols. 454–455.

In translating Augustine's Latin one must deal with the meaning of the crucial verb he uses to designate the spouse's departure. It is *discedere.* In the cultural context of Augustine's society it at least implied dissolution of the marriage. But inferring from his clear judgment that even after a Christian spouse's *discessus* the bond of his or her first marriage is not dissolved, and that an attempted remarriage is adultery, we can say safely that by *discedere* Augustine means no more than a separation from bed and board.

62. *Ibid.,* Cols. 455–456.
63. *Ibid.*
64. *Op. cit.,* Col. 473.

10. FROM AUGUSTINE
TO THE CANONISTS
OF THE TWELFTH CENTURY

Some modern Catholic authors have explained the history of divorce and remarriage in the Church during the seven centuries from Augustine until Gratian and the other twelfth-century canonists as a protracted and disobedient refusal by newly converted barbarian peoples, and their ethnic bishops meeting in isolated regional councils, to accept the orthodox doctrine worked out by Augustine and the single, unambiguous discipline promulgated by the Popes of these centuries.[1]

What is accurate in this interpretation is that across the expanse of continental Europe, and across the span of these seven centuries, bishops—and sometimes their lay colleagues with them—met and published canons and decrees on divorce and remarriage that formed a mosaic of inconsistency and disagreement. But to ascribe this to recalcitrant refusal to accept orthodoxy emanating from a single and central authority is not accurate. For one thing, even if we understand the papacy during these centuries to have functioned as a central authority, it sent indecisive messages to the bishops and synods in the provinces, as we shall see. And in the two preceding chapters we have already seen copious evidence that when the provincial bishops turned to the written authorities on divorce and remarriage, to the Fathers and the teachers of the first four centuries, they found among them even more thorough disagreement.

How could it have been otherwise? For when the earlier authorities to whom the regional synods looked for guidance had themselves turned to their guiding sources, the New Testament traditions, they found there the disagreement and indecision we have already examined. I think we shall see in this chapter that where a synod of bishops or a Pope or an influential canonist-scholar enunciates a single, unambiguous judgment on the permissibility or even the possibility of divorce and subsequent remarriage, this is because that authority chooses Luke's and Mark's version of Christ's instruction in preference to Matthew's, or Paul's in preference to these Synoptics', or even Augustine's patchwork interpretation of the Synoptics and of Paul as a kind of single source, along with his barely-ventured theology of the sacrament. And rarely if ever is the reason for choosing one authority in preference to his equals other than that the one rather than his equals is needed as the more effective instrument of reform.

During the centuries from Augustine onward there were other obstacles to the forming of a single doctrine and discipline of divorce than this unclarity in the sources. One of these must be mentioned briefly if only because it is almost universally overlooked. Unitary doctrine has ordinarily been the product of theological crises met and resolved by keen and active intellects. But after Augustine in Europe and North Africa the political and social peace usually needed for theologizing was torn up in the West, and later in the East as well. Where the local churches confronted invading tribes—for example the Vandals in North Africa, the Huns in northern Italy—their task was that of surviving at all. Where they confronted indigenous and relatively peaceful tribes—the Franks, the Allemands, the Saxons—their task was one of instruction, conversion and civilizing. None of these projects is the incubator of theology.

Moreover, the period of the great heresies, whose resolution produced the Trinitarian and Christological theologies and the theology of original sin, justification and grace that have lasted in the traditional churches to our own day, had come to an end. With the great doctrinal challenges gone, gone too was the stimulus needed to awaken potentially great minds. Whatever else it was, the disagreement about divorce and remarriage was perceived as far more a disciplinary challenge. As a doctrinal question it had to wait for its doctrinal resolution until the appropriation of an agreed exegesis of the New Testament divorce passages. Jerome and Augustine notwithstanding, that agreement never arrived. We shall see later that the disciplinary settling of the issue in the end simply forged an exegetical answer as a needed instrument.

During the same century after the death of Augustine in 430, the century during which the splintering of thought and practice accelerated in the West, unity was being achieved in the Eastern Church. Somewhat ironically the cause of this was an earlier version of the much later cause of unity in the West, a powerful central authority. But in the East the authority was not that of the Bishop of Rome, but of the emperors, most notably of Theodosius II in the fifth century and of Justinian in the sixth, as we have seen. And their elected interpretation of the New Testament passages fixed as a principle the assumption that Matthew's is the most authentic, that its exceptive clause comes from Christ himself; and that this at least implies that dismissal of a wife for her adultery dissolves the marriage and frees the husband to marry again.

Political and social history in the West ran an opposite course. The Western Roman empire crumbled and disappeared during the two centuries following Augustine's death, and with it vanished any possibility of a single, central and effective ecclesiastical government. As I have already hinted, regionalism became the form of ecclesiastical life in the West. Unlike their counterparts in the Eastern empire and Church, who lived under a series of powerful theocratic emperors, the Christians in the West were governed by local synods and regional councils of bishops. We know, with the benefit of hindsight, that a single and universal discipline for divorce and remarriage was not to find success in the West until a jurisdiction powerful enough to impose it came to power.

A peculiar interval of legal division and identity following the barbarian invasions and the crumbling of Roman authority made the installing of a single divorce discipline in Europe especially difficult. After the Teutonic invasions of the fifth and sixth centuries, that law in the newly formed kingdoms that bound a person was the law proper to his race. Thus a double jurisdiction grew up. Men and women belonging to the old, indigenous Roman population lived under Roman law. The barbarian invaders lived under their own laws. In some cases the new non-Roman rulers promulgated two laws, one for their own "new people," the other for the Romans. For example there were the Roman Law of the Visigoths (*Lex romana Visigothorum*) and the Barbarian Law of the Visigoths (*Lex barbara Visigothorum*), the Roman Law of the Burgundians and the Barbarian Law of the Burgundians.

These companionate systems of law were installed after the conversion of the barbarian tribes to Christianity. And divorce was easily available under both systems. Those under the Roman system ruled their marrying and divorcing by the Theodosian Code and Justinian's emendation of it.

Among the Germanic tribes divorce was designed to fit their conception of marriage. The latter regarded marriage as a transfer of the woman (of her *mundium*) from the authority of her father to that of her husband. By this transfer the latter gained absolute authority over her. For her adultery he could kill her or have her killed. He could dismiss her without naming the grounds for doing so provided he paid to her family a compensatory fine. Among these tribes the Burgundian code, the *Lex Gundalati* of c. 517, allowed a husband to dismiss his wife without compensation if he could prove against her adultery, poisoning or the violation of sepulchres. The *Pactus Alamanorum* of c. 600 acknowledged divorce by mutual consent. But among the Germanic tribes a wife had generally no right to divorce. The same *Lex Gundalati* prescribed that a wife who tried to dismiss or abandon her husband could be executed by drowning.

Chindaswind, in the *Lex barbara Visigothorum,* allowed a wife to divorce her husband because of unnatural vice on his part or in reprisal for his trying to force her into adultery. This was his ruling of c. 650, a half-century after the conversion of the Visigoths to Christianity.

Among the Lombards a husband who tried to kill his wife forfeited authority (his *mundium*) over her and she could divorce him. The consequences were the same if he accused her falsely of witchcraft or permitted another man to do violence to her. And according to a statute of the year 688 a wife's parents could reclaim *mundium* over her, and she could divorce her husband, if he kept a concubine in their house.

The Anglo-Saxons practiced divorce at the time of their conversion in the sixth century, and there is no evidence that the conversion ended a practice so rooted in their tradition. Among the laws of King Ethelbert (560–616) Article 79 allowed a woman who wished to abandon the marriage and take her children with her to have half her husband's property to support them. But Article 80 stipulated that if the husband kept the children, the departing wife was to have a portion of his property equivalent to one child's inheritance.

The form of divorce common to these non-Roman traditions in which the wife was considered the husband's possession was that of dismissal. But by the seventh and eighth centuries the Franks and Visigoths, in the *Pactus Alamannorum,* gave the wife a measure of equality by acknowledging divorce by mutual consent for those couples in their territories who lived under Roman law. And by this time these tribes become kingdoms had been Christian for three and four centuries. It is striking that the paragraph of the *Formula* (Book 2, Paragraph 30) authorizing this divorce names as the warranting cause for it the spouses' inability to heal the discord grown up between them and to return to peace. After dissolving their marriage they could either enter monastic life or remarry.[2]

It is understandable that divorce practices rooted so deeply in ancient tradition and law—and newly supported by Roman codification in the fifth and sixth centuries—would be ended neither soon nor easily. A powerful central authority would be needed to even begin to change them. Charlemagne created this jurisdiction at the end of the eighth century and the beginning of the ninth, but its success was limited and brief. Such a jurisdiction was not to be created until a series of powerful Popes did it three centuries later.

Two other agencies would also have to become effective. For one, a dominant jurisprudence would have to build up and be made the ruling jurisprudence of the Western Church by the central authority just mentioned. It was to be a jurisprudence formed of an application of the Roman tradition on marriage and its indissolubility applied in resolution of conflicts among the early medieval nobility, most of them Frankish and Germanic. Hincmar of Rheims in the ninth century, Yves of Chartres in the eleventh, and Gratian and Alexander III (Rolando Bandinelli) in the twelfth were to be the most influential of these jurists.

The other agency was to be a theological doctrine concluding that the marriages at least of Christians cannot be dissolved, and providing a religious logic leading to this conclusion. Augustine sowed the seeds of this theology in those of his essays we have just examined. But these were to lie dormant until the essays began to be read in the schools of the West thanks to the work of the early medieval monk-copyists, and until the marriage of Greek-Arabic metaphysics with the pertinent passages from the Scriptures and the Fathers could bring an authentic theology to birth in the thirteenth century.

Part I: From Augustine to the Carolingian Reform

There is an evident advantage in dividing this examination of the seven centuries from Augustine until the twelfth-century canonists into two periods, the first of them comprising the three and a half centuries until the Carolingian reform. The examination of this first period will in turn be divided topically into an inspection of the canons and decrees of councils held in various regions of Europe, interspersed by the few statements of the period coming from the Popes, and then an examination of the divorce discipline enshrined in the widely popular penitential manuals.

It is significant that the first in sequence of these regional councils came in the end to be the most far-reaching in influence because the substance of its severe ruling on divorce and remarriage is the one finally adopted in the Western Church. It came to be quoted by later councils and ecclesiastical writers as a model and an ancient authority. This was the Eleventh Council of Carthage, held in June of 407 as one of a series of synods of the North African churches that began in 393 under the presidency of Aurelius, bishop of Carthage.[3] Although no mention is made of his presence, Augustine must have attended as bishop of Hippo. Certainly the council's ruling on divorce and remarriage reflects his mind. This is concentrated in its Canon 8.[4]

> We decree that according to the evangelic and apostolic discipline neither a husband dismissed by his wife, nor a wife dismissed by her husband may marry another; but that they are to remain as they are or to be reconciled to one another. If they despise [this law] they are to be subjected to penance. And on this subject an imperial law ought to be promulgated.

The first clause of the canon refers in sequence to the Synoptic instruction (the evangelic discipline) and then to the Pauline (the apostolic discipline). Here there is an adaptation of meaning, since neither instruction mentions a wife's dismissing her husband.

The canon takes no notice of the Matthean exceptive clause. That it does not will later be taken as evidence of the absoluteness of the canon's prohibition of true dissolution and subsequent remarriage. There is, of course, no explanation offered for the omission despite the clause's belonging to the "evangelic discipline" in that one of the four Gospels that Augustine himself considered the earliest authored and the source itself of

Mark. The bishops' expressed desire to have imperial legislation embody this canon's discipline is evidence that they wanted the incumbent legislation (still pre-Theodosian) to be replaced.

The consequence that the canon names for those who disobey it is a prolongation of the unclarity we became used to in the earlier canons and in the writings of the Fathers. Perhaps it is too much from the viewpoint of the twentieth century to expect fifth-century bishops to have pronounced clearly and unambiguously on the possibility itself of dissolving a marriage and then of creating a second marriage. Their concern was rather with the permissibility of doing either. So they do not declare on this possibility. They say rather what spouses *must not* do, i.e., dismiss one another. Then they say what they *must* do if disobedient on that first count, i.e., they must either remain celibate or must be reconciled to one another. And finally they say in the canon what spouses must do if disobedient on this second count as well. They must do penance.

The bishops do not, in the canon, say that a marriage is not dissolved by the dismissal they have in mind. Nor do they say that second marriages after such dismissal are null and void; and consequently they do not say also that they are null and void because, despite the dismissal, the spouses are still married to one another. (And on our part, if we see this early writing of law to be crippled because it fails to rule in a matter so clear to our minds that are attuned to validity and invalidity in divorcing and remarrying, we must get used to it.)

A regional council of Frankish bishops met in Angers (France) in October 453 under the presidency of Thalacius, bishop of that city. Its Canon 6 ruled as follows:

> Those who under the name of marriage abuse the wives of other men while the latter are still alive are to be barred from communion.[5]

The abusing in question is almost certainly the men's taking as wives women who had been dismissed by their husbands or who had abandoned their husbands. In any case, public opinion formed according to both Roman and Frankish law held second unions after both dismissal and abandonment to be marriages. The canon implies that they are not, as long as the husbands of the first unions are still alive, in ruling that the men in the second unions (although not the women) are excommunicated.

But again exactness is wanting. The canon could have said that the attempted second unions are null and void. It does not, but only veers close to this by saying that they have "the name of marriage."

Between 450 and 460 Patrick and his suffragan bishops of Ireland met in two synods. The first of these, in 456, published two canons on divorce and remarriage.[6] Canon 19 ruled: "A Christian woman who, after accepting a man in honorable marriage, later departs from her first husband and joins herself in adultery [to another] is to be excommunicated." And Canon 22: "If anyone gives his daughter in honorable marriage, but she comes to love another man, and he gives consent to his daughter and accepts the [second man's] dowry, for this both are to be excommunicated."

Canon 19 looks expressly to a limited instance, that of a woman abandoning her husband and going to another man. It calls this second joining an adultery (presumably because the woman is still married to the first man), and for it the woman is excommunicated. But Canon 22 leaves ambiguity: Why is the second union in this case envisioned here not also called adultery? It may be that the marriage contract in question is not completed, but has got no further than betrothal. If this is so, the excommunication is punishment for the violation of betrothal. In any case the canon is formulated with less than the needed exactness.

Whatever the severity of these two canons, it was mitigated in two others coming from the Second Synod of St. Patrick (whose date within the same decade is uncertain). In these canons the Irish bishops addressed the case, already so commonly disputed in the churches of Mediterranean Europe, of the husband whose wife has committed adultery. In their Canon 26 they ruled as follows:

> It is unlawful for a man to dismiss his wife except for her fornication—and if he says it is for that reason. Hence if he marries another, as if after the death of the first, it should not be forbidden.

And Canon 28:

> First vows and first marriages are to be observed in the same way, that the first not be made void for the second unless they have been stained with adultery.[7]

Both canons presume the authenticity and effectiveness of the Matthean exceptive clause, and understand it to permit a man's dismissing his wife for her adultery, and then his remarrying. And these canons have a special significance coming from the fact that the Irish churches had not been Romanized, but were still Celtic in Patrick's time. Hence the canons do not embody a confrontation of New Testament traditions with Roman custom and law concerning divorce. They are rather a Celtic confrontation with the New Testament traditions, and are withal predictably uncertain about how to accept them with and despite the discordances. Just as predictably the synod's simple and unnuanced reading of the traditions results in a concern only for the conduct of a husband having an adulterous wife. The bishops show no concern for a wife with an adulterous husband.

Pope Leo I

The most significant declaration on dissolution and remarriage coming from a Pope in the fifth century is from Leo I. Attila the Hun's invasion of northern Italy in 452 was a disaster for the Roman army. Its defeat led to captivity for thousands of its officers and men. Some later returned from captivity; some did not. But in either case the bishops of the devastated north were faced with decisions about the painful situation of the wives of the captured soldiers. Could those whose husbands had simply disappeared without verification of death remarry? And what were those wives to do who after remarrying found their husbands returning from captivity?

Bishop Nicetas of Aquileia referred the second of these questions to Leo. The latter wrote in reply that the second unions must be ended, but since the wives had acted in good faith, they were not to be punished. However those who remained with their new consorts and refused to return to their husbands were to be excommunicated.[8]

This reply of course answers a question simply different from that posed by a spouse's infidelity or desertion. But what it does is to rule that mere indeterminate and involuntary absence of a spouse does not of itself dissolve a marriage. However Leo answered the easier of the two questions posed by the husbands' absence in captivity. On the record he said nothing to help wives whose husbands did not return but whose deaths were never verified.

The Councils of Vannes and Agde

An assembly of Frankish bishops titled the Council of Vannes met at Tours in 465 under the presidency of Bishop Perpetuus, with its principal intent to end the abuse that had angered both Jerome and Augustine fifty years earlier and helped to fix them in their judgment on divorce and remarriage. The abusive practice saw Christian husbands, with little or no evidence to sustain the charge, accuse their wives of adultery in order to dismiss them and remarry, or, even worse, force them into adultery for the same purpose.

The council's Canon 2 set a severe penalty for this fraudulence:

> Those also who have abandoned their wives [*relictis uxoribus suis*], except for the cause of fornication, as the Gospel says, and without proof of their adultery have married others, we decree are excommunicated, lest their sins overlooked through our indulgence entice others to the license of error.[9]

If we take the canon as it is written, it says that excommunication awaits a husband who dismisses his wife and remarries her only if he has failed to prove adultery against her. It seems then to imply that the husband who does prove it will not be thus punished for dismissing his wife and remarrying. The council's interpretation and use of the Matthean clause here is obvious.

Forty-one years later, in 506, another regional council of Frankish bishops, held at Agde in Narbonne, attacked the same abuse by threatening the same penalty of excommunication. But it refined the demands on the husband who accused his wife of adultery and sought to dismiss her. In its Canon 25 the council ruled that a man was not to separate from his wife without the consent of his bishop and not before her condemnation by the civil judges on some serious charge (whose nature the canon does not specify). The canon's awkward formulation is the following:

> Those laymen who with grave fault dare to abandon the marital union or have even done so, and in order to take up an illicit or adulterous union desert their marriages without alleging a cause therefor in a fitting manner, if they do this before alleging the cause of their departure before the bishops of their province, and dismiss their wives before these have been condemned by judicial sentence—they are to be excluded from communion in the Church and from the holy company of the people because they defile their trust and their marriages.[10]

Again the nettlesome exceptive clause seems to have a decisive place in this ruling even though it is not cited. The punishment threatened for husbands who dismiss their wives is contingent on their doing so without formal allegation of a justifying cause before ecclesiastical and civil authorities. But what if they should charge their wives with adultery and prove it against them? As the canon is written the husbands would at least escape the punishment it sets.

Pope Gregory I

In order to block yet another fraudulent tactic used by Christian husbands to get rid of unwanted wives Pope Gregory I (590–603) ruled that forcing these wives into monastic life in order to gain the wanted dissolution in virtue of the monastic vows is against the law of God. The husbands in these cases took advantage of a reverse interpretation of Roman civil law, for in his Novel 22, Paragraph 5, Justinian had ruled that if one spouse wished to enter monastic life and did so even against the will of the other, their marriage was dissolved by this entry. These husbands sought to exploit the seeming principle allowing one spouse's will to override the other's.

Gregory set forth his ruling in three of his letters, and most clearly in his Letter 45, *Ad Theoctistam* (the sister of Emperor Mauritius). He went to the root of the matter and denied that the entry of a spouse into monastic life dissolves a marriage in any case. Civil law may allow this but divine law forbids it. Those who defend the practice are un-Christian.[11]

But then in his Letter 50 to Adrianus, the notary of Panormae, he returned to a real-life instance of a husband's using the Justinian law in order to end his marriage, and about it passed an ambiguous judgment.[12] A Christian wife, Agathosa, represented to him that against her will her husband had left her in order to take the vows of monastic life. Gregory's immediate response was to order an examination of the facts of the case. At the same time he ruled that if the woman had committed no serious fault in the marriage justifying her husband's departure, he was to return to her even if he had already taken the monastic tonsure. The reason for this ruling: "For although human law rules that a marriage can be dissolved by one spouse's going into religious life [*conversionis gratia*] even against the other's will, the divine law forbids this."[13]

At this the letter stops—disappointingly. Gregory does not say if religious vows taken by one spouse *with* the approval of the other dissolves the marriage. Nor does he say in this, Agathosa's case, what would be his judgment if the examination of the facts were to verify serious fault in her. We do not find out if he would rule her marriage dissolved by her husband's departure even against her will.

The Council of Hertford

Under the presidency of the archbishop of Canterbury, Theodore of Tarsus, an assembly of English bishops met at Hertford in 673 to legislate on moral matters for the Christians of their country. Their Canon 10 was intended to regulate conduct regarding marriage, and is yet another example of the carelessly written law of the time.

> Regarding marriages: no one is to have any but a legally recognized marriage [*legitimum connubium*]. No one is to commit incest. No one is to abandon his own spouse unless, as the holy Gospel teaches, he does so because of fornication. But if anyone dismisses a spouse joined to him legitimately in marriage, if he wishes truly to be a Christian he is to be united to no one else but is either to remain as he is or to be reconciled with his own spouse.[14]

The canon uses two verbs to designate what is forbidden in the matter of divorce. These are "to abandon" (*relinquere*) and "to dismiss" (*expellere*). To do either is forbidden except in the case of *fornicatio*. The implication then is that this sin justifies doing both. But nothing is said about the consequences of doing either if not justified by *fornicatio*. The canon simply forbids doing either to an innocent spouse.

Then it turns to the consequences of dismissing a spouse generally. If one does this yet wishes to be truly a Christian (*si Christianus esse recte voluerit*), he must not take another consort but must take one of the two options Paul proposed in 1 Corinthians 7:11, either to remain celibate or to return to the spouse. But if one does not truly wish to be a Christian, may he then take another spouse? Or even if he does wish truly to be a Christian, but takes a second spouse notwithstanding, does he truly create a second marriage albeit disobediently? The canon says nothing about these issues it could not help raising, however unwittingly.

The Twelfth Council of Toledo

The same vague writing appears in a decree of the Twelfth Council of Toledo convened in 681 under the presidency of Archbishop Julian of that city.

> It is the command of the Lord that a wife must not be dismissed by her husband except because of fornication. There-fore whoever goes beyond the guilt of this crime and leaves his wife for just any reason . . . is to be deprived of ecclesiastical communion and excluded from the community of Christians until such time that he returns to the society of the wife he abandoned.[15]

The canon is an obvious attempt to apply the Synoptic tradition to the divorcing and remarrying of Christians in these Spanish bishops' terri-tories. They choose the Matthean version of this tradition and rule as a consequence that only a wife's *fornicatio* justifies her husband's dismissing her. If a husband dismisses her, according to the ancient Hillel jurispru-dence, "for just any reason," he is to be excommunicated until he takes her back. The canon says nothing about the consequences to the husband of dismissing his wife for her *fornicatio,* leaving the impression that these bishops thought there were none, or that there was at least not the consequence that the husband must accept either of the Pauline alterna-tives of celibacy or reconciliation.

Pope Gregory II

When Pope Gregory II sent his legates to Bavaria in 716 to help the local bishops restore religious discipline, he sent with them a letter of instruction that contained the following:

> This, then, the Apostle said: "You are bound to a wife? Do not seek to be loosed. As long as your wife lives, do not seek to pass over to carnal relations with another woman."[16]

Within this careless quoting of 1 Corinthians 7:27 the instruction is simple and absolute. It recognizes no exceptions to the permanence of at least a Christian marriage. But that this was not Gregory's doctrinal stance is evident in his letter of November 22, 726 to Boniface, apostle of the Saxons, written to answer his question asking what a husband ought to do if his wife can no longer have intercourse with him because of some permanently disabling illness. Gregory's reply, in his *Epistola 3,* plainly though reluctantly approves of remarriage for the husband in these straits.

> It would be good if he could remain as he is and live a life of continence. But this requires great virtue. So if he cannot live chastely, it is better that he remarry. But let him not cease to support her [his first and incapacitated wife].[17]

Again like so many authoritative instructions of the time, Gregory's letter fails to address other crucial issues raised by the problem that inspired the letter to begin with. What, for instance, of this husband's relationship with his first wife? In order to marry the second woman may he dissolve the first marriage by dismissing the incapacitated wife whom he must nevertheless continue to support? Or does Gregory here imply the permissibility of bigamy by saying nothing about the dissolving of the first marriage? In any case he clearly allows the second marriage.

The Council of Soissons and Pope Zachary

Twenty-three Frankish bishops gathered at the Council of Soissons in 744, invited by Pepin the Short to work at reforming the morals of his kingdom. The bishops decreed that no husband or wife was to remarry while the other still lived, " . . . because a husband must not dismiss his wife except for her being apprehended in adultery."[18]

Because this decree was inconclusive about a husband's dismissing his wife and remarrying in the event he did apprehend her in adultery, Pepin wrote to Pope Zachary asking for a judgment in this and in related matters of discipline. On January 5, 747 Zachary addressed a letter of reply to Pepin himself, the mayor of the royal palace, to the Frankish bishops and to the abbots and nobles of the realm. The substance of his answer was to simply cite Canon 8 of the Eleventh Council of Carthage of three centuries earlier (along with Number 47 of the Apostolic Canons).[19] We recall the wording from Carthage.

> We decree that, according to the evangelic and apostolic discipline, neither a husband dismissed by his wife nor a wife dismissed by her husband may marry another; but that they are to remain as they are, or to be reconciled to one another. If they despise [this law], they are to be subjected to penance. . . .[20]

If Zachary had omitted the last clause from the canon he would perhaps have conveyed to the Franks his judgment that no cause justifies the dismissal of a spouse that is a true dissolution of the marriage. But, as with Carthage itself, since the stated consequence of dismissing is (only) that the spouse who does this must complete an assigned penance, the question at the heart of the matter remains unanswered: Even if no cause for dismissal is justifying, does the dismissal nevertheless dissolve the marriage?

The Council of Verberies

Nine years later, in 753, the Frankish bishops legislated in the Council of Verberies (Vernon-sur-Seine) with apparent unconcern for what Pope Zachary had written in reply to Pepin. Typically in an age when civil and ecclesiastical jurisdictions enjoyed only blurred boundaries or were thought of as twin manifestations of a single authority, the members of the council included not only the bishops but laymen as well, and its decisions had the force of royal capitularies. These were later included in the many collections of the Frankish church.

The council ruled, in its Canons 2, 10, 11 and 18, that a marriage must be dissolved when it is violated by a certain kind of adulterous incest. The innocent party may remarry, but the guilty party never. Canon 5 ruled that if a wife conspired against her husband's life, he could divorce her and remarry, but she could not. Canon 9 ruled that if a husband were forced to leave his country but his wife refused to accompany or follow him, if he could not live a life of continence apart from her he could take another wife after doing an appropriate penance. But the council ruled in its Canon 21 that if a husband permitted his wife to take the vows of monastic life, he could not remarry.[21]

The Council of Compiègne

How divergent the canonical rulings on marriage could be from council to council in these centuries becomes evident if we compare the canons legislated at Verberies with those of another council of Frankish bishops that met at Compiègne three years later, in 756. With them met two legates sent by Pope Stephen III, George of Ostia and John Sacellarius, who apparently approved the council's legislation. From their inclusion in later collections of regional canons by Benedict the Levite, by Regino of Prümm and by Burchard of Worms, it is evident that these canons of Verberies and Compiègne were considered authoritative in and by the Frankish church.

Canon 9 of Compiègne ruled that in the event a vassal followed his lord to a new fief, but then this first lord died and a new lord gave him a wife, and the vassal later returned to the household of his first and now deceased lord and took a second wife, the latter marriage was to remain intact.

Canon 11 ruled that if a wife committed incest with her brother-in-law, her husband must separate from her, and with the right to remarry.

Canon 15 ruled that separation was obligatory if the husband contracted spiritual affinity with his wife by acting as godparent to his stepchild at its confirmation. In this case neither the husband nor the wife could remarry.

Canon 16 ruled that if one spouse permitted the other to pronounce the vows of monastic life, he or she could remarry.

Canon 19 ruled that if one spouse contracted leprosy, the marriage could be dissolved by mutual consent, with remarriage permitted to the healthy spouse.

Canon 21 ruled that compulsory flight from one's country did not give the right to remarry.[22]

The Synod of Aachen

Still the back-and-forth went on as the eighth century ran to its close. The Synod of Aachen met in Charlemagne's palace in 789.[23] About the possibility of remarriage after dissolution of a marriage by one of the spouse's dismissing the other it did nothing more than to quote Canon 8 of the Eleventh Council of Carthage (but thereby added jurisprudential strength to this severe though inconclusive canon of three and a half centuries earlier).

The Council of Friuli

The Council of Friuli met in northeast Italy under the presidency of Paulinus of Aquileia in 791. It was the first synod in Catholic history to rule explicitly, in its Canon 10, that despite the wife's dismissal on the ground of adultery, the marriage remains in existence and remarriage is therefore forbidden. How the bishops of the council came to this determination is evident in the means they used to resolve their doubt about the interpretation of the Matthean exceptive clause, the words that for seven centuries had served as the warrant for the practice they finally interdicted. They went to the then acknowledged master of New Testament interpretation, Jerome, explaining,

> We ordered that the book of commentaries of that most expert and blessed man, Jerome, be inspected carefully, hurrying eagerly to find out how this most renowned teacher would use his subtle genius to clarify the meaning of these sacred words of the Lord.[24]

The bishops found Jerome saying, in his Commentary on Matthew, Chapter 19, that Jesus meant that the husband of an adulterous wife could do no more than dismiss her; he could not remarry after dismissing her. And the reason he could not was that the possibility of remarriage would open the way generally to husbands' slandering faithful wives, or even to their forcing them into adultery. The bishops of Friuli apparently found no difficulty in using Jerome's reason of pastoral prudence to resolve what was at heart a question of Christian doctrine.

The Penitential Manuals

In their efforts to install an effective rigorous discipline of divorce and remarriage the European bishops met no counterforce more intractable than the habitual use by priest confessors of the later penitential manuals. These were literally handbooks for confessors to guide them in assigning to their confessants penitential acts fitted to the sins they confessed. Their significant place in the Western Catholic history of divorce and remarriage is that for the sin of dismissing or abandoning a spouse the most influential of the manuals assigned severe penitential acts, but did not demand separation from the new spouse and return to the abandoned or dismissed spouse. In effect they acknowledged the possibility of dissolving marriage by divorce and then remarrying, much as they punished the realizing of this possibility.

A background sketch of the origin of these manuals will help in understanding the spread of their use and influence in Europe from the sixth century through about the eleventh. The manuals embodied the second in sequence of the traditional penitential practices in the Western Church. The first dated from as early as the third century, was in vigor through the fourth, declined in the fifth, and had virtually vanished by the middle of the sixth century. Its decline and fall were both the occasion and in part the effect of the discipline of the manuals.

According to the first penitential discipline a Christian who, having sinned, subsequently sought forgiveness that included reconciliation with the Christian community, must confess his sins publicly, to and before the community with the bishop at its head. The immediate sequel to this public confession was not that the confessant received absolution from his or her sins and reintegration with the community, but had imposed on him or her publicly a penitential conduct that must be carried out publicly. As this discipline developed and became systematized, four stages of progress through the penitential conduct were established. The first was that of "the weepers" (*synkláiontes*), whose place during public worship was at the church door. The second was that of "the hearers" (*akouómenoi*), who worshiped from the church vestibule but were dismissed from the Eucharist after the lesson and homily. The third were "the kneelers" (*hypopiptóntes*), who could join the congregation for all of the Eucharist but who must remain at the rear of the church and must kneel when the others stood. The fourth and last were "the co-standers" (*synistámenoi*), who could mingle with the eucharistic congregation but could not receive the consecrated bread and wine.

These stages were not themselves the penitential conduct. This conduct could vary from the lenient (prayers to be recited) to the truly severe (fasting on bread and water for years; exile; enforced sleeplessness in prayerful night vigil; for the married the denial of sexual intercourse). And withal there was the public humiliation consequent on the revelation, through the public confession, of sins that were personally disgracing.

In these first centuries four sins were regarded as capital, and rigorists such as Origen, Tertullian and Novatian denied they could be forgiven by the Church's penitential discipline. These were idolatry (participation in pagan cult), apostasy (formal and public rejection of the Christian religion), murder, and adultery. The rigorists who denied that these sins could be forgiven by the penitential discipline generally insisted also that other serious sins could be forgiven by it only once. Recidivists, like apostates, idolaters, murderers and adulterers, must seek private and uncertain forgiveness from God's mercy alone.

But no early teacher insisted that all sins, even the most venial, must find forgiveness through public penitential acts. The confessing of them by itself sufficed to forgive them, according to common opinion.

It is obvious that such a religious practice contains within itself the cause of its own eventual destruction. These causes began to be clearly effective from about the year 400, and they were rendered all the more effective because by then a good half-century had gone by since the citizens of the empire and others had begun flooding into the Church for reasons of political or economic advantage, or both. Such fainthearted conversion did not lead zealously to and through the rigors of the incumbent penitential discipline.

One pair of historians has discerned the following proximate causes of the demise of this discipline.[25] First and most predictably (as I have said) the anguish of public humiliation and protracted austerity was too much for most Christians to bear. Analogously with Augustine's protracting his catechumenate and putting off baptism until sexual passion would lose its imperious hold on him, many Christians put off repentance and the required penitential discipline until old age, when compassion would acknowledge their feebleness and lessen the rigor of the discipline.

Some among the bishops cooperated with this cause by mitigating severe penances even for those in the vigor of life. The usual mitigation was to commute the traditional self-castigation to prayers or good works completed privately. It is to be expected that the names of these more lenient pastors would get about and that their ministration of penance would be sought to the neglect of that of others who were more demanding.

Even as a larger and larger portion of the Christian population came to their religious demands with less and less fervor, a seriously disruptive cultural invasion overtook the penitential discipline. Apostasy under torture, or marital infidelity to a spouse vanished in exile, could be understood humanly and forgiven by all but the most rigorous in the established Christian population of the old empire. But the new barbarian Christians—the Franks, the Lombards, the Visigoths, the Teutons—brought with them cultural habits that were truly shocking, which stretched the reconciling capacity of the traditional discipline perhaps beyond its limits. The most flagrant such habit was that of the vendetta, the law of vengeance even to killing in order to redress injury done to one's person or to one's family. Along with this came the accessory crimes of bribery and betrayal, of hypocrisy and deception, and the consequent cruelty to wives and children as the vendetta included them among its victims. In our own day we have seen structures and procedures of law broken by the uncaring cruelty of a population. We should not be surprised that the Christian moral structure, which supposes a responsible care for one's neighbor, would crumble under the cruelty native to the vendetta.

Finally there was a cause quite foreseeable in a civilization and a polity which distinguished only slightly between civil and religious jurisdictions, between civil power and religious. From the end of the second decade of the fifth century, after the Visigoths had taken Rome and pillaged it in 410, Roman civil authority crumbled irretrievably. With it crumbled the public sense of government and the readiness of persons to submit to it. Rejected along with other facets of public authority was the compelling authority of the bishops that brought sinning Christians to the penitential discipline.

The summary effect of all these causes was, as I said above, that by the middle of the sixth century the first of the Church's penitential disciplines had virtually vanished. It was kept alive as an ideal by some bishops; it was kept in practice by almost no one. It was into this religious vacuum that the second tradition of penitential discipline, that which produced the penitential manuals, made its entry.

The Origin and Nature of the Manuals

These handbooks used by priest confessors in guiding repentant Christians in the practice of penance, either as an internal element of sacramental confession or apart from it, were most of them written in Latin, with a few done in the vernacular. The earliest were produced in Welsh and Irish monasteries to guide the monastic confessors and spiritual directors in their imposing of penitential acts on the monks. As for dating the earliest of them, the first that belongs beyond doubt to the category of penitential manuals is ascribed to a series of Welsh synods of the sixth century held under the guidance of St. David. But the earliest book sufficiently comprehensive to serve as a guide for confessors was the Irish Penitential of Finnian dating from before 650.

These manuals were religious instruments produced by the Celtic church, by a Christian people who had never been Romanized and had therefore never experienced the first penitential disciplines belonging to the Western as well as to the Eastern Christian churches. They were the product of a religious fervor led by Irish and Welsh monks, and the earliest of them contained transparent evidence of the extraordinary austerity of which these men were capable. They were Celtic also in that they carried forward within themselves Celtic religious practices that were pre-Christian, such as satisfaction made to the relatives of an injured party, the redemption of assigned penance by money payment, exile as a religious punishment, fasting, and nocturnal singing.

The early monastic manuals, Welsh and Irish, became the progenitors and models for generations of manuals for popular confessors in Ireland, England and the Continent. In general their use moved in sequence from Ireland to the Frankish lands in the sixth century, taken thither by the Irish missionaries to the Franks, then to England in the late seventh century, to Italy in the late eighth century, and finally to the Spanish Visigoths by the beginning of the ninth century.

Ecclesiastical authorities on the Continent, the bishops and the abbots, were generally opposed to the spread of the Celtic manuals and their imitators. They held against them that they came from anonymous foreign sources and could show no sponsorship by recognized authority. There lingered too among the Continental authorities vestiges of their own ancient Roman penitential discipline. Thus local councils here and there sought to suppress the use of the Celtic manuals, in part by trying to revive the old discipline—a move that proved unsuccessful against the new manuals used so conveniently by itinerant as well as parochial confessors. In England no such resistance was raised because the old Roman discipline had never been established there.

Much of the popularity of the new manuals lay in the method of penitential discipline that they offered. Unlike the Roman discipline this was private at every step. Indeed the confessor was bound most seriously to secrecy. Disclosure of a confession was regarded in some places as a sin for which there could be no forgiveness. Confession, instead of made publicly to a church community presided over by its bishop, was made privately to a priest. (Early in the history of the manuals' use confession to a person reputed for holiness, whether priest or not, was an alternative, and this included confession to holy women. St. Brendan confessed in the sixth century to St. Ita of Cluain Credill.)

The confession was made in exact detail, after the manner of a monk rendering an account of conscience to his abbot. The penitential acts following the confession were imposed privately and at least in intent were to be carried out privately. But given the nature of the acts they often simply could not be kept private. Yet in principle this conduct was not, as in the Roman discipline, something done in reference to the community as an apology and reparation to it. Also as a principle this discipline supposed that penitential conduct could be carried out whenever a person sought to repent of his or her sins, whatever their gravity.

The kinds of penitential conduct imposed most commonly were borrowed from the monastic practices. Among these the most common were the recitation of psalms and fasting. There were also deprivation of sleep in nocturnal prayer vigils, praying with the arms extended to form a cross, corporal self-flagellation, and the more severe forms such as demotion from ecclesiastical rank, exile in pilgrimage (sometimes in a foreign monastery), for the married abstinence from sexual intercourse, and slavery to a family to make amends for the murder of one of its members. A system of substitutions for the longer penances grew up, of *arrea* that were thought to compensate for length because of their brief severity. Rigorous fasting was one of these, as were sleeping in water, on nettles or with a corpse.

Another reason for the popularity of the new discipline was that its manuals fulfilled the need of priests for a convenient guide in imposing penitential acts. In a Christian society whose people took universally for granted that the relationship of human beings to God is a forensic one—he both plaintiff and judge, they the guilty accused—it was inevitable that God's vicar in the penitential discipline must function as a judge. And if this vicar lacked in education and intelligence, as he so often did, he needed a handy guide in his work of judicial sentencing. The manuals served as just this guide.

Thus they proliferated, with little control and therefore with much disagreement from manual to manual, and with easy presumption by anonymous authors in claiming the names of renowned churchmen for their titles.

The manuals had necessarily to deal with marriage, and specifically with the question of dissolving marriages and remarrying after the dissolution. The summary evidence they offer testifies to the simultaneous insistence by some authors that divorce and therefore remarriage are impossible; by others that though both are possible, either both are forbidden or at least remarriage is forbidden; and by still others that divorce and remarriage are both possible and permissible for specific serious reasons.

A note on the quality of testimony in these manuals is important. From one point of view this quality is minimally valent as a source and cause of Catholic doctrine and discipline on divorce and remarriage because the manuals were the product of monks, clerics and bishops writing privately and outside the mainstream of the Church's authoritative teaching. The manual having the most authoritative name for its author, that of Theodore, archbishop of Canterbury from 668 to 690, is considered by most scholars a collection of penitential norms done by an anonymous editor who forged the archbishop's name to it. Nevertheless it has this credibility, that Theodore was from the Greek church in Tarsus, St. Paul's birthplace in Silicia, and the manual's permissive attitude toward divorce and remarriage reflects the Greek discipline accurately.

On the other hand these manuals have better than minimal quality as witness because of their wide use in Ireland, Wales, Scotland, England and on the Continent. This acceptance had a mirroring effect. The manuals formed the thinking of confessors and penitents who used them, and this general use reflected the spirit of receptivity of the believing Church. Since in fact the manuals as a collection gave ambiguous and contradictory instructions about the possibility and the permissibility of divorce and remarriage, they helped generously to continue the changing and inconsistent discipline in this domain into the second half-millennium of the Church's history.

The Early Celtic Penitentials

The earliest of the Celtic manuals, those produced by the Irish monks, were severe in forbidding divorce and remarriage, and in this respect were akin to the church in Visigothic Spain. Three examples will suffice to show this severity, the first of them from the Penitential of Finnian dating from c. 525–550.

Finnian of Clonnard was a monk and a founder of monasteries. He wrote a most inclusive penitential, and he claimed at its close that he had written it in accord with the Scriptures and with the opinions of very learned men. With this he implied that he was no innovator, but that what he had done was to codify the practices of penance in his time that he thought most useful. His Penitential has three canons that speak directly and tersely to the matter of divorce and remarriage.

> Canon 42: We declare against separating a wife from her husband; but if she has left him, we declare that she remain unmarried or be reconciled to her husband according to the Apostle.
>
> Canon 43: If a man's wife commits fornication and cohabits with another man, he ought not to take another wife while his wife is still alive.
>
> Canon 45: . . . a woman, if she has been sent away by her husband, must not mate with another man so long as her former husband is in the body; but she should wait for him, unmarried, in all patient chastity, in the hope that God may perchance put patience in the heart of her husband. . . .[26]

Canon 42 is obviously inspired by 1 Corinthians 7:10–11. Finnian does little more than to quote Paul at this point. Canon 43 addresses the matter of a husband's dismissing an adulterous wife, and ignores the Matthean exceptive clause in commanding what the dismissing husband must not do. Finally Canon 45 disposes of the fate of the guilty and dismissed wife. Neither may she remarry. Withal Finnian's is among the clearest and most exact statements coming from the first six Christian centuries.

A manual dating from a century later (c. 650) and attributed to Cummean, bishop of Iona, forbade a husband to divorce his wife because of her sterility, but obliged them to live a life of continence together. It directed too that if a wife left her husband but then sought to return to him, he was to take her back without demanding a new dowry, while she was to do penance for a year.[27] And if in the meantime the husband had taken another wife, he was to dismiss her and likewise do penance for a year. Exempting the penitent wife from the new dowry indicated that despite her absence she was still married to her husband.

The Penitential of Adamnan, abbot of Iona a generation after Cummean, designated a woman a prostitute if she abandoned her husband and remarried. And even if a wife did this, the penitential forbade the husband to remarry as long as she lived. This is in the manual's Canon 16:

> Of a wife who is a harlot [it is said], "She will be a harlot who has cast off the yoke of her own husband, and is joined to a second or third husband; and her husband shall not take another [wife] while she lives . . ."[28]

The Penitential of Theodore

But this Celtic severity began to thaw under the influence of a prelate mentioned above who brought with him from his home in the Eastern Church the more permissive discipline of that Church. This was Theodore of Tarsus, appointed to the archbishopric of Canterbury by Pope Vitalian in 668, a see that he held until his death in 690.

The Penitential of Theodore as it was read and and used in England and later on the Continent was not the work immediately of the archbishop (but there is no doubt that he did compile a manual which served as the source for the Penitential that has survived). What the Penitential itself claims to be is an inventory of answers given to the presbyter Eoda, and after an interval edited by an anonymous scribe who took the pseudonym *Discipulus Umbrensium*. He was possibly a native of Northumbria who had been a disciple of Theodore, or more likely an Englishman of southern birth who studied under the northern scholars.

The Penitential's relevant canons are, first of all, in Book I, Chapter 14:

> Canon 8: He who puts away his wife and marries another shall do penance with tribulation for seven years or a lighter penance for fifteen years.
>
> Canon 13: If the wife of anyone deserts him and returns to him undishonored, she shall do penance for one year; otherwise

for three years. If he takes another wife, he shall do penance for one year.[29]

It is obvious that the manual accepts that a husband's dismissing his wife, or her deserting him, dissolves a marriage. The dismissing is seen as a sin for which penance must be done; so also is the deserting; and so also is the husband's remarrying after being deserted. But nothing is hinted about the second marriage's being void because of the perdurance of the first.

In Book II, Chapter 12, Canon 5 prescribes more in detail for both the husband and the wife in the case where he has dismissed her for her adultery.

> Canon 5: If the wife of anyone commits fornication, he may put her away and take another; that is, if a man puts away his wife on account of fornication, if she was his first, he is permitted to take another; but if she wishes to do penance for her sins, she may take another husband after five years.[30]

Canon 6 makes a conventionally Eastern and literal application of the Matthean Synoptic tradition. And it names the respected Eastern source from which it takes its entire attitude.

> Canon 6: A woman may not put away her husband, even if he is a fornicator, unless perchance for [the purpose of entering] a monastery. Basil has so decided.[31]

Canons 7 and 8 prescribe in the matter of dissolving a marriage by the consent of both spouses. The first of these is not a return to the Roman law that allowed a dissolution *mutuo consensu,* but is a setting of the principle that guides the directive in Canon 8.

> Canon 7: A legal marriage may not be broken without the consent of both parties.
> Canon 8: But either, according to the Greeks, may give the other permission to join a monastery for the service of God, and [as it were] marry it, if he [or she] was in a first marriage; yet this is not canonical. But if such is not the case, [but they are] in a second marriage, this is not permitted while the husband or wife is alive.[32]

Canons 9, 24 and 25 rule in cases in which one spouse is deprived of the other against the former's will. The Penitential permissively allows remarriage; and even where (as in Canon 25) the wife once kidnaped is restored to her husband, he has no obligation to take her back if he has remarried in the meantime. The Penitential has none of the compassion for the returned exile that Pope Leo I showed in his Letter 94 to Bishop Nicetas of Aquileia.

> Canon 9: If a husband makes himself a slave through theft or fornication or any sin, the wife, if she has not been married before, has the right to take another husband after a year. This is not permitted to one who has been twice married.
>
> Canon 24: If an enemy carries away a man's wife, and he cannot get her again, he may take another. To do this is better than acts of fornication.
>
> Canon 25: If after this the former wife comes to him again, she ought not to be received by him if he has another, but she may take to herself another husband, if she has had only one before. The same ruling stands in the case of slaves from over sea.[33]

And Canon 20 returns to the situation addressed earlier in Book I, Chapter 14, Canon 18, that of a husband deserted by his wife. But this canon directs the conduct of a husband whose wife refuses to return to him. He may remarry, with his bishop's consent, after five years. But she, unlike the wife dismissed for her adultery, may not remarry even after doing penance (see Canon 5 above).[34]

The Later Penitential Manuals

The later Penitential of Pseudo-Egbert, along with other Anglo-Saxon manuals, concurred in allowing a husband to take a second wife if his first were kidnaped or taken captive in war, and to remain with the second wife to the exclusion of the first even if the latter were returned to him. The legal principle thought to warrant this was that prisoners become slaves, thus disqualifying them from marriage with a citizen or freedman.

From this point it will be helpful to turn to a topical review of the penitential manuals, to what they prescribed regarding dissolution and remarriage in varied cases in addition to dismissal or desertion. Thus the Penitential of Theodore itself, in Book II, Chapter 12, Canon 12, prescribed that if either husband or wife suffered permanently from a repulsive illness, the other spouse could remarry as long as both consented. This was repeated in the *Capitula Dacheriana,* Chapter 111.[35]

Impotence on the husband's part, according to the Penitential of Theodore, constituted grounds for his wife's divorcing him and remarrying, but only provided she could prove his impotence.

> If a husband or wife are united in marriage, and afterwards the wife says of the husband that she cannot have intercourse with him, if she can prove this is true, she may take another husband.[36]

Not all the penitentials agreed with Theodore in permitting a husband to take a second wife if his first were kidnaped. The Confessional of Pseudo-Egbert disagreed, requiring (in its Canon 26) that the husband take back the once captured but now returned wife. But in agreement were the *Capitula Dacheriana* (Chapter 36)[37] and the Canons of Gregory (Canon 72). The *Iudicium Clementinum,* composed by an anonymous author of c. 700–750, agreed and added that the returned wife too could remarry.[38]

If a wife simply tired of her husband and abandoned him, some manuals (for example the Penitential of Theodore in a canon we have already seen; the Canons of Gregory, Canon 70; the *Capitula Dacheriana,* Chapter 159) permitted her husband to remarry after an interval of two to five years, but only with the permission of his bishop. Other texts, instead of stating explictly the husband's right in such a case, inflicted a light penance on him if he entered a second marriage.[39]

Entrance into monastic life by one of the spouses, according to the Anglo-Saxon Penitentials, provided if done with the other's consent, freed the latter to enter a second marriage (thus too the Penitential of Theodore, Book I, Chapter 14, Canon 7, and Book II, Chapter 12, Canon 8).[40]

While the marriages of Christians with pagans were severely discouraged during these centuries, such marriages did occur and led to the discord about which St. Paul felt obliged to counsel in 1 Corinthians 7. The Confessional of Egbert, in its Canon 17, followed his lead, and it left the question of dissolution just as imprecisely answered as he had left it. It began by addressing the situation of a man and a woman, married as pagans, who separate and then are both baptized.

> If any heathen man puts away a heathen woman who is in his power, after they are baptized it matters not whether he has her or not. If one of them is a heathen, the other baptized, the heathen may leave the baptized, as saith the Apostle, "If the unbeliever departs, let him depart."[41]

The Penitentials of the seventh and eighth centuries generally permitted remarriage for both parties if they had divorced by mutual consent. Ordinarily there was a reason for such a divorce, but there is no evidence that one was required in order to gain the right to remarry. Thus the Penitential of Theodore, Book 2, Chapter 12, Canon 8, and the Canons of Gregory, Canon 84. But the *Iudicium Clementinum* in its Canon 15 set a severe limitation on the use of this divorce: "Legal marriage may not be dissolved unless there is an agreement of both [parties] that they shall remain unmarried."[42]

About dismissal for adultery and subsequent remarriage, we have already seen the permissive Eastern discipline with which Theodore of Canterbury softened the severe Celtic stand. Those who came after him for the most part agreed with him, although there was little agreement about the steps in the path through dissolution and remarriage. Some of the manuals permitted the husband of an adulterous wife to enter a second marriage without any limitation of time after dismissing her, and without penance (thus the *Capitula Dacheriana,* Chapter 163). Others allowed the husband to remarry in such a case only if the wife he was leaving was his first wife (The Confessional of Pseudo-Egbert, Canon 19 and the Canons of Gregory, Canon 82). Adultery on the part of the husband gave no right to the innocent wife to remarry. According to the Penitential of Theodore (as we have seen in its Book 2, Chapter 12, Canon 6), if a wife left an adulterous husband, she had only the recourse of entering monastic life. But inconsistently an adulterous wife abandoned by her husband was allowed by the same manual to remarry after doing penance for five years (Canon 5).[43]

Thus apart from the earliest Celtic manuals there were few in the Church who held to an inflexible denial of the possibility of remarriage after dissolution by dismissal for adultery. One of these was the learned Anglo-Saxon Benedictine monk of the monastery at Jarrow, St. Bede (672–735). In Chapter 10 of his Commentary on Mark he wrote,

> For a wife to be dismissed there is only one carnal cause, and this is fornication; there is only one spiritual cause, and this is the fear of God, as it is read that many have done for religious motives. But there is no cause allowed by the law of God whereby a man may marry another woman while the wife he has deserted is still alive.[44]

Part II: From the Carolingian Reform
Until the Canonists of the Twelfth Century

I have already suggested that nothing effective could be done to reduce this confusion concerning divorce and remarriage until a central authority could assert itself and, armed with a coherent legislation and a reasonable jurisprudence, could simply rule and punish disagreement out of existence. Although the union of these forces—the authority, the legislation and the jurisprudence—was not to be completed for three and a half centuries, it did begin at the end of the eighth century with the coming of Charlemagne to the head of the Frankish kingdom and his crowning, on Christmas Day of 800, as head of the newly invented Holy Roman Empire. He provided the single authority in overpowering measure as he virtually took over the Church from the Lowlands in the north to the border of the newly erected (by himself) papal state in the Italian peninsula.

Charlemagne considered himself a second Constantine. He sincerely thought himself chosen by God to govern the Western Church in companionship with the Pope, whose protector he was anyway both from the recently broken Byzantine power in Italy and from the recently defeated

Lombard nobility in the north of the peninsula. And in his mind, which harbored a naive synthesis of Augustine's City of God, the Church and the Christian state were hardly distinguishable. To strengthen his empire from within he established a centralized juridical system, again indistinguishably both civil and ecclesiastic. In it he personally legislated, among other things, the conduct of bishops and abbots and their monks, public worship, private prayer, doctrinal belief, personal and societal morals, and family relationships—including, of course, marriage. He severely opposed any local-regional legislation, and either suppressed it or superimposed on it his imperial legislation.

He had a divided mind about divorce and remarriage. Personally and in practice he must have approved of both, as his succession of four wives and ten to twelve mistresses attests. So if his mind was touched by his reading of Augustine on divorce and remarriage, it was touched only in its legislative enterprise. Not as a point of principle but apparently as a device for legal control in his empire he adopted a discipline drawn from Roman sources after rejecting that of the permissive Frankish councils we have just reviewed. In 774, six years after he had succeeded his father Pepin on the Frankish throne, he had been sent by Pope Hadrian I a collection of canons on ecclesiastical discipline first formed in the fifth century by Dionysius Exiguus. Because of both the editor of the collection and the giver of it as a gift, this is known as the Dionysio-Hadrian Collection.

Included in this collection was the by then famous Canon 8 of the Eleventh Council of Carthage, which ruled that despite the separation of husband and wife by divorce, neither could remarry while the other lived. In 789 Charlemagne published a capitulary, an official instruction, admonishing the bishops of his realm to see to the better observance of the canons already promulgated. This general admonition was followed by eighty-one *capitula* singling out points of discipline about which the bishops should be especially vigilant. *Capitulum* 43 was worded to reproduce closely the wording of Canon 8 of Carthage: "In the same council [it was decreed] that a woman dismissed by her husband must not take another as long as the first still lives; and the man must not take another wife as long as the first still lives."

But when Charlemagne died in 814, after dividing his empire among his three sons, the contesting for authority started all over again. It was only as his empire began to do its own crumbling, and later when vigorous Popes arose, that the latter could claim exclusive competence over marriages against the claim of civil rulers. They did this most effectively by creating a separate ecclesiastical jurisdiction, with which Catholic princes later interfered in their self-appointed role as patrons and protectors of the Church. The churchmen's taking of exclusive competence over marriage was hastened in Italy by the distant Carolingian rulers' actually granting to bishops civil authority to rule in their territories. Some historians (for example Gabriel LeBras in the *Dictionnaire de Théologie Catholique*[45]) say that the exclusive competence of the Church in marriage matters was accomplished everywhere in Europe by 1000, with the exception of England. Lay competence held on only in scattered parts of Italy and France.

The full strength of papal authority would be felt in Europe only with the reform of Gregory VII (1073–1085) in the last quarter of the eleventh century. But even so, his reform was concerned only minimally with matters of marriage over against its concentration on the abuses of simony, Nicolatism and clerical concubinage.

It is obvious that if the reform of the marriage discipline in the direction of severity were to succeed, the European clergy's use of the penitential manuals would have to be brought under control. It is not only that these were permissive of divorce and remarriage by comparison with the canons newly promulgated by Charlemagne and by his son and successor Louis the Pious. But in their variety and discoherence, in their anonymous and even pseudonymous authorship, in their unauthorized copying and circulation, they troubled pastors and bishops; and they challenged exactly the two qualities Charlemagne wanted most, a single and centralized authority, and a single, homogeneous discipline.

A feature internal to the penitential practice supplied by the manuals made it especially difficult to suppress. In the first place the Frankish and Germanic peoples simply refused to accept the Roman practice, even at its near-vanishing point. What the Mediterranean peoples had found distasteful and difficult about it—the public accusation, the public imposition of penitential acts and their public performance—these northern peoples found simply unacceptable. But their bishops had nothing effective to offer in its place. Rabanus Maurus, abbot of Fulda and later archbishop of Mainz, wrote his *Poenitentium liber* c. 842 in an effort to supply a substitute for the old Roman discipline and at the same time over-ride the manuals of Celtic origin. But it was too general, and, in the circumstance of sparse religious education, too sophisticated to compete with the handy and crudely simple manuals.

So gradually but persistently measures were taken to suppress these manuals. Already in 813, a year before Charlemagne's death, the Council of Chalons had ordered the Frankish clergy to impose penances only according to the official canons: "The kind of penance imposed on those who confess should be determined by the teaching of the ancient canons, by the authority of the Holy Scriptures, or by ecclesiastical custom—rejecting and paying no attention to the booklets called penitentials, whose errors are as certain as their authorship is uncertain."[46]

Louis the Pious continued the effort to move to the more rigorous discipline. In 829 he convened a synod at Paris for the express purpose of reforming abuses among the faithful. Book III, Chapter 2 of the *acta* of this council states that the people " . . . should understand that marriage was created by God . . . and that, as the Lord said, a wife is not to be dismissed except for her fornication, but is to be kept and sustained; and that those who take second wives after dismissing the first for their fornication are by the Lord's sentence to be declared adulterers." Louis ordered the bishops to inspect the penitentials used in their dioceses and to confiscate and burn those that disagreed with the authorized canons.[47]

In the same year Louis convened synods at both Worms and Nantes. The former repeated almost verbatim the canon from Paris that I have just quoted. The synod at Nantes expanded the ruling in its Canon 12:

> If a man's wife shall have committed adultery, and this has been discovered and made public by the man, let him dismiss his wife, if he wishes, because of the fornication. The wife, however, is to do public penance for seven years. But the husband cannot in any way marry another while his wife still lives. But he has permission to be reconciled with his adulterous wife if he so chooses. In this case, however, he must do penance with her, and when penance is completed after seven years, both may take communion. The same procedure is to be followed by the wife if her husband commits adultery against her.[48]

A second arm of the strategy designed to defeat the penitential manuals coming from the Celtic tradition was to supply the European clergy with substitutes for them, but substitutes that would revive the abandoned Roman discipline of penance. The use of the latter would then be imposed on clergy and people at the same time as the Celtic-Frankish manuals would be interdicted.

Thus at the urging of his friend Ebo, archbishop of Rheims, Halitgar, the bishop of Cambrai from 817 to 831, compiled his Five Books on the Assigning of Penances (*Libri 5 de Ordine Poenitentium*).[49] Ebo's motive was the one I have just cited—to have a simple, authentically Roman penitential manual available to replace the multiple popular penitentials whose discordance with one another was producing such confusion of consciences among his people.

Nothing of Halitgar's own thought is in his compilation, since it is just that—a compilation of others' decrees. Nor is it authentically Roman, since much of it is taken from decrees of councils and authorities nearly contemporary with himself.

It is in Book 4 that he set forth his "On the Selecting of Penances for the Laity" (*De judicio poenitentium laicorum*). He devotes two canons, or *capita,* to the question of divorce and remarriage. *Caput 10* is nothing other than a verbatim repetition of Canon 8 of the Eleventh Council of Carthage—still more evidence of the far-reaching effect of the unqualified and severe decisions reached in that fifth-century Visigothic-Catholic synod.[50]

In *Caput 11* he does little more than quote Chapter 27 of Innocent I's Letter to Exsuperius.

> Those who, even though their marriages seem dissolved
> [*conjugia dissociata*], go to another union [*copula*] while their
> wives are still alive, cannot be considered other than adulterers;
> in such a way that the persons themselves too with whom they
> are united are considered to have committed adultery, according
> to what we read in the Gospel: "A man who dismisses his wife
> and marries another commits adultery." Therefore all who do
> this are to refrain from communion with the faithful. About their
> parents or their friends nothing can be decreed unless they are
> found to have urged these illicit unions.[51]

A similar attempt at replacing the popular manuals by composing a
traditional Roman substitute was made by Rabanus Maurus, in 841. This
was his *Poenitentiale*.[52] In its Chapter 21 he dealt with divorce and
remarriage under the heading, "Concerning Those Who Commit Adultery" (*De his qui adulterium commitunt*).

Like Halitgar he carefully omitted from his compilation the canons of
the Frankish councils we have reviewed. And like Halitgar he took care to
cite, as the first of his traditional canons, Canon 8 of the Eleventh Council
of Carthage (although he calls it "Chapter 69 of the African Council"). He
begins, "Likewise . . . it was decreed concerning those who dismiss their
wives or their husbands, that they remain as they are . . ." From this point
he simply quotes the canon verbatim.

He then turns to the letter of Pope Innocent I to Exsuperius, and first
to its Chapter 24. Again he does little more than quote it. He reports:
"There it is prescribed that men are not to come together with women who
are adulteresses." Then he quotes Innocent's rhetorical query: "And we
would like to know why men who take communion are not to come
together with adulterous women, while women seem permitted to remain
with men who are adulterers."

When he cites Innocent's Chapter 27 he again hardly more than
quotes it, as we have just seen Halitgar do: "About this question, your
worship, concerning men who take [dismissed or deserting] wives while
their husbands are still alive . . . (then the quotation)."[53]

Finally he quotes the first half of Canon 9 of the Council of Elvira:

> A Christian woman who has left an adulterous husband and
> has sought to marry another is forbidden to do so. If she does
> take another, she is not to receive communion until the husband
> she left has died, unless serious illness should demand she do so.[54]

Papal Intervention

But as early as the Carolingian reform itself, and even before it, Popes
had begun to apply their authority in favor of the severe marriage discipline. Pope Zachary wrote in 747 to Pepin, to the bishops and abbots of

the Franks, and to their nobility, to explain the Western Church's teaching on divorce and remarriage. What he used for his explanation was a harbinger of later papal instruction and legislation. He simply quoted Canon 48 of the Apostolic Canons, and the familiar Canon 8 of the Eleventh Council of Carthage. The former decreed excommunication for a husband remarrying after dismissing his wife, and for a man marrying a dismissed wife.[55]

Both a Pope and a scholar made their voices heard in favor of the Roman discipline when they intervened in behalf of justice for a ninth-century wife mistreated by her royal husband. In 855, at the age of seventeen, Charlemagne's grandson, King Lothair II of Lorraine, married Teutberga, daughter of the duke of Burgundy. But within three years of the wedding he sought to dismiss her and to marry Waldrada, earlier his mistress. He tried to justify the dismissal by charging Teutberga with incest consummated before the marriage with her brother Hubert, abbot of St. Maurice in Vallais. According to Frankish law the conduct was a crime that invalidated any subsequent attempt at marriage.

At a council of bishops and nobles assembled in Aachen in 860 Teutberga was forced to confess to the incest. The council convicted her of the crime and declared her marriage to Lothair null. But she escaped the monastic imprisonment intended for her and found refuge in the realm of her uncle, Charles the Bald. From there she appealed to Pope Nicholas I.

In 862 Lothair summoned another council at Aachen to secure from it permission to remarry, but this time on the double and internally contradictory pleas of his wife's premarital incest (which would have voided his attempted marriage) and her adultery (which presumed his valid marriage to her). The second of these crimes, according to Frankish law, would allow him to dismiss her and remarry. This council acted rather on his first allegation again, and declared his marriage to Teutberga null.

At the same time in answer to her plea Pope Nicholas sent two legates to complete a new investigation and process in a council held at Metz. But the legates, Rodoald de Porto and John of Ficaclae, accepted bribes from the court of Lorraine and with the other prelates and nobles at Metz confirmed the decision handed down earlier at Aachen.

Then Nicholas took personal action. He suspended the bishops who had concurred in the fraudulent judgment against Teutberga, and denied both of Lothair's claims. But he did so not because he disagreed with the Frankish law on premarital incest or on dismissing adulterous spouses (although he did indeed disagree with it), but because he was sure that both of Lothair's charges were false. He excommunicated Waldrada and compelled Lothair under threat of excommunication to dismiss her and to take Teutberga back. Lothair did this, but only briefly before dismissing her again. In her weariness and discouragement she asked Nicholas to declare her marriage with Lothair null, but the latter's reply to this request was that this was impossible. Nicholas died in 867, Lothair in 869.

Hincmar of Rheims and the Canonical Compilations

The scholar who had a hand in the investigation of Lothair's accusation against Teutberga was Hincmar, archbishop of Rheims. Before the second assembly at Aachen in 860 he was asked by Lothair's partisans to declare in favor of the king and the charge against his wife. He was asked also to take part in the assembly, but pleaded poor health in order to avoid participating in that travesty. The party of Lothair tried to represent his reluctance as tacit approval, and this drew from Hincmar a document in which he offered a most detailed judgment of the case. It is titled "Concerning the Divorce of King Lothair and Queen Teutberga" (*De divortio Lotharii regis et Teutbergae reginae*).[56]

In character the document is a not very expert amalgam of philosophy, Scripture, theology and law concerning divorce and remarriage. In it Hincmar devised a plan of twenty-three *interrogationes* to himself by which he meant to cut to the heart of Lothair's case against Teutberga. His *responsiones* to each of the twenty-three *interrogationes* make up the amalgam mentioned just above. Perhaps the most valuable trait of the whole is that it is the earliest attempt in Christian history at a comprehensive ingathering and arranging of the judgments, or *sententiae,* of synods, prelates and scholars on the question of divorce and remarriage. For Hincmar over-answers each of his *interrogationes* at dismaying length. He uses each of them as the occasion for reviewing the history of Christian judgments on the point queried in it.

Thus his *De divortio Lotharii regis* is a compilation. And that it was not done with dispassionate scholarly collecting and arranging as its goal becomes evident if one notices the *sententiae* that he omits from his compilation in contradistinction to those he includes. The omitting and the including seem carefully biased to build the case against the permissive discipline promoted by the Celtic and Anglo-Saxon penitential disciplines, the permissiveness at whose door one could at least in part lay responsibility for Lothair's arrogant and cruel treatment of his young wife. He includes a wealth of rigorous rulings from the Roman and African churches; he carefully skirts the permissive decrees from the Frankish synods.

In *Responsio 2* he lays down the principle that Christians live by a different law than does the rest of the human race.[57] He insists, with St. Paul in 1 Corinthians 7:27, that a wife is bound to her husband as long as he lives, and that she is free to marry again only after his death.

He adds that a man may not dismiss his wife for just any reason, but only for her *fornicatio.* Then the assertion of his own mind regarding the crucial next question: even if a husband dismisses his wife after proving *fornicatio* against her, he may not remarry as long as she lives, nor may she as long as he lives. The reason for this severe restriction is found in Christ's words, "What God has joined man must not separate." And here Hincmar draws a theological interpretation from his scriptural sources:

God has joined husband and wife in this inseparable way by making them two in one flesh. Perhaps he himself can "separate" them, but even when he does so, this is only that they may abstain from intercourse for a while so that they may engage in prayer. But once they separate by dismissal for adultery, they are either to remain as they are or are to be reconciled to one another.

In *Interrogatio 5* he gets at the same issue by asking, this time in detail, how and for which causes, according to the authorities, marriages once joined can be separated, without which causes they should not be separated, and whether after separation the husband and wife may seek second unions while the other spouse still lives, and whether they both come equally under the judgment of sinning if they remarry.

His *responsio* here is a repetition of that he made to *Interrogatio 2,* a review, in prolix and flawed Latin, of the subject beginning with the ancient Fathers, Popes and earliest synods. His one addition to the consensus that he had brought together in *Responsio 2* is aimed clearly at Lothair: no dismissal of a spouse or desertion of a marriage may be done without the permission of one's bishop.

He then turns to Paul's metaphor, in Ephesians 5, of the husband and wife as one body, with the husband as head of this body, ruling his wife with love. But even though he calls the marriage of two Christians a *mysterium* of Christ and the Church, he does not draw from the metaphor that this marriage is indissoluble. He insists rather that because of the intimate love in such a relationship Christian husbands must treat their wives fairly and with compassion.[58] But he does not extend the fairness and compassion to the husband's keeping his wife even despite her infidelity. (Thus the Matthean exceptive clause still triumphs over the metaphor in Ephesians.)

In his *Responsio* 10 Hincmar denies that entry into monastic life by one of the spouses against the other's will dissolves their marriage.[59] And in his *Responsio* 21 he reiterates that one spouse can dismiss the other only for adultery and—among Christians only—for the sake of a life of continence.[60] But in either case to attempt remarriage is adultery. He quotes Chapter 1 of Augustine's *De nuptiis et concupiscentia* where it says that the substance (*res*) of the *sacramentum* in the marriage of two Christians is that they persevere together inseparably as long as both are alive. And even if they separate and enter new "marriages," they are still married to one another rather than to their new partners.

Hincmar's compilation of canons and of *sententiae,* as I have intimated, was only the earliest of a series that was to continue through at least four centuries. But as weapons of reform to be used against the chaotic and permissive divorce discipline of central Europe they could be effective only if they resisted the temptation to the scholarly virtue of inclusiveness, only if they winnowed the Western tradition in such a way as to make the severe discipline the authentic one. But for whatever reasons, damaging inclusivity got into more than one of these compilations, and synods such as Verberies and Compiègne and the Penitential of Theodore found honored places in them.

For one, Benedict the Levite, a deacon of the church of Mainz, compiled his *Collectio Capitularium* between 847 and 850, a work of pretended scholarship which nevertheless had considerable influence. He came down on the side of rigor in denying that the dismissal of a spouse because of adultery frees the innocent party to remarry, and in denying that one spouse's entry into religious life, even with the other's permission, frees the latter to remarry. All that these allow is separation, and these are the only causes justifying separation. This he wrote in Book II of his *Collectio*. But he confused the issue of indissolubility by quoting, in Book I, the Council of Compiègne's Canon 11, which allowed divorce and remarriage if one spouse had incestuous intercourse with the other's blood relative (an intercourse which created, in the legal vocabulary of the time, "supervenient affinity"). But in Book III he qualified this by stating that the husband (and apparently he alone) could remarry only when his wife died.[61]

Regino of Prüm

Another compilation was done by Regino, abbot of Prüm in Lorraine from 892 until his expulsion from that office in 899. He was then engaged by Rathbod, archbishop of Trier, to provide him a personal guide in the governing of his diocese. This was Regino's On Ecclesiastical Discipline (*De ecclesiasticis disciplinis*), in two books, composed in 966, and like Hincmar's *responsiones* a collection of canons, decrees and patristic teachings.[62]

As it was with Benedict the Levite, so with Regino the concern for inclusiveness undermined any effort at reform in the direction of Roman rigor. His canons and *sententiae* on marriage are found mainly in Book 2. But he did not begin well in Canon 200 of Book 1, where he said of husbands who dismiss their wives and subsequently take other men's wives for their own only that they must do penance for seven years.[63] Perhaps he meant at this point that the second union is adultery; but if he did, in quoting his source, an anonymous penitential's prescription, he carelessly failed to say so.

In Book 2, Canon 118 he cited Canon 5 of Verberies which allows a man whose wife has plotted against his life to kill the would-be assassin, to dismiss his wife and then to remarry, while she is obliged to do penance and to remain unmarried for the rest of her life. And in Canon 124 he cited the same synod's Canon 9 which stipulates that if a wife refuses to follow her vassal husband when he is taken into a foreign duchy or province by his lord, she is to remain celibate as long as her husband is alive; but that if her husband leaves her in this way because he is compelled to, and he has no hope of returning to her, he may take another wife.[64] And in Canon 127 he completes his citation of Verberies on this point by recording that when such a vassal marries his first wife in a foreign land, but is separated from her on being returned to his homeland and there remarries, he may keep this second wife.[65]

But in Canon 131 of Book 2 he quotes Canon 21 of the Council of Nantes, which decreed that even if a man apprehends his wife in adultery (for which she must do the seven years of penance), though he may dismiss her, he may not remarry as long as she is alive. The same holds for a wife who can prove adultery against her husband.[66]

One wonders what sort of help for Archbishop Rathbod's effort to bring order into the marriage discipline at Trier this compilation could have been. It quoted or cited canons which tugged in contrary directions about the permissibility of dissolving marriages and remarrying, and, more seriously, undermined any conviction that Christ's words about men's not separating what God has joined could point to a fundamental indissolubility of marriage.

What is yet more striking is that one of the points on which Regino advised bishops to satisfy themselves when holding a visitation of their dioceses was that their priests have and use a penitential manual of recognized authority—for example that of Bede, or the Roman Penitential, or that of Theodore of Canterbury.

> . . . whether he has the Roman Penitential, or that compiled by Theodore the bishop, or by the venerable priest Bede, so that he may question his confessant according to the contents of [one of] these manuals, or impose on his confessants the proper penance.[67]

That the move toward a strict discipline was making little headway even by the middle of the eleventh century is evident in two major canonical compilations of the first half of that century. The Petrine Excerpts from Roman Law (*Petri exceptiones legum romanorum*) was produced by the jurists of Ravenna shortly before 1050. It shows the influence of classical and post-classical Roman law in Italy after seven centuries of established Christianity. It is in fact an attempt to adapt that law to early medieval life. It consists principally of extracts from the *Epitome* of the Roman jurist Julian.[68]

In its Book 1, Chapter 37, titled On the Dissolving of Marriage (*De solutione matrimonii*), it sets down the condition for remarriage after dissolution for adultery: "In the case of adultery the innocent party is not forbidden to form another marriage . . . when the separation of the previous union has been decreed in both the civil and ecclesiastical courts."[69]

Burchard of Worms

Burchard was elevated from the rank of deacon to the archbishopric of Worms in the year 1000, and held that office until his death in 1025. He was a scholar and writer as well as prelate. His most extensive work is The Book of Decrees (*Decretorum liber*) written c. 1008–1012, a rich compilation of synodal and papal decrees and scholarly judgments on Church government.[70] Burchard compiled it originally to meet the needs of his own clergy, but its usefulness eventually won it wide circulation among canonists of his own and of succeeding generations.

Even as the most developed compilation of the eleventh century, The Book of Decrees drew from earlier compilations, and most evidently from Regino of Prüm's Ecclesiastical Discipline, and from a late ninth-century Italian collection known as the *Anselmo dedicata*. The spirit of inclusiveness triumphed with Burchard too, as he combined Celtic and Anglo-Saxon penitential canons with Roman—with the predictable effect of prolonging through and beyond his generation the European Church's indecisive divorce discipline.

He divided the compilation into twenty "books" (1,785 chapters in the *Patrologia Latina*). Book 9 he devoted to "non-consecrated women."[71] In it he showed a clear preference for indissolubility in marriage, but he just as clearly allowed dissolution for specific causes, and subsequent remarriage. On the side of permanence of the marital union he set down in his Canon 9 that a Christian married to a non-Christian is, according to the instruction of Paul in 1 Corinthians 7, not to dismiss him or her.[72]

In Canon 28 he says that if a man and a woman are both of sound mind when married, but one later becomes insane—or blind or maimed— the marriage cannot for this cause be dissolved.[73] Masters cannot dissolve the marriages of their slaves (Canon 29).[74] If a woman can prove in a judicial hearing that she cannot have intercourse with her husband because of his impotence, she may take another husband, but the husband may not remarry (Canons 40, 43, 44).[75] In Canon 54 he repeated Chapter 6 of the Council of Worms decreeing that a vassal who follows his lord into a foreign duchy, marries there a wife provided for him by his lord, but because of the latter's abusive treatment returns to his native land, he may remarry a woman of his own choice.[76]

To the Close of the Eleventh Century

The seesaw struggle that had begun with the Carolingian reform continued through the second half of the eleventh century. On one side were the territorial bishops (often installed by their secular lords) and the local synods, who sought to preserve the permissive discipline of the Celtic and Anglo-Saxon penitential manuals. On the other were the Popes and the monastic reformers who sought to replace it with the more severe discipline coming from the Roman, Spanish and African synods. Despite all efforts to suppress them the manuals continued in widespread use. We have seen how even an acknowledged reformer, Regino of Prüm, at the end of the ninth century had recommended for common penitential use the most permissive of the Anglo-Saxon manuals.

That these manuals and others sharing their spirit were still in common use a century later is evident in the scathing denunciation of them by the Italian ascetic and reformer, Peter Damien (1007–1072). In it he addressed to Pope Leo IX a treatise that was later titled formally his *Opusculum septimum* (Minor Work no. 7), but informally by Peter himself *Liber Gomorrheanus* (The Book of Gomorrha).[77] It is an inventory and a denunciation of most of the abuses of conduct that Peter saw in the Western Church of his time, particularly of those of clerics and monks. He criticized with especial bitterness their laxity in the administration of penance and their use of haphazardly discoherent and lenient penitential manuals. He leveled against the penitential manuals the serious charge that they were of dubious, even spurious authorship—unauthorized and therefore illicit as instruments of penitential discipline. He all but demanded that the only authentic disciplinary canons be those coming from the Pope.

> For who compiled these canons? Who dared to sow in the royal groves of the Church such spiny and stinging thorns? For it is surely evident that all truly authentic canons have been voted in the venerable synods as promulgated by the holy Fathers of the apostolic see. No individual person by himself can issue canons. This privilege belongs alone to the man who presides in the chair of Peter.
>
> But these spurious and upstart canons of which we speak are known to have been excluded by those holy councils, and have been proved foreign to the decrees of the Fathers. It follows therefore that no rules are to be included among the canons which have not come from either the decretal edicts of the Fathers or from the sacred councils. For what is not included among any of the species is certainly alien to the genus.
>
> But if the name of the author of many of these canons is sought, no one can produce it because it cannot be found consistently in the various editions [codices]. For in one it is said "Theodore says"; in another "the Roman penitential says"; in another "the Canons of the Apostles." The citation reads one way here, another way there. And since they cannot verify a single exact author, they simply forefeit all authority. For canons that wander so uncertainly among various authors claim none with clear authority. So it follows necessarily that canons which raise such a cloud of doubt in the minds of their readers must without doubt be removed and give way to the light of Sacred Scripture.[78]

Peter's appeal to the principle of a single primatial authority was well-timed. It was at this moment, in the closing decades of the eleventh century, that the Popes themselves began to take an effective personal part in resolving the conflict, and resolving it, of course, on the side of the Roman discipline. By then the Carolingian interference with papal authority had been beaten back. The Cluniac reform of Benedictine monasticism in France had spread an enthusiasm for reform in all facets of Christian life. The compilations of canons and *sententiae* in which tradition could be concentrated were beginning to serve as instruments of rational decision, despite their including the ambiguous and contradictory elements of the tradition.

Even before Cardinal Hildebrand came to the papacy as Gregory VII in 1073 papal authority was felt personally in central Europe. In 1049 Leo IX went to France and convened the Council of Rheims as part of the work of reform of the French church. The council's Canon 12 ruled without qualification: "It is unlawful for any man to abandon his legitimate wife and marry another."[79]

Eleven years later the papal legate, Cardinal Stephan, convened a series of synods in France in order to continue the reform there. One of these was the Council of Tours, which pronounced excommunication on all Christians who had sought to dissolve their marriages under civil authority and then remarry, and threatened excommunication for all who would do so in the future. But this Canon 9 of the council was the same kind of ambiguous formulation that had for centuries been keeping alive the very permissive discipline that the council was trying to suppress. Its first clause said that "any man who dismisses his wife without the judgment of the bishop and marries another, until he gives himself over to penance effectively, is to be excluded from the body and blood of Our Lord Jesus Christ." The phrasing leaves the suggestion that if the husband dismisses his wife *with* the approval of his bishop, he avoids excommunication and perhaps is even free to remarry. The canon implies a second qualification where it says ". . . until he has given himself over to penance effectively, he is to be excluded, etc." Once he has done the penance imposed on him is he then free to keep his second wife and return to communion?[80]

Again in 1072 a council held at Rouen published two canons dealing with dissolution and remarriage. Canon 17 ruled that a man whose wife has taken the vows of religious life could not remarry during her lifetime. Canon 18 forbade a woman whose husband has left for a foreign country, and not returned, to remarry until she has received definite word of his death. As a move against husbands' abandoning and even murdering their wives in order to gain freedom to marry a mistress, Canon 16 ruled that if it were commonly known that a man had committed adultery, he could not marry his accomplice even after the death of his wife.[81]

Yves of Chartres

The most representative of all the compilations of canons and *sententiae* until the great reform of Church law in the twelfth century were the two completed by Yves, bishop of Chartres from 1091 until his death in 1116. These are his *Decretum,* completed in 1095, and his *Panormia,* completed shortly afterward.[82] He was incomparably the most accomplished canonical jurist of his age. He belonged to the mainstream of the post-Gregorian reform of the European Church; he strove mightily for the recognition of the papacy's preeminent authority.

But none of this kept him from being a faithful heir of his Frankish ancestry. For while accepting the Gregorian reform in principle and substance, he insisted on preserving among the ancient disciplinary norms included in his compilation those of his own Frankish tradition. Or, more accurately, he insisted on their inclusion in his *Decretum.* He sought to fuse the strict juridical principles of Roman-Gregorian law and the particular legislation of the Frankish-German tradition. What this produced was an evolved and gentled Roman rigorism. His vast and encyclopedic knowledge of his predecessors showed him the inadequacy of the central European law for ruling Christian life. At the same time it convinced him that the Roman-Gregorian law was too rigid for ruling that life. What he sought was to amalgamate the two traditions with each qualifying and bettering the other. The material for this amalgam he drew from Burchard of Worms' *Decretum,* from his own earlier and sparser collection, the *Tripartita,* from an anonymous collection of papal decrees, from the text of Justinian's Roman law, from multiple texts of the Fathers and ecclesiastical writers, from the texts of Carolingian civil law, and from historical texts in the *Liber pontificalis.*

Yet Yves' *Decretum* worked its influence on later generations indirectly, through his third compilation, the *Panormia.* For the latter not only drew the overwhelming portion of its material from the *Decretum,* but it was a careful systematization of the wholly unsystematic *Decretum.* The *Panormia* was, so to speak, Yves' second effort, an orderly emendation of a first and mountainous project of text-gathering.

It is significant that Yves was educated in England, a pupil of Lanfranc and a fellow student with Anselm of Canterbury. This early familiarity with the discipline of the Anglo-Saxons and the Franks had its gentling effect on him. For while he saw the necessity for reform in the life of eleventh-century Europe, he was unable to appropriate the rigidity and the absolutism of the Roman-Gregorian reform. He favored tradition and progress simultaneously; he tried to fuse them discreetly.

Because Yves' *Panormia* is so clearly a careful selection from and rearrangement of the material in his *Decretum,* we may take for granted that the *Panormia* comes closest to an expression of his own mind on dissolution and remarriage. But in both documents his argument for a restrictive law is evident. He rejects the compiler's inclusiveness that most of his predecessors had exercised. Instead he simply omits the permissive legislation from the Frankish councils and the canons from the Celtic and Anglo-Saxon penitential manuals.

The following traits of the *Decretum* are worth noting.

Yves does not at all points use his sources accurately. For example, he prefers to cite some of the *loci communes* from the Scriptures rather than quote them. In some places this results in his skewing their meaning.

His knowledge of the Fathers does not seem comprehensive. Although he reaches as far back as Hermas' Shepherd, Mandate 4, he concentrates his research on Jerome, Ambrose, Augustine, Isidore and Gregory. Either he did not know the Eastern Fathers, or he avoided them because including certain of their key passages would have undermined his case against the permissive discipline.

If his intent in both documents is to bring the minds of the ancients to bear on marital questions in his own generation, he apparently thinks this can be done by producing a mere catalogue of their decrees and *sententiae*. At no point does he attempt an interpretation of their minds by studying their statements in context. This enables him, for one thing, to quote restrictive decrees from Theodosius II and Justinian, who in general proposed a most permissive divorce legislation, as we have seen.

Despite Yves' tendentious motive he is not entirely careful in avoiding passages that contradict one another. On a point tangential to dissolution and remarriage, in Part 8, Chapter 153 he cites Augustine's homily 49 in which the latter asserts that no man may with moral rightness keep a concubine.[83] But he also cites the First Council of Toledo's Canon 17, which rules that if a man does not have a wife, he may take a concubine.[84]

He perpetuates some of the ancient uncertainties about the reasons for the impermissibility of dissolution, and beyond this keeps alive the uncertainty about the possibility itself of dissolving a marriage. For example he quotes Augustine's insistence, in his On the Good of Marriage, Chapter 7, that dismissal does not dissolve the marital covenant, but then he includes Augustine's rhetorical addition that "only in the city of our God, on the Holy Mountain, is such the case with a wife"—which implies that only in the marriages of Christians does dissolution not dissolve the marital covenant.[85]

He records Jerome's judgment in the latter's Commentary on Matthew, Chapter 19, that only for adultery may husband or wife dismiss the other, but even so both are to remain unmarried. But then he adds Jerome's reason for the husband's remaining unmarried, that his wife may have the opportunity to repent and return to him.[86]

The issue, therefore, of marriage's natural indissolubility he leaves inconclusive. Again, he accounts for Christian marriages' invulnerability to dissolution by citing Chapter 10 of Augustine's On Marriage and Concupiscence, where the latter argues that even after dismissal there remains in the souls of the Christian spouses *quiddam coniugale*—a certain marital something—in the same way that the *sacramentum* of baptism remains in the soul of an apostate Christian.[87]

He continues this doubt about marital indissolubility as well as about the impermissibility of dissolution by quoting Gregory II's *Epistola* 13 to Boniface, which ruled that if a man has a wife with whom he cannot have intercourse, it is better for him to remain celibate, but since this demands heroic conduct, he may take a second wife while continuing to provide for the first.[88]

In the same quarter he quotes the Theodosian Code, Chapter 19, which decrees that if a husband is still impotent after two years of marriage, his wife or her parents may dismiss him.[89] And his one citation from the Council of Verberies is in his Chapter 179, where he cites from its Chapter 17 that if a wife swears on the cross that she has never had intercourse with her husband, she may separate from him and remarry.[90] It is to be noted that in these permissions for remarriage in the case of impotence, this is allowed not after a declaration of nullity, as in modern Church law, but after a true dissolution by dismissal. In the last-named canon, from the Council of Verberies, there is no question of impotence but simply of non-consummation of the marriage.

The *Panormia*

Yves' *Panormia* may serve well as a précis of the Western Catholic discipline for dissolution and remarriage as it stood at the brink of the twelfth century. And within the discipline are cited the sources of the doctrine undergirding it. I list here in reasonably succinct order the substance of this discipline and the *fontes* from which Yves draws it.

1. A wife's sterility is not sufficient cause for her husband's dismissing her, even if having children was the motive for their marrying (Augustine, On the Good of Marriage, Chapter 7).[91]

2. A marriage may not be dissolved so that one or both spouses may take up monastic life and pronounce its vows (Letter of Pope Gregory I to Theotista).[92] And even if both spouses do pronounce these vows, their marriage remains (Pope Eugene I in Chapter 36 of an unidentified synod).[93]

3. Wives whose husbands have been taken captive in war may not remarry unless the deaths of the former have been verified (Letter of Pope Leo I to Bishop Nicetas of Aquileia: Leo's *Epistola* 77; Pope Innocent I's *Epistola* 9 to Bishop Rola; The *Pandecta,* Book 24, Title 2).[94]

4. If a wife refuses to follow her husband into a foreign land when he is compelled to go there, she must not remarry as long as he is alive (Council of Verberies).[95]

5. Spouses who are sane and in good health at the time their marriage is created may not dissolve it because of later insanity, ill health, blindness or maiming (Letter of Pope Nicholas to Bishop Charles of Mainz).[96]

6. A woman once taken as wife is to be kept no matter what illness or deformity befalls her (Augustine, The Sermon on the Mount, par. 32).[97]

7. A Christian is not to dismiss a spouse because the latter is not a Christian (St. Paul, 1 Corinthians 7).[98]

8. No man may dismiss his wife for any cause without first proving

this cause before a court of bishops (Fourth Council of Carthage, Chapter 30).[99]

9. A man may not dismiss his wife except for her *fornicatio* (generally understood as her adultery) (Jerome's letter to Oceanus concerning the remarriage of Fabiola).[100]

10. A man who dismisses his wife except for her *fornicatio* is to be excommunicated (no reference).[101]

11. Although a wife may be dismissed for her *fornicatio,* the bond of her marriage remains, just as the *sacramentum* of baptism remains in the soul of a Christian despite his apostasy (Augustine's On Adulterous Marriages, Book 2 Chapter 4).[102] Even though civil law permits dismissal for adultery, for Christians such dismissal does not dissolve the marriage bond (Augustine, On the Good of Marriage).[103]

12. If a husband or a wife leaves the marriage because of this *fornicatio,* both spouses are forbidden to remarry (Augustine, Commentary on 1 Corinthians).[104]

13. A man who marries a dismissed wife commits adultery (Augustine, The Sermon on the Mount).[105]

But one ought not infer that any of these canons, decrees or *sententiae* compiled and arranged by Yves declares the radical indissolubility of marriage, the simple impossibility of its dissolution by human agency. The notion itself of radical indissolubility was not current in the minds of churchmen and canonists at the end of the eleventh century. Their understanding was concentrated on the permissibility and impermissibility of any human agency's attempting such dissolution. For a number of them stated unambiguously a cause which justifies one spouse's dismissing the other, or at least his or her departing from the marriage. Yves cited unhesitatingly those authorities who said that a wife can leave her husband and remarry if because of his disability he cannot have intercourse with her (The Theodosian Code, Book 5, Chapter 19, Title 10, and Chapter 20, Title 7).[106] The same prerogative is available to a husband if his wife cannot have intercourse (Letter of Pope Gregory II to Bishop Boniface).[107]

And those spouses who are impotent because of curses and sorcery must seek through penance and contrition to be restored. But if these fail, they may depart from the marriage and remarry (Hincmar of Rheims; no source named).[108]

The *Panormia*'s one citation from the Frankish Council of Verberies records its decree in Canon 27 that allowed a wife to depart from the marriage if she swore on the cross that she had never had intercourse with her husband.[109]

And again it is most important to note that these canons and decrees declare not that impotence in a spouse is an impediment to his or her creating a marriage, an impediment causing the nullity of the attempt to do so. They say rather that impotence is a cause justifying the dissolution of a marriage until that moment presumed real. But the *Panormia*'s one citation from Verberies (above) expands even this cause for dissolution, as we have seen. For this canon allows a wife to depart from the marriage if she will swear on the cross not that her husband is impotent, but that she has never had intercourse with him. So in her case the ground of dissolution is not impotence but the simple fact of non-consummation.

Conclusion and Reflections

As we bring this brief examination of the history of the doctrine and discipline of divorce and remarriage in the Roman Catholic Church to the threshold of the high Middle Ages, let us set aside for the moment the question asking which of the two traditions about divorce and remarriage is the accurate one—the Roman or the Eastern Orthodox (and the Reformation Protestant). For one thing, answering the question depends on the criterion for accuracy that one adopts. The adopting is simplified by this, that both sides surely say that accuracy in this case is gained by finding out the mind of God on the subject. But on the other hand the adopting is complicated by the fact that the one access to the mind of God which both sides have agreed to use is the Scriptures, which at least seem to convey uncertain and discordant versions of God's mind as this is expressed in Christ's teaching. And the adopting is complicated profoundly by the fact that the interpreters of the Scriptures whom both sides accept—the Fathers and other ecclesiastical writers of the first four Christian centuries—themselves disagreed on how to interpret the passages from the Scriptures. That a primatial authority vested in one person should be ultimately their interpreter has been, of course, unacceptable to the Eastern Catholics and to the Protestants. The former of these, in company with the major episcopal churches, accept that a primatial authority vested rather in the *collegium* of bishops is the authorized (but not infallible) interpreter.

What is more to the point at this juncture is to reflect on the means used by the Roman Church during the eleventh century to accelerate its movement toward the divorce and remarriage discipline it now has. But first we must glance again at the causes that dragged heavily on the movement and retarded it during the preceding centuries.

There were first of all the uncertainties about the divine sources mentioned just above.

Then when the Church penetrated and took root in the European peoples its marriage discipline, already uncertain because of the uncertainties in these sources, collided with the ancient pre-Christian traditions. Two interlocked features of these traditions set a mighty resistance against any rigorous doctrine or discipline. First, among the central and northern European peoples marriages were created when fathers (or their surrogates) gave their daughters to other men as possessions passing from their ownership to the others'; and, second, it was taken for granted that either set of men was to have full and free authority in disposing of their possessions. The Frankish, Lombard and Germanic laws were designed primarily to protect this authority. For the Church to tell a husband in one of these societies that he could no longer dismiss his wife if he found her seriously lacking was to demand that he abandon his own culture and appropriate a new and strange one. And such a husband, who had become Christian mainly because his king or lord had done so and fealty demanded the same of him, could think of no compelling reason for making this change.

Moreover, the Christianity that first came to the Europeans was Roman, and brought with it Roman law. We have already seen that this could serve a bishop only poorly in establishing a rigorous discipline of divorce and remarriage in his missionary diocese.

Christianity came to so many of the Europeans just during those decades of the fifth and sixth centuries when the Roman empire and its centralized authority dwindled and disappeared. With them disappeared a system of roads and communication, a central judicial system, and a peace-keeping army (despite its intermittent mutinies). Even if there had been formed by this time a single clear and certain doctrine and discipline, there was little chance they could have been disseminated and imposed.

The form that Church government took was instead local-regional. The bishops of a kingdom or province met in regional synods and legislated for the people of only their regime. If different minds on points of discipline throve in different regions, the synods produced the mosaic of discordant legislation that we have seen. And if a spouse in one province wished to exploit the permissive discipline thriving in another, provided he could afford to do so he could move there, establish residence, secure his divorce, and then return to his own and marry a woman who, unlike his first wife, was his own choice and not that of his father.

And complicating all else were the superimposed and even fused ecclesiastical and civil jurisdictions that we have already seen. It was not so much that from the beginning two independent jurisdictions had, each with its own judicial system, wrestled for exclusive competence over marriage, with first civil jurisdiction triumphant, then ecclesiastical. So long as the Roman empire had been intact, there had been a single imperial jurisdiction, first held by pagans, but with these gradually replaced by Christians.

But as the empire crumbled the Christians who exercised this jurisdiction in the courts came more and more to be the bishops. Among the Franks and Germans in the fifth century and later, a similar situation obtained. Powerful Merovingian then Carolingian rulers become Christians set up courts and staffed them sometimes with churchmen, sometimes with laymen. The contest then for centuries was not between two competing jurisdictions but over who would have the authority to legislate and to appoint judges within the one Christian civil-ecclesiastical jurisdiction. While at his apogee Charlemagne did both, and this with the approval of the Popes who welcomed him as their protector against both the Lombards and the Byzantines. But when his empire too splintered and its centralized authority dwindled, the contesting started up again. And by this time princes were quite used to holding this jurisdiction, to appointing lay judges as well as clerical, and were not ready to give these prerogatives up easily. Only when the two jurisdictions were distinguished and divided once for all by the end of the tenth century, and as strong a Pope as Gregory VII in the eleventh could assert the Church's authority over significant sectors of Christian lives, was the condition born in which a single, coherent discipline could be imposed in the Western Church. Even so, the Church's taking exclusive competence over marriage in Christian Europe was accomplished only gradually and at different paces from region to region. Success in this came to Church authority in England, for example, only at the end of the eleventh century.

I have said that what occurred in Europe was that authority in the Church imposed a discipline of divorce and remarriage. I mean this in a kind of exclusive sense, to suggest that which was not done to bring order to the fragmented rule of divorce and remarriage.

This authority did not develop, as an instrument of order, a theology of marriage's indissolubility among Christians. That such a theology existed at least in germ was hinted at again and again as the compilers repeated Augustine's assertion that only in the city of God, only in the Christian Church, does a marriage survive the spouses' attempt to dissolve it because sterility keeps from it the children for which it was created to begin with. Fewer compilers reported that Augustine had said that even in a spouse who deserts the marriage a certain conjugal something remains, in the way that the *sacramentum* of baptism remains in the soul of a Christian who has apostatized. But no one among the authorities strove to explain what this *quiddam coniugale,* this *sacramentum* of marriage is, or how it causes the marriage of two Christians to be indestructible. And none of them drew from Ephesians 5 that because the marriage of two Christians mirrors on earth (or ought to mirror there) the indestructible union of Christ and the Church, this marriage too is (or ought to be) indestructible.

Only the early Scholastic theologians worked at this understanding, but it was not their understanding—which we shall examine in a later chapter—that brought order into the Western Church's discipline. Certainly it could not have in any case. Bringing order to the situation of marriage in the eleventh and twelfth centuries was but a part of the huge task of bringing order to a Europe only then recovering from the devastation of the barbaric invasions, from the disappearance of a societal structure and the consequent breakdown of authority. Authority is reestablished by the exercise of authority, and the instrument of order typical to authority is not theology, not philosophy, not scriptural exegesis, but law and a judicial system.

So neither was it a satisfactory exegesis of the New Testament divorce texts that brought order. The compilers' treatment of them was to simply quote or cite them as divine authority backing the ecclesiastical canons.

The Matthean exceptive clause was presumed without question to be authentically from Christ himself. Where it was thought to be in contradiction with Christ's Synoptic *logion*—"What God has joined man must not separate"—no way was found to resolve the contradiction. And the authorities in the West knew well enough that their counterparts in the Eastern Church used it to justify the dismissal of adulterous spouses that allowed remarriage at least for the innocent parties. If they sought, then, to use the New Testament teaching as an instrument for reform, for ending the discoherence and installing a single rigorous discipline, they had to make a selection from among these passages that were in *prima facie* disagreement. Obviously they had to confine this use to Mark, Luke and 1 Corinthians 7. Thus, for example, in all the books and chapters of Yves of Chartres' *Decretum* and *Panormia* on divorce, Matthew is mentioned not once.

And if the authorities in the eleventh and twelfth centuries were to enlist the help of earlier authorities in interpreting the disagreeing New Testament passages—that of the Fathers and other ecclesiastical writers— again they would have to choose among disagreeing authorities. They would have, for example, to choose between Basil and Ambrosiaster on the one hand, and Jerome and Augustine on the other. The evidence shows, of course, that they chose the latter. Basil is cited but rarely; the passages from the Ambrosiaster never.

The temptation, then, of one who considers this history is to conclude that with no ground for the severe discipline of divorce and remarriage more solid than the disagreeing canonical traditions in Europe and uncertain scriptural interpretation, no agency could bring the clergy and people of Europe to accept this discipline other than a powerful papal authority that would simply force it on them. But the evidence shows that if this is true, it is only partly so. How the entwined issues of the permissibility of divorce and the possibility of it for Christians were invaded in the eleventh and twelfth centuries from a surprising quarter by an even more troublesome marital issue—and how this invasion opened the way to a partly unforeseen resolution of the divorce-remarriage issue—is the substance of the following chapter.

NOTES

1. This is a theme running through G.H. Joyce's volume published in a revised edition in 1948, *Christian Marriage, An Historical and Doctrinal Study,* Chapter 8, pp. 304–361; and is an at least implicit judgment in Anthony Bevilacqua's essay of 1967, "The History of the Indissolubility of Marriage," in Proceedings of the Twenty-Second Annual Convention, The Catholic Theological Society of America, Vol. 22, pp. 253–308.

2. For a survey of these non-Roman, European traditions of divorce and remarriage, see Joyce, *op. cit.,* pp. 336ff.

3. The canons promulgated by this council are in Migne's *Patrologia Latina*, Vol. 67, in the collection *Codex Canonum Ecclesiasticorum* first completed by Dionysius Exiguus, but later titled *Codex Canonum Vetus Ecclesiae Romanae.* The canons from these synods at Carthage are in Cols. 181–230.

4. This numbering of the canon is proposed by Hefele-Leclercq, *Histoire Des Conciles,* Vol. 2, p. 158, although it is known also as Canon 102 of the entire series of synods. Mansi lists it also as Canon 17 of the Second Council of Mileve held in 416. It is in P.L., Vol. 67, Cols. 215–216: "Placuit ut secundum evangelicam et apostolicam disciplinam, neque dismissus ab uxore, neque dismissa a marito, alteri conjugetur, sed ita maneant, aut sibimet reconcilientur; quod si contempserint ad poenitentiam redicantur, in qua causa legem imperialem petendam promulgari."

5. In H.T. Bruns, *Canones Apostolorum et Concilorum Saeculorum IV, V, VI, VII* (Berolini, 1839, 2 vols), Vol. 2, p. 138. "Hi quoque qui alienis uxoribus, superstitibus ipsarum maritis, nomine conjugii abutuntur, a communione habeantur extranei."

6. In Bruns, *op. cit.,* Vol. 2, p. 303.

Canon 19: "Mulier christiana quae acceperit virum hónestis nuptiis et postmodum discesserit a primo et junxerit se adultero (seu adulterio), etc. . . ." Canon 22: "Si quis tradiderit filiam suam viro honestis nuptiis, et amaverit alium, et consentit filiae suae et acceperit dotem, ambo ab acclesia exclundantur."

7. In Bruns, *loc. cit.,* p. 308.

Canon 26: ". . . Item, non licet viro dimittere uxorem, nisi ob causam fornicationis, ac si dicat ob hanc causam, unde si ducat alteram velut post mortem prioris, non vetant."

Canon 28: "Eadem ratione observanda sunt prima vota et prima conjugia, ut secundis prima non sint irrita, nisi fuerint adulterata."

8. This reply is in *Epistola 94,* Chapters 1 and 4 (in P.L., Vol. 54, Cols. 1136–1137): "We hold it necessary that the legitimate union be restored. Strive with all diligence that each man receive that which is his own."

Chapter 3 of this letter introduced into the case one of the ambiguities so typical of the decrees of these centuries: "Therefore if the men who return after long captivity still so persevere in love of their spouses that they desire to have them back in marriage, that which was compelled by need is to be overlooked, and judged innocent; and that which fidelity demands is to be restored" (Col. 1137). Taking Leo at his word one could interpret him as setting the condition that if the returned husband wants or demands it, his wife must return to him—leaving the implication that if he does not, she is free to stay with the second husband.

9. In Bruns, *op. cit.,* Vol. 2, p. 143.

"Eos quoque qui, relictis uxoribus suis, sicut in evangelio dicitur, excepta causa fornicationis sine adulterii probatione alias duxerint, statuimus a communione similiter arcendos, ne per indulgentiam nostram praetermissa peccata alios ad licentiam erroris invitent."

10. In Bruns, *op cit.,* Vol. 2, p 151.

"Hi vero saeculares qui conjugale consortium culpa graviori dimittunt vel etiam dimiserunt et nullas causas discidii probabiliter proponentes propterea sua matrimonia dimittunt ut aut illicita aut aliena praesumant: si antequam apud episcopos comprovinciales discidii causas dixerint, et prius uxores quam judicio damnentur abjecerint, a communione ecclesiae et sancto populi coetu pro eo quod fidem et conjugia maculent excludantur."

11. In P.L., Vol. 77, Cols. 1156–1164.

The pertinent clauses in the letter are these: "For this was pronounced against them because they have dissolved their marriages by exploiting religious vows. . . . And if there are those who seriously think this and hold to it, there is little doubt that they are not Christians. I and all the Catholic bishops with me—and indeed the entire Church—anathematize them because they think things contrary to the truth and say things contrary to it."

Again there is ambiguity. For Gregory accuses these men of having dissolved their marriages—making his case against them not that they have attempted the impossible, but that they have done the impermissible.

12. In P.L., *loc. cit.,* Col. 1169.

13. *Ibid.*

The pertinent part of the letter reads as follows: "But if you know that the aforesaid woman has committed none of these things, nor any kind of *fornicatio* that justifies a husband's leaving his wife, lest his conversion (to monastic life) should become an occasion of damnation for his wife left in the world our will is that even if this husband has already taken the tonsure he is to return to her without excuse. Because even if the secular law prescribes that for the sake of monastic vows a marriage can be dissolved by either spouse's entry, yet divine law does not permit this. For it is not granted a man to dismiss his wife except because of her *fornicatio,* because by their joining in marriage husbands and wives become one body; and one part of this body cannot enter monastic life while the other remains in the world."

If it seems ironic to the modern reader that the Roman civil law of Gregory's time should defend a spouse's dissolving his or her marriage in order to take monastic vows, while a Pope condemned this as un-Christian, consider that easy consciences could use this point of the law to escape from unwanted marriage—and perhaps even into a wanted one. For even then monastic vows once taken could later be dispensed.

14. In Bruns, *op. cit.,* Vol. 2, p. 310.

"Decimum pro conjugiis, ut nulli liceat nisi legitimum habere connubium; nullus incestum faciat, nullus conjugem propriam nisi ut sanctum evangelium docet fornicationis causa relinquat; quod si quisque propriam expulerit conjugem legitimo sibi matrimonio conjunctam, si Christianus esse recte voluerit, nulli alteri copuletur, sed ita permaneat aut propriae reconcilietur conjugi."

15. In Bruns, *op. cit.,* Vol 1, p. 328.

"Praeceptum domini est, ut excepta causa fornicationis uxor a viro dimitti non debeat. Et ideo quicumque citra culpam criminis supradicti uxorem suam quacumque occasione reliquerit, quia quod deus conjunxit ille separare disposuit, tamdiu ab ecclesiastica communione privatus et coetu omnium Christianorum maneat alienus, quamdiu et ad societatem relictae conjugis redeat."

16. *Epistula 26 ad Probum* (in Bevilacqua, *op. cit.,* p. 284).

17. *Ibid.*

The Latin formulation of Gregory's concession is ". . . sed quia hoc magnorum est, ille qui se non poterit continere, nubat magis."

18. In P.L., Vol. 96, Col. 1506.

The maimed Latin of the decree is this: "Similiter constituimus . . . nec marito viventem sua mulier alius non accipiat, quia maritus muliere sua non debet dimittere excepto causa fornicationis deprehensa."

19. The eighty-five Apostolic Canons are a collection drawn from the more

numerous Apostolic Constitutions, which date from the end of the fourth or the beginning of the fifth century, and were produced in either Syria or Palestine by a single author whose name has been lost; they are drawn also from the councils of the first four centuries. They treat of obligations and the qualities of persons in the Church, of the ordination of clergy, of delicts and penalties and other disciplinary headings. Despite the Eastern Church's rejection of the Constitutions because of their apocryphal authorship, they were taken into the compilation of Dionysius Exiguus and gained acceptance throughout the Western Church. But in the Council of Trullo in 691 the Eastern Church accepted that part of the Constitutions that makes up the Apostolic Canons.

20. *Zachariae Papae Epistola VII ad Pippinum Majorem Domus itemque ad Episcopos, Abbates et Proceres Francorum,* Canon 7, Cap. 12 (In Bevilacqua, *op. cit.,* p. 287).

21. *Pippini Regis Capitulare Vermeriense,* Canones 2, 5, 9, 10, 11, 18, in P.L., Vol. 96, Col. 1506.

22. *Pippini Regis Capitulare Compendiense,* Canones 9, 10, 11,16, 19, 21, in P.L., Vol. 96, Cols. 1513–1515.

23. *Karoli Magni Capitularia: Capitulare Ecclesiasticum,* Canon 43 (in Bevilacqua, *op. cit.,* p. 296).

24. In Mansi, *Sacorum Conciliorum Nova et Amplissima Collectio,* Vol. 13, p. 849.

25. The historians are John T. McNeill and Helena M. Gamer, in *Medieval Handbooks of Penance* (Records of Civilization, Sources and Studies No. 29), N.Y., 1938.

26. In McNeill and Gamer, *op. cit.,* pp. 95–96.

Canon 45 adds the consequences for persons who have committed the kind of sin that raises the question of dismissal: "But the penance of these persons is this— that is, of a man or woman who has committed fornication: they shall do penance for an entire year on an allowance of bread and water separately, and shall not sleep in the same bed" (*ibid.,* p. 96).

27. *Op. cit.,* p. 105.

28. *Op. cit.,* p. 133.

29. *Op. cit.,* p. 196.

30. *Op. cit.,* p. 205.

31. *Ibid.,* pp. 208–209.

32. *Ibid.*

33. *Ibid.,* pp. 209–210.

34. *Ibid.,* p. 210.

35. In Bevilacqua, *op. cit.,* p. 303.

36. Book II, Chapter 12, Canon 32. The Confessional of Pseudo-Egbert in its Canon 20 concurred with this ruling.

37. In Bevilacqua, *ibid.*

38. In McNeill and Gamer, *op. cit.,* p. 273.

39. In Bevilacqua, *op. cit.,* p. 304.

40. *Ibid.*

41. In McNeill and Gamer, *op. cit.,* p. 246.

42. In Bevilacqua, *op. cit.,* p. 302.

43. In McNeill and Gamer, *loc. cit.*

44. In P.L., Vol. 92, Col. 230.

45. In Volume 9 of the 1926 edition, Col. 2123.

46. In Mansi, *op. cit.,* Vol. 14, Col. 101.
47. *Op. cit.,* Vol. 14, Col. 596.
48. In Bevilacqua, *op. cit.,* p.298.
49. In P.L., Vol. 105, Cols. 651–718.
50. *Loc. cit.,* Col. 682.
51. *Ibid.,* Col. 683.
52. In P.L., Vol. 110, Cols. 467–494.
53. *Loc. cit.,* Col. 988.
54. *Ibid.*
55. See note 20, above.
56. In P.L., Vol. 125, Cols. 619–772.
57. *Op. cit.,* Cols. 613–615.
58. *Op. cit.,* Col. 657.
59. *Loc. cit.,* Col. 686.
60. *Loc. cit.,* Col. 732.
61. In P.L., Vol. 97, Cols. 760–771–773.
62. In P.L., Vol. 132, Cols. 184–400.
63. *Loc. cit.,* Col. 249.
64. *Loc. cit.,* Col. 307.
65. *Ibid.,* Col. 308.
66. *Ibid.,* Col. 309.
67. Book I, Canon 95 (*op. cit.,* Col. 191).
68. Quoted in Joyce, *op. cit.,* pp. 613–614.
69. *Ibid.*

This chapter names the three causes for which a marriage may be dissolved, and shows clearly the adaptation to contemporary conditions that was made of Roman law. These causes were adultery by either spouse, the husband's impotence lasting for at least two years, and the choice of monastic life by either or both spouses.

70. In P.L., Vol. 140, Cols. 537–1058.

The title page makes this claim for the *Decretum:* "Compiled from the decrees of the orthodox Fathers, as also from the synods of various nations, i.e., from all the common sources—a compilation that includes, in splendid brevity, the ancient disciplines of the churches."

71. *Op. cit.,* Cols. 815–830.
72. *Loc. cit.,* Cols. 816–817.
73. *Ibid.,* Col. 819.
74. *Ibid.*
75. *Loc. cit.,* Cols. 821–822.
76. *Ibid.,* Col. 821.

A contemporary of Burchard, Fulbert of Chartres, wrote in about 1020 that a man whose wife had abandoned him because of his cruelty toward her could remarry provided she entered a convent and there pronounced the vows of religious life (in P.L., Vol. 141, Col. 223).

77. In P. L., Vol. 145, Cols. 161–190.
78. *Op. cit.,* Col. 172.
79. In Joyce, *op. cit.,* p. 359.
80. In Joyce, *ibid.*
81. *Ibid.*
82. The *Decretum* is in P.L., Vol. 161, Cols. 47–1046; the *Panormia* in *op.*

cit., Cols. 45–1344. In the *Decretum* Yves treats of marriage in Part 8 (Cols. 585–656) under three hundred and thirty-four *capita.* The *Panormia* treats of it in Book 6, Cols. 1243–1278, and in Book 7, Cols. 1279–1304, with special attention to dissolution and remarriage in Cols. 1275–1282.

83. *Op. cit.,* Col. 617.
84. Chapter 64, Col. 597.
85. Chapter 9, Col. 506.
86. Chapter 43, Col. 593.
87. Chapters 12 and 13, Col. 586.
88. Chapter 78, Col. 600.
89. Chapter 79, Col. 600.

He also quotes on this point the letter of Pope Gregory to John of Ravenna, that if a husband is impotent, his wife may dismiss him and remarry.

90. Col. 621.
91. Book 6, Chapter 28, Col. 1251, and Chapter 105, Col. 1271.
92. Book 6, Chapter 78, Col. 1259.
93. Book 6, Chapter 76, Col. 1259.
94. Book 6, Chapters 86–90, Cols. 1263–1264.
95. Book 6, Chapter 91, Col. 1264.

Omitted from the *Panormia* are the canons from the Frankish councils which allowed a husband in this circumstance to take a second wife.

96. Book 6, Chapter 93, Col. 1264.
97. Book 6, Chapter 104, Col. 1271.
98. Book 6, Chapter 94, Col. 1265.
99. Book 6, Chapter 106, Col. 1272.
100. Book 7, Chapter 3, Col. 1279.
101. Book 7, Chapter 1, Col. 1279.
102. Book 7, Chapter 3, Col. 1280.
103. Book 7, Chapter 6, Col. 1280.
104. Book 7, Chapter 2, Col. 1279.
105. Book 7, Chapter 4, Cols. 1279–1280.
106. Book 7, Chapter 113, Col. 1273.
107. Book 7, Chapter 112, Col. 1273.
108. Book 7, Chapter 117, Cols. 1275–1276.
109. Book 7, Chapter 118, Col. 1276.

11. DEVELOPMENT OF THE LAW THROUGH THE THIRTEENTH CENTURY: GRATIAN AND PETER LOMBARD

What this examination has turned up thus far could leave the impression that divorce and remarriage posed the only problem concerning marriage that troubled the authorities in the medieval Church, or that it was even the problem that troubled them the most grievously. This was not true in either case. Until early in the twelfth century the authorities wrestled with another problem, one that seemed for a time equally as intractable as that of divorce and remarriage. And divorce and remarriage may well have seemed to them a facet and even an effect of this other more inclusive problem.[1]

The problem came to life as an inevitable consequence of the meeting, of the colliding and conflicting, of two cultures, the Roman and the European. The conflict bore upon the question, "Which act of human agency creates a marriage?" And the conflict came to life in the following way.[2]

Classic Roman law interpreted marriage as a *consortium* established by the reciprocal consent of the man and woman, and by no more than this consent.[3] The marriage was said to be a *consortium* whose interior *forma* is the spouses' *maritalis affectio,* their will to be married.

This conception of and this law concerning marriage spread gradually into the West. The Theodosian Code and its revised version promulgated by Justinian in the sixth century was preserved and applied by the canonists of Italy and of the French Midi. But outside these territories the Church and its appropriated Roman law came into conflict with local ethnic traditions.

This conflict, as I have said, was inevitable and was bound to become a conscious challenge from the side of the local traditions. For each of the major ethnic groups entering the inclusive Christian community had its own understanding of the nature of marriage, unformed and inarticulate though the understanding may have been. And especially each had its own conviction concerning the agency that creates a marriage, the process that brings a marriage into existence. None of these groups—the Lombards, the Franks, the Germans—was of a mind to simply relinquish its own tradition and adopt the Roman.

The element in the process of marrying common to all these European peoples appears to have been some form of conveyance, of a handing over, a *traditio*. This did not necessarily exclude from the process the parties' reciprocal consent. But it lessened the sufficiency of the consent for creating the marriage; it made the consent only one part of a multi-step process of marrying, and left uncertainty concerning its exact function there.

Lombard custom required that before the nuptial celebration the couple exchange consent in the presence of the community, and before an *orator,* a layman chosen by the parents. The latter asked and received the spouses' consent. Where the *mundium,* the dowry used in negotiation of the betrothal, was in full use, the marriage was contracted between the *mundoaldus,* acting as agent for the girl's father, and the groom-to-be. But in this case the essential step in creating the marriage was held to be the *traditio,* the handing over of the girl to her husband by the *mundoaldus.*

Where the tradition of the *mundium* was neglected, the beginning itself of cohabitation replaced the *traditio* as the moment creating the marriage. In this case it was said of the bride, *ambulavit ad maritum—* "she has walked (or gone over) to her husband."

This practice, as well as that of the *traditio,* was discordant with the Roman marriage by reciprocal consent of the parties. The point of insistence in Lombard custom was that a transfer, a conveyance, was required for a valid marriage, either the *traditio* of the bride, or this *traditio* preceded by the *mundium.* Thus the obvious contractual character of this Lombard custom. Although the consent of both bride and groom was asked, it is not clear that it was required for creating the marriage.

In the Frankish tradition the bride received an endowment from her husband-to-be, and her father in turn gave the *mundium* to him. Even where there was no *mundium* the endowing of the bride was obligatory. If the latter was not done, there was a firm presumption against the existence of the marriage.

Among the Germanic peoples too a conveyance lay at the essence of marriage. This was a transfer of authoritative guardianship of the girl from her father to her new husband. A *mundoaldus* arranged with the girl's father for the transfer. She in turn had little choice about whom she married, into whose authority she was transferred. The husband, as the one holding the *mundium* following the transfer, became his wife's new *mundoaldus.* After she had been handed over to him ceremonially he led her to her new home. If a marriage was to be accepted as a *matrimonium legitimum,* one that would give to the children the right of inheritance, it had to be created according to this ceremony. Without the ceremony a woman could be taken as a wife, but her marriage was not considered legitimate. She was called a *concubina,* and her children could not inherit.

The Roman Procedure in Marrying

It was not that the Romans had failed to produce a multi-step ceremony even in face of the fact that no one was obligated to use it. By the time of Pope Nicholas I in the middle of the ninth century the ceremony consisted of the following four main elements. First there was the betrothal, the *promissa foedera,* a consent given by both parties in consideration of the future marriage, a consent which could be given only with the consent in turn of the parent or the legal guardian. Then there was the *desponsatio* wherein the wedding pledges, the *arrhae,* including the bride's ring, were exchanged and the deed of financial settlement was given to the bride. Next came the nuptial Mass wherein the spouses received the Church's blessing. And finally there was the departure from the church and entry into the new home to begin married life.

But Roman law and tradition held that among these steps it was the reciprocal consent of the bride and groom, however it was manifested, that created the marriage. Even if other parts of the ceremony, or even if the entire ceremony were omitted, the creation of the marriage by the consent alone was acknowledged. A secondary consequence of this acknowledgment was that in Roman tradition there was nothing in the process of marrying that warranted calling the marriage, the effect of the process, a contract.

The Roman canonists shared a virtual consensus that the reciprocal consents which create a marriage do not produce a contract because they have for their object not the producing of reciprocal obligations. This object, the intended effect of the consenting, is rather to produce a state, to bring the *consortium* of the spouses into existence, to produce the *individua vitae consuetudo,* the undivided sharing of life. This, according to the Romans, is neither a real contract in which the transfer of the woman's *mundium* would be the object, nor a consensual contract in which the spouses would commit themselves to exchange a service.

But the main point of the conflict between authorities in the Roman tradition and those in the European was not that the latter regarded marriage as a contract while the Romans did not. In the ninth and tenth centuries neither had come to these expressly conflicting judgments, however contractual the marriage transaction in the Lombard, Frankish and Germanic uses may have been. The object of the Roman resistance was the European treatment of the bride as a virtual chattel conveyed in a contractual exchange to the man whose negotiation through a *mundoaldus* most pleased her father or guardian. The European resistance in turn was directed at the Roman concession that the consent of the parties could create their marriage apart from any witnessing ceremony—a Church-vindicated permissiveness that undermined the European father's authority over his children and voided his chance to use them to improve the fiscal and perhaps social standing of his family.

When the dispute drew to a close early in the thirteenth century its formulation included a serious question about the place of sexual intercourse in creating a marriage. The Roman side of the argument was capsulized in the axiom, *Nuptias non concubitus sed consensus facit*—"Not intercourse but consent creates a marriage." If this side were to win out, yet another European tradition would be voided. This held that the combination of sworn promise to marry in the future (the betrothal oath) and subsequent intercourse could together create the marriage. And they could do so even without the intervention of the marital consent itself. They were taken, in combination, as a manifestation of marital consent. Apparently voided too would be the tradition that until the first act of intercourse a marriage is not fixed in indissolubility. And an ancient avenue of escape from unwanted marriages—entrance into a religious order permitted if the marital consent were not consummated by intercourse—would be closed off.

What was to complicate the complicated disagreement even more was this, that while Popes from the time of Nicholas I canonized the principle in Roman law that it is the consent that creates the marriage, the Popes of the eleventh century did not always distinguish clearly the two acts of consent possible in the process of marrying. Sequentially the first of these was the consent to marry in the future, called the *promissa foedera,* or the *desponsatio,* or the *consensus de futuro.* The second was the *consensus de praesenti,* also at times called carelessly the *desponsatio.* It was not that anyone thought seriously that the *consensus de futuro* by itself could create the marriage. But this consent, since it was clearly an expression of the will to marry, if followed by a manifested execution of this will—for example in sexual intercourse—was thought to be effective in creating the marriage.

How the question of divorce and remarriage is a facet of this more inclusive question concerning the agency that creates a marriage is clear enough. Granted that Christ's words remembered in the Synoptic Gospels, "What God has joined man must not separate," forbid any spouses' dissolving their marriages. Granted too that Christ's instruction conveyed by Paul in 1 Corinthians forbids at least a Christian wife's abandoning her marriage and her husband's dismissing her (and supposing that his words not only forbid these but make them impossible). But there remains the question: If marrying is a multi-step process, at which step do the impermissibility, and perhaps even the impossibility, of dissolving it take hold? Or to reformulate the question, Christ's command, "What God has joined man must not separate," seems a logical conclusion to his earlier assertion that when a husband joins to his wife they are no longer two but become "one body." At which point then in the process of marrying does God's joining the man and the woman produce that which no man may separate? At the moment of exchanged consent? If so, at which of the two consents we have noted just above? Or not at the moment of either consent, but in a later act that completes the consent? If so, what is this act? At what point do a man and woman become the "one body" that defies human separating? If at the moment of consent, how can this consent alone make them "one body"? Does this not have to wait until they become in some physical way one body in sexual intercourse?

There was a further refinement of the question brought by the theology of indissolubility of Christian marriages thought to be implicit in Ephesians 5. If, concluding from Paul's premise, the marriage of two Christians is indestructible because it images the indestructible union of Christ and the Church, at which point in its history does a Christian marriage begin to do this imaging? Surely, a provisory and generic answer would have it, when the marital union is most complete. But could this completion come from consent alone? Must it not wait for at least the first intercourse? And if it must, it follows that Christ's Synoptic instruction must refer only to the consummated marriages of Christians, even though he nowhere hinted at this qualification.

Yves of Chartres

Let us go back to Yves of Chartres at the end of the eleventh century to see how one scholar's indecision and perhaps carelessness could contribute to the tangling of the effort to resolve the dispute. Yves seems to have been the first to attempt to sort out and to evaluate the several components of the process that in his society created a marriage.

In Book 6, Chapter 14 of his *Panormia* he seems to have set forth his own theory in the matter: What the reciprocal consents of the parties do is to *begin* their marriage (*in desponsatione conjugium initiatur*).[4] But it is not clear that by this consent he meant other than the betrothal promise, for in the succeeding chapter he says that from the first promise to marry the parties are truly to be called spouses (*a prima fide desponsationis conjuges verius appellantur*).[5] If there is a first promise, there is a second. And since no other second promise was known than the marital promise itself (the consent *de praesenti*), by the first promise here he must mean the betrothal promise (the consent *de futuro*). Therefore, he concludes in still the next chapter, consummation by intercourse is not needed for the creating of the marriage. But seven chapters later, in Chapter 23, he asserts that the relationship is not a *true* marriage (*verum matrimonium*) until the first intercourse.

He confirmed his judgment about this efficacy of the betrothal promise (and by his choice of words further confused the issue) where, in his *Epistola 99,* he wrote that through this promise a marriage is for the most part concluded by a reciprocal expression of wills (*ex majori parte fuerit conjugium ex utrorumque voluntate compactum*).[6]

Indeed in Yves' mind there seemed no difference between sworn betrothal and a non-consummated marriage. In his vocabulary both *desponsatio* (according to *Epistolae 99* and *246*)[7] and *pactum conjugale*

(*Epistolae 134, 198, 161, 167* and *246*)[8] signified either of them. But whichever of the two he referred to by these terms, betrothal or unconsummated marriage, he was clear in his mind that the principal element in the creating of a marriage is the sworn promise.

How did this bear upon the dissolubility and the indissolubility of marriage? In his *Epistola 167* he says that the sworn betrothal (the *promissa foedera*) is irrevocable. If this seems to allow the ambiguity that though the product of this oath may be dissolved, the oath itself may never be withdrawn, Yves clears up the point elsewhere (in *Epistolae 147, 161, 216*) by asserting that even before the first intercourse a marriage (which he has already insisted can be created by the betrothal oath) is indissoluble.[9] And in two other letters he refined the point, turning to the theology of the sacrament. With the exchange of conjugal consent there is a union of souls. But this has just as effective a part as the union of bodies has in mirroring the relationship of Christ and the Church (*Epistola 134*). In fact this mirroring is truly present only in the union of charity in the spouses' wills (*Epistola 242*).[10] Therefore his conclusion: because this mirroring may take place even before the first intercourse, the marriage at least of two Christians is invulnerable to dissolution before the first intercourse. How little in agreement Yves was on this last point with many of his successors we shall soon see.

The first of these successors was Anselm of Laon, who wrote his Treatise on Marriage (*Tractatus de Matrimonio*) shortly before his death in 1117. He agreed with the Roman law and tradition that it is the expressed agreement of the parties' wills that creates a marriage, although true to his European heritage he insisted that there are other elements that are needed to bring a marriage to its completeness. Thus only a consummated marriage realizes the union of Christ and the Church. And this has consequences for the possibility of dissolving a marriage: "If a man is impotent, his marriage is not complete. His wife may dismiss him and marry another" (*Si frigidae naturae est vir, non perfectum est conjugium. Dimittat ipsa eum et nubat alteri*). And again it is to be noted that the husband's impotence, as Anselm understands it here, is not a cause of nullity in his attempt to marry; rather it grounds the possibility of his marriage's dissolution, since it keeps his marriage from being *perfectum*.

Toward the end of his *Sententiae* William of Champeaux posed the problem concerning marital consent that was to become a common paradigm in which the canonists set forth the distinction they hoped would resolve this problem. He asked if a man who has already pledged himself under oath to marry one woman can marry another. Obviously he was asking if the sworn betrothal creates a marriage. By way of answering he distinguished two kinds of promise (*fides*)—the *fides pactionis* by which a man promises that he will on a future date take a woman as his wife, and the *fides conjugii* by which a man actually takes the woman as his wife, whether within the wedding ceremony or before it.

William was decisive in his judgment that the *fides pactionis* does not create the marriage, but that the *fides conjugii* does. For the man in question must keep the second of the women because his *fides coniugii* made with her has made them spouses. But because of his violated oath to the first woman he must do penance. Not even before consummating his marriage with her may he dismiss the second woman in order to keep his promise to the first, because the *fides conjugii* with the second woman is inviolable. If he were to try to return to the first woman, he would be obliged to dismiss her and return to the second, to whom he is truly married.[11]

In his *Epitome Theologiae Christianae* William's pupil, Peter Abelard, repeated his mentor's distinction but in different terms. First there was the agreement to contract a marriage in the future (*foederatio de conjugio contrahendo*), then the agreement to marry (*foederatio conjugii*). The latter consists of words which express the *traditio* at the moment it takes place, as though the spouses were to say to one another, "I give myself over to you for the use of my body, so that as long as you live I shall not marry another" (*Trado me tibi ad usum carnis meae, ita ut quamdiu vixeris, non me alii conjungam*).[12] Thus for Abelard not only was it the second of the two promises that creates the marriage, but it creates it in such a way that apparently even without consummation the way is barred to a second marriage until one of the spouses dies.

Gratian's *Decretum*

During the six decades from about 1090 until 1150 the canonists of Europe gathered and published the richest volumes of *sententiae*, collections (often without commentary) of statements on religion, morals and law coming from earlier Christian teachers, and of decrees by Popes and councils touching the same issues. The two most active centers of this work were the two universities of Bologna and Paris. In the former worked the most thorough collector of them all, the Camaldolese monk, Graziano de Clusio, known in history simply as Gratianus (anglicized as Gratian). His *Concordantia discordantium canonum* (Concordance of Discordant Canons), compiled during the years 1127–1140, became the handbook of that epoch for students of canon law. To them it was known as Gratian's *Decretum,* the name by which it has been known ever since. Along with his colleagues at Bologna Gratian taught that more than just the reciprocal consent of the parties is needed to create a marriage. What he thought that more is we shall see presently.

The University of Paris was the home of Gratian's counterpart as a collector of ancient *sententiae,* and, although not a canonist, his amiable adversary in the interpretation of the marriage in this essentially juridical debate. He was Peter Lombard. His *Libri IV Sententiarum,* compiled during the years 1155–1158, became the handbook during the following century for students of philosophy and theology in the schools of Europe. Perhaps paradoxically, despite Peter's residence in Paris, he and his colleagues there were the champions of the Roman interpretation that the consent of the parties alone is sufficient to create a marriage.

Gratian's *Decretum* took its place in the long line of those medieval collections that sought to bring scattered ecclesiastical and learned opinions into manageable order. With only qualified success did it accomplish what its formal title claims it to be, "A Concordance of Discordant Canons." Gratian's own judgments on the disputed issues appear in his attempts to work out concordance among the disagreeing judgments making up the disputes. But he makes his place in the history of Catholic marriage law because he was the most able representative of the Bolognese side of the debate about the agency needed to create a marriage. He argued, against the Roman position (championed by the theological faculty of the University of Paris), that the consent of the parties by itself is insufficient to create a *matrimonium perfectum,* a completed marriage; but insisted rather that consent at some stage and in some form only if followed by sexual intercourse constitutes the agency needed for creating a completed marriage. His judgment on the possibility and permissibility of dissolving a marriage flows as a necessary consequence from this judgment.

For Gratian the dispute concerning the agency needed to create a marriage came to a point in this question: Are a man and a woman who have declared their intention to marry—declared it whether by *consensus de futuro* or by *consensus de praesenti*—truly married before first intercourse?

He acknowledged the consequences of the two possible contradictory answers to the question. If a man and a woman thus promised are not married before their first intercourse, it follows that Mary and Joseph (who according to Christian tradition lived a virginal relationship) were never married. But if a man and a woman are truly married before their first intercourse, it follows that a brother and a sister can marry and do so innocently provided they never have intercourse. It was in preparing for his own answer to this question that he assembled in dialectical fashion the pertinent texts answering in one way or the other.[13]

To reconcile as far as possible the disagreeing texts among those he had gathered, and to propose his own solution, he borrowed a distinction that his congenial adversaries at the University of Paris had already made. This was the distinction between the *matrimonium initiatum* (the inchoate marriage) and the *matrimonium ratum* (the ratified or completed marriage). It said accordingly that a marriage is constituted inchoately by the *desponsatio* but is made complete by the first intercourse.

As I have suggested, Gratian did not pluck this distinction out of midair. And true to his jurist method he drew support for it from a typical marriage case that had been adjudicated in council by the bishops of Toledo.[14] One man had kidnaped and raped another's fiancée; he was sentenced to public penance and forbidden ever to marry. If the woman had not consented to the crime she was not to be denied marriage. But if the partners to the rape later presumed to marry, they were to be excommunicated.

Gratian reasoned from the decision as follows. The woman could not have been a wife to anyone despite being betrothed, since while her betrothed was still alive she was not forbidden to marry another. And he asked how the betrothed could through history have been called spouses by the Fathers when they were not yet married. His answer to this carries his key distinction: What is to be understood from the Fathers, as also from the logic of the Toldeo decision, is that by the *desponsatio* the marriage is only begun. But for its completion it must await the first intercourse.[15] His exact words are these:

> It seems therefore that that woman was not a wife to whom permission to marry was not denied even while her spouse (*sponsus*) was still alive. How can it be then that Ambrose and the other Fathers call them spouses but yet all these reasons show they are not? To understand this, note that a marriage is begun by the *desponsatio* but is completed by intercourse. Hence between spouse and spouse (*inter sponsum et sponsam*) there is marriage, but [only] inchoate marriage (*conjugium initiatum*). But between those who have had intercourse there is ratified marriage (*conjugium ratum*).[16]

But Gratian's use of the distinction failed at the solutions he hoped for from it because of the obviously ambiguous reference he leaves in his use of the term *desponsatio*. He fails to make clear whether the word as he uses it refers to the act of betrothal (the consent *de futuro*) or to the wedding vows (the consent *de praesenti*). Elsewhere in this Question 2 he says that the *desponsatio* by itself does not create a marriage. Here he apparently means the wedding vows, because he goes on to say that these vows, insufficient by themselves to create the marriage, nevertheless have this effect, that with the ensuing intercourse the marriage does come into existence. In other words, for creating a marriage the consent and the subsequent intercourse act as necessary co-causes, each insufficient without the other, but in cooperative tandem producing their effect.[17]

Then, commenting on the ancient axiom, "It is not intercourse that creates a marriage, but consent that does so," he continues:

> . . . this is to be understood in the following way: intercourse without the intent to contract a marriage, and the deflowering of a virgin without the exchange of consent, do not create a marriage. But an antecedent intent to contract marriage and the exchange of consent has this effect, that in the losing of her virginity, or in her intercourse, a woman is said to marry her husband, or "to celebrate their marriage."[18]

One consequence of his ambiguous use of *desponsatio* that Gratian almost certainly did not intend was the possibility that the act of betrothal followed by intercourse could create a marriage equally with the wedding vows followed by intercourse. But whichever meaning he intended for this term, he insisted that by itself the *desponsatio* creates only an inchoate marriage.

And for Gratian this becomes the pivot of his judgment on the dissolubility and indissolubility of marriage. A marriage can be dissolved, but only during its inchoate stage. Once it is completed by intercourse it becomes invulnerable to dissolution. How he applied this principle emerges as one reads through those passages in the *Decretum,* Causes 27 through 33, in which he assembles the Christian teachings on marriage that had come down to his day.

There is no need to examine every one of these passages in detail. They contain what we have seen and have become familiar with since the Synoptic Gospels. Where we shall linger for closer inspection is at those passages in which Gratian offers his own judgment on disputed questions.

He first broaches the question of dissolving a marriage when he asks, in Cause 27, Question 2, whether a maid betrothed (*desponsata*) to one man can renounce this commitment and transfer it to another man. And he divides this question into two: Are this maid and her first espoused married to one another? If they are, can they depart (*discedere*) from one another?—which is to ask if they can dissolve their marriage.[19]

Gratian first cites two sources in favor of their being married. The first is the commonly accepted definition of marriage coming down from Ulpianus: "Marriage is the joining of a man and woman who live in an undivided sharing of life" (*Sunt enim nuptiae sive matrimonium viri mulierisque conjunctio, individuam vitae consuetudinem retinens*). The second source is multiple, the repeated judgment of the Fathers and Christian writers in history that it is the consent of the parties, not sexual intercourse, that creates this undivided sharing of life.[20] Against this judgment he quotes (in Chapter 16 of this Question 2) the dictum attributed erroneously to Augustine, "There is no marriage between persons who have not been united by the commingling of the sexes."

The judgment that Gratian himself passes on this question we have already seen. Here it is repeated (in Chapter 45) where he distinguishes between inchoate marriage and completed, or consummated, marriage. Therefore his judgment too on the paradigm with which he introduced this issue: the girl's *desponsatio* with the man created only an inchoate marriage with him.

Immediately he turns to the second of the subquestions: Where there is this *desponsatio* can a girl break it and transfer her commitment to another man? In reply he cites the ruling that Pope Siricius had made in his letter to Bishop Himerius of Tarracona: The departure of the betrothed from betrothed is a marital separation (*conjugalis separatio*); and Siricius had forbidden and anathematized the marriage of the girl to the second man after such a separation because the priest's blessing upon her marriage was considered by the faithful a kind of sacrament.[21]

But Gratian points out that this prohibition and condemnation by Siricius touched the case of a girl who had already been veiled, had been blessed and had been led into her new home, while the girl in the case adduced by himself had gone through none of these ceremonies. Therefore Siricius' judgment in no way forbade her marriage to the second man. In short she was not married indissolubly to the first man by reason of her *desponsatio* with him. This indissolubility must wait for intercourse or perhaps (accepting the authority of Siricius) for the nuptial veiling and blessing and the leading of the bride into her new home.

Along the way to this conclusion at the end of Cause 27 Gratian had taken up and weighed other traditional causes for the separating and dismissing of spouses. Thus in Chapter 28 he offered his judgment about the dissolving of marriages by one or both spouses' vowing a life of continence in a religious order. He reasoned in reverse order from the fact that one spouse can end the union in this way even against the will of the other, to the conclusion that they were never husband and wife (*coniuges*) to one another to begin with because, according to the apostle Paul, neither has the right to dispose of his or her own body, but the other has.[22]

Evidently his reason for denying the reality of the marriage in this case was that one or the other had not given over the right to his or her body in its sexual acts. Implicitly then Gratian held that the reciprocal exchange of this right is essential to the creating of a marriage. One spouse's taking up the life of the vows against the other's will seemed, for Gratian, to be evidence that that spouse had never granted this right.

Chapter 29 contains his judgment on the possibility of dissolving a marriage because of the husband's impotence.[23] If this impotence appears after the spouses have once had intercourse, it does not dissolve the marriage (*Ecce, impossibilitas coeundi, si post carnalem copulam inventa fuerit in aliquo, non solvit conjugium*). His unstated reason for this is that even a single act of intercourse makes of the union a completed marriage. But from such a marriage no spouse is allowed to depart.

But if the impotence is verified before the first intercourse (and this may be done by the wife's swearing on the holy relics before seven witnesses chosen from her own family), she may abandon her impotent partner and marry another. And this marriage will not be her second but her first. For here, in offering his justifying reason for the departure and taking of a second partner, Gratian parts company with generations of his predecessors. Where they had said simply that a marriage unconsummated because of impotence can be dissolved, he says that non-consummation because of impotence keeps the union from being a marriage at all (*Si vero ante carnalem copulam* [*impotentia coeundi*] *deprehensa fuerit, liberam facit mulierem alium virum accipere. Unde apparet illos non fuisse conjuges*).[24] And he clinches his reasoning with two arguments from consequence. First, the partners could not have been husband and wife to begin with, since if they had been, they would not have been allowed to abandon the marriage except because of adultery (*fornicatio*). Second, if a woman were truly married to an impotent man, her departure from him would be a divorce. Gratian takes for granted that to admit the last-named is false.

The reason at the back of Gratian's mind for his calling a marriage incomplete until consummated by the first act of intercourse surfaces in Chapter 39 of this Question 2.[25] There he asks why according to custom a betrothed woman (*sponsa*) is not given over to her husband immediately on the completing of the betrothal agreement (the *pactum*). The reason he offers had become so traditional in the Europe of his time that its formulation was by then a witty jingle: *Ne vilem habeat maritus datam quam non suspiraverat sponsus dilatam* ("Lest husband think he had a common maid for not having sighed through pleasure delayed"). Immediately he uses the question to reiterate his pivotal distinction. The pseudo-Augustinian axiom that a woman is not truly married to her spouse unless she has had intercourse with him he says is true only of *matrimonium perfectum*, a completed marriage. But here he says what it is in a marriage itself that makes it to be complete, and consequently what it is that intercourse does to complete it. This completeness is found in its being a *sacramentum* of Christ and the Church. This *sacramentum* therefore is what intercourse puts into a marriage.

Immediately he anticipates the objection that if this is so, one must say that the marriage of Joseph and Mary was not complete. His reply is a distinction conventional in his time: the completeness of a marriage may be found in its dutiful vocation (its *officium*), which is fulfilled by intercourse, or it may be found in those qualities which are concomitant with a marriage, namely fidelity, progeny and the *sacramentum*. Mary and Joseph's marriage was complete in the latter sense. And he finishes the thought with this summation.

> Everything that has been adduced about not dissolving a marriage is understood of a complete marriage, one which has begun by the joining in espousal and has been consummated by fulfilling the duty of bodily intercourse. Those arguments which show that a marriage is dissoluble apply to an inchoate marriage, one which has not yet been completed by the exercise of this duty.[26]

Thus Gratian helps to fix in Catholic tradition the judgment that a non-consummated marriage may be dissolved. But this is not the only kind of marriage he considered vulnerable to the desire for dissolution. In his introduction to Cause 28 he adduces the case of a married pagan who is converted to the Christian faith, but whose wife abandons him out of hatred for this faith. Subsequently this man takes a Christian woman for his wife, and after her death he becomes a cleric, and eventually because of his virtue and intelligence he is elected a bishop. About this case Gratian asks three questions: (1) whether there can be marriage among pagans, (2) whether this man can take a second wife while his first wife still lives, and (3) whether a man who has had one wife before his baptism and another after it is to be deemed a *bigamus* (and is therefore disqualified from election as a bishop).[27]

Gratian cites opinions on both sides in answer to Question 1 but records his own judgment in the affirmative. This is in Chapter 17 of this Question 1, and he here offers an inventory of the kinds of marriages:

> Although it is a marriage, a marriage that omits God (as Augustine says) is not a ratified marriage [*matrimonium ratum*]. For a marriage may be legitimate but not ratified, another ratified but not legitimate, yet another both legitimate and ratified. A legitimate marriage is one contracted according to the laws and customs of one's land. But among pagans this is not a ratified marriage because it is not firm and inviolable. With the giving of the writ of dismissal they can separate and remarry, following the law of the courts, not that of the city [of God]. But among Christians marriage is ratified because once they enter a marriage they cannot dissolve it. Of these ratified Christian marriages some are legitimate, as in the marriage wherein the woman is given over by her parents, she receives the dotal gifts from her husband, and she is blessed by a priest. Such a marriage is called both legitimate and ratified. But those marriages which have disdained all such solemnities and are created only by the parties' manifestation of will [*solo affectu*], these are not legitimate but are said only to be ratified.[28]

About Question 2 he again cites opinions on both sides, but now on further divisions of the question. One such opinion is that a Christian spouse is permitted to abandon a pagan because the latter is an occasion of sin for the Christian. In support of this judgment he cites Augustine's saying, in his The Sermon on the Mount, that since idolatry is fornication in the spiritual sense, and Christ permitted a husband to dismiss his wife for her fornication, a husband may dismiss an idolatrous, which is to say a pagan, wife. And by logical extension a Christian wife too may dismiss a pagan husband.[29]

After citing other opinions in favor of dismissing a pagan spouse Gratian offers his own judgment, and it necessarily involves his making a distinction.

> It is one thing to dismiss a spouse who wishes to continue the marriage [*volentem cohabitare*]. It is another to not follow a spouse who abandons the marriage. It is permitted to dismiss a pagan spouse who wishes to continue the marriage, but not to

take a second spouse while the first one still lives. But this holds only for those who have wedded while both were still pagans.

But if both spouses are converted to the Christian faith, or if both were joined in marriage as Christians, but in the course of time one abandons the faith, and out of hatred for the faith abandons the marriage, the abandoned spouse is not to live with the other. And as long as the apostate still lives, the abandoned spouse may not remarry because the marriage between them is *ratum.* And this can in no way be dissolved.[30]

Here is another paragraph in Gratian's and eventually the Church's doctrine and discipline of divorce and remarriage. A Christian spouse may dismiss a non-Christian—to save himself or herself from perhaps fatal temptation, if we draw on Gratian's earlier reasoning borrowed from the Fathers. But in this case the Christian may not remarry. He or she may not because the scriptural and patristic passages permitting remarriage refer not to this case but to one in which the pagan spouse abandons the Christian. This permission then is what warrants the remarriage where the pagan spouse takes the initiative and abandons the Christian. But it is the lack of ratification that establishes the radical possibility of its dissolution, a possibility that Gratian apparently considers realized by the pagan's act of abandoning the Christian.

But where both spouses are Christian, and one of them apostatizes and abandons the marriage out of hatred for the faith, the reason why the abandoned Christian cannot remarry is different. Here no scriptural or patristic permission rules the case. Now the reason is that the marriage, though sundered socially and physically, has been ratified. It has been made a sacrament by the spouses' sexual intercourse. And nothing that either spouse can do, not even hate-motivated rejection of the faith, the faith that was one of the causes creating the sacrament, can obliterate the sacrament and release its effect that is the indissolubility of the marriage. And in real life the agency producing this inviolability was the reciprocal consent of the parties and at least one subsequent act of sexual intercourse.

Clearly visible in Gratian's summary here are the elements of what has come to be known in Catholic marriage law as the Pauline Privilege.

As for Question 3—whether a man who has one wife before his baptism and another after it is a *bigamus,* and whether, if he is, he may be elected a bishop—Gratian gives it only brief consideration.[31] Apparently his concern is with obedience to Paul's prescription in 1 Timothy 3:2 that a bishop must be a man of one wife. He recalls Jerome's opinion that this refers only to wives taken by a man once he has become a Christian, since in baptism all things old are dismissed and everything is made new.

But Gratian judges that those who think more sharply on the matter deny that such a man may be elected bishop. For in baptism that which is done away with is a person's earlier sins. A marriage entered before that baptism is not dissolved by it, just as a woman who gives up her virginity while a catechumen cannot be accepted for consecration as a virgin after her baptism. (Apparently the reasoning here is that baptism does not change ontological conditions, and a marriage is as ineradicably an onto-logical condition as the state of non-virginity.) Thus a man who had one wife before his baptism, but, presumably after abandoning her, takes another on being baptized, is rightly deemed a *bigamus* and cannot be elected a bishop—despite his excellence in holiness and in knowledge.

Gratian does not here consider that perhaps the first wife may as a pagan have abandoned the man in question. Or if he does suppose this, he may hold that the man is a *bigamus* nonetheless. Not to be passed over is his neglecting to say that whatever the cause of the first marriage's being abandoned, the man is not required to give up the second wife (and despite having taken the second wife he may indeed be holy). The only conse-quence is that he is barred from the episcopate.

In Cause 32 Gratian takes up the question about divorce that had been the focus of attention for centuries: "May a spouse dismiss an adulterous spouse and marry another?" But he takes it up in an altered formulation that is bound to qualify his answer to it: "May an adulterous husband dismiss an adulterous wife, and may this husband remarry while his dismissed wife is still alive?"[32]

Gratian's own answer is a no to both questions. But his answer to the first of them is qualified by the fact of the husband's own adultery. So the answer is not the answer to the ancient query born of the Matthean exceptive clause. His answering goes even further astray in that the reason he offers for his judgment is not that "What God has joined man must not separate." It is rather that husbands and wives must be bound by the same demands of justice. Indeed, he says, since the husband is the head of the wife, his adultery is more grievous than hers.[33]

He does not suggest that by this equal justice a wife ought to be able to dismiss her adulterous husband as readily as he can dismiss her. He implies rather that because both are guilty, justice rules that neither may dismiss the other. (Thus the punishment for their infidelity is ironically that they must remain together.)

He adds a second perplexing qualification that if an adulterous hus-band is intent on dismissing his wife for her adultery, he must first be *purgatus* of his own sin. Then, apparently again in consideration of equal justice, he applies the same qualification to an adulterous wife seeking to dismiss her husband for his adultery.[34]

To the second of these questions as it is asked in this simple form— "May this husband remarry while his dismissed wife is still alive?"— Gratian's answer too (in Chapter 16) is simple, drawn as it is from a carefully one-sided selection of Fathers and Christian writers: "By these authorities it is most clearly (*evidentissime*) proved that a man who dismisses his wife for her adultery cannot remarry while she is still alive, and that if he seeks to do so, he is guilty of adultery."[35]

But in Chapter 18 he essays an interpretation of two patristic texts that must have been the cause of disagreement and dispute among the canonists of his generation and before.[36] The first was a commentary on 1 Corinthians 7 attributed for centuries to Ambrose. The passage as Gratian read it contained a curiously expanded version of verse 10.

> "A wife is not to depart from her husband [here follows the expanding phrase] except for his *fornicatio*; and if she in fact departs, she is either to remain unmarried or is to be reconciled with her husband. And a husband is not to dismiss his wife." [Paul] did not apply to the husband what he said of the wife because a husband is allowed to take a second wife.

The other passage was from Gregory II's Epistle 4 to Bishop Boniface answering the latter's question asking how to rule in the cause of a husband whose wife could no longer have intercourse with him because of her illness. We recall Gregory's judgment in the case: Boniface was to urge the man to stay with his wife and live a life of continence. But because this was a demand for heroic conduct, if the man could not live such a life he was to be allowed to remarry while continuing to support his infirm wife.[37]

Gratian's judgment on the passage attributed to Ambrose is brief: "What is attributed here to Ambrose is said to have been interpolated by falsifiers." By Gratian's time the inauthenticity of the passage was beginning to be taken for granted. The suspected interpolater was later to get the sobriquet The Ambrosiaster.

His judgment on Gregory is nearly as succinct but markedly more severe: "The judgment of Gregory is simply contrary to the sacred canons, indeed to the Gospel and to the apostolic teaching."[38]

Then he turns back to the passage from the Ambrosiaster to subject it to a most singular exegesis.

> But some, desirous of saving Ambrose's opinion, hold that it refers not to just any kind of adultery, as though because of any kind a man may licitly dismiss his wife and remarry. But they say it refers only to incestuous adultery, as when a man's wife publicly prostitutes herself to his father or his son, or to his brother or uncle, or to someone like them. And this woman, because she has thus rendered herself illicit to her husband in perpetuity by her intercourse with his blood relatives that established affinity with him in the first, second or third degree, may be licitly dismissed; and while she is still alive her husband may take another wife.[39]

At this point Gratian offers his own explanation.

> One who urges this explanation ought to understand that it is allowed no more to a man than it is to a wife if her husband

should commit adultery in the same way. For Ambrose has in mind a person who is a man not according to gender but according to strength of soul; and he has in mind a person who is a woman not according to gender but according to weakness of mind (*mollitia mentis*). But because no authority allows that a second wife may be taken while the first still lives, Ambrose's judgment must be taken to apply to the above-named kind of adultery. However it is not as though a man could remarry while his first wife still lives; it is rather that after the death of an adulterous husband or wife (of whom both, as noted above, are called women because of their lust), the spouse who is innocent of adultery, whether this be husband or wife, may remarry; while the adulterous spouse, if he or she is the survivor, may absolutely not remarry.[40]

In Cause 33 Gratian takes up the issue of dismissing a spouse because of impotence. But here he poses the question in anything but its usual formulation. The paradigmatic case he adduces has the husband impotent as the victim of sorcery. About him he asks, first, whether because of his impotence his wife *ought* to leave him, and, second, whether, after her departure, she can marry a man with whom she had committed adultery during her marriage.[41]

His replies are not at all points on the target of his questions. First he cites the reasons against the impotent husband's dismissing his wife, principal among them Christ's command that a wife may be dismissed only for her adultery, and Paul's command (from Christ) that a wife is not to leave her husband as long as he still lives.

But Gratian's own judgment draws predictably on his distinction between inchoate marriage and completed marriage.

A marriage is completed by intercourse [*conjugium confirmatur officio*] . . . ; so after a marriage has been completed by intercourse a husband is not permitted to dismiss his wife, nor a wife permitted to leave her husband, except because of adultery. However, before completion the impotence itself dissolves the bond of marriage [*impossibilitas officii solvit vinculum conjugii*].[42]

As for the wife of this impotent husband, Gratian quotes with approval (in Chapter 1) Pope Gregory II's letter to Bishop John of Ravenna ruling that if the wife can prove in due process that she has been unable to have intercourse with her husband, she may leave him and remarry.[43] But in Chapter 3 Gratian makes a distinction demanded by the formulation of his original question. Gregory had ruled what is to be done if the husband's impotence comes from natural causes. But in this case his impotence is the effect of sorcery. May the wife in the latter case leave her husband and remarry?

In reply he quotes Hincmar of Rheims' ruling that this couple must make a general confession, pray, do penance, and even seek exorcism. But if even these measures do not restore the husband's potency they may separate and she may remarry. And if the husband later regains his potency, they cannot return to one another. Gratian points out the disagreement here with Gregory's ruling that when the husband regains his potency the wife must return to him. He leaves the issue at this unsatisfactory point.

Note that, as I have said, Gratian sees the possibility of dissolution and remarriage in this case to lie in the marriage's incompletion. And since he must acknowledge that, if the wife is to truly leave and remarry, the marriage must be dissolved, he must name the cause of the dissolution. He selects the impotence itself as this cause (in contrast to the later ruling that it is of nullity that the impotence is the cause).

This seems Gratian's most significant bequest to the developing Catholic doctrine and discipline concerning divorce and remarriage: he took the by then accepted attenuation of Christ's command that a husband must not dismiss his wife nor a wife leave her husband—the attenuation saying that this command refers only to a consummated marriage—and decided that in departure or dismissal because of impotence there is a true dissolution. Indeed it is the impotence itself that does the dissolving, so that the consequence (which he never draws) should be that not only is the dismissal or departure permitted, but it is obligatory. We shall see now that Peter Lombard, as the representative of the Roman mind centered in the faculty of theology at the University of Paris, both agreed with Gratian and the Bolognists at one point and disagreed with them at another.

Peter Lombard

Peter Lombard completed his four books of *Sententiae* at Paris between 1155 and 1158, only a little more than a decade after Gratian had completed his *Decretum* at Bologna. (In the language of medieval Scholasticism *sententiae*, as I explained briefly above, are statements, opinions, intellectual positions on arguable issues in philosophy and theology taken by teachers in the history of Christianity beginning with the apostles and coming down to perhaps a generation before the compiler. The editor of a book of *sententiae* was just that, a compiler. Today we would call his work "selected readings." However his selections were seldom longer than a paragraph and frequently as slight as a single sentence. The purpose for such compilations was to gather and in some degree arrange these sayings under headings so as to make them more available as sources, principles and examples of theological reasoning. A compiler and editor of *sententiae* also had the prerogative of offering his own interpretations and conclusions. They are Lombard's interpretations and conclusions in which we are mainly interested here.)

Like the work of his predecessors Lombard's is, as I have said, a compilation, except that it is the work not of a jurist but of a philosopher-theologian. It is therefore not, as theirs are, an informal corpus of laws but a more inclusive compendium of Christian teaching that includes *sententiae* of Popes, councils, Fathers and other Christian writers, many of which *sententiae* were already fixed in Catholic legislation. But Lombard was not only a gatherer and arranger. He was an analyst and critic who sought to answer the questions handed down to his generation in the *sententiae* he gathered and arranged. Again, they are his answers that mainly interest us here.

It is in Book 4 of his *Libri Sententiarum,* Distinctions 26 through 42, that he treats of marriage.[44] The most important among these passages are Distinction 26, which deals with the defining of marriage and the function of marital consent and of intercourse in constituting a marriage; Distinction 27, on the betrothal promise and on the content of marital consent; Distinction 28, on freedom of consent; Distinction 31, on the goods of marriage; and Distinction 34, the *locus* of our keenest interest, on the severing of the marriage bond.

Little of the material in these passages is the product of Lombard's original search among the sources. He borrowed virtually all of it from Gratian and from another near-contemporary, Hugh of St. Victor. The value of his work lies in its arranging the borrowed material in the most manageable form it had ever found. The fact that virtually all the significant scholars of Europe in the generations following Lombard's included among their works a *Commentarium in IV Libros Sententiarum Petri Lombardi* attests to his epoch's respect for the utility of his collection of Christian teaching.

It will help for later understanding Lombard's judgment on the solubility and indissolubility of marriage to review briefly his answer to the question asking which kind of act or acts create a marriage.

His answer to the question is unambiguous and simple. In Distinction 28, Chapter 3 he says, "What creates a marriage is not the consent to cohabitation nor the carnal copula; it is the consent to conjugal society that does so."[45] He has already said in Distinction 26 that what creates a marriage is the reciprocal consent of the parties, whether expressed in words or in other and equivalent signs. Like Gratian he insisted that all the traditional conditions and liturgy surrounding the marriage are non-essential, however much they are mandated by custom and some of them by law. The consent of the parents and their ceremonial giving over of their daughter are non-essential. So too are the religious ceremonies, including the priestly blessing.

In saying that the act creating a marriage is the parties' reciprocal consent to conjugal society, he makes the careful distinction that Gratian did not, between the parties' *consensus de futuro* and their *consensus de praesenti.* Both are consents to marriage, but the *consensus de futuro* establishes only the betrothal but not the marriage itself, even when it is made under oath. What creates the marriage is the separate *consensus de praesenti,* and it creates it before and separately from sexual intercourse. The *consensus de futuro* followed by intercourse, with the *consensus de praesenti* omitted, cannot create the marriage. And the *consensus de praesenti,* by itself and even without the subsequent intercourse, makes any subsequent attempt at another marriage invalid, since this consent creates the marriage about which Christ said that no man must divide it.

Consistently with the traditional method he inherited Lombard touched the question of divorce first in his consideration of the good of marriage that is the *sacramentum.* He notes in his Distinction 31, "The goods of marriage are mainly three, according to Augustine in his *De Genesi ad Litteram....* In the *sacramentum* it is established that the marriage not be separated, and that the husband or wife once dismissed is not to marry another for the sake of children."[46]

By reproducing Augustine's rhetoric all too faithfully at this point Lombard slips into carelessness. He appears to say that a husband or wife is not to remarry if dismissed (he thereby leaves open the question about remarriage after other forms of dissolution). And he implies that neither husband nor wife is to remarry for the sake of having children (he here leaves open the question of possible remarriage for other motives).

In the same passage he records the kinds of separations that are predicated of marriage.

> Separation can be of two kinds, corporeal and spiritual. Spouses can be separated corporeally because of adultery, or by mutual consent in order to enter religious life, whether for a time or permanently. But they cannot be separated sacramentally as long as both live, provided they are married legitimately. For the marital bond remains between them even though, on separating, they should seek to marry other partners.[47]

Again the thinking is faithful to Augustine's own. The severing of a marriage that involves no more than the ending of cohabitation—a severing unknown to ancient Roman law—seems in this passage the only kind possible. For despite such separation the most tenacious of Augustine's three goods, the *sacramentum,* survives. The thought is the same whichever way one translates Lombard's *sacramentaliter vero separari non possunt* ("But they cannot be separated sacramentally ...")—whether "the *sacramentum* makes a true separation impossible" or "the *sacramentum* cannot be dissolved" or, as I have it here, "... they cannot be separated sacramentally."

Here Lombard identifies himself as a sponsor of the distinction that was to become useful in later Catholic marriage legislation, the distinction between the marriage (*conjugium*) and the marital bond (*vinculum conjugale*), or perhaps between married life and the marital bond.

He cites Augustine's claim in the latter's On Marriage and Concupiscence (*De Nuptiis et Concupiscentia*), Book 1, Chapter 11, that despite dismissal of or abandonment by a spouse, the marriage survives because there remains *quiddam conjugale*—a certain marital something—that continues to bind the spouses to one another. This "something" is analogous to the *sacramentum* of faith that remains in the soul of a Christian even if he apostatizes, and keeps him a Christian willy-nilly. It is not yet clear that this something is, to Lombard's mind, identical with the bond, or that the bond and the *sacramentum* are identical. But what is certain and clear to him is that this "something" is both distinct and separable from cohabitation and survives even the latter's irreversible destruction. He adds in confirmation of this that this *vinculum* is not broken between two spouses who after their wedding and even after its consummation agree to live a married life of sexual continence.

In addition Lombard makes clear that neither is the marriage itself identical with the *sacramentum*.

> And note that the third of these goods is called the *sacramentum*, not in the sense that it is the marriage itself, but because it [the marriage] is a sign of the same sacred reality, namely of the spiritual and inseparable union of Christ and the Church.[48]

I quote this passage partly because it is a transparent example of a medieval theologian's taking the meaning of marriage's *sacramentum* well beyond the point at which Augustine had left it. We recall that the latter held it to be resident in every marriage, Christian and non-Christian, since he included it among the goods inherent in marriage that makes marriage itself good, against the Manichees' contention that it is evil. And for Augustine the primary meaning of the term *sacramentum* was the sworn commitment of the spouses never to separate as long as both lived, a commitment made either singly to one another or jointly to God.

But here Lombard says that the meaning of *sacramentum,* precisely as one of the three goods of marriage named by Augustine, is its quality as an image of the union of Christ and the Church. It is, Lombard asserts, the *sacramentum* thus understood that makes a marriage indissoluble as long as both spouses live—as it was the *sacramentum* according to Augustine's understanding of it that made it, to his mind, just as indissoluble. Or, to read Lombard's interpretation more finely, if we assume that in his mind the marital bond and the *sacramentum* are one and the same, it is the *sacramentum*-bond, understood as the image of the union of Christ and the Church which is imperishable. It survives even if the marriage understood as *coniugium* is destroyed by dismissal or abandonment.

Here the several ingredients of the later theology of radical indissolubility are laid out clearly enough. And a new opening has been created.

Whereas by Lombard's time it was long accepted that a true marriage could be dissolved provided it were not consummated, now one only need draw an easy and obvious conclusion to say that a true marriage can be dissolved if it has not in it the *sacramentum* understood as Lombard understands it here. And it is one more slight step to conclude that this dissolution is possible even if the marriage minus *sacramentum* is consummated.

His judgment that it is the *sacramentum* of marriage that causes its indissolubility Lombard confirms where he insists that the *sacramentum* is the only one of the three goods of marriage that is not separable from the marriage. He notes that some persons are married even though one or both of the other two goods of marriage are lacking in it. To sustain his opinion he cites the common experience of the married. For example, the failure of fidelity (*fides*) in a marriage does not annihilate it, ". . . because a wife who is an adulteress is not for that reason no longer a wife; for unless she were a wife, she would not be an adulteress. So when she commits adultery she sins, but the *sacramentum* of her marriage is not thereby destroyed."[49]

Neither does the absence of offspring (*proles*) keep the union from being a marriage. What the term *bonum prolis* designates is not the actual production and presence of children, but the spouses' hope for or expectation of children so that they may be nurtured in the Christian religion. Lombard says that this good is rooted not in the marriage itself but in the marital intent and desire of the spouses. (But he does not sustain his reasoning carefully when he goes on to say that the elderly can marry [how could they hope for children?], and that spouses can agree to a life of sexual continence [wherein they expressly void the desire and the intent to have children].)

But he insists it is quite different with that good of marriage that is the *sacramentum*. And again he repeats Augustine's claim for it.

> But the *sacramentum* is rooted so inseparably in a marriage of legitimate persons that it seems that without it there is no marriage at all, because as long as they live there remains between them the marital bond. Hence even though there be divorce [*divortium*] because of adultery, the firmness of the marital bond is not dissolved. . . .[50]

Again Lombard neglects to explain whether this *sacramentum* makes a marriage imperishable because it is identical with the marital bond that Augustine had said cannot perish while both spouses live, or whether it is distinct from this bond but is a quality of the marriage that makes the latter's destruction impossible as long as both spouses live.

In Distinction 34 he makes clear what he means by "legitimate persons."[51] There he distinguishes two degrees of qualification for marriage and one disqualification.

The fully (*plene*) legitimate are those who are not impeded from marriage by a vow of chastity, by sacred orders, by disparity of religious belief, by in-lawship, by impotence, or by the social condition of slavery.

At the opposite extreme are the fully illegitimate, those who are blocked by one of these impediments from marrying.

The qualifiedly legitimate (*mediate legitimi*) are those impeded by the conditions of slavery or impotence. If certain conditions, which Lombard does not name, are verified, they can marry; if they are not, they cannot. But his judgment about the effect of impotence on the attempt to marry is unclear. He seems to agree with a tradition saying that if a wife claims that she married in order to have children, but that she has been unable to have intercourse with her husband because of his impotence, and if she will swear in the presence of seven of her own kinfolk that she and her husband have never had intercourse with one another, she may remarry. But it is not clear, as Lombard explains this, whether the wife is freed for the second union because the impotence impeded the creating of her first marriage (and, being still single, she is free to marry), or whether the first marriage is dissolved because not consummated (and thus the wife is freed by this dissolution for a second marriage). If Lombard means the first of these, his choice of words is careless, for he says: *Tunc videtur mulier secundas posse contrahere nuptias*—"It seems the woman can then contract a *second* marriage."[52]

Lombard's final consideration of marital dissolution is in Distinction 36, where he asks whether because of slavery (*extrema conditio*) a wife can be separated from her husband and vice versa.[53]

He replies, after reviewing the current opinions on the matter, that if a free person marries a slave knowingly, he cannot dismiss her. But he can dismiss her if he has married the slave unwittingly, either by an innocent mistake or as the victim of deception. The same is true for a woman. He quotes the eighth-century Council of Verberies on this point and seems to agree with it.

> If a free man takes another's handmaid as his wife thinking that she too is free, if she is subsequently put into slavery, he may redeem her from this if he can. But if he cannot, he may take another wife if he wishes.[54]

It is unclear here whether the man was married at all to the handmaid he thought to be free, or whether he could finally marry her after buying her freedom from slavery. The latter is almost certainly Lombard's judgment, since the alternative would have him permitting dissolution of a true marriage followed by remarriage, and this is not because of the wife's deception but simply because of her slavery. There is nothing in Lombard's writings that suggests this permissiveness, this cruelty to a legitimately married woman.

Summary

In the thinking of Yves of Chartres, Gratian and Peter Lombard we see the coming together of the elements that were to make up the Catholic explanation of which kinds of marriage are indissoluble and which are the causes of their indissolubility.

The early medieval dispute over which act or acts create a marriage produced as a by-product the distinction between the consummated marriage and the unconsummated. This distinction opened the way in turn to a distinction in indissolubility. Now it could be said where indissolubility is to be found, namely in the consummated marriage—but only there.

The reason given for finding indissolubility only in the consummated marriage was that it alone is a true and complete image of the union of Christ and the Church. This prepared a convergence with the theology of marriage the sacrament that was then being drawn from Augustine's inconclusive reflection seven centuries earlier on the *sacramentum*. The "certain conjugal something"—the *quiddam coniugale*—that he had insisted survives, even though all else disappears from the union of a husband and wife, came to be identified in the twelfth-century canonists' minds with precisely this *sacramentum*. Thus this *sacramentum* lost its identity as Augustine had suggested it, as the unbreakable pledge of the spouses to one another, and came to be the marriage's imaging the relationship of Christ and the Church.

With this the elements of the theology of indissolubility were all in place and ready to be fixed: Only a marriage that is a sacrament is indissoluble, because it alone images the unbreakable union of Christ and the Church. And only a marriage that is consummated as well as a sacrament is indissoluble, because it alone images that union truly and completely.

Thus near the end of the twelfth century the Catholic reformers' efforts to install a rigorous discipline of divorce in the Western Church met the canonists' and theologians' determination of the acts that create a marriage, with the consequence not that it became impossible to dissolve a marriage in the Church, but that the possibility of dissolution was isolated in a careful corner of marriage where presumably it could be carefully controlled.

NOTES

1. This problem and its resolution belonged mainly to what is now called the classical age of Catholic canon law, an age that extended approximately from the Gregorian reform at the end of the eleventh century until the end of the thirteenth century. It is no exaggeration to say that the work of resolving this problem helped to produce the law that is now called classical.

2. See Chapter 6 of my earlier volume *What Is Marriage?* for a more detailed examination of this conflict and its resolution. Here I am drawing on the resources of that chapter and quoting much from it verbatim.

3. We recall that Ulpianus' judgment, *Consensus facit nuptias*—"It is the consent that creates a marriage"—had been embodied as axiomatic in Roman law, specifically in the Theodosian Code (V, 17, 8) and in Justinian's Digest (17, 30). It made its way into the medieval collections of canons at approximately the beginning of the twelfth century, the epoch in which classical Roman law was recovered by the Church in the West. It is found in the collection of that time called the *Polycarpus* and in the *Collectio Caesaraugustana,* where it is reformulated slightly but significantly, *Nuptias non concubitus sed affectus facit*—"It is not intercourse but the will to be married [rather than marital consent] that creates the marriage."

4. In P.L., Vol. 161, Cols. 1246–1247. That is the title of the chapter, quoted from Ambrose's On the Instruction of Virgins, Chapters 5 and 6. The entire chapter reads as follows: "When a woman is *desponsata* to a man she receives the name 'spouse.' For when the marriage [*conjugium*] is begun, the name belonging to marriage [*nomen conjugii*] is taken. The deflowering of the girl is not what creates the marriage but the marital consent [*pactio conjugalis*]. Thus when the girl is joined [to her husband] there is a marriage, not when she has intercourse."

5. *Loc. cit.,* Col. 1247.

6. Quoted in D.T.C., Vol. 9, Col. 2138.

7. *Ibid.*

8. *Ibid.*

9. *Loc. cit.,* Col. 2139.

10. *Ibid.*

11. *Loc. cit.,* Col. 2142.

12. *Loc. cit.,* Col. 2144.

13. This he did in Cause 27, Question 2 of his *Decretum* (in P.L., Vol. 187, Cols. 1392–1414).

14. *Ibid.,* Chapter 34, Col. 1406.

15. This distinction Gratian repeated immediately in Chapters 35 and 36, which are little more than headings taking the form of consecutive axioms: "Behold, in the *desponsatio* a marriage is begun, not completed"; and "It is by the intercourse of the conjoined that a marriage is completed" (Cols. 1406–1407).

16. *Loc. cit.,* Chapter 39, Col. 1407.

17. Gratian reasons in this way: "From all this it is evident that the betrothed are called spouses by reason of their hope of future things, not by reason of the reality of present things. But how is it that they are *called* spouses [*conjuges*] from betrothal if a woman deemed betrothed is not considered a wife [*conjunx esse negatur*]? The answer is that persons are called spouses from the time of betrothal not because in that betrothal they become spouses, but because from the commitment that they owe one another by virtue of the betrothal they subsequently become spouses—just as sins are said to be forgiven by faith not because they are thus forgiven before baptism, but because faith is a cause of our being cleansed from sin by baptism . . ." (Col. 1407).

18. *Ibid.*

19. *Op. cit.,* Col. 1392.

20. *Ibid.,* Cols. 1392–1397.

21. *Op. cit.,* Col. 1412.

22. *Op. cit.,* Col. 1403.

23. *Ibid.,* Col. 1404.
24. *Ibid.*
25. *Loc. cit.,* Col. 1407.
26. *Ibid.,* Cols. 1407–1408. "Cuncta ergo quae de non separando conjugio inducta sunt, de perfecto intelliguntur, quod sponsali conventione est initiatum, et officio corporalis commixtionis est consummatum. Illa vero, quibus separabile conjugium ostenditur, de initiato intelliguntur et quod nondum officio sui perfectum est."
27. *Op. cit.,* Col. 1413.
28. *Op. cit.,* Cols. 1427–1428.
29. *Ibid.,* Col. 1429.
30. *Ibid.*
31. *Ibid.,* Cols. 1429–1430.
32. *Op. cit.,* Col. 1463.
33. *Op. cit.,* Cols. 1493–1494.
34. *Ibid.,* Col. 1493.
35. *Loc. cit.,* Col. 1500.
36. *Ibid.,* Col. 1501.
37. *Ibid.*
38. *Ibid.*
39. *Ibid.*
40. *Ibid.,* Cols. 1501–1502.
41. *Loc. cit.,* Col. 1505.
42. *Loc. cit.,* Col. 1507.
43. *Ibid.,* Col. 1508.
44. These distinctions are in P.L., Vol. 192, Cols. 908–943.
45. *Op. cit.,* Col. 915.
46. *Loc. cit.,* Col. 918.
47. *Ibid.,* Cols. 918–919.
48. *Ibid.*
49. *Ibid.*
50. *Ibid.,* Col. 919.
51. *Loc. cit.,* Cols. 926–927.
52. *Ibid.,* Col. 927.
53. *Loc. cit.,* Col. 930.
54. *Ibid.*

12. THE FORMING OF THE LAW BY DECRETISTS AND DECRETALISTS

The nearly simultaneous publishing of Gratian's *Decretum* and of Peter Lombard's *Libri Sententiarum* at the middle of the twelfth century provided the sources for two streams of development in the Church's teaching on divorce and remarriage. The *Decretum* inspired a development in two major stages. The first of these was worked out by a group centered at the University of Bologna and called understandably the Decretists. These were pupils and successors of Gratian. They wrote commentaries on his text, *glossae* as well as full-scale *summae*. Principal among these decretists were Huguccio (later bishop of Ferrara), Stephen of Tournai, Paucapalia, Omnibene, Rufinus Bazianus, John of Faenza, and especially Rolando Bandinelli, who was to become Pope Alexander III and to put a busy hand to the shaping of the marriage law.

These scholars and writers followed Gratian in making the crucial distinction between the *matrimonium initiatum* (the inchoate marriage) and the *matrimonium perfectum* (the completed marriage). The effect of this distinction on subsequent divorce legislation was to fix as a principle that the inchoate marriage can be dissolved for certain causes, but that the completed marriage is impervious to dissolution. The decretists added little to the theology of the sacrament of marriage. They were canon lawyers, not theologians. But following Gratian they did find in the distinction between consummated and non-consummated marriage the added distinction between a marriage that images the indestructible union of Christ and the Church and one that does not. The recognition of this imaging as a cause of indissolubility—and the lack of it as a possibility of dissolution—they left as a bequest for their juridical heirs to pick up and put to rich use.

The second stage in this juridical line of development arrived with the legislative work of Pope Gregory IX (1227–1241). He published his *Liber Decretalium*—the Book of Decretals—in 1234.[1] A more accurate designa-

300

tion of this work would put the title in the plural, *Libri Decretalium,* since it is divided into five "books." Like Gratian's *Decretum* these make up a collection, but what is collected here is much narrower in species. Where Gratian reproduced statements from Fathers, councils, Popes, canonists, and theologians, Gregory limited his collecting to juridical statutes and judicial decisions—literally decretals—coming from councils and Popes. Where Gratian produced a source-book to be mined for statutes and decisions, Gregory produced a corpus itself of statutes and decisions. Those having to do with marriage are in Books 3 and 4, but mainly in the latter. The title within it most pertinent to our study is Title 19, On Divorce (*De Divortio*). Other related but less pertinent titles are Title 1, On Betrothal and Marriage; Title 8, On the Marriage of Lepers; Title 9, On the Marriage of Slaves; Title 15, On the Impotent, the Hexed, and Those Incapable of Intercourse.[2]

The value in combination of the *Decretum* and the *Liber Decretalium* is immense. They provide the student with a thorough and reasonably organized compendium of the Roman Catholic teaching on divorce and remarriage through the first third of the thirteenth century. The decretals of the Popes preceding Gregory by a few decades—notably those of Alexander III (1179–1181), Urban II (1185–1187) and Innocent III (1198–1216)—find their way to us thanks to his collecting and editing.[3]

Worth noting here first and almost parenthetically is Gregory IX's contribution to the most serious of the debates concerning marriage during the twelfth and thirteenth centuries, a debate, we recall, that was not about divorce and remarriage. It was, again, about the precise moment in the process of marrying at which the marriage comes into existence, about the human act or acts that are both needed and suffice to create the marriage.

Where Alexander III accepted the Roman-Parisian consensual theory, over against the Bolognese, that the reciprocal consent of the parties suffices, but did so hesitantly and ambiguously, Gregory accepted and installed it as Catholic law. The parties' *consensus de praesenti* creates their marriage, and no other act is needed for this creating. Yet his legislation kept a place for sexual intercourse in judicial determinations about marriage. Intercourse after consent *de praesenti* could confirm it where it had been vitiated by error or fear in the mind of one or both of the parties. It could bring an end to the effect of a suspensive condition placed by one of the parties at the time of consenting and thus bring the marriage into existence. If it were truly a oneness in flesh—truly the *unitas carnis* of Genesis and of Christ's quotation of it—it could make an engaged couple husband and wife. An impotent person, one incapable of intercourse, is incapable of marrying. And of course Gregory kept the distinction between a non-consummated marriage and one consummated by intercourse.

The other line of development began after the middle of the twelfth century, springing from Peter Lombard's treatment of marriage in Book 4 of his *Libri Sententiarum.* This was the first attempt at a philosophical anthropology of marriage, the first attempt at any kind of theology of it in the seven centuries since Augustine, and the first serious and disciplined attempt at a theology of it in history. This work was undertaken by theologians at last prepared to do it because they were also, and perhaps first of all, philosophers. We shall examine in the following chapter the thinking on divorce and remarriage of the four whose influence has come down most strongly through the centuries. They are Hugh of St. Victor, Thomas Aquinas, Bonaventure and John Duns Scotus.

The shaping of the law on divorce and remarriage done by the decretists and decretalists, and by the Popes numbered among or recorded by them I shall set forth here topically. It will be helpful to divide their epoch, from about 1150 until 1250, into two periods: from the appearance of Gratian's *Decretum* in 1140 until Alexander III's death in 1181; then from this date until about the middle of the thirteenth century.[4]

I. From the *Decretum* Until the Death of Alexander III
The Dissolution of Unconsummated Marriage

The possibility itself that a marriage already created by the consent of the parties but not yet consummated by their sexual intercourse may be dissolved can be drawn logically from both Gratian's Bolognese interpretation of the acts needed to create the marriage, and from Peter Lombard's Roman-Parisian interpretation. From the former it can be drawn because it said that the consent of the parties produces only the *matrimonium initiatum,* but that not until the first intercourse after consent is there the *matrimonium perfectum.* Insert into this logic the assumption that Christ had only consummated marriages in mind when he declared that what God has joined no man must separate, and permissibility of dissolution is added to possibility. Add, finally, the Church's application of its supreme authority, its power "to bind and to loose," and a capable agency completes the mechanism needed for marital dissolution.

From Lombard's interpretation too could be drawn the possibility of this dissolution, although not so immediately. To his interpretation must be added Christ's other words, those that give the apparent reason internal to marriage for God's forbidding the human separating of what he has joined. This is that husband and wife become two in one flesh. But when this reason is added as the ground of God's command, the way is opened to saying that husband and wife become two in one flesh only in their first intercourse, and is opened thence to the conclusion that only after they have thus become one flesh does their marriage come unqualifiedly under God's command that it not be separated.

Thus by the end of the twelfth century Catholic discipline held that a marriage not yet consummated can be dissolved by authority held in the Church. This was the discipline because it was also the doctrine. And the possibility of this dissolution came to be realized under the following conditions and for the following causes.

Dissolution Because of Entry into Religious Life

The most obvious instance in which the supposed indissolubility of marriage created by the consent alone of the spouses could be put to the test is that in which one spouse sought to take the vows of religious life. No disability is at issue in such an instance, no delinquency, but simply the will of at least one of the spouses to end the marriage in order to take up the life of the evangelical counsels. And if this spouse could end the marriage, how was this ending to be understood? As no more than a separation that leaves the marriage intact? As a true dissolution that annihilates the marital bond? And whichever the kind of ending, may the other spouse remarry?[5]

Pope Alexander III was successively of two different minds about this. At first he was apparently influenced effectively by Peter Lombard's interpretation of the act that creates a marriage. In a decretal of 1170 or 1171 he gave this ruling to the bishop of Sant'Agata de' Goti in Italy: A woman took the oath of betrothal; her fiancé wished to hold her to this, but she subsequently sought to be released from the oath in order to take the vows of religious life. Alexander ruled that she could do this only *si conjuncti non fuerint*—only "if they have not yet been joined." Otherwise she was to consummate her marriage.[6] The phrase "if they have not yet been joined" did not refer to the marriage's consummation, but to the *verba de praesenti,* the parties' consent that creates the marriage. Thus Alexander implied in this ruling that entry into religious life is permitted after the betrothal, that is, after the *verba de futuro,* but not after the *verba de praesenti* even though the marriage this consent creates has not yet been consummated.

But he did not persevere in this judgment drawn from Lombard's interpretation. He was a disciple of Gratian and admitted the consequences of the latter's interpretation gradually into his judicial decisions. In 1173 or 1174, in a decision addressed to the archbishop of Sens, he ruled that once the *verba de praesenti* are pronounced, the marriage bond exists and blocks any subsequent attempt at marriage; but this bond is not indestructible because it can be dissolved for good cause by the authority of the Church.[7] But during at least the early years of his papacy Alexander did not include a spouse's entry into religious life among these causes. Even if a spouse, because his or her marriage was not consummated, were granted permission to take religious vows, the marriage bond was thought to remain; and the other spouse, being also of course still married, could not enter a second marriage.

But by 1179 Alexander began to make full use of the conclusion logically deducible from Gratian's interpretation. Before that date he had addressed a decision to the bishop of Brescia: "If the wife has not had intercourse with her husband, she is permitted to enter religious life."[8] He reasoned here that the impermissibility of divorce taught by Christ refers only to a consummated marriage. He did not say expressly that the husband could remarry, but he did say that the wife's pronouncing the vows of religious life dissolved the marriage and did so because theirs was not a consummated marriage.

Thus by using Gratian Alexander went beyond what Lombard had taught. Just as for the latter the vows of religious life could dissolve the bond formed by sworn betrothal, the *verba de futuro,* but not the marital bond formed by the *verba de praesenti,* so for Alexander these religious vows could dissolve the marital bond but not such a bond completed by sexual intercourse. If we may use a spatial metaphor at this point, Alexander in effect moved the indissolubility barrier one more step inward toward the center, yielding more ground to dissolubility as he did so. The ruling made in this decretal to the bishop of Brescia soon became a part of classical canon law.

The reasoning by which Alexander justified this shift of position from Lombard's to Gratian's I have already pointed out. It was that Christ's command, in Matthew's Gospel, that husbands not dismiss their wives (except for their *fornicatio*) was given because in marriage spouses become two in one flesh; but they become two in one flesh not by the *verba de praesenti* but only by sexual intercourse after that consent has created their marriage.[9] His reasoning on this point is set out more fully in a decretal recorded in the *Collectio Claustroneoburgensis* (n. 317).

> Our origin and forefather Adam, when first seeing the rib that had been taken from his side and formed into the woman, was moved by prophetic spirit to say "For this reason a man will dismiss [sic] his father and his mother, etc." By these words he intimated that a man and woman could become one flesh by no other way than by clinging to one another in carnal copula. We cannot see, then, how a man who has not been proved to have had intercourse with his wife within their marital covenant, can become one flesh with his wife through the mere pronouncing of their marriage vows [*propter nuda sponsionis verba*].[10]

But what of the *consummated* marriage of two Catholics, one or both of whom wish to enter religious life and pronounce its vows? By Gratian's time it was established in Catholic law and custom that this entry is permissible, but only on condition that either both spouses do it by mutual agreement, or that if only one wishes to do so, he or she have the consent of the other.

But it was acknowledged from the beginning that the pronouncing of religious vows does not dissolve a marriage once consummated, and no voice has ever been heard claiming that it does. The spouse whose consent allows the other to enter religious life may not afterward take another spouse, because he or she still has one. He or she is presumed to have accepted a life of perpetual continence because the marriage still exists and his or her spouse is living a life of perpetual chastity. It follows too that if the spouse who vows evangelical chastity is later released from this vow, both may resume normal married life with one another.

By a series of decretals Alexander established rules for conduct in this circumstance. Thus from the moment a marriage is consummated spouses can take up religious life only by mutual agreement. Either both are to take the vows of religious life, or the one who does not is to take a vow of continence outside this life.

As long as one or the other has not taken the respective vows, he or she can demand the other's return to the marriage, even after having first agreed to the separation. In ruling thus Alexander appealed to a quasi-principle:

> As long as the two have become one body in the marital union, it is incongruous that one part [of this body] should be converted to religious life and the other remain in the world. Nor could God accept the conversion to religious life of a man whose marriage would end in [his wife's] prostitution.[11]

But Alexander ruled too that if the spouse who remains outside religious life is aged and beyond suspicion of unchastity, he or she may live with family without taking the vow of perpetual chastity.

If a husband wishes to take sacred orders apart from life in a religious order, the same demand holds. He may do so only with his wife's consent. And he may be ordained only after his wife has taken the veil in a religious convent.

But Alexander insisted that in any case, once the marriage had been consummated, entry into religious life could effect no true dissolution. It involves no more than the physical separation of the spouses, so that ". . . from a carnal joining a spiritual marriage may ensue (. . . *et fiat deinceps de carnali copula spirituale coniugium*).[12]

Dissolution Because of Prolonged Absence

The question of a spouse's prolonged absence as a ground for dissolution is complicated by this, that either the absence may be considered such a ground in itself (as it is in many modern civil codes), or the prolongation of the absence may be taken as evidence of the probable death of the absent spouse. It was as the latter species of evidence that such absence was treated in the developing Catholic marriage law of the twelfth century.

Alexander III permitted remarriage in such a case by an exercise of authority that is truly perplexing. In an undated decretal (in the *Collectio San Germanensis,* Lib. 9, Cap. 13) he ruled on a petition from a woman in

Hastings, England.[13] At the age of eleven she had been married, but she had never lived with her husband and they had not consummated their marriage. After a short time he had dismissed her and gone to Jerusalem, telling the girl's father that he would return after two years. When five years had passed without his returning, and it was no longer certain that he was still alive, Alexander was petitioned to rule in the case because the now sixteen-year-old girl wished to marry another man.

Alexander replied by first requiring a longer wait, but concluded that if the husband did not return, and if even his returned companions could not verify that he still lived, the girl would be free by dispensation to remarry. What is perplexing here is that in other decretals Alexander permitted remarriage because of prolonged absence and probable death even where the first marriage was consummated, but with the understanding that if the absent spouse were to return, the first marriage was to be restored. (In the latter event it seems that the first marriage had never been dissolved and the second had never been created, since the latter's consent had been qualified by the condition—the death of the first spouse—that turned out not to have been realized.)

But in the case of the English girl Alexander granted a dispensation. What was its object? It could not have been other than the bond of her unconsummated marriage. This object was not permission to remarry because of the presumed death of her husband, because if his death had been presumed there would have been no room and no need for a dispensation. Consequently in this case Alexander did not simply declare the girl free to remarry by authoritatively presuming her husband to be dead. He freed her to remarry by dissolving her first marriage by dispensation.

In this matter of dissolution for prolonged absence—an urgent and painful matter when so many thousands of European husbands went off to the Crusades and simply vanished—Alexander was perplexed and hesitant. Early in his papacy, in 1170 and 1171, a case came to him from the bishop of Vicenza. It concerned a woman whose husband had been absent in Constantinople for ten years. When the wife asked Bishop Aribert for permission to enter a second marriage, he authorized a search for her absent husband. After this had proved futile he pronounced a judgment of dissolution and granted the wife permission for the second marriage. Alexander's surprising and ambiguous judgment on the case was to issue a decretal ordering the bishop to declare legitimate any children born of the second marriage.[14]

The primary intent of this decretal is not clear. It may have been simply to declare the children legitimate because of the parents' putative marriage contracted in good faith. But at least Alexander seems to have accepted a presumption of the death of the absent husband. That such a presumption was the key to his judgment here and not the intent to dissolve a consummated marriage merely because of prolonged absence becomes clearer from a letter he wrote on July 6, 1171 to King Canute of

Sweden. The letter was virtually a doctrinal treatise in miniature. The burden of it was that a consummated marriage simply cannot be dissolved.

> It is forbidden to a husband to dismiss his wife except for her adultery. And if, after dismissing her, he takes another while she still lives, he will be called an adulterer, and so too will the woman he takes.[15]

He added that when one spouse is taken into captivity, the other cannot remarry as long as it is known that the captive still lives. If the other remarries on evidence of the probable death of the captive, but the latter is subsequently freed and returns, the first marriage must be restored to cohabitation because it still exists and the second union is not a marriage. If the parties persist in the second marriage, they live in adultery.

Thus Alexander was both as stringent as modern Catholic marriage law in denying that a spouse's absence of itself, no matter how prolonged, constitutes ground for dissolution and remarriage; and he was more lenient in allowing that a reasonable presumption of the absent spouse's death warrants a declaration of the right to remarry. But his successors did not continue even this leniency. They demanded proof of the death of the absent spouse before permitting remarriage. Between 1181 and 1185 Pope Lucius III wrote a decretal addressed "to all Christians in Saracen captivity" that evidences the haste with which the survivors of these captives remarried. Lucius interdicted their second marriages as long as there was no convincing evidence of the captive spouse's death. But he did not demand separation of the second unions already contracted provided the death of the captive spouse was at least probable. As a further and curious stricture on the second union he ruled that the partners could have sexual intercourse if it were demanded of one by the other, but he forbade either to make the demand. He ruled, however, that if the captive spouse were freed and returned, the first marriage must be restored because it had never ceased to exist.[16]

And when, in the Spanish diocese of Saragossa, a number of wives whose husbands had been absent over seven years and whose fate was unknown asked permission to remarry, alleging their youth and their "weakness of the flesh," Pope Clement III (1187–1191) replied in the words of St. Paul, "A woman is bound to her husband as long as he lives." His decision in the case was that no matter how long a spouse's absence, there can be no second marriage for the other without evidence of certain death.[17] This has remained the Roman Catholic law in the matter.

Dissolution Because of Supervenient Affinity

This concept so strange to modern Christian minds—*affinitas superveniens*—calls for explanation. In the medieval marriage law it designated an impediment to a man's and woman's marrying because they become relatives-in-law to one another after having become engaged, and even an impediment to *remaining* married because they become relatives-in-law after having contracted marriage. The way in which they become relatives-in-law was interpreted according to the ancient assumption that when a man and woman have sexual intercourse with one another the act establishes them in a kind of oneness of legal and moral personhood. The assumption is found in 1 Corinthians 6:16–17 where Paul declares the two-in-one-flesh consequences not of the intercourse of spouses but of the man and the prostitute to whom he goes: "Do you not know that a man who goes to a prostitute is one body with her?" And he applies the words of Genesis to this fornication: " 'For', it is said, 'the two become one flesh.' "

This legal-moral oneness of partners in intercourse was thought to have, as a second consequence, that they become relatives-in-law to one another's blood relatives. Thus a married man having intercourse with a girl not his wife became a kind of son-in-law to her parents. Where the impediment of supervenient affinity became a lively issue in Catholic marriage law was in those cases in which, for example, an engaged man had intercourse with his fiancée's mother or sister. This was thought to make him a relative-in-law of his fiancée because of his two-in-one-fleshness with the latter's blood relative. But according to the extant law and custom relatives-in-law could not marry. Thus he was impeded from marrying his fiancée.[18]

This legal snarl was only worsened where the fornication was committed after the exchange of marital vows but before the consummation of the marriage. This was thought to have the remarkable effect of turning the new husband's bride into his sister-in-law. Thence the question: Was he permitted to consummate his marriage with his new sister-in-law? Or could this unconsummated marriage be dissolved?

Early in his pontificate Alexander III accepted as established by the authority of the Church that if one spouse in an unconsummated marriage had intercourse with the blood relative of the other, this constituted him or her the relative-in-law of the other spouse, and if this affinity were public and notorious it had the effect of dissolving the marriage.[19] This was an extension and application of Gratian's explanation that a man's or woman's intercourse with a blood relative of the betrothed established his or her affinity with the betrothed; and this in turn had the effect of dissolving the betrothal and impeding the marriage of the erstwhile partners in betrothal—whether they thought to marry by consent *de praesenti* or by intercourse during betrothal.

This is what Alexander accepted in principle. But true to his indecisive nature and changing mind, he qualified its application. The case was brought to him of a man in Worcester, England who had dismissed his wife and taken one of her relatives in her place. Alexander ruled that if the latter were related to the wife within the second degree of kindred, the man was to be separated from both women and forbidden ever to remarry. (Here it seems that he was only separated from his first wife, but not that his marriage with her was dissolved.) But if the two women were related no more closely than in the third degree, the man was to return to his first wife and then do penance for his sin. The record of the case does not show that Alexander asked if the first marriage were consummated.[20]

That Alexander considered the impediment of supervenient affinity to be a thing of ecclesiastical law was evident in his qualifying the law so that if the incest were not both public and notorious, the spouses in the unconsummated marriage could continue to cohabit.

His early decretals resolving such cases took no note of either the consummation or the non-consummation of the marriages in question, although we know that in principle he held to the radical indissolubility of consummated marriage. But his later rulings show a gradual development in his thinking. As long as he held to Peter Lombard's theory that the consent *de praesenti* of both parties is sufficient to create the marriage, he refused to accept that supervenient affinity *after* this consent dissolves the unconsummated marriage. But once he came to accept his teacher Gratian's interpretation that a marriage is incomplete until consummated after the consent that creates it, he held that this affinity dissolves an unconsummated marriage once the incest creating the affinity becomes public and notorious. Both parties may subsequently remarry, but the one guilty of the incest must secure an ecclesiastical dispensation to do so. This he or she must do because the punishment for incest established by law was that the sinner was impeded from contracting any subsequent marriage at all.

Alexander's rulings concerning supervenient affinity brought about by incest after the consummation of a marriage underwent further development. Beginning, as I have said, with his principle that no created cause can dissolve a marriage once consummated, he ruled in the following ways in a decretal addressed to the bishop of Worcester.[21]

If the husband's incest is with the mother, sister or daughter of his wife, and is public and notorious, the guilty husband must separate from his wife and is deprived in perpetuity of the right to return to her. This separation is obligatory even against the will of the innocent wife.

If the incest is secret and unverifiable, a penance must be imposed on the guilty husband, and during as well as after the period of penance he must render the marriage debt to the innocent wife if she demands it.

If the incest is with the wife's blood relative of the third degree or beyond, separation is not obligatory, but an appropriate penance is required of the husband.

If the wife commits incest with any of her husband's blood relatives, she must be separated from him even if the incest is secret. She may never remarry, but her husband may remarry after her death.

In general, if the incest is committed within the third degree of the spouse's blood relationship and is public and notorious, the spouses must separate. They may not have intercourse (although this stricture could be relaxed). The guilty spouse could never remarry, while the innocent spouse could remarry only after the death of the guilty.

II. From Alexander III to the Middle of the Thirteenth Century Dissolution by Entry into Religious Life

What Alexander III had fixed as a principle, that by divine law only a consummated marriage is radically indissoluble, was accepted without question by his successors in both papal rule and in the work of forming the law. Therefore they accepted also in principle that an unconsummated marriage is dissoluble. And in practice they accepted as one of the causes dissolving an unconsummated marriage one or both spouses' taking the vows of religious life.

The rationale justifying this discipline was set forth variously.[22] An unconsummated marriage was said to image no more than the union of the Christian soul with God by faith and love. But since this union can be dissolved by sin, the marriage that images it is itself not invulnerable to dissolution. (Whereas the consummated marriage images the union of either Christ and the Church or the union of the two natures in Christ, or both. And both are indestructible.) Since the unconsummated union is perishable, it can be dissolved, so the reasoning went, in favor of the higher good which is religious life.

Such was the main theological justification for dissolving an unconsummated marriage for entry into religious life. Alan of Lille offered also a juridical reason: an unconsummated marriage and its indissolubility reside within the purview of ecclesiastical authority, while a consummated marriage and its indissolubility reside within divine law. So the determination that an unconsummated marriage can be dissolved by religious vows is an exercise of papal authority.

Or the difference was explained by a distinction in the degree of ownership rights. It was said that before consummation a husband has not taken full ownership of his wife's body, nor she of his. But when he or she pronounces religious vows, the husband or wife is owned completely by the religious superior, who is in the place of God. Thus the religious profession prevails over the rights of marriage because it enjoys actual and full possession. (We shall see that the theologians of the thirteenth century were impatient with the latter, juridical explanation here. But whether they provided a more convincing explanation by distinguishing between primary and secondary demands of natural law remains to be seen.)

Pope Innocent III accepted the discipline established by Alexander that an unconsummated marriage is dissolved by religious vows, but did so with regret, and only in order to not overturn the law written by his predecessors. What is more, this was the only cause for dissolving a marriage that he accepted. This he made clear in a decretal addressed to the archbishop of Lund on January 2, 1206. In the same document he made his own the opinion of Bishop Huguccio of Ferrara that only definitive entry into religious life—only actual entry into a monastery, the taking of the religious habit there, and the pronouncing of the vows— dissolves an unconsummated marriage. The taking of the vow of chastity alone, or the taking of it along with the religious habit, does not dissolve the marriage if the spouse remains in his or her home.[23]

Boniface VIII (1294–1303) ruled, finally, that an unconsummated marriage is dissolved by religious vows only when these are the solemn vows of a religious order approved by the Holy See, the papal government itself. He accepted as equivalent to these vows the taking of sacred orders. This too dissolves an unconsummated marriage.[24]

Dissolution Because of Supervenient Affinity

A number of Alexander's contemporaries and of his early successors in the papacy rejected the lenient conclusion about dissolution because of supervenient affinity that he had drawn from Gratian's teaching. They denied that this affinity is a cause for dissolution, even if the marriage is unconsummated. Huguccio criticized the practice severely, insisting that unconsummated marriages are as invulnerable to dissolution as consummated. He pointed out that the Gospel allows dismissal of a spouse only for adultery (apparently not noticing that the incest in question is also adultery), and that the apostle Paul had at least offered the spouses two choices, reconciliation as well as a life of forced continence. He urged too that the spiritual relationship of marriage is stronger than a blood relationship, as the Book of Genesis teaches in saying that a man must leave even his father and his mother in order to join to his wife. A fortiori then a marriage is stronger than the affinity created by incest and ought not be made its victim.[25]

Huguccio contended that the choice in this discipline was between Pope Alexander's decrees and the Gospel. And his conclusion defended the innocent party whom Alexander would force into a life of sexual continence. He or she has the right to the marriage and to sexual intercourse, while the guilty spouse must accede to a demand for the act but must not demand it.

Pope Urban III (1185–1187), in a decretal addressed to the archbishop of Bordeaux, confirmed the dissolving power of supervenient affinity on betrothal created by the consent *de futuro*. And he denied a financée's claim to have her betrothed in marriage if it were commonly known in their territory that (as he claimed) he had had intercourse with one of her blood relatives during the betrothal.

It was Innocent III who finally and definitively rejected supervenient affinity as a cause of dissolution. From his time forward the consequences of this affinity for an unconsummated marriage were the same as those for a consummated marriage. These were hardly different from those established by Alexander III outlined above.[26]

Dissolution of Unconsummated Marriage
Because of Supervenient Leprosy

Pope Urban III authorized the dissolution of an unconsummated marriage because of *lepra superveniens* (this in a decretal directed to the bishop of Florence) where Alexander III had rejected it as a cause for dissolution. Urban's decision was given in an answer to the question asking if, after the *sponsalia* but before the beginning of cohabitation, one of the parties contracts leprosy, the other shall be obligated to consummate the marriage and thus render it indissoluble, or may the other spouse remarry. His reply was that the spouse in good health is not to be obliged to remain in the marriage "because the marriage has not yet been consummated."[27]

In a decretal addressed to the archbishop of Canterbury, Innocent III rejected this ground of dissolution. He had heard that husbands and wives afflicted with leprosy had been abandoned by their spouses. His answer to the question concerning this was: "Since a husband and wife are one flesh, and neither should be for long without the other, we command . . . that husbands and wives are to remain with their spouses when these are afflicted with leprosy and take care of them with marital affection. . . . If you cannot bring them to do this, you are to order them that so long as their spouses still live, they are to persevere in sexual continence. But if they refuse to obey you, you are to excommunicate them."[28] The wording of the decretal indicates clearly Innocent's will both to protect spouses afflicted with leprosy from abandonment and to insist on the invulnerability of marriage to the attempt to dissolve it even under duress as grievous as leprosy.

The canonist Raymond of Peñafort made a convenient distinction in Pope Urban's formulation permitting dissolution because of leprosy. He said that by the word *sponsalia* the Pontiff meant not the marital consent itself but the betrothal promise, the consent *de futuro*. Consequently the authorized dissolution because of leprosy was not of an unconsummated marriage but of a betrothal.[29]

Dispensation Without Cause from an Unconsummated Marriage

It is clear that the decisions of Alexander III that we have reviewed led to the conclusion that an unconsummated marriage can be dissolved by papal dispensation. Pierre de Sampson, a canonist who taught at Bologna from 1230 to 1260, wrote of a prince-husband in an unconsummated marriage who sought to exploit this conclusion by asking Innocent III to dispense him to contract a second marriage. He adduced no cause for his petition that was recognized in the Church; he simply appealed to Alexander III's judgment that the Gospel's prohibition against dismissing a wife applies only to consummated marriages.[30]

Innocent is said to have answered the prince, "Cursed be he who has taught you this." But Pierre remarked that this left unclear whether Innocent nevertheless granted the dispensation.

The decretalists following Gregory IX simply refused to recognize Alexander's dissolution of an unconsummated marriage because of prolonged absence, and thus cleared the territory of one cause for dissolving unconsummated marriages. But others kept the issue alive by arguing that the regulation of unconsummated marriages belongs not to divine law but to positive ecclesiastical law. These canonists—Vincent of Spain, Tancred, Bernard of Parma among them—in effect turned the question into the domain of ecclesiology by posing it as one of papal authority: How far does the power to bind and to loose extend? To the marriages of all Christians? To all of them, or only to those that are unconsummated? If only to these, what is it about consummated marriages that puts them beyond this power? It would be by an indirect route to the center of the theology of the sacrament of marriage, but eventually this question about the reach of papal authority, that was raised by the need for a judicial discipline, would eventually help to produce that theology.

Dissolution of Marriage by Mutual Dissent

The decretalist Hostiensis introduced a refinement of this question about papal authority to bind and to loose in marriages. It was interlocked with the question about the power of the spouses themselves to dissolve their unconsummated marriages by mutual dissent. This hinted at a return to classical Roman law which included just such dissolution. Holding, as it did, that the parties create their marriage by their mutual consent (sufficient in itself to do so apart from any other agency), and that their marriage perdures by the perdurance of this consent, Roman law concluded that the parties could also dissolve their marriage by mutually withdrawing this consent—by mutual dissent (again sufficient in itself apart from any other agency).

Hostiensis proposed to modify and Christianize this philosophy of creating and annihilating marriage by bringing the latter half of it under papal control. He reasoned that because even the unconsummated marriages of Christians are sacraments, they come under ecclesiastical authority. But the determination of what makes a marriage ratified, what creates it despite its being unconsummated and therefore dissoluble, belongs to papal authority. Therefore the conclusion: it is within this authority to dissolve unconsummated marriages by withdrawing its ratification or by establishing the agency that can do this. Here the mutual dissent of the parties would enter. Papal authority could authorize the spouses to dissolve their unconsummated marriage by this dissent.[31]

But Hostiensis did not intend that this mechanism for dissolution be available for indiscriminate use. He added another condition, namely that it be used only in the case wherein one of the spouses enters religious life and pronounces its vows. Apparently he intended this procedure to bring with it a more reasonable accounting for the dissolution effected by the pronouncing of these vows. He also proposed that papal power dissolve an unconsummated marriage even without the withdrawal of consent by one of the spouses where that spouse has fallen into heresy.

But this proposal and the theory purporting to justify it found no support in Hostiensis' own or later generations. It disappeared thanks mainly to the influence of the thirteenth-century theologians. These, as we shall see, found the cause of marriage's indissolubility—even that of unconsummated marriages—elsewhere than in the authority of the Church. In fact, being also philosophers, they found two causes of it, in the law of nature and in the demands of the sacrament. They went with the tide of Christian tradition that accepted dissolution of unconsummated marriages by the vows of religious life. But they explained this dissolution by a cause other than papal authority. This was that because an unconsummated marriage is no more than a spiritual union of the spouses, it can be dissolved by the spiritual death, the vows in religious life, of one or both of the spouses.

Dissolution Because of a Spouse's Heresy

Pope Celestine III, and perhaps Urban III before him, sought to introduce into Roman Catholic law the dissolution of a marriage because of the lapse into heresy of one of the spouses. Celestine's intent was that even a consummated marriage be dissolved for this cause.

The medieval estimation of the effect on a marriage of a lapse into heresy was borrowed from a judgment we have already seen come from Augustine. He assimilated apostasy or heresy to adultery, calling it "spiritual adultery." In this he followed the metaphor used so commonly by the Hebrew prophets Hosea, Jeremiah, Isaiah and Ezekiel in portraying Israel's religious defection as adultery committed with the enemies of the Lord God, Israel's (metaphoric) husband.

A case which Celestine decided in this way involved a husband who had abandoned his wife, had abandoned the Catholic faith, and had sought to take an unbaptized woman as his second wife. An archdeacon of the diocese of Florence declared the first marriage dissolved and permitted the abandoned wife to remarry. Celestine approved of this, and himself declared that even if the apostate husband were to return to the Catholic faith, the wife's second marriage would remain. She would not be obliged to return to him; he was no longer her husband.[32]

Celestine's justification for this ruling was the case's analogous relationship to the situation among the Corinthian Christians about which St. Paul had instructed, "If the non-believing spouse separates, let him separate" (1 Corinthians 7:15). From this Celestine reasoned that if Paul allowed his converts in Corinth to dismiss their non-believing spouses who would not live in peace, a fortiori should a Catholic spouse be allowed to dismiss a husband or wife who has apostatized, since apostasy is a worse evil than mere recalcitrant non-belief? (Like so many users of 1 Corinthians 7:15 Celestine failed to notice that Paul did not counsel the Christian spouses to dismiss the non-Christian, but to not hinder the latter if they wished to depart. Moreover it is significant that Celestine deemed the effect of what he thought to be the dismissal counseled by Paul to be the dissolution of the marriage.)

In 1199 Bishop Huguccio consulted Innocent III about a case that had come to light in the former's diocese of Ferrara. One spouse had lapsed into heresy and had abandoned the other. Was the marriage thereby dissolved? Could it be dissolved because of the heresy and abandonment? Could the abandoned and still religiously faithful spouse remarry?

Innocent's reply was a firm no. He insisted on the absolute indissolubility of a marriage that is both a sacrament and consummated. And he rejected the contrary decision that had been made by "one of my predecessors." He added that the use of the Pauline privilege could dissolve only the marriages of non-believers, for even though theirs are true marriages, they are not sacraments. Innocent added that insistence on this point would close off any attempt at fraud whereby a Catholic would pretend a lapse into heresy so as to be able to abandon one spouse and take another. It is helpful to quote most of Innocent's decretal directed to Huguccio because it constitutes one of the primary authoritative sources for the installation of what has come to be called the Pauline privilege.

> In your letter Your Fraternity intimated that with one of two spouses going over to heresy, the other wishes to marry again and to have children. You asked Our judgment whether this is permitted by our law.
>
> Answering your question according to the common mind of Our brother bishops, We make a distinction (even though a certain one among Our predecessors has passed a different judgment) between the case of two non-believers, one of whom is converted to the Catholic faith, and that of two Christians, one of whom falls into heresy or into unbelief.
>
> If one of two non-believing spouses is converted to the Catholic faith but the other is not converted at all, or is converted but not without blasphemy of the divine name, or wishes to continue cohabitation so as to draw the convert into mortal sin, the convert may, if he or she wishes, marry again. In this case we recall what the Apostle said, "If the unbeliever departs, let him depart. In such cases the brother or sister is not to play the slave"; and the rule which says that "Contumely toward the Creator dissolves the marriage of the spouse who is left [in the faith]."
>
> But if one of the two Christian spouses falls either into heresy or into unbelief, We do not think that in this case the

spouse who is left can enter a second marriage as long as the other lives, even though in this case there seems more grievous contempt of the Creator. For even though there exists a true marriage [*matrimonium verum*] between non-believers, it is not a sacrament.[33]

In this decretal Innocent informs Bishop Huguccio not only that where one of the spouses is unbaptized they may separate, but that with their separation accomplished their marriage is vulnerable to dissolution. He does not make a condition of this vulnerability that their marriage not be consummated; he does not mention consummation at all. And the subsequent use of the privilege in Catholic law has never made non-consummation a condition for this use.

I have explained the elements of the Pauline privilege briefly in Chapter One of this volume. The only matter calling for explanation here is the central point of difference that makes the marriage of two non-believers vulnerable to dissolution but leaves that of two believers, one of whom apostatizes, invulnerable to it. This difference will also bring to light Innocent's difference of judgment from that of St. Paul about the causes of the vulnerability and invulnerability in question.

Innocent insists that despite the apostasy of one of them, the marriage of the two Christians cannot be dissolved because it is a sacrament. He implies that it remains so despite the one spouse's abandoning the Christian faith. He also points out why he authorizes the eventual dissolution of the two non-believers' marriage. It is not a sacrament. But this is not the reason Paul had given that warranted the Corinthian Christian spouses' letting the non-believing spouses depart. His reason was that Christian spouses are not to play the slave in their marriages since, in answering the call of Christ, they had answered a call to peace. Assuming that Paul himself later wrote the Letter to the Ephesians and there likened the husband-wife relationship to that of Christ and the Church, at the time he wrote 1 Corinthians this likeness had apparently not yet occurred to him. Or if it had, the absence of it from a religiously mixed marriage had evidently not seemed to him the reason for this marriage's dissolubility. Innocent's thinking that it is, and conversely that the presence of the likeness in two Christians' marriage is the cause of its indissolubility, shares the inference that later Catholic theology has drawn from Ephesians 5.

Thus where Paul urged that Christian spouses' love for one another *ought* to image the love of Christ and the Church, Innocent concluded that their baptism *makes* of their marriage such an image and an indefatigable sharer of the Christ-Church relationship's indestructibility.

Two years later, in 1201, Innocent made what appears the same determination in a case presented to him by the bishop of Tiberias in the Latin kingdom of Jerusalem. His decretal reads as follows (in translation from its convoluted Latin).

A man who has dismissed his legitimate wife according to his rite, since in the Gospel Truth [Christ] has forbidden this dismissal, may not take another woman to wife as long as his dismissed wife lives, even if he is converted to the faith of Christ; unless after his conversion she refuses to cohabit with him; or, if she consents to cohabit, will not do so without contempt of the Creator, or does so in order to lead him into mortal sin ... because, according to the Apostle, in such matters the brother or sister is not to play the slave. But if the first wife too is converted, he is to be compelled to accept her before he takes a legitimate second wife for the reasons just stated.[34]

Here Innocent helps with the interpretation and adaptation of Paul's disciplinary strategy that has become a feature of the Pauline privilege. I have pointed out a number of times, and just above, that Paul's instruction in 1 Corinthians 7:15 does not counsel the Christian spouse to dismiss a vindictive unbelieving spouse. Dismissal is not to be the Christian's reaction to the other's refusal to live in peace. He writes there that the Christian is to let the other depart if he or she wishes to do so. The Christian is not to take positive action but is to not hinder action on the other's part. The destroying of marital peace that Paul wanted to avoid would ensue if the Christian tried to force the unbelieving spouse to stay against his or her will.

But in this decretal Innocent writes expressly of the newly converted Christian spouse's dismissing the other. And he introduces a new interpretation of the non-Christian's departure, one that is religious-moral and will soon become juridical. He holds that the latter "departs" if, despite wanting to continue cohabitation, he or she acts in contempt of the Creator, or tries to draw the Christian into mortal sin. Here Innocent understands the destroying of the marital peace to be initiated by the non-believing spouse. He sees the fact of this destruction of peace offering the reason that justifies the Christian's dismissing, where Paul saw the fear of the loss of this peace as the reason for not holding the non-believing spouse to cohabitation.

But that the ruin of marital peace is not a compelling reason for dismissal and dissolution Innocent makes clear in the last sentence I have quoted from this decretal. If the first and non-believing wife is converted to the Christian faith along with her husband, the latter either may not dismiss her, or, if he has already done so, he must take her back and cannot take a second wife. One may wonder if Innocent thought this conversion of a dismissed or almost dismissed wife would restore peace to the marriage. But one need not wonder about Innocent's measure of the strength of the sacrament in marriage. He was convinced that once it is there because of the baptism of both spouses, it makes the marriage invulnerable to at least the dismissal he thought he saw Paul allowing in his advice to the Corinthian Christians.

"Separation from Bed and Board"

In an earlier chapter I pointed out that the separation of spouses known in Roman Catholic law as *separatio a mensa et toro* (translated colloquially as "separation from bed and board") was unknown in classical Roman law. The ground of possibility itself of such a separation was inconceivable to the Roman mind. This ground in Roman Catholic law is the assumption that a couple can cease life together, can even withdraw their wills to be married, can reject and hate one another, but that their marriage goes on as a juridical bond existing apart from their day-to-day lives, apart from and even in contradiction to their minds and wills.

But such a separation was lodged in Roman Catholic marriage law in the twelfth and thirteenth centuries, and two opinions coming from men of authority made the lodging of it there possible.

We have already seen that Jerome innovated an interpretation of the Matthean exceptive clause in a way that was to last in Catholic history with decisive effect.[35] He took for granted that the clause was authentically from Christ. But rather than admit that Christ permitted a husband's dismissing an adulterous wife in a way that ended the marriage, he insisted that he had permitted only the husband's banishing the wife from cohabitation.

The second opinion took the form of a distinction authorized, if not innovated, by Pope Alexander III in his *Stroma* (Cause 32, Question 7). This acknowledged two distinct bonds in a marriage. One is the *ligamen,* the juridical bond that survives any attempt at dissolution once the marriage as a sacrament is consummated, the bond whose existence is an effective obstacle to any attempt at a second marriage as long as both spouses live. The other bond Alexander understood more in the nature of a moral obligation, the bond by which "a man is obligated to render the marriage debt to his wife when she demands it of him." This is the bond that can be broken by a spouse's conduct. Combining this distinction with Jerome's interpretation one may say that this is the bond broken by a spouse's adultery, and the breaking of it justifies the innocent spouse's dismissing the adulterer in the way that Jerome understood this dismissal. But of course the other and juridical bond, the *ligamen,* remains.

Indeed Huguccio defined this *separatio a mensa et toro* as "the separation, brought on by adultery, from the bond of rendering the marriage debt"—*separatio quoad debitum reddendum causa fornicationis facta.*[36] He went on to explain that by this separation there is no dissolution of the marriage, but the moral bond is loosed. The innocent party is freed from the *servitus* (from the service, and even the servitude) that marriage brings—the paying of the marriage debt and cohabitation. He understood this to be an application of the moral maxim, "There is no obligation to keep a promise to one who himself fails to keep the promise and even breaks it"—*Non servanti imo frangenti fidem non tenetur fidem servare.* He added that since the adulterer sins directly against the marriage, it is just that he or she should be punished by being deprived of the marriage act.

The jurisprudence of the early thirteenth century worked out further traits and conditions of this separation. It was understood to be a medicinal punishment in the same sense as excommunication is such a punishment. As excommunication does not destroy the excommunicant's membership in the Church but only bars him or her from communion in its sacraments, so this separation does not destroy the marriage but only bars the guilty spouse from the marriage act and, in its severest form, from cohabitation.[37]

Since the innocent spouse too is deprived by this separation from cohabitation and from sexual intercourse, he or she must be provided for, must be compensated for the backlash from the punishment meted out to the guilty spouse. The canonical mind considered the former sufficiently compensated by being allowed to enter religious life and take its vows, even against the will of the guilty spouse. And the latter might not remarry, since he or she was still married. (Could the guilty spouse too enter religious life? The more common opinion came to be that he or she could, but not without the consent of the innocent spouse, since the latter retained the right to demand reconciliation.)

Still in the interest of the innocent party, since the decision to separate was deemed a right accruing to him or her because of the adulterer's violation of the marriage, there was no obligation to separate, especially if the adultery were not known publicly. The innocent spouse had the right to demand reconciliation. And if the guilty party refused this, he or she could be constrained to it by Church authority.

Alexander III did not inaugurate the *separatio* as a substitute for dismissal or other forms of dissolution. He seems rather to have understood it as a disciplinary measure to be used when a marriage consummated and thus invulnerable to dissolution was violated. Thus he allowed the *separatio* only where the marriage in question was consummated. And he allowed it for only three exactly specified causes. The first was adultery by one spouse. If the innocent spouse did in fact dismiss the adulterer into *separatio,* he or she had either to later accept reconciliation or to take the vows of religious life. But the separation was not allowed if the adultery had been incited by a refusal to have intercourse. And if the dismissing spouse later committed adultery, he or she was obligated to take back the one dismissed.

Another cause for separation was one spouse's plotting against the life of the other.[38] The third was the attempt to force or to lead the spouse into adultery, presumably so as to gain cause for separation. By a kind of logic of equivalence Alexander allowed separation for any other attempt to incite a spouse to crime.

As the jurisprudence of separation developed in the early thirteenth century adultery remained the principal cause warranting it, since it was thought to be named such expressly in the Gospel. The conditions warranting it were refined. As Alexander III had ruled, the adultery must be *singulare,* that is, committed by only one of the spouses. It must be culpable, which it was not if a spouse were deceived into it or incited to it. It must be notorious, that is, amenable to judicial verification.

Conversely the right to separation for adultery was forfeited by both spouses if both committed it.[39] The innocent spouse forfeited it also: if he or she had abandoned the adulterous; if the former had refused marital intercourse; if because of the other's long absence the adulterer had in good faith presumed the other's death and attempted remarriage; if the wife were deceived into having intercourse with a man she thought mistakenly to be her husband (a deception not impossible in a society where, thanks to betrothal and marriage completed by proxy, a woman might meet her husband for the first time some weeks or months after becoming his wife); if the wife were physically forced into adultery; if the innocent spouse, while knowing of the other's adultery, effected reconciliation implicitly by having intercourse with him or her.

A spouse's involvement in crime did not of itself justify dismissal and separation. A decretal of Alexander III ruled explicitly that a wife could not leave her husband for his brigandage or equivalent crime, nor could a husband leave his wife. But each could leave if the other tried to draw him or her into criminal activity and tried to corrupt the spouse's religious faith. In this case separation was permitted. But even so neither could take a second spouse, since the marriage continued in existence despite the separation.[40]

We saw above Celestine III's proposal that a Christian spouse be allowed to dissolve the marriage if his or her spouse fell into apostasy or heresy, and Innocent III's contradiction of the proposal. What Innocent established instead was the right of the religiously faithful spouse, short of dissolution, to dismiss the other and to make use of the *separatio a mensa et toro.*[41]

He offered as a reason justifying this dismissal and separation that the apostate or heretic sins against the author of marriage, which is more grievous than to sin against the marriage itself. Here again the logic of *a fortiori* is evident. If infidelity to the marriage justifies dismissal and separation, much more so does infidelity to the author of marriage.

The conditions for separation because of lapse into heresy showed contrasts with those warranting separation because of adultery. Whereas a single act of adultery justified separation, the heresy must be repeated and continued, since it is by nature not a single injurious act (as adultery may be) but a consciously taken religious attitude, and an attitude in turn is an abiding state. Thus the heretic must be contumelious. That is, he or she must reaffirm the newly taken heretical attitude after being given the opportunity to return to orthodox belief.

The spouse who remained religiously faithful was, in this jurisprudence, obligated to separate from the heretic in order to avoid religious perversion, where the innocent spouse of an adulterer was free to either demand separation or to seek reconciliation.

Whereas separation for adultery could be perpetual, by contrast if the heretical spouse returned to the orthodox faith, he or she could demand reconciliation. In separation for adultery the guilty spouse, once repentant, could not demand reconciliation but could only request it.

Summary

This epoch of legislation by papal decretal saw two principal developments in the Catholic doctrine and discipline. Indeed it appears that the discipline, the legislation, produced the doctrine.

The first development was to fix as a principle that an unconsummated marriage can be dissolved by Church authority. Crucial for this was Alexander III's interpretation-by-fiat that when Christ commanded that no man separate what God has joined, he referred only to consummated marriages.

The jurists provided a theological undergirding for this: since the reason within a marriage for Christ's forbidding such separation is that a husband and wife become "two in one flesh," the jurists reasoned that they do so only in completing sexual intercourse.

The reverse correlate to this determination came naturally in the principle that a marriage once consummated is indissoluble; it can be dissolved by no authority on earth. Thus was the permissive discipline of Europe's regional councils since the fifth century shut down.

A theological tour-de-force expanded the explanation here. It said that a consummated marriage can be dissolved while an unconsummated cannot because the former images only the union of the Christian soul with Christ, a union vulnerable to destruction by the Christian's sin, while the latter images either of two indestructible unions, that of Christ with the Church or that of the two natures in the person of Christ.

What was left to do after this legislating of the theological principle was to legislate the causes for which unconsummated marriages may be dissolved. Disagreement here was inevitable. Supervenient affinity, supervenient leprosy, and the spouses' mutual withdrawal of their marital consent were all proposed but rejected. Entry of one or both spouses into religious life was accepted; so too was antecedent sexual impotence until this was reinterpreted as a cause of nullity in attempting marriage.

The second major development in this epoch was the establishment of the "separation from bed and board" as an option of an aggrieved spouse in a damaged marriage. Uncritical acceptance of Jerome's interpretation made this establishment possible—his interpretation that such separation was what Christ allowed in the Matthean exceptive clause's determination concerning treatment of an adulterous wife. Locked into this establishing of the *separatio* was the insistence that despite even permanent separation the marriage survives because the *ligamen,* the marital bond, survives.

Here too surfaced for the first time decisively the useful juridical distinction between the marriage as a human relationship and the marital bond.

Finally Innocent III's justification of the Pauline privilege strengthened the growing theology of indissolubility. He reasoned that a first marriage of two unbaptized spouses can be dissolved precisely because it is not a Christian sacrament. Conversely, because a marriage of two Christian spouses is a sacrament, it cannot be dissolved, not even (as in the cases he adjudicated) if one of the spouses lapses into heresy or abandons the Christian religion entirely.

NOTES

1. For the examination of the most pertinent of the decretals on marriage recorded by Gregory I have used *Corpus Iuris Canonici,* Editio Lipsiensis Secunda, the Leipzig edition edited by Emile Friedberg, 1881. The *Liber Decretalium* is in *Pars Secunda: Decretalium Collectiones.*

2. In Friedberg, *op. cit.,* pp. 720–725.

3. As Gratian inspired the continuation of his own work in the group of scholars called the Decretists, so Gregory was the intellectual parent to the Decretalists. To us the best known of these are Vincent of Spain, Hostiensis, Bernard of Parma (author of the *Glossa Ordinaria*), Bartholomew of Brescia, and, the best-known of all, Raymond of Peñafort, actual author of the *Liber Decretalium,* although it bears Gregory's name.

4. For this examination I shall borrow substantially from and adapt the information in Jean Dauvillier's *Le Mariage Dans le Droit Classique de L'Eglise,* Paris, 1933.

5. That these were not idle questions, and that they needed authoritative answering, is evident from the popular histories of the twelfth century. Before 1167 Marie de France told, in one of her lays, how Guildeluc lost her husband Ileduc's love to his mistress. Guildeluc's reaction was to found a monastery and then to take religious vows in it. Ileduc subsequently married his mistress, apparently persuaded that his wife's taking religious vows had dissolved their marriage.

In his *Ile et Galeron* Gauthier of Arras recorded how the Breton knight, Ile, married and the father of several children, fell in love with Gunor, the daughter of the emperor of Rome. His wife Galeron thereupon entered a monastery, and Ile subsequently married Galeron—in a wedding at which the Pope (unnamed in the poem) officiated. Gauthier insisted that his account, unlike the popular lays of his time, was not full of falsifications. (In Dauvillier, *op. cit.,* p. 282.)

6. In *Quinque Compilationes Antiquae . . .* Instruxit Aemilius Friedberg, Graz, 1956; Compil. I, Lib. 3, Titul. 28, Cap. 9, p. 39.

7. *Op. cit.,* Compil. I, Titul. 4, Cap. 4, Par. 5, p. 46.

8. "Si mulier non fuerit a viro cognita, licitum est sibi [sic] ad religionem transire." (*Liber Decretalium,* Lib. 3, Titul. 32, Cap. 32, Friedberg, *op. cit.,* Col. 579)

The part of this decretal that is decisive for the jurisprudence of dissolution because it interprets Christ's prohibition against dismissal is this: "Certainly what the Lord says in the Gospel, that a wife is not to be dismissed except for her adultery, is to be understood, by interpretation of Sacred Scripture [*sacri eloquii*], to refer to those whose marriage has not been consummated by sexual intercourse—intercourse without which a marriage cannot be consummated. Hence if the wife has not had intercourse with her husband, she is permitted to enter religious life." (See also Lib. 4, Titul. 4, Cap. 3, *op. cit.,* Col. 681.)

   9. *Ibid.*
   10. In Dauvillier, *op. cit.,* p. 292.
   11. *Liber Decretalium,* Lib. 3, Titul. 32, Cap. 15 (Friedberg, *op. cit.,* Col. 579).
   12. *Ibid.*
   13. In Dauvillier, *op. cit.,* pp. 301–303.
   14. *Liber Decretalium,* Lib. 4, Titul. 17, Cap. 8 (Friedberg, *op. cit.,* Cols. 712–713).

Alexander's disposition of the case came in these words: "Therefore because the truth of the matter has not, to our mind, been established, we command . . . that you investigate the matter carefully, and if you find that the bishop has in fact pronounced the judgment of divorce between them, you are to judge legitimate the children she has borne of the second husband (to marriage with whom she came by the authority of the aforenamed bishop, without question or prohibition on the part of the Church); and that you not allow them for this cause to be deprived of their inheritance."

   15. In Migne, P.L., Vol. 200, Col. 1259 (Dauvillier, *op. cit.,* p. 306).
   16. *Liber Decretalium,* Lib. 4, Titul. 21, Cap. 2 (Friedberg, *op. cit.,* Col. 730).

"By apostolic authority we reply, concerning the marriages that certain among you have contracted without having verified the death of your spouses, that none of you presume to take up a second marriage until you have established with certainty that your spouse has died. If any of you has to date not observed this, and regards the death of your first spouse as still doubtful, you need not deny the marriage debt to your second spouse if he or she demands it, but you yourselves are not to demand it. But if after this your spouse is verified as alive, you must leave your illicit and adulterous unions and return without delay to your first spouse."

   17. *Liber Decretalium,* Lib. 4, Titul. 1, Cap. 19 (Friedberg, *op. cit.,* Col. 668).
   18. A medieval European male of elastic conscience and irresistible charm could exploit this customary law to block his being forced by his parents into a marriage he did not want. If he could succeed in having intercourse with his unwanted fiancée's sister or even her mother, he could make of the first-named his sister-in-law and then claim in his favor the impediment barring the marriages of relatives-in-law.
   19. The terms "public" and "notorious" belong to the vocabulary of the Church's criminal law, or indeed to any criminal law. A criminal act is deemed public if it is known generally in a given territory, or, if not yet known, circumstances lead reasonably to the judgment that the act can and will readily become known. An act is *notorious in law* if it has been judged by a competent ecclesiastical court, or if the perpetration of the act has been confessed in open court. An act is *notorious in fact* if it is publicly known and the circumstances of its perpetration were such that it cannot be concealed from a court and no legal defense can excuse it.
   20. In *Compilationes Antiquae,* Compil. 1, Lib. 4, Titul. 13, Par. 2 (Friedberg, *op. cit.,* pp. 49–50).
   21. *Op. cit.,* Compil. 1, Lib. 4, Titul. 20, Par. 6 (Friedberg, *op. cit.,* pp. 52–53).

22. In Dauvillier, *op. cit.,* pp. 296–298.

23. *Liber Decretalium,* Lib. 3, Titul. 32, Cap. 14 (Friedberg, *op. cit.,* Cols. 583–584).

24. *Liber Sextus Decretalium,* IV, 15, 1.

Given the establishment of this discipline, the authorities had to decide the question asking how long a spouse could delay the consummating of the marriage in consideration of possible entry into religious life. Inevitably the opinions on this point differed. Alexander and Huguccio fixed in the jurisprudence on this point that the spouses have a right to sexual intercourse, and have it from the moment of marital consent; and that they must either grant the exercise of the right to one another or exercise their other right, namely to dissolve the marriage by taking the vows of religious life. They set two months from the date of the marital consent as the limit of delay of consummation. Innocent IV (1243–1254) interpreted this period as a probation during which the spouses were to decide either to remain in their marriage or to enter religious life. He added that the spouses' bishop could either lengthen or shorten this period, but that at the end of it he could compel them to decide one way or the other, and compel them also to execute their decision. The probationary period has in subsequent centuries borne the name *privilegium bimestris,* the "privilege of the two months."

25. Dauvillier, *op. cit.,* pp. 329–330.

26. *Liber Decretalium,* Lib. 4, Titul. 13, Cap. 6 (Friedberg, *op. cit.,* Col. 698).

27. *Liber Decretalium,* Lib. 4, Titul. 8, Cap. 3 (Friedberg, *op. cit.,* Col. 692). This decree clearly made non-consummation a condition of dissolution. Accordingly it contradicted early rulings that did not. For example, before 1187 the assizes of the lower court of the Latin kingdom of Jerusalem ruled that where a wife becomes leprous or suffers an equivalent physical defect, ecclesiastical authority might dissolve the marriage. This freed the husband to remarry, and the wife could enter religious life. In this ruling the court agreed with the law of the Byzantine Church.

28. *Liber Decretalium,* Lib. 4, Titul. 8, Cap. 1 (Friedberg, *op. cit.,* Cols. 691–692).

In another decretal addressed to the bishop of Bayonne Innocent returned to the principle that a spouse may be dismissed only for adultery, expanded his prohibition to include dissolution for any illness at all, and forbade even separation because of it. He added that the leprous may marry, and that a leprous spouse has the right to demand intercourse with the other, and the latter the obligation to accede to the demand (*ibid.,* Col. 692).

29. Dauvillier, *op. cit.,* p. 329.

30. *Op. cit.,* p. 331.

31. *Loc. cit.,* p. 332.

32. *Liber Decretalium,* Lib. 3, Titul. 33, Cap. 1 (Friedberg, *op. cit.,* Col. 588).

33. *Liber Decretalium,* Lib. 4, Titul. 19, Cap. 7 (Friedberg, *op. cit.,* Cols. 722–723)

The fifteenth-century Sicilian canonist, Panormitanus (Nicolò de' Tedeschi), explained succinctly why the marriages of the unbaptized can be dissolved: "But the marriage of non-believers does not have this signification (namely, of the union of Christ and the Church), because they deny the Incarnation. Thus marriage among them is not as firm and indissoluble because it lacks the reason [or cause] of indissolubility" (*Lectura in Decretales,* Lib. 4, Titul. 19, Cap. 7).

34. *Liber Decretalium,* Lib. 4, Titul. 19, Cap. 8 (Friedberg, *op. cit.,* Cols. 723–724).

I say that this decretal seems to repeat what Innocent wrote to Huguccio in 1199. But its formulation suggests a difference whose importance is hard to estimate. The husband's conversion is not said clearly to be from non-belief, because Innocent writes of the dismissal of his wife "according to his rite" (*secundum ritum suum*). On the face of it this could indicate conversion from one of the Eastern Catholic churches to the Roman Catholic. But it could as well refer to dismissal according to Jewish law and custom. This interpretation is helped slightly by Innocent's writing of the husband's conversion "to the faith of Christ." It is not likely that he would think the man's passing from Eastern to Roman Catholicism marked his first conversion to the faith of Christ. The phrase more realistically describes his passing from Judaism to Christianity.

35. See Chapter Six.

36. In Dauvillier, *op. cit.,* p. 340.

37. *Ibid.,* pp. 340ff.

38. The Council of Worms in 847 had ruled as follows concerning a wife whose husband committed homicide in defending himself against an attempt on his life arranged by her. If it could be proved that the wife had so plotted, the husband could dismiss her. She was to be subjected to severe penance, and she could never remarry. But neither could the husband remarry until after the wife's death (*Liber Decretalium,* Lib. 4, Titul. 19, Cap. 1; Friedberg, *op. cit.,* Col. 720).

39. Alexander III issued a decretal showing that this was his judgment, but with the variation that a husband who had justifiably dismissed his adulterous wife but had later committed adultery himself was obligated to take her back because of his own sin. This is indirect evidence that Alexander did not consider the separation a dissolution of the marriage. (The decretal is in *Liber Decretalium,* Lib. 4, Titul. 19, Cap. 5; Friedberg, *op. cit.,* Cols. 721–722.)

40. *Liber Decretalium,* Lib. 4, Titul. 19, Cap. 2 (Friedberg, *op. cit.,* Col. 720).

41. *Liber Decretalium,* Lib. 4, Titul. 19, Cap. 7 (Friedberg, *op. cit.,* Cols. 722–723).

13. THE MEDIEVAL THEOLOGIANS ON DIVORCE AND REMARRIAGE

I have already suggested that from the death of Augustine in 430 through the next seven centuries the development of the theology of marriage was so slight as to be virtually non-existent. Surely, as we have seen, everyone knew the sacred texts that are the primary sources of such a theology. Augustine himself was only one of the latest in a succession of Fathers who took the exhortation in Ephesians 5 that a husband's love for his wife ought to be modeled on Christ's love for his Church and raised it to a declaration of fact that the marriage of every Christian couple is an image of that love. He insisted that the root of imperishability of the marriage of two Christians is the *sacramentum* in their souls. And all the *loci classici* from the Scriptures were repeated century after century to build the *doctrina,* the authoritative teaching, and the discipline of divorce and remarriage in the Western Church.

But little theologizing was done from these sources. For example, one searches in vain among the scholarly writings of these seven centuries for a serious attempt to explain how it must follow that because the relationship of Christ and the Church is indestructible, so too must the marriage of two Christians be the same—that is, how the link of analogy between the two relationships reproduces the first relationship's indissolubility in the second of them.

Everyone repeated the claim, and the sheer accumulated momentum of repetition came naturally to serve not a theological development but the building of a juridical position, just as repetition by authority builds a legal precedent. Here and there an esoteric and novel interpretation of a passage from the Scriptures was seized on and added to the process of building. One thinks immediately of Augustine's assurance that the dismissal of the adulterous wife permitted in the Matthean exceptive clause was only her banishment from bed and board, and of Alexander III's insistence that Christ's command that a husband not dismiss his wife refers only to consummated marriages, and that this is why, if a marriage is not consummated, one spouse's taking the vows of religion can dissolve it.

One memorable effect of this form of development was the persuasion among some canonists of the early thirteenth century that (as Dauvillier notes) the invulnerability of marriage to dissolution, at the point where it is in fact invulnerable, is not so much a characteristic of marriage itself as a quality of conduct commanded by divine positive law.[1] In other words, they were persuaded that indissolubility is not ontologically in marriage but deontologically from God.

This interpretation helped explain to them some otherwise unassimilable facts. Among them was the dismissing of wives commanded (or permitted) in the law of Moses, carried on by arguably good Hebrew men, and permitted by some unquestionably holy Christian teachers (Basil the best-known of them). Another such fact was the one we saw just above, the fact that one and the same Christian marriage could up to a certain point be dissoluble, but beyond this point—its consummation by first intercourse after consent—be indissoluble. The answer in both cases was that it is willed to be so by divine authority, and because the Church has been endowed with this authority on earth, those who hold it in its highest form can contract and expand the perimeters of marriage's indissolubility.

But as Dauvillier also points out, the theologians of the late twelfth and thirteenth centuries were not satisfied with this explanation. He does not say why they were not, but one may guess at the reasons. Two of these, closely interwoven, seem evident. Precisely as theologians they had learned philosophy, since they understood that it is impossible to do theology without using a conceptual system and language provided by philosophy (as we know it is impossible to do physics without using a language provided by mathematics). But the philosophy that these Catholic philosophers came to use was that of Plato first, and that of Aristotle too as the latter's works became known in the Latin West thanks, paradoxically, to their introduction there by the Muslim occupiers of otherwise Catholic Spain.

What the theologians read in Plato and Aristotle about marriage must have challenged them to meet these great pagan thinkers on their own ground. Aristotle especially, as we have seen, deemed marriage an *officium,* an instrumental relationship of men and women; it is for the supplying and nurturing of citizens for the state. The need and the obligation of spouses to stay together is measured, therefore, by the needs and demands of this *officium.* They are to stay together as long as this is needed for the nurture of their children and as long as they are needed for the support of one another.

The theologians could start with this assumption that marriage is indeed an *officium,* but could argue against Aristotle that he had understood it in too confined a sense. Marriage may exist for the gaining of goods outside itself, but for more goods, and goods demanding more permanence, than he acknowledged.

But more than this, the study especially of Aristotle deepened the theologians' understanding of what was hinted at transparently by the Stoics. These insisted that there is possible in human conduct that which is natural for men and women, and that which is unnatural for them (as intercourse during pregnancy is unnatural). This points at a reality that is nature, a complex ensemble of sensate and insensate beings, an ensemble having its inherent needs, its inherent patterns of conduct, its inherent laws and paths of development. This perception of nature is a *Weltanschauung*, a point of view, quite different from that of the Hebrews. They saw the material universe as a kind of a performance stage of a benevolent God, a kind of playground whose only "law" is that it be amenable to his will, that it be wholly responsive to his strategies for disclosing his presence and carrying out his mighty acts in it.

Putting these two concepts of nature together the theologians became curious to know what is natural about marriage, what is inherent in it and put there by God, and to know especially what nature and the Creator of it demand about the perseverence of a man and a woman in their marriage once they have formed it.

This focused curiosity in the thirteenth-century theologians about the demands of marriage's nature helps account for a surprise awaiting the student who reads them. One finds more a philosophy of marriage in them than a theology. When one looks for their arguments in favor of marriage's permanence these are drawn mainly from the law of nature. Why this is so one can account for again only by informed conjecture. There were reasons of historical circumstance. Lacking a necessary instrument for New Testament interpretation, a command of the *koine* Greek in which these Scriptures had been written, they could not get behind what the Western Fathers had passed on to them in Latin. So one does not find them critically curious about what the texts of the Gospels and Epistles really said.

Again, Aquinas' study of marriage is incomplete. He died in 1274 before getting to the sacrament of marriage in his most thoroughly theological work, the *Summa Theologiae* (*Pars Tertia*). What we have from him on marriage is almost exclusively in two works. The first is his commentary on Book IV of Peter Lombard's *Libri Sententiarum*. He was only thirty years old when he did this commentary between 1254 and 1256 as a *Sententiarius* at the University of Paris. So in it we find very little of his own thought, nothing of his later speculative adventuring. The other work is his handbook for Dominican missionaries working among the Muslims of Spain, the *Summa Contra Gentes*. His one brief chapter on the indissolubility of marriage there in its Book III betrays that it is intended to instruct and perhaps change non-Christian minds. It is hardly theology.

Yet well before the turn of the thirteenth century one theologian did essay a forthright theological treatise on marriage. He sought to interpret marriage as a sacrament; what he said about the indissolubility of the marriages of Christians is drawn from the demands of the sacrament. This theologian was Hugh of St. Victor, a canon regular of St. Augustine who taught in Paris at the College of St. Victor (as his name tells). He was the first Christian thinker of his time to write an independent and integral treatise on marriage—in fact the first since Augustine almost eight centuries earlier.

This treatise is Hugh's *De Sacramento Conjugii* (On the Sacrament of Marriage), which is Part 11 of Book 2 of his summary treatise *De Sacramentis Christianae Fidei* (On the Sacraments of the Christian Faith), which he completed between 1130 and 1143.[2]

The definition of marriage that Hugh offered—and he offered it not obliquely or implicitly, but as a formal effort to define—was in almost all its parts uniquely his own. He had presented it first in an earlier work *De Beatae Mariae Virginis Virginitate* (On the Virginity of the Blessed Virgin Mary).[3] It lacked the exactness of the ancient Roman jurists' definitions in the Digest and the Institutes. But it reached back behind them to long-neglected biblical sources, and at the same time hinted at the distant future in proposing that a marriage is a relationship of self-giving love.

> What else is marriage, but the legitimate association between a man and a woman, an association in which each partner owes (*debet*) himself to the other by virtue of equal consent. This owing can be considered in two ways, that one reserve oneself for the spouse, and that one not refuse oneself to the spouse. That is, he reserves himself in that after giving consent he does not go now to another union. He does not refuse himself in that he does not separate himself from that mutual association of one with the other.

Even a first brief inspection of this definition shows that Hugh has written permanence, and perhaps indissolubility, into the very definition of marriage; they are owed by the spouses one to the other by virtue of the kind of consent that creates a marriage. Whether this goes beyond the holding power even of the objective *bonum* of marriage that is the *sacramentum* remains to be seen. But clearly it is an early suggestion of what will be stated explicitly by the bishops of the Second Vatican Council, that the source within a marriage of its permanence lies in the kind of commitment the spouses make to one another.

Like every other Christian of his time Hugh took for granted that God had created marriage, and had done so in the garden of Eden when he gave the first woman to the first man (according to the Garden parable in Genesis 2 and 3), to help him in the propagation of the human race (according to the creation poem in Genesis 1).[4]

Hugh saw two distinct institutions of marriage, separated in time, but at each institution made a sacrament. The first took place in the garden before the sin of the first parents. Then and there it was instituted to carry out an *officium,* a functional duty, which is the multiplication of the human species. In its nature it was instituted as a pact of love (*foedus dilectionis*).[5] And because it was made such it could also be the sacrament it was intended to be, a sacrament of the relationship between God and the human soul. So marriage was made by God to be this, a pact of love, distinctly from any goods it could realize or any ends it must attain. And apart from any of these it has been made a sacrament. In saying this Hugh clearly went aside from the mainstream of medieval thought that did little more than repeat Augustine and the other Fathers.

But this first institution intended also that marriage fulfill its *officium* through sexual intercourse. By doing this it could also, and subsequently, become the sacrament of the love relationship between Christ and the Church. In saying this Hugh rejoined the ranks; he shared the opinion of most of his contemporaries, and anticipated that of many of his successors, that the marriage of two Christians becomes a sacrament of the new law when the spouses have their first intercourse, and only then.

Marriage's second institution took place after the sin of the first parents (although Hugh does not try to identify the time or the place of this second institution). This institution, after the first parents' sin, brought no diminution of the pact of love. On the contrary, it reinforced marriage's nature as such a pact. It did so by providing a *remedium* for the weakness and the evil in the spouses, or more exactly in their sexuality, by giving it an excuse. This excuse is found in the goods that marriage yields. And here Hugh had in mind the three goods that Augustine proposed, fidelity, offspring and perseverance in the martial commitment. Thus with the second institution there comes an addition to the *officium* given marriage in the first, in that the healthy procreation (belonging to the first) becomes also the *remedium* (belonging to the second).[6]

How central Hugh thought sacramentality is to the nature of marriage—central to it even in its original state, at its first institution, before the sin of the first parents and before the coming of Christ and its second institution—is evident in his reason for insisting that this "natural" sacramentality can be present even if intercourse never takes place. For even without intercourse marriage is a sacrament in its mirroring the relationship of God and the soul. The transparent implication here reiterates what he had said earlier: a marriage is a relationship of spiritual love between the spouses; it is this relationship which makes it a sacrament and, in the logical sequence of his reasoning, therefore a marriage.

> ... the very association which is preserved externally in marriage by a compact or covenant is the natural love of souls which is guarded in turn by the bond of conjugal society and agreement.[7]

Given that Hugh disagrees with so many of his contemporaries in denying that intercourse is needed either for completing the marriage or for forming the sacrament, what place did he then see for it in marriage? He saw it as an act of love which is a *remedium*, a protection against the sinful effects of concupiscence.

It is in his consideration of the three goods of marriage named by Augustine and lodged at the heart of the understanding of marriage by his time that we find Hugh's judgment concerning the possibility and the permissibility of dissolving a marriage. He called the three goods "blessings" and said that they *accompany* (*comitantur*) a marriage. He named them fidelity (*fides*), hope of progeny (*spes prolis*) and the sacrament (*sacramentum*).[8]

About these three blessings Hugh asked (in Chapter 8) whether they are inseparable from a marriage.[9] He was confident that two of the three, fidelity and hope of offspring, are separable from it. About fidelity he says that since this consists of having no intercourse outside one's marriage, and since its violation consists of adultery, it is evident that this blessing inheres in a marriage in such a way that its presence makes the marriage better, but that its absence does not destroy the *sacramentum* of the marriage. An adulterous spouse is still a spouse. And his reasoning here suggests clearly that there is some more stable reality underlying the contingent fidelity, a reality that is not lost by the loss of fidelity. This reality seems to be the good that is the *sacramentum*.[10]

He continues, saying that the hope of progeny too is separable from the marriage. For men and women advanced in years and therefore sterile can and do marry. If the blessing of progeny were inseparable from marriage, they could not.

But he insists that the *sacramentum* is the one blessing of the three that is not separable. Without it a marriage cannot exist. Or, said more exactly, it is so inseparable that without it the relationship would not be a marriage. In saying this he is consistent with his earlier defining of any and every marriage as a sacrament.

In the latter half of this Chapter 8 he resumes his exposition of the subject. In a marriage there are two components which are distinct one from the other. One is the marriage itself, which is the *legitima societas*—the legitimate society, or union. The other is the *officium*, the functional duty belonging to a marriage, and this is sexual intercourse. It is to the first of these that the *sacramentum*, the demand for permanence, belongs, while fidelity and the hope of offspring belong to the second. The latter can be absent from a marriage while yet leaving the *legitima societas* and its *sacramentum* intact.

From this much Hugh reasons in the following way: since the *sacramentum* is in the marital union (the *societas*), and this union cannot be dissolved as long as both spouses live, then the *sacramentum* lasts as long as does the union. Clearly he does not reason as later generations of canonists and theologians were to reason, that *because* a marriage of two Christians is a sacrament it is an indissoluble union. He seems rather to reason in the counter-direction. Starting with the assumption that the marital union is of its nature undivided, he concludes that the *sacramentum,* which is inseparable from it, lasts until at least one of the spouses dies. For, as he says at the end of this Chapter 8, "those have the *sacramentum* of marriage who by reciprocal consent have joined together to conserve indivisibly that society that God has instituted between man and woman."[11] Taking this at its literal value one finds Hugh saying that they are the spouses who effect the *sacramentum* in their marriage by coming together with the intent to maintain their union permanently. We shall see presently that without noting explicitly that he does, he draws from this the conclusion that they are the spouses who by this same intent cause the indivisibility of their marriage.

But it is not evident that he held that because every marriage is an *indivisa societas,* an undivided union (and thus a *sacramentum* of Christ's relationship with the Church), it is invulnerable to any attempt to dissolve it. He addresses this issue implicitly by getting explicitly at a different question, one whose formulation is unique in the inventory of questions that exercised the canonists of his age. This is found in the title of Chapter 11 of this same treatise: "Whether that [relationship] is to be called a marriage which can sometimes [or subsequently] be dissolved (*Utrum conjugium dicendum est quod aliquando dissolvi potest*).[12] (In the concluding sentence of this Chapter 11 he repeats this question he believes he has just answered, but this time as his side of a dialectic: "I have said all this to counter those who think that in no way can one call a marriage that [relationship] which can sometimes [or subsequently] be dissolved.")[13]

One may wonder how Hugh came to examine and try to answer this singular question. Perhaps its origin may have been something like the following. Since he held that sexual intercourse is not necessary for either the creating of a marriage or its completion, but that the parties' consent is sufficient for both, he must then necessarily say that the otherwise permitted dissolution of a non-consummated marriage (for example, on the ground of impotence) is not the dissolution of an incomplete marriage but of a completed one. The recently and painfully formed discipline forbidding such dissolution in the Western Church forbade dissolving completed marriages. Therefore Hugh must have been challenged to be consistent and to admit that dissolution according to his interpretation would not be dissolution of a marriage at all, but the separation of an invalid union. Hence his way of phrasing the question here: "Whether a relationship that can be dissolved is to be called a marriage."

This seems at the same time a backdoor entry to the question asking whether a marriage can be dissolved, and likewise a slightly disguised posing of the broader question, "Is marriage dissoluble or indissoluble?"

He begins his examination of the question by noting that there are those who flatly deny that a relationship that can be dissolved is to be called a marriage. He acknowledges that they draw this judgment from what they read in the Scriptures and in certain of the Fathers. He takes special notice of Augustine's insistence in The Good of Marriage that despite its supposed dissolution a marriage survives because the marital covenant is the interior substance (the *res*) of a certain *sacramentum.*

But Hugh rejoins, "However at least for now it is not clear to me how they can prove that the power of the marital *sacramentum* can bring it about that the union is [or must be] undivided by both parties as long as they live, and prove therefore that a relationship that can sometimes [or subsequently] be divided is not a marriage."[14]

He cited the argument he has heard these writers and teachers offer. It is this, that for a relationship to be a marriage it must have all those properties belonging essentially to the nature of marriage. But indissolubility is such a property. Therefore if the relationship is in fact dissolved, it could not have been a marriage.

His rejoinder is that this reasoning is conclusive to a point, namely that when a relationship is all that a marriage should be, it *ought* to have in it the *individua societas—quia hanc* [*individuam societatem*] *conjugium habere debet quando scilicet est ubi esse debet.* For this undivided union belongs to marriage, and marriage demands it, or rather produces it, insofar as it can—*Haec enim conjugii est et hanc conjugium exigit, sive potius confert, quantum in se est.*[15]

He then sets out to clarify this by an analogy. In the same way it is true to say that it is the nature of baptism to cause the remission of sin. It is true to say that it is the nature of the Eucharist to cause union and participation with Christ. But it is also true that an adult who merely pretends to receive baptism does not in fact have his sins forgiven by this sacrament, as also a person who receives the Eucharist unworthily is not in fact united with Christ. Nevertheless—and here Hugh applies the point of his rebuttal—even when these two sacraments fail to produce their effects no one denies it is the nature of baptism to forgive sin, or denies it is the nature of the Eucharist to unite persons with Christ. In the same way one need not deny that the *individua societas* belongs to the nature of marriage even though we at times find a marriage that does not produce it as its effect.[16]

At this point he anticipates his opponents' counter-attack. If they say that in such a case the marriage is at least not a sacrament, then by the same logic they must say that where baptism does not, because of the person's pretending, produce forgiveness of sin in him, it is not a sacrament and the pretender is not baptized. Or where because of unworthiness the Eucharist does not produce union with Christ, neither is it a sacrament and thus the body of Christ is not truly present because the person fails in spiritual participation with Christ.

So again, one who says that a marriage *has* the *individua societas* really ought to say rather that *when* it has all that it ought to have, it has this. Where a marriage lacks it, it is not for this reason any less a sacrament while it exists, although it is less helpful to the persons joined in this marriage. And he reiterates his conclusion in the following way.

> In this way I think that certain marriages can truly be called marriages as long as they are considered ratified according to the mind of the Church, even if later, with the surfacing of legally justified causes, they are rightly dissolved. And if they are subsequently maintained presumptuously and against the Church's decision, they are deemed illicit and illegitimate [invalid?] unions.[17]

The form of Hugh's argument in this passage is clear enough. He makes a distinction in the predictability of the term "natural" in its designating indissolubility's relationship to a marriage. He sees his adversaries saying that indissolubility, the *individua societas,* belongs to the nature of marriage as one of its essentially constitutive properties (with the consequence that where it is absent from a man-woman relationship, this cannot be a marriage). But he insists that indissolubility is natural to marriage in the sense that it is an effect that marriage as a sacrament by nature produces when this marriage-sacrament is able to work its effect fully (as it is of the nature of baptism as a sacrament to produce forgiveness of sin when it can work its effects fully). Thus, he is convinced that he has, by this distinction, saved (1) the nature of marriage as *individua societas,* (2) the status of indissolubility as a good of marriage the sacrament, (3) the undeniable fact that some marriages are dissolved—and (4) perhaps his own teaching that even after consent alone but before intercourse a marriage is complete. And one should not fail to notice, between the poles of his distinction, that Hugh has advanced the suggestion, startling for its time, that indissolubility is not something a priori and simply given in a marriage, but where it is present in a marriage it is there as an effect of the spouses' intent to preserve their marriage as an indivisible union. That is, indissolubility is not in a marriage as a cause working in the spouses the effect of binding them in an unbreakable bond. It is there (when it is there) as an effect produced by the will of the spouses to live their marriage to its fullest. (Eight centuries later the bishops of the Second Vatican Council were to say that a cause of a marriage's indissolubility is the spouses' irrevocable personal consent that is needed to create the marriage.[18])

How widely this argument was ever read by the canonists of his own and succeeding ages we have no way of knowing. That it was set forth futilely is evident in the eventual coming to pass of what Hugh probably suspected was happening in his day, namely that marriage was entering a history of being defined, and the definition was beginning to include among its essentially constitutive elements the quality of indissolubility. As he said, he did not see how anyone could prove from the scriptural and patristic sources that this is true. If anyone noted this challenge, no one at least in his century tried to meet it with counter-arguments.

Thomas Aquinas

In his teaching on divorce and remarriage Thomas Aquinas (1225–1274) shows clearly the two distinct categories of examination to which many Scholastic theologians submitted the issue. He dealt with it in the two works authentically his own that I named earlier, in his commentary on the fourth book of Peter Lombard's *Libri Sententiarum,* and in the third book of his *Summa Contra Gentiles.* I will here examine the latter work first, keeping in mind the date of its completion in 1264, some eight years after Thomas had completed his commentary on Lombard's *Libri Sententiarum.*[19]

In his *Summa Contra Gentiles* Thomas does not take up directly the question of divorce and remarriage. He gets at it only indirectly as a product of his arguing for his thesis, in Chapter 123 of Book 3, "That marriage ought to be indissoluble" (*Quod matrimonium debet esse indivisibile*). I hesitate about this translation of the adjective *indivisibile.* Thomas does use the term *indissolubile* in his reply to the question. While the term is understood in modern Catholic marriage law to designate a marriage's inherent invulnerability to being dissolved by divorce, it is not clear that in the *Summa Contra Gentiles* Thomas tries to demonstrate such invulnerability.

Here in the *Summa Contra Gentiles* he examines marriage as the natural association of a man and a woman, not as this association become sacrament in the marriage of two Christians. He does invoke the divine law formulated in the Christ-Church analogy of Ephesians 5, and he seems to see this formulation in the law applying to marriage generally, not only to the marriages of Christians. But he says of this formulation that "it adds a certain reason" to the regulating of marriage. He does not in this passage argue that the analogy has probative and obligating force. That is, he does not say that *because* the relationship of Christ to the Church is indestructible the marriage of a Christian husband and wife is indissoluble.

What then is his mode of argument? It is a philosophical *argumentum quia.* It begins with an assumed understanding of marriage taken from the Platonic-Aristotelian tradition. This understanding is that a marriage is an *officium,* a dutiful vocation. Its principal good is utilitarian; a marriage exists and functions primarily for the attaining of goals outside itself— goals which are arranged tributarily and therefore hierarchically. That is, marriage is principally for the good that is procreation and nurture of offspring. This in turn subserves the good of civil society and ecclesiastical society. Hence the pivot of Thomas' argument: permanence is needed in marriage for the good of nurture, and thence for the good of these societies. This is also a demand of *aequitas* for both the offspring and their mother. Conversely the dissolving of marriages is damaging to offspring (an *inaequitas* to them) and thence damaging and an *inaequitas* to the societies mentioned above. Whether Thomas succeeds in demonstrating that dissolution of marriage is unexceptionably an *inaequitas* in these senses—whether it is always and in every imaginable case so damaging to offspring, mother and society as to be proscribed without exception—the reader will have to decide.

At the end of this ethical argumentation Thomas does cite the familiar Synoptic passages in which Christ forbids the dismissing of wives. And he quotes from 1 Corinthians 7:10 Paul's command (from Christ) that wives are not to depart from their husbands. But he does this only to confirm what he considers already proved. He also, along the path of his ethical argument, appeals to the love and friendship of the spouses as a reason against dissolution, an appeal that calls for closer examination in its place.

To understand Thomas' argument here in Chapter 123 we must back up and first examine what he says in Chapter 122, because Thomas himself says that it is there, in his argument that sexual intercourse of the unmarried (*simplex fornicatio*) is sinful, that one finds the beginning of his argument that marriage ought to be indissoluble: "If one thinks carefully on it, the foregoing argument [in Chapter 122] leads not only to the conclusion that the association of a man and a wife that is called marriage ought to be long-lasting (*diuturnum*), but to the conclusion that it should last the lifetime of the spouses."

His argument that fornication is sinful is rooted, as in a principle, in what is needed by offspring, and in what is needed by them, in turn, for the good of human nature. He begins with what he takes for granted to be self-evident about the male anatomy: that semen by nature serves a useful good—it is for the purpose of generation. But, he proceeds, the act of generating would be frustrated unless it were followed by nurture, since without nurture the child produced by generation could not survive.

Hence the rightly ordered emission of semen demands both that conception be possible (since this is what semen is for) and that the child once conceived be nurtured (since without nurture the emission of semen would be frustrated in its purpose). Thus it follows that any emission of semen in such a way that conception cannot ensue is contrary to the good of man, is against human nature. However, Thomas holds that this is true only if conception is impossible because of the way the emission itself is procured, but is not true if conception is impossible for some other reason—for example because of the woman's sterility. In the latter case the futile emission of semen is not against nature and thus is not a sin.

Thus too the emission of semen in circumstances such that though conception can result yet nurture is impossible is contrary to the good of man.

From this preliminary conclusion Thomas subsumes immediately as a point of fact what must have been a common persuasion in his society. This is that a woman by herself is manifestly incapable of nurturing her child. There are necessities of life which she cannot by herself procure for it. Hence the conclusion: it is according to human nature that the father remain with the mother beyond the conception and birth of the child in order to secure these necessities for the child. (And he insists that this argumentation is not refuted by the fact that this or that woman, because of her wealth, can provide by herself for the child. His reason for saying this is that "natural rectitude in human acts is not measured by what happens apart from the normal [*per accidens*] in one person, but by that which affects the entire human species.")

What is more, Thomas continues, children have an extended need for instruction of the soul, not only for education but also for the repression of their unruly passions. But a woman left to herself is not capable of this instruction. Therefore the father must remain with her until it is completed. And this association of the man and woman for the procreation and nurture of children is called marriage.

It is at this point that his argumentation thus begun continues into Chapter 123 and into his thesis that a marriage ought to be *indivisibile*—that it ought to be not only long-lasting in an unspecified duration, but for the lifetime of the spouses.

He adduces several reasons that demand this perpetuity. For one, when a woman is taken into marriage by a man, she is taken for the sake of procreation. As he had said in the preceding chapter, Thomas here repeats that husband and wife must stay together as long as their children need nurture, since the wife cannot provide this by herself. But if the husband were allowed to dismiss his wife later, after her beauty has faded and her fertility ended, he would treat her with serious unfairness. All the more would this be unfair because she is forbidden a second marriage.

Nor can a wife either dismiss or abandon her husband. She is by nature subject to him as to her ruler (her *gubernator*), and one who lives under the authority (*potestas*) of another cannot depart from this authority. For the wife to do this would be contrary to the natural order of things. But if the husband could abandon the wife, this would, again, be unfair to her; she would be a kind of slave to him.

Thomas sees a reason for the permanence of marriage in the friendship that is natural to a husband and wife. For the more intense a friendship becomes the more enduring and lasting (*firma et diuturna*) it is. But the friendship of a husband and wife is the most intense of friendships. "A man will leave even his father and mother and will cling to his wife." And husband and wife are joined not only by sexual intercourse, which creates a certain tender union even among brute beasts, but also by the sharing in the entire life of the home.

The natural need for the retaining of private possessions argues too for the permanence of marriage. A father cannot live perpetually to keep possessions within his family; he must do this through his sons. But he can do this only if his care (*sollicitudo*) for his sons endures until the end of his life. And, Thomas implies, he can maintain this care only if he remains within the marriage that produced these sons.

This solicitude of fathers for their children is the source for Thomas of another argument for permanence. In men there is a natural solicitude for knowing who their children are. So that whatever destroys this certitude is contrary to a natural instinct of the human species. But if a husband could dismiss his wife, or she him, and both could take another spouse, a woman would have intercourse with plural husbands and the certitude of paternity would be lost—which, again, is a violation of natural instinct.

Finally Thomas argues for the permanence of marriage because it is needed as tributary to the good moral conduct of persons as individuals, as members of families, and as members of civil society. The principle he draws from here is that marriage is oriented by nature not just to procreation but to the goodness of life both individual and social.

This being so, marriages must be permanent because if they were not, serious harm would come to persons, to families and to civil society. On the other hand, where husbands and wives know they are joined permanently, their love for one another is more faithful. They will take more faithful care of their homes and possessions. A cause of conflict between a husband and his wife's family is removed if he cannot dismiss her, and affection among relatives in law is strengthened. Finally the temptation to adultery is removed because, knowing that they must remain together, neither husband nor wife can, while still married to one another, solicit other spouses.

Thomas sees divine revelation in the Scriptures entering these reasons for permanence of marriage via moral philosophy. Revelation impinges on this permanence thanks to the place of law in governing society. Thomas begins by pointing out that among the acts natural to human beings only generation is oriented to the common good—to that which human beings as a collectivity need by virtue of their nature. For only generation among all natural acts is in itself oriented to the preserving of the human species.

It follows that generation must preeminently be ruled by law, since this is the purpose of law, to procure the common good. Now if these are human laws, they must proceed from human instinct. And since it is human instinct that the sexual joining of human beings be that of one man and one woman, and this permanently, human law must mandate these traits of exclusivity and permanence. (*Instinctus humanus* here in Thomas' thought designates something more than a genetically coded and preconsciously impelled pattern of conduct. It does designate that, but at a more fundamental level it designates something that is needed to both sustain human life and to bring it to completion. He sees the function of this instinct vis-à-vis human law to be this, that it inspires the formulation of the law and grounds its obligating valence, while the law in turn gives the *instinctus* its compelling effect in society.)

But where the law in question is divine law, its function is not only to "explain," to make clear what *instinctus humanus* urges. Its function is also to supply what is deficient in this instinct. Here is the point of entry Thomas sees for divine revelation: it adds a confirming reason to the natural demand for permanence in marriage. This confirming reason is found in marriage's signifying the relationship of Christ and the Church, a relationship which consists of a single pair of spouses, and which is indestructible (*inseparabilis*).

Thomas does not argue this point explicitly; he seems to presume that *because* a marriage is a sign of the indestructible relationship of Christ and the Church, it too must be indestructible. (Nor does he take up the question that vexed some of the early Fathers, the question that asks why it does not follow that since the relationship of Christ and the Church is not vulnerable to death, human marriages ought, in order to signify this indestructibility, be also invulnerable to death.) And somewhat strangely Thomas does not, in this passage, make this signifying of the relationship of Christ and the Church a function of Christian marriages alone. Reading him strictly in this passage, one finds him affirming this function of marriage generally. Consequently he at least implies that the same cause of permanence is found in non-Christian marriages as in Christian. Multitudes of his predecessors, contemporaries and successors in the Church did not and do not agree with him on the point.

But he makes the necessary distinction between Christian and non-Christian marriages in Book 4 of this *Summa Contra Gentiles*. There in Chapter 78 he explains briefly how the marriages of Christians are sacraments.

> Just as in the other sacraments something spiritual is imaged (*figuratur*) by an exterior and observable action, so in this sacrament the union of Christ and the Church is imaged by the union of husband and wife, according to what the Apostle says in Ephesians 5: "This is a great sacrament. I say this in regard to Christ and the Church."

Then comes the crux of his argument for the indestructibility of marriages that are sacraments.

> Therefore because the union of husband and wife images the union of Christ and the Church, the image must correspond to the reality imaged. But the union of Christ and the Church is of one person with one person, and it is to last in perpetuity.

And at this point he makes the distinction between marriages general-ly and the marriages of Christians.

> Therefore it must be (*necesse est*) that a marriage, because of its character as a sacrament of the Church, must be of one man having one woman in an indissoluble union (*Necesse est igitur quod matrimonium, secundum quod est Ecclesiae sacramentum, sit unius ad unam indivisibiliter habendam*).

Thomas adds that this permanence and unicity belong to the Chris-tian faith by which the husband and wife are committed and bound (*obligantur*) to one another. By exclusion then the unicity and permanence may not belong to those not living in the Christian faith. And we may see here the real conclusion to all Thomas' reasons adduced for permanence in marriage in Book 3. They came to only this, that a husband and wife (whether Christian or non-Christian) *must not* dissolve their marriage because either private persons or civil society or the human race generally would be harmed by the dissolution. But here he seems to say that husband and wife who are Christian *cannot* dissolve their marriage be-cause it is an image of the indestructible union of Christ and the Church. Or does he only adduce a powerfully reinforcing cause why they must not dissolve their marriage, a cause drawn from the Christian spouses' com-mitment in faith and from their vocation to image the union of Christ and the Church? I think this question here remains unanswered—this question about the radical indissolubility of a sacramental Christian marriage, about the impossibility of dissolving it as well as the impermissibility.

And let me point again to what I said earlier. This is that Thomas here in his *Summa Contra Gentiles* writes permanence into his understand-ing of marriage in a way quite different from that of the later canonists. They will make it an inherent characteristic of the contract of marriage; they will simply prescribe that this contract is non-voidable, and imply that if the parties reject this non-voidability, they cannot make the con-tract to begin with. If Thomas claims that permanence is a trait intrinsic to marriage, he finds the intrinsicity (to coin a word) in the natural needs of men and women who engage in sexual intercourse with one another, in the natural needs of their children, and in the natural needs of civil society that are consequent on their children's entering this society.

Thomas' Commentary on the Fourth Book of the *Libri Sententiarum*

Years earlier, in composing his commentary on Book Four of Peter Lombard's *Libri Sententiarum* Thomas invoked as a reason for marriage's invulnerability to dissolution the nature itself of marriage as this had been defined by the canonists and theologians of the two generations preceding his own.[20]

In Distinction 31 of his commentary he examined the three tradition-ally named goods of marriage, *fides* (fidelity), *proles* (offspring) and the *sacramentum*. In Article 3 of this distinction he asks if the *sacramentum* is the most valuable (*principalius*) of the three goods. To answer his question he makes a set of distinctions. In order of value (*dignitas*), as distinct from the order of essentiality, the *sacramentum* is of greatest worth among the three goods because it confers grace, which has greater worth than nature.

But when one looks to the essentiality of marriage, another distinction is in order. If one speaks of the use of marriage, of the conduct essential to it, fidelity and offspring are of greater value because they belong to this *usus* of marriage. But if one speaks not of marriage's use, but of marriage itself, the *sacramentum* is of greatest value. The reason he offers for this tells much about the definition of marriage in the young Thomas' mind.

> But indivisibility, which the sacrament brings, belongs to marriage itself in its own nature [*secundum se*]. For from the fact that through their marital agreement [*per pactionem conjugalem*] the spouses give authority [*potestas*] over themselves to one another in perpetuity, it follows that they cannot be separated. Hence it is that marriage is never found without its inseparabil-ity, while it can be found without fidelity and offspring, since the existence of a thing does not depend on its being used.[21]

This passage answers some questions that the treatment in the *Sum-ma Contra Gentiles* left pending (if we may reverse the historical sequence of Thomas' examination of marriage, and at the same time raise the question whether, after composing his commentary on this book of the *Libri Sententiarum,* he changed his mind). But here he says clearly what his predecessors had said and what the 1917 Code of Canon Law will say seven centuries later. Inseparability (indissolubility) is an essential trait of marriage itself. And its essentiality is found, in turn, in the essential contractuality of marriage. That is, *because* husband and wife have ex-changed their authority over their own bodies, and this exchange is made in perpetuity, their marriage cannot be separated. That is, again, *because* this marital contracting is non-voidable, the marriage itself is indissoluble.

It is striking in a modest way that Thomas finds the *sacramentum* thus understood to be a trait of marriage generally, not only—as Augus-tine had said—a trait characteristic of and unique to the marriages of Christians. It is striking too that, as the reader may already have noticed, Thomas did not repeat this reason for holding marriage generally to be *indivisible* when arguing for the latter in Question 123 of Book 3 of the *Summa Contra Gentiles.* Had he then changed his mind about the contrac-tual irreversibility of marriage? This natural irreversibility would have been a suasive kind of evidence in a handbook meant for missionary work among non-Christians, on whom the Christian sacrament's demand for permanence presumably would have been wasted.

What Thomas means by the natural indissolubility of marriage emerges more clearly in Distinction 33, Question 2, Article 1, where he asks if the *inseparabilitas* of a wife belongs to the law of nature (*Utrum inseparabilitas uxoris sit de lege naturae*). His answer to the question is affirmative; his explanation for the answer is the following.

> According to nature's intent marriage is oriented to the nurture of offspring, and this not for a limited time but for the entire lifetime of the offspring. Thus it is according to the law of nature that parents save for their children and that children be heirs to their parents. Therefore, since offspring are the good of both husband and wife together, the latter's union must remain permanently, according to the demand (*dictamen*) of the law of nature.[22]

To the fourth objection in this article—that a husband ought to be allowed to dismiss at least a sterile wife because with her he cannot realize the primary end of marriage—Thomas replies in a way that shows his reasoning at this stage of his thinking is hardly existential. That is, his moral conclusions are ruled not by what is good for persons in their concrete, real-life circumstances, but by what is good for either marriage and human society understood in a hypothetical ideal, or by what is good for them understood in a kind of concrete abstraction, marriage taken in the generality of cases.

> Because of its primary end marriage is oriented primarily to the common good. And this primary end is the good of offspring. True, by reason of its secondary end it is oriented to the good of the persons contracting the marriage—for example in the matter of remedying concupiscence in them. Therefore in the laws governing marriage there is procured that which is helpful for all rather than that which can be advantageous for the individual. Therefore too the inseparability of a marriage may block for one man the realizing of the good that is offspring, but it helps to secure this good taken simply (*simpliciter*).[23]

The last clause here reveals the object of Thomas' ethical reasoning at this point. It is not human beings in their existential singularity, in their real-life circumstances. It is human nature, human society, taken ideally while existing in the race conceived of as a generality.

If that tells us what "nature" means in Thomas' thinking here, Article 2 under the same Distinction 33, Question 2, tells more clearly what he means by the "law of nature." Here he asks whether it can be licit by dispensation that a man dismiss his wife (*Utrum licitum esse possit per dispensationem uxorem dimittere*). His reply deserves quotation in full.

I reply that a dispensation in commands [or in laws—*in praceptis*], especially in matters that belong in some way to the law of nature, is like a change in the course of a natural entity. This change can happen in two ways. In one way it is made by the intervention of a natural cause. One natural cause impedes another in its natural course, as occurs in all things in nature which happen occasionally and by accident. But this kind of changing changes the course in nature not of those things that happen always, but only of those things that happen frequently.

Another kind of change is worked by a cause that is entirely supernatural, as occurs in miracles. In this way there can be changed not only the course of nature that is ordered to frequency of occurrence, but even that which is ordered to occur always, as happened in the sun's halting in its course during the time of Josue. . . .

This kind of dispensation in the rules [*in praeceptis*] of the law of nature takes place sometimes among lower causes. In this case the dispensation affects secondary precepts of the law, but never primary, because the latter stand permanently, as is said concerning plurality of wives, and similar matters. But sometimes such a dispensation takes place among the higher causes, and here the dispensation can by divine will be against even the primary precepts of the law of nature—and this for the sake of some divine mystery intending to reveal or to signify itself, an intent that was evident in the command given Abraham to kill his innocent son. Such dispensations are given not commonly and to all, but only to individual persons, as happens in the case of miracles.

Therefore, if the indissolubility of marriage is included among the primary precepts of the law of nature, only in this second way will it come under dispensation. But if it is included among the secondary precepts, it could have come under dispensation even in the first way. And it seems rather to be included among the secondary precepts. For the indissolubility of marriage is ordered to the good of offspring (who are the primary end of marriage) only to the extent that parents provide for their children throughout the lifetime of the latter by making available to them the necessities of life. But the appropriation of these necessities is not required by nature's primary intention, that intention by which all things are for human beings in common.

Consequently the dismissing of a wife seems to be not against a primary intention of nature, and consequently not against a primary precept of the law of nature, but against a secondary precept. Hence those who dismiss a wife can come under dispensation even in the first sense [a dispensation made by a secondary cause, such as human authority].[24]

I think the following interpretation of "natural indissolubiiity" is evident in this passage written early in the history of Thomas' thinking on marriage.

The indissolubility, the *inseparabilitas,* of marriage belongs to marriage's nature not in the way that a clause essential to a definition belongs to this definition—in such a way that if the clause were removed, the definition would no longer define what it had defined before the removal.

Rather, this indissolubility belongs to marriage's nature as the fulfillment of a need that is natural to it. That is, marriages produce children as the realization of their primary natural end; children naturally require nurture; and nurture can be provided (in the generality of cases) only if both parents stay with one another. But Thomas admits a distinction in this need, a distinction that he makes in his response to Objection 1 in this Article 2. Supplying some needs of the offspring is an obligation under a primary precept of the natural law. These needs are procreation itself, then nutrition and instruction until the children become self-sustaining adults. But the supplying of other needs comes under only a secondary precept of the law of nature. Such a need is the passing on to the children of their inheritance and similar goods. It is from such a secondary precept of the law of nature ruling marriage that dispensation is possible. In short, as Aristotle had reasoned centuries earlier in his Nicomachean Ethics, because they are the needs of the children that demand the inseparability of the parents, once these needs are met the demand relaxes. Or, to include Thomas' distinction, once those things needed by the children for their very existence and for their fundamental happiness have been provided—such needs as can be supplied only by the parents—the demand for the parents' inseparability relaxes. This demand can be dispensed even by created causes, namely by persons having the authority to dispense. (In this matter Thomas must have had in mind the history of papal dispensation as well as the Old Testament law allowing the dismissing of wives.)

Consequently the young Thomas Aquinas is not rightly accused of a divine voluntarism regarding marriage, as though he were saying that because God designed and rules marriage, he can do with it what he wills, making it indissoluble when he wants, but suspending (or dispensing) this indissolubility when he wants. To begin with, as I have already pointed out, Thomas does not reserve to God this authority to dispense. But more substantially, the dispensability from indissolubility is a quality found in marriages themselves. It is in the temporariness of the children's need for both parents' providing certain necessities of life for them.

In a few other passages in this fourth book of his commentary Thomas offers this judgment on facets of dissolution that we have seen discussed down through the centuries.

In Distinction 34, Question 1, Article 2 he asks whether impotence in a person impedes his or her marrying (*Utrum frigiditas matrimonium contrahendum impedit*).[25] His answer to the question is ambiguous. At one point in his response he says that a sexually impotent person cannot marry because in marriage the partners form a contract "to render to one another the carnal debt." But an impotent person, if his impotence is permanent, will never be able to render this debt, and therefore cannot form the contract. But later in this *Solutio,* where he explains the Church's discipline in his time that allowed spouses three years during which to try to have intercourse, he says that if the attempts fail, the Church dissolves the unconsummated marriage. But if there is a marriage to be dissolved, the impotence is not, as Thomas first decided, an impediment to marriage. Indeed, he adds, if after the three years the supposedly impotent party succeeds at intercourse with a second presumed spouse, he or she is to be sent back to the original marriage, which still exists, immune to the mistaken ecclesiastical dissolution.

In Distinction 35, Question 1, Article 1 he asks whether a husband is allowed to dismiss his wife for adultery (*Utrum propter fornicationem liceat viro uxorem dimittere*).[26] Thomas' judgment is affirmative. A husband may do this except in the following circumstances: if he himself has committed adultery; if he has forced his wife into prostitution; if the wife has remarried thinking, because of the husband's long absence, that he is probably dead, whereas he still lives; if she has had intercourse with another man who has deceived her into thinking that he is her husband; if she has been raped; if by having intercourse with her after her adultery the husband has in effect taken her back.

From the words themselves that Thomas uses to designate the husband's action it is not clear if he understands that the dismissal is a true dissolution. *Dimittere* is his verb for the husband's dismissing the wife. He also calls the dismissal *divortium.*

But in the third and fourth objections under this Article his use of synonyms for these terms betrays that he does not have a true dissolution in mind. These synonyms are *separatio* and *separatio a toro* (separation from the marriage bed). This interpretation is reinforced in Article 3 where Thomas explains that a husband can dismiss his wife in either of two ways: he can exclude her from sexual intercourse, or he can bring cohabitation with her to an end. About this he says expressly, "This dismissal is what is called *divortium.* "[27] And finally in Article 5 he answers the question, "Can a husband remarry after divorce?" (*Utrum post divortium vir alteri nubere possit*).

> ... Nothing happening subsequently to a marriage [once formed] can dissolve it. Hence adultery does not make a true marriage to not be a true marriage. For, as Augustine says (in his *De nuptiis et concupiscentia,* Chapter 10) the marital bond between the spouses remains while they both live, a bond that neither separation nor union with another can end. Hence as long as the spouse still lives it is not permitted to enter a second marriage.[28]

But Thomas reserves this indissolubility to a consummated marriage. For in Distinction 31, Question 1, Article 2, in the answer to the third objection, he had made a significant distinction.[29] He pointed out there that marriage is said to be indissoluble (*inseparabilis*) because it cannot be dissolved in this life. But it can be dissolved by death—by physical death following physical joining (*per conjunctionem carnalem*), or by spiritual death following spiritual joining. That is, once a marriage has been consummated by intercourse, by physical joining, it can be dissolved only by physical death. But it can be dissolved by spiritual death—by the spouses' taking the vow of chastity—if it has been no more than contracted, that is, if it has been joined only spiritually, but has not been consummated.

I would finish this examination of Thomas' thought with a return to his *Summa Contra Gentiles.* Although his treatise on the sacraments in his *Summa Theologiae,* Part 3 stopped short of the sacrament of marriage, he did complete a treatise-in-miniature on the sacraments in Book 4 of the *Summa Contra Gentiles.* It is found there in Chapters 56 through 78; and the one chapter on marriage is the last of the group.[30] Despite its brevity its value is considerable because it offers in concentrate the theology of marriage's radical indissolubility as this was taught during the apogee of Scholastic thought in the thirteenth century.

At the halfway point in this Chapter 78 Thomas explains how it is that marriage is a sacrament in the Christian Church.

> But in so far as marriage is oriented to the good of the Church, it must be subjected to the Church's government. But those things which are dispensed to the people by the Church's ministers are called sacraments. Therefore marriage, in so far as it consists in the union of a man and woman who intend to procreate and nurture children to the honor and worship of God, is a sacrament of the Church. Hence a certain blessing is given to the spouses by the Church's ministers.

I believe that thus far Thomas has answered two implicit questions. The first would ask why marriage is numbered among and is called one of the Church's sacraments. He answers this in a most general way, that this is because marriage is oriented to the good of the Church and is consequently governed by the ministers in the Church. However satisfactory or unsatisfactory this explanation, the second implicit question would ask what marriage consists of. The answer is that it is the union of a man and a woman who intend to procreate and nurture children for the honor and worship of God.

From this point Thomas goes on to explain of what the sacramentality of marriage consists. He does so by applying to marriage the theology of sacraments generally, namely that in them a created and sensate reality images a spiritual reality.

And just as in the other sacraments a spiritual reality is imaged by a sensate action, so in this sacrament the union of Christ and the Church is imaged according to what the Apostle wrote to the Ephesians: "This is a great sacrament. I say this in reference to Christ and the Church."

Then Thomas accounts for the vertical linking of the imaging marital union with Christ and the Church. This linking is effected by the grace of the sacrament. He hints that this is a healing and sustaining grace.

And because the sacraments effect what they image, we must hold that grace is conferred on the married through this sacrament, grace through which they belong to the union of Christ and the Church. And this is very necessary to them so that they may strive that in earthly and bodily affairs they not be separated from Christ and the Church.

Then comes the fuller theology of Christian marriage as the image of the union of Christ and the Church.

Therefore because the union of husband and wife images the union of Christ and the Church, the image must correspond with that which it images. Now the union of Christ and the Church is a union of one person with one person, and a union that is perpetual . . . for Christ will never be separated from his Church. As he himself says in the last chapter of Matthew, "Behold, I am with you even unto the end of the world. . . ." It follows necessarily then that a marriage, in so far as it is a sacrament of the Church, must be of one man and one woman, and must be a union that is indissoluble. And this belongs to the fidelity by which the husband and wife are bound.

Thus the goods of marriage are three in so far as it is a sacrament of the Church, namely the offspring (which are to be accepted and nurtured for the honor and worship of God); fidelity, in that the man is bonded to one wife; and the sacrament, in that the marital union is indissoluble for being an image [*sacramentum*] of the union of Christ and the Church.

The following seem some of the assumptions that produce and rule Thomas' reasoning here. First, he takes for granted that in his Letter to the Ephesians Paul did not exhort the spouses of that community to image the love of Christ and the Church in their love for one another, but that he said that every marriage of two Christian spouses is in fact such an image.

Thomas assumes too that nothing more is needed in the two Christian spouses to make their union an image of the union of Christ and the Church than the fact of their being Christian.

He also assumes that the Christian marital union as an image of the Christ-Church union must and simply does correspond to the latter in its characteristics of monogamy and indestructibility. This correspondence is not something that must be striven for but is something there and given automatically. The cause of this ontological correspondence he seems to assume is the fact itself that the marriage is such an image—the fact that it is a sacrament, and is a sacrament in the way it is. That is, the marriage of two Christians cannot not be indissoluble. Yet he does not take care to claim this only of consummated marriages, and therefore does not explain how consummation of a sacramental marriage finally causes its radical indissolubility. That is, he does not here explain how the first sexual intercourse after marital consent completes the imaging of Christ's union with the Church.

Bonaventure

In his commentary on the fourth book of Peter Lombard's *Libri Sententiarum* Bonaventure takes up the question of dissolving marriage under three distinct titles.[31] The first of these is in his commentary on Distinction 27 where he elaborates a complex definition of marriage; and as part of this elaboration he asks about the indissolubility of marriage. The second title is in Distinction 31 where he examines the three traditional goods of marriage, the *sacramentum* among them. The third is in Distinction 35 where he examines the possibility and permissibility of one spouse's dissolving the marriage by dismissing the other because of the latter's adultery, and of a second marriage by the innocent spouse after the dismissal.

Under the first title he divides the question and asks about two degrees or stages of marriage whether both are indissoluble. He asks this first in Distinction 27, Article 3, Question 1: "Whether a consummated marriage is indissoluble" (*An matrimonium consummatum sit insolubile*);[32] then about a non-consummated marriage the same question, whether a marriage of souls is indissoluble (*An matrimonium animarum sit insolubile*). (That "a marriage of souls" here designates a non-consummated marriage is confirmed in the introduction to this Article 3 where he asks this question about indissolubility *quantum ad matrimonium animarum sit insolubile*—regarding a ratified marriage—as distinct from the *matrimonium consummatum* that he already named.) What Bonaventure means by the adjective *insolubile*, which is etymologically closer to later Catholic marriage law than Aquinas' *inseparabile*, emerges in his argumentation.

In answering the first question he makes a necessary distinction between the indissolubility of a consummated marriage and its perpetuity. The first of these qualities indicates that no human agency can end a marriage short of the death of one of the spouses. The second indicates the simple imperishability of a marriage even beyond death. Thus Bonaventure reasons in the Conclusion of this question: as long as both parties to the marriage live it is indissoluble. But if one of them dies, the marriage ends because of the fact that a bond between two persons demands that both persons bonded continue to live. A marriage ends with death because a marriage engages bodies in an essential way, since, in turn, it is a sexual union. Thus because of human mortality marriage is said not to be perpetual. But it is by nature indissoluble.

As for the causes of this indissolubility, Bonaventure names three kinds. The first is the authority of God revealed in the words of Christ, "What God has joined man must not separate." And those thus joined are joined inseparably because what he has joined God does not separate.

This divine authority is revealed in another passage: "They are no longer two but one flesh." And here there is not only a divine command but a divine revelation about marriage's nature. In it two persons become one. But this oneness defies separation because separation is possible only where there are plural separables making up a union. Bonaventure says this cause of marriage's inseparability is the *effective* cause whose agency *makes* it indissoluble.[33]

The second kind of cause of marriage's indissolubility is found in its nature expressed in its definition. The definition that Bonaventure quotes here is that of Ulpianus recorded in Justinian's *Instituta:* "... *viri et mulieris coniunctio, individuam consuetudinem vitae continens*" (the union of a man and woman containing an undivided sharing of life). Along with many of his medieval contemporaries Bonaventure replaces the final word, *continens,* with *retinens*—apparently to get the notion of permanence that he wants into the definition.

Of the third and last cause Bonaventure says that marriage's indissolubility comes from it *dispositive.* This cause is marriage's function as a sign, an image on earth of the union of Christ and the Church. But this union is an inseparable union; therefore it disposes marriage too to be inseparable. Like Thomas Bonaventure does not reserve this imaging function to the marriage of Christian spouses but seems to predicate it of any and all marriages, which he says do this imaging in that by nature they are fitted to do so, *secundum conformitatem naturae.* Consistently with his calling God's decree that marriage be indissoluble its *effective* cause, he does not bother to explain the dynamics of the kind of ontological causation coming from marriage's imaging the inseparable union of Christ and the Church. That is, he does not here explain how it is that the inseparable *signatum,* the indestructible union of Christ and the Church, brings it about that the *signum,* the marriage on earth, not only *ought not* be dissolved but *is in fact* invulnerable to dissolution. And the student must also wait until later in Bonaventure's commentary for his explanation of what it is in the consummation of the marriage of two Christians that makes this marriage image the inseparable union of Christ and the Church. We shall find him saying there, in Distinction 35, that it is a different indestructible union that the consummated Christian marriage principally images. This is the union of the human and the divine natures in Christ.

What of the other kind of marriage that Bonaventure has noted, the marriage of souls? Is it too indissoluble? When he says that it is, but in its own way that is a lesser way, we are reminded again that in all this discussion the medieval mind understands this adjective in a qualified sense. The modern mind would say that marriage is either indissoluble without qualification or is dissoluble. But Bonaventure and his contemporaries are not really discussing the nature of marriage itself. They are discussing the efficacy of the causes of dissolution whose causation in dissolving a marriage is part of the religious-canonical heritage with which they must deal in dealing with marriage at all.

The way in which he formulates his Response to the question, "whether the marriage of souls is indissoluble," is revealing.[34] He says that indissolubility accompanies *(consequitur)* this kind of marriage too. It is because of this that such a marriage is ratified *(ratum)*—because it has indissolubility, albeit an indissolubility proportioned to itself. For just as the bond of a consummated marriage is indissoluble as long as the persons bonded live in corporeal life, and it is not dissolved except by corporeal death, so too a marriage that is a union of minds and souls cannot be dissolved except by a spouse's dying spiritually to this world. This is done when a spouse dies "to the work of the flesh" *(operi carnis)* by entering a religious order and pronouncing there the vow of chastity.

When, in Distinction 31, Bonaventure discusses the three traditional goods of marriage, he says, in the Conclusion of Article 1, Question 1, that the *sacramentum,* the inseparability of marriage, belongs to the genus of good that is the delectable or pleasurable good,[35] because so strong is the union of husband and wife that a man will leave even his father and mother in order to form this union, and will become one body with his wife. Clearly Bonaventure sees the *bonum sacramenti* to be in marriage generally, not only in the marriages of Christians. And he reinforces this by saying, in the Conclusion to Question 2 of this Article 1, that the *bonum sacramenti* is in a marriage by reason of its divine institution. But then he mixes the natural and the supernatural, the secular and the religious in marriage, by adding that this *bonum* is the work of grace, for it signifies the union of Christ and the Church. What is more, all three of the traditional *bona,* when taken together, signify this union fully. For the *bonum fidei* images the union of the one Christ with his one Church. The *bonum prolis* images that this union generates its own sons and daughters. And the *bonum sacramenti* images the indestructibility of Christ's union with the Church.

He adds that of these goods the *bonum sacramenti* is the principal good and the only good inseparable from marriage. For obviously this or that marriage could lack children or could fail in fidelity. This indissolubility is consubstantial to marriage; a marriage cannot exist without it. (In the Conclusion to Question 3 of this Article 2 he says that *bonum sacramenti* is *de necessitate* in marriage.[36] For this good, this indissolubility, comes from the spouses' binding themselves to one another, from the divine creation and design of marriage, and from the marriage's imaging the union of Christ and the Church.)

But he does not explain why the *bonum sacramenti* is not separable from marriage as the other two goods are. For if one judges the nature of marriage and its good on experiential evidence, as he does the *bonum prolis* and the *bonum fidei,* and this evidence shows that some marriages lack children and some fail in fidelity, evidence shows also that some spouses separate from one another permanently. He seems rather to find the *necessitas* in marriage of the *bonum sacramenti* simply in God's will, in his incontrovertible design for marriage. And further unclarity is brought into this examination by his saying all this, again, not about the marriages of Christian spouses but about marriage generally.

Bonaventure and Dissolution by Dismissal for Adultery

Before taking up the question (in his Distinction 35) asking whether one spouse may dismiss the other because of adultery, he glances briefly (in Distinction 33, Article 3) at the practice in Mosaic law of husbands' dismissing their wives.[37] His judgment on this is that it was conceded to the Jewish husbands as the lesser of two evils, lest they rid themselves of their wives by murder. Consequently, although they were not without fault in this practice, they were not punishable because they were availing themselves of what their law permitted.

Bonaventure offers his definitive judgment on the radical indissolubility of marriage when he examines the question that the Matthean exceptive clause had bequeathed to Christian tradition, to the perplexity and the indecision of generations of councils, canonists and theologians. In Distinction 35, in Question 1 of its single article, he asks in a general way if there can be divorce because of adultery (*An causa fornicationis possit esse divortium*).[38]

His immediate answer to this question is almost an "Of course." Taking the exceptive clause as coming authentically from Christ, he gives as the simple reason for his opinion that Christ allowed such divorce. He explains immediately why Christ allowed it—but without volunteering the evidence for this explanation of Christ's motives. The reason for Christ's permission is that no one is bound to keep a reciprocally made promise to the partner in promise who has already broken it. He adds that the justice of marital law demands this permission because by the adultery the adulterer withdraws the right to his or her sexual acts earlier given over to the spouse. Finally, because the adulterer sins directly against the marital act, this sin is to be punished in the marital act.

From these reasons, he continues, it is evident that not just any *fornicatio* merits the permission for divorce. It must be culpable and it must be unilateral. So if both spouses have committed adultery, neither may dismiss the other. The same is true if the husband prostitutes his wife or in any other way forces her into adultery, or if one spouse commits adultery with the other's approval. In these cases both are participants, so that no injustice is done to either.[39]

Moving thence to the crucial issue of remarriage after dismissal for adultery, Bonaventure asks, in Distinction 35, Article 1, Question 4, whether once the divorce (for adultery) is completed, the husband can take another wife (*An divortio celebrato, possit vir aliam uxorem ducere*).[40] He also asks immediately in the sub-title, ". . . or can the wife take another husband?"

Again his reply is a series of distinctions. And in them we find what the word *divortium* means to Bonaventure as an act permitted an innocent spouse who has suffered the injustice of the other's adultery. First, where the parties were *illegitimae ad contrahendum* (impeded by law from marrying to begin with), both can remarry after the *divortium*. But where there is true adultery (which presupposes a valid marriage) neither an innocent husband nor wife can take another spouse after dismissing the adulterer. Why not? Because binding the spouses is the *vinculum sacramenti,* the bond of the sacrament. And this is an indissoluble bond. Here appears Bonaventure's understanding of the *divortium* permitted now in this circumstance. It is not the sundering of the sacramental bond, but is only a separation, a relaxation of the obligation to the marital act and to cohabitation.

In his reply to Objection 1 under this Question he makes an important distinction concerning the sacrament as the cause of indissolubility at which I hinted earlier. He does so in replying to the objection that since a marriage is a sacrament insofar as it is an earthly image of God and his people, and in Hosea 2:2 God is quoted as saying about his people, "She is not my wife, and I am not her husband," it follows that the union of God and his people can be sundered. It must then follow too that since this invisible reality can be sundered, the visible reality which images it on earth—the sacramental marriage of husband and wife—can be sundered.

Bonaventure replies that the union of God and his people is not what is principally imaged in the sacrament of marriage. What is principally imaged in it is the union of the divine and human natures in Christ. And since this union can never be sundered, the image of it in the sacrament of marriage can never be sundered.

Since he gives this as the reason for the impossibility of dissolving marriage generally, and makes no mention of restricting this cause of indissolubility to the marriages of Christians, it seems that he implies that any and all marriages are sacraments because images of the union of the two natures in Christ and of the union of God and his people. But later, in Distinction 39, Article 1, Question 2, he clears up the point in his answer to the question, "Whether between non-Christian spouses there is the sacrament of marriage" (*An sacramentum matrimonii sit inter infidelem et infidelem*).[41] His answer is that there is not. For whereas the marriages of baptized spouses image the two unions we have named just above, in the marriages of non-Christian spouses there is only an aptitude for this imaging. Thus the conclusion that must follow from this: the marriages of non-Christian spouses are indissoluble but not perfectly so.

He gets at this in Question 4 of the same Article.[42] There he asks whether a man who contracts one marriage before his baptism and a second after it is a bigamist (*An bigamus sit, qui ante et post baptismum contrahit matrimonium*). In reply he acknowledges the disagreement on this point between Jerome and Augustine seven centuries earlier. Jerome said that the baptism of one spouse dissolves a marriage contracted earlier when both were unbaptized, because baptism voids the old and makes all things new. But Augustine insisted that marriage even among the unbaptized is instituted by God, is therefore good, and is not voided by baptism.

But then in Article 2, Question 1 of this Distinction 39[43] Bonaventure asks whether, if one of two unbaptized spouses accepts the (Christian) faith, the marriage is dissolved for the new Christian (*An altero infidelium veniente ad fidem, solvatur matrimonium quoad fidelem*). And once again his reply involves a series of distinctions.

A dissolution may consist of a sundering of the bond (*vinculum*) or it may consist of the ending of cohabitation and mutual service. The second of these dissolutions the newly Christian spouse can effect.

But a dissolution that is a sundering of the bond? The spouse remaining unbaptized may wish to continue cohabitation or not. If he or she wishes this, it may be with blasphemy of the name of Christ or without it. If without it in the cohabitation, he or she may yet seek to draw the newly Christian spouse back to religious infidelity.

If the non-Christian spouse wishes to cohabit without blaspheming the name of Christ and without seeking to lead the Christian spouse back to infidelity, the marriage is not to be dissolved.

But if the non-Christian spouse wishes to depart, or though wishing to continue cohabitation does so with blasphemy of the name of Christ or while seeking to lead the Christian back to religious infidelity, in any of these three cases the Christian can dismiss him or her. And because of the contumely directed at God and at the marriage, the bond can be dissolved and the Christian spouse can afterward marry another.

Bonaventure then explains the three causes that in this case effect the dissolution and free the Christian spouse to marry.

The first is the *imbecillitas* of such a marriage, its frailty. It is incomplete, not *ratum*. This *makes possible* its dissolution.

The second cause is the *disparitas cultus,* the disagreement and even contradiction regarding the Christian faith. For when one spouse becomes Christian a stronger bond enters and begins to command his or her life. This adds to the possibility of dissolution a *disposition* for it.

Finally there is the *injuria,* the contumely, done to God and the marriage. For if the non-Christian despises God and the marriage, this contradicts the Christian's bond with God. Thus with the possibility and the disposition for the dissolution already established by the first two causes, this third cause finally dissolves the bond of marriage itself. Of the three causes Bonaventure says that it is the concurrence of them that effects the dissolution. And even if the marriage in question has been consummated, since because of the lack of Christian faith in one of the spouses the marriage is an incomplete image, it is vulnerable. That is, without Bonaventure's saying exactly this, it is a marriage's imaging the unions of the two natures of Christ and of God and his people imperfectly that keeps it short of radical indissolubility—as the perfect imaging of them brings the radical indissolubility. And he seems satisfied that the baptism of both spouses, and the perdurance in their souls of the baptismal character, are sufficient to produce the complete and perfect imaging.

He confirms this obliquely in Question 3 of this Article 2[44] where he replies to the question asking if a marriage is dissolved where one of two Christian spouses abandons the faith. His answer adds a significant term to the question. He says that no, ". . . if one of the spouses lapses into infidelity the *sacramentum* of marriage is not dissolved." We see immediately why he adds the noun *sacramentum* as he gives the three reasons for his reply. The first and least reason is that if a lapse into infidelity brought dissolution, the way would be open to the evils of pretense and deception.

The second reason is a demand of the truth of the case—*est secundum veritatem.* The *sacramentum* of marriage between two Christians is indissoluble because it images an indissoluble union and images it perfectly *(perfectam habet significationem).* Third—and again *secundum veritatem*—because the *sacramentum* of marriage is rooted *(fundatur)* in the *sacramentum* of baptism, which imprints an indelible character in the soul, the *sacramentum* of marriage is indissoluble.

This is to date the most developed and theologically sophisticated accounting among Christian scholars for the claim of radical indissolubility in marriage—for the impossibility of any human agent's dissolving it. A marriage has this indissolubility where both spouses are baptized Christians, and only with them. And with them it is radically indissoluble for two reasons: because their being baptized Christians makes the *sacramentum* of their marriage a perfect image of an indissoluble union (Bonaventure takes for granted that such an image of such a union cannot be other than indissoluble), and because the marital *sacramentum,* being rooted in the indelible baptismal character of the two spouses, must because of this indelibility be indissoluble. He neglects to add the last refining point that many of his contemporaries and the later Catholic magisterial teaching add, that the imaging of the imperishable unions is complete only when the marital *sacramentum* of two Christians is completed by consummation, by complete sexual intercourse.

John Duns Scotus

A generation after Thomas and Bonaventure the Franciscan philosopher-theologian John Duns Scotus (a Scotsman as his sobriquet tells) wrote two treatises on marriage in the same format they had used, in a commentary on Book 4, Distinctions 26 through 37 of Peter Lombard's *Libri Sententiarum.* (Scotus lectured and wrote on Lombard's work twice during his years of teaching. He did so first at Oxford in 1297–1301. The commentary coming from this period is his *Opus Oxoniense.* He taught as a *sententiarius* again at the University of Paris in 1302–1304, where he used and revised his lectures from Oxford. His commentary on Lombard from the Paris tenure is titled *Reportatio Parisiensis.* He was only twenty-one years of age when he began teaching at Oxford.)

To get first at his commentary on Book 4 of the *Libri Sententiarum* in the *Opus Oxoniense,* we find Scotus rooting marriage's indissolubility in ground that Thomas and Bonaventure had barely touched. This is the contractual nature itself of marriage.

Scotus did indeed define marriage explicitly and formally (and it is curious that of the definitions of marriage set forth by the great medieval theologians it is his that is most nearly repeated in the Catholic Code of Canon Law of 1917).

What he said most explicitly and formally (in his commentary on Distinction 26, Question 1, Article 8),[45] is that marriage is a contract. He even played on the Latin noun in the definition to make clear what he meant: *matrimonium dicitur contractus, quasi simul contractus duarum voluntatum*—"Marriage is called a contract in the manner of a drawing together—the con-tracting—of two wills."

He stated this contractual nature of marriage more clearly yet in his commentary on Distinction 30, Question 2. There he set forth a formal, two-part definition—or more accurately two consecutive definitions.[46]

> Marriage is an indissoluble bond between a man and wife arising from the mutual exchange of authority over one another's bodies for the procreation and proper nurture of children.
>
> The contract of marriage is the mutual exchange by a man and wife of their bodies for perpetual use in the procreation and proper nurture of children.

Note first that in these definitions he does what Bonaventure did in his: he makes an implicit distinction between the marriage as *conjugium,* as the lived relationship, and marriage as the *vinculum,* the juridical bond. This distinction will serve later generations of canonists well because if, with Bonaventure and Scotus, they lodge marriage's indissolubility in the bond, they can insist that this remains invulnerable to whatever erodes or even destroys the *conjugium.* And with the indissoluble heart of marriage now identified by Scotus as the bond, marriage is well on its way to being understood in Catholic law as a juridical entity before all else.

In the first of these definitions Scotus names the cause that most proximately creates the marital bond. It is the parties' mutual consent, a consent in which each gives to the other authority over his or her own body. The thought repeats that of Paul in 1 Corinthians 7:4—"A wife has no authority over her own body, rather her husband has it; just as a husband has no authority over his own body, but his wife has it." Therefore the consent that creates the marriage is a contractual consent, and marriage itself a consensual contract. It is not clear that Scotus also intends that the indissolubility of marriage has as its proximate cause the same reciprocal contractual consent. That the indissolubility has this consent as its cause is indeed hinted in the second of the definitions. But the first of them hints equally that the indissolubility is simply a given and fixed element of the kind of bond that a marriage is, that it is simply marriage's nature to be indissoluble.

That Scotus' mind settled into the latter interpretation is evident in a later examination of the subject in his *Reportatio Parisiensis*. There he says that if one understands marriage as the marital bond, indissolubility belongs to it *ex se formaliter*—formally, essentially, of its very nature. The contract-bond is indissoluble from the instant the parties create it by making their reciprocal consent. The indissolubility does not come from the marriage's consummation by sexual intercourse. "One can no more conceive of a marriage that is not indissoluble than one can conceive of a being that has no nature, no form of being."[47]

There could be no clearer example of a thinker's verifying the indissolubility of marriage by simply putting it into the definition of marriage. Because of this one would expect Scotus to deny the very possibility of dissolving a marriage—of dissolving any marriage from the moment it is created by the parties' consent. Accordingly one would also expect him to challenge the discipline (and the implicit doctrine), built up since Alexander III and earlier, that a marriage is indissoluble only after it is consummated and because of its consummation.

But Scotus makes neither the denial nor the challenge. His reasoning in explanation of why he makes neither tempts the student to find him proposing a divine voluntarism, and proposing as well a kind of nominalism, about the nature of marriage. My grounds for this two-ply suspicion are found in Scotus' treatment of two pertinent questions in the *Supplementum* to his *Summa Theologica*.[48] In Question 67, Article 1, he asks whether "the inseparability of a wife" derives from the law of nature— *Utrum inseparabilitas uxoris sit de lege naturae.*[49] In Article 2 of the same Question 67 he asks whether it could have been licit that a wife be dismissed by dispensation—*Utrum potuerit esse licitum per dispensationem uxorem dimittere.*[50] (The formulation here contains an ambiguity. One could read it to ask whether it could have been licit by dispensation to dismiss a wife. But I am satisfied from what follows in the text that the author(s) intended the first rendering that I have given.)

Note that three significant elements have joined Scotus' examination since he first took it up in the *Opus Oxoniense.* He now asks not about the indissolubility of the marital bond, but whether a wife can and may be dismissed. This different formulation of the conventional question is appropriate to the work in which it appears, a *summa theologica,* a summary of theological analysis. Such an analysis properly takes its questions from theology's primary source, which is the Scriptures. Scotus has obviously drawn this question from the practice, recorded in the Scriptures, of Hebrew husbands' dismissing their wives.

The second new element is the law of nature. It appears where Scotus identifies this law's demand, that wives not be dismissed, with marriage's natural indissolubility. And here we will find the singular understanding of "nature" and of "natural indissolubility" that suggests the nominalism and the divine voluntarism I mentioned above.

The third new element is the authority of the Church to dispense, in this case to dispense from the law of nature's demands on marriage. That Scotus does not here mean (or mean only) the divine power to dispense men and women of the Old Testament from this law's demands, but also the Church's possession of divine power to dissolve marriages by dispensation, will also soon become evident. Equally evident will be the perplexing question about Scotus' understanding of marriage's essential indissolubility when we find him acknowledging that divine authority exercised in the Church can indeed dispense from the law of nature's demand that a wife not be dismissed.

In his Response, in Article 1, to the first of the questions above he says what he had said in the *Opus Oxoniense,* Book 4, Distinction 26. He makes a crucial distinction, one whose first facet is the following:

> . . . the inseparability of the wife—that is, that marriage is an indissoluble bond of husband and wife—does not belong to the law of nature where this law is a principle of conduct whose truth is known by an analysis of its terms, nor is it a principle clearly deduced from these terms . . .[51]

Then the other facet follows:

> . . . But it is quite true that it [this inseparability, this indissolubility] is concordant with the law of nature.[52]

Then from a surprising source comes supporting evidence for this distinction and for the truth of both its facets. This evidence is the statement of Christ containing the positive command from God. This command it is that makes marriage to have what indissolubility it has by nature.

> That marriage is indissoluble comes from Christ's statement coming in turn from the command of God, in Matthew 19, where the Savior, after abrogating the dismissal that the Law of Moses permitted, brought marriage back to what it had been at its institution, saying "But what God has joined man must not separate."

At this point Scotus makes the distinction between the primary and secondary precepts of the law of nature that Thomas and Bonaventure had made (and at the same time suggests that Christ's own awareness of this distinction helped evoke from him this command).

> For that which belongs to the law of nature as a principle self-evident to all need not be commanded and imposed through positive law. And if it is commanded, it admits of no dispensation. . . . Therefore the inseparability of the wife does not derive strictly [*proprie*] from the law of nature, in the sense of something evident to all by the natural light of reason. Nevertheless it is clearly concordant with this law, as I have said . . .[53]

Here Scotus crosses the border dividing philosophy and scriptural exegesis in order to summon and apply his evidence. That is, he says we know from two points of evidence that marital indissolubility does not belong to the law of nature as one of its self-evident principles. First, such principles need not be commanded by positive law—whereas in fact God has commanded indissolubility. Second, such principles cannot be dispensed from, even by divine authority—whereas in the law of Moses God did dispense from marriage's natural indissolubility.

Having satisfied himself that indissolubility is not in marriage as either a self-evidently true principle or as a conclusion drawn self-evidently from such a principle, and having said instead that indissolubility is only clearly concordant with natural law thus understood, Scotus then seeks to account for how indissolubility is related to marriage itself. This is a procedurally necessary accounting, since, as we have seen in the *Opus Oxoniense,* he said that indissolubility belongs to the nature of marriage; that one can no more conceive of marriage without indissolubility than one can conceive of a being without its formal nature. In reading this accounting we find him also naming the causes that put indissolubility into a given marriage. He insists again on the point: indissolubility belongs to marriage formally and of its nature—*Itaque haec indissolubilitas convenit matrimonio ex se formaliter.*

Therefore this indissolubility belongs to marriage formally and of its nature, and by the nature of the marital contract that marriage is. It arises from the reciprocal expression of the wills of the contracting parties, but comes effectively [*effective*] from the [divine] Legislator's institution, from him who designed this indissolubility into this contract . . .[54]

Scotus completes this response by enlisting the law of nature's demand for indissolubility according to a second understanding of this law—the understanding that Thomas Aquinas had used.

> . . . although as far as it itself is concerned the contract could be an exchange consisting of only a single act or be meant to hold for only a limited time. However, from the divine author the indissolubility has gained this, that once the marriage is consummated, it becomes permanent and perpetual and admits of no exception because this is highly concordant with the law of nature because of the good of the offspring and of the family, and of civil society.[55]

The reasoning here contains surprises. For Scotus clearly says that although indissolubility belongs to marriage's very nature, it belongs to it in such a way that (1) it is only concordant with the marital contract; in such a way that (2) a marriage could be contracted for only a limited time; and in such a way that (3) indissolubility found in marriage as really permanent and perpetual is found only in consummated marriages, because then indissolubility becomes concordant with the law of nature in that only then do the goods of children, family and society need it. And even in this last case such permanent and perpetual indissolubility is found only because God wills it to be there. In even shorter formulation, indissolubility is in marriage of the latter's nature; it is God who puts it there; and he can put there either indissoluble indissolubility or dissoluble indissolubility.[56]

Having come to these conclusions about marriage as to usable principles for resolving other questions, Scotus moves easily to answer the question he poses in Article 2 of this Question 67: "Whether it could have been licit for the husband to dismiss his wife by dispensation" (*Utrum potuerit esse licitum per dispensationem uxorem dimittere*). The reply here is taken over from the earlier *Opus Oxoniense,* Book 4, Distinction 26, numbers 1–4.

> It could have been licit that the husband dismiss his wife by means of the [divine] Legislator's dispensation—from him who has determined precisely that the marital contract brings upon the contracting parties the perpetual obligation that neither leave

the other. For those [obligations] which do not derive from the law of nature taken in its primary and strictest sense because they are not principles of conduct known self-evidently, and where those obligations are not conclusions drawn self-evidently from such principles, but are said to belong to the law of nature only insofar as they are concordant with its self-evident principles or are conclusions from them—those obligations admit of exceptions made by the legislator who established them.

But that marriage brings upon the contracting parties the obligation of perpetuity is of the law of nature understood in that secondary sense, insofar as this perpetuity is concordant with the law of nature taken strictly. . . .

Therefore that which is now illicit—namely to dismiss one's wife—could be licit by the intervention of the authority of the legislator dispensing from marriage's indissolubility.[57]

That his minor premise here is true—namely that marriage's bringing upon the contracting parties the obligation of perpetuity belongs to the law of nature only in its secondary sense—Scotus verifies by citing from the Old Testament those instances in which God did in fact dispense from obligations deriving from the law of nature taken only in its secondary sense. Such examples include God's commanding Abraham to kill his son Isaac, his commanding the Israelites to steal from their Egyptian masters as they departed on their exodus from Egypt, and his commanding the prophet Hosea to have children of the prostitute Gomer.

In his reply to Objection 3 under this article Scotus brings to light another facet of his theory of the law of nature.[58] The objection has it that the obligation to not dismiss a wife derives from the Second Table of the Decalogue (from those commands, beginning with the command to honor one's father and mother, that rule conduct involving other human beings). But those acts forbidden by divine command are forbidden because they are in themselves evil. They are not evil because they are forbidden by the divine command. Therefore, the objection concludes, since dismissing a wife is forbidden by God because it is evil, not even he can dispense a man to dismiss his wife licitly.

Scotus' reply to this is to insist that conduct ruled by the law of nature in its secondary sense is either good where and because God wills the conduct to be executed, or evil where and because he wills it to be withheld. Hence the same conduct which is prohibited at one time as evil could be good if allowed by God by dispensation at another time. What is more, if the commands of the Second Table of the Decalogue had their rectitude necessarily and prior to the divine will, the divine will would have to be conformed to them in order to have its own rectitude, and God's knowledge concerning human conduct would be determined from outside himself by conduct subject to human will—all of which is false. In short, any time he thought it prudently advisable, God could dispense a man to dismiss his wife with normal goodness, although ordinarily it is evil for the man to do so.

Scotus and the Remarriage of the Dismissed

But may wives dismissed by their husbands subsequently remarry? Or, to reask this question within the historical context that Scotus chooses in article 4 of this Question 67, was it permitted that the Israelite wives who were dismissed according to the law of Moses might remarry? (*Utrum liceat uxori repudiatae alium virum habere*).[59] We shall see that one of his two answers to this question is applicable to wives in any society living under any law.

For Scotus divides his answer, making its alternatives depend on differing causes warranting the dismissal of the wife. If the wife's dismissal was or is warranted by God's dispensation from the obligation of indissolubility, there was and is no mortal sin in the act of dismissing. Consequently this woman is free to contract a second marriage and can do so without sin, just as she was free to contract the first marriage and could do so without sin.

But if the law of Moses permitted Israelite husbands to dismiss their wives only in order to avoid a greater evil than the dismissal—specifically the greater evil of the husbands' ridding themselves of their wives by murdering them (the accuracy of Jerome's ascribing this conduct to Israel's husbands is here taken for granted)—then the dismissed wife could not remarry. She could not because no woman can have two husbands, for this would be harmful to marriage's primary goal, the procreation and nurture of children. The wife dismissed only in order to avoid the greater evil of her murder is still married to the husband who dismissed her.

As for Christ's words in Matthew's Gospel, chapters 5 and 19, affirming that a man who seeks to marry a dismissed wife commits adultery in doing so, Scotus says that these words belong to the epoch of the law of the Gospel. Christ revoked the dispensation to dismiss and he forbade polygamy in order to bring the marital contract back to the nature it had had when first instituted (*reductus est matrimonialis contractus ad naturam primaevae suae institutionis*).[60]

This claim does not help for clarity in understanding the nature of marriage and the place of indissolubility in it. The claim can be construed ambiguously. Scotus may mean by Christ's bringing the marital contract back to its original nature by revoking the dispensation to dismiss and to take plural wives, only that Christ put an end to the practices themselves of dismissal and polygamy without his altering the fact that both could be reinstated by his renewed dispensation. If this is what Scotus means here, he does not state his mind well by saying Christ returned the marital contract to the *nature* it had had in the beginning. For Christ's revocation in this case would change nothing of marriage's nature, but only a temporary and particular conduct regarding marriage. But if Scotus means that Christ restored marriage to its primeval nature by removing the very possibility of dispensing spouses to dismiss one another and remarry, then he implies that this possibility was not there when marriage was instituted. And one is left wondering indeed what he means by the "nature" of marriage. Whatever he means, he appears to have seen this nature as most pliable to the will of God to make of it what he will in the course of human events.

NOTES

1. *Op. cit.,* p. 322
2. This is in PL, Vol. 176, Cols. 479–520. The best available translation of it in English is *Hugh of St. Victor: On the Sacraments of the Christian Faith,* by Roy J. Deferrari, Cambridge, Mass., 1951. Book 2, Part 11 is in pp. 324–369.
3. This brief treatise is in PL, Vol. 176, Cols. 857–880; the definition is in Col. 859.
4. Deferrari, *op. cit.,* p. 325.
5. This significant term appears early in Chapter 1 of Part 11 of the *De Sacramento Conjugii* (PL, Vol. 176, Col. 481).
6. Deferrari, *loc. cit.,* p. 325.
7. *Loc. cit.,* p. 326.
8. In Chapter 7 of *De Sacramento Conjugii* (PL, Vol. 176, Col. 494).
9. *Ibid.,* Cols. 494–496.
10. *Ibid.,* Cols. 494–495.
11. "Sacramentum autem conjugii habent, qui pari consensu ad eam quae a Deo inter masculum et feminam instituta est societatem indivise ad invicem conservandam convenerunt" (*ibid.,* Col. 496).
12. In Cols. 497–499.
13. "Haec autem dicta sunt contra illos qui putant conjugium omnino dici non posse quod aliquando dissolvi potest" (*ibid.,* Col. 499).
14. "Sed mihi interim non apparet qua ratione possit probari quod ad virtutem sacramenti conjugalis pertinent, ut individua ab utrisque societas, quamdiu uterque vivit conservetur; propterea conjugium non fuisse quod aliquando dissolvi potuit" (*ibid.,* Col. 498).
15. *Ibid.*
16. *Ibid.*
17. "Ad hunc modum putamus quaedam conjugia vere dici posse, quamdiu secundum judicium Ecclesiae rata habentur, quae tamen postmodum emergentibus causis legitimis recte solvuntur, et si postea, contra Ecclesiae probationem pertinaci praesumptone tenentur, illicitae et illegitimae copulationes judicantur" (*ibid.,* Cols. 498–499).
18. In *Pastoral Constitution on the Church in the Modern World* (*Gaudium et spes*), Art. 48.
19. There is an examination of the issue in the *Supplementum* of the *Summa Theologiae,* Question 68 (*De Libello Repudii*—"On the Writ of Dismissal"). But this and the entire treatment of marriage in the *Supplementum* (Questions 41–68) is no more than a rearrangement, according to the method of the *Summa,* of

Thomas' examination in his commentary on Book 4 of Lombard's *Libri Sententiarum* and completed by Reynaldo of Piperno after Thomas' death.

For my examination of the treatment in the *Summa Contra Gentiles* I use the *Editio Leonina Manualis,* Rome, 1934. Book 3, Chapter 122 is in pp. 373–375; Chapter 123 is in pp. 375–376.

20. Here I use the Parma edition of 1858 (reprinted in 1948), *Sancti Thomae Aquinatis Opera Omnia,* Tomus VII: *Commentum in Quatuor Libros Sententiarum Magistri Petri Lombardi,* Volumen Secundum.

21. *Op. cit.,* pp. 955–956.

22. *Op. cit.,* p. 972.

23. *Ibid.*

24. This is the *Solutio* to *Quaestiuncula* (subquestion) 4, p. 973.

25. *Op. cit.,* p. 984.

26. *Op. cit.,* p. 989.

27. *Loc. cit.,* p. 990.

28. *Loc. cit.,* p. 992.

29. *Loc. cit.,* pp. 954–955.

30. *Editio Leonina Manualis.* p. 543.

31. For this examination of Bonaventure's thought I have used the edition, S.R.E. *Cardinalis Bonaventurae Opera Omnia,* Sixti V . . . Iussu Diligentissime Emendata Editio . . . A.C. Peltier, Tomus 6. Parisiis, L. Vives editor, 1866.

32. *Op. cit.,* pp. 233–234.

33. In his reply to the third objection in this Article 3 Bonaventure must surely have taken aim at the Roman tradition of dissolution by mutual consent of the spouses. This objection has it that the cause creating a marriage, the mutual consent of the spouses, is perishable. But where a cause is perishable, so also must its effect be perishable.

Bonaventure's reply to this is drawn from a distinction in the relationship of causes to their effects. One kind of cause both initiates the existence of its effect and preserves this existence. Another kind of cause only initiates the existence of its effect, and this causation can cease while leaving its effect in existence. The parties' consent is this second kind of cause relative to their marriage.

34. This is in his Response to Article 3, Question 2 of Distinction 28, *op. cit.,* pp. 234–235.

35. *Op. cit.,* 273–274.

36. *Op. cit.,* p. 275.

Bonaventure has a sense for fairness in the form of equality of treatment of husband and wife in the matter of dismissal for adultery. In the Exposition of the Text for Distinction 35 he says that a husband who has himself committed adultery secretly is morally reprehensible if he dismisses his wife whose adultery he can prove—unless he has already done penance for his sin. But if his adultery too is known and provable (public and notorious), he cannot dismiss his wife for hers. The reasons he offers justifying an adulterous wife's contesting, in the law, her husband's dismissing her are the same reasons that Aquinas enumerated in his commentary on Book 4 of the *Libri Sententiarum.*

An interesting glance at the cultural mores and attitudes of his age is in his asking and answering the question, "Who sins more seriously in adultery, the husband or the wife?" A reason for saying that the husband sins more seriously lies in this, that the male sex is by nature more stable (*habilior*) and therefore ought to rule the wife. Because of this he sins more seriously when he commits adultery. On the other hand the wife belongs to the traditionally more modest sex. She is not as driven by sexual desire as is the male sex. Therefore her excuse is less and she sins more seriously, and is certainly more seriously condemned in society (pp. 337–338).

37. *Op. cit.,* pp. 315–319.

38. *Op cit.,* pp. 339–341.

39. As to whether dismissal for adultery is a matter of precept, Bonaventure answers in Question 2 of this article with a series of distinctions. If the adultery is secret, dismissal is not permitted because the adultery cannot be proved. If the adultery is commonly known (public), but the guilty party repents and ceases the adulterous conduct, the innocent spouse may dismiss but is not obligated to do so. But if the adulterous spouse continues his or her conduct publicly, the innocent spouse must dismiss because of the scandal and in order to bring the guilty spouse to repentance. Even so the dismissal is to be temporary, and the innocent spouse must meanwhile live a life of sexual continence.

40. *Op. cit.,* pp. 343–344.

41. *Op. cit.,* pp. 396–397.

42. *Op. cit.,* p. 400.

43. *Op. cit.,* pp. 401–403.

44. *Loc. cit.,* p. 404.

45. *Opera Omnia, Quaestiones in Quatuor Libros Sententiarum,* Vives edition, Vol. 19, p. 176.

46. *Op. cit.,* p. 186.

47. Quoted in Dauvillier, *op. cit.,* pp. 322–323.

48. There is serious doubt about the immediate authenticity of this *Supplementum.* Like Thomas Aquinas Scotus died in mid-career (in Cologne in 1308, when he was only forty-two). He left much of his work unfinished, and his pupils set about to finish it from his own notes. So what we read here in these two questions from the *Summa* may be Scotus' only at one remove. But I make this the object of close examination because it appears to represent the finished version of Scotistic thought on marriage's indissolubility. And the editor establishes close, point-for-point concordance of the argumentation in the *Summa* with the same in the *Opus Oxoniense* and the *Reportatio Parisiensis.*

49. In the *Editio Sallustiana,* Romae, 1903, pp. 652–653.

50. *Loc. cit.,* pp. 654–655.

51. Respondeo dicendum, inseparabilitatem uxoris, seu Matrimonium esse vinculum perpetuum et indissolubile maris et foeminae, non esse de lege naturae, quatenus proprie lex naturae est principium practicum ex terminis notum, et conclusio inde evidenter deducta . . . (*op. cit.,* p. 653).

52. . . . bene tamen esse id apprime consonum legi illi (*ibid.*).

53. *Ibid.*

54. Itaque haec indissolubilitas convenit Matrimonio ex se formaliter, et ex natura talis contractus matrimonialis; et oritur ex mutua voluntate contrahentium; sed effective est ab institutione Legislatoris, qui indidit huic contractui indissolubilitatem . . . (*op. cit.,* p. 653)

55. *Ibid.*

56. Evidence surfaces in Scotus' response to the first objection in this article that confirms this interpretation of his way of thinking about the law of nature. There he says that God has commanded by positive law that a man must cling to

his wife perpetually and inseparably. God could have commanded or at least permitted that a man cling to his wife precisely as long as or until she gives him children. *Therefore* God put indissolubility into the marital contract as something more concordant with the law of nature. But the inseparability of wife and husband is not in marriage according to the law of nature in the other sense, that is, as a trait found there necessarily and self-evidently. If I understand him, Scotus says that though indissolubility is in a marriage, it is there not because demanded unqualifiedly by the law of nature but because God puts it there. He in turn puts it there because it is concordant with the law of nature taken in its strict sense—as he could have left it out if he had thought it insufficiently concordant.

57. *Op. cit.,* pp. 654–655.
58. *Ibid.,* p. 655.
59. *Op. cit.,* pp. 660–661.
60. In the reply to Objection 2, *ibid.,* p. 661.

14. SECULAR CHALLENGE, THE PROTESTANT REFORMERS, AND TRENT

By 1350 there was every reason to think that the Roman Catholic doctrine and discipline of divorce and remarriage had come to the end of their long course of development, that they were by then fixed and permanent. But however much they may have then seemed so to the clergy and people of Europe, they were susceptible to challenge at two vulnerable points. And these were challenges that could cross over, and both of them strike first one point of vulnerability then the other.

The first vulnerability was the Catholic authorities' reading of the New Testament divorce passages. Few of these bishops and teachers seemed aware of Jerome's own uncertainty about his reading of the passages, an uncertainty expressed to his friend Eusebius for whom he completed his commentary on the Gospel of Matthew in less than two weeks. The charge that the authorities' interpretation invited, and the charge against it that was later made, was that it was simply inaccurate. The doubt that never stopped festering lay in the interpretation of the Matthean exceptive clause. Could it not be interpreted to say that the dismissing of a spouse for adultery truly dissolves a marriage and frees at least the innocent party to remarry? Or could one not at least say that Jerome's interpretation that in it Christ allowed only the separating of the guilty spouse "from bed and board" is a doubtful interpretation, and that the issue is therefore still open?

Thence came a second challenge to the Catholic reading of the divorce passages, and perhaps a distinct third challenge as well. The interpretation had been a *tour de force,* in modern terms not an exegesis of the passages but an eisegesis—not an interpretation that is a bringing forth of what lies in the texts, but a reading into the texts of what one wants them to say. The Church had had to fashion a divorce discipline in order to reduce the marital chaos in an empire crumbled under barbarian invasions and in order to protect the defenseless in the chaos. Now, having already fashioned the discipline, the authorities had to build a doctrinal foundation under it. They had done so by interpreting the New Testament passages in such a way as to support the discipline. The Protestant version of the challenge was to be one that applied its own doctrinal principle that what Christians are to believe is found only in the Scriptures. The challenge from them was to be that in forming the Catholic teaching on divorce and remarriage mere men had presumed to twist and to fit the word of God to accommodate human convenience.

The second point of vulnerability to challenge was hardly an inch distant from that one. This was the Catholic bishops' exercise of authority in regulating marriages. Until the sixth and seventh centuries secular authorities had regulated the marriages of Christians. The bishops had taken this for granted and had never challenged it. The regulation had gone over to them only by default at the disintegration of the Roman empire and its judicial system. What is more, because marriage in the human race antedates the Church, it is a secular reality belonging within the purview of secular authority. It may have had its origin in the will of God and may be susceptible of religious celebration. But it is pre-ecclesiastical and therefore not properly a creature of ecclesiastical authority.

At this point the first of the challenges could return and reinforce the second. Churchmen already overstepping the limits of their authority even in presuming to regulate the marriages of Christians were using the New Testament divorce passages—dubiously interpreted at that—as a disciplinary instrument. Indeed their misuse of authority, their over-reaching of it, was found in their closing down arbitrarily the discussion of the difficult passages' meaning in order to use them in applying that same authority to the regulating of marriages.

These came in fact to be the principal challenges of the sixteenth-century Protestant reformers. But the points of vulnerability were detected well before that century and were attacked with varying degrees of seriousness by Catholics who never left in schism. By the fourteenth century the secular rulers of Europe were recovering from the defeats dealt their fathers by such powerful Popes as Innocent III, Innocent IV and Gregory IX. Feudal Europe was breaking up. The conglomerate of princedoms and duchies called the Holy Roman Empire was disintegrating, and the powerfully centralized Church was losing its control over the people of Europe. Boniface VIII's attempt to cling to the medieval vision of the Pope as a supreme authority over Christendom and his long and disastrous feuding with Philip IV of France, the secular monarch who contested his effort most violently, ended with papal power over secular life broken for good.

The Church's hold on the lives of Europe's Catholics was weakening at every point. That hold had saved Europe and kept it at least in some degree civilized through six centuries of barbarian invasion. Thanks to great bishops and monks the barbarians had been converted and civilized rather than that they had destroyed a civilization. But now after so many centuries of near-fiefdom to the Church—and in some cases of actual fiefdom to her—the unchurchly side of Europe's Catholics was asserting itself and demanding its freedom.

Most pertinently for us, the secular intelligence of Europe began demanding its right to speak and to be heard on the subject of marriage. Layfolk, the married who had personal experience of marriage, began to speak and to write about it outside the confines of Scholastic philosophy, theology and canon law. What they said about it suggested that they did not experience marriage at all points exactly the way it was assumed to exist or intended to exist by ecclesiastical regulation. (Perhaps the Wife of Bath was speaking for more than herself among Europe's women when, in the prologue to her tale in Chaucer's *Canterbury Tales,* she insisted that the genital anatomy has more purposes than procreation, and that pleasure is one of the more—as she had found out in at least the last two of her five marriages. Or, to put it more accurately, the earthy lady was speaking Chaucer's mind and thereby conveying his perception of what women were thinking and feeling about their sexuality and marriage circa 1385. Chaucer's contribution was to give public expression to these thoughts and feelings. In no way do they confirm what one reads in Gratian, Lombard, Alexander III, Aquinas, Bonaventure or Scotus. The discrepancy is sharp enough. That Chaucer, whose writing shows that he knew something of what these scholars had written, felt free to make the discrepancy public is the point I have in mind.)

Where the Wife of Bath told enthusiastically of marriage, others of Chaucer's age and after wrote satirically and pessimistically about it. There was Francesco Barbaro's *De re uxoria* (On Wifely Matters) of 1415. In 1472 the German Albrecht von Eyb wrote his *Ob einem Mann sey zu nemen ein eheliches Weib* (Whether a Man Ought To Take a Wife). In France one could read *Les Arrêts d'Amour* (The Disappointments of Love).

The earliest recognizable secular effort to regain control over the marriages of European Catholics was put forth at the very height of ecclesiastical control of them. This was made in the twelfth century by those Italian communes that contested the control of the German emperor from the north, of the Pope from the center of Italy, and of the foreigner king of Sicily from the south. Milan and Florence were principal among these communes. Along with their attempts to end clerical privilege and clerical exemption from civil law, they tried to end ecclesiastical control over marriage cases, especially over the setting of impediments and the dispensing from them. This legislation reserved to the civil courts the examining and resolving of marriage cases. The *Statutes of Pistoia,* drawing on Lombard law, were the most obvious effort to take away from the Church courts the ruling on and the dissolving of betrothals, the decreeing of nullity, the ordering of separation, the settling of property after annulment or separation, and the determining of legitimacy and of the liceity of relationships in marriage.

The most vivid attempt to take control of Christian marriage matters away from the Church was made toward the middle of the fourteenth century by the emperor, Ludwig of Bavaria, during the papacy of John XXII. Ludwig wished to marry his son to a wealthy noblewoman, Margrete Maultasch, who was already married to Johann Heinrich of Bohemia. With an eye to gaining her considerable fortune for his family Ludwig claimed that her marriage was unconsummated and therefore dissoluble. He demanded that John XXII dissolve it.

When the latter refused, Ludwig in 1342 declared himself juridically competent in the matter and decreed the dissolution of Margrete's marriage. At John's protest two "publicists"—two defenders of the authority of secular princes—used the occasion to set forth the philosophic justification for Ludwig's claiming and exercising authority as he did. These were William of Occam and, predictably, Marsilius of Padua.

In his *Tractatus de Jurisdictione Imperatoris in Causis Matrimonialibus* (Treatise on the Emperor's Jurisdiction in Marriage Cases) Occam asserted two points of fact. First, the Roman emperors had exercised legislative and judicial authority over the marriages of their subjects, and during the empire the Church had acquiesced to this without complaint. The Holy Roman Empire is the continuation of the Roman empire and continues its authority. (Occam's implied conclusion was obvious: as emperor, Ludwig held this authority coming down to him from Constantine, from Theodosius I and II, and from Justinian.) The second fact Occam asserted was that it is the office of the emperor to protect the public good in his realm. Therefore whenever obedience to ecclesiastical law would injure this good, the emperor can exempt himself from this law and rule according to his wisdom.

Occam's express conclusion drawn from these alleged facts as from principles was that Ludwig had judged Margrete Maultasch's case validly and justly. Since the non-consummation of her marriage was verified, she was by divine law freed from this marriage, and the emperor could authorize her marriage to his son, even over the Church's objection. Underlying this appraisal of the case was Occam's assumption that a Christian emperor is subject only to divine law. Consequently his authority can regulate marriages when the public good demands it. Ecclesiastical authority can no more than apply to marriage the details of the divine law.

Marsilius of Padua concurred in this theory. Ecclesiastical authority can no more than define the dispositions of divine law, can only say what these are. But coercive power in regard to this law belongs to the emperor alone. Only he, since he knows the facts of the case, can decide the dispositions of divine law in particular instances. Luther's interpretation a little less than two centuries later was to differ hardly at all. He was to insist that marriage is *ein weltliches Geschäft*—a secular affair. Therefore it comes properly under the authority not of churchmen, but of Christian princes. He was confident that the princes ruling the marriages of Europe's Christians would themselves always be Christian.[1]

Challenge to the Interpretation of the Divorce Passages

The man of this epoch most qualified to question the conventional interpretation of New Testament passages on marriage and divorce was the humanist, Erasmus of Rotterdam. He took the time to learn the *koiné* Greek in which the passages had originally been composed.[2] And as well as the limited archeological resources of his time allowed, he informed himself about the history of their composition, the setting in which Christ and St. Paul spoke their minds, how their audiences' real-life perplexities revealed and qualified the meaning of their instructions. And especially was Erasmus' interpretation of these passages not done *parti pris;* his interpreting mind was not already made up by the use his authoritative predecessors in the Church had made of these passages.

When commenting on 1 Corinthians 7 in his *Annotationes in Novum Testamentum* (1515) Erasmus devoted twelve quarto pages to his interpretation of this key divorce passage. He said first of all that he hardly intended a definitive judgment, although he felt justified in examining Paul's words anew. He questioned whether the words of Christ that Paul passed on to his readers are really a command binding consciences; he suggested that these words rather no more than counsel an ideal that Christians should strive to realize. He pointed to many practices approved in and by the Church that assumed as such counsel words of Christ recorded in the Gospels as commands. Apparently, Erasmus suggested, Paul understood Christ's words about divorce in this way when allowing "separation"—that is, divorce—to a Christian convert whose pagan spouse refused to live in peace.

> Because of the human weakness that the Church has in so many of her members no one is forbidden to defend his rights under the law; no one is forbidden to take oaths provided he does so seriously and does not perjure himself; no one is forced to be obligated to those who cannot be trusted. So why do we make of everyone and anyone this one demand in regard to divorce? If, because of their hardheartedness, the Jews were permitted to dismiss their wives for any cause lest they turn to more serious faults; and we see among Christian spouses crimes that go far beyond continual feuding—crimes such as murder, poisoning, the laying on of curses—if their ills are the same, why may we not use the same remedy? . . . When Christ recalled his followers to the original innocence of marriage he did not want divorce because he did not want hardness of heart. Yet Paul indulges human weakness by mitigating the command of the Lord in many places. Why could not the Roman pontiff do the same?[3]

Erasmus was especially concerned about the compassion that the Pope and the bishops could exercise in the case of lives ruined by entrapment in a disastrous marriage. Especially during his sojourn in England he personally had seen many men whose lives had been models of virtue until they were caught in a miserable marriage. Since there was no escape for them they had simply gone their own way in defiance of the law.

> I had only pity for the men whom I saw bound in such unbreakable chains. I knew many of them, especially in England where I first drafted this essay. I saw men who had once held to the most orthodox teaching and had lived lives of holiness, whom not even the Gospel or the words of Paul could keep from divorce.[4]

In his *Paraphrasis Novi Testamenti* (1517–1524) Erasmus apparently took a definitive stand on the effect of adultery on a marriage. He was of the opinion that the act of adultery itself dissolves a marriage. When the faculty of theology at the University of Paris, led by Noël Beda, issued a formal condemnation of a series of propositions drawn from the *Paraphrasis* and others of Erasmus' writings, the latter explained that he did not intend to say that with the act of adultery the bond of marriage is severed. He meant only that the guilty spouse has forfeited all claim to the rights of a husband or wife, even all claim to be regarded as such.

He added that while he considered it his prerogative to state the arguments favoring the interpretation that adultery dissolves a marriage, however, since the meaning of the pertinent passages is not unambiguously clear, he was willing to submit to the authority of the Church in the matter. Here is a point at which Luther was to differ. Because the meanings of the divorce texts were to him also not clear, he protested and finally rebelled against the Catholic authorities' coming down on a fixed and definitive interpretation of them.

Erasmus was not the only Catholic of his century to go back to Basil and others of the Fathers for the interpretation that in Matthew's Gospel Christ allowed true divorce because of adultery. In his *Commentarium in Evangelium Sancti Matthaei,* xix: 9, the theologian and churchman Cardinal Cajetan (Tomasso de Vio Cajetano) came to the same opinion as Erasmus before him and Luther at his own time: the meaning of the passages is not entirely clear. But they do admit of a reading that finds in them Christ's allowing a husband to dissolve his marriage by dismissing his wife because of her adultery. Cajetan made the point that this is the first and clear sense of the passage in Matthew 19.

> But if you insist, and object that the words of Jesus mean that a man who dismisses his wife because of her adultery and in marrying another does not commit adultery, I reply that this is how the text reads according to its clear literal sense.[5]

Like Erasmus Cajetan was, because of the inch of doubt about the exact meaning, prepared to defer to ecclesiastical authority, especially in the face of centuries of theological and canonical tradition that had accumulated in support of the authorized interpretation of these divorce passages.

> But because I do not dare oppose such a flood of theologians and ecclesiastical judges, I have said that the text says nothing decisive about the dismissing of an adulterous wife. Therefore my position is this: according to the law of Our Lord Jesus Christ a Christian man is permitted to dismiss his wife because of her adultery and to marry another. But I submit this to the judgment of the Church—which until now has not been definitive.[6]

Ambrosius Catharinus was a second Catholic theologian who shared Erasmus' doubts about the accepted Catholic interpretation, but who also, because his was only a doubt and not a contradictory certain judgment, was willing to defer to the ecclesiastical authorities in the application of the passages to real-life marriages.

In his *Annotationes contra Cajetanum* of 1542 he urged that the Gospel according to Matthew at least does not forbid remarriage where adultery is proved against a wife. He suggested that the unqualified prohibition against remarriage is justified papal legislation needed to prevent the increase of adultery as an escape from unwanted marriages. Because this prohibition is only a product of papal authority, this authority can grant exceptions to its own legislation.

Later, in his *Commentarium in I Corinthios 7* he wrote more hesitantly even while holding to the same view. He confessed that the will of Christ about divorce and remarriage remained still unclear to him. He wished that he could have from the Church a final decision in the matter. But he had a severe judgment about Erasmus' published opinion.

> Finally, this place [the teaching on divorce and remarriage in the New Testament] remains still obscure. Therefore I would so gladly welcome a definitive interpretation from the Church. . . . But I cannot avoid saying how carelessly, indeed how very petulantly Erasmus has written about these passages in his Annotations. Surely because of the scandal they have brought to so many they ought to be consigned to the flames.[7]

The Eastern Catholic Churches

Before going on to examine in detail Luther's challenge and the Roman Catholic response to it in the Council of Trent, it will be revealing to look briefly at the Roman treatment of the centuries-old disagreement with the Eastern Catholic Churches on the possibility and the permissibility of divorce and remarriage.

With the success of the first Crusade, and the capture of Jerusalem from the Muslims in 1099, those of the Western Christian armies that remained in Palestine formed the Latin Kingdom of Jerusalem. A Roman Catholic hierarchy was set up alongside the Orthodox and Monophysite Churches there. And despite the cruelty of the Crusaders toward the Eastern Catholics, the Maronite Church of Syria entered into permanent union with Rome, while for two centuries the other emperors and patriarchs of the East carried on discussion about reunion. The most notable of these discussants was the Byzantine emperor of the second half of the thirteenth century, Michael Paleologos. Consideration of reunion went as far as Pope Clement IV's proposing to him, in 1267, a profession of faith to be required as a condition of reunion. The same profession was proposed by the Second Council of Lyons in its fourth session, on July 6, 1274, during the papacy of Gregory X.[8]

Beyond these efforts a multitude of marriages among Latin Catholics and their Eastern counterparts came into existence. So inevitably the two doctrines and disciplines concerning divorce met, and met in conflict over the questions "How shall disagreement be dealt with in light of the reunion desired by both churches? Shall there be compromise, with each side yielding at points? Shall the Orientals be required to give up their far more permissive teaching and practice? Shall the Roman Church yield from its hardening severity?"

By the middle of the thirteenth century the doctrine and discipline of the Byzantine Church, the most numerous among the Eastern Catholic Churches, was the following.

Where a marriage is indissoluble this comes of its being a sacramental marriage of two Christians. But even this indissolubility yields to divine dispensation as this was expressed by Christ in the exceptive clause recorded in Matthew 5:32 and 19:9. The clause was interpreted independently from Christ's teaching as this is reported in Mark, Luke and 1 Corinthians. In the circumstances envisioned by the Matthean passages the Church was thought to be authorized to separate the spouses, to dissolve their marriage in the name of and by the authority of God. (This interpretation was adapted from early interpretations of Matthew made by some of the Eastern Fathers, most especially by Basil.) *Pornéia* in the exceptive clause was taken to designate adultery; dismissal was taken to designate the dissolution of the marriage.

But the adultery warranting dismissal and dissolution was understood to be not the only cause, but to be only a sample and a point of departure for other and equivalent causes. It was taken as self-evident that other crimes are possible to spouses that injure their marriages with equal or greater severity. Abortion and attempted murder of the spouse were only two of these.

All the Eastern Churches permitted divorce and remarriage. For the discipline of the Byzantine Church Justinian's Novel 117 was the basis; all the causes named there to justify dismissal of a spouse were named in this discipline. Since the tenth century they were included in the Byzantine

Nomocanon under fourteen titles. The great canonist of the fourteenth century, Theodore Balsamon, cited in Title 13, Chapter 5 of this commentary on Byzantine law all the causes for dismissal listed in Novel 117.

One significant difference surfaced in the law of the Byzantine Church. Whereas the Justinian Code of the sixth century permitted divorce without cause, the Church's Council of Constantinople in Trullo of 680–681 had rejected it. Divorce by mutual consent was also rejected by this Council and later by Balsamon. A marriage could be dissolved only by the authoritative action of the Church, and only for just cause.

But the Byzantine law did not restrict itself to the causes for dissolution named in Novel 117. Scholars have counted twenty-six causes introduced into this law from the ninth century through the middle of the fifteenth. One example of these is closely akin to the supervenient affinity accepted in the Roman Church as a cause by Pope Alexander III. Thus if a spouse acted as godparent to his or her own child in baptism, this was held to create an in-law relationship with the other spouse. According to the Council in Trullo named above, this had the effect of dissolving the marriage. To note the obvious, this point of law must have offered spouses a most convenient escape from an unwanted marriage.

According to the same Council a priest's elevation to the episcopate dissolved his marriage. But his wife, now equivalently a widow, could not remarry. One spouse could take up monastic life and its vows even without the consent of the other, and this had the effect of dissolving their marriage "by reason of religious piety." But here at least the other spouse could remarry.

Different Byzantine jurists—Leo the Philosopher, Patriarch Emmanuel II, Patriarch John III Glykos—suggested different causes justifying dissolution. Among them were the insanity of the husband if this lasted three years; abortion procured by the wife; lapse of one of the spouses into religious infidelity or heresy; a wife's fraudulently concealing a physical defect from before the marriage vows; the wife's hatred for her husband brought on by his cruelty or his forcing her into sodomy; irreconcilable discord of spouse from spouse.

The Roman Catholic Reaction

In 1218 Pope Honorius III was asked by his legate to the Byzantine Church, Cardinal John, how to deal with that Church's law and its broad permissiveness about dismissing spouses and remarrying. The Pope's response, of August 18, was that there was to be no compromise, no dispensation from the law of God as the Roman Church understood it, because indissolubility of the marriage bond is God's law equally for believers and unbelievers, for Greeks as well as for Latins.

In light of this decision it is surprising that twenty-seven years later, when the First Council of Lyons attempted to write legislation for the reunion of the two Churches, the Roman bishops paid no attention to this major disagreement about divorce and remarriage. They confined their work mainly to divergencies in ritual and religious custom.[9] But when the Second Council of Lyons convened two summers later (from May 7 to July 17, 1274), the profession of faith proposed to the Byzantine emperor, Michael Paleologos, did address the questions of remarriage in widowhood and of polygamy. In that part of the profession dealing with the sacraments is the following passage.

> It [the Roman Catholic Church] teaches concerning marriage that no man may have plural wives simultaneously, nor a woman plural husbands. But if a legitimate marriage is dissolved by the death of one of the spouses, it teaches that a second or a third or more marriages are licit as long as no canonical impediment blocks them.[10]

Some interpreters say that implicit in this paragraph is the assumption that only death can dissolve a legitimate marriage. Others say that the Council chose to skirt the entire matter of divorce and remarriage as a territory of conflict. But at least the bishops manifested a reluctance to attack directly and deny explicitly the Greek discipline of divorce and remarriage. This reluctance was to be repeated a century later in the Council of Florence, and again a century after that in the Council of Trent.

The Council of Florence

The ecumenical council which bears the name Council of Florence was the Council of Basel transferred first to Ferrara in 1438, thence to Florence in the following year. Its participants were equally Greeks and Latins—among the former the Byzantine emperor John VIII Paleologos, the patriarch of Constantinople Joseph II, twenty metropolitan bishops, and deacons, monks and courtiers. All who came from the East numbered about seven hundred. There were in attendance one hundred and eighteen Latin prelates, with Pope Eugene IV at their head. The purpose of the Council was to bring the Greek and Latin Churches together in unity, an ambition motivated in the Greeks partly by their desire for help in defending themselves against the Turks.

The main issues of discussion and dispute were the Latin addition of the term *filioque* to the Nicene Creed (to indicate that in the trinity of persons in God the Spirit proceeds from the Son as well as from the Father); the Eucharistic bread (whether this is to be leavened or unleavened); the supremacy in Church government of Pope over Council; and the nature of the suffering experienced by the souls in purgatory. A statement of union was signed by the principal representatives of the two Churches while the Council was in session. But the union collapsed soon afterward, partly because of the failure of the Western nations to send to the Greeks sufficient military help against the Turks.

Curiously, and perhaps surprisingly for the student of the history of Christian marriage, the severely differing disciplines for divorce and re-marriage were not seen as a territory on which the disagreement of the two Churches would have to be reconciled if the desired reunion were to be realized. There is no evidence from the Council that either side thought the hoped-for union demanded as one of its conditions a resolution of the disagreement about divorce and remarriage. Whether both sides were quietly willing to allow the other its position, or whether both thought the dispute peripheral to their truly serious concerns—to this question we have no answer. The issue is not so much as hinted at in the *Decretum unionis Graecorum,* the Decree of Union of the Greeks, promulgated by the Council on July 6, 1439.[11]

But the issue got substantial attention in another decree, one that came from the Council later the same year. Just as the Greek representa-tives were leaving Florence on August 2, representatives of the Armenian Orthodox Church arrived. Three months later, on November 22, a decree of union of the Roman Church with the Armenians was signed. Its Part 5 is a quite full statement of the acknowledged Roman Catholic doctrine of the sacraments at that time. Following conciliar tradition the paragraph concerning marriage is the last in this part 5.

> The seventh sacrament is the sacrament of marriage, which is a sign of the union of Christ and the Church, according to the words of the Apostle, "This is a great sacrament; in this I refer to Christ and the Church." The efficient cause of a marriage is ordinarily the mutual consent expressed through the words *de praesenti.*[12] A three-fold good of marriage is acknowledged. The first is offspring to be procreated and nurtured for the worship of God. The second is fidelity, which each spouse owes to the other. The third is the indissolubility of the marriage deriving from the fact that it images the indissoluble union of Christ and the Church. And though because of adultery a separation from sexual union is allowed, it is not allowed that this be followed by a second marriage, since the bond of a legitimately contracted marriage is permanent.[13]

The modern Roman Catholic theology of indissolubility is encapsu-lized almost perfectly here. There is the cause of a marriage's indissolubil-ity drawn from natural law, namely that a marriage rightly contracted is by nature permanent. The decree does not say so, but this affirmation is referable to any marriage and strictly speaking explains nothing about marriage *qua* sacrament. But the "theological reason" is the familiar one: because a marriage that is a sacrament is such in that it images the indissoluble union of Christ and the Church, the marriage also is indissolu-ble. The image replicates ontologically that which it images. One must notice here too the interpretation of Augustine's third among the goods of marriage. Where he had called this good the *sacramentum,* the decree names it as the indissolubility (*indivisibilitas*) of the sacramental marriage. That is, where Augustine had named as the third good the cause whose effect he saw to be indissolubility, the decree names the effect itself.

Finally, the decree consecrates Jerome's interpretation of what Christ permitted in the exceptive clauses of Matthew 5 and 19: the dismissal for adultery supposedly allowed there does not dissolve the marriage, but no more than separates the spouses "from bed and board."

The Challenge from the Protestant Reformers

Like Erasmus and Cajetan, the Augustinian monk and provincial superior Martin Luther had serious doubts about the accepted Catholic interpretation and use of the New Testament divorce passages. But he differed from them in what he did about his doubts. Instead of deferring to authority in the Church because he was uncertain, he determined to challenge this authority in the most radical and thorough way. He went far beyond the accuracy of the authoritative interpretation to challenge, as I hinted in the first paragraphs of this chapter, the right itself of the Popes and bishops to interpret the word of God in the Scriptures. He did this not because he considered the prelates contemporary with him to be ignorant men (which he did) but because he believed almost doctrinally that they were claiming an authority that was not theirs.

The earliest Reformers made their case against the Roman Catholic doctrine and discipline on divorce and remarriage on two interlocked issues. One of these was the authority of ecclesiastics to regulate Christian marriages to begin with—the authority not only of Roman but of any ecclesiastics. Grounding their challenge to this authority was their denial, doctrinal in nature, that marriage among Christians is a sacrament instituted by Christ. Thus their logic: because the marriages of Christians are not sacraments, ecclesiastical authorities have no reason in these marriages for claiming jurisdiction over them. As we have seen and shall see again, Luther claimed that marriage is a secular business, a thing of this world. Therefore it belongs rightly under the jurisdiction of secular rulers.

The second issue, necessarily interlocked with that one concerning jurisdiction, was the accuracy of the Catholic interpretation of the New Testament marriage and divorce passages. If it were to be shown that the authorities were wrong in teaching that the marriages of Christians are sacraments, it must be shown that they read the key New Testament passages inaccurately. Beyond this, if it were to be shown that apart from such marriages' being sacraments, and apart from the ecclesiastics' having jurisdiction over them, the Catholic discipline itself of divorce and remarriage is mistaken, it must be shown to involve a misinterpretation of the New Testament divorce texts. The Reformers were confident that they could show this as well.

As with so many of his quarrels with the Catholic authorities, Luther's indictment of them for their illegitimate regulation of marriage was inspired by his experience of abuses in this regulation. He saw churchmen tangling the marriage plans and the married lives of the faithful by irresponsibly creating impediments in the law and cancelling them, by applying them to couples and then dispensing them with infuriating ease— and much of this for venal motives, since the securing of a dispensation demanded the paying of a fee.

> But what shall we say concerning the wicked laws of men by which this divinely ordained way of life has been ensnared and tossed to and fro? Good God! It is dreadful to contemplate the audacity of the Roman despots, who both dissolve and compel marriages as they please.[14]

What Luther refers to here as the dissolving of marriages was almost certainly the practice of dissolving unconsummated marriages on the many grounds reviewed in earlier chapters of this volume. He continues in this essay and gets at both the legitimacy of ecclesiastical authority and at the motives for arrogating and using it.

> Who gave this power to men? Granted that they were holy men and impelled by godly zeal, why should another's holiness disturb my liberty? Let whoever will be a saint and a zealot, and to his heart's content, only let him not bring harm upon another, and let him not rob me of my liberty. . . . These laws of men seem to have sprung into existence for the whole purpose of serving these greedy and rapacious Nimrods.[15]

To the Catholic regulation of dissolution and dispensation by arrogated ecclesiastical authority he opposes another authority available to any sincere Christian. This is the authority of the Gospel. And Luther is confident, at least in this essay, that the Gospels assert clearly enough that the dissolving of marriages is beyond human authority. (That this confidence wavers at other times we shall see in a moment.)

> I ask and urge all priests and friars when they encounter any impediment to marriage from which the pope can grant dispensation but which is not stated in the Scriptures, by all means to confirm all marriages that may have been contracted in any way contrary to the ecclesiastical or pontifical laws. But let them arm themselves with the divine law which says, "What God has joined together, let no man put asunder" [Matt. 19:6]. For the joining together of a man and a woman is of divine law and is binding, however much it may conflict with the laws of men; the laws of men must give way before it without hesitation. For if a man leaves father and mother and cleaves to his wife [Matt 19:5]

how much more will he tread underfoot the silly and wicked laws of men, in order to cleave to his wife! And if pope, bishop or official should annul any marriage because it was contracted contrary to the laws of men, he is Antichrist, he does violence to nature and is guilty of treason against the Divine Majesty, because this word stands: "What God has joined together, let no man put asunder" [Matt 19:6].

Besides this, no man has the right to frame such laws, and Christ has granted to Christians a liberty which is above all the laws of men, especially where a law of God conflicts with them.[16]

Having rescued the regulation of Christian marriages from the wrongful hands of churchmen, Luther claims two things about it which at first reading may sound contradictory. First he insists that marriage the human institution has its origin in God. It is he who first invented it.

Marriage itself, being a divine institution, is incomparably superior to any laws, so that marriage should not be annulled for the sake of the law; rather the laws should be broken for the sake of marriage.[17]

On the other hand, even though of divine invention, marriage is not a religious institution, not at least in a way that makes it an element of ecclesiastical organization and polity. It is a secular affair, instituted as such by God. And because it is secular it comes properly under the authority of secular rulers.

What is the proper procedure for us nowadays in matters of marriage and divorce? I have said that this should be left to the lawyers and made subject to the secular government. For marriage is rather a secular and outward thing, having to do with wife and children, house and home, and with other matters that belong to the realm of government.[18]

We neither commend nor forbid divorce, but leave it to the government to act here, and we submit to whatever the secular law prescribes in the matter.[19]

Whichever the Christian authority to whom he commended the regulating of marriage and divorce, Luther could not have been unaware that this regulating involves inescapably the interpreting of the pertinent New Testament passages. Yet, having scolded the Roman ecclesiastical authorities for their arrogating and misusing the authority to divorce, without anxiety he turns this authority over to the secular Christian princes, and along with it, in effect, the prerogative of interpreting those passages.

The same advice—that marriage matters should be left to the Christian secular authorities—Luther repeated in his essay, *On Marriage Matters.* Here he repeated, too, his denial to the Pope of any jurisdiction over Christian marriages, but in a way more emphatically and colorfully than in the passages we have just seen.

> Now inasmuch as imperial law has concerned itself with marriages as a temporal affair and codified and interpreted it, my dear pope should rather have left it at that and not interfered in another's office that was not committed to him, for that is the same thing as taking it by force and robbery.[20]

Again he gives a full vote of confidence to the ability of secular rulers and magistrates to administer wisely the teaching of Christ concerning divorce and remarriage—of Christ who was himself not a lawyer and had no intention to regulate marriage juridically.

> ... we should not tamper with what government and wise men decide and prescribe with regard to those questions [divorce and remarriage] on the basis of the laws and of reason. Christ is not functioning here as a lawyer or a governor, to set down or prescribe any regulations for outward conduct; but he is functioning as a preacher, to instruct consciences about using the divorce law properly, rather than wickedly and capriciously contrary to God's commandment.[21]

This insistence that the regulation of Christian marriages belongs rightfully to secular authorities passed beyond Luther's private criticism of established Catholic practice in his time. It became fixed Lutheran teaching, although in a form tempered and qualified from Luther's polemic extreme. This teaching holds that marriage indeed needs regulating by law, and that this regulating may be done by ecclesiastics. But—and this is the capital point—when ecclesiastics regulate marriage they do this as an exercise not of divine but of human right. And secular rulers can exercise this authority with equal right, and must exercise it where ecclesiastics neglect to do so. Thus Article 29 of the Augsburg Confession:

> Whatever other power and jurisdiction bishops may have in various matters (for example, in matrimonial cases and in tithes), they have these by virtue of human rights. However, when bishops are negligent in the performance of such duties, the princes are obliged, whether they like to or not, to administer justice to their subjects for the sake of peace and to prevent discord and great disorder in their lands.[22]

This position is elaborated more fully in the Smalcaldian *Treatise on the Power and Primacy of the Popes*. Intended as a supplement to the Augsburg Confession, this treatise was officially adopted as an element of the Lutheran confession of faith.[23]

> There remains jurisdiction in those cases which according to canon law pertain to ecclesiastical courts (as they call them), especially matrimonial cases. This, too, the bishops have by human right only, and they have not had it for long, for it appears from the *Codex* and *Novellae* of Justinian that decisions in matrimonial cases had formerly belonged to the magistrate. By divine right temporal magistrates are compelled to make these decisions if the bishops are negligent. This is conceded by the canons. Wherefore it is not necessary to obey the bishops on account of this jurisdiction either. And since they have framed certain unjust laws concerning marriage and apply them in their courts, there is additional reason why other courts should be established. For the traditions concerning spiritual relations are unjust, and equally unjust is the tradition which forbids an innocent person to marry after divorce. Unjust, too, is the law that in general approves all clandestine and underhanded betrothals in violation of the right of parents. It is enough to have pointed out that there are many unjust papal laws on matrimonial questions and that on this account the magistrates ought to establish other courts.[24]

The Reformers' Denial of the Sacrament

Luther's personal challenge to the Catholic doctrine of marriage's sacramentality among Christians is found predictably in his assessment of the New Testament source from which this doctrine was drawn at this time. He comments on the passage, Ephesians 5:29–32, in his *Babylonian Captivity of the Church*. He first makes a point on which Pauline scholars have come to agree, namely that where, in Ephesians 5:32, Paul writes, "This is a great sacrament [or mystery]," he refers to the union of Christ and the Church, not to the union of husband and wife that images it on earth.

> Therefore, sacrament or mystery, in Paul is that wisdom of the Spirit, hidden in a mystery, as he says in I Corinthians 2 [7–18], which is Christ. . . . the preachers he calls stewards [I Corinthians 4:1] of these mysteries because they preach Christ, the power and the wisdom of God [I Corinthians 1:24], yet in such a way that, unless you believe, you cannot understand it. There-

fore, a sacrament is a mystery, a secret thing, which is set forth in words, but received by the faith of the heart. Such a sacrament is spoken of in the passages before us: "The two shall become one. This is a great sacrament" [Ephesians 5:31–32], which they understand as spoken of marriage, whereas Paul himself wrote these words as applying to Christ and the Church, and clearly explained them himself by saying, "I take it to mean Christ and the Church. . . ." See how well Paul and these men agree! Paul says he is proclaiming a great sacrament in Christ and the church, but they proclaim it in terms of a man and a woman! If such liberty in the interpretation of the sacred Scriptures is permitted, it is small wonder that one finds here anything he pleases, even a hundred sacraments.[25]

In that last jibe Luther makes a charge to which the bishops at Trent would respond explicitly (although regarding a different New Testament passage), the charge namely that they and the teachers in the Catholic tradition have falsified the meaning of the Scriptures.

Luther goes on to deny expressly that marriage among Christians is a sacrament, offering his principal reason for the denial: The very passage that the Catholics use as evidence calls a sacrament not the marriage of Christian spouses but the union of Christ and the Church.

Christ and the church are, therefore, a mystery, that is, a great and secret thing which can and ought to be represented in terms of marriage as a kind of outward allegory. But marriage ought not for that reason to be called a sacrament. The heavens are a type of the apostles, as Ps. 19 declares; the sun is a type of Christ; the waters, of the peoples; but that does not make those things sacraments, for in every case there are lacking both the divine institution and the divine promise, which constitute a sacrament. Hence Paul, in Eph. 5 [29–32], following his own mind, applies to Christ these words of Gen. 2 [24] about marriage; or else, following the general view, he teaches that the spiritual marriage of Christ is also contained therein, when he says: "As Christ cherishes the church, because we are members of his body, of his flesh and his bones. 'For this reason a man shall leave his father and mother and be joined to his wife, and the two shall become one.' This is a great sacrament, and I take it to mean Christ and the church." You see, he would have the whole passage apply to Christ, and is at pains to admonish the reader to understand that the sacrament is in Christ and the church, not in marriage.

Granted that marriage is a figure of Christ and the church; yet it is not a divinely instituted sacrament, but invented by men in the church who are carried away by their ignorance of both the word and the thing.[26]

With the way cleared of the Catholic interpretation that Christian marriages are sacraments, and of the Catholic claim to ecclesiastical jurisdiction over these marriages, what doctrine and discipline of divorce and remarriage did the Lutherans erect in the clearing?

Here again the student of this history must distinguish between Luther's occasional statements, which are so frequently polemic rhetoric and therefore not carefully formulated, and the official confessional statements of the Lutheran Church.

In his *Babylonian Captivity of the Church* Luther was uncertain and troubled about a discipline of divorce and remarriage that would obey the New Testament instructions. About the two major parts of this instruction—Matthew 19 and 1 Corinthians 7—he had no doubt that the former's exceptive clause concludes to a true dissolution. He assumed too that this passage names the only ground for dissolution allowed by Christ, and concluded therefore that the Popes err when they dissolve marriages—unconsummated marriages—for other causes. He read 1 Corinthians 7 to interpret Paul's saying that when a Christian wife is separated from her husband there too the marriage is dissolved. In the light of these two passages interpreted in this way he could not understand why the spouses should not be allowed a second marriage.

> As to divorce, it is still a question for debate whether it is allowable. For my part I so greatly detest divorce that I should prefer bigamy to it; but whether it is allowable, I do not venture to decide. Christ himself, the Chief Shepherd, says in Matt. 5 [32]: "Every one who divorces his wife, except on the ground of unchastity, makes her an adulteress; and whoever marries a divorced woman commits adultery." Christ, then, permits divorce, but only on the ground of unchastity. The pope must, therefore, be in error whenever he grants a divorce for any other cause; and no one should feel safe who has obtained a dispensation by this temerity (not authority) of the pope. Yet it is still a great wonder to me, why they compel a man to remain unmarried after being separated from his wife by divorce, and why they will not permit him to remarry. For if Christ permits divorce on the ground of unchastity and compels no one to remain unmarried, and if Paul would rather have us marry than burn [I Cor. 7:9], then he certainly seems to permit a man to marry another woman in the place of the one who has been put away. I wish that this subject were fully discussed and made clear and decided, so that counsel might be given in the infinite perils of those who, without any fault of their own, are nowadays compelled to

remain unmarried; that is, those whose wives or husbands have run away and deserted them, to come back perhaps after ten years, perhaps never! This matter troubles and distresses me, for there are daily cases, whether by the special malice of Satan or because of our neglect of the Word of God.[27]

He continues and concludes with a careful insertion of the rule of equivalency into his interpretation of what Paul taught in 1 Corinthians 7, with a denial again of Popes' and bishops' authority to regulate divorce and remarriage, and with a choice instead of acceding to the wise judgments of learned men. Does this leave the reader to conclude that Luther thought divorce and remarriage would get along better if freed from all authoritative regulation? If so, Luther's memory fails when he later urges putting them under the authority of Christian princes and magistrates.

> I, indeed, who alone against all cannot establish any rule in this matter, would yet greatly desire at least the passage in I Cor. [7:15] be applied here: "But if the unbelieving partner desires to separate, let it be so; in such a case the brother or sister is not bound." Here the Apostle gives permission to put away the unbeliever who departs to set the believing spouse free to marry again. Why should not the same hold true when a believer—that is, a believer in name, but in truth as much an unbeliever as the one Paul speaks of—deserts his wife, especially if he intends never to return. I certainly can see no difference between the two. But I believe that if in the Apostle's day an unbelieving deserter had returned and had become a believer or had promised to live again with his believing wife, it would not have been permitted, but he too would have been given the right to marry again. Nevertheless, in these matters I decide nothing (as I have said), although there is nothing that I would rather see decided, since nothing at present more grievously perplexes me, and many others with me. I would have nothing decided here on the mere authority of the pope and the bishops; but if two learned and good men agreed [Matt. 18:19–20] in the name of Christ, I should prefer their judgment even to such councils as are assembled nowadays, famous only for numbers and authority, not for scholarship and saintliness. Therefore I hang up my lyre on this matter until a better man confers with me about it.[28]

But as Luther continued his writing and speaking on the subject he appeared to grow less tentative in his judgments. In 1522, two years after completing *The Babylonian Captivity of the Church,* he wrote and delivered *Die Predigt vom Ehelichen Leben,* his Sermon on the Estate of Marriage.[29] In Part 2 of the sermon he approved generally of three grounds for divorce: impotence, adultery and refusal of a spouse to fulfill the conjugal duty of sexual intercourse. About adultery he interpreted the Matthean exceptive clause to say that Christ permitted the dismissing of an adulterous husband as well as wife, with the consequence that the marriage is dissolved and the innocent party has the right to remarry.[30]

As for the ground of divorce that is a spouse's refusal to cohabit or to have sexual intercourse, where it is the wife who thus refuses the husband must warn her two or three times. If she remains obdurate, he is to inform the evangelical community and dismiss her. Luther's reasoning here is that the wife's refusal robs the marriage, for in 1 Corinthians 7:4 Paul instructed that neither husband nor wife has authority over his or her own body, but the spouse has it. This violation of rights cuts to the heart of marriage and even dissolves it. The husband may even ask the civil authorities to compel his wife to have intercourse with him; and if she still refuses, these authorities may put her to death. But if they fail to do so, he may dismiss her and take another wife.[31]

Luther is noticeably more merciful about two other sources of trouble in marriage, for one of which the Popes had legislated for centuries. Where the wife is an invalid and because of her illness cannot have intercourse, her husband cannot dismiss or leave her. He must keep her and care for her. As for the continence forced on him, God will give him the grace to survive this.[32] Where the trouble is discord apart from the refusal to have intercourse, this justifies the spouses' separating after the manner proposed by Jerome and Augustine. That is, the separated spouses must, according to Paul's instructions in 1 Corinthians 7:10–11, either be reconciled or live in continence. (After only two years Luther either forgot that he had said in *The Babylonian Captivity of the Church* that in this passage Paul allows dissolution of the marriage, or he simply did not worry about his contradicting that earlier interpretation.)

The Council of Trent

The formal Catholic response to this multi-front challenge was made in the Council of Trent's decree on marriage promulgated in its twenty-fourth session, which ended on November 11, 1563. The decree was formulated in such a way as to counter the Lutheran challenge at its crucial points. It took the conventional conciliar form of an expository statement setting out the Catholic position, followed by several canons tightening this teaching to exactness by condemning, each of them, an error about marriage. The linking of the Catholic position with its claimed sources in the Scriptures is done in the prior statement; the exact and formal Catholic doctrine on divorce and remarriage is in the seventh of the twelve canons.[33]

But the history of Trent's statement on marriage began as much as eighteen years earlier, in 1547, when the Council was convened at Bologna. Discussion of the doctrine concerning marriage began there on April 26 of that year; the problem of clandestine marriages occupied the period from August 29 to September 6. A series of canons began formulation on September 9, but little progress was made in the next five years, and in 1552 Pope Julius III prorogued the Council. It was not to meet again until reconvened by Pius IV in 1561. Even then the discussion of marriage did not resume until February of 1563. On the ninth of that month the assisting theologians (the *theologi minores*) began an examination of eight articles containing the main challenges coming from the Reformers. (These theologians were to guide the bishops in the latters' formulating of the decree and the canons.) Among these articles-to-be-condemned the third read as follows.

> A man is permitted to contract a second marriage after dismissing his wife because of her adultery even while she still lives. The error in the matter is to grant divorce outside the case of adultery.[34]

The second of the clauses here clearly refers to Luther's denial that Catholic authority is competent to dissolve unconsummated marriages. This competence would be reasserted by the Council in its condemnation of the article in both its clauses.

Five months later, on July 20, the *theologi minores* had ready for the bishops' discussion eleven canons *De Sacramento Matrimonii.* The proposed teaching on divorce and remarriage was formulated in Canon 6.

> If anyone shall say that a marriage can be dissolved because of adultery by one of the parties, and that it is permitted to both, or at least to the innocent partner who gave no cause for the adultery, to marry a second time; and [if anyone should say] that a man who, after dismissing his adulterous wife, marries another, and the woman who, after dismissing her adulterous husband, marries another, are not [themselves] guilty of adultery—let him be anathema.

At this point the ancient uncertainty and indecision among the Church's teachers came back to life. Although the great majority of the bishops approved of the canon as worded, some hesitated to anathematize in it an opinion they believed held centuries earlier by Basil and Ambrose (they were not aware that the writings of the Ambrosiaster came not from the great Latin Father), an opinion approved by such regional Councils in the Roman Church as Arles, Compiègne and Verberies. The future Pope Urban VII himself, Archbishop Giambattista Castagno of Rossano, shared this hesitation. It would be one thing for the Council to propose Catholic doctrine; it would be quite different and shocking to declare heretics two men listed among the Doctors in the calendar of the saints. A few of the bishops, most notably those of Segovia and Modena, even proposed that

marriage's invulnerability to dissolution is not itself a matter of faith but is
no more than a law of the Church. The bishop of Modena explained his
reluctance in the following way.

> I vote against Canon 6. Never has the Church applied an
> anathema except against what is contrary to the common con-
> sensus of Catholics. What Christ did was to mitigate the law in
> Deuteronomy in punishment of the adulterous wife. He ruled
> that rather than being executed she is to be dismissed. In Ori-
> gen's time a man could take a second wife because of his first
> wife's adultery. Basil held the same opinion. . . . Consequently we
> can proceed in this cause as the bishops of Segovia and Lucca
> have suggested.[35]

What the bishop of Segovia had suggested was that Canon 6 be
amended to read, "If anyone shall say that the Church has erred in
teaching that marriage is not dissolved by adultery, let him be anathema."
The bishop of Modena wished to qualify the matter even further. He
recommended that the canon do more than simply condemn those who
maintain that the Church has not authority to prohibit from marrying a
second time spouses who have dismissed a partner because of adultery.[36]
His intent was apparently to take out of the domain of doctrine the
possibility of divorce and remarriage, but to establish in that domain
instead the authority of the Church to rule in the matter. In this way
Luther's denial of the Pope's authority would be caught directly in the
condemnation and his favoring dissolution for adultery would be caught
indirectly. Thus the bishop of Segovia introduced an anathema by indirec-
tion, a strategem that the Council was to use in a fullsome way that we
shall see presently.

But these compromises found only minority favor among the bishops.
In the revised schema submitted to them on August 7 Canon 6 was
unchanged. Such might have been the definitive formulation of Trent's
canon on divorce and remarriage had the Republic of Venice's representatives at the Council not made an extraordinary intervention. They pointed
out that at the time the inhabitants of the islands of Crete, Cyprus,
Cephalonia, Corfu and Ithaca were subjects of the Republic. They had for
centuries held to the Greek discipline for divorce and remarriage. The
bishops of these islands were appointed by Rome, but they had thus far
chosen not to challenge this discipline among their peoples. The Venetian
ambassadors urged that with patience on the part of the Roman Church
these Aegean and Ionian peoples might eventually be led to accept this
Church's discipline. But if the tradition and practice of divorce on the
ground of adultery were anathematized by the Council, they might rebel
and break away for good. The ambassadors proposed and even begged that
the canon embody a circuitous and softened condemnation in a form such
as the following.

> If anyone shall say that the Holy Roman and Apostolic Church, which is the teacher of all other churches, has erred or does err when she teaches that because of the adultery of one of the spouses, etc. . . .

This hinted clearly at a tactical problem now facing the bishops at Trent. It was how to not catch in the same target area with Luther, who had accused the Roman Catholic Church of teaching error, the Greek Catholics who had never made that accusation; yet at the same time to assert doctrinally the Roman Catholic discipline on dismissal because of adultery over against that of the Greeks. This was a delicate, simultaneously positive and negative maneuver. If it failed on the one side and the Greeks came out anathematized, the consequences would be severe. The Council of Florence had apparently produced a reunion of belief and practice between the Roman and some of the Orthodox Churches of the East, the Armenian principal among them. Apparently by design the representatives at Florence of Rome and the Eastern Churches had omitted any discussion of divorce and remarriage, leaving everyone to conclude, as I said above, that agreement or disagreement on this point was not significant for reunion. For Trent to now turn about and anathematize these Orthodox Churches—and with an anathema that meant excommunication—would do incalculable harm, and not alone to the Republic of Venice.

The great majority of the bishops favored the Venetians' proposal. That they did so is evident in the Canon 7 that was finally approved for promulgation on November 11. It was intended to anathematize Luther's position but spare the Orthodox, and apparently succeeded in doing both. But before examining it in detail it will be helpful to look at the theological statement that prefaced it. It takes care to counter Luther's attack on Catholic teaching at every significant point of the attack. It clearly intends to validate its counter-case by drawing it at every point from the Scriptures, since this had been one of Luther's principal grievances, that the Catholic teaching is no more than a human invention.[37]

> The first parent of the human race, inspired by the Divine Spirit, declared the bond of marriage to be permanent and indissoluble when he said, "This now is bone of my bone and flesh of my flesh. For this reason a man will leave his father and mother and cling to his wife, and they shall be two in one flesh."
> Christ the Lord taught yet more clearly that no more than two persons are joined in this bond when, after he had repeated these words as coming from God—"Therefore they are not two, but one flesh"—he immediately sealed [*confirmavit*] the strength of this bond that had been only declared by Adam, saying, "Therefore what God has joined man must not separate."[38]

This is not yet a dogmatic decree; that will come presently in the canons anathematizing the Lutheran challenge in its several points. But it is a doctrinal statement. It says what is the Catholic teaching on the subject. It says specifically that marriage's indissolubility is of divine origin; and it says implicitly that this indissolubility is the kind understood by the Popes and by the Catholic Church's other bishops in 1563—the kind that can yield to dissolution if the marriage is not consummated. Therefore it implies as well that the inspired words of Scripture—those from Adam as well as from Christ—refer only to consummated marriages, as Pope Alexander III had said three and a half centuries earlier.

The statement then turns to the challenged issue of Christ's having made marriage among Christians a sacrament of his new law. And again it seeks to draw its theology from the Scriptures.

> Christ himself, he who instituted and perfected the holy sacraments, has by his passion merited the grace which completes this natural love [of husband and wife], which seals the spouses' indissoluble unity and sanctifies them. The Apostle Paul intimated this when he said "Husbands, love your wives as Christ loved the Church and gave himself up for her," and then added shortly afterward, "This is a great sacrament; I say this in regard to Christ and the Church."[39]

That this paragraph has the sacramental grace sealing, or confirming, marriage's "natural" indissolubility reveals the understanding of indissolubility the bishops had in mind in the preceding paragraphs. Here the current Catholic doctrine of marriage's *radical* indissolubility is stated succinctly: such ultimate and *indissoluble* indissolubility is found only where a marriage is a sacrament, and is consummated as a sacrament. The way is kept open too for the discipline, soon to expand, whereby papal authority can dissolve even consummated marriages provided they are not sacraments.

The statement's final paragraph begins with a forthright assertion that marriage in the new law is a sacrament, and with a not entirely defensible claim that the Fathers and Councils of the Church have always taught this, indeed that this has always been the Church's tradition.

> Therefore since, thanks to the grace of Christ, marriage in the law of the Gospel surpasses the marriages of old, the Fathers, the councils, indeed the tradition of the universal Church has always rightly taught that marriage is to be included among the sacraments of the New Law. . . ."[40]

The concluding lines of this paragraph then declare the Council's intent to single out the most glaring among the Reformers' errors concerning marriage and to condemn them. These last lines were written with a care that apparently had the Venetian ambassadors' pleas in mind. They say that the anathemas to come will reply to the errors "of impious men of this world who have used a pretext of the freedom warranted by the Gospel to mislead the faithful"—an accusation phrased to catch exactly the Lutherans' claim that their position was a return to the Gospel teaching, back beyond the dictates of mere men, of Popes and bishops.

Trent's Canons on Marriage

These canons function as a set of lenses focusing that doctrinal statement on the Lutheran challenge part by part.[41] They apply the doctrine of this statement to these points in a literally critical way to judge and condemn them as false. Of the twelve canons I will quote only the three that are most pertinent to the purposes of this volume. Of these Canon 7 is the most pertinent because it condemns the Lutheran challenge to the Catholic teaching on divorce and remarriage. I will go immediately to Canon 7.

The canon takes a circuitous route in its counter-attack on Luther's challenge because in it, as I have explained, the bishops sought to strike with their anathema Luther's challenge while at the same time sparing from it the Greek doctrine and discipline. Thus it begins, as the abandoned Canon 6 had done, *Si quis dixerit ecclesiam errare* . . . "If one should say that the Church errs . . ." This formulation points at a significant difference of the Greeks from Luther. While the former disagreed with the Roman Church in discipline and doctrine, it had never condemned these. But Luther had done exactly that. He had condemned the Roman discipline as erroneous because legislated without competence, because Popes and bishops had gone beyond their authority in pretending to resolve once for all and immutably an issue left inconclusive in the Scriptures—and worst of all to resolve it by judicial ruling. A fine point here: since Luther had accused the Roman Church of error in juridical practice, this is what Canon 7 itself means in anathematizing those who accuse it of error on the point in question. That is, the canon's anathema skirts those who accuse the Church of error in doctrine but strikes those who accuse it of error in juridical discipline.

The next clause of the canon is just as carefully worded: . . . *errare cum docuit et docet iuxta evangelicam et apostolicam doctrinam* . . . ". . . errs when it has taught and when it still teaches according to the doctrine of the gospels and of the apostles . . ." The last substantive here refers most probably to 1 Corinthians 7. The clause carefully distinguishes the New Testament sources from the theological and juridical tradition that had been built up during the centuries preceding Trent. But this tradition is brought into the clause where it says "when it has taught and when it still teaches." This claims the historical fact that the Church's canons and the papal decretals have always taught that not even adulterous marriages can be dissolved by human authority, and that they still so teach. And the claim of the canon to this point is that in so teaching they have not erred.

The prepositional phrase, "according to the doctrine of the gospels and of the apostles," shows a careful choice of words. Where some of the bishops at the Council wished to claim that the Roman Church teaches exactly what these sources taught, others, whose judgment prevailed, insisted on nothing more than that the Church's teaching and discipline do not contradict the sources. For the choice of the preposition *iuxta* ("according to") suggests clearly that this teaching and discipline are drawn from and are inspired by the New Testament teaching, and of course do not contradict it.

... *propter adulterium alterius coniugum matrimonii vinculum non posse dissolvi*— ". . . teaches that the bond of marriage cannot be dissolved because of the adultery of one or other of the spouses." The original phrasing of this clause was ". . . teaches that *a marriage* cannot be dissolved . . ." The noun "bond" was added in order to do two things. The first was to avoid saying that a marriage itself is essentially indissoluble, a claim that would contradict the Catholic practice of dissolving unconsummated marriages. The second intended effect of adding the noun "bond" was to deny that a marriage *ipso facto,* because of the adultery, dies of itself, or that the partners can in their own consciences decide to end the marriage (which is what Luther favored). Or to put it in language drawn from the canon law textbooks, by the addition of "bond" the clause deliberately though implicitly sustains the instrinsic indissolubility of marriage. But by saying nothing about "extrinsic indissolubility" it keeps the way open for the Popes' use of the "power of the keys" to dissolve marriages.

Adding the noun "bond" also widened the jurists' useful distinction between marriage as a lived relationship—the sharing in all of life that classic Roman law once called it and the bishops of Vatican II were to call it again—and the juridical bond.

The last clauses are the longest of the canon but add the least of substantial meaning. They round off and conclude the thought of the preceding clause. That is, the Catholic Church does not err in teaching that a marriage cannot be dissolved because of a spouse's adultery, neither does it err in teaching (1) that neither spouse, even the innocent one who gave no cause for the adultery, cannot remarry as long as the other lives, and (2) that if the innocent spouse does attempt remarriage after dismissing the guilty, he or she commits adultery in doing so (. . . *et utrumque coniugum, vel saltem innocentem, qui causam adulterii non dedit, non posse, altero coniuge vivente, aliud matrimonium contrahere moecharique eum qui dimissa adultera alteram duxerit, et eam, qui dimisso adultero, alii nupserit*).

The bishops sought to incorporate here two quotations from Luther so that they could anathematize them rather than his person, in accord with the Council's comprehensive strategy of dealing with heretical doctrines rather than with heretics themselves. This accounts at least in part for the intricate weave of this clause.

But over the objection of some of the bishops and of the commission that had written this Canon 7 the Council decided to maintain the anathema "for those who should assert the contradictory of the canon." They did this because they wished, by using the severe penalty of anathema, which means excommunication, to make clear that they were teaching "dogma."

This indicates at least what "dogma" did not mean in the vocabulary of Trent. The term did not refer solely to a truth revealed directly by God, as the First Vatican Council was to define the term three centuries later. The term at Trent could also designate Church teaching embodied in theological and juridical tradition, provided it was at least drawn from the Scriptures and was accepted universally in the Western Church. It is significant that the anathema, the excommunication for heresy, did not affect the Greek Catholics in their practice of permitting divorce and remarriage after proved adultery. And it seems to have left also untouched their practice of dissolving marriages for the whole repertory of causes drawn from Justinian's Novel 117.

Trent's Answer to Luther's Challenge to Catholic Jurisdiction

Insofar as conciliar decrees are thought to meet challenges, the bishops of Trent were no doubt satisfied that their Canon 7 met Luther's challenge to the Catholic Church's accuracy in interpreting the New Testament passages on divorce and remarriage. But as we have seen, Luther had challenged Catholic authority in another quarter, this one a territory of mixed doctrine and discipline. The bishops answered this challenge too, but may have suspected only faintly that it was the harbinger of a much more serious challenge and conflict yet to come, when powerful princes and parliaments of nations would rise up to contest the Church's claim to exclusive jurisdiction over the marriages of Europe's, and Europe's colonies', Catholic peoples.

Where they saw Luther aiming this other challenge is disclosed in the phrasing of their Canons 1 and 4, but especially of Canon 12.

Canon 1 anathematizes those who seek to undermine the Catholic Church's compelling reason for claiming jurisdiction over the marriages of all Christians. This reason is that Christ made the marriages of Christians sacraments, and the Church of its nature has jurisdiction over all Christian sacraments and sacramental institutions. Thus the canon anathematizes those who deny that Christ constituted marriages (among Christians) as a sacrament.

If anyone shall say that marriage is not truly and in the proper sense of the word one of the sacraments of the law of the

Gospel instituted by Christ, but has been invented in the Church by men, and that it does not confer grace—let him be anathema.[42]

Canon 4 anathematizes those who deny that the Catholic Church has authority to establish invalidating impediments to marriage, and those who say that it has erred in doing so.[43]

Finally Canon 12 fixes on the challenge that was the harbinger of the greater conflict to come. It anathematizes those who deny that marriage causes (we would say marriage "cases") brought for adjudication belong properly to the jurisdiction of ecclesiastical judges. Let us recall Luther's logic on this point—a logic which was, in modified form, to become the logic two centuries later of philosophers, jurists, princes and parliaments. Granted marriage is a religious insititution (a point that the most influential of the later philosophers did *not* grant). But it is not by nature an ecclesiastical institution. It had existed centuries before there was ever a Church and its authority. Even during the first one thousand years of Christianity marriages of the members of the Church had been ruled by civil authority (even though bishops had exercised this authority), and the Church had accepted this peacefully. The Popes had erected no separate judicial system claiming a separate and higher jurisdiction over marriage. Thus Canon 12 in reply:

If anyone should deny that marital causes belong to [or are under the authority of] ecclesiastical judges, let him be anathema.[44]

Apostolic Constitutions and the Dissolving of Non-Sacramental Marriages

Even while the bishops at Trent were rejecting, with the most severe counter-charge at their command, Luther's denial of Catholic authority to rule in marriage cases, this authority began to be exercised in a way that was to surprise even orthodox Catholics. We saw in the preceding chapter the history of speculation and decision about the causes that justify the Church's dissolving unconsummated marriages. After the turmoil and indecision that came to a climax during the papacy of Alexander III the practice of dissolving such marriages was brought under severe control by Gregory IX. Not until the papacy of Martin V (1417–1431) is there record of dissolutions granted on the other grounds that had been acknowledged earlier. Gregory appears to have allowed dissolution only by the pronouncing of the vows of religious life.

But because the principle that unconsummated marriages can be dissolved was now long since accepted in the Church, the canonists and theologians were never to allow the issue to rest. In fact they could not. Too many questions attending the issue still awaited an answer. For one there was the question that had been dominant from the beginning of the practice: Which are the causes that justify the dissolving of an unconsummated marriage? That is a juridical question. But behind it hid the theological question: Why can an unconsummated marriage be dissolved, but a consummated marriage cannot? We have seen the two most common answers to this second question. First, that Christ's own reason for forbidding a man's dismissing his wife is that they are two in one flesh; but they do not become one flesh until their marriage is consummated by their first sexual intercourse. Then the second reason, that speaks only to the sacramental marriages of Christians: because the consummated marriage of two Christians images the union of Christ and the Church or the union of the two natures in Christ, both of which are indestructible unions, a sacramental marriage cannot be dissolved. But an unconsummated marriage images only the union of the human soul with God, a union that is not indestructible because it can be destroyed by sin. Therefore this unconsummated marriage fails of indissolubility.

But the question to which a negative answer could have undermined the practice itself of dissolving unconsummated marriages was a hybrid of theology and law. It asked if the supreme authority in the Catholic Church, "the power of the keys" vested in the Pope, was competent to dissolve such marriages. Does the power to bind and to loose include the loosing of the bond of a marriage that is not consummated? Opinions in the matter were divided in the sixteenth century. Some—theologians principal among them, following Aquinas and Bonaventure—said no. They did not deny this authority explicitly, but only implicitly by contending that the dissolution of an unconsummated marriage by the pronouncing of religious vows is not an exercise of authority. In this case authority is exercised only by the granting of permission to take up religious life. But by a metaphoric extension of the principle that as a marriage is dissolved only by the death of one of the spouses, the pronouncing of religious vows is a spiritual dying that ends a marriage.

The canonists of the three centuries from Gregory IX until Trent were divided in their answers to the question. We have seen that Alanus of Lille defended the Church's authority to dissolve by theorizing that a merely vowed but not consummated marriage (*matrimonium ratum*) has the effects of marriage, including its indissolubility, solely by ecclesiastical law; that of its own nature it is not really a marriage, and as a consequence the Church has the authority to loose the bond which is created by its authority. Alanus was alone in proposing this thesis that was to be adopted later in secular form by the governments of Europe.

Those canonists who defended the Church's authority to dissolve offered two conjoined reasons for doing so. Unconsummated marriages are fundamentally dissoluble because they fall short of the full imaging of any indestructible divine union (as we saw just above); and the Popes have in fact dissolved unconsummated marriages.[45] Durandus of Mende (d. 1296) asked explicitly, "Can the Pope dissolve a marriage contracted by the *verba de praesenti* which has not been consummated by intercourse?" He answered by calling to mind Alexander III's letter *Ex publico* to point out that this had been done. Then, insisting that a later Pope can grant a dispensation that overrides a law framed by one of his predecessors, Durandus urged that one or more of Gregory IX's successors had done just this in dissolving unconsummated marriages.[46]

Johannes Andreae (d. 1348) agreed with Hostiensis when interpreting Alexander III's practice of dissolution. But a century later Panormitanus (d. 1445) showed considerable hesitation, not denying the Pope's authority, but urging that it be used only in extreme cases. Two other canonists of the fifteenth century, Antoninus of Florence (d. 1459) and John of Turrecremata (d. 1468), shared Panormitanus' negative judgment. But while recording the arguments on both sides, and though personally siding with the theologians who denied that the Popes have this authority, both pointed to the evidence that eventually closed the case in favor of the papal power to dissolve. They acknowledged that Popes Martin V and Eugene IV had in fact dissolved unconsummated marriages. Antoninus admitted having seen bulls of dissolution issued by both Popes.[47]

The logic by which the dispute was ended seems to have been the following. The Church was in a state of honest doubt concerning the extent of its power, vested in the Popes, to bind and to loose—whether it reached as far as unconsummated marriages of the faithful. Rather than be stalled by this doubt a number of Popes used it as an opening. They in fact dissolved unconsummated marriages. It was then left for the canonists and theologians to explain after the fact how the now established practice was possible.

The Apostolic Constitutions: Paul III's Altitudo

It may be that the pragmatic resolving of the doubt in the sixteenth century that we are going to examine was spurred by Luther's expressly denying, in his *Babylonian Captivity of the Church,* the Catholic Church's authority to dissolve marriage for any other cause than adultery (while insisting on the lawfulness of true divorce for this one cause). Whether this challenge played a role or not, a decision was almost forced upon certain Popes of the sixteenth century by some unique circumstances of missionary activity in the Spanish and Portuguese colonies in Africa and the Indies. Pope Paul III was the first to have to decide about the use of his papal authority, in 1537, eight years before the convening of the Council of Trent. He did so, using his authority to dissolve multiple marriages by issuing on June 1 of that year his apostolic constitution *Altitudo.* But a striking feature of this constitution and its use of authority is that it presumed the marriages in question to be dissoluble not because they were unconsummated but because they were not sacraments. Because of this the dissolutions were at the time interpreted as extensions of the use of the Pauline privilege. That Paul instead used the power of the keys to bind and to loose in these cases is a later interpretation of his action.

Altitudo looked to the case of polygamous native husbands in the Indies who sought to convert to the Catholic faith. That they remain in their polygamous unions was simply irreconcilable with the Catholic way of life that they sought. Not that polygamous marriages are merely reprehensible morally. They are also impossible, according to the Church's understanding of God's word in Genesis, ". . . they shall be two in one flesh." Therefore ostensible polygamy really involves marriage to one wife and concubinage with the other pseudo-wife or wives—which is to say adultery.

The constitution prescribed that if the husband seeking conversion could recall which of his "wives" he had married first, he was to keep her, since she was his one true spouse, and dismiss all the others. If he could not recall which he had married first, he could keep the woman of his choice and dismiss the others. The Pope's authoritative application of the Pauline privilege would, on petition, dispense him and his unidentifiable wife from their marriage.

> We decree concerning their marriages that men who, before their conversion, had plural wives (according to their custom) and cannot recall which of them they married first, once they are converted to the faith they may keep that wife from among them whom they choose, and may contract marriage with her by the *verba de praesenti,* as is customary. But those men who can recall which wife they married first are to keep her and dismiss the others.[48]

(The second exchange of marriage vows had, of course, to wait for the dispensation, because until the latter was granted the man was not free to remarry. If the wife he chose among the several women for his second marriage happened, without his knowing it, to be the one he had first married, there ensued something unique in the Catholic experience of marriage: since the papal dispensation dissolved his first marriage to her, he ended by marrying the same woman a second time. The availability of this dispensation is also reported to have been the cause of suspicious failures of memory on the part of men who not unexpectedly preferred a younger wife.)

Despite being called at the time an extension of the Pauline privilege, the use of this constitution was more likely something quite other than that—the inauguration of a new ground for dissolution. For one of the elements essential to the use of the Pauline privilege was missing. That is, there was here no evidence that one spouse remained unbaptized and refused to live in peace with the other after his conversion and baptism. What is more, the first and only wife may have also accepted baptism or may not have. If she had not, then the possibility for papal dissolution was grounded in the marriage's not being a sacrament. But if she had accepted baptism and thus made of her marriage a sacrament, then this possibility was grounded in her marriage's not being consummated *as a sacrament.* But whichever the case, Paul's constitution was clearly a use of papal authority to dissolve marriages that were either not sacraments or were unconsummated as sacraments.[49]

Pius V's *Romani pontificis*

Pope Pius V's constitution *Romani pontificis* of August 2, 1571 looked to a singular difficulty within the inclusive difficulty of accepting for baptism polygamous males of the Indies. One difficulty arising in a polygamous society has already been suggested in Paul III's constitution: a native husband seeking baptism was to keep his first wife if he could recall which of several she was. If he could not, he could keep the wife of his choice. But this liberality opened the way to obvious difficulties. Not only could a converted Indian husband conveniently forget which of his partners he had married first, but where he honestly remembered and identified her, she could well be a pagan who insisted on remaining a pagan. Thus the husband's honesty kept him joined to a pagan wife despite his wanting a sacramental marriage with a Christian.

In addition problems of conscience were created for the missionaries themselves in the Indies. They were driven to wonder if it is really so easy to dissolve a marriage. Ought there not be firmer ground on which to do so than that presumed by Paul III's constitution? Pius V found this ground in the possibility that the marriage a native convert kept might become a sacrament. Thus, though the converted husband could keep only one of his women, this could be the one among them who would accept baptism along with him.

> Since plural wives are permitted to the natives of the Indies as long as they remain pagan ... what has come about is that those men who receive baptism are permitted to remain with whichever woman receives baptism along with the husband. And since this woman often turns out to be not the first whom the husband had married, both the ministers of the sacrament and the [local] bishops are bothered by the most serious scruples, thinking that this is not a true marriage. But because it is a cruel thing to separate such a man from the woman with whom he received baptism; and because it would be most difficult to find and identify his first wife ... therefore of Our own will and initiative [*motu proprio*] and from Our clear awareness of the fullness of Our apostolic power, We declare that the natives of the Indies ... who have been baptized or who shall be baptized may remain, as with their legitimate wife, with that woman who

has been or will be baptized with them after dismissing the others
. . . and We declare that such marriages between them are legitimate.[50]

It may be to the point to make clear that the exact object of the
exercise of papal authority here is the dissolution of the one true marriage
in those cases where the woman who received baptism with the husband-
convert was other than his first and legitimate wife. Here again the effect
of the exercise of authority is the dissolution of a marriage considered
dissoluble not because it is unconsummated but because it is not a sacrament. And the reason for its dissolution is that it stands in the way of a
second and sacramental marriage. The latter enjoys privilege under the
law, a privilege that was subsequently to be termed "the privilege of the
faith."

An extraordinary feature of this constitution is found in Pius' claiming expressly that it was apostolic power and authority that enabled him to
specify which woman is the legitimate wife in the case of converted native
husbands, and that therefore he, Pius, had the authority to dissolve any
other marital bond affecting the man in question. As Plöchl remarks,
"This was a decisive step in the development of Church law."[51] One could
add that it was just as decisive a step in the development of the theology of
papal power to bind and to loose, and in the theology of marriage's
indissolubility as well. Pius formulated his claim thus: ". . . of Our own
will and initiative [*motu proprio*] and from Our clear awareness of the
fullness of Our apostolic power, We declare . . ."

Perhaps because of the extraordinary claim of power and authority
lodged in this constitution the canonists of the time thought to confine it
within a limited interpretation and to explain it as an added use of the
Pauline privilege, and to control its use by subordinating it to the incumbent Decretal law concerning divorce. This interpretation found favor in
the Roman congregations of the Holy Office, of the Sacred Propaganda,
and of the Council—the congregation established by Pius IV immediately
after Trent to interpret that Council's decrees. They urged generally that
the constitution could be applied only in those cases in which the unbaptized first wives of the native converts could not be found or identified.
This would at least keep papal authority from dissolving *known* consummated marriages and would consequently confine the authority to dissolve
non-sacramental marriages to non-verifiable instances of the same.[52]

Gregory XIII's *Populis ac nationibus*

The third of these apostolic constitutions was Pope Gregory XIII's
Populis ac nationibus, issued on January 25, 1585. It was published in
consideration of the consequences of the growing slave trade that tore
thousands of Africans from their homeland and removed them across the

Atlantic to "the Indies."[53] Many of these had been married before being enslaved; many of their now abandoned spouses sought Christian baptism and wished to marry again. So too did the spouses taken into slavery. By implication the constitution restated the authority to dissolve non-sacramental marriages asserted in Paul III's *Altitudo* and in Pius V's *Romani pontificis.* But what it did explicitly was to dispense the newly baptized Catholics from what was in fact impossible to them. This was the otherwise obligatory inquiry and questioning (the interpellation) of the distant and inaccessible spouse to determine his or her will to continue the disrupted marriage. The first paragraph of the constitution reveals the benign motive for granting the dispensation and exercising the power to dissolve.

> There is compelling reason for favoring the freedom of those peoples and nations recently converted from pagan error to the Catholic faith. We do this lest persons who are scarcely accustomed to a life of continence may perservere less willingly in the faith and lest others be deterred by their example from embracing the faith.
>
> It happens frequently that many of both sexes—but especially those of the male sex—are taken captive after being married according to their pagan custom, and are removed from their native lands and their wives into distant countries. As a consequence both the captives as well as those who remain behind, if they are later converted to the faith, cannot, as justice demands, ask their far distant and still unconverted spouses if they wish to cohabit without contempt of the Creator ... [54]

Then Gregory states the canonical-theological possibility for his exercising the power to dispense from the otherwise obligatory interpellation of the still pagan spouses' will to continue the marriages peacefully.

> Understanding that these marriages contracted by pagans are true marriages but are not considered ratified [not sacramental marriages] to the point that they cannot be dissolved if necessity urges ... We grant to the local Ordinaries and to pastors ... the authority to dispense the Christians of both sexes in the aforesaid territories [from the interpellations]—men and women who have contracted marriage before being baptized and who have later converted to the faith; so that they may, even while the other spouse still lives, licitly contract marriage with any baptized person of whichever rite. This they may do even without asking the consent of the first spouse or without waiting for his or her reply. They may solemnize their second marriage in the Church, and after consummating them they may remain in

these marriages as long as they live. [This may be done] provided
it is established, even if only summarily and extra-judicially, that
the absent spouse cannot be informed according to the law, or
that even though informed has not manifested his or her will
within the time stated in the informing communiqué.[55]

Thus far in the constitution it is evident that the kind of marriage
Gregory deems dissolved under the conditions he sets down here is a non-
sacramental marriage. He assumes too that this is the point of its vulnerability to dissolution, that it is not a sacrament. Finally he all but says
expressly that the most religiously warranted reason for exercising his
authority to dispense and to dissolve is "in favor of the faith"—so that the
newly converted Christians may enter into a second and sacramental
marriage. For he says that the new converts in question "may licitly
contract marriage *with any baptized person . . .*"

But Gregory was aware of what could happen in such circumstances
to change the ground of possibility for the dissolution. Sometimes both of
the spouses in question were baptized after being separated. According to
the incumbent theology and law this made their marriages sacraments,
despite the distant and permanent separation. The last clauses of the
constitution provide for this contingency.

Even if it should later come to light that the earlier and
pagan spouses could not declare their will [to resume cohabita-
tion] because they were unjustly prevented from doing so; and
even if they should be converted to the faith at the time the
[absent spouse's] second marriage is contracted, We decree nevertheless that these second marriages are never to be rescinded
[that is, found null] but are to be held valid and perpetual [*firma*]
and that children born of them are to be legitimate.

Since the conversion to the Catholic faith of the second spouse
rendered the original marriage a sacrament, then the possibility of dissolution had, without Gregory's saying so, changed significantly. Now it had
to be lack of consummation. But granted the original marriage had been
consummated before either spouse's baptism, the ground must now be
ultimately that marriage was not consummated *after* becoming a sacrament—was never consummated *as a sacrament.*

It is no exaggeration to say that with this the papal power to bind and
to loose came to its longest reach in the history of the Catholic regulation
of marriage. And the attenuating of Christ's command, "What God has
joined man must not separate," had reached its most elastic extreme. In
this constitution Gregory interpreted that command to hold only in the
case of two Christians who have created a sacramental marriage and have
consummated it as a sacrament. No other kind of marriage is finally

indissoluble. (To be sure, the theology that validates this attenuating says that in these papal constitutions it is not that men separate what God has joined, but that the divine authority given to Peter and his successors by Christ is what separates it. If this distinction were formulated epigrammatically it would read, "What God has joined God can separate—through his vicar on earth." The cross-over point in the theological validating is the assumption that this power to separate is included in the "power to loose.")

Plöchl explains well the issue that has now been brought to center stage in the continuing drama of Catholic treatment of divorce and remarriage.

> Inevitably this constitution [Gregory XIII's *Populis ac nationibus*] provided the stimulus for continuing theoretical debate. Does it really involve only an application of the Pauline privilege and dispensation from the interpellations? Or does it involve a new application of the papal power to dissolve the bond of marriage under specific conditions?
>
> These two questions—and they really are two distinct questions—never got their theoretical answer at this time. Indeed to this day they remain the object of discussion and debate. In any case the argument favoring the view that the pope actually has an authority to dissolve that goes beyond the Pauline privilege has shifted ground decisively. Today this exercise of authority is called—over the technical objection of some, but in a way to emphasize the difference—the "Petrine privilege."
>
> For the historian of law there is an even more significant issue involved. The constitution *Populis* marks the first point of arrival in a developing theory—a theory making it a part of law that the pope has the authority under specific conditions, and quite apart from the Pauline privilege, to dissolve the bond of marriage. . . . This decisive difference [between the exercise of authority and the use of the Pauline privilege] was hardly noted or was noted not at all. It is indisputably certain that a marriage, first created while both spouses are pagan, becomes a sacramental and consummated marriage *(matrimonium ratum et consummatum)* after both these spouses are baptized. It becomes a Christian sacramental marriage. But here there is a question of a marriage that was consummated beforehand, and became a sacrament only through baptism; and because of circumstances [the separation of the spouses] could never be consummated [as a sacrament]. Thus the kind of marriage in question was consummated and [later] a sacrament [*consummatum et ratum*]. The newly sacramental marriage could not be brought to completion. Therefore it could be dissolved thanks to the papal authority to do so.[56]

NOTES

1. Gabriel LeBras discusses this case in his essay on marriage in *Dictionnaire de Théologie Catholique*, Vol. 9, Cols. 2221–2222.

2. Johan Huizinga, in his *Erasmus and the Age of Reformation*, reports that Erasmus spent almost three years (1499–1502) doing little else but learning Greek, and learning it without the help of a teacher. At the end of that time he could write it fluently. He had put himself through this agony expressly so that he might read the New Testament in its original language and therefore read it accurately—so that he might, in turn, work at the reform of theology in his time (p. 49).

3. *Opera* (Basel, 1542), Tomus 6, p. 499 (quoted in G. H. Joyce, *op. cit.*, p. 391, note 1).

4. *Ibid.*, p. 505 (G.H. Joyce, *loc. cit.*, p. 392).

5. G.H. Joyce, *loc. cit.*, p. 393.

6. *Ibid.*

7. *Ibid.*

8. This profession is quoted in Denzinger-Schönmetzer, nn. 851–861, pp. 275–277.

9. The Council's main legislation is recorded in Denzinger-Schönmetzer, nn. 830–839, pp. 270–272.

10. Denzinger-Schönmetzer, n. 860, p. 277.

11. In Denzinger-Schönmetzer, nn. 1300–1308, pp. 331–332.

12. "Ordinarily" in this sentence translates the Latin adverb *regulariter*. It is in the text in order to allow that the consent can be manifested in other ways than verbally.

13. In Denzinger-Schönmetzer, n. 1327, p. 336.

14. "A Prelude of Martin Luther on the Babylonian Captivity of the Church," in *Luther's Works*, Jaroslav Pelikan and Helmut Lehmann, general editors; Vol. 36, edited by Abdel Ross Wentz, Philadelphia, 1959, p. 96.

15. *Loc. cit.* p. 97.

16. *Loc. cit.*, pp. 98–99.

17. *Ibid.*

18. "Sermon on the Sermon on the Mount," in *Luther's Works*, Vol. 21, edited by Jaroslav Pelikan, St. Louis, 1956, p. 93, used by permission of Concordia Publ. House, © 1956.

19. *Loc. cit.*, p. 96.

20. *Op. cit.*, Vol. 46, "The Christian in Society III," edited by Robert C. Schultz, p. 316.

By the time he wrote this Luther must have forgotten that, as we saw just above, he had absolved marriage from any regulation by law: "Besides this, no man has the right to form such laws, and Christ has granted to Christians a liberty which is above all the laws of men especially where a law of God conflicts with them." The imperial law he refers to here is that of Theodosius II and Justinian, not that of Charles V.

21. "Sermon on the Sermon on the Mount," *op. cit.*, p. 98, used by permission of Concordia Publ. House, © 1956.

22. In *The Book of Concord, The Confessions of the Evangelical Church*, edited by Theodore C. Tappert *et al.*, Philadelphia, 1959, p. 85.

23. The representatives of the Lutheran Smalcald League, meeting in February of 1537, were asked to draw up a statement of the nature and limits of papal

authority. This was to fill a lacuna in the Augsburg Confession, left there in order to not offend the Catholic emperor, Charles V, when there was still hope that he and the Catholic prelates on one side, and the Lutheran reformers on the other, might, in the Diet of Augsburg in 1530, work out a peaceful reconciliation of their differences.

24. *The Book of Concord,* p. 333.

25. "Sermon on the Sermon on the Mount," *op. cit.,* p. 94, used by permission of Concordia Publ. House, © 1956.

26. *Ibid.,* pp. 95–96

Philip Melancthon then makes the denial more succinctly and crisply in his *Apology of the Confession of Augsburg,* published in April 1531 as the Lutheran response to the Catholic reply to the Confession of Augsburg, the *Confutatio Romana.* Although it was first regarded as Melancthon's private publication, it became part of the Lutheran confession when it was signed, along with the Augsburg Confession, at Smalcald in 1537. It is important as a contemporary commentary on the Confession by the principal author of that document.

"Matrimony was first instituted not in the New Testament but in the very beginning, at the creation of the human race. It has the command-ment of God and also certain promises, but these apply to physical life and not strictly to the New Testament. If anybody therefore wants to call it a sacrament, he should distinguish it from the preceding ones which are, in the strict sense, 'signs of the New Testament,' testimonies of grace and of the forgiveness of sins. If matrimony should be called a sacrament because it has God's command, then many other states or offices might also be called sacraments because they have God's command, as, for example, governments." (*The Book of Concord,* p. 213)

27. *Op. cit.,* pp. 105–106.

28. *Ibid.*

29. This is in *Luther's Works,* Vol. 45, *The Christian in Society II,* edited by Walther O. Brandt, Philadelphia, 1962, pp. 17–49.

30. *Op. cit.,* p. 30.

He accounted for God's permitting divorce through the law of Moses in the Old Testament as one of the "worldly laws" given only in order to put a limit on evil conduct. That is, to gain the lesser of two evils the law of Moses allowed husbands to dismiss their wives "for any reason" lest they rid themselves of them by murder. But Christ called the law back to severity by limiting the right of dismissal to the husband cheated by adultery. He reasoned further that where the wife's adultery is secret, her husband may correct her if he chooses. But to dismiss her and remarry publicly he must ask the civil authorities to investigate and verify her guilt; or if this authority will not do so, then he may appeal to that of the evangelical community. Thus a control is put on husbands' desire to dismiss their unwanted wives. As for the party proved guilty of adultery, Luther counseled that he or she be put to death by the civil authority; or if this authority refuses to do so, the guilty party must leave for a distant land. There he or she may remarry if unable to live in continence. But if after public verification of guilt the innocent spouse wishes to keep the guilty, the latter must do penance after being publicly rebuked. Luther's sense of justice had the effect of putting the life of the guilty spouse squarely in the hands of the innocent, there to test his or her Christian compassion (*ibid.*, pp. 32–33).

31. *Ibid.*, p. 33
32. *Loc. cit.*, p. 35
33. The decree is in Denzinger-Schönmetzer, nn. 1797–1816, pp. 415–418.
34. *Concilium Tridentinum,* Tomus 9, p. 380.
35. *Op. cit.*, p. 675.
36. *Op. cit.*, p. 658.
37. This theological statement is in Denzinger-Schönmetzer, nn. 1797–1800, pp. 415–416.
38. *Ibid.*, nn. 1797–1798, p. 415.
39. *Ibid.*, n. 1799, p. 415.
40. *Ibid.*, n. 1800, p. 415.
41. The canons are in Denzinger-Schönmetzer, nn. 1801–1812, pp. 416–417.
42. Denzinger-Schömetzer, n. 1801, p. 416.
43. *Op. cit.*, n. 1804, p. 416.
44. *Op. cit.*, n. 1812, p. 417
45. Thus Hostiensis in *Summa Aurea,* Lib. 3, "De Conversione Coniugatorum."
46. In G.H. Joyce, *op. cit.*, pp. 435–436.
47. *Ibid.*, p. 437.
48. Denzinger-Schönmetzer, n. 1497, p. 363.
49. This constitution was not at the time applied to the universal Church; it was directed to the bishops of the West Indies and of Latin America—to those territories that had been opened to Spanish colonization. Therefore it belonged to particular law in the Church, not to universal law.
50. Denzinger-Schönmetzer, n. 1983, p. 438.
Nothing is said in this constitution to resolve the difficulty consequent on two or more of these men's wives' wanting to be baptized along with them.
About Pius' constitution there arose the question whether, like Paul III's, it belonged only to the Church's particular law. In fact its area of reference was inexactly stated, since it was applied to "the Indies." Did this refer only to the West Indies, as did *Altitudo,* or to the East Indies as well? The question was answered in practice because *Romani pontificis* was included among the privileged faculties accorded the religious orders—mainly Franciscans, Dominicans and Jesuits—active in missionary work throughout the world. Through the "communication of privileges" the constitution came to be applied in any missionary territory in the world, including North America. (Plöchl, *Geschichte Des Kirchenrechts,* Wien, 1965, p. 314)
51. *Op. cit.*, p. 315.
52. *Ibid.*
53. Denzinger-Schönmetzer, n. 1988, pp. 439–440
This constitution was applied to Angola, Ethiopia and Brazil, as well as to persons living "in other regions of the Indies."
54. *Op. cit.*, p. 315.
55. *Ibid.*
56. *Op. cit.*, pp. 316–318.

15. THE AGE OF SECULARIZATION

It is obvious that within a decade after the Council of Trent adjourned in December of 1563 the Roman Catholic teaching concerning divorce and remarriage was linked inextricably with the Church's teaching concerning the sacramentality of marriage. If the former teaching were to stand and to be kept believable even to Catholics themselves, the latter would have to be held firm and be vindicated in a way understandable to Catholics themselves. For if Paul III and Pius V could extend the use of the Pauline privilege—or, said more accurately, if they could use their power "to bind and to loose"—to dissolve even consummated marriages, they must have seen marriage's indissolubility to lie elsewhere than in its being a non-voidable contract, and even elsewhere than in its being consummated as such a contract. The only other trait of marriage in which indissolubility could be located is its sacramentality, where a given marriage is in fact a sacrament.

But even this was not enough, as we have seen. The Church had already for centuries acknowledged the dissolution by entry into religious life of the sacramental marriages of Catholic spouses, but only where they could be verified as unconsummated. So by 1580 the locus of indissolubility, the fortress where it lived and survived, was its consummated sacramentality. Only that marriage was held to be finally indissoluble, even against papal power to dissolve, where it is a sacrament and is consummated as a sacrament. It thus became essential for its marital regulation that the Church be able to verify which marriages are sacraments and which are consummated as sacraments.

To accomplish this it was crucial that the doctrine of marriage the sacrament be fixed, stand firm, and be explained in a way that might convince at least interested Catholic minds. The doctrine was fixed clearly enough, as we have seen in the first of Trent's canons on marriage. But if its standing firm as a rule of conduct in the Catholic countries of Europe depended on its being explained convincingly, the explanation never came. The causes of this failure were multiple, and one of them could hardly be

405

laid as a charge against the theologians. Along with the Protestants there were Catholics in Europe who were beyond being convinced by any reasoning coming from the Church. In their souls the passion for independence, for the assertion of national autonomy and the unhindered regulation of their own lives, swept away any other consideration.

But most importantly, the theology of marriage was at this moment in its history once again coopted by and made an accessory to another Catholic dispute. We have already seen the beginning of this in Marsilius of Padua and in Occam, and in the conduct of Ludwig of Bavaria. The dispute belonged properly to ecclesiology; it centered in the division between Church and state of power and authority over the Catholic peoples of Europe, and by now of Europe's colonies. The Church had claimed and exercised almost exclusive authority over marriage matters for centuries. Now the secular rulers—the Catholic secular rulers—set about reclaiming the authority that they pointed out accurately had been theirs before the disintegration of the Roman empire and its judicial system. Their case for retaking this authority and the Church's counter-case were what subsumed the theology of marriage the sacrament. For no reasonably faithful Catholic would deny that the Church has the right to regulate its sacraments. But precisely there the Catholic princes concentrated their claim: the marriage of two Christians is not all and only a sacrament. It is first a secular reality, a contract—a natural and then a civil contract. This contract can be deemed a sacrament and celebrated as such. But this does not void its nature as first a civil contract. And who could deny that such contracts come properly under civil authority? It is for this authority to say which are the impediments that block the forming of the contract, to establish such impediments, to dispense from them, and, where they are removable, to remove them.

It took no keen prescience to foresee that divorce and remarriage would sooner or later be in the lists. For underlying the secular claim to authority over the contract of marriage was the assumption that in Christian marriages the contract and sacrament are separate. This necessarily demanded an answer to the question asking how the separable sacrament is related to the contract, and an answer to the question asking what the sacrament is. Both questions were to be answered in a way that would in consequence destroy the sacrament's holding power.

Here is the concern of this chapter: first to detail briefly the history of the Catholic challenge to the Church's claim to exclusive authority over Christian marriage contracts; then to examine the explanation of the relationship between contract and sacrament offered by the secular rulers to justify their claiming authority over the contract; finally to examine a few of the typical explanations by both Popes and theologians intended to show the inseparability of contract and sacrament, and intended to show thence the holding power of the sacrament that creates the indissolubility of Christian marriages.

The Royalist Challenge

The name "royalist" designates those Catholics—jurists, philosophers, theologians and statesmen of the seventeenth and eighteenth centuries—who sought to establish secular jurisdiction over the marriages of Europe's Catholic peoples. It is not accurate to see their precursors in Marsilius of Padua, Occam, Ludwig of Bavaria or the Protestant reformers. These all challenged the authority of the Catholic bishops at its root. The royalists never did this. They acknowledged that authority, but they sought to restrict it to religious and spiritual matters. And insisting that the marriage contract is not a religious but a secular entity, they logically sought to take it under secular jurisdiction. Their real precursors were the Scholastic philosophers and jurists, among them some of the fathers of Trent—with Melchior Cano principal among these—who had drawn too resolute a distinction between the sacrament in marriage and the contract.

One of the first and most influential arguments for the royalist position was made in 1620 by the archbishop of Spoleto, Marcantonio de Dominis, in his essay *De Republica Christiana.*[1] He reasoned his case from two assumptions, but came from both to the same conclusion. First, assuming marriage is now a sacrament, yet in the beginnning of the race God instituted it as a natural contract. Christ later sought to restore marriage to its original monogamy and to make it indissoluble. But these are only accessory characteristics of a marriage. Christ did not try to change its nature, which is that of a contract—first natural and then civil. The regulation of civil contracts belongs by nature to civil authority. The Church's authority is limited to only what is religious about marriage, and this is something accessory to the contract. The sacrament and its indissolubility, being religious entities, are accessory to the contract.

Or if one begins with the assumption that marriage is not now a sacrament, the same conclusion follows. (In fact de Dominis did not consider the marriages of Christians to be sacraments. He thought St. Paul's mind in 1 Corinthians 7 had been misinterpreted; he did not think Christ's forbidding the dismissing of wives instituted sacramentality.)

Whichever assumption one took, implicit in the obvious conclusion was a second and not-so-obvious conclusion. If the civil marital contract stands by itself distinctly from the sacrament, which is only a religious accessory to it, and if, as Catholic doctrine has it, indissolubility is in this or that marriage only because it is a sacrament, it follows that indissolubility is not a trait of the contract itself. It too is no more than something accessory to it, only a religious imposition on the contract. And it is a trait with which secular authority is by nature unconcerned.

In France this theory was applied to conduct by the monarch himself. When Gaston of Orleans, the younger brother of Louis XIII, married the daughter of the king's hated enemy, the Duke of Lorraine, Louis feared that the succession might pass to the house of Lorraine. He declared his brother's marriage null before the Parliament of Paris on September 5, 1634. Gaston challenged this ruling, and Louis took his case to the Assembly of the Clergy, which supported his decree of nullity. The discussion and debate which followed the ruling and the approval created the Gallican theory of jurisdiction in marriage matters. As outlined by Hennequin, a professor at the Sorbonne, it hardly differed from that of de Dominis.

Hennequin insisted that in making marriage a sacrament Christ changed nothing in the civil contract.

> In elevating the contract to the dignity of a sacrament Our Lord Jesus Christ only grafted the sacrament into the civil contract, which was in turn already grafted into the natural contract. He no more than imposed, attached, inserted it as something accessory to an essential foundation . . . but even after this elevation that contract remained unchanged.[2]

In his *Regia in Matrimonium Potestas* (The Royal Authority over Marriage) another Gallican theoretician, Jean Launoy, explained that a marriage is a contract, like a sale, and that in the matter of contracts secular authority rules all conditions demanded by the common good. In the following century Léridant, in his *Examen de Deux Questions Importantes sur le Mariage concernant la Puissance Civile* (1753), repeated the same theory, adding that the sacrament is found in the nuptial blessing. It was this that Christ added to the contract to sanctify it and to confer grace on the spouses. And it is over this alone, the sacrament understood as the nuptial blessing, that the Church has authority. Its most important exercise of authority is to determine if the parties are worthy of the nuptial blessing.

Neither Launoy nor Léridant was given pause by Canons 4 and 12 of the Council of Trent asserting the juridical and judicial authority of the Church over Christian marriages. They held that these are only disciplinary canons, that the term "Church" in Canon 4 refers not to churchmen but to the Christian sovereigns,[3] and that in any case the canons and decrees of the Council had never been allowed promulgation in France and consequently were ineffective there.

The Philosophers of the Enlightenment

The men of the Enlightenment were concerned not to profit by the distinction between sacrament and contract in marriage and claim thence authority for civil rulers over the latter. What they did was to take matters the obvious next step and widen the distinction to separation.

Michel Montaigne set the emotional tone of this challenge in the eighteenth century, writing in Book 2, Chapter 15 of his *Essais:*

> We have thought to knot more firmly the bonds of our marriages by getting rid of every way to dissolve them. But the more the bond of constraint has been tightened, ⟨ ⟩ more the bond of will and affection has been loosened and debased. By contrast that which kept marriage among the Romans so long in honor and security was the freedom to dissolve it if they wished. They loved their wives all the more because they could lose them. And with full license to divorce, more than five hundred years passed before anyone made use of it.[4]

In fact these philosophers did not so much reason that because marriage is fundamentally a civil contract it is vulnerable to dissolution, and that the civil authority to which marriage belongs can dissolve it. They argued rather that the love which holds spouses together transcends the control of law. No authority can create, compel and preserve husbands' and wives' regard for one another. To compel them to stay together—to demand of a cuckolded husband that he live a life of sexual continence—is to contradict nature and to offend against justice. Obviously this took the challenge right to familiar Scholastic ground, beyond the religious reasons against divorce. Aquinas, Bonaventure, Scotus and the others had argued for permanence in marriage as a demand of nature. Now the philosophers argued that this same nature demands the availability of divorce.

In the *Dictionnaire de Philosophie* (1764) under the term *Adultère,* Voltaire pled the cause of divorce, invoking in its favor equity, history and the favorable example of every people "except the Roman Catholic people." Helvétius in his treatise *De l'Esprit* and d'Holbach in his *Christianisme Dévoilé* (Christianity Unmasked) (1767) and his *Morale Universelle* (1776) called for a reform in civil law that would establish the availability of divorce. Their thesis in support of the demand was that love enjoys a natural freedom from civil regulation. And Montesquieu added with tender irony (in his *Lettres Persanes,* n. 116) that nothing would contribute more to spouses' mutual attachment than their awareness that either of them could dissolve the marriage.[5]

Others, espying a threat to the needs and rights of children, argued for spouses' right to divorce, but only when their children had been reared. In his *Social Contract* Rousseau wrote that " . . . the oldest of all societies and the only natural society is the family. . . . A child is bound to its father only as long as it needs him for survival. But as soon as this need ends, this natural bond is dissolved." And again in his *Encyclopédie,* under the word *Mariage,* he wrote, "A husband should remain with his wife until their children are grown and of an age to survive by themselves or on their inheritance; . . . although the child's needs demand that the marital union of wife and husband last longer than that of other animals, there seems to me nothing in the nature and goods of this union demanding that husband and wife be obliged to remain together all their lives after having reared their children and left to them the means by which to live."[6]

Clearly enough, while Voltaire and Rousseau met head-on the Scholastic teaching that the needs of spouses and children demand permanence in marriage, by arguing contrarily that these needs are not permanent and at times even demand dissolution, they also sought, at least by implication, to simply cut the ground from under a kindred Catholic position. This was the philosophic-juridical establishment of indissolubility-by-definition, the Scholastic jurists' invention anew of the very nature of marriage that put the trait of indissolubility into its definition. These philosophers refused to think of the definition, and the "nature" in whose defense they argued was the nature not of marriage but of the spouses. Theirs was a humanism echoing faintly that of Erasmus in the sixteenth century, but intoning more clearly a humanism that was to be taken up by Catholics in the second half of the twentieth century. This would be a humanism grown into a personalism that asks not "What is good for marriage?" but "What is good for the man and the woman in the marriage?"

The Philosophers of Natural Law and the Law of Nations

Outside France this "naturalizing" of marriage in Europe—as a first step toward its eventual secularizing—was taken up by the School of Natural Law. This school's founder was Hugo Grotius. But its moral and social philosophy was worked out most systematically by another German, Samuel von Pufendorf, in his *De Jure Naturae et Gentium* (On the Law of Nature and of Nations) of 1672 and in his *De Officio Hominis et Civis* (On the Duty of Man and Citizen) of 1673.

Book 6 of the *De Jure Naturae et Gentium* opens with a long chapter on marriage. The main elements of its position are, first, that the right ordering of human society requires that the race be propagated according to the laws of marriage. Men and women have an obligation to contribute to this propagation, but they are to fulfill it variably according to positive civil law. This law can establish impediments but not in such a way as to hinder natural freedom. Polygamy is not absolutely contrary to the law of nature, but the surer way to have peace in families is that each man have but one wife. Pufendorf condemns acts contrary to nature and promiscuous and irresponsible sexual conduct.

Thus far he disagrees with nothing in Catholic doctrine. But the agreement ends when he declares his mind on divorce and remarriage.

He begins with the assumption about marriage's nature that the later Scholastics had handed down, that marriage is a contract. Given this nature, he is fundamentally opposed to divorce, not only because in almost every instance it would violate the contract, but because the divorce he knows of—the dismissing of one spouse by the other—is legally impossible except for one kind of cause. One party to the contract is not free to void it simply on his or her unilateral initiative. Moreover, until the children born to the marriage are able to survive on their own, the parents have a natural obligation to maintain the family and sustain them in it.

> As is supposed at the outset, every pact implies that one party cannot depart from it but with the consent of the other, or if the other has violated it. Therefore, it will be repugnant to natural law if one of the married pair leaves the other against his will, when the latter has violated no part of the marriage pact; and this merely to better his position, or because it suits his fancy.[7]

But as Pufendorf hints here, there are exceptions to this restraint. When one party to a contract violates one or more of its substantial conditions, the other is no longer held to it. So it is with the marital contract. The innocent spouse is not bound to it if the other violates it, for example by adultery. And here, to reason his case, he makes use of the patristic commonplace concerning the primary end, or goal, of marriage. It is for the reproduction of offspring. Therefore serious offenses against marriage's nature at this point violate the contract and justify the innocent spouse's freeing himself or herself from the marriage.

> We must inquire, further, whether what is common to all other pacts also holds true of marriage, namely that when the primary articles, at least, of the pact have been violated by one of the parties the other secures thereby the power to withdraw from the marriage. It appears that this can safely be answered in the affirmative in the case of the principal articles. For the bond is entered into for the procreation of offspring, which end requires the mutual service of their bodies. Therefore, by mere natural law one of the two will be freed from the marriage bond when the other is guilty of malicious desertion, as well as of obstinate and voluntary refusal to perform the due rights of marriage.[8]

Adultery violates the marital contract in the same way because a man has the right to gain marriage's end by procreating offspring he knows with certainty to be his own.[9]

At this point Pufendorf emphasizes his claim that his argument draws only on the law of nature. He denies that the right of divorce for the causes he has just named is one given by divine positive law (he almost certainly has the exceptive clause in Matthew 19 here in mind). He adds the flourish (this time with the Catholic interpretation of Matthew's dismissal in mind) that divorce in this case truly frees the innocent party to remarry.

It appears, then, that the reason why adultery and malicious desertion are recorded as a sufficient cause for divorce is not due to a special positive law of God, as though these were the two exceptions added to the absolute stability of marriage, but to the fact that the common nature of pacts is such that when one party does not abide by the agreements, the other is no longer bound by them. So much so that not only is the injured party no longer required to cohabit with such a perfidious consort, but he or she may marry again. Whatever the canon law urges to the contrary is nonsense.[10]

For Pufendorf deciding that much was easy. But now he takes up a purported cause justifying divorce that must have been the more difficult to judge because it was probably the more commonly adduced in his society. What if one spouse treats the other cruelly and neglectfully? Must the victim bear this patiently and until the death of one of them ends the marriage? Or has he or she the right to end the misery by divorce?

In dialectical fashion he first offers the reason arguing against divorce in these circumstances. A person enters marriage for its primary end, procreation, and this can be realized even despite the cruelty of one's spouse. Being loved or being despised and mistreated is a secondary condition in marriage. This is especially true where a marriage is contracted expressly for the distinct ends of procreation and (in Scholastic language) of mutual help. This is a contract made for multiple goods. But a contract can still bind under one of these (especially if it is the principal good) even if it be violated under another (especially if this in turn is a secondary good).

But now the other facet of his dialectic enters and carries the argument, and it does so by joining psychology to law. For granted that securing the primary end of marriage is theoretically possible even with a cruel spouse, yet in real life no man or woman would *want* or seek to have intercourse with a spouse who acted with habitual contempt or cruelty. Consequently the contractual good which is cooperation in procreation involves inextricably the good of love and respect. And consequently too the destroying of the bond of respect and love inevitably involves the violating of the contract to cooperate in procreation.[11]

Pufendorf proposes this second facet of the dialectic in the following way.

> Now if the marriage was contracted in this form [as a contract of several goods], it is apparently possible for the performance of the dues which pertain to the bringing forth of issue to be continued, even when the wife has by her vexatious manners rendered herself no longer suited to constant cohabitation. But since it is not likely that she with whom association is intolerable can fit herself for the debt, or that a man will not turn from a

body which houses so crabbed a guest, since a man will scarcely
want issue of one whom he hates, it is the regular custom for
husband and wife to make an agreement, by one and the same
pact, regarding the two goods of the mutual service of the body
and association of family life, which are so inextricably bound
together that the breaking off of the one appears to involve the
severing of the other.[12]

At this point he abandons the cool detachment of the philosopher-
jurist to insist with vehement rhetoric, as well as logic, that if the marital
contract is violated in its primary end, the innocent spouse is free to
remarry after dissolving the marriage, and that it is a violation of natural
law to demand that he remain unmarried on the assumption that his first
marriage still exists despite the impossibility of continuing to realize in it
this primary end.[13]

Therefore it is repugnant to natural law for husband and
wife to separate from the association of table and bed, because of
intolerable manners and incompatible temper, and yet to maintain the bond of marriage which prohibits them from changing
their position for the better.... For it is absurd to say that the
bond of a pact still holds when no part of the debt which flows
from that pact can or should be performed. And although we
concede that the party on whose shoulders rests the blame for
separation is perhaps justly punished by this method, yet the
innocent is injured, being forced to pay for another's sins, and
compelled to a life of celibacy, perhaps highly inconvenient and
intolerable.[14]

Now disagreement with the Catholic teaching on indissolubility is at
its most radical. Now it is not a conclusion drawn from the distinction
between contract and sacrament, and thence from their separability. It is
not the product of a discrepant reading of the New Testament divorce
passages. Neither is it merely claimed as an escape route whose availability
is needed as flight from a miserable marriage. It is almost—although not
quite—a pointed contradiction of the Catholic philosophic-juridical definition of marriage that wrote indissolubility into marriage as a natural
institution. This disagreement rewrites the definition once again, but this
time writes indissolubility out of it and puts dissolubility in its place. It
goes back to what the Greek philosophers and the Roman jurists of their
classical epoch took for granted about marriage's dissolubility. For them
marriage was an instrumental relationship-institution; that is, it exists in
order to realize a good outside itself. Spouses must remain together as long
as the full realizing of this goal—procreation and nurture—is for them
both possible and needed for the good of society. But when realizing its
goal is no longer either possible or needed, the reason for their remaining

together lapses. There is no reason blocking the dissolution of their marriage.

In 1689 John Locke published a most transparent version of this "natural law" of dissolubility in his Essay Concerning the True Origin, Extent and End of Civil Government (Of Civil Government, Second Treatise). His argument was exactly drawn from natural law as he understood it. Thus, the natural end of marriage is the procreation and proper nurture of children. To realize this end husband and wife must remain together until their children are duly educated, provided for, and able to live on their own. But once all this is accomplished the reason demanding that they stay together lapses, and they may dissolve their marriage.

> But though there are ties upon mankind which make the conjugal bonds more firm and lasting in man than the other species of animals, yet it would give one reason to inquire why this compact, where procreation and education are secured, and inheritance taken care of, may not be made determinable, either by consent, or at a certain time, or upon certain conditions, as well as any other voluntary compacts, there being no necessity in the nature of the thing, nor to the end of it, that it should always be for life—I mean to such as are under no restraint of any positive law which ordains all such contracts to be perpetual.

The Final Secularizing of Marriage

We have seen thus far the slow but persistent process by which marriage in Christian Europe was brought to the status of a secular institution, in which it was stripped gradually of its character as a religious relationship lived under the authority of the Church, and turned over to civil authority as a purely human relationship, a civil contract. And in this newly asserted public identity marriage was also stripped of its one dimension—the sacrament—that even the Church considered the cause of its indissolubility. It lay vulnerable to the combined will of the parties and authority of the civil rulers to dissolve it by divorce.

This process was substantially completed during the last quarter of the eighteenth century, although with varying degrees of thoroughness in the different states of Europe. Indeed the completing was done mainly during the eleven years from 1781 to 1792.[15]

In the Catholic Austro-Hungarian Empire Joseph II instituted his rule of enlightened despotism. His vice-chancellor Cobenzl declared that marriage is an entity that is mainly civil and only accessorily religious. Accordingly in 1781 Joseph made a first move toward asserting control over it by claiming for the bishops of his realm the authority to grant dispensations from impediments without having recourse to Rome. Subsequently he reserved to imperial authority everything that concerned the civil contract. All judicial determinations of marriage were given to the civil courts. Priests who blessed marriages (in Joseph's mind this was the conferring of the sacrament) were said to do so under civil authority.

In 1786, Joseph's brother, Leopold II, established the same secular reform in Tuscany.

The first obvious step toward secularization in France at this time was the edict of the Parliament of Paris in November of 1787 that allowed Protestants to marry either before a priest functioning as a civil magistrate or before a civil judge. The same edict stated that judicial actions affecting Protestant marriages were henceforth to come from civil courts.[16] (If the modern student should wonder that this be considered a step in stripping the Church of its authority, it helps to recall that still two centuries after the Protestant reform Protestants were regarded by Catholic authorities as dissidents within the one Church, and therefore still subject to this Church's authority.)

The secularizing was brought to a climax during the final deliberations on the Constitution of 1791. Between September 3 and 14 the assembly wrote Title 2, Article 7: "The law holds marriage to be only a civil contract." This much established the principle whose practical application was formulated in two statutes a year later, on September 20. One of them, determining the mode in which civil contracts are established, in its Title 4 formulated a purely civil legislation for marrying. The other legislated the availability of divorce. It derived this availability constitutionally from the assumptions first of civil liberty for persons, and then of the civil contract character of marriage. Religious ceremonies at a wedding were not forbidden, but they were to have no civil effect; the parties to the ceremony were not to be considered married in virtue of them.

Although Napoleon Bonaparte undid much of this work of the French Revolution and in a sense "re-established" the Catholic religion in France, he kept the substance of the marriage legislation incorporated in the Constitution of 1791, and included it in his own *Code Civil.* This was but a part of his intent to make the Church a creature of his state and to make it serve his own ends. Thus Article 191 of the *Code* declared the following:

> Any marriage that has not been contracted publicly and has not been solemnized before a competent civil magistrate can be attacked by the spouses themselves, by the parents, by the ascendants, by all those who have a natural and current interest in it, as well as by a public minister.

Bonaparte's legislation on marriage was completed between 1801 and 1803; it became Title 5 of the *Code.* (Marriage was to be regulated by Articles 63–76 and 144–228.) It maintains the separation of the contract and the sacrament, and it establishes the availability of civil divorce. And in his *Code Pénal* (Articles 199 and 200) he ordered that the civil witnessing of marital consent was always to precede any religious ceremony.

Most of the other nations of Europe fell into line during the nineteenth century, all of them influenced in some degree by the *Code Napoléon* to establish marriage in their laws as a civil contract. Italy put this legislation in its civil code in 1866, Switzerland in 1874, Germany in 1875. The French introduced it in Holland in 1795, where it was incorporated in the new code of 1833. Belgium did the same after its separation from Holland in 1830. Spain did not adopt this legislation until the ascendancy of republican government in 1931. Until then civil marriage was permitted only if the parties declared themselves to be not members of the Catholic Church. In 1929 the concordat between the Italian government of Premier Mussolini and the Roman see recaptured for the Church authority over the sacrament of marriage, and marriage under this authority was conceded full civil effects. The Church's courts were acknowledged to have exclusive competence over cases alleging nullity and those seeking the dissolution of unconsummated marriages. But the state retained civil marriage, so that in Italy a Catholic can make marital consent before civil authorities which is accepted by the state as creating a marriage.

In all these states except Spain and Italy it was taken for granted that with marriage established as a civil contract ruled by civil authority, dissolution by this same authority is both possible and available. In 1976 this availability was finally put into Italian law by national referendum—over the long but futile objection of Pope Paul VI and the other bishops of Italy.

Further Development of the Supporting Theory

However much or little the changing theory of marriage spurred the change in attitude of Europe's Christian rulers, we have already seen the beginnings of this theory in the sixteenth century and its elaboration in the seventeenth by such scholars as Pufendorf and Locke. The development continued at a slowing pace into the eighteenth century and the early nineteenth, and halted there. In the Empire the Josephist jurists, Pehem, Rieger, Eybel, applied to marriage the *ius maiestaticum,* with the familiar consequence of separating sacrament from contract and laying the latter open to dissolution.

Immanuel Kant devoted Part One of his *Metaphysics of Morals* to a study of the theory of rights.[17] There he defined marriage nearly as Scotus had defined it in the fourteenth century, as the union of two persons of diverse sex who grant to one another reciprocal rights over their bodies for the duration of their lives. Each acquires a real and personal right over the other; each possesses the other as a thing but must treat the other as a person—for the principle of freedom would be violated if they tried to possess a person as a person, or if one person treated the other as a thing.

But in his defining of marriage Kant omitted an element the Scholastics held essential. This was the primary end of marriage that is procreation and nurture. Without saying that a marriage is a civil contract vulnerable to dissolution by civil authority, Kant nevertheless omitted from his definition of marriage the principal reason for permanence claimed for it since the classical Greeks, namely the need of children that the parents remain together.

The man whose theory of marriage broke with virtually all of the European past, except—and unbeknownst to himself—with what Hugh of St. Victor had written in the twelfth century, was Georg Wilhelm Friedrich Hegel. And by a kind of irony-in-prospect, the twentieth-century understanding of marriage that was to most closely replicate his was— again unbeknownst to its author—that of Pope Paul VI in his encyclical letter of 1968, *Humanae vitae.* For Pope Paul a man and a woman in marriage "through the gift of their selves that they make to one another, a gift unique to themselves . . . work toward a communion of their beings for the sake of a shared personal perfection. . . ."[18] The love that Paul described as specifically and even uniquely marital ". . . is not . . . simply a movement of instinct and emotion; it is also and especially an act of free will. This love is meant to last and to grow by means of the joys and sorrows of everyday life, to such a point that the husband and wife become one in heart and soul, and together realize their human fulfillment."[19]

A union of persons in which human perfection is attained was for Hegel too the epitome of his understanding of marriage. In his dense prose he defined marriage descriptively in a way that contained the leitmotif of all his philosophy, that is, development by evolution of consciousness through ever higher forms of spiritual existence.

> As an immediately accessible kind of moral relationship marriage involves, first of all, the dimension that is physical life; and as a substantive relationship, life in its totality—namely the actuality of the race and its life-process. But beyond that, marriage as this purely private, self-existent, external unity of the sexes is, in self-consciousness, transformed into a spiritual, self-aware love.
>
> Added reflection: Marriage is essentially a moral relationship. In the past it has been regarded, especially in the major theories of natural law, only from its physical aspect, only from that which belongs to it from nature. It was dealt with as a sexual relationship. Consequently any path to a higher perception of it was closed off.
>
> It is just as crude to conceive of it as a mere civil contract, a conception of it that even Kant harbored. This is a conception in which the parties commit themselves by reciprocal acts of will to a contract; and marriage is debased to a reciprocal contractual exchange and contractual use.
>
> A third damaging conception of it saw marriage only as

love. For a love that is only an emotion delivers marriage over to passing caprice, to a character in which morality can find no place. . . .[20]

Hegel does not deny that this is what marriage has been and still in his time is for many persons. But there can be a dimension of it in some persons that transcends the physical, the juridical, the emotional. This dimension develops where two wills consent to form a oneness of persons.

> From the subjective side marriage can have as its source the unique attraction of the two persons who enter the relationship. . . . But its objective source is in the free consent of the persons—most especially in their will to make of themselves one person, to give over their natural and individual personhood into this oneness. From the conventional point of view this oneness seems a denigration of the self. But it is really a freeing of the selves because in it they rise to their substantive self-consciousness.[21]

It is hardly necessary to point out that when Hegel writes of the union of persons in marriage, he goes far beyond the union that Paul VI had in mind. For the latter the union leaves the persons distinct; it takes place in their interaction of intellect, emotion, will, body—none of which is the substance itself of a person. For Hegel these uses of consciousness are precisely what are substantive in a person, so that when union in them is realized, the persons become one in a substantive way.

But this extraordinary conception of marriage as a fusing of the two persons into one, what does it say of permanence, even of indissolubility? What must have alarmed the Catholic authorities who came to know it was its locating of indissolubility at the level, and even at the moment in the history of a marriage that it does. It does not find indissolubility in the definition itself abstractly antecedent to any real-life marriage. It does not find it in the needs of children born to a marriage, and certainly not in the sacrament, which Hegel never mentions. (His view of all of reality as evolving consciousness would not let him see any sensate conduct as an imaging of higher, supra-sensate reality, since for him these were not two distinct dimensions of reality. Neither could he acknowledge any sensate conduct as an instrumental medium through which a transcendent Creator sanctifies human beings. He acknowledged no creation and no transcendent Creator—indeed no transcendence other than the goal toward which evolving consciousness continally strives, and in so striving transcends itself. Therefore he acknowledged no elevation, no holiness coming from outside this evolutionary process as a gracious gift to the conscious entities involved in it.)

For Hegel indissolubility was, rather, a quality of a marriage realized when the two distinct persons, fused into one person, reach an exquisite level of consciousness. It is not something prior and given in all marriages; it is a state attained by some persons' striving toward and attaining a certain quality of union. It is a property of the moral reality of a marriage, and this is a reality created by the spouses themselves. They *make* their marriage indissoluble—those who trust, love and share at a certain intensity.

> The moral dimension of marriage consists in the persons' consciousness of this unity as their substantive goal; and consists therefore in their love and their trust, and in their sharing of their entire existence as individual persons.
> In this attitude and in this reality their sexual desire diminishes to a mere physical feature, to a desire that will vanish in its very satisfying. But the spiritual bond takes its rightful place as the substance of the relationship. It rises above the caprice of the passions and the transience of infatuation to an inherent indissolubility.[22]

Inherent indissolubility? This would find a fervent welcome in Catholic circles, except that the inherence is not in a contract itself nor in a contract-become-sacrament. It is in a union of two exquisitely developed consciousnesses. It is an indissolubility realized by a man and a woman at the end of a process of becoming one. Brought down to earth, of course, Hegel's vision of marriage leaves questions about the permanence of the ordinary marriages of ordinary men and women, marriages which never reach the fusion into oneness where he alone finds indissolubility.

The Catholic Reaction

What Luther presumed in challenging the Catholic Church's claim to jurisdiction over all Christian marriages, and in seeking to move that jurisdiction back to princes and civil judges, was that these princes and judges would themselves be faithful Christians. He sought to break Roman ecclesiastical power over these marriages but intended also that they move over under civil authority wielded by Christians.

What he did not reckon with was the birth of that creature of first the Enlightenment and then of the French Revolution—the secular state. And once unreligious and even anti-religious men in civil society conceived as secular interpreted marriage as an institution that has been developed through the centuries in order to provide offspring for this society, these men logically saw no reason why the legitimate authority in such a society should not command exclusive authority over this institution.

It was a part of the same logic for them to think that since marriage is a human invention, there are no characteristics or exigencies within it transcending the authority of the secular state. When this authority on investigation agrees with the plea of the parties in a marriage that prolongation of their relationship is damaging to them, to their children, and through their children damaging to civil society, there is no cause overriding the authority's decision to dissolve the marriage.

If the parties in a marriage happen to have a religious affiliation and wish to form their relationship in a religious ceremony, the secular authorities would not object provided all understood that the ceremony asserts no exercise of ecclesiastical authority *in place* of the secular authority of the state—unless the state wishes, as it does in the United States, to enfranchise religious ministers with its own civil authority to witness and verify the marriages of its citizens.

Obviously if the Catholic *magisterium* were to break this logic and its consequences, it had to begin by disproving its major premise, namely its assumption that marriage as a natural human relationship is non-religious and secular. The disproof would have to consist of a proof of marriage's natural religiousness. And the most obvious evidence sustaining this was the record in Genesis of God's inventing marriage when creating the first human beings as a heterosexual pair and commanding them to populate the earth and to master it and care for it as a pair. This is evidence that the Protestants themselves could not dispute.

Unfortunately for the effectiveness of the disproof this evidence was cited just at the time that biblical scholars, ironically the best of them confessing Lutherans, were beginning to undermine the historical factuality of the Genesis creation poem and Garden parable. It was no help either that the newly developed sciences of anthropology and paleontology were gathering evidence that the human race had begun unimaginably earlier than 4000 B.C. and possibly not in the Middle East.

The Papal Documents

The direct and serious Catholic moves to break the secularist logic came from the Popes of the nineteenth century. They were directed at the secularizing of marriage in the so-called Catholic countries of Europe and Latin America and the consequent opening to civil divorce. But these moves had been preceded in the eighteenth century by four minor documents. On April 11, 1741 Pope Benedict XIV had sent his encyclical letter *Matrimonii* to the bishops of Poland recalling them to the discipline of indissoluble marriage. He repeated the scriptural interpretation, traditional by his time, that in declaring and commanding every marriage's indissolubility with his words, "What God has joined man must not separate," Christ made of marriage a sacrament—when contracted in the Church.

> The lasting and indissoluble bond of marriage—the sanctity of which was declared in the beginning by Adam, and confirmed graciously by Christ with these words ... so elevating it by evangelical grace and making it a great sacrament in the Church—has now been brought to Our attention as being easily

dissolved. This is so in some Catholic regions of the world, especially in that flourishing kingdom of Poland, as if marriage were not contracted under the guardianship of the natural and divine law, the evangelical precepts and the approved canons.

On November 23 of that same year Benedict issued an apostolic constitution on the same subject, titled *Dei miseratione.* In it he reiterated God's invention of marriage as well as the natural demand for its permanence.

Since the matrimonial contract was instituted by God, inasmuch as it is a natural institution whose aim is the education of the offspring and the conservation of the other benefits of marriage, it is suitable that it be perpetual and indissoluble.

On September 16, 1747 he issued the constitution *Apostolici ministerii* aimed at ending the practice whereby some male Jewish converts to Catholicism in central Europe divorced their wives after their baptism and did so according to rabbinic law. For them he recommended the use of the Pauline privilege when their wives would not live peacefully with them after the baptism. But he made it clear that the use of the privilege, not the rabbinic divorce, dissolved their first marriage.

The fourth document was Pope Pius VI's letter *Deessemus nobis* of September 16, 1788, to the bishop of Motula in the kingdom of Naples. The latter had been authorized by the king to serve as judge in a civil court, and serving in this capacity the bishop had handed down judgment in a nullity trial. Pius' correction consisted of assuring him that Canon 12 of Trent's twenty-fourth session reserved absolutely all marriage cases of Catholics exclusively to ecclesiastical judges, even when, as in the case in question, there was no more at issue than the finding of a fact.

The first substantial Catholic counter-attack against the secular encroachment on ecclesiastical authority in marriage cases was the same Pius VI's apostolic constitution *Auctorem fidei* of August 28, 1794. It was substantial in scope, being directed "to all the faithful" instead of to this or that bishop or prince or region. What first provoked Pius was the memorandum of Leopold II, archduke of Tuscany, sent to the bishops of his duchy in 1786. It contained fifty-seven articles by which Leopold proposed to reform ecclesiastical discipline. The archbishop of Tuscany, Scipio Ricci, gathered a synod of the bishops of Tuscany which met from September 18 to 28 that same year. It took the name "Synod of Pistoia" and published "The Acts and Decrees of the Synod of Pistoia," a document dominated by Jansenist and Febronian thinking.

Pius' reaction to the document and its articles was to publish the above-named constitution. It listed eighty-five propositions coming from the synod, slightly changed from their original formulation, and condemned them. Proposition 59 in Pius' list contains the denial of the

Church's essential right to establish and to dispense from impediments in the marriages of Christians, and the counter-claim that this right belongs by nature to the civil ruler.[23]

Pius' reaction to Pistoia touched only by faintest implication the matter of divorce and remarriage. But it bore immediately upon the claim over marriage by civil authority in Europe and elsewhere. And this was an authority that was soon to understand itself as secular in a sense not intended by Archduke Leopold and the Tuscan bishops, the secularity of non-religion and even anti-religion.

When, just under a century later, a secular government in this sense was established in Italy itself by Garibaldi, Mazzini and Cavour, Pope Pius IX published his *Syllabus of Errors,* on December 8, 1864. This is an inventory of eighty theological, religious, philosophical, anthropological and political propositions, arranged in ten sections, all condemned as in some degree contrary or harmful to Catholic belief or conduct.[24] Section 8 is titled "Errors Concerning Christian Marriage." It condemns ten propositions, six of them containing the philosophical and juridical thinking about marriage that warranted civil authorities' claim to be able to divorce even Christian marriages.[25] These six are the following:

Proposition 65: "That it can in no way be verified that Christ has raised marriage to the dignity of a sacrament."

Proposition 66: "That the sacrament in marriage is no more than something accessory to the contract and is separable from it; and that the sacrament itself consists of nothing more than the nuptial blessing."

Proposition 68: "That the Church has no power to establish invalidating impediments, but that this power belongs to civil authority, by whom the extant ecclesiastical impediments ought to be abolished."

Proposition 69: "That only in later centuries did the Church begin to establish invalidating impediments, and did this not by its own authority but by using authority lent it by civil rulers."

Proposition 73: "That a marriage in the true sense can be formed between two Christians by a merely civil contract; and that it is false to say either that the marriage contract between two Christians is in every case a sacrament, or that there is no contract where the sacrament is excluded."

Proposition 74: "That marriage cases and betrothals belong of their very nature under civil jurisdiction."

The Syllabus gets at the issue of divorce and remarriage in its proposition 67. It does so by reasserting the natural indissolubility of any marriage and denying the authority of civil rulers to divorce any—and does these, in turn, in the mode peculiar to a *syllabus errorum* by condemning the contrary opinions: "That the bond of marriage is not by the law of nature itself indissoluble, and that in various cases divorce properly so called can be executed by civil authority."

The condemnatory statement is careful to say that it is the bond of marriage that is indissoluble by virtue of natural law. This leaves the way open for the established Catholic teaching that the bond can nevertheless be dissolved by the authority in the Church that transcends nature and its law.

Implicit here also is a *processus* of legal logic that runs as follows. Where a marriage is a sacrament the bond is not separable from it. Therefore the bond is indissoluble by civil authority for two reasons: its own nature as indissoluble and its added character as a sacrament. But because the bond and the sacrament are, though not separable, nevertheless distinct, ecclesiastical authority is incapable of dissolving a sacramental marriage not because of the natural indissolubility of the bond but because of the supernatural inviolability of the sacrament. This caution is implied again in the second clause of the condemned proposition, where the opinion condemned is that civil authority is competent to dissolve marriages by divorce. Nothing is said there about, and the way is left open for, the competence of Catholic ecclesiastical authority to dissolve certain marriages.

Since the social philosophy of the time said that civil authority can dissolve marriages because as a matter of history marriage had existed as a secular reality ages before churchmen began to claim it as a religious contract subject only to their own authority, it was crucial to the Popes to verify the religiousness of marriage from its beginning in the human race. Especially crucial was it, at least for marriage in the Catholic countries, to reassert that Christ has made *all* Christian marriages sacraments, and that he did so by elevating the natural contract itself to the condition of a sacrament, and that as a consequence—to repeat a thought advanced above—the contract and the sacrament are inseparable.

Pope Leo XIII

This is what succeeding documents show the Popes doing. In his encyclical letter *Quod apostolici* of December 28, 1878, Leo XIII said that marriage "was instituted by God as indissoluble from the beginning of the world."[26]

In his fullest and most formal statement on marriage, the encyclical letter *Arcanum divinae sapientiae* of February 10, 1880, Leo set forth both the claims stated above.[27] First he recalled the institution of marriage by God himself at the beginning of creation.

> We recall what everyone knows, and what no one can doubt, that after God had formed man from the mud of the earth on the sixth day of creation, and had breathed into his face the breath of life, he wished to give to him a companion. In miraculous fashion he took her from his side while he slept. In his most provident care God thus intended that this married couple be the natural origin of all human beings.[28]

Leo had full confidence that the first two chapters of Genesis record actual events. And he had no hesitation about combining the creation poem of Genesis 1 (which tells of the Lord God's creating the first man and woman together in a single creative act) with the Garden narrative of Genesis 2 in such a way as to have Yahweh form the man alone from the earth on the sixth day of creation and afterward draw the woman from his body. He also read the Church's canonical definition of marriage back into this conflated account of marriage's origin, and found the definition's two "essential properties" in God's original design.

> And so that this union of husband and wife might cooperate more effectively with God's providential plan, it has from the very beginning contained two especially valuable and deeply ingrained characteristics, namely exclusivity and perpetuity.[29]

Did Leo see in the Yahwist author's comment on the union of the first man and woman—"For this reason a man shall leave father and mother and cling to his wife, and they shall be two in one flesh"—evidence of God's will that every marriage be indissoluble? He did, but not in virtue of the comment's coming from the Yahwist. It is such evidence, Leo implies, because Christ used the comment to declare his own mind on marriage's indissolubility and sealed it with his own judgment, "Therefore what God has joined man must not separate." Of Christ's declaration Leo said the following.

> In the Gospel we see Christ's authority declaring and verifying this clearly. He witnessed to the Jewish people and to his apostles that from its very institution marriage is to be of only two persons, the husband and wife; and that the bond of marriage is by God's will so closely and strongly joined that no human being can either dissolve or separate it.[30]

Leo then went on to recapitulate briefly the traditional theology of indissolubility—that Christ has raised the natural union among Christian spouses to the dignity of a sacrament, that this union is a sacrament because it images the marital love of Christ and the Church, and that therefore the natural permanence of this union is made all the more firm.

He then cited the *locus classicus* in 1 Corinthians in which Paul passed Christ's command on to that early Christian community: "To the married I proclaim—it is not I who do so, but the Lord—that a wife is not to be separated from her husband. And if she is in fact separated, she is either to remain unmarried or is to be reconciled to her husband (verse 10). . . . A wife is bound to the law as long as her husband lives; but if he dies, she is freed (verse 39)."[31]

Moving on to interpret this passage he inserted immediately the critical verse from Paul's Letter to the Ephesians, making it "It is for these reasons that marriage is 'a great sacrament' . . ."—misreading the meaning of the phrase but following the Scholastic tradition that finds evidence of marriage's sacramentality in its indissolubility. (He also, apparently without noticing it, came up against the difficulty created by saying, on the one hand, that any and every marriage is indissoluble, and implying on the other that Christ made marriage a sacrament by affirming its indissolubility. Did Leo mean to imply, as a logical consequence, that any and every marriage is a sacrament? And if he did, how might he have reconciled this with the Church's practice of dissolving some marriages on the ground that they are not sacramental?)

As civil divorce became the law and the custom in the secularized governments of traditionally Catholic countries it was inevitable that Catholic judges bound to administrate such law would be caught between the constitutional demands of their office and the religious demands of their Church. A decree of May 27, 1886 by the Congregation of the Holy Office ruled for French Catholic judges caught in just such a conflict. The decree is set out sequentially in an *expositio,* three *quaestiones* and a *responsum.* [32]

> *The Exposition:* The following *dubia* have been proposed to the Holy Roman Inquistion on June 25, 1885. The . . . Inquisition instructed all the Ordinaries in France and its territories concerning its law of civil divorce: "Taking into consideration the serious conditions of times, places and things, and granting that those who hold the office of magistrate and act as advocates in marriage cases need not resign their offices," the instruction set down conditions for this toleration, the second of which is this, that "[they may continue to function in office] provided that when they are compelled to judge the validity or nullity of marriage, as well as decide for separation from cohabitation, they never urge or render or defend a judgment that is repugnant to divine or ecclesiastical law."

> *The Questions:* (1) Is the following interpretation of this instruction that has been printed and published throughout France the correct one? Does a judge satisfy the instruction above when, in regard to a marriage valid in the eyes of the Church, he simply prescinds [in his decision] from such a true marriage and, in applying the civil law, decides that a divorce is possible and advisable, but in doing so intends no more than to apply civil effects and to dissolve the civil contract, and the terms of his judgment refer to these effects alone? In other words, does such a judgment handed down in this way not violate ecclesiastical law?

(2) After the judge has determined the possibility and the advisability of divorce, can the mayor, looking only to the civil effects and the civil contract (as explained above), hand down a decree of divorce even though the marriage remains valid in the eyes of the Church?

(3) Once the divorce has been decreed, and one party from that divorced marriage attempts a second marriage, can the mayor witness this marriage even though the first marriage remains valid in the eyes of the Church and the other spouse is still alive?

The Replies (confirmed by Pope Leo himself): Negative to all three questions.

Two years later, on September 24, 1888, the Sacred Penitentiary issued a reply that eased considerably the plight of a Catholic judge caught in such a conflict. This body determined in a particular case that a mayor who would otherwise be removed from office could hand down a decree of civil divorce after a civil judge had ruled that divorce was possible and advisable provided the former fulfilled two conditions:

(1) that he explain publicly the Catholic doctrine on marriage, and explain too that marriage cases belong exclusively under the jurisdiction of ecclesiastical judges; and (2) that in the divorce decree itself, and speaking as a public magistrate, he declare that he is ruling only in regard to the civil contract and the civil effects, and that before God and before his conscience the bond of marriage remains otherwise unaffected.[33]

Throughout the last two decades of the nineteenth century and into the first three years of the twentieth Leo XIII kept up a counter-attack against the secular (and, to him, secularist) repossession of marriage in the traditionally Catholic countries of Europe and in their one-time colonies. Leo interpreted this takeover as the work of the Freemasons, and he directed his entire encyclical *Humanum genus,* of April 20, 1884, against this society. In the letter he offered a synopsis of the secularism he condemned:

As regards domestic society, here in brief is the Naturalists' doctrine. Marriage is only a civil contract. It can be rescinded legitimately by the free will of the partners. To the State belongs the power over the matrimonial bond. No religion is to be imposed on the children when educating them. When they are older, each one is free to choose that religion which pleases him most.[34]

If he had published a brief enchiridion of the "Naturalists' " destructive and evil conduct deriving from such theory as that, it would have included the following:

In the governments they control they claim primary jurisdiction over all marriages, even over those of Catholics.

They impose by force of law a sequentially prior civil marriage even on Catholics.

Accordingly they relegate the sacrament to a subsequent and marginally significant ceremony, claiming that the marriage contract has already been created by the earlier civil ceremony.

They have established civil divorce and by it purport to dissolve even the sacramental marriages of Catholics, since they regard marriage as a civil contract coming under their jurisdiction.

On this subject Leo wrote in protest to the president of the French republic on May 12, 1883; to the bishops of Hungary the encyclical letter *Quod multum* of August 26, 1886, and to the bishops of Italy in the encyclical letter *Dell'alto* of October 15, 1886; his letter, *Il divisamento* of February 8, 1893, again to the Italian bishops; another encyclical on September 2, 1893, to the Hungarian bishops; the encyclical *Caritatis* of March 19, 1884 to the bishops of Poland; the letter *Longinqua* of January 6, 1895 to the American bishops; the letter *Dum religiosa* of August 10, 1898 to the bishops of Peru; and the letter *Dum multa* of December 24, 1902 to the bishops of Ecuador.

NOTES

1. De Dominis' theory is explained in D.T.C., Vol. 9.
2. *Op. cit.,* Col. 2267.
3. Recall the wording of this canon: "If anyone should say that the Church has not had the authority to impose invalidating impediments, or that it has erred in doing so, let him be anathema."
4. Translated from *Essais De Messir Michel De Montaigne* . . . Tome 4me, Paris, 1928, p. 87.
5. Montesquieu's observation was: "Nothing would contribute more to mutual attachment than the availability of divorce. A husband and wife would be brought to bear patiently the troubles of domestic life knowing that they could bring an end to them; and they would often keep this power in hand all their lives without using it, only because they know they could use it any time they wish." Editions Renaitre, Lausanne, 1967, p. 218.
6. D.T.C., *loc. cit.*
7. In *The Classics of International Law,* edited by James Scott Brown; the translation of the 1688 edition by C.H. and W.A. Oldfather, N.Y., 1964; Liber 1, Caput 6, p. 875.
8. *Loc. cit.,* p. 877.
9. *Ibid.,* p. 878.

10. *Ibid.,* p. 879.

11. Is this a remarkable foreshadowing by almost three centuries, and by a Protestant philosopher, of Pope Paul VI's thesis in his encyclical letter *Humanae vitae* that the two meanings of sexual intercourse in marriage, the unitive and the procreative, are joined so inextricably that the violation of one of these inescapably involves the violation of the other?

12. *Loc. cit.,* p. 880.

13. One may wonder if Pufendorf was any more aware than was Paul VI how much his argument depended for its validity on an assumption—in his case on the assumed inseparability of the two ends of marriage, as in Paul's case on the assumed inseparability of the two meanings of marital intercourse.

14. *Ibid.,* pp. 880–881.

15. D.T.C., *loc. cit.,* Col. 2272. This history is also narrated in Joyce, *op. cit.,* pp. 255–262.

16. D.T.C., Col. 2272; Joyce, *op. cit.,* pp. 263–266.

17. His discussion of marriage is in Part I of "The Metaphysical Elements of the Theory of Right, Section 1: Private Right, Chapter 2, On Acquiring Something External; Section 3, Rights *in rem* Over Persons; Paragraphs 28 and 29: Marital Rights."

18. Par. 8.

19. Par. 9.

20. *Grundlinien der Philosophie des Rechts,* in G.W.F. Hegel, *Sämtliche Werke,* Herausg. von Hermann Glockner, Stuttgart, 1938, 7er Band, s. 239.

21. *Op. cit.,* p. 240.

22. *Ibid.,* p. 241.

23. The propositions are in Denzinger-Schönmetzer, *op. cit.,* numbers 2600–2700. Proposition 59 (number 2659) is the following: "The Synod's teaching that 'to the supreme civil power alone does it belong to establish impediments to the marriage contract that render it null and are called diriment.' This 'natural right' is said also to be linked essentially to the right to dispense. And the Synod adds that given the assent and the cooperation of princes, the Church may justly establish diriment impediments to marriage, as though the Church has not always had, and still has, the power and its own authority to establish impediments to the marriages of Christians and to dispense from them—impediments which not only impede the marriage bond but also render it null, and which bind Christians even in pagan territories. This teaching subverts canons 3, 4, 9 and 12 of the twenty-fourth session of the Council of Trent, and it is heretical."

24. The Syllabus is in Denzinger-Schönmetzer, *op. cit.,* numbers 2901–2980.

25. *Loc. cit.,* numbers 2965–2974.

26. In *Papal Teachings: Matrimony,* edited by Michael J. Byrnes, Boston, 1963.

27. Unlike most documents of its kind, this encyclical was published in an official organ of the Roman see, *Acta Sanctae Sedis,* before its formal dating. It appears in Volume 12 (1879), pp. 385ff. The name of this organ was changed in 1909 to *Acta Apostolicae Sedis.*

28. *Op. cit.,* p. 386.

29. Atque illa viri et mulieris coniunctio, quo sapientissimis Dei consiliis responderet aptius, vel ex eo tempore duas potissimum, easque in primis nobile quasi alte impressas et insculptas prae se tulit proprietates, nimirum unitatem et perpetuitatem (*ibid.*).

30. *Ibid.*

31. In the Latin text of his encyclical Leo followed Jerome's Vulgate rather than the original Greek text, thus having the wife "depart" (*discedere*) rather than having her "be separated" (in verse 10), and having her "bound to the law" rather than simply "bound" (in verse 39).

32. These are in Denzinger-Schönmetzer, *op. cit.*, numbers 3190–3191, and in *Acta Sanctae Sedis*, Vol. 22 (1889–1890), pp. 635–636.

33. In Denzinger-Schönmetzer, *op. cit.*, number 3192.

34. In *Papal Teachings: Matrimony*, pp. 167–168.

16. CATHOLIC TEACHING IN THE FIRST HALF OF THE TWENTIETH CENTURY

We have seen how at different junctures in the history of the Catholic Church its appointed teachers have drawn the line of indissolubility at different places in the multi-phase process of creating a marriage. One would conclude at the end of the first Christian generation, if one were to read only the divorce passage in the Gospel according to Mark, and read it simplistically, that authority in the Christian community allowed no divorce with the possibility of remarriage for anyone under any circumstances. Had one also read St. Paul's First Letter to the Corinthians one would have found Paul saying the same thing, but with this single exception, that if the still-pagan spouse of a new Christian convert refused to live peacefully in the marriage and wished to abandon it or had already done so, he or she should be allowed to go, and the newly freed Christian spouse is so freed as to be able to marry again, but this time only "in the Lord." One would almost surely have inferred thence that it is only when a marriage is of two Christians that true dissolution is absolutely impossible.

If about ten years later than Mark one were to read Matthew's version of Jesus' statement, he would find Matthew saying that Jesus had forbidden divorce and remarriage for all, but with one exception, and this different from the exception allowed by Paul. If a wife were found guilty of conduct deemed *pornéia,* her husband could dismiss her, thereby dissolve his marriage to her, and could remarry without committing adultery. As the decades and centuries went on observers could then watch the Greek and the Latin halves of the Christian Church diverge farther and farther in their interpretations of this exception, with the Greeks by the ninth century unquestioningly divorcing marriages because of adultery, in such a way as to free the innocent spouse to remarry, but with the Latin sector of the Church, across a full millennium of slowly growing conviction gnawed at always by residual doubt, finally shutting off, universally and once for all, adultery in marriage as a ground for divorce—but at the same time

430

gradually attenuating marriage's presumed indissolubility at a different juncture. By this I refer to the practice, already flourishing in the twelfth century, of permitting a Christian spouse to leave his or her marriage in order to take up monastic life provided the marriage were not yet consummated, and then dissolving the marriage by taking the religious vow of chastity.

In the sixteenth century he would find the two Popes, Paul III and Pius V, professedly extending the use of the Pauline privilege to dissolve marriages of unbaptized spouses separated from one another by captivity in slavery, so that one, now baptized, could enter a sacramental marriage with another Christian. But the interpretation of these dissolutions as a use of the Pauline privilege remained always doubtful because only by torturing the meaning of words could one say that the spouse remaining unbaptized had "departed from the marriage" unwilling to live in peace with the newly baptized spouse. Even less likely an extension of the Pauline privilege was Gregory XIII's untangling the confusion of the polygamous marriages of newly baptized husbands in Africa and India by dispensing them from whichever bond of marriage happened to be authentic among their plural consorts. All too often the woman least wanting to leave in anger and most wanting to stay on in peace and receive baptism herself could have been the authentic spouse.

These apostolic constitutions were used with great caution. They were in practice applied only to certain persons in certain places. They were never published formally, so that they never gained the character of decrees setting precedent for universal application. Even under restricted use they were applied with careful variations. In 1631 a missionary in Latin America asked that native converts living in polygamous relationships be dispensed from their one marriage so as to be able to marry the consort of their choice. After at first refusing, the Congregation for the Propagation of the Faith six years later relented and granted the dispensation in each case on one condition, that the wife taken first in sequence had been asked to accept baptism and had refused.

The power to dissolve asserted in these constitutions denied its own use in the so-called Florentine case of 1680. An Italian Jewess converted to the Catholic faith; her husband divorced her according to rabbinic law, and subsequently remarried under the same law—a divorce and remarriage deemed null by Catholic law. Later the Jewish husband and his second wife themselves both became Catholics, making the marriage to his first wife, which was still in existence according to Catholic law, a sacrament. The first wife insisted that he return to her. He reacted by petitioning a dissolution of his marriage to her on the ground that as a sacrament it had never been consummated. But the Holy See refused to dissolve it, and insisted that he return to the wife he had married first.

Among the Catholic missions of the Far East a yet different situation arose in the eighteenth and nineteenth centuries. More women than men were being converted to the Catholic faith, so that many of them, in order to marry at all, had to secure a dispensation to marry an unbaptized man. From 1708 until 1874 the Holy See refused to dissolve their non-sacramental marriages and thereby free the convert wives to remarry, claiming that even if a marriage is contracted while both spouses are unbaptized, it is by nature indissoluble, and that the bond of marriage can be dissolved only by the Pauline privilege. It was this thinking that drove the canonists of the epoch on in their effort to link the dissolutions permitted by these apostolic constitutions of Paul III, Pius V and Gregory XIII to the Pauline privilege—but link them perforce only by a long subtle trail of association.

It was at this point in the history of the Church's treatment of marriage that an element of theology extraneous to marriage entered its law and became decisive in determining how far dissolution of marriage could go, and in determining reciprocally what juncture in the religious completion of a marriage would be the point beyond which no power on earth could dissolve it. In 1891 Pietro Gasparri, the canonist who was to be mainly responsible for the codifying of Catholic law between 1904 and 1916, returned to a point of doctrine that had already been suggested by earlier canonists. It was a point that could spare the Popes the dubious effort at linking the dissolution of non-sacramental marriages with the Pauline privilege. In substance this doctrine was that of "the power of the keys" to bind and to loose. (In chapter 16, verse 18 of the Gospel according to Matthew Jesus is pictured as vesting this authority in Peter alone; in chapter 18, verse 18 Matthew has Jesus vest the same authority in an unspecified number of his disciples.)[1] Gasparri urged that this authority could be extended to the binding and loosing—to the creating and dissolving—of the bond in marriages that enjoy less than the absolute indissolubility of a consummated sacrament. He reasoned that it was this power of the keys that the three sixteenth-century Popes had employed in their apostolic constitutions (although they may not have been aware of this at the time). Accordingly when designing the marriage law in the Code of Canon Law, Gasparri took care to write this doctrine into it. In Canon 1125 he had the authority of the three apostolic constitutions extended universally, to the entire world, wherever the circumstances originally inspiring the constitutions might prevail.

> Canon 1125: Those points that look to marriage in the constitution *Altitudo* of Paul III (June 1, 1537), *Romani pontificis* of Pius V (August 1, 1571) and *Populis* of Gregory XIII (January 25, 1585), which were decreed for particular places, are extended to other regions where the same conditions are found.[2]

This is how the indissolubility of marriage and the ecclesiastical authority to dissolve this indissolubility met in compromise in the Church's first Code of Canon Law.

The Formulation of the Code of Canon Law

It may come as a surprise to the students of Catholic history to find that the Church's law was first codified only within the first two decades of the twentieth century. To be sure, the Church had regulated its life by law for centuries, from the earliest regional councils of bishops. But until the Code was drafted during the years from 1904 to 1916, and promulgated on Pentecost Sunday of 1917, this law remained only a body of law, a *corpus iuris*. It was a collection—or, more accurately, a collection of collections—of decrees and decretals. The development of this law dates properly from the twelfth century with the publication, circa 1140, of Gratian's *Decretum*. This became the source and model for subsequent collections of decrees of Popes and of Councils, of papal congregations and of learned commentaries. The most used of the later collections were Gregory IX's *Quinque Libri Decretalium* (edited by Raymond of Peñafort in 1234), to which Boniface VIII added his *Liber Sextus Decretalium* in 1298; then Jean Chappuis' *Corpus Iuris Canonici,* published in Paris in 1500, and containing the above-named collections, along with Clement V's constitutions (the *Clementinae*), the twenty added decretals of John XXII (the *Extravagantes*) and the seventy more decretals of subsequent Popes (the *Extravagantes Communes*). This was the juridical instrument of self-regulation that the Roman Catholic Church had in 1545 and the Council of Trent.

In their twenty-third session the bishops of Trent ordered a revision of the law, but despite several attempts by groups of canonists put or invited to the task by Popes—most notable among them the commission appointed by Gregory XIII in 1582—no revision was accepted.

But when in the nineteenth century the European states one by one developed their codes of law under the inspiration of the Code Napoléon, and with it as a model, the demands of the Catholic bishops for a code of Catholic law grew more and more insistent. The demand reached its climax in the preparation for the First Vatican Council, which convened on December 8, 1869. But even this general Council failed to get seriously at the task, crippled and then abruptly cut off as its work was by the Piedmontese conquest of the papal states and of Rome itself in 1870.

Finally Pope Pius X, in his encyclical *Arduum sane munus* of March 19, 1904, created the Pontifical Commission for the Code of Canon Law. Gasparri, by then a cardinal, was appointed secretary of the commission. It was charged with the task of revising the Church's law radically, of producing a coherent code of statutes, and was given twenty-five years within which to accomplish this immense task. But thanks mainly to Gasparri's genius as organizer, scholar and jurist, the commission completed its work in just twelve years, and delivered its draft of the Code to Pope Benedict XV on December 4, 1916.

The Code is divided into five books.[3] Book 5—*De Rebus* (Concerning

Things)—has as its Title 7, *De Matrimonio.* This consists of one hundred and thirty-one statutes, or canons, from Canons 1012 through 1143.

The Defining Canons

In a manner probably unique in a code of law the first canons of Title 7 are a transparent reaction and riposte to a recent attack in the territory of doctrine. Europe's philosophers, jurists, princes and parliaments had just claimed authority over the marriages of their Catholic citizens, and they had staked this claim on the theological ground that marriage is in essence a civil contract that is not only distinct but separate from the sacrament where the marriage is of two Christians.

Canon 1012, paragraph 1 is a flat denial of the latter half of that claim, the theological ground for the assertion of civil authority. And it makes its denial by asserting an event in Christian history—again a clause unique in the codification of law.

> Christ Our Lord has raised the marital contract itself, where it is of baptized persons, to the dignity of a sacrament.[4]

Paragraph 2 of the canon asserts the consequences of this event for the marriage of two Christians—for any marriage of any two Christians.

> Consequently, where it is of baptized persons there can be no valid marital contract without its being by that very fact a sacrament.[5]

Some explanation of both these clauses is in order. First, because the Code of Canon Law is not an essay, it offers no explanation identifying the time and the place of Christ's raising the marriages of all Christians to the dignity of a sacrament. But one may note that if the writers of this canon had in mind Christ's asserting, in the Synoptic passages we have examined in an earlier chapter, the invulnerability of marriage to the dissolving power of civil authority, he made this assertion to all his Jewish hearers about their Jewish marriages. It is not evident that he confined its reference to those among his hearers who were, or were to become, his followers and thus religiously Christian.

The clause at least implies that, though the contract and the sacrament are distinguishable (as they must be, since it implies also that the marital contracts of the unbaptized are not sacraments), where the spouses are Christians the contract itself becomes the sacrament. What the sacrament is, is nothing other than the contract raised to the capacity of a grace-giving instrument of Christ in the Church. The sacrament is not something added to the contract *ab extrinseco.*

This has serious consequences for the understanding of the sacrament, for every one of the Christian sacraments has as its matrix some kind of human act. Baptism has as its matrix a bathing, or at least a washing, with water. The Eucharist has as its matrix the blessing, sharing and consuming of bread and wine. What is claimed implicitly in this canon is that for the sacrament of marriage the matrix is the human contract. The same man who supervised the writing of the canon, and who perhaps himself formulated it, had already specified that the contractual good exchanged in the marital contract is each spouse's right to his or her sexual acts. It then follows logically that what the sacrament as elevated contract is, is a grace-giving, sanctifying exchange of this right. Because Catholic canonists along with theologians had been saying for centuries that a Christian marriage is a sacrament in that it images the love relationship of Christ and the Church, the formulation of this canon left on the formulator's hands the task of explaining how a contractual exchange of rights images that love. There is no evidence that Cardinal Gasparri ever took up this task.

The second paragraph's assertion, that where in a marriage both parties are baptized, there can be no marital contract without this contract's being a sacrament, does not mean that in such a marriage the contract must come up to the quality of a sacrament in order to be a marital contract—so that if it fails to attain the quality of sacrament it fails to be even a marital contract.

What it means rather is that the marital contract of two baptized persons is automatically a sacrament by reason of their having been baptized and by reason of the baptismal character abiding in their souls. In short, the baptism of both spouses guarantees that their marriage is a sacrament. It is not likely that the paragraph intends the simple symmetry of saying that the marriage of two Christians cannot be one—either contract or sacrament—without being the other. Although it intends this meaning in effect, what it intends more immediately is to say that nothing more is needed to make their marital contract a sacrament than that both spouses have been baptized. It is not the added priestly blessing, nor even the solemnizing ceremony, that does it.

Canon 1013 is the first of three "defining canons" about marriage. Sacramentality aside, it declares certain features of every marriage's nature.

> 1. The primary end of marriage is the procreation and nurture of offspring; its secondary end is mutual help and the remedying of concupiscence.
> 2. The essential traits of marriage are unity and indissolubility, which in a Christian marriage gain a special firmness by reason of the sacrament.[6]

Although it may not intend to do so expressly, paragraph 1 of this canon supplies the reason for permanence in marriage that the Greek and Roman philosophers, the medieval philosopher-theologians, and the seventeenth- and eighteenth-century philosophers of natural law acknowledged.

This is that marriage is an instrumental contract-institution; it exists for the gaining of a good beyond itself—or, more accurately, according to the wording of this paragraph, it exists primarily for the gaining of such a good. This good, named as an end, or natural goal, is the procreation and nurture of children. (Even though the stated secondary end, mutual help and the remedying of concupiscence, seems to be goods internal to the marriage, so that the marriage is not an instrument for their attaining, that is not so. The marriage is instrumental in their regard too. As long as one puts the essential heart of the marriage in the contract, as we shall see these canons doing, and as long as one thinks of this contract's ends, one is thinking of what it is *for* beyond the formation and existence of the contract. This makes it an instrument.)

This said, one would expect paragraph 2 to begin with "Therefore," to indicate that the claimed essential traits of marriage that are unity (combined monogamy and sexual exclusivity) and indissolubility are in a marriage because it is for the procreation and nurture of children— because this procreation and nurture demand the exclusive and permanent union of the spouses.

But, presuming the formulators of the canon thought of this, they knew that they could not write the "therefore" into the second paragraph and still get as an essential trait of marriage the kind of permanence that is the indissolubility they wanted. They surely knew of the ancient philosophic conclusion, that once children are able to survive on their own, the compelling reason for the permanence of their parents' union vanishes, especially where this union is on other counts not supportive but destructive for the parents.

So they set the two paragraphs as logically independent of one another. And this leaves the student of their work to wonder about the philosophic and anthropologic warrant for their insisting that (to single it out) indissolubility is a trait essential to marriage. Why is it? What is the cause of this indissolubility in a marriage? Given their readiness to reach into Christian history, as they did in Canon 1012, and use Christ's institution of the marital sacrament as a cause, one would expect them here to cite Christ's words, "What God has joined man must not separate." But this would not have sufficed because these words say nothing about marriage's nature; they say only what men must not try to do to marriages.

And a defining statement of marriage's nature is what was wanted in this canon. Consequently a student curious about the logic of method here can conclude only that this second paragraph (indeed the first as well) is a prescription for what the formulators of the canon wanted marriage to be. That is, they got indissolubility into marriage's nature by simply writing it into their prescriptive definition of it.

The final clause of the second paragraph—"[unity and indissolubility] which in Christian marriage gain a special firmness by reason of the sacrament"—reveals, as much as anything in these canons does, that their formulators were looking not within the pale of philosophy or of anthropology nor within that of theology's reasons in Canon 1012. What they were doing rather was arranging abstract juridical categories in order to get an internally coherent statement. For what does it mean to say that indissolubility in marriage can gain a special firmness? One expects that indissolubility admits of no degrees, that a human relationship is either indissoluble or it is not.

But here again the writers of these canons were antecedently committed to defending an already taken position. The Church had for three and a half centuries been dissolving marital contracts, and holding as finally invulnerable to dissolution only those contracts that become sacraments in the marriages of Christians. So if the canon wishes to say that the marital contract is by nature indissoluble, it must nevertheless both allow for the dissolubility of this natural indissolubility, and allow as well for the role of the supernatural sacrament in making this natural indissolubility finally and in fact indissoluble. In the end, what the terms "indissoluble" and "gain special firmness" really refer to is not indissolubility itself, but the marital contract's vulnerability or invulnerability to the authority to dissolve. The canon really means by marriage's natural indissolubility that any and every marital contract is invulnerable to dissolution by civil authority, but that it becomes invulnerable to ecclesiastical dissolution as well only when it becomes a sacrament in the marriage of two Christians.

Canon 1081 is the second of the defining canons, even though its express intent is to define the kind of act needed to create a marriage. Its first paragraph proceeds from the assumption that a marriage is a contract, and prescribes that only the legally manifested consent of the contractants themselves can create the contract. The canon's historical thrust is against those cultural customs, the Germanic principal among them, that acknowledged the authority of parents, guardians and even of princes to put men and women into marriage. It seeks to protect the freedom of the parties about marrying at all, and their freedom in marrying spouses of their own choice.

> 1. A marriage is created by the legally manifested consent of persons who are capable according to the law of consenting; and no human authority can substitute for this consent.[7]

With the act needed to create a marriage thus clearly identified, paragraph 2 of the canon goes on to prescribe the traits of the act. It specifies by which of the human faculties the act is made (by the will); the kind of act it is (it is an exchange); what is exchanged (this is a right held initially by each contractant); the content of this right (it is the right to their sexual acts that are of themselves apt for conceiving); and finally two qualities of this exchange of rights (it is perpetual and it is exclusive to the contractants).

2. Marital consent is an act of the will by which each party gives and receives a right to his or her body, a right that is perpetual and exclusive, a right ordered to acts that are of themselves apt for the conceiving of offspring.[8]

Our interest is obviously concentrated in the quality of the contractual marital consent that is its perpetuity. But it is not unimportant to know that this paragraph contains the fruit of a centuries-long effort to define marriage exactly by naming with pinpoint precision how it differs from any other human relationship.[9] In the language of Scholastic philosophy this was a search for marriage's ultimate specific difference. This point of difference, according to the canon, lies in the object of marriage's contractual exchange. This is the parties' right to their sexual acts that are apt for conception, that is, their right to those acts of each person that can be the components of sexual intercourse. It is most significant historically, and indeed doctrinally for Catholic tradition, that the object of this marital contractual exchange be not the conduct itself of sexual intercourse, but only the right to one's contribution to this conduct. Only by thus limiting the object to the right could this canon and the reasoning that produced it avoid contradicting the tradition holding both that Mary, the mother of Jesus, was truly married to Joseph, and that she nevertheless lived a life of perpetual virginity. That is, the canon preserves an interpretation of Mary's and Joseph's intent at the time they made their marital consent: they exchanged the right to their sexual acts (and thus were truly married) while at the same time intending never to exercise this right.[10]

To return to the territory of intent in this canon, note that we have in its second paragraph a kind of correlate to the statement in Canon 1013, paragraph 2 that one of marriage's essential traits is indissolubility. There marriage's permanence, understood as its indissolubility, is said to be a trait of the contract itself. But here in Canon 1081, paragraph 2 the permanence enters as a trait of the act that creates the contract. And it is prescribed as an essential trait of the act, as indissolubility is prescribed in Canon 1013 as an essential trait of the contract. That is, if from his or her contractual intent in consenting one of the parties excludes this permanence, the consent does not create a marriage. This invalidating defect of intent is made a point of the law in Canon 1086, paragraph 2.

1. The internal consent of mind is always presumed to conform to the words or signs that are used in the wedding ceremony.

2. But if either party or both parties by a positive act of will exclude the marriage itself, or every right to the marital act, or some essential trait of marriage [the indissolubility of Canon 1013.2 is intended here], they consent invalidly.[11]

This contractual consent prescribed as necessary for creating a marriage is unique in the history of law. It is of the nature of contractual consent that it be made freely by the contractants themselves. Canon 1081 legislates this, and Canon 1086 presumes it. It is also traditional in law that the contractants retain a measure of control over their contract, a control that includes the right and the authority to modify it once made, and to void it by mutual agreement. But the second paragraphs of Canon 1081 and 1086, taken in combination, legislate a literally singular kind of contract. The former says accurately that the parties' right to their own sexual acts is perpetual. It also implies that each party's giving over of this right to the other has this perpetual effect, that neither giver can take it back and neither recipient can give it back—not even if both recipients will freely to return this right to its giver.

And Canon 1086.2 says that if one or both contractants exclude from their marital consent the irreversible alienation of this right (although the right is named only generically and obliquely as one of marriage's essential traits), they fail to create the contract. Thus they are free to enter the act of contracting (no one can force them to marry). They are presumably free in the act of contracting (this act must be an exercise of their own wills for which no one else's will can substitute). But they are not free about continuing or discontinuing the effect created by their free act (once they have formed their marital contract it escapes their power to undo it).

Again, because these statutes are not jurisprudential essays they do not explain the historical origins and reasons for the laws that invent this unique kind of contracting, nor do they offer either the philosophic or the theological principles whence this contracting is derived as from its sources and warrant, even though the earlier Canon 1013 is careful to name its own religious-historical warrant in Christ's elevating the marital contract to the level of a sacrament.

And unless I am mistaken, these Catholic jurists' unique irreversible marital contract in face of the established papal practice of dissolving both unconsummated and non-sacramental marriages creates an anomaly in the law. Canon 1086.2 states that a cause of invalidity in contracting marriage is the exclusion of the marriage's indissolubility from one's contractual intent. Canon 1081.2 states that the contractual right whose exchange creates a marriage is a right held perpetually, with the consequence that the exchange is presumably perpetual and irreversible. But in fact the exercise of papal power to dissolve marriages gainsays this. By the dissolving of unconsummated and non-sacramental marriages the once-given-over right is returned to the giver. Thus in marrying the contractants are held to give over irreversibly a right whose giving can nevertheless be reversed. In other words, the contractants, in order to marry, are held to intend indissolubility, but it is an indissolubility that does not exist.

In light of this the student of the Catholic marriage law may be forgiven if he or she suspects that in these canons there is a concentrate, a miniature, of the eighteenth- and nineteenth-century conflict between ecclesiastical and secular authorities over the possession of the right to control Christian marriages juridically and judicially. For in these canons those who wish to contract marriage are told that they must intend indissolubility, that they must give over irreversibly the contractual good and can neither give it nor take it back. But the Catholic tradition of papal dissolution tells them also that there exists an authority which can dissolve their marriages, which can give back to them their once irreversibly given contractual good.

Pope Pius XI and *Casti connubii*

Thirteen years after Benedict XV had promulgated the Code of Canon Law, Pius XI sent his encyclical letter *Casti connubii* to the Catholic bishops throughout the world.[12] His motive for doing so he explained to the bishops. It was little different from the motive which had produced Leo XIII's *Arcanum divinae sapientiae* fifty years earlier. In Pius' view the condition of marriage in the world had deteriorated sadly. He was writing to call it back to the dignity God intends for it.

> We observe—and you, Venerable Brethren, cannot but share Our sorrow as you also observe—that there are many ignorant of the sanctity of marriage, who imprudently deny it, who even allow themselves to be led by the principles of a modern and perverse ethical doctrine to repudiate it with scorn. As these pernicious errors and degraded morals have begun to spread even among the faithful. . . .[13]

The immediate occasion for the letter is said to have been the declaration by the Anglican bishops in Lambeth Conference in the spring of that year that the members of that church were free to follow their own consciences about using contraceptive methods for birth control.

Part Two of the encyclical is a brief encyclopedia of the evils Pius had in mind: companionate and trial marriages, contraception, abortion, sterilization, adultery, the emancipation of women, religiously mixed marriages, and divorce. Underlying all these evils, and functioning as the cause of them, was the fundamental evil, the secularizing of marriage. About the proximate cause of this secularization, and in a sense an inverted doctrinal cause of it, Pius agreed with his predecessors. It was the denial of what he and they regarded as a fact of history, namely that God instituted marriage—and did so almost in the act itself creating the first man and woman—and the substituting for this biblical account the theory that marriage is a product of social evolution devised for the survival of the clan. Logically deducible from this theory taken as a premise is the conclusion that since men have invented the relationship, they can form and reform it according to their own perceived needs. It has no permanent and immutable nature fixed by a transcendent Creator. (Pius' counter-case was not strengthened by the opinion then solidifying among scholars of the Old Testament that neither narrative of creation, in the first and second chapters respectively of the Book of Genesis, is a factual account of God's forming the world and bringing into existence the first human couple.)

The secular interpretation that Pius confronted held that for most of recorded history men have seen a need to keep marriage a stable relationship between a man and his wives, and more recently between a man and his wife. But they have also seen a real need to keep this relationship a flexible one—to keep every marriage dissoluble in case the good of either or both spouses, or of their children, or of larger society should require its dissolution. After all, the idea of dissolution for the good of the spouse was no stranger to the Catholic mind. Popes since the eleventh century had agreed that the idea was at work in Paul's mind when he wrote what are now verses 12 through 16 of 1 Corinthians. Thus, with one side claiming overtly and the other admitting tacitly that marriage the natural relationship is dissoluble, the real issue bore upon the authority to do the dissolving and who owns it.

Pius XI contradicted the secular premise explicitly:

> Let this stand as a fixed and inviolable principle, that marriage was created and established not by men but by God. Not men but God, the author himself of nature, and Christ the restorer of this nature, provided, strengthened and ennobled marriage with its laws. Consequently these laws can in no way be vulnerable to the wills of men, not even to the spouses' withdrawal of their covenanting wills.[14]

In the words that follow immediately Pius offers as unequivocal and emphatic a statement that a point of Catholic teaching is essential dogma as a Pope could offer short of a solemn, *ex cathedra* statement itself.

> This is the teaching of the Sacred Scriptures; this is the unchanging and universal tradition of the Church; this is the solemn definition, which teaches and affirms that the perpetual and indissoluble marital bond, and its unity and firmness, come from God himself as their author as expressed in the words themselves of Sacred Scripture.[15]

It is hard to resist the temptation to suggest that Basil, Ambrose and even Augustine himself would have been surprised to read that this natural indissolubility of marriage the natural union is taught by the unchanging tradition of the Church, as the modern student must be surprised to read about this naturally perpetual and indissoluble bond when the Popes themselves have been dissolving it for centuries either where it is unconsummated or, though consummated, is not a sacrament. One must suspect that the words "perpetual and indissoluble" either have a meaning not shared by men and women in their common parlance, or that they belong to the vocabulary of a jurisprudential discipline that does not deal immediately with marriage as lived in real life.

Pius goes on to insist that indissolubility is not something invested in this or that marriage by spouses who seek this quality for their relationship. It is a quality of any and every marriage designed into it by God. When a man's and a woman's consent creates their marriage it creates an indissoluble bond.

> Therefore in marriage souls are joined and made one, and this is accomplished before any union of bodies, and more firmly than in such a union. It is done not by any passing inclination of senses or emotions, but by a resolute decision of will. Thus from this joining of souls there arises, by God's decree, a sacred and inviolable bond.[16]

As so many of his predecessors had done before him Pius proceeds in his interpretation of the nature of marriage by reviewing Augustine's explanation of the three blessings or *bona* of marriage. And like those predecessors he locates these *bona* in a significantly different relationship to marriage from that which Augustine had assigned them. The latter had meant, in replying to the Pelagian charge that he despised marriage as evil, that he saw marriage as good because it contains and produces three goods, the third of them apparently unique to Christian spouses. The first two are offspring and fidelity; the third is the *sacramentum,* ". . . which signifies that the bond of marriage shall never be broken, and that neither party, if separated, shall form a union with another, even for the sake of offspring."[17] Pius turns the meaning to make the *sacramentum* a natural trait of every marriage. And in this he repeats the by then predictable anachronism of reading marriage the non-voidable contract invented in the twelfth century back into Augustine's fifth-century essay.

But that is not Pius' only modification of Augustine's sense of the word *sacramentum.* Whereas the latter meant that the *sacramentum* designates the pledge, the commitment made by the spouses, their promise that they would never for any reason try to dissolve their marriage bond, Pius reads a later theology of the sacrament into the term and explains that the word ". . . designates both the indissolubility of the marital bond and the consecration and elevation of this contract by Christ to become a sign which is a cause of grace."[18]

Once again reading indissolubility as an inherent characteristic of every marriage anachronistically back into the New Testament he has Christ declare every marriage indissoluble in the familiar Synoptic logia, "What God has joined man must not separate," and "Every man who dismisses his wife and marries another commits adultery. . . ."[19]

As he must in consideration of the Church's own practice of dissolving indissoluble marriages throughout much of its history, Pius then begins the expected series of qualifications.

> But this inviolable permanence [*firmitas*] belongs to every true marriage, although not with the same perfection to each of them. For the words of Christ—"What God has joined man must not separate"—were spoken of the marital union of the first parents, the prototype of every subsequent marriage. Therefore they apply to every true marriage.[20]

Pius then reasons that these same words that had been spoken of Adam's and Eve's marriage at the beginning of history had the effect in Jesus' time, by his repeating them, of restoring marriage generally to its original inviolability after the concession to human stubbornness in the law of Moses had diminished this inviolability.

> But in virtue of his authority as supreme legislator Christ rescinded this concession and restored the law to its original integrity through those words that must never be forgotten, "What God has joined man must not separate."[21]

At this point he reaches back one hundred and forty years, to July 11, 1789, to quote from a rescript of Pope Pius VI, one that in the heat of the dispute with the Josephists and the framers of the new constitution of the French commune had to make two distinctions. One of these was obvious and acknowledged by all Catholic thinkers of the time; the other was subtle and not so widely acknowledged. The first of these distinctions is between the marital contract and the sacrament, the second apparently between the contract and the marital bond. If both Piuses intended the second distinction, they nevertheless intended too that, though distinct, the contract and the bond are inseparable. The effect of this is that even in pagan marriages, where there is no sacrament as a cause of indissolubility, there is nevertheless the indissolubility of the naturally indissoluble bond.

> Therefore, even though the formality [or the concept—*ratio*] of the sacrament can be separated from the marriage, as in the case of the unbaptized, nevertheless in their marriages, because they are in fact true marriages, there persists that permanent bond [*perpetuus ille nexus*] which from the very beginning has been by God's law so inseparable from marriage that no civil authority has power over it. Therefore any marriage that is said to be contracted is either contracted as a true marriage, with the consequence that that perpetual bond is joined to it which by divine law inheres in every true marriage, or it is presumed to be

contracted without this perpetual bond, in which case it is not a marriage but an illicit union objectively repugnant to the divine law. . . .[22]

This careful formulation with its subtle distinctions, we know by now, had its origin in marriage's long career in the Church's battle to set a doctrine and discipline against the incursions of civil rulers and of philosophers in just those territories of the doctrine and discipline which, by their indecision and ambiguity, invited the incursion.

Neither Pius wanted to say that where a marriage is a sacrament, the sacrament itself is separable from the marriage, because this would concede the argument to the Josephists and the Gallicans. So they said, Pius XI quoting Pius VI, that it is the *ratio* of the sacrament—its formality or concept—that is separable from the marriage. (The signification of the verb used here is sufficiently vague. It is *seiungere*—to separate, to sever, to disjoin. Yet it is significant that neither Pius used the term *distinguere*—to distinguish.) But neither wanted to concede to the Philosophes and to the framers of Europe's secular constitutions beginning with the French Revolution that just because among the unbaptized the contract is not a sacrament, it is vulnerable to dissolution by civil authority. Therefore they apppealed to the ancient interpretation that indissolubility is God's law even for non-sacramental marriages. Here Pius XI at least seems to have in mind the oft-quoted verse from the Garden parable in Genesis—"What God has joined, etc. . . ."—since he has already quoted it several times in this part of the encyclical.

This distinction between the marriage itself and the indissoluble bond adhering to it is easily made when one thinks of marriage as a juridical category. We shall see in the final chapter of this volume how Paul VI made use of it in 1976 when he felt compelled to explain how a marriage continues to exist when every element that *Gaudium et spes* (and he himself in *Humanae vitae*) said belongs to a marriage has vanished. We shall see too that he added a precision that Pius did not, namely that the essence of marriage is found in the juridical bond, and since it remains despite the disappearance of all else, the marriage remains.

Pius goes on predictably to acknowledge that in some cases a marriage, although by nature indissoluble, is nevertheless in fact dissoluble. That is, there are certain merely natural marriages contracted between the unbaptized, or marriages between Christians that are ratified (are sacramental contracts) but are not consummated. He explains that the power that Christ has given the Church in the person of the Pope can dissolve such marriages, but adds: ". . . no such dissolving power can for any cause be exercised upon a Christian marriage ratified *and consummated*."[23] The reason for this ultimate indissolubility is that because in this marriage the marital covenant is brought to its full perfection, by God's will it manifests the fullest perpetuity [*firmitas*] and indissolubility which no human authority can put asunder."[24]

The explanation he offers for this is traditional: it is not the fact alone that the marriage of two Christians is a sacrament that makes it indissoluble even against the papal power to dissolve. The ground of this indissolubility is that the contract has been finally brought to completion by sexual consummation. Where one may find revealed God's will setting exactly the consummated sacrament and it alone as the cause of such indissolubility, Pius does not explain. But he does see the need to verify a still more secure cause for such final indissolubility.

> And if we wish ... to seek out reverently the reason at the depth of the divine will for this indissolubility, we shall find it readily in the mystical meaning of a Christian marriage, a meaning that is found fully and perfectly in the consummated marriages of Christians. For the Apostle says, in the Letter to the Ephesians (at which we have hinted here from the beginning), that the marriage of two Christians images that most perfect union that joins Christ and the Church: "This is a great sacrament. I mean in Christ and in the Church." This is a union that no separation can ever dissolve as long as Christ shall live and the Church lives through him.[25]

Pope Pius XII

Because Pius XII spoke so frequently and copiously about marriage during the twenty years of his pontificate one may study his statements on divorce and remarriage best, I think, by reviewing them topically rather than in their calendar sequence. Almost all his themes repeated those of his predecessors. But as we shall see, one was a significant innovation that the bishops of Vatican II and later Pope Paul VI put at the heart of their considerations of marriage.

By 1939 when Pius became Pope civil divorce was an established practice in most Western countries. Nowhere was it more available and more used than in the United States. In his encyclical *Sertum laetitiae* of November 1, 1939 he addressed the Catholic Church in the United States, dwelling on its strengths, its trials and its temptations. One strength he acknowledged was the freedom and the prosperity enjoyed by the American Catholic Church. But he pointed out that in the same freedom the American Catholic Church is tested most severely by the habit of divorce and the effects of divorce in this country.

> Oh, if your country had known from the experience of others and not from its own the immense damage caused by divorce. Let reverence toward religion and love for the great American people counsel energetic action to cure this perverse disease at its very root.[26]

At this point Pius spelled out his diagnosis of the American situation by citing from Leo XIII's encyclical *Arcanum divinae sapientiae* the social evils consequent on easily available civil divorce.

Beginning with his earliest public discourses Pius reinforced the notion, long since introduced by his predecessors, that in a marriage there is a bond, and that this bond is indissoluble.[27] He does not explain the distinction, if any, between the marriage itself and this bond. He uses the term "bond" as an item of accepted vocabulary. What he develops is a quasi-history and bits of a philosophy of this bond. He says that the first marriage bond was formed in the Garden of Paradise, and that it was of this first marriage bond that Christ later said: "What God has joined man must not separate."[28] The reason for not separating the partners in the bond is not only that they have been joined by God, but that they are "two in one flesh."[29] That is, Pius seems to identify two causes blocking the separation of the partners, an external cause which is God's will, and a cause internal to the bond, which is the union of the partners.[30] About the second of these causes he says, "In the unity of the marriage bond you see stamped the seal of indissolubility."[31]

He comes again to the idea of the marriage bond's internal and self-established indissolubility when noting the function of the partners' wills in forming the bond. Only the human wills of the partners can create the bond. But these same wills are powerless to dissolve it once it is created. Why? Because as causes what their wills produce is an effect whose nature contains indissolubility. More than that, because the effect of their act of will, of their consent, is the perpetual bond, their consent itself is perpetual. It cannot be revoked. In short, in the act of will creating a marriage, the nature of the effect determines a serious quality of the cause, namely irrevocability of that cause's act which has produced the effect.

In a tightly woven statement Pius offers a resume of all the human causation entering the creation of the marriage bond:

> The "yes" pronounced by your lips through the impulse of your will unites you by the marriage bond and ties your wills together forever. Its effect is irrevocable: sound, the sensible expression of your consent, passes away, but the consent, formally established, does not pass away; it is perpetual because it is a consent established in the perpetuity of the bond, while a consent exchanged for only a certain period would not constitute between the parties true matrimony.[32]

But faithful to by now established Catholic discipline Pius insists, in the same discourse, that the power to bind and to loose invested by Christ in the successors of Peter can dissolve this indissoluble bond where it is either not a sacrament or, though a sacrament, is not consummated.

Earlier he had referred to this power to dissolve as his "ministerial power."[33]

In that same earlier discourse he identified two norms of judgment to be applied in the decision to dissolve a marriage or not. At one pole there is the norm of God's will expressed in Jesus' prohibiting command, "What God has joined man must not separate." At the other pole there is the norm set by the apostle Paul, "The brother or sister is not to play the slave in these matters, for God has called us in peace." Thence it is for the Pope in the exercise of his ministerial power to apply in particular instances the over-arching norm which is the *salus animarum*—that which is needed for the salvation of souls—to decide what is necessary for the souls involved in the particular decision.[34]

Where Pius develops as much of a theology of indissolubility as is appropriate for his popular discourses, he is just as traditional as in his philosophy. Apparently without distinguishing between the marriages of the unbaptized and those of the baptized, since he claims a sacramental function for the indissolubility found, according to Catholic tradition, in *any* marriage, he says: "The intimate and inviolable wedding bond is a sign and a symbol of the indissoluble union of Christ with the Church."[35]

In a discourse eight months later he filled in explicitly the causal nexus of the marriages of Christians with the love relationship of Christ and the Church. Pius takes as given what he said in the earlier discourse, that such marriages in fact represent, are images on earth of, the Christ-Church relationship. He reasons that *because* they are, and *because* the Christ-Church relationship is perfect, is imperishable, it follows that the marriages of Christians must be perpetual and even indissoluble.[36]

In 1959 he returned to this traditional interpretation but reinforced it in a way unique at that point in papal teaching. He takes as a given premise that the relationship of Christian husband and wife is to mirror that of Christ and his Church. To this he links as a kind of minor premise Paul's instruction to the Ephesian spouses in which he tells the wives that they are to be subject (according to Pius' interpretation) to their husbands *as* the Church is subject to Christ. The logic he finds here is that since the Christian wives are to be subject to their husbands as the Church is subject to Christ, it follows that the bond between Christian husbands and wives is as unbreakable as that between Christ and the Church.

> In raising to the dignity of a sacrament the marriage of baptized persons, Christ conferred on the spouses an incomparable dignity and assigned a redemptive function to their union when he affirmed that women must be subject to their husbands as the Church is to Christ. St. Paul establishes a very clear difference between the spouses, but by that very fact he illustrates the force of the bond which unites them with one another and maintains the indissolubility of the link which joins them.[37]

Marital Love and Indissolubility

I said above, when beginning this review of Pius XII's teaching, that he introduced, or at least first brought to vivid use, a reason for marriage's permanence that had been absent or subdued in the writings of earlier Popes, and that the bishops of Vatican II and then Paul VI later set this reason at the heart of their teaching on marriage's permanence. This reason Pius finds in the kind of love that creates a marriage, in the expression of this love that is the act of creating a marriage. Pius calls this expression a gift of the self, a gift which (and this is essential) must be total. And its totality must include irrevocability, for without irrevocability there is no totality.

> Such is Christian marriage, modeled, according to the famous expression of St. Paul, on the union of Christ with his Church. In the one as in the other, the gift of self is total, exclusive, irrevocable. . . .[38]

Pius' development of the thought is really an interpretation of marital love. He insists that the love which leads a couple into marriage *wants* to be perpetual. This is simply a truth about human nature in men and women. Hence God's will for marriage's permanence and his grace enabling it only to strengthen and bring to completion what human nature already desires.

> But what does nature say about this perpetuity? While grace with its salutary action does not change nature, even if it always and in every case perfects it, would it perhaps encounter an enemy that hinders it? No: God's art is wonderful and gentle; it is always in accordance with nature, of which he is the author. That perpetuity and indissolubility, which the will of Christ and the mystical signification of the Christian marriage require, is required by nature also. Grace fulfills the desire of nature and gives it strength to be that for which it greatly longs.[39]

In what follows immediately Pius explains, poetically and emotionally, what he refers to by the term "desire of nature":

> Question your hearts' desires, beloved newlyweds. . . . If you recall to mind the moment in which you felt your affection respond fully to another love, does it not seem to you, perhaps, as if from that instant the "yes" pronounced by you both in front of the altar there had been an advance hour by hour, steps taken in anxious hope and fearful expectancy? Now, that hope is no longer in waiting but a rose fully flowered, and that expectation awaits other joys. Has your dream vanished perhaps? No: it has

become reality. What has transformed it into a reality of union before the altar? Love, which has not disappeared but has remained, has become stronger, firmer, and in its firmness has made you cry out: "This love must remain unchanged, intact, inviolate forever!" ... Thus you attribute to your nuptial love without realizing it, We would say, with holy jealousy, that characteristic sign which the Apostle Paul ascribed to charity when, exalting it, he exclaimed, *Caritas numquam excidit*— "Charity never fails."[40]

At this point Pius takes a logical step that may in fact be a leap. He says that *because* authentic married charity never fails, it follows that the marriage it produces is, and apparently must be, indissoluble.

> The indissolubility of marriage is therefore the fulfillment of an impulse of a pure and incorrupt heart, of the *anima naturaliter christiana* [of the soul naturally Christian], and ceases only with death.[41]

The reader may have noted how here the flow of causation has reversed direction from what it was in Pius' earlier reasoning. There he explained that because in the marital consent a person wills to enter a contractual relationship that is of its nature indissoluble, the consent must, as an effect of the given indissolubility, be itself irrevocable. Here in the 1942 discourse he explains that it is the imperishable nature of married love that produces, as its effect, the indissoluble marriage relationship.

Toward the end of this discourse Pius pursues the thought of the spouses' "natural desire" for indissolubility under the heading of their personal dignity:

> But the indissolubility of matrimony is demanded by nature for yet another reason. Such a quality is needed to protect the dignity of the human person. Married cohabitation is a divine institution rooted in human nature as a union of two beings made to the image and likeness of God, who calls them to continue his work in the preservation and propagation of mankind.[42]

Were he rehearsing only what is referred to in Catholic tradition under the demands of personal dignity, he would have taken an immediate negative turn and listed the socially degrading effects of divorcing and being divorced. He comes to this quickly enough, but this degradation is not his primary referent here. What he has in mind is the spouses' fundamental need for permanence in their love, at least (or perhaps especially) after they have begun the intimate communication native to marriage.

From its most intimate expressions such cohabitation appears as something of extreme delicacy; it ennobles, sanctifies and makes souls happy when it rises above sensible things with a movement of mutual and simultaneous spiritual and unselfish devotion of the two married persons.[43]

Then he names the ground and cause of their dignity specifically as married partners, and the warrant demanding that they not be subjected to the indignity of divorce. In doing so he moves into the kind of psychology of married love that will become the epicenter of both the Vatican II bishops' and Paul VI's reasoning about marriage.

There is rooted and living in the consciousness of both husband and wife a desire to belong totally one to the other, to remain faithful to each other in all the changes and chance of life, in the days of happiness and sadness, in health and sickness, in their first years together as in their later years, without limit or conditions, until God wishes to call them to eternity. In this consciousness, in these intentions, human dignity is exalted, matrimony is exalted, nature is exalted which sees itself and its laws respected. . . .[44]

Pius here speaks in a sense for the married; he says what they want in the matter of permanence in their marriages, perhaps even in the matter of indissolubility. Or does he perhaps imply that this imperishability of their marriage is what they want after their love reaches a certain strength and intimacy? Or does he even say that the kind of love whose dignity is safeguarded only by an unbreakable commitment is the kind of love that is proper to marriage—and is indeed as a cause indispensable for forming a marriage? If this last is what he says at least implicitly, he anticipates what the bishops of Vatican II will also imply, but much more clearly, and what Paul VI will say expressly—that only if a man's and woman's union is the product of a love wanting and intending permanence until death is this union a marriage.

Those students of marriage's history in the Church who have urged that what the bishops of Vatican II said about the centrality of love in marriage began in the mind of Pius XII have the evidence in these statements on their side. If it was not born there alone, but also in the minds of certain Catholic scholars and churchmen of central Europe, a Pope's concern to put love at least near the center of marriage was the overture of a new age in the Church's understanding of this relationship. And far more than Pius realized, or more than even the bishops of the Council seemed to realize, putting love near the heart of marriage compelled yet another re-examination, in the long history of re-examinations, of the causes of marriage's permanence.

NOTES

1. Jesus' recorded words of investiture are: "Whatever you shall bind on earth will be bound in heaven. . . . " In the first of these passages the Greek verbs translated as "to bind" and "to loose" (*déein* and *lúein*) are used in the singular number. In the second of the passages they are in the plural.

2. "Ea quae matrimonium respiciunt in constitutionibus Pauli III *Altitudo,* 1 Jun. 1537; S. Pii V *Romani pontificis,* 2 Aug. 1571; Gregorii XIII *Populis,* 25 Ian. 1585, quaeque pro peculiaribus locis scripta sunt, ad alias quoque regiones in eisdem adiunctis extenduntur."

3. These are Book I, General Norms; Book II, Concerning Persons; Book III, Concerning Things; Book IV: Concerning Processes; Book V, Concerning Crimes and Penalties.

4. 1. Christus Dominus ad sacramenti dignitatem evexit ipsum contractum matrimonialem inter baptizatos.

5. 2. Quare inter baptizatos nequit matrimonialis contractus validus consistere quin sit eo ipso sacramentum.

6. 1. Matrimonii finis primarius est procreatio ateque educatio prolis; secundarius autem mutuum adiutorium et remedium concupiscentiae.

2. Essentiales matrimonii proprietates sunt unitas ac indissolubilitas, quae in matrimonio christiano peculiarem obtinent firmitatem ratione sacramenti.

7. 1. Matrimonium facit partium consensus inter personas iure habiles legitime manifestatus; qui nulla humana potestate suppleri valet.

8. 2. Consensus matrimonialis est actus voluntatis quo utraque pars tradit et acceptat ius in corpus, perpetuum et exclusivum, in ordine ad actus per se aptos ad prolis generationem.

9. My earlier volume, *Marriage in the Catholic Church: What Is Marriage?,* details at length the history of this effort.

10. Cardinal Gasparri was almost certainly the formulator of this precision in the canon. I say this because it reflects faithfully what he had written in the 1891 edition of his *Tractatus De Matrimonio.*

11. 1. Internus animi consensus semper praesumitur conformis verbis vel signis in celebrando matrimonio adhibitis.

2. At si alterutra vel utraque pars positivo voluntatis actu excludat matrimonium ipsum, aut omne ius ad coniugalem actum, vel essentialem aliquam matrimonii proprietattem, invalide contrahit.

12. A satisfactory translation of the encyclical is in *Papal Teachings: Matrimony,* pp. 219–291. The officially published document is in AAS, Vol. 22 (1930), pp. 539–592.

13. *Papal Teachings: Matrimony,* p. 220.

14. AAS, Vol. 22, p. 541.

15. *Ibid.*

16. *Ibid.,* p. 542.

17. *On the Good of Marriage (De Bono Coniugali),* Chapter 2, n. 32.

18. AAS, *loc. cit.,* p. 550.

19. *Ibid.*

20. *Ibid.,* p. 551.

21. *Ibid.*

22. *Ibid.*

The Latin text of this passage is the following: "Itaque licet Sacramenti ratio a matrimonio seiungi valeat, velut inter fideles, adhuc tamen in tali matrimonio, siquidem verum est matrimonium, perstare debet, omninoque restat perpetuus ille nexus [the bond] qui a prima origine divino iure matrimonio ita cohaeret ut nulli subsit civili potestati. Atque ideo quodcumque matrimonium contrahi dicatur, vel ita contrahitur ut reapse sit verum matrimonium, tumque *adiunctum habebit perpetuum illum nexum divino iure omni vero matrimonio cohaerentem;* vel contrahi supponitur sine illo perpetuo nexu, tumque matrimonium non est, sed illicita coniunctio divino legi ex obiecto repugnans . . . (italics mine).

23. *Ibid.,* p. 552.

24. *Ibid.*

25. *Ibid.*

26. *Papal Teachings: Matrimony,* p. 308.

27. Allocution to the Roman Rota, October 1, 1940 (in *Papal Teachings: Matrimony,* p. 314).

28. Allocution to newlyweds, March 5, 1941 (in *Papal Teachings: Matrimony,* p. 321).

29. Allocution to newlyweds, August 13, 1941 (in *Papal Teachings: Matrimony,* p. 330).

30. Allocution to newlyweds, April 22, 1942 (in *Papal Teachings: Matrimony,* pp. 340–342).

31. *Ibid.,* p. 342.

32. *Ibid.*

33. Allocution to the Roman Rota, August 20, 1941 (in *Papal Teachings: Matrimony,* p. 337).

34. *Ibid.,* p. 338.

35. Allocution to newlyweds, August 13, 1941.

36. Allocution to newlyweds, April 29, 1942 (in *Papal Teachings: Matrimony,* p. 347).

37. Allocution to the World Union of Women's Organization, September 19, 1959 (in *Papal Teachings: Matrimony,* p. 501).

38. Allocution to newlyweds, October 23, 1940 (in *Papal Teachings: Matrimony,* p. 315).

39. Allocution to newlyweds, April 29, 1942, *op. cit.,* p. 347.

40. *Ibid.,* p. 348.

Here Pius means "never fails" in the most serious sense of the words. In the paragraph immediately following this one he explains that although marriage the sexually expressed human relationship, the contract oriented to procreation, ends at the death of at least one of the spouses, yet the married love of the spouses for one another need not end at death: "If, however, married love in this its peculiar manifestation ends with the cessation of the purpose for which it was established on earth, nevertheless, inasmuch as it has acted in the souls of the married couple and has bound them to each other in that great bond of love which united their hearts to God and with each other, such a love remains in the other life, as endure the souls wherein such love had its abode here below" (*ibid.*).

41. *Ibid.*

42. *Loc. cit.,* p. 349.

43. *Ibid.*

44. *Ibid.*

17. THE SECOND VATICAN COUNCIL AND THE REVISED CATHOLIC MARRIAGE LAW

By the time Pope Pius XI published his encyclical letter *Casti connubii* on the last day of 1930, the contest between Catholic authorities and the civil governments of once-Catholic Europe over the regulation of marriages was at an end. The Catholic authorities had sought an unqualified victory, and on this scale had lost. In every country except Ireland, Spain and Italy marriage under secular authority was established constitutionally. And in Italy authority had been returned to the Church only a year earlier by the Vatican concordat with the Mussolini government. Moreover, in most of these countries marriage under civil authority was obligatory. If a couple wished to have their marriage acknowledged by this authority, a religious ceremony was not enough. They could have this ceremony, but since the Church's authority was not recognized by the government, they had also to exchange their wedding vows before a civil magistrate.

Since its beginning in the seventeenth century this contest over the authority to regulate, which was then minimally doctrinal and mainly juridical, had become the vehicle for the far more serious doctrinal dispute about the dissolubility of marriage. While the civil authorities had at first wanted jurisdiction mainly so as to control the setting of and dispensing from impediments to marriage, this motive elided gradually into that of establishing the availability of divorce. Here too they carried the battle. By 1920 every one of the Western European states in question, again excepting Ireland, Spain and Italy, had made civil divorce available to their citizens, Catholics included.

It is easy to explain this victory of secular authority over ecclesiastic as the simple repossession by main force of a right once held by Roman secular magistrates but handed over to the Church by default as the empire disintegrated in the fifth and sixth centuries. But this is hardly an inclusive accounting for the causes at work. It is not likely that by the eighteenth and nineteenth centuries the Catholic peoples of Europe would have tolerated the secular taking of authority if their understanding of marriage had not shifted massively by that time. For their governments to establish divorce so universally without popular protest, the people had to have seen this as a favor to themselves. It is most unlikely that they would have seen it as such if their way of life, its culture and especially its economy, had remained rural and agricultural. Easy and sanctioned break-up of marriages is a mortal enemy to a people who live mainly on the land and from it. Holding the land depends on continuity of family. Acknowledged or not by Catholic Europe, its people's understanding of marriage as a natural union of man and woman was of a device for continuing family and land. The perception was firm that these two survive together or fall together. If the family falls apart, the land as a source and sustainer of life is lost.

But what must happen to an entire society's understanding of marriage when this society becomes industrialized, when fewer and fewer of its people live either on or from the land? A transforming logic becomes active in their minds. Not only do family and land-holding no longer survive or fall as one, but men and women begin to have a different reason for marrying. Children as the future holders of patriarchally bequeathed land are no longer central in their motivation. *Therefore* marriage begins to be seen and felt as a different kind of institution, even if the difference is barely articulated in the popular mind. Parents have less and less reason, and excuse, for putting their children into marriage for the sake of the patriarchal family. The children gradually slip free to marry for their privately felt reasons and with spouses of their private choosing.

In other words, in this transition men and women see marriage less as an instrument for securing a good outside itself. Now in their minds marriage becomes a good in its own right. Said somewhat less abstractly, they get married in order to be married, to gain and to enjoy what this sexual relationship can yield to them as persons.

This yield can be interpreted selfishly, although not inevitably so. It can also be interpreted variously, according as men and women understand happiness in various ways. But once men and women begin to view marriage as a good-in-itself, it is inevitable that they begin also to view differently two facets of marriage in which the Catholic Church has always taken a keen interest. These are the purpose of sexuality in their marriages and the possibility of ending their marriages short of the death of one of the spouses. Certainly these two issues are bound up inextricably with the happiness sought for in marriage. But as doctrinal questions concerning marriage these two issues were, by 1930, thought by the Catholic authorities to have been settled once for all.

The New Catholic Challenge

Perhaps it is one of the ironies of Catholic history that just as victory on this doctrinal front, after defeat on the juridical front, was thought secure, even this victory began to be undermined by Catholics who were on all other counts thoroughly loyal to the Church and to its teachings. These were German and French scholar-writers deeply influenced by the phenomenology of Edmund Husserl, Max Scheler and Maurice Merleau-Ponty. Of these the best known to English-speaking Catholics were the Germans Dietrich von Hildebrand and Heribert Doms. The former's essays still retain some currency in the United States. Doms' popularity in these and other countries waned once his most influential work, *The Meaning of Marriage,* was withdrawn from publication in the early 1940's by order of the Congregation of the Holy Office. Hardly known at all among English-speaking Catholics, probably because they entered the challenge-become-debate almost a decade later than von Hildebrand and Doms, were Bernardin Krempel and Ernst Michel.

At the time these men brought their challenge the popular mind saw it directed at the traditional Catholic teaching concerning contraceptive intercourse. This was not quite accurate. Their challenge was directed first of all at the understanding of marriage fixed in the minds of Catholic authorities by the beginning of this century and enshrined in the Code of Canon Law promulgated in 1917. Only derivatively, only by necessary consequence, did their challenge strike the teaching concerning contraception. By a still further consequence, one that von Hildebrand, Doms and the others never intended, it also struck the Catholic doctrine and discipline concerning divorce and remarriage.

The Quasi-Definition of Marriage in Catholic Law

To understand the challenge and its consequences we must review briefly the quasi-definition of marriage legislated in the Code of Canon Law. One must keep in mind that this is a prescription for the marriages not of Catholics alone, nor even of only Christians. It is a statement of the nature of marriage universally, in all times, of all places and peoples.

Thus it says that marriage is a contract—not a real contract, in which the contractants exchange a consumable good, but a consensual personal contract, in which they exchange a personal service.

The contractants in a marriage are and can be only one human male and one female who are capable of creating and fulfilling this kind of contract. With this specification polygamous marriage is defined into impossibility; so too is homosexual marriage. (Since the definition intends all marriages in all ages as its referents, it raises an obvious difficulty about the purported polygamous marriages of the Hebrew patriarchs.)

The marital contract is created by a reciprocal consent of will by both contractants, and can be created only by them. No other persons' consent can substitute for this.

The object of their contractual consent, the contractual good that they exchange, is a personal right that each possesses by nature. As we saw in the preceding chapter, this right is specified exactly. It is the right to one's sexual acts, to control them and to exercise them. More exactly yet, it is the right to those sexual acts which are apt for conception.

The contract has as its natural and innate goals, or ends, the three goods of marriage that Augustine claimed for it. Primary among them is procreation and nurture. Secondary, and together making up a single goal in the law's formulation, are the remedying of the spouses' concupiscence and their mutual help.

The contract has also two natural and innate characteristics. These are unity (the contractual right can be exchanged with only one heterosexual partner) and indissolubility (the contract once created is non-voidable, even by the contractants themselves).

No affect, no emotional contribution is needed for creating the contract other than perhaps whatever emotional resolve is needed to reinforce the initial contracting will to subsequently deliver the contractual good that is sexual intercourse, to deliver it on demand by the spouse, and to confine one's intercourse to the spouse.

Since the object of the contractual consent, the good that is exchanged, is only the spouses' right to their sexual acts, they can create the contract while yet agreeing in advance to never exercise this right. (This explains *ex post facto* how a few Christian spouses, Mary and Joseph among them, could live virginal marriages that were truly marriages. That these spouses intended not to realize marriage's primary end posed no evident difficulty for the formulators of the definition.)

Indeed because of this narrow and exactly defined object of contractual consent in marrying, the spouses need not even live together. And this denial of cohabitation can be made unilaterally and even against the other spouse's will without voiding the contract, since the right to cohabitation is not included within the object of contractual marital consent. Combine this forgoing of cohabitation with the agreement to never have intercourse, and two strangers who never in their lives meet could become spouses to one another by exchanging consent through the service of proxies.[1] It goes without saying that, as hinted just above, in the forming and sustaining of a marriage there is no need for love in any sense acknowledged by men and women of the Western world who marry for reasons of love.

The Point of the Catholic Challenge

Especially Heribert Doms objected that this triumph of exact juridical writing prescribes a marital relationship that is unrecognizable to the men and women whose marriages it purports to define. Even allowing for the fact that it is a prescriptive rather than a descriptive definition, it prescribes a kind of marital relationship that is unrecognizable to the very persons who are presumed to create it and live it.[2]

Doms concentrated his challenge especially at that point in the definition that has procreation and nurture as marriage's primary end. He objected that at least this ignores the meaning of their marriages that men and women in Western society experience as first and central. This is a meaning that is in their minds prior to any goal. It is a meaning that they realize *within* the relationship, not a goal outside it whose realizing makes the marriage an instrumental reality.

This meaning Doms called *Zweieinigkeit,* the becoming-one of two persons. If one would describe realistically what men and women do in marrying, one must say that they *get married* in order to *be married.* Even if they have a goal in view that lies in their future as they marry, this goal is not a product or a state outside their relationship. It lies within the relationship; it is the completing of themselves in their sexual natures as man and woman—a completing that is possible precisely because they are reciprocally masculine and feminine. At the same time it is the completing of their two-in-oneness as a man and a woman.

Doms continued, saying that even if one insists on thinking of goals in marrying, there is no need to distinguish two separate goals of either marriage itself or of marital intercourse. Intercourse's first meaning—or goal—is to effect and complete the spouses' union. It is the most thorough way in which they can give and accept one another's entire persons. This is, again, marital intercourse's first meaning, its first value.

The bringing of this union to reality is in turn oriented to two further goals, the fulfilling of the husband and wife as persons, and the conceiving of a child. But while the primary meaning of intercourse is realized objectively in every sexual act, not in every case are the two further goals attained, despite intercourse's natural orientation to them.

To express this relationship of meaning and goals in marital intercourse still more precisely, Doms said that marriage attains these goals in and by realizing its meaning. That is, this meaning which is the union of husband and wife is not *for* some goal beyond itself; it is not an instrumental means to such a goal. Rather, the conception of the child is related to the uniting of husband and wife at this union's natural completion. It is the full flowering of their unreserved self-giving and acceptance.

The child is first of all a gift from both husband and wife to one another. Their personal sexual fulfillment leads them to give this gift. Its giving is the most specific completion of their union. And while the child enriches their union it also completes them as distinct persons. Its prolonged need for nurture, if they accept this need and provide for it, matures them as man and woman.

I cite this, Doms' interpretation of marriage, not because it was the only one of its kind to appear in the 1930's, but because it was the most detailedly worked out that also got widest publication. It was the substance of his volume *Vom Sinn Und Zweck Der Ehe* (On the Meaning and Goal of Marriage) that he published in 1935 while a theologian and Privat-Dozent and a priest at the University of Breslau. Two years later the essay was published in French translation as *Du Sens Et De La Fin Du Mariage,* and in 1939 in English as *The Meaning of Marriage.*[3]

It was inevitable that such a thesis about marriage should attract the attention of authorities in the Church and awaken their concern. We shall see presently the form and the effectiveness of the authoritative reaction. But it is clear enough that from the beginning of this dissent the focus of the authorities' concern was on Doms' and his peers' defining marriage not according to its traditionally asserted goals, and thence on his and their implied challenge to the primacy of procreation and nurture among these goals.

There were consequences from this challenge if it should ever succeed, and succeed by displacing from Catholic teaching the primacy of procreation and nurture among marriage's goals, and replacing it with union of the spouses as its most valuable meaning. To judge from the Catholic authorities' reaction, the consequence that worried them most would be found in the Church's negative moral judgment on contraceptive intercourse. The freshest formulation of this judgment at the time was in Pope Pius XI's encyclical letter *Casti connubii.* It is clear from Pius' own words that his condemnation of contraception depended for its validity on first accepting that procreation and nurture are a natural, innate goal of marriage.

> But there is no reason at all, not even the most serious, that can make what is inherently contrary to nature conform to nature and thereby morally good. The marital act is by its very nature oriented to the procreation of children. Therefore those who in performing it intentionally block its natural capacity and efficacy act contrary to nature and do something which is degrading and intrinsically immoral. Wherefore ... We proclaim once again: any use of marriage at all in the exercise of which the act is deprived, by human intervention, of its natural capacity to procreate life, is an offense against the law of God and of nature, and that those who do this are guilty of serious sin.[4]

What raised alarm among Catholic authorities was, as I have already said, not the more veiled, because implied, threat to the traditional Catholic teaching concerning divorce. It was the explicit denial that marriage is to be understood according to its natural goals, and thence the implicit denial that procreation and nurture is primary among these goals. For if there is no such primacy because there is no such goal—or at least if such a goal does not belong to the essence of marriage—contraceptive intercourse could not be said to contradict an essential goal of marriage. The case against contraception would either have to be dropped or would have to be argued on different ground.[5]

But the Congregation of the Holy Office's order halting the distribution of Doms' essay did not halt what was by the early 1940's a tide of disagreement among Catholic European philosophers and theologians. By the spring of 1944 the same Roman congregation was sufficiently alarmed to apply a far more vigorous braking action to their challenge. On April 1 of that year it published a decree condemning certain unnamed "lucubrations" that deny that procreation and nurture are the primary end of marriage, that deny that the secondary ends are subordinate to it, and that say instead that marriage's primary end is the personal perfection and mutual fulfillment of the spouses.[6]

But this decree too was ineffective in ending the intramural challenge to the established Catholic teaching. So seven years later Pope Pius XII condemned the challenge even more vigorously and in finer detail. This he did in the best-remembered of his many discourses on marriage, delivered to the union of Italian Catholic Obstetricians on October 29, 1951.

Because it is a discourse and not a decree his statement is less lapidary and considerably more humane than that of the Congregation of the Holy Office. He was concerned to keep within the Catholic understanding of marriage the "personal values" that Doms *et al.* proposed as central in the meaning of marriage. But he also proposed to keep them in their place—subordinated to procreation and nurture.

> "Personal values" and the need to respect such are a theme which, over the last twenty years or so, has been considered more and more by some writers. In many of their works even the specifically sexual act has its place assigned, that of serving the "person" of the married couple. The proper and most profound meaning of the exercise of conjugal rights would consist in this, that the union of bodies is an expression and the realization of personal and affective union. . . . If from the complete reciprocal gift of husband and wife there results a new life, it is a result which remains outside, or at most on the border of, "personal values"—a result which is not denied, but neither is it desired as the center of marital relations. . . .
>
> Now if this relative evaluation were merely to place the emphasis on the personal values of husband and wife, rather than on that of offspring, it would be possible, strictly speaking, to put such a problem aside. But, however, it is a matter of a grave inversion of the order of values and of the ends imposed by the Creator himself. . . .[7]

That much is a statement of Pius' understanding of the Catholic personalists' challenge and of the reasons for his anxiety concerning it. To it he opposed his restatement of the Church's accepted teaching concerning the nature of marriage. The restatement comes as close as Pius ever did to offering his definition of marriage.

Now the truth is that matrimony, as an institution of nature, in virtue of the Creator's will, has not as a primary end the intimate and personal perfection of the married couple but the procreation and upbringing of new life. The other ends, inasmuch as they are intended by nature, are not equally primary, much less superior to the primary end, but are essentially subordinated to this.[8]

Pius then located the personal values of marriage in what he considered their right relationship to procreation.

Would this lead, perhaps, to our denying or diminishing what is good or just in personal values resulting from matrimony and its realization? Certainly not, because the Creator has designed that for the procreation of new life human beings made of flesh and blood, gifted with soul and heart, shall be called upon as men and not as animals deprived of reason to be the authors of posterity. . . .

All this is therefore true and desired by God. But on the other hand, it must not be divorced completely from the primary function of matrimony, the procreation of offspring. Not only the common work of external life, but even all personal enrichment—spiritual and intellectual—that in married love as such is most spiritual and profound, has been placed by the Will of the Creator and of nature at the service of posterity.[9]

Despite the fact that Doms *et al.* nearly ignored the question of divorce and remarriage in their challenge to the traditional Catholic understanding of marriage, and despite the Sacred Congregation of the Holy Office's and Pius XII's ignoring the question altogether, was there nevertheless something in the challenge that touched also the traditional teaching on divorce and remarriage?

There was, although not immediately and explicitly. By 1951 the Catholic case against divorce was argued in three domains that in part shared the same terrain. Divorce was said to offend against the nature of marriage because it cripples and even ruins this nature by hindering the nurture of children, but it is to their nurture that marriage is by nature oriented—as we see Pius XII insisting at length in the discourse we have just quoted. (One may call this the philosophic-anthropologic case against divorce.) It was said to offend against the nature of marriage also because it denies one of marriage's essential traits, which is its indissolubility. (This is the juridical case against divorce and like the philosophic-anthropologic was considered valid against the dissolving of any and all marriages.) Finally it was said to be simply impossible to dissolve the consummated marriage of two Christians because, since it is a sacrament, this marriage images the indestructible union of Christ and his Church, and by imaging this indestructibility, also appropriates it. (Here obviously is the theological case.)

But—and this is the implicit pertinence to divorce and remarriage of the challenge led by Doms and von Hildebrand—what would happen to these *argumenta* if all concerned, the Catholic authorities included, were to acknowledge that they had for centuries misunderstood marriage and that they had misdefined it? To point at the obvious, if marriage's invulnerability to dissolution had for centuries been said to grow out of marriage's nature, would the invulnerability still be there if it were admitted that this nature had been misunderstood, and if a new understanding of it were worked out?

Doms had in fact faced this question, although only briefly and, in comparison with his long and detailed attention to the meaning of marriage, almost only in passing. He held to marriage's permanence. But where he located it—or more accurately where he relocated it from its traditional place in the needs of the children and in the definition of marriage the contract—was a harbinger of something the bishops of Vatican II were to say thirty years later.

Doms found the source of marriage's permanence in the spouses' love that expresses itself in sexual intercourse. He reasoned that when this intercourse is an authentic sexual union of the spouses, it is the complete giving of their selves to one another. Spirit in them, desiring this completion and expressing this desire, seeks its fulfillment in flesh, in bodily union.

But this desire cannot seek honestly for fulfillment, this mutual self-giving cannot reach honestly for completion, if they are intended to be temporary. To realize marriage's, or married love's, meaning, the man and woman must will their union to be permanent.[10]

Already the shift of locus is evident. Doms finds the source of marriage's permanence elsewhere than in the needs of the children (since not all marriages can produce them, and frequently the spouses know this in advance), elsewhere than in the objective nature of the marital contract (Doms did not think marriage a contract). Even in Christian marriage he located this source not quite in the sacrament itself, since he considered that the love that seeks completion in permanence must be already there and must be brought by the spouses to their sacrament.

Relocating the cause of marriage's permanence from the nature of the contract to the will of the spouses, and even to the quality of their love for one another, must have grievous consequences. Despite the absence from their statements of any hint of worry about these consequences, Pius XII and the members of the pertinent Roman congregations cannot have been unaware of them. What they surely did not suspect was that a little more than a decade later the bishops of the Second Vatican Council would do the same relocating that Doms had—but with consequences for Catholic doctrine and discipline somewhat more thorough and lasting.

The Second Vatican Council

On January 25, 1959, in his homily during Mass on the feast of the conversion of St. Paul, Pope John XXIII announced his intention to convene the Second Vatican Council. A major part of the preparation for this general Council of the Roman Catholic Church consisted of the gathering, by the Central Preparatory Commission, of suggestions from persons and groups around the Catholic world. This the Commission did early in 1960. Bishops and other prelates were asked to submit suggestions (*consilia*) and make known their recommendations (*vota*), the Catholic universities and faculties their studies (*studia*) and recommendations. The congregations of the Roman curia were asked to submit their recommendations and advice (*monita*).[11]

Two of these Roman congregations proposed that the general Council treat of marriage. One of them, the Sacred Congregation for the Discipline of the Sacraments, prepared two statements on marriage, neither of which was accepted by the Central Preparatory Commission.

The other was the Congregation of the Holy Office. It proposed the Council's examination of marriage in its *Schema Pro Concilio Oecumenico*, which was in substance and in mood an exhortation to the bishops soon to convene that they condemn the new errors against reason and against the Catholic faith that had gained currency since the First Vatican Council's condemnation of the errors current in 1869 and 1870. What this *Schema* exhorted the bishops of Vatican II to say is in its Part 4, Paragraph 24.

> It is most opportune to recall, clarify and reconfirm the main headings on the doctrine of marriage: its origin, its ends, its essential properties, its use. Then it should examine and define in the matters of birth control, periodic continence, *amplexus reservatus,* artificial insemination, consummation (penetration and semination), and the Petrine privilege, so called. There should be a careful examination of the validity of marriages in general of the baptized, and of the conditions of this validity.[12]

This brief paragraph proved to be the seed of a comprehensive text that almost certainly had as its principal author the prefect of the Holy Office, Cardinal Alfredo Ottaviani. The text came to the Central Preparatory Commission under double sponsorship because Cardinal Ottaviani was not only prefect of the Holy Office, which produced the brief paragraph. He was also president of the Theological Commission set up, under the supervision of the Central Preparatory Commission, to help prepare the agenda for the Council. It was the Theological Commission which developed the lengthy schema that was born in the brief paragraph quoted above.[13]

The Theological Commission proposed this schema to the Central

Preparatory Commission early in 1962. (The full Council was to meet in four approximately ten-week sessions, with the first convening on October 11, 1962, and the last adjourning on December 8, 1965.) Its title was *De Castitate, virginitate, matrimonio, familia.* In preparation for the Central Preparatory Commission's first discussion of it on May 7, 1962 Cardinal Ottaviani had sent to this commission a *relatio* in which he pointed out that the schema was meant to be a *constitution* voted and accepted by the full Council, " . . . a constitution pastoral, but pastoral and doctrinal, not pastoral-disciplinary. Consequently the Theological Commission has set out the objective order, that which God himself has willed in instituting marriage. Only in this way can the modern errors that have spread everywhere be vanquished."[14]

In Part 2, Chapter 1 of this schema-constitution—"The Divinely Established Order of Marriage"—the Theological Commission set forth the interpretation of marriage it intended for the entire Council to establish in the Church by doctrinal decree. The interpretation is encapsuled in the sixteenth and last paragraph of this Chapter 1, a paragraph titled "Errors Condemned," where, in a method imitating that of earlier Councils, it proposed to teach doctrine by anathematizing exactly phrased contradictions of the doctrine in question.

> The Holy Synod knows how greatly the health of the Mystical Body of Christ depends on a right acceptance of the divine order ruling marriage. In order to protect this health it is constrained before all to condemn those radical errors according to which marriage, in its order and constitution, is a mere social phenomenon undergoing continual evolution; those errors that deny it comes from God and from Christ, and deny that it is subject to the authority of the Church.
>
> It likewise condemns those errors holding that the marriage of Christians is not a sacrament or that the sacrament is only something accessory to and separable from the contract itself. It condemns the opinion asserting that marriage is a specific means of attaining that perfection by which man is truly and properly the image of God and of the Blessed Trinity. Likewise it condemns the opinion of those who hold either that the marital state is in the objective order superior to the state of virginity or to celibacy taken up for the Kingdom of God. . . .
>
> It condemns severely the errors and theories denying that there is an immutable divine order regarding the properties and ends of marriage. And it rejects explicitly as a supreme calumny the assertion that the indissolubility of marriage comes not from God but is something invented cruelly by the Church and cruelly held to. What is more, it condemns the theories which subvert the right order of values and makes the primary end of marriage

inferior to the biological and personal values of the spouses, and proclaims that conjugal love is in the objective order itself the primary end.[15]

What the Theological Commission wished the Council to decree concerning divorce and remarriage it set forth in Chapter 2, "On the Rights, Obligations and Virtues Proper to Marriage," in Paragraph 21, "Obligations Regarding Indissolubility" (the *bonum sacramenti*), and in Paragraph 22, "On Civil Divorce." Paragraph 21 reads as follows.

> The *bonum sacramenti*, "which designates the indissolubility of the bond and the elevating and consecrating of the contract as an efficacious sign of grace," is the most valuable of all the goods of marriage. And it brings with it serious duties. The Christian faithful have before all else the duty not to set aside the religious wedding prescribed by the Church and instead wed only in a civil ceremony, and by this juridical act have themselves declared married in this sense only, that in civil society they gain merely civil rights and duties. The faithful should understand that from the mere civil union alone, insofar as it contradicts the invalidating prescriptions of the Church, they enter into no marital bond or sacrament valid before God. For this reason those who attempt marriage invalidly against the laws of the Church are rightly and deservedly considered public sinners; and the Church has the right to declare its erring children such publicly, and to apply to them canonical penalties.[16]

This declaration must have been intended as the latest salvo in the two-centuries-old battle with the governments of Europe that claimed authority to regulate the marriages of their Catholic citizens. It got at the hither end of this claim by denying that Catholics can even create a marriage in a civil ceremony, and by threatening ecclesiastical penalties for those who try to do so nonetheless.

Paragraph 22 then gets at the further end of the civil governments' claim by denying their authority to dissolve marriages, and by forbidding Catholics to seek dissolution of their marriages by civil magistrates.

> The faithful are seriously forbidden to seek so-called civil divorce—divorce in the sense of a dissolution in the literal sense, as if the valid bond established before God could itself be dissolved by civil authority. Moreover no others are allowed to cooperate directly and formally in this civil divorce. For no reason or motive—even if not infrequently there be serious and painful cause for it—are the faithful allowed to dismiss a spouse and marry another as long as their sacred bond lasts, as the Lord

himself clearly teaches (Mark 10:11), even though civil authority sometimes allows this, though invalidly.

But at times the faithful can petition a "civil divorce" itself, with the permission of Church authority, and with the understanding that the marriage bond still goes on. Neither is simple separation of the spouses to be done without a serious, just and proportionate cause.[17]

It was the fate of this schema of the constitution to not only not be adopted and promulgated by the Council; it was not even accepted by the Central Preparatory Commission to be presented to the Council. For while most of the cardinals making up the Commission found it substantially satisfactory, four of them did not. These were Cardinal Julius Döpfner of München-Freising, Cardinal Emile Léger of Montreal, Cardinal Bernhard Jan Alfrink of Utrecht, and Cardinal Leo Joseph Suenens of Malines-Bruges. They found the schema seriously unsatisfactory, not only in some of its parts but in its inclusive point of view and even in its presumably pastoral attitude. If one can isolate the core of their negative criticism, this appears to be that the schema proposed an understanding of marriage that missed the mark of reality. It was an understanding foreign to the Christian married themselves; it was a taut, juridical definition of a relationship that the married do not experience.

Cardinal Döpfner's critical comment was by far the longest and most detailed (it occupies twelve pages in the *acta* of the Preparatory Commission's examination of the schema). Among other matters he objected to the misunderstanding of marital love and its omission from the schema's interpretation of marriage—a potential source of disedification for the Christian married.

> The bishops of the Church surely cannot be ignorant of how many damaging mistakes have been made in our pastoral practice under the inspiration of those textbooks treating this matter in an exclusively negative and juridically analytic way rather than in a spirit of charity and concern. We need not be surprised that so many of the faithful have been scandalized by the practice of confessors (so many of whom disagree with one another) interpreting sexual intercourse in a way looking only to the animal nature of men and women, while either ignoring the aspect of personal union in it or relegating it to a secondary status.
>
> Our faithful, who must give and want to give witness to the Christian life in marriage, but in most difficult circumstances, seek from the Council above all a synthesis that is truly constructive and attractive, in which marital love consecrated by their sacrament has a visible role. For such love it is that bears the

fruit that is chastity and fertility for this life and the next. It is this love which sustains fidelity and all the marital virtues.

The draft says a number of things in a beautiful way about the mystery of marriage, and about charity and love. But from a first reading of some of its parts one gets the impression that what it must say about marital love it says in a grudging way, more in order to warn against its dangers (which are, of course, not to be ignored), and more to point out its falsifications than to present it in its authentic nature. For example, in the entire chapter, "The Divinely Established Order of Marriage," nothing more is said about married love than the condemnation, at the end of the chapter, of the opinion of " . . . those who claim that marital love is the primary end in the objective order."

One must be grateful that the draft does not insert marital love into the order of marriage as a secondary end, as some have done, and to the considerable scandal of the educated faithful. But does not marital love, in the objective order itself and according to God's intent, somehow constitute the very form and soul of marriage, in such a way that without true marital love the ends themselves of marriage can neither be conceived of nor be rightly attained?[18]

It is of course not to be expected that in a statement so preliminary to the Council's full examination of marriage, and aimed mainly at blocking the acceptance of the Theological Commission's schema at least in its first formulation, Cardinal Döpfner would take notice of the consequences to marriage's permanence of his suggesting that ". . . marital love, in the objective order itself and according to God's intent, somehow constitutes the very form and soul of marriage in such a way that without true marital love the ends themselves of marriage can neither be conceived of nor be rightly attained." If this is true of marital love, what conclusion must be drawn about a marriage whose history shows that in the beginning it was indeed formed in and with love, but that this love later sickened and died, and did so irrecoverably? With the "form and soul" of the marriage gone from it—so that not even its ends can be attained or even conceived of— what remains of the marriage itself? (Nine years later the judges of the Catholic diocesan marriage court in Cardinal Alfrink's Utrecht were to put just this question concerning a presumed marriage that showed this history. And, as we shall see later in this chapter, they gave what seemed to them the logically necessary answer.)

Cardinal Alfrink continued and expanded the negative criticism of the schema. His intervention occupies almost three pages in the *Acta*. What follows seems the most significant part of it.

What the constitution says about the ends of marriage, specifically in its Part II, paragraph 13, "The Ends of Marriage," is in general true. But it will bring little light to the contemporary discussion of the subject. There are a certain confusion and disagreement in these discussions because so many of today's Catholics think and speak in a way quite different from those who talk in traditional terms of the primary and secondary ends of marriage. They do not understand one another because they speak different languages—one of them a juridical language which considers marriage merely as a contract, the other a language of psychology—a human and, unless I am mistaken, also a theological and biblical language. This second group understands marriage primarily as a sharing of life by two human beings who love one another and seek to bring children into the world.

One senses a most urgent need that through this constitution the Council bring light into this quite confused discussion. But I am afraid that this constitution will deceive and disappoint many because it does nothing but set forth the traditional way of thinking.

Without doubt it ought to present an uncompromised Catholic teaching on marriage. But the question is whether this juridical way of thinking really belongs to Catholic doctrine. Marriage is, to be sure, a contract. But is it only a contract? Or does it have other very important components? And is it not possible to set forth Catholic teaching in some other mode of thought?[19]

From this questioning of the contractual model's ability to make marriage understandable to modern Catholics, Cardinal Alfrink went on to do what Cardinal Döpfner had done, to demand that marital love have a place in the interpretation of marriage. He pointed out that the Book of Genesis declares that " . . . a man shall leave father and mother and cling to his wife," and he offered a brief exegesis of the passage, pointing out that it bespeaks a psychological love-union of husband and wife.

This passage speaks of a marital love which surpasses the love of parents and drives a man to his spouse. Here marital love seems to be understood not as a consequence of marriage but as its cause. Men and women who are about to marry do so *because* they love one another. Marital love is rather an element making up marriage itself than a consequence of a marriage.

Precisely because of this marital love marriage is universally in the Old Testament and in the New Testament a symbol of the relationship between Christ and his Church. Surely this is because of marital love which is the image of the love of Christ for his Church.

Sacred Scripture sees this bond of marital love not as the

end of marriage—as neither its primary nor its secondary end. It sees it rather as a constitutive element of marriage itself, not in the sense that without it the marriage would be invalid, but in the sense that it would be in some way defective, imperfect, incom- plete. Marital love belongs to marriage itself, at least if marriage be considered not merely as a juridical contract. And the prima- ry end of this bond of marital love remains in the objective sense the offspring conceived of this love, even though in the conjugal act the spouses do not have the child as their primary end.

Unless I am mistaken, this is the modern Catholic's way of thinking, a way of thinking that is more psychological, more human, as well as more theological-biblical.[20]

Cardinal Alfrink here touched momentarily an issue that was later to perplex and divide authorities and scholars in the Church. He says that marital love is a constituent element of marriage, yet not so constituent that its absence makes an attempt at marriage null, but only leaves the marriage incomplete. This may not have been the time and place for him to explain his understanding of the word "constitutive." But even if he stopped short of saying that love is essentially necessary for a marriage's existence, he did say that it is necessary for its completion. So even if love's absence does not keep a relationship from being a marriage, its absence seems to block its consummation. Would this then leave the marriage a candidate for dissolution by the papal power to dissolve? The answer to this question had to wait for a definition of consummation fitted to the new understanding of marriage's nature for which Cardinal Alfrink was arguing.

It is surprising that in their forty-six pages of critical comments on a document that was intended to concentrate and publish the Catholic Church's teaching concerning marriage in the twentieth century, the cardinals of the Preparatory Commission had virtually nothing to say about the schema's statements on divorce in paragraphs 21 and 22 of its Chapter 2. Even if they agreed with these statements, as they apparently did, one would expect them to say something pastorally helpful about the serious difficulty in leading a Christian life thousands of devout Catholics experience when living in enforced celibacy after a civil divorce. The most that any of them say is that these, like men and women who have never married, live under the moral obligation of perfect continence, and that God's grace is available to help them do so. There is in all these pages no evidence of an understanding proportioned to the size and severity of the problem in Western society.

The Pastoral Constitution on the Church in the Modern World

But the labor of research and writing expended by Cardinal Ottaviani and the Theological Commission in writing the schema, and the time and labor spent by the cardinals of the Preparatory Commission in reading and criticizing it, went for naught. When the cardinals voted to accept or reject the schema at the end of this, the sixth of the sessions in which they reviewed the agenda for the Council, it was obvious that they were unwilling to send it to the Council without substantial revision. Of the Commission's sixty cardinals only ten voted unqualified approval (a vote of *placet*). While only one voted unqualified disapproval, the others so hedged their approval (with a vote of *placet iuxta modum*)—some with substantial amendments, others with the request that the document be rewritten entirely—that the Commission had in effect rejected it. What is more, thirty-five of the sixty cardinals sided expressly with the criticisms leveled by Cardinals Döpfner, Alfrink, Léger and Suenens. Cardinal Augustine Bea's summary comment following his vote pointed to where the deep dissatisfaction lay: "The text ought to be less juridical—more positive and constructive. Let it use Sacred Scripture more fully and let its language be less technical."[21]

A second document on marriage intended for the Council's consideration met an equally futile fate. This was a decree, *Decretum de Matrimonii Sacramento,* prepared by the Conciliar Commission for the Discipline of the Sacraments by July of 1963. Even in its revised form it dealt with no more than the impediments to marriage, with the problem of religiously mixed marriages, with the form of marriage (the manner of exchange of marital consent), and the pastoral preparation for marriage. The fate dealt it during the Council's third session (dealt it on November 20, 1964, to be exact) was to remand it to Pope Paul VI for consideration by the yet-to-be-established commission that would eventually revise the Code of Canon Law, including its Title 7, *De Matrimonio.* (At the same time he announced his intention to convene the Council Pope John XXIII announced that the Code would be revised thoroughly.) Nothing more was ever heard of this document.

The document concerning marriage that the bishops of the Council eventually gave to the Church and to the world is the product of drafts and of revisions of drafts, of debate in the fourth session of the Council in the fall of 1965, of amendments, of procedural maneuvering and even of behind-the-scenes manipulation. Divorce and remarriage were not among the document's points of most intense concern. Such points were, first of all, the place of procreation and nurture as the primary end of marriage, with the subordination of all other ends and traits of marriage to this primary end, and, linked inseparably with this hierarchical arrangement of ends and traits, the moral judgment on contraceptive intercourse.

But though these two were the items of most serious concern, they were no more than that. It would be misleading to describe this last session of the Council as a debate and decision about the ends of marriage and about birth control. As its title indicates, the document the bishops produced, "The Pastoral Constitution on the Church in the Modern World," was immensely more than that. Even its one chapter on marriage,

"Fostering the Nobility of Marriage and the Family" (which is Chapter 1 of the document's Part II, "Some Problems of Special Urgency"), was in substance a change in the Catholic Church's very understanding of marriage. It is this changed understanding that produced the Council's judgment on the hierarchy of ends in marriage, and would have produced its judgment on birth control if Pope Paul had permitted the Council to make it.

And while the constitution speaks most briefly about marriage's permanence, and even about its indissolubility, what it says derives from the same changed understanding. The consequences of this change for permanence and indissolubility have proved more serious than the bishops may have anticipated.

The history of *Gaudium et spes'* production (this is the abbreviated title of the constitution taken from its opening words) is worth recounting briefly because it reveals the two mentalities among the bishops that met over the constitution and clashed there. In consideration of marriage's indissolubility this history is worth recounting also because it shows that neither group of bishops—not the tradition-minded conservatives such as Cardinals Ottaviani, Ruffini, Browne and Larraona, nor the progressive-minded such as the cardinals mentioned earlier—seemed much concerned about the consequences for indissolubility of this changed understanding of marriage. The conservatives were heartily, and some even bitterly, opposed to the change, but minimally because they saw in it any consequences for indissolubility. Their anxiety was concentrated in the change's consequences for the moral judgment on birth control. The progressives as well seemed to pass quietly over the consequences of the change for the traditional teaching on indissolubility. At least this is the impression one draws from studying the record of the debate in the Council on this chapter of *Gaudium et spes.*

The Production of *Gaudium et spes*

Like all the documents promulgated by the Council, the first draft of *Gaudium et spes* was written by a subcommission gathered and appointed especially for this task. It did its work under the supervision of Cardinal Suenens and a mixed commission consisting of the Theological Commission and the Commission for the Apostolate of the Laity. The subcommission first met in the spring of 1963, between the Council's first and second sessions. But because parts of the constitution, called at that time by a kind of code name, *Schema 17,* was not ready for distribution to the bishops by the summer of 1963, nothing of it was discussed in the Council's second session, in the fall of that year. It was worked at during the winter and spring of 1964, and was finally sent to the bishops at home in July of that year—but now, following the reordering of all the Council's documents, as *Schema 13,* "The Church in the Modern World."

The conflict that attended its gestation and birth—with the conservative prelates of the mixed commission wanting in it a repetition of the traditional teaching set forth earlier in the 1962 document prepared by Cardinal Ottaviani and the Theological Commission—seemed to end in a victory for those who wanted a gentler, pastoral statement.

This draft sent to the bishops in the summer of 1964 treated of marriage at two different places within itself. In its chapter 4, "The Special Tasks To Be Accomplished by Christians in the Modern World," paragraph 21 was titled "The Dignity of Marriage and the Family." The passage was brief, consisting of not more than eight paragraphs of moderate length.[22] Clearly dominant in it was the desire to understand sympathetically the difficulty of sustaining marriage in a Christian and even human manner in the modern world, and the desire to help men and women in this sustaining. It showed especial concern for the burden of bringing children into and rearing them in this world. And evident throughout it was the foundational shift in the understanding of marriage itself that I have already mentioned, the shift that so alarmed Cardinals Ottaviani *et al.*

Thus a statement early in the passage seemed to demote procreation and nurture, as ends of marriage, to parity with its more pastorally conceived goals.

> For God, in the wisdom of his love, designed marriage not only for procreation and nurture and for the husband's and wife's mutual help in earthly matters [the remedying of concupiscence is not mentioned], but also for the mutual sanctification and shared glorifying of God. Thus through them their children, even their neighbors and the environment in which the family finds itself, are helped along the road to holiness and salvation.[23]

Following closely on this opening declaration is the first sign of the shift in the understanding of marriage. This is the insertion of marital love near the center of this understanding. And it is within the passage's descriptive definition of this love that marriage's permanence and indissolubility make their first appearance.

> Since in our time so many exalt the love of husband and wife, it is the work of Christian spouses to show the world the true nature of this marital love. . . . True marital love is a mutual and free gift of the self made by each spouse to the other into one spirit and one flesh. It is a mutual interior conformation of one to the other. It is proved by tender affection; it far exceeds mere passing infatuation, which vanishes quickly and sadly when it is exploited in selfishness. This love, committed and declared in faith, and sanctified in the love of Christ, is indissolubly faithful through all of life's joys and trials.[24]

Here, at its first mention, the traditional characteristic of marriage that is its indissolubility is introduced not as a trait of marriage the contract, but as a trait of marital love. What is more, the marital love seems to gain its indissolubility not from anything to which it impels the spouses. Rather it is when it brings them to join in the sacrament and to live by the grace of Christ that this love gains its indissolubility. (The Latin of the passage is *Qui amor, fide ratus et in Christi amore sanctus, est indissolubiliter fidelis. . . ."* The word *ratus,* apparently drawn from the vocabulary of Catholic marriage law, designates a publicly acknowledged sacramental marriage of two Christians.)

Then comes a fair rebuff to the centuries-old interpretation of marriage as an institution serving the good of civil and ecclesiastical societies instrumentally. And here indissolubility is predicated for the first time of marriage itself as one of its traits.

> Marriage is no mere instrument of procreation. Rather the nature itself of the indissoluble covenant between the persons, and most especially the good of the children, demand that the spouses truly love one another. And even if the marriage has no children, it is in no way deprived of its fundamental value, of its indissolubility. But such is the character of marital love that marriage is of its nature oriented to the procreation and nurture of children.[25]

One can understand the anxiety of the conservative members of the mixed commission that received this draft on reading the last clause here. For centuries procreation had been said in and by the Church to be the natural end of marriage, and said in recent centuries to be its primary end. But here the necessity of children is grounded not in the nature itself of marriage but partly in marital love and partly in an orientation of marriage. The hint is there too that love is the source of the orientation.

The other place in the text of *Schema 13* that spoke of marriage was in one of the *adnexa,* or appendices, to the body of the text. This was *Adnexum 2,* "On Marriage and the Family."[26] What it said about the centrality of married love, on the place of love as the source of marriage's orientation to children and of its fidelity and indissolubility, is added evidence of the shift of understanding that created the anxiety among the conservative prelates that I have already mentioned.

Thus the first mention of indissolubility in this *adnexum* is of a characteristic of marital love.

> . . . While discerning the signs of the times the Council seeks to instruct the Christian faithful how they may, while standing by the truth, through their marriages and families witness for the world to the effective presence of Christ, and take part in the

renewal of this world. The first thing to consider in this divinely established vocation is the holiness of marriage and its sanctifying power. This done, and within an understanding of the new and changed conditions of life, the Council will treat of marital and family love, then of the characteristics that manifest and prove true marital love, namely the spouses' fidelity to one another and the unity and indissolubility of marriage. . . .

Then follows a brief sketch of marriage's history in the human race. Of this history the document says that Christ restored marriage's original unity and indissolubility. This is a return to the traditional thinking that sees indissolubility to be one of marriage's natural traits. And this natural indissoluble unity is strengthened by the grace of the sacrament—as the Council of Trent taught.[27]

In paragraph 4 of the *adnexum* appear clearly the elements of the dispute that began with von Hildebrand and Doms, that aroused the minds and emotions of Cardinals Döpfner, Alfrink, *et al.* in the May 1962 meeting of the Central Preparatory Commission, that complicated and exacerbated the dispute over *Schema 13* in the Council itself, and that continues in Catholic marital jurisprudence to this day. The dispute turns on the exact place of love in a marriage. Is its presence there essentially necessary, so that its absence would keep the couple from ever forming a marriage?

The inadvertent answering of this not explicitly asked question had begun earlier, in paragraph 2, with a statement that called marriage itself a covenant of love (*amoris foedus*). And the statement again located indissolubility in marriage as one of its traits. Joining the two predicates, one finds the statement saying of marriage that it is an indissoluble covenant of love.

> God, seeing that it was not good for the man to be alone . . . created them male and female from the beginning. He joined them in a covenant of love. He blessed them and said, "Increase and multiply and fill the earth." By blessing them he called them, so that "in one flesh"—joined, that is, in a single and indissoluble union—they might co-work with him and glorify him in the procreating of the human race.[28]

Back again in paragraph 4 of this *adnexum* one finds an answer to another implied question. Again the answer seems to say that love is essentially necessary to marriage, and again indissolubility is identified as a quality inherent in marriage—either as one of its "specific traits" or as one of its "essential goods." The question asks this time about the object of the consent needed to create a marriage. To what must a man and a woman consent if their consent is to make them spouses to one another?

Marital consent of its essence intends the unity of this covenant, its indissolubility and the love that is devoted to the service of life. The stronger and purer the marital love, the more strongly and perseveringly will the spouses accept and realize marriage's specific traits and its essential goods.

... No one is unaware of how seriously necessary it is that love be fully present in the act of consent, and increase throughout the entire married life. For love will fulfill and cause to be fulfilled what the consent has said and has promised.[29]

The answer to the question concerning the essential necessity of love in marriage sits unsatisfactorily in the last two sentences here. One of the sentences seems to say that love must be in the consent; the other seems to take this away, implying that love is only a cause needed to bring to fulfillment what is already created by the act of consenting.

In paragraph 5 the subcommission that drafted this *schema* went in detail through the interwoven issues of marital fidelity and indissolubility in a way that was not to be duplicated in the final and approved draft of *Gaudium et spes*. Because it was not, it will be enough at this point to record cursorily what it said.

First, it is according to God's original intent for marriage that it be indissoluble. But as a sacrament of the new law this original indissolubility becomes an image of Christ's fidelity to his Church, and through it the Christian spouses participate in this fidelity and become witnesses to it on earth.

Then the role of marital love is identified: of its very nature it intends an irrevocable fidelity.

Where a marriage is consummated as a sacrament it cannot be dissolved even by the authority of the Church. But for serious reasons this authority can dissolve the bond of a non-sacramental marriage, or of a sacramental marriage that is not consummated, but only within the limits of the authority set by Christ. (The claims here are virtually a recitation of the incumbent Canon Law. No explanation is offered of the limits of the authority set by Christ.)

The recitation concludes with a statement of "the privilege of the faith" in regard to a doubtful first marriage. That is, where two persons wish to be baptized but are already living in what is apparently a second marriage, the Church does not insist, as a condition of their baptism, that the persons leave this second union provided they had entered it in good faith. And the Church will baptize them despite the doubt about the validity of this second marriage consequent on the probable survival of the first. In a word, the obligation to fidelity grounded in the fact of natural indissolubility (of the first marriage) yields to the higher value found in the creating of a sacrament in the second union. Indeed natural indissolubility itself yields, in dissolution, to the subsequent sacrament.

The Debate on *Gaudium et spes*

Neither of these statements about marriage—not Chapter 4 nor *Adnexum* 2—survived to be included in the final version of *Schema* 13 (by that time become *Gaudium et spes*). Both the statements stirred resistance by the conservative-minded bishops too intense to allow the *schema* serene passage to promulgation. They were not the clauses concerning indissolubility that did this, since little notice was taken of indissolubility's quiet migration from among the qualities of a non-voidable contract into those of a covenant formed by a specific marital love. The negative and sometimes bitter criticism was aimed at what was deemed the document's indecisive mind on the place of procreation in marriage, at its ignoring what Cardinal Browne insisted was by then the certain doctrine of the Church about this place.

As a consequence of the disagreement and dispute in the Council's third session, in the fall of 1964, the *schema,* though approved in principle, was sent back to its authors for substantial revision. (Part of this revision during the winter and spring of 1965, between the third and the fourth session of Vatican II, was a major structural redrafting of the *schema.* The *adnexa* chapters were put into the body itself of the text, and this was divided into two parts. Chapter 1 of Part Two became "On Fostering the Nobility of Marriage and the Family.")

Despite returning to the Council in revised form in September of 1965, the *schema* met the same severe resistance. For the revising had removed none of its personalist conceptualization and vocabulary of marriage. It still refused to say that procreation and nurture are marriage's primary end. Indeed it avoided any discussion of the ends of marriage and therefore mentioned no hierarchy of ends. It refused to call marriage a contract and thus called into doubt the exchange of rights to sexual acts as the object of marital consent. It thus also removed the non-voidable contract as the locus of marriage's indissolubility. It insisted again on marital love's having a central place in marriage now understood as the marital covenant.

The bishops debated the entire text of the revised *schema* from its introduction at the start of this fifth session, on September 21, until October 8. They urged several emendations, or *modi.* Subcommission 6, headed by Archbishop Charles Dearden of Detroit, and working under the authority of the Mixed Commission on the final drafting of the chapter on marriage and family, completed its own revising by October 17 and on that date turned its results over to the Mixed Commission.

On November 12 the bishops in full session took up what was by then the sixth version of the constitution and debated it yet again for three days. The voting on its several parts occupied another three days, November 15, 16 and 17. Predictably the greatest number of rejecting (*non placet*) votes was directed at the chapter on marriage and family. But even so this chapter was accepted by an overwhelming majority of the bishops on the second day of the voting, November 16.[30]

Again there was no significant objection to what *Gaudium et spes* said concerning marriage's permanence and even indissolubility. The objections were again aimed carefully at the constitution's apparent change of teaching concerning the nature of marriage and its hierarchy of primary and secondary ends, and at its refusal to repeat the Church *magisterium's* earlier explicit condemnation of contraceptive practice, especially the condemnations written in Pius XI's encyclical letter *Casti connubii* and in Pius XII's discourse of 1951 to the Union of Italian Catholic Obstetricians.[31]

Detailed Statement in *Gaudium et spes*

En route to this analysis of *Gaudium et spes'* teaching about marriage I have suggested more than once that this teaching shifts the site as well as the cause within marriage of its claimed indissolubility from what they had been until 1965. That is, I think this teaching has introduced changed answers to the two questions, "Assuming marriage is indissoluble, what is it among its plural facets that is in fact indissoluble?" and "Whence comes this indissolubility? from which cause or causes?" Or to stake my claim more modestly, if *Gaudium et spes* did not shift decisively the site and the causes of indissolubility, it at least clearly suggested that other sites and causes than those traditionally acknowledged are possible. To make my case for this claim demands scanning carefully what the constitution says of the nature of marriage. What it says does not constitute a formal definition of marriage in the rigorous sense of "definition." It does not designate the genus of reality to which marriage belongs (which is a relationship), nor does it designate the species of relationship within this genus.

The constitution offers rather a descriptive definition of marriage, abundant, in places metaphoric, in other places diffuse and even imprecise. But from all this there emerges, I am convinced, a decisive understanding of marriage's nature—substantially unchanged from the understanding of it proposed in the 1964 draft of what was then *Schema* 17, but substantially changed from the understanding proposed in the Theological Commission's rejected 1962 document, the understanding that was a prolongation of the contractual definition coming down from the twelfth century.

Let us look first at the predicates that the bishops applied to marriage, at an inventory of the substantives they predicated of it. They first refer to it (in Article 47) as a community, as a community of love (*communitas amoris*).[32]

Then (in Article 48) they call marriage an intimate partnership—a community, or sharing—of marital life and love (*intima communitas vitae et amoris coniugalis*). They call it an institution (*institutum matrimonii*), and (in Article 49) the marital covenant (*foedus coniugale*).

Their understanding of marriage's nature emerges more clearly as they designate, or describe, the kind of act that creates a marriage. And they begin the relocating of indissolubility within marriage where they say (in Article 48) that marriage, which they have already called an intimate community of marital life and love, is created by a marital covenant, that is, by an irrevocable personal consent (*foedere coniugali seu irrevocabili consensu personali instauratur*). Here is the biblical notion of the act of covenanting. It is this, they say, that creates a marriage. Parties who covenant thus do so by consenting to an exchange. And here the bishops say that the consent is irrevocable, so that what is exchanged cannot be either taken back or given back.

What the bishops say is exchanged in the marital covenanting marks as clear a departure from the Church's juridical definition of marriage as does their calling marriage a covenant instead of a contract. It is not each spouse's right to his and her sexual acts. It is their very persons that they give over to one another ". . . in this human act by which the spouses reciprocally give over and accept one another (. . . *actu humano quo coniuges sese mutuo tradunt et accipiunt*).

The bishops come back a second time, here in Article 48, to this marital giving over of the spouses' persons to one another. Referring again to marriage as intimate union, they call it a reciprocal gifting of two persons to one another (*mutua duarum personarum donatio*).

Marital love has its function in this giving over of the selves, although the bishops do not say exactly what this is. They do say of it (in Article 49) that such love leads the spouses to make a free and mutual gift of themselves, and it pervades the whole of their lives (*talis amor . . . coniuges ad liberum et mutuum sui ipsius donum . . . conducit totamque vitam eorum pervadit*). What the bishops do not decide here is the question that exercised the cardinals of the Central Preparatory Commission in their meeting of May 1962 and alternately smoldered and flamed up since that meeting: Granted the serious need for such love in a marriage, is it also essentially necessary, so that its absence keeps the relationship from being a marriage?

Gaudium et spes and Marriage's Indissolubility

While the bishops were inconclusive about the essentiality for marriage of a specific love, they were both decisive and indecisive about marriage's indissolubility. The decisiveness was clear and emphatic; they said in many places and in different ways that marriage is indissoluble. Their indecisiveness appears to have been unwitting; they located this indissolubility now in one place, now in another in the multifaceted nature of marriage and among the causes needed to create a marriage.

I have already pointed out that *Gaudium et spes'* first predication concerning marriage, in Article 48, affirms that ". . . this intimate community, or sharing, of marital life and love is created by the marital covenant—by an irrevocable personal consent." Assuming that the last phrase here is in apposition to the one preceding it, the entire clause says that irrevocability is an essential quality of the consent needed to create a marriage. Logically, then, if one or both spouses intend against this irrevocability, they create no marriage despite their attempt at covenanting.

The sentence that follows points out a necessary effect of this covenanting that is an irrevocable consent. It creates an institution that is permanent—*institutum firmum*. This is God's design, and no human choice can change it—*non ex humano arbitrio pendet.*

The demand for marriage's permanence coming from the needs of the spouses and of their children appears too in this Article 48, the "defining article," of the chapter. But where the argument from natural law used by the Scholastics looked first to the good of the children as the source of this demand, here the bishops look first to the kind of union that a marriage is. *Because* this union is a reciprocal self-gifting of the spouses' persons, it demands both their fidelity and the union's indissolubility. This is not yet to simply define indissolubility into the covenantal union itself. But it comes very close to this. It says that both the act which creates the union, and its principal fruit, which is children, require that indissolubility be one of its traits.

What is not yet clear is whether the indissolubility thus predicated this early in the chapter is identical with the "natural" indissolubility predicated in the Code of Canon Law—the kind of indissolubility that is vulnerable to dissolution by papal authority, or the radical indissolubility said to be found only in marriages consummated as Christian sacraments. Since until this point in the chapter the sacrament has not been mentioned, it is accurate to conclude that the former is what the bishops have in mind.

But it soon becomes evident that behind the bishops' thinking even about marriage as the natural human relationship is a religious-historical assumption. It challenges the sharp distinction that a by now secularized Western mentality makes between the secular and the sacred. For the bishops say simply that men's and women's authentic marital love has as its model, and draws its meaning and its strength from, God's love for his human creatures. This love has been realized most concretely first in God's love for the people Israel, and now in Christ's love for his Church. Ultimately it is for its subsumption into the people of God and the Church that marital love exists.

And here, in précis, is the traditional theology of indissolubility, but with a new variation. Marriage's permanence is a derivative of marital fidelity; spouses remain together because their love for one another is faithful. But here the bishops skirt a much-needed precision, as it is skirted in so many other authoritative documents. What the bishops say is that "Christ abides in the spouses, so that just as he has loved the Church and has given himself up for it, so the spouses, by their mutual self-giving, may love one another with perpetual fidelity."

The desired but lacking precision is needed to answer a question concerning the relationship of the spouses' unfailing love for one another to the unfailing love of Christ for his Church. Is the spouses' love for one another unfailing (where it is) only as an imitation of its model found in Christ's unfailing love? The Latin *quemadmodum*—"just as"—can be interpreted to mean this. Or does Christ's unfailing love demand deontologically, by a moral imperative, that the spouses' love too be unfailing because the former is the model for the latter? Or where the love of two spouses is unfailing, is it so because Christ "abides in them," even as he abides in his Church with an unfailing love? One may acknowledge that *Gaudium et spes* is not a theological analysis, and that these questions probe for a fine point of such an analysis of indissolubility. But having an answer for them from the bishops, the teachers in the Church, is seriously important for Christians, and others, who want to know *how and why* marriages consummated as sacraments cannot be other than radically indissoluble.

In Article 49, which is an express and detailed examination of marital love, the bishops say more about the link between this love and marriage's permanence.

> This love, when committed in mutual trust, and especially when bonded and strengthened by Christ's sacrament, remains indissolubly faithful in body and in mind through the light and dark [of married life], and consequently remains a stranger to adultery and divorce.

It is anything but easy to ferret out exactly what the bishops mean to say here. Part of the risk in the search for their intent is to look for a fineness of meaning that they did not intend. But what is clear is that they affirm a causal function for marital love in producing a marriage's indissolubility. What they seem to say is this: marital love is faithful—faithful in the sense of invulnerable to adultery and to divorce—when it produces an unbreakable tie and because it does so through a personal commitment, and, by having produced an unbreakable tie through the personal commitment, it makes of the marriage a Christian sacrament.

If this complicated cause-effect linkage is what the bishops have in mind here, they simultaneously say something familiar and expected and do not say something familiar though expected. The familiar but expected thing they do not say is that the spouses' commitment creates a bond that is of its nature indissoluble, but a bond that is more firmly indissoluble where it is a sacrament. The familiar and expected thing they say, although only implicitly, is that for a marriage to be finally indissoluble, it must be a Christian sacrament.

But they also at least seem to say something that is both unfamiliar and unexpected. And here is where I detect the shift in the location of indissolubility within a marriage, a shift that I have already mentioned more than once. They seem to say that indissolubility is created in a marriage when marital love impels or leads the spouses to commit themselves in mutual trust, and the love and the commitment are also subsumed into the sacrament.

This may sound like nothing different from the earlier interpretation of marital consent which held that the spouses' consent can create a marriage only if both intend marriage with all its essential traits, indissolubility included. But there is a difference. That traditional interpretation never said that the spouses' consent causes the indissolubility of their marriage, much less that their love does so. But here in *Gaudium et spes* the bishops may say that the spouses' love does create their marriage's indissolubility—that their marriage is indissoluble if their love can produce a commitment that makes it so.

If this is what the bishops say here, then they unintentionally bring to life an issue of validity and nullity in marriages. To put it succinctly, if one insists, borrowing from those parts of the chapter which say that the marital union is in itself and of its nature indissoluble, it follows that couples whose love cannot bring them to make a commitment for indissolubility fail to marry.

The bishops' last remarks concerning indissolubility do assume that it is a trait of the marital union itself. Article 50 is a statement about the natural fertility of marriage and about the moral obligations attending this fertility. At the end of the article there are two needed qualifications concerning the essentiality of procreation in marriage—the second one needed lest it be thought that infertility because of age or other causes makes marriage impossible. The bishops insist that despite sterility a marriage exists and survives as the spouses' sharing, or communion, in all of life, and keeps its value and its indissolubility (. . . *suumque valorem atque indissolubilitatem servat*).[33]

The first of these qualifications points out that while procreation is natural to marriage, marriage exists for more than that. Two values demand also that the spouses show love for one another, and grow and mature in this love. These two values are the good of the children and the fact that their marriage is an indissoluble covenant.

> . . . but the character itself of the indissoluble covenant
> between persons, as well as the good of the children, demands
> that the mutual love too of the spouses be rightly oriented, that it
> grow and mature.[34]

Here the lines of causation reverse direction from what they are in the chapter's earlier statements linking marital love and indissolubility, although the reversal hardly contradicts the earlier causation. Here it is not that marital love impels the man and woman to an irrevocable covenanting. Rather their covenant, which is by nature indissoluble, demands a specific love in their marriage. So, although again allowing for the imprecision to be expected in a document that is not theological analysis, we find the bishops reiterating the traditional Catholic understanding that indissolubility is a characteristic of the marriage relationship itself, at least logically antecedent to the love that the spouses bring to their marriage.

But the bishops themselves are responsible for sowing in the Catholic consciousness a curiosity that asks about the precise link of causation between a marriage's invulnerability to dissolution and marital love. The curiosity peers at two questions, and the answer to the second depends for both its reference and its accuracy on the answer to the first.

Must the spouses exercise a specific love, marital love, if they are to create a marriage? And is the exercise of this love a necessary agent in the causing of the indissolubility of their marriage? The second of these questions can seem redundant, for if the answer to the first is affirmative, it follows that without such love no indissolubility is effected because no marriage is created. But by no means all Catholic authorities agree today that a man and woman must be able to love in a specific way in order to create a marriage.[35] Their denial hardly results in their denying marriage's indissolubility. But it does leave them to assume that indissolubility is not a characteristic found in a marriage because the spouses love one another in a specifically marital way, and to assume that it is found there not because the act that creates a marriage is a covenanting. They say what the Code of Canon Law says, that indissolubility is simply a given trait of marriage the contract—already there for the man and woman to accept if they choose to marry.

The Encyclical Letter *Humanae vitae*

Gaudium et spes was promulgated by the bishops of Vatican II, and the Council was adjourned on December 8, 1965 without the bishops' having declared their minds expressly on the principal marital question that engaged them, the morality of contraception as a method of birth control. They did not reverse the centuries-old Catholic proscription of this method. They reiterated it, but their reiteration was generic. They insisted only that a couple's decision about methods of regulating their fertility must be determined by objective standards, and that methods must not be used which are proscribed by the teaching authority of the Church.[36]

What the bishops refused to do was to single out which methods fall under this proscription, although the condemnations by Pius XI and Pius XII were already on record. This restraint was the consequence of Pope Paul's reserving to his own judgment the identifying of the methods of fertility control which were to be condemned anew as morally reprehensible. But this he did not want to do until he had received the report from the work of a study commission set up originally by Pope John XXIII in March of 1963, and enlarged by himself in June of 1964. This commission for the study of the problems of population and the regulation of births was made up of specialists in many fields—moral theologians, demographers, sociologists, psychologists among them. The commission sent its report to Pope Paul in June of 1966, recommending that the Church could relax its moral condemnation of individual instances of contraception while continuing its condemnation of marriages dominated by a contraceptive mentality, by a deliberate, persistent exclusion of children.

Paul deliberated, even agonized over the matter for more than two years. Finally, on July 25, 1968 he published his encyclical letter *Humanae vitae*, "On the Regulation of Birth."[37] In it he rejected the study commission's conclusion. He repeated the condemnation of single acts of contraceptive intercourse as morally disordered. What he said exactly about the moral obligation regarding individual acts is found in his paragraph 11.

> . . . The Church, calling men back to the observance of the norms of natural law, as interpreted by its constant doctrine, teaches that each and every marital act (*quilibet matrimonii actus*) must remain open to the transmission of life.[38]

Then in paragraph 14 he identified the methods of birth control that he considered morally disordered. First he identified acts that are physically contraceptive, along with abortion.

> . . . We must once again declare that the direct interruption of the generative process already begun, and, above all, directly willed and procured abortion, even if for therapeutic reasons, are to be absolutely excluded as licit means of regulating birth.[39]

Following this he singled out conduct intended directly to prevent conception by rendering one or other spouse sterile.

> Equally to be excluded, as the teaching authority of the Church has frequently declared, is direct sterilization, whether of the man or of the woman. Similarly excluded is every action which, either in anticipation of the conjugal act, or in its accomplishment, or in the development of its natural consequences, proposes, whether as an end or as a means, to render procreation impossible.[40]

The relevance of this condemnation to the Church's doctrine of marriage's permanence is admittedly distant. But I think it is real. It surfaces in Paul's reply, early in the letter, to those who argue that an accurate understanding of love and responsible parenthood leads to the conclusion that contraception is morally permissible if used within the context of a fundamentally fruitful marriage, one that does in fact produce children.[41]

Paul got his moral reasoning in refutation of this claim under way by offering "the true concept" of both marital love and responsible parenthood. (It is apparent that in offering it he also offered, although only informally and by implication, his definition of marriage.)

> And since, in the attempt to justify artificial methods of birth control, many have appealed to the demands of both conjugal love and of "responsible parenthood," it is good to state very precisely the true concept of these two great realities of married life. . . .[42]

Paul says first of all, about marital love, that it comes to men and women from God as from its source. He also implies that it is this love that leads them to marry, with a consequence that he notes explicitly, namely that in marrying a man and a woman are to carry out God's providence in the world.

> Marriage is not, then, the effect of chance or the product of evolution or unconscious natural forces; it is the wise institution of the Creator to realize in mankind his design of love.[43]

With this much set as a context he then offers his quasi-definition of marriage. He does so by identifying two kinds of causation that enter the creating of a marriage, the first the kind of act that creates it, and then the intent or goal of this creating. He plainly borrows from *Gaudium et spes* that a man and a woman marry by covenanting, by making to one another a personal gift of their selves. He goes beyond the constitution's "intimate community of marital life and love" (*intima communitas vitae et amoris coniugalis*) when naming this other kind of causation that enters the creating of a marriage, the final or motivational cause. Along with procreation and nurture he identifies the spouses' "communion of their being."

> By means of the reciprocal personal gift of self, proper and exclusive to them, husband and wife tend toward the communion of their being in view of mutual personal perfection, to collaborate with God in the generation and education of new lives.[44]

What Paul does not say here about the creating of a marriage is important. Consistently with *Gaudium et spes* he does not call marriage a contract. Therefore the man and woman do not create their marriage by making a contractual exchange. Therefore too indissolubility is not in their marriages as the non-voidability of a contract.

He does not follow *Gaudium et spes,* in its Article 48, in saying that the spouses' gift of their selves to one another is irrevocable. Even where he closes his paragraph 8 by adding that "for baptized persons, moreover, marriage invests the dignity of a sacramental sign of grace, inasmuch as it represents the union of Christ and of the Church," he does not add that a sacramental marriage's being the image of the unfailing love of Christ and the Church causes it too to be unfailing, or to demand that it be unfailing.

Where Paul might most opportunely have inserted his mind about marriage's indissolubility, he refrained from doing so. This is in paragraph 9 that follows immediately, wherein he explains the characteristics of marital love that he apparently considers essential to it. Where the issue of marriage's permanence could be found seminally in Paul's discourse is here in his explanation of these characteristics.

By the first of these, marital love's humanness, he means that it is both sensate and spiritual, that it is not only a rush of instinct or of affection, but is also—and is especially—a free act of the will. The act tends to this goal, that by the persevering and growing strength of this will (or act) the spouses become one in mind and affection, and together realize their human completion.

> This love is first of all fully *human,* that is to say, of the senses and the spirit at the same time. It is not, then, a simple transport of instinct and sentiment, but also, and principally, an act of the free will, intended to endure and to grow by means of the joys and sorrows of daily life, in such a way that husband and wife become one only heart and one only soul, and together attain their human perfection.[45]

Is it fair to conclude that an act of volitional love having this goal demands that the spouses stay permanently with one another?

The second characteristic of marital love that Paul sees is its totality. He says that this makes such love a unique form of friendship in which the spouses share everything. It is an essentially giving love, one by which the spouse is loved not only for what he or she can give, but in and for his and her own person. Paul returns to *Gaudium et spes'* concept of marriage's covenantal nature: the totality of marital love impels the spouses to make gifts of their own persons to one another.

> Then this love is *total,* that is to say, it is a very special form of personal friendship, in which husband and wife generously share everything, without undue reservations of selfish calculations. Whoever truly loves his marriage partner loves not only for what he receives, but for the partner's self, rejoicing that he can enrich his partner with the gift of himself.[46]

Odd it is, however, that in this characteristic of totality Paul does not include temporal totality—the permanence of marital love. Is this a deliberate stopping short, a cautious reluctance to suggest that marriage's indissolubility has its cause, or even one of its causes, in the spouses' love?

The third characteristic is the marital love's fidelity and exclusivity until death.

Again, this love is *faithful* and *exclusive* until death. Thus in fact do bride and groom conceive it to be on the day when they freely and in full awareness assume the duty of the marriage bond.[47]

If Paul had here named only marital love's fidelity, one would be tempted to infer that he has in mind the virtue that keeps spouses from going to other sexual partners. But he seems to designate this virtue by the term "exclusive," and thus leave the way for fidelity to mean a quality of the spouses' love that keeps them together for as long as both live. If this distinction of meanings is what he intends, this, his most apposite statement about marriage's permanence, locates this permanence in the love that brings a man and woman into marriage. Does he go so far as to say that their marriage is permanent because they love one another with authentic married love? No, I think he does no more than set in juxtaposition the elements of a psychology of marriage that could produce this conclusion.

He names the fourth and last of the characteristics of marital love as its fecundity. By this Paul means that the spouses' love is not contained and perhaps cannot be contained within the communion, or sharing, that is central to their marriage, but this love exceeds the limits of this communion and overflows into the producing of new life in their children. He quotes at this point the beginning words of Article 50 in *Gaudium et spes'* chapter on marriage.

And finally, this love is *fecund,* for it is not exhausted by the communion between husband and wife, but is destined to continue, raising up new lives. "Marriage and conjugal love are by their nature ordained toward the begetting and educating of children. Children are really the supreme gift of marriage and contribute very substantially to the welfare of their parents."[48]

I return again to the significance of Pope Paul's not repeating certain magisterial assertions available to him in this, his effort to explain in what way men's and women's artificial controlling of their fertility is morally disordered. He omits readily and completely what the bishops of Vatican II omitted only after difficult debate and in a compromise statement, namely any defining of marriage according to ends apart from itself. Where the bishops refused only to speak of a hierarchy of marriage's ends, he refused to speak of ends at all.

It was essential to his argumentation in demonstrating contraception's moral disorder that he define marriage, since this disorder is demonstrable only if contraception in some way offends the nature of marriage. But instead of referring any defining predicates to marriage as an institution or relationship he referred them to the act that creates a marriage (the spouses' gift to one another of their persons), and to the realization internal to a marriage for which it exists (the spouses' communion meant to grow into their mutual completion—which includes their collaborating with God in producing and nurturing new life).

But more than all else, he drew Catholic awareness to, and fixed it on, marital love. For in a feature of his logic that has not always been noticed by students of *Humanae vitae,* Paul sought to demonstrate the moral disorder of contraceptive intercourse by showing that it offends not immediately against the nature of marriage itself, but against the nature of marital intercourse, and that it offends against this nature by damaging intercourse as the spouses' expression of a communion in love unique to themselves. Thus he postulated that marital intercourse has two meanings, the procreative and the unitive, that these two meanings are equal in value, and that they are morally and psychologically inseparable in conduct. That is, he took for granted that if any act of intercourse is to be truly unitive, it must be also procreative, and, reciprocally, that if it is to be truly procreative, it must be also unitive. In short, he reasoned that contraceptive intercourse offends against marriage because it offends against marital love. It inhibits, it constrains, it shrinks the natural fruitfulness of this love.

No one need be surprised then if Catholic students of marital matters—students of indissolubility as well as of fertility and its control—should take Paul's cue and reason about them mainly within the context of marital love.

The Revised Marriage Law

During the same homily on January 25, 1959 in which he announced the future convening of the Second Vatican Council Pope John XXIII announced also that the Catholic Church's Code of Canon Law would be subjected to a thorough revision. We recall that the Church's first code of law had been promulgated only in 1917. Pope John's reason for deciding to revise it from beginning to end after only forty-two years was to make it reflect the Church's developed understanding of itself in the middle of the twentieth century, an understanding that was to be expressed in the Council he had convened.

The revising was done under the supervision of the Pontifical Commission for the Revision of the Code of Canon Law. Under this supervision several subcommissions, called *coetus* in the vocabulary of Catholic administration, each worked at the revising of the several parts of the Code. (The subcommission that worked until the spring of 1978 on the revision of Title 7 of the Code, *De Matrimonio,* had Monsignor Guillaume Onclin as its secretary and Fr. Pieter Huizing as its *relator,* the person who prepared the subcommission's work sessions.)

In the revision the canons regulating marriage have been relocated from Book 3 of the 1917 Code, titled *De Rebus* (On Things), to the more appropriate Book 4, The Sanctifying Office of the Church, Part 1, The Sacraments. There the canons on marriage are under Title 7.

The *coetus* that revised these canons began its work in 1966. On their way to final revision the canons passed through multiple reformulations at many hands. The same disagreements about the nature of marriage and of marital consent that caused fervent debate in the fourth session of Vatican II continued among the persons and groups that had a hand in their revising. The successive and tentative versions of the canons published from 1971 until their promulgation in final and definitive form on January 25, 1983 reflected the back and forth surge of the debate. But this is not the place to examine that brief but complicated history. I shall limit this examination to the canons in their now definitive form.[49]

The Defining Canons

We recall that the two canons in the 1917 Code that define marriage, although informally, are Canons 1012 and 1013. It will help, in explaining the new and revised defining canons, to see the old canons once again.

1012.1 Christ Our Lord has raised the marital contract itself, where it is of baptized persons, to the dignity of a sacrament.
2 Consequently, where it is of baptized persons there can be no valid marital contract without its being by that very fact a sacrament.

1013.1 The primary end of marriage is the procreation and nurture of offspring; its secondary end is mutual help and the remedying of concupiscence.
2 The essential traits of marriage are unity and indissolubility, which in a Christian marriage gain a special firmness by reason of the sacrament.

The canons in the revised Code that state the nature of marriage are Canons 1055 and 1056. They show both significant changes from and significant replications of the older canons.

1055.1 The marriage covenant, by which a man and a woman establish between themselves a partnership of their whole life, and which of its very nature is ordered to the well-being of the spouses and to the procreation and upbringing of children, has, between the baptized, been raised by Christ the Lord to the dignity of a sacrament.
2 Consequently a valid marriage contract cannot exist between baptized persons without its being by that very fact a sacrament.
1056 The essential properties of marriage are unity and

indissolubility; in Christian marriage they acquire a distinctive firmness by reason of the sacrament.[50]

To note first the replications, Canon 1055.1 reaffirms what is asserted, in the older canon, as an historical event, and has been subsumed into Catholic doctrine, that Christ brought it about that the marriage of any two baptized Christians, at any time and in any place, is a sacrament. This is a reaffirmation of the disputed "automatic sacramentality" of the marriages of the baptized. Canon 1055.2, which repeats old Canon 1012.2 word for word, reasserts both that two Christians cannot be married at all unless their marriage is a sacrament, and that what their sacrament is, is the marital contract. Here there is an at least apparent inconsistency in the revised formulations, for Canon 1055.2 says that it is the marital contract that becomes the sacrament, whereas Canon 1055.1 calls marriage not a contract (as old Canon 1012.1 does) but a covenant. Consistency, it seems, would demand that new Canon 1055.2 say also that it is the marital covenant that becomes the sacrament.

In any case, by legislating once again the inseparability of the contract (or covenant) from the sacrament in Christian marriages the revised law keeps a tight grip on the reason for holding such marriages to be radically indissoluble, namely that they are inescapably sacraments.

Catholic critics were heard around the world when shown this first draft of the revised marriage canons, with old Canon 1012's automatic sacramentality left unchanged in new Canon 1055.2. But both the subcommission and the supervising commission were unyielding on this point. They offered for their adamant stand an explanation that I shall review toward the end of this chapter.

New Canon 1056, because it simply repeats old Canon 1013.2, also reiterates its prescriptive insertion of indissolubility into the definition of marriage. The new canon also means by indissolubility what the old canon did: not that marriage is by nature impervious to any attempt to dissolve it, but, as we know from the larger context and history of indissolubility, that no authority other than that of the Pope can dissolve a marriage. This unique because dissoluble indissolubility is evident in the last clause of the canon, which repeats that it is when the indissoluble contract or covenant becomes a sacrament that its indissolubility finally becomes indissoluble even in face of papal authority—that it gains its "distinctive firmness."

Surely new Canon 1055's most significant change from old Canon 1012 lies in its saying no longer that what a man and woman do in marrying is to contract with one another. It says rather that they covenant; its key term is not *contractus* but *foedus*. If the import of this changed predication is not immediately evident in the canon itself, it becomes so in new Canon 1057.2 There the man and the woman were said to create their marriage not, as in old Canon 1081.2, by giving over to and accepting from one another the right to sexual intercourse. That is the exchange fitted to a contract. But with new Canon 1055.1 now naming marriage a covenant, Canon 1057.2 identifies that which the spouses give to and accept from one another in their marital consent as their persons. We shall look more closely at the significance of this in a moment.

To note a refinement of meaning in Canon 1055.1, it does not name marriage a covenant. It seems to predicate this term, *foedus,* of the act by which the spouses create their marriage, since it says that by this covenant they create a "partnership of their whole life." The covenant seems the instrument of their creating, the partnership the product of it.

What Canon 1055.1 understands marriage to be emerges if we review briefly the sequence of selection and rejection of substantives in the history of its revision. If we take this history inclusively, the revision began in the Second Vatican Council's *Gaudium et spes.* In the first clause of its Article 48 (of Part II, Chapter 1) the constitution calls marriage an intimate community, or sharing, of marital life and love (*intima communitas vitae et amoris coniugalis*). This community is there said to be created by the spouses' covenanting.

In the first draft of its proposed revision, published in 1971, the subcommission designated the nature of marriage as a man's and woman's intimate conjoining of their entire lives (*intimam totius vitae coniunctionem inter virum et mulierem*). The apparent reason for replacing the constitution's *communitas* with *coniunctio* was that the commission sought to designate the act by which a marriage is created rather than the abiding effect of the act, namely the marriage. The Latin substantive *coniunctio,* ending as it does with the letters *tio,* refers to an action rather than to a state. Why designate the act of marrying rather than the state of marriage? Because if the covenanting that is, according to *Gaudium et spes,* the cause of a marriage should fail, it would follow not that the marriage would vanish from existence, as some far-seeing and adventuresome Catholic marriage courts were willing to conclude—as we shall see in the following chapter. It would follow only that the couple had failed to create a marriage at all.

And most emphatically was *Gaudium et spes'* designation of marriage as an intimate community of love left out of the formulation of Canon 1055.1. There was to be nothing in it from which the conclusion could be drawn that with the vanishing of the spouses' love from the marriage, the marriage itself has vanished.

After five years of study and criticism of the proposed revision of these canons on marriage, the subcommission presented, in the spring of 1978, its final formulation of this defining canon (which was at the time numbered Canon 242). There the spouses were said to create, by their covenanting, an intimate communion, or sharing in all of life (*intimam inter se constituunt totius vitae communionem*). Again the formulation shows, in its principal substantive *communio,* that it intends to declare not the nature of marriage as a state, a stable relationship, but the nature of the act by which the spouses create their marriage. This formulation obeyed the injunctions of the most authoritative of the revision's critics, the plenarium of cardinals in the commission supervising the revision of the entire canon law. They convened in Rome in May of 1977. I quote here from my earlier volume to explain what the cardinals instructed about the new canons that were to define marriage in the revised Code, and why they did so.

The cardinals of the *plenarium* proceeded in their deliberation on this canon ... by putting to themselves the following three *quaestiones de natura matrimonii:*

(a) Whether a concept of marriage ought to be included in the code. If so ...

(b) Whether the definition ought to include the element of "conjoining of life" (or "communion," or "sharing" of life) as an expression of the personal aspect of marriage (*Gaudium et spes,* no. 48). If so....

(c) What should be the valence of this element in determining the validity of a marriage?

They voted that, yes, a concept of marriage ought to be included in the revised code. But they urged that it take there a form both oblique and descriptive, presumably in preference to a formal definition. They added the qualification that explains their keeping the substantive *coniunctio* instead of *communitas.* They wished the defining concept to refer to a marriage *in fieri,* to a marriage in its creation at the moment of consent. But what a marriage is in its nature as an abiding state they apparently wished the law not to say. Knowing what the Code's definition was likely to be, they meant it to refer only to the act which creates a marriage. With this vote went the admonition that expressions leading to false interpretations be kept out of the canon.

In their second vote the cardinals drew that much definition to a finer focus. They agreed, although with a weaker majority, that the element "conjoining of life" (or "sharing" or "communion" of life) be included in the definition. But again a kindred caution was urged, namely that in the final phrasing of the canon expressions be avoided that could open the way to false interpretations of the canon in jurisprudential practice of the Church's marriage courts.

Answering the third and last of their own questions, about the valence of the element of communion, or sharing, in determining the validity of marriages, the cardinals voted by a still smaller majority that this element have valence in so determining. But again they urged their earlier qualification that this valence be limited to judging the validity of the consent creating a marriage, but that it have no valence in judging the validity of a marriage *in facto esse,* once it is established in existence. They wanted nothing in the Church's law vulnerable to the interpretation that once the "intimate sharing in all of life" disappears irretrievably from a marriage, the marriage dies out of existence.[51]

But following a meeting of the *plenarium* of cardinals again in the fall of 1981, and apparently according to its instructions, the wording of this canon as it was published in the spring of 1982 (by then it had been given the number 1008) had *consortium* as its key substantive. With this the intent apparently shifted back to declare the nature not of the covenanting act that creates a marriage, but the nature of the relationship that the covenanting act creates, the state of marriage. Apparently too the worry lest this canon's formulation be vulnerable to the conclusion that a marriage could end by the failure of the spouses' covenantal love has been put aside. In any case, the law's part in making marriage invulnerable to dissolution is evident in two other canons we have already seen. The first is new Canon 1056, which simply repeats old Canon 1013.2 in declaring that indissolubility is an essential trait of marriage. The other is new Canon 1057.2 which replaces old Canon 1081.2 in stating exactly the nature of the act which creates a marriage.

Definition of the Act That Creates a Marriage

The entire Canon 1057 reads as follows:

> 1 A marriage is brought into being by the lawfully manifested consent of persons who are legally capable. This consent cannot be supplied by any human power.
> 2 Matrimonial consent is an act of will by which a man and a woman by an irrevocable covenanting mutually give and accept one another for the purpose of establishing a marriage.[52]

Paragraph 2 reproduces, although not verbatim, a key phrase from Article 48 of *Gaudium et spes:* "The intimate community [or sharing] of marital life and love ... is created by the covenant of marriage, an irrevocable personal consent."[53] The paragraph seems to intend the following things about the nature of the act that creates a marriage, all of them bearing, with varying significance, on the indissolubility of marriage.

First, that which creates a marriage is two persons' acts of will, their conjoined decisions. It is not an attitude in them, not a condition of emotional union. When expressed in the way prescribed by law it can be verified in time and in place, can be verified as completed once for always. Therefore, since it is a causative act, when it produces its effect, the marriage, this production too can be measured within a verifiable time and place. Therefore too the producing of the marriage is not a process whose nature is to be continuous, so that if the process halts the marriage vanishes.

That which is designated as the covenant is not the effect of the consent, the marriage itself. The Latin noun for covenant, *foedus,* is here used in the ablative case, *foedere.* Syntactically it is an ablative of means. Thus the adjective that modifies it, *irrevocabili,* designates not an indestructible marriage-effect. It designates an irrevocable consent on the part of the spouses. This is the correlate to the trait of marriage named in Canon 1056 as its indissolubility. The indissoluble marriage is produced by an irrevocable consent. It is also the analogue to the consent which in old Canon 1081.2 was said to have as its effect the spouses' exchange of their right to sexual intercourse. That consent was not called irrevocable; it was said rather to exchange the right in perpetuity. Here in new Canon 1057.2, while the spouses are said to give over their persons to one another (*sese mutuo tradunt*), the permanence is predicated not of the effect of the exchange, but of the exchanging act itself. It is an irrevocable covenanting.

Thus once the spouses make this gift of their persons to one another they can neither take it back nor accept it if the other tries to give it back. Whence comes this irrevocability? Since it is predicated of marriage universally, not only of Christian marriages, it cannot be said to come from the latters' sacramentality. Rather it seems simply defined into marriage by the bishop-definers of marriage in their writing of *Gaudium et spes,* whence in turn this formulation is borrowed by the revised law. *Gaudium et spes* offers as its apparent warrant for this irrevocability Christ's repetition (in Mark 10:8 and Matthew 19:6) of the Genesis declaration that once a man and woman are spouses "they are no longer two . . . but one body." If my finding of the cause-effect relationships here is accurate, Canon 1057.2 concludes, via multi-link causation, that the consent creating a marriage (the cause) is irrevocable because the marital union (the effect) is indestructible. Hence a unique reciprocal causation: The consent-cause produces a marriage-effect which in turn, because it is indestructible, makes the consent to be irrevocable.

But despite all this there persists the Catholic understanding that marriage as a natural human relationship is not really indestructible. Provided it has not been consummated as a sacrament it can be dissolved, which is to say destroyed, by papal authority. Consequently while the canon defines irrevocability into the marital consent, it does not account for its being there. In a disguised and oblique way it simply repeats the traditional locating of the authority—and lack of authority—to dissolve marriages. Repeating this location seems to be its unacknowledged intent.

The Indissoluble Bond of Marriage

The last of the defining canons in the 1917 Code is in its Chapter 9 of Book 3. The chapter is titled "The Effects of Marriage" (*De Matrimonii Effectibus*). The canon, 1110, is worded as follows:

> From a valid marriage there arises between the spouses a bond which is of its nature perpetual and exclusive. Moreover a Christian marriage confers grace on spouses who put no obstacle to this conferring.[54]

New Canon 1134 of new Chapter 8 is the revised formulation of this statement. It leaves the first clause untouched, but it alters the second to say, in the words of *Gaudium et spes* (Article 48), "Moreover, in Christian marriage the spouses are by a special sacrament strengthened and, as it were, consecrated for the duties and the dignity of their state."[55]

The first clause, which reads so routinely, has in it one word that can be crucial in all theoretical argument concerning the indissolubility of marriage and in the disciplinary regulation of divorce and remarriage. It makes its first appearance only here among the last of these defining canons. The word is *vinculum*—"bond." Set in the wording of the canon it is meant to designate the effect of the cause that is there named *matrimonium*. In context the latter must signify the marital consent which creates the marriage. Therefore in using the term *vinculum* the canon means to say what it is that the marital consent creates, and in effect says what a marriage is. It is a bond. And the two adjectives that modify it—"exclusive" and "perpetual"—simply repeat the essential characteristics of marriage as these are named in old Canon 1013.2 (which is reproduced in turn in new Canon 1056). It is not that the canon defines so exactly as to say that it is the marital consent that causes the exclusivity and the perpetuity. Rather, what is assumed in the canon is that the consent, acting as a cause, produces its effect, the bond, which in and of itself has the characteristics of exclusivity and perpetuity.

I said just above that the term "bond" is crucial in the Catholic doctrine and discipline of divorce and remarriage. In the next and concluding chapter we shall see how this is so, how Pope Paul VI was able to use it distinctly from *Gaudium et spes'* predicates concerning marriage— covenant, community, communion, sharing—and even in contra-distinction against them to assert that even though all these realities should disappear from a marriage, it nevertheless survives in existence. The reason it does so, he explained, is that that which is the essence of a marriage, the bond, is invulnerable to the failure of the covenant, etc. It survives despite their failure. Hence the marriage survives. Thus if one be tempted to think that the bond, which the canon says arises from the *matrimonium*, is a reality distinct from the marriage, Pope Paul at least has countered the suspicion by affirming that the bond is itself the essence of the marriage. Thus he clearly though implicitly insisted that the community, the sharing, the covenant, the community—all of which can fail and vanish—do not belong to the essence of marriage. This essence is in the indestructible bond. Therefore the marriage cannot fail and vanish.

The Canons Ruling Divorce and Remarriage

This review of the proposed revision of the Catholic marriage law may come to an appropriate end with an examination of those canons which rule the dissolution of marriage. The proposed revision of these canons appears to keep unchanged in essentials the wording of the 1917 canons, despite the urging by critics among the consultative groups that they be changed at certain points. The changes that have been made in these canons are confined to their less than essential parts.

Old Canon 1118 continues unchanged, in the proposed revision, in new Canon 1141.

A marriage which is ratified [sacramental] and consummated cannot be dissolved by any human authority or by any cause other than death.[56]

While this formulation may seem at first reading to contain a reiteration of marriage's natural indissolubility, it does not. We shall see soon enough that in context it is, among other things, an introduction to the canons which state who can, by Catholic doctrine and in Catholic law, dissolve marriages. On the other hand, this canon says not so much who cannot dissolve, but which kind of marriage cannot be dissolved by anyone. It thus prepares the way for saying which kinds of marriages can be dissolved by those empowered in the Church to dissolve.

It is evident from what has gone before in this essay that the canon encapsulates centuries of history. It says what the authorized teachers in the Church thought, by 1917 and still in 1984, is the inner inviolable barrier of marriage's claimed indissolubility. Finally and immovably that marriage and it alone is beyond the reach of any cause save death to dissolve which is a sacrament and which has been consummated as a sacrament.

Where the canon's claim is arguable, and where the invited critics did argue between 1975 and 1978, is in the assumptions lying behind the terms *ratum* (sacramental) and *consummatum.* These assumptions are that, first, a marriage is a sacrament by the mere fact that both spouses are baptized, and, second, that this marriage is consummated provided the spouses have had a single act of complete sexual intercourse following their marital consent.

What is arguable within these two assumptions is, first, that all that is needed to make a marriage a sacrament is that the parties to it have received Christian baptism. It takes for granted that no Christian faith, no Christian trust or love, is needed at the time of marrying nor during the marriage. Both parties could be atheists by the time they marry. Yet the automatically surviving baptismal "character" in their souls makes their marriage automatically a sacrament, an imaging on earth of the love of Christ and his Church.

Almost as arguable here is the assumption concerning the act that is sufficient to consummate a sacramental marriage. The act fitted to the consummating of a contract—a single, complete exercise of the contractually exchanged right—is kept from the 1917 Code and asserted to be the act which completes a marriage as this has been defined by the bishops of Vatican II: a community, a sharing, of marital life and love. The one act consummates, which is to say that it completes, this sharing as it is subsumed into Christian sacramentality. The one act is said to complete the spouses' imaging of the love of Christ and his Church for one another.

Cardinal Felici and the revising subcommission acknowledged such criticisms as these. Their reply to them contained a curious methodology of ecclesiastical legislation. They admitted that the issues under criticism are theological and theologically disputed. But precisely because they are, and because the subcommission wanted no juridical decision to seem to resolve this theological dispute, it determined that the 1917 legislation in their regard is to be kept unchanged—as though this legislation were not already a decision made in their regard.[57]

New Canon 1142 repeats old Canon 1119, but with one significant omission and one significant change. Canon 1119 reads as follows:

> A marriage of baptized persons that is not consummated, or a marriage of one baptized person and one unbaptized, is dissolved, by virtue of the law itself, by solemn religious profession, or by a dispensation granted for a just cause by the Apostolic See, and granted at the request of both parties or of one of them, and in the latter case even against the will of the other party.[58]

New Canon 1142 is this:

> A non-consummated marriage between baptized persons or between a baptized party and an unbaptized party can be dissolved by the Roman Pontiff for a just reason, at the request of both parties or of either party, even if the other is unwilling.[59]

This canon continues both an assumption and a claim that are by now familiar. The assumption is that only a sacramental marriage that has been consummated specifically as a sacrament is finally invulnerable to even dissolution by papal authority. The claim is that the papal "power of the keys" to bind and to loose given by Christ to Peter and to others of the disciples can "loose" marriages provided they are either not consummated or are not sacraments, or are neither.

There are familiar theological issues that trouble this canon. These issues are, first, the assumption that a marriage is a sacrament merely because of the baptism of the spouses. Then there is the assumption that a marriage is consummated by the first act of complete sexual intercourse after the marital consent. A complicating element added to the first of these difficulties surfaces in the contingency pictured in the following hypothetical example.

Let us say that two spouses, both unbaptized, separate by civil divorce. Two years after the separation one of them is baptized a Roman Catholic. Four years after it the other attempts a second marriage. Twelve years after it, and at a distance of three thousand miles, this other spouse receives Christian baptism in a Protestant community that accepts civil divorce. According to the theology of sacramentality enshrined in the Catholic law this second baptism makes a sacrament of the original marriage, which still exists despite the civil divorce. But still it can be dissolved by papal authority because it has not been consummated since becoming a sacrament.[60]

In the new Canon 1142 the ancient dissolution of unconsummated marriage by the pronouncing of solemn vows in a religious order is omitted. So too is the more recent extension of this juridical tradition to the dissolving of non-sacramental marriages by the same profession.

There is another difference in the revision of these canons, the last to be mentioned for now. Old Canon 1119 specified that the use of the papal power of the keys to dissolve these marriages is specifically a dispensation. Implied there was a qualification of this claim concerning papal power, namely that it does not so much dissolve marriages directly as dissolve them by dispensing the parties from one of the effects flowing from the natural indissolubility of the marriage bond. The new Canon 1142 omits this qualification. It says nothing about dispensation, but simply asserts the papal power to dissolve. The reason given for the change is, again, the unwillingness of the subcommission to take up a theological dispute and resolve it by legislation. But this time the unwillingness results in a change from the incumbent law instead of a continuation of that law.

The Revised Canons Concerning the Pauline Privilege

Five canons in the revised law regulate the use of the Pauline privilege in dissolving marriages and thereby freeing the parties for a second marriage. The first of these, new Canon 1143 (a revision of old Canon 1120), in its first paragraph defines the nature itself of the privilege and states how its use dissolves an extant marriage. Its paragraph 2 explains the conditions under which the privilege can be used.

1 In virtue of the Pauline privilege, a marriage entered into by two unbaptized persons is dissolved in favor of the faith of the party who received baptism, by the very fact that a new marriage is contracted by that same party, provided the unbaptized party departs.

2 The unbaptized party is considered to depart if he or she is unwilling to live with the baptized party, or to live peacefully without offense to the Creator, unless the baptized party has, after the reception of baptism, given the other just cause to depart.[61]

The possibility of dissolving a marriage by use of the Pauline privilege is the fact that the prior marriage was not a sacrament. The warrant for the privilege's use is, we recall, the interpretation of 1 Corinthians 7:15 which has it that St. Paul instructed the Christian spouses of Corinth to let their non-Christian spouses depart if the latter wished to do so—and that this departure results in the dissolution of the marriage. The new Canon 1143 modifies this historical interpretation by specifying exactly that it is the subsequent marriage that dissolves the first marriage when this privilege is used.

An entirely innovated new Canon 1147 states that for a serious cause the ordinary of the place can permit that by the use of the Pauline privilege the baptized party can contract a second marriage with a baptized non-Catholic or even with an unbaptized person, provided the Catholic law concerning religiously mixed marriages is observed.[62]

With this the meaning of the terms "dissolved by the Pauline privilege in favor of the faith" expands to intend not only that the baptized party may enter a second marriage that is a sacrament, but also that he or she may enter a second marriage simply, with no qualification set for the kind of marriage that he or she may enter.

The Law's Retention of the Sixteenth-Century Apostolic Constitutions

I wish to notice here at the close of this chapter a curious reformulation of old Canon 1125 which set in the law the use of the apostolic constitutions issued by Popes Paul III, Pius V and Gregory XIII in the sixteenth century. We recall that these constitutions ruled on the remarrying by polygamous natives who sought baptism in Catholic missionary territories, and on the remarrying by slaves who, after being separated from their spouses of a pagan marriage, were baptized and sought to marry again as Catholics. Old Canon 1125 did no more than to extend the use of these constitutions to any territory on earth wherein the situations regulated by the constitutions are verified. But new Canon 1148.1 goes beyond this into exact detail in resolving the problem of a convert to Catholicism who is already married polygamously.

> When an unbaptized man who simultaneously has a number
> of unbaptized wives, has received baptism in the Catholic
> Church, if it would be a hardship for him to remain with the first
> of the wives, he may retain one of them, having dismissed the
> others. The same applies to an unbaptized woman who simulta-
> neously has a number of unbaptized husbands.[63]

The canon is an amalgam of both Paul III's constitution *Altitudo* of
June 1, 1537 and of Pius V's *Romani pontificis* of August 1, 1571. Its
formulation is curious, first because its wording implies that an unbaptized
person can be really married simultaneously to plural spouses, and this in
face of the assertion in new Canon 1056 (and in old Canon 1013.2) that
one of marriage's essential features is its unicity—that it is of one man and
one woman. If the subcommission drafted new Canon 1148.1 with this in
mind, it stretched the meaning of unicity most elastically to include "one
set of spouses."

But perhaps the subcommission did not think that the first marriage,
while the convert-to-be was still unbaptized, was truly of one husband with
multiple wives, or of one wife with multiple husbands. For in paragraph 2
of this same canon it is required that to create the second and monogamous marriage, and this with one of the women to whom he is already
"married," the man must exchange wedding vows before the required
witnesses. The same holds for a woman marrying the man of her choice
from among her multiple unbaptized husbands. This requirement would
be without purpose, and indeed illicit, if the consultors of the subcommission thought the man or woman were already married to the several
spouses, including the one he or she chooses for a monogamous partner
following baptism. If this was the thinking of the subcommission, it used
language carelessly in saying of the first multiple relationship that in it the
man has plural wives (*uxores*) and the woman plural husbands (*maritos*).

The canon is curious also because it allows the man or woman, in
choosing and keeping from among the multiple spouses (or consorts) the
one he or she wishes, to get rid of the unwanted and first such spouse (or
consort) by *dismissing* him or her. No dissolution by papal authority is
mentioned. A reviviscence of the ancient dissolution by unilateral dismissal seems countenanced here. And it does no good to say that the canon
implies that the dismissal simply rids the person of a consort to whom he
or she is not married. The purpose itself of the canon is to allow a convert
to free himself or herself from a first spouse with whom *durum est . . .
permanere*—with whom it is difficult to remain.

The canon assumes, of course, that a non-sacramental marriage is
fundamentally dissoluble. It is apparently presumed to be dissolved here
by the papal power of the keys through application of the aforementioned
apostolic constitutions. But the canon nowhere says this. And this is not
oversight, because it in fact replaces old Canon 1125 that did say it.

Finally new Canon 1149 puts in statutory form what Pope Gregory

XIII authorized in his constitution *Populis ac nationibus* of January 15, 1585.

> An unbaptized person who, having received baptism in the Catholic Church, cannot re-establish cohabitation with his or her unbaptized spouse by reason of captivity or persecution, can contract another marriage, even if the other party has in the meantime received baptism, without prejudice to the provisions of Canon 1141.[64]

This canon makes no mention of the exercise of papal authority as the cause of the first marriage's dissolution. Indeed nothing at all is said about the dissolution of the marriage. The canon says only that in the circumstance envisaged the person "can contract another marriage," leaving the strict reader of the statute to conclude that it permits polygamy.

This criticism is irrelevant, of course, if the canon supposes that it is an application of the Pauline privilege. But this would be to turn back on the interpretation of the use of these apostolic constitutions to dissolve marriages, the interpretation that took hold in the Church during the intervening centuries. This is that their use is an exercise of the papal power of the keys. And to now interpret their use as that of the Pauline privilege could claim only the most fragile link with Paul's instruction in 1 Corinthians 15. Read as it is worded, Canon 1149 says that under the circumstances named therein an already married person who is now newly baptized as a Catholic can take a second spouse. It does not even say that this second spouse must be a Christian so that the second marriage may be a sacrament.

We have in these new canons of the revised marriage law the Roman Catholic Church's latest interpretation, extension and adaptation of the primitive Christian teaching concerning divorce and remarriage. Assuming that the revision of the law is not a once-for-always and settled enterprise but is ongoing and continually open to criticism, one may ask in what degree these canons continue the intent of the primitive teaching, and may ask also what the intent of the contemporary Catholic legislators has been in rewriting the marriage law as they have.

These two questions will dominate the following, and concluding, chapter of this historical examination—a chapter of critical reflections.

NOTES

1. If this set of consequences seems far-fetched, consider the following petition for nullity accepted on appeal by the Roman Rota on December 11, 1943, and eventually denied.

This judgment was on the petition by a young Italian male that his presumed marriage of September 19, 1931 be declared null on the two grounds of simulated marital consent by his partner and of consent on his part invalidated by force and grave fear. The court of first instance denied his petition on December 10, 1942. The Roman Rota accepted the case on appeal a year later, but on the single ground of simulated consent.

The young man had had sexual intercourse with his consort before their wedding. Then he found out that she had a contagious and incurable disease, and that he had got her pregnant. He fled to a different city, but at the plea of his own mother and under threats from the girl's relatives he returned to Rome and married her. He claimed subsequently that he had never intended to consummate the marriage (which he could do only after the wedding), and the two of them were able to prove that they had never cohabited following the wedding.

The Rota denied the petition for nullity on the one ground it considered, simulated consent. But it did secure from the Pope a dissolution of the marriage after satisfying itself that it had never been consummated.

The point here is that in denying the man's petition for nullity the Rota affirmed that he had been truly married, despite his having intended never to have intercourse with his wife nor even to live with her. He had got himself married by exchanging with the woman nothing more than the right to sexual intercourse.

2. As its name indicates, a descriptive definition describes a reality that is in existence before the definer sets about defining it. If accurate, his definition is an accurate description of it.

A prescriptive definition does what its name indicates. It prescribes what the reality in question, which does not yet exist, shall be when it is brought to existence. The definer comes first, as a design engineer comes before and produces his design. A prescriptive definer is concerned not with accuracy but with the effectiveness of the thing designed in producing the results he wishes from it.

3. This English title lost the cutting edge of the German original and of the French title, since what Doms intended was precisely the contrast between marriage understood according to meaning and the same understood according to goals. In the early 1940's the Church's Congregation of the Holy Office ordered that the volume be taken out of circulation and not reprinted.

4. Translated from *Acta Apostolicae Sedis,* Vol. 22 (1930), pp. 559–560.

5. This is exactly what happened after the bishops in the Second Vatican Council reduced procreation and nurture to parity with the other goals of marriage toward the end of the Council, in December of 1965. This they did in *Gaudium et spes,* Art. 50. Two and a half years later, in his encyclical letter of July 25, 1968, *Humanae vitae,* Pope Paul VI proscribed contraceptive intercourse not because it is contrary to the natural goal of marriage but because it offends against the nature of sexual intercourse by trying to separate in conduct its two inseparable meanings, the procreative and the unitive.

6. This is in *Acta Apostolicae Sedis,* Vol. 36 (1944) p. 103.

7. This translation is taken from *Papal Teachings: Matrimony,* pp. 422–423.

8. *Ibid.*

9. *Ibid.*

10. *The Meaning of Marriage,* pp. 52–53.

11. All these are in *Series I (Antepraeparatoria), Vol. 3* of *Acta Et Documenta Concilio Oecumenico Vaticano II Apparando.* Romae, 1960.

12. *Op. cit., Series I,* p. 13.

13. The schema is published twice in the *acta* of the Council, and in perfect synonymity. It is in pages 40–134 of *Series II (Praeparatoria), Vol. 3, Pars 1,* which

contains the *acta* of the Preparatory Commission's secretariats. It is also in pp. 893–937 of *Series II* (*Praeparatoria*), Vol. 2, the *acta* of the Central Preparatory Commission, *Pars 3*.

14. *Op. cit., Series II, Vol. 2, Pars 3*, p. 937.

15. *Loc cit.*, p. 910.

16. *Ibid.*

17. *Ibid.*

Paragraph 24, the last of this Chapter 2, and titled "Some Errors Are Condemned," states: "It is the duty of the Sacred Synod [the Council] to condemn severely that relationship which is called a 'temporary marriage' or 'an experimental marriage' or 'a marriage of friendship' " [*matrimonium amicale*]. And in footnote 35 the document quotes from Pius XI's *Casti connubii* to make clearer the kinds of relationships it wishes to condemn at this point: "Drawing from these principles some have come to the point of devising new kinds of relationships, which they consider more accommodated to present conditions—relationships which they nevertheless wish to call new kinds of marriage. Such are 'temporary marriages,' 'experimental marriages,' 'marriages of friendship.' They wish these to have the full rights and privileges of marriage, but wish to exclude indissolubility and offspring from them unless the partners subsequently convert their community and sharing of life into marriage in the full, legal sense of the term."

18. *Op. cit.*, pp. 947–948.

19. *Op. cit.*, pp. 960–961.

20. *Ibid.*

21. *Op. cit.*, p. 978.

22. It is in *Acta Synodalia, Vol. 3, Periodus 1, Pars 5*, pp. 131–133.

23. *Ibid.*, p. 131.

24. *Ibid.*

25. *Ibid.*, p. 132.

26. *Op cit.*, pp. 158–168.

27. *Ibid.*, p. 159.

28. *Ibid.*

29. *Loc cit.*, p. 161

30. The distribution of votes on the five paragraphs of *Gaudium et spes* was the following:

Paragraph 46, Preface: *Placet* 2106; *Non placet* 39.

Paragraphs 47–49, on the nature of marriage and of marital love: *Placet* 2052; *Non placet* 91.

Paragraphs 50–51, responsible parenthood: *Placet* 2011; *Non placet* 140.

31. The constitution's strange history, from the time its acceptance was voted, on November 16, until December 3 and the eve of the Council's adjournment, I have detailed in pages 263–265 of my earlier volume, *Marriage in the Catholic Church: What Is Marriage?*

32. I draw here from the Latin text of *Sacrosanctum Oecumenicum Concilium Vaticanum II, Constitutiones, Decreta, Declarationes*, Roma, Città del Vaticano, 1966, pp. 753–766.

33. *Op. cit.*, p. 761.

34. *Ibid.*

35. See my volume mentioned earlier for an examination of some decisions of judges in the Roman Rota, the Catholic Church's ordinary appellate court for marriage litigation, who deny the need for this love in the creating of a marriage.

This examination is in the volume's Chapter 11, "The Defining of Marriage Since Vatican II and *Humanae vitae*."

36. This is in *Gaudium et spes,* Art. 51: "Therefore the moral character of conduct, where the issue is that of reconciling marital love with the responsible transmission of life, depends not only on sincere intention or the weighing of motives. This moral character must be determined by objective criteria drawn from the nature of the person and of his or her acts. These are criteria which preserve the meaning of self-donation and of human procreation in a context of true love."

37. In *Acta Apostolicae Sedis,* Vol. 60 (1968) pp. 481–503. It is available in English translation in the Paulist Press edition, *Encyclical of Pope Paul VI, Humanae Vitae, On the Regulation of Birth* . . . 1968.

38. English-language edition, p.9.

39. *Op. cit.,* p. 11.

40. *Ibid.*

41. This is in paragraphs 7 and 8, pp. 6 and 7.

42. *Ibid.,* p. 7.

43. *Ibid.*

44. Par. 8, p. 7.

45. *Ibid.,* p. 7.

46. *Ibid.*

47. *Loc. cit.,* p. 8.

48. *Ibid.*

49. But it is helpful to see at least a sketch of this history of the revision that got under way in 1966.

1966–1973: The subcommission revising the marriage law completed the first version of the canons concerning marriage. This draft was published in the Pontifical Commission's journal, *Communicationes,* Vol. 3 (1971) pp. 68–81 and Vol. 5 (1973) pp. 73–90.

This first and informal publication of the revision drafts drew criticism, though published also informally, from various persons around the Catholic world.

Spring 1975: The entire draft of The Discipline of the Sacraments was sent formally to various consultative persons and groups for criticism: to individual bishops, to national conferences of bishops, to the Roman dicasteries (members of the papal curia), to pontifical faculties of canon law, to regional canon law societies, and to the International Union of Superiors General of religious orders. These persons and groups were asked to return their criticisms to Cardinal Pericle Felici, Secretary General of the Pontifical Commission, by the end of the year.

February 1977 through February 1978: The subcommission drafting the marriage canons met twenty-four times to rework the 1975 version of these canons in light of the criticisms coming from the consultative groups.

May 22–28, 1977. The *plenarium* of cardinals making up the Pontifical Commission met in Rome to evaluate and criticize the formulation of the marriage canons. Its criticisms were included among those sent to the subcommission.

Spring 1978 to summer 1981: Following the subcommission's completion of its work, the revised marriage canons were in the hands of the Commission itself. A select group of prelates in the Vatican *curia,* aided by consultor experts in marriage law, worked at refining the revised canons. In the spring of 1980 the product of this group's work was distributed to appropriate persons throughout the Church.

October 1981: The *plenarium* of cardinals met again in Rome to review the revising and refining to date. It made further amendments.

Spring 1982: The canons reworked to incorporate the *plenarium's* amendments were included in a volume containing the draft of the entire revised Code, a volume that was authoritative but whose printing and distributing were not a promulgation. The distribution was limited to authorized persons.

Fall 1982: A mini-commission made up of a few members of the Pontifical Commission, assisted by canonical experts, continued the editing of the text of the marriage canons.

January 25, 1983: Pope John Paul II promulgated the revised Code of Canon Law in its entirety.

November 27, 1983: The revised Code went into effect, replacing the 1917 version.

50. 1055.1 Matrimoniale foedus, quo vir et mulier inter se totius vitae consortium constituunt, indole sua naturali ad bonum coniugum atque ad prolis procreationem et educationem ordinatum, a Christo Domino ad sacramenti dignitatem inter baptizatos evectum est.

      2 Quare inter baptizatos nequit matrimonialis contractus validus consistere quin sit eo ipso sacramentum.

1056 Essentiales matrimonii proprietates sunt unitas ac indissolubilitas, quae in matrimonio Christiano peculiarem obtinent firmitatem ratione sacramenti.

51. Mackin, *op. cit.,* pp. 290–291.

52. 1 Matrimonium facit partium consensus inter personas iure habiles legitime manifestatus; qui nulla humana potestate suppleri potest.

      2 Consensus matrimonialis est actus quo vir et mulier foedere irrevocabili sese mutuo tradunt et accipiunt ad constituendum matrimonium.

53. Intima communitas vitae et amoris coniugalis . . . foedere coniugii seu irrevocabili consensu personali instauratur. (*Sacrosanctum Oecumenicum Concilium Vaticanum II, Constitutiones,* etc., p 754.)

54. Ex valido matrimonio enascitur inter coniuges vinculum natura sua perpetuum et exclusivum; matrimonium praterea Christianum coniugibus non ponentibus obicem gratiam confert.

55. . . . in matrimonio praeterea Christiano coniuges ad sui status officia et dignitatem peculiari sacramento roborantur et veluti consecrantur.

56. Matrimonium ratum et consummatum nulla humana potestate nullaque causa, praeterquam morte, dissolvi potest.

57. The subcommission stated this, its counter-critical stance, in its journal, *Communicationes,* Vol. 7.1 (1975), p. 28. Rev. Thomas J. Green comments on it in his essay, "The Revised Schema *De Matrimonio*: Text and Reflections," in *The Jurist* (1980, no. 1), p. 65.

58. Matrimonium non consummatum inter baptizatos vel inter partem baptizatam et partem non baptizatam, dissolvitur tum ipso iure per sollemnem professionem religiosam, tum per dispensationem a Sede Apostolica ex iusta causa concessam, utraque parte rogante vel alterutra, etsi altera sit invita.

59. Matrimonium non consummatum inter baptizatos vel inter partem baptizatam et partem non baptizatam a Romano Pontifice dissolvi potest iusta ex causa, utraque parte rogante vel alterutra, etsi altera pars sit invita.

60. Canonists and theologians who fantasize worst-case scenarios have pointed out that according to the sense of the law at this point—and especially because

of the merely juridical interpretation of the act that consummates a marriage—the following can happen. Years after the two partners in the example given here have separated and have accepted baptism, but still before the papal dissolution of their marriage, they meet by sheer coincidence. Let us say that this is at a convention in an out-of-town hotel. They have sexual intercourse—a consequence of which is that they consummate their now sacramental marriage (a consequence which would ensue even if they should somehow not recognize one another). The marriage thus becomes invulnerable to papal dissolution.

61. 1 Matrimonium initum a duobus non baptizatis solvitur ex privilegio paulino in favorem fidei partis quae baptismum recepit, ipso facto quo novum matrimonium ab eadem parte contrahitur, dummodo pars non baptizata discedat.

2 Discedere censetur pars non baptizata si nolit cum parte baptizata cohabitare vel cohabitare pacifice sine contumelia Creatoris, nisi haec post baptismum receptum iustam illi dederit discedendi causam.

62. Ordinarius loci tamen, gravi de causa, concedere potest ut pars baptizata, utens privilegio paulino, contrahat matrimonium cum parte non catholica sive baptizata sive non baptizata, servatis etiam praescriptis canonum de matrimoniis mixtis.

63. 1 Non baptizatus qui plures uxores non baptizatas simul habeat, recepto in Ecclesia catholica baptismo, si durum ei sit cum earum prima permanere, unam ex illis, ceteris dimissis, retinere potest. Idem valet de muliere non baptizata quae plures maritos non baptizatos simul habeat.

64. 2 Non baptizatus qui, recepto in Ecclesia catholica baptismo, cum coniuge non baptizato ratione captivitatis vel persecutionis cohabitationem restaurare nequeat, aliud matrimonium contrahere potest, etiamsi altera pars baptismum interea receperit, firmo praescripto can. 1141.

We recall that new Canon 1141 affirms the radical indissolubility of a marriage that is a sacrament and has been consummated as a sacrament—that it can be dissolved only by death.

18. SOME CRITICAL REFLECTIONS

Let us begin critical reflection on the history of the Roman Catholic doctrine and discipline of divorce and remarriage by returning to the paradigm which begins the introduction to this volume.

We recall that the person in the paradigm is a woman fifty-two years of age. Two years earlier she had been abandoned by her husband after twenty-nine years of marriage. Both were baptized in the Roman Catholic Church. Therefore their marriage is presumed in Catholic law to be a sacrament. That it is also consummated as a sacrament is concluded from the evidence of the four children born of the marriage. All of these are now adults living independently of their parents.

The husband has made clear that he has no intention of resuming married life. Two months after leaving her he began civil divorce proceedings, which she did not contest. And when the final decree of divorce was handed down he entered a second and civil marriage.

She and another man, a widower also a Roman Catholic, are seriously attracted to one another, have experienced a beginning happiness as companions, and wish to marry. Our question concerning them asks whether, according to the Catholic doctrine and discipline of divorce and remarriage, they may do so.

The answer is that they may not; they are morally obligated not to attempt marriage with one another. If they were to attempt marriage knowing of this obligation and flouting it freely, they would be deemed to sin seriously and would continue in a sinful state in presuming to live as though married to one another.

Why this negative obligation? Whence the sinful act and sinful state?

To these questions the answer is that the woman's marriage to her husband continues in existence. Being still his wife she would commit adultery in attempting to live as though married to the man. There is also this refinement in the answer to the question, that she may not attempt the second marriage because this marriage is an impossibility. It would be immoral for her to pretend to do what is impossible. The reason for this impossibility is that Catholic marriage law, as we have seen, defines marriage in such a way as to make polygamy impossible. It is not that a person is forbidden plural simultaneous marriages, but that such simultaneity is impossible.

But the answer to the question that asks why the woman in the paradigm cannot marry a second time is both more detailed and more simple than to say that she is still married to the man with whom she pronounced wedding vows twenty-nine years earlier and with whom she brought four children into the world.

If neither she nor her husband had been baptized Christians at the time they pronounced their vows, but she had become a Christian since that time, the use of the Pauline privilege would be granted to her so that she could enter a second and sacramental marriage with the Catholic who wants her as his wife. (It is certain from her husband's seeking civil divorce and remarriage that he has abandoned their marriage and has no desire to resume it.) But because both she and her husband were baptized Christians at the time of their vows, their marriage is presumed a sacrament, and therefore the Pauline privilege is not available to her.

If she could prove that her marriage, though presumably a sacrament, had never been consummated, she could petition from papal authority a dissolution of her unconsummated marriage. But with consummation understood in Catholic law to be accomplished by the first complete sexual intercourse after the marital consent, the fact of her four children simply removes consummation from consideration.

If she alone had been unbaptized at the time of their wedding and she were still unbaptized, while her husband was a non-Catholic Christian, papal authority could dissolve her non-sacramental marriage in consideration of her desire to enter a second and sacramental marriage, and of her desire to accept baptism in order to do this. But again, one element of her situation is that both she and her husband were baptized Roman Catholics at the time of their wedding vows. Consequently their marriage is presumed to be a sacrament, and this use of the papal power to dissolve—the use, colloquially, of the Petrine privilege—is not available to her.

Let us say that this woman has an inquiring and critical mind. This impels her to ask two questions of the Catholic authorities. In the first she asks, "In what way am I still married to my husband of twenty-nine years?" In the second she asks, "How can it be that our marriage is still a Christian sacrament?"

She may propose the first question in more detailed form, and thereby reveal the cause of her critical curiosity in asking it. She points out that her husband left her and has no intention to return. He has withdrawn his will to be married to her and has done so permanently. Since his abandoning her and because of it, she has withdrawn her will to be married to him. More than this, his will is to have a different woman as his wife, and he regards himself as married to her.

This woman lives at a distance of two thousand miles from the man she first married. They have not communicated in any way in eighteen months and have determined on no communication ever in the future. Their will is to be functional strangers to one another. The woman admits to anger and even bitterness at being abandoned. Love for her husband, apart from the most detached and cold wishing the best for him, is impossible for her.

She continues her questioning in the context of the bishops' understanding of marriage in the Second Vatican Council. They deemed marriage a community of love, an intimate sharing of marital life and love, a sharing of the whole of life. Therefore she asks, "How is it that with love gone irretrievably, with any sharing of life, any community destroyed forever, we are still considered married? With these obliterated, what is there of our marriage that still exists?"

About her marriage as a sacrament she first points out what is a commonplace in Catholic teaching, that a marriage of two Christians is a sacrament in that it images the love of Christ and the Church. So she asks, "With my husband's going now to another woman after having abandoned me, with our love destroyed, and with us now deciding to be strangers to one another, how does our marriage still image the love of Christ and his Church? In what way is it still a sacrament?" And she adds, not without anger, "It seems to me that the only real meaning of the Catholic teaching about the indissolubility of marriage, its only real effect that a man and woman experience in their lives, is that of an obstacle to a second marriage. The authorities have acknowledged mine and my husband's separation. No one has said I have an obligation to call him back to *live* our marriage. All they say is that I cannot marry again. It appears that without being aware of it, one of the things I did when pronouncing my wedding vows was to also pronounce a vow of celibacy."

The Utrecht-Haarlem Case

The authoritative Catholic answer to the woman's first question—"In what way am I still married to my husband of twenty-nine years?"—was given, or rather repeated, during the years 1971 to 1976. The question which was answered during these years was not this woman's verbatim. But the issue was substantially the same as hers, the perdurance of a marriage despite the final, irreversible abandonment of the wife by the husband. The issue was raised in the ecclesiastical province of Utrecht in Holland in the following form.[1]

A native-born Italian couple came to Holland and exchanged marriage vows in Arnhem on February 12, 1963. A child was born of the union three months after the wedding. A month later the husband deserted the wife and went to Switzerland. In May 1970 the tribunal of Utrecht accepted the woman's petition for a decree of nullity on the ground of defect of marital consent on the part of her supposed husband. She alleged that he had never intended to form a permanent union with her, therefore any marital union at all. On August 12, 1971 the Utrecht tribunal ruled formally on her petition, declaring: "It is evident that this marriage was null and void on the ground of defect of consent, that is, of moral impotence." (By the latter term the court meant that the supposed husband had been incapable, at the time of the exchange of vows, of making a consent specifically marital, a consent sufficient to create a marriage.)

The tribunal of Haarlem heard this first-instance decision on routine appeal, and on September 28 of the same year sustained it. It agreed that the couple's attempt at marriage had been invalid because of the moral impotence of the supposed husband and on the subsidiary ground of his defect of marital consent.

These decisions would probably have vanished into the obscurity of tribunal records had not two unusual elements entered their history. One of these derived from the fact that the husband and wife were both Italian citizens. Because of this the tribunal of Utrecht on September 5, 1972 communicated the favorable decision to the Congregation of the Sacred Signatura in Rome to be transmitted to the Italian authorities for the implementing of its civil effects. Thus the judges of the Signatura examined this decision that might otherwise have not come to their attention.[2]

The second unusual element was one that the Signatura judges came upon when they examined the Utrecht decision. This was the *in iure* argument, the jurisprudential application of the law, worked out by the judges of that court in coming to their decision. We shall see why the Signatura judges took alarm on examining this reasoning. Among its main elements the first spoke directly to the first question posed by the woman in our paradigm.

The argument of the Utrecht judges was that, according to the teaching of the bishops at Vatican II in *Gaudium et spes,* a marriage is an intimate community of life and of marital love. Therefore, because both the community can disintegrate and the love can erode and vanish, the marriage itself can erode, disintegrate and come to an end.

The other elements of this *in iure* reasoning are less relevant to our paradigm but add nonetheless to the causes of the *Signatura* judges' alarm. Because a marriage is a communion, a sharing, the ancient axiom in Roman law, "It is the consent of the parties that creates a marriage," takes on an unusual meaning. Because a marriage is a communion, which is a continuing process, the consent that creates it is no longer to be understood as a juridical act completed in an instant, not an instantaneous exchange of juridical rights given once for always. This consent has more the nature of a continuing commitment to a sharing of lives.

Had the next element of the Utrecht court's argument been verifiable in our paradigm, the woman could have urged not that her marriage had come to an end, but that it had really never come into existence, and that as a consequence her supposed marriage of twenty-nine years could be found null. The judges of the court reasoned that for a marital union to be brought into existence, the parties must really will it in all its fullness.

Thus, in order to verify the defect of marital consent in a particular case it is enough to verify that one or the other party has not really willed it in all its fullness.

What is the evidence for this deficiency of marital will? If a couple has really willed a union of lives, this will show itself gradually, as the marriage evolves. But if the relationship is flawed from the beginning, and with the passing of time deteriorates in an obvious way—with its qualitative curve going downward rather than upward—there arises a strong presumption for defect of marital intent, and consequently for the nullity of the supposed marriage.

How thoroughly a developmental philosophy of marriage influenced the Dutch judges' decision is evident in a key clause in the favorable appellate decision rendered by the Haarlem court: "Reading this case one comes to the spontaneous conclusion that this short-lived union (of hardly four months) could not have been a marriage. *It did not have the chance to develop to the point of becoming a normal community of life and love*" (italics added).

The Signatura's Critical Judgment

These lower-court decisions evoked two major reactions on the part of Catholic authorities in Rome. The first in sequence was that of the Congregation of the Signatura itself.

On reading the Utrecht-Haarlem decisions in the fall of 1972, Cardinal Dino Staffa, prefect of the congregation, and others of its judges asked for the *acta* of the case from the Dutch courts. And having studied the *acta* Cardinal Staffa asked the Apostolic See to appoint an *ad hoc* commission of Signatura prelates to study, in third instance, the merits of the two lower-court decisions. Pope Paul VI authorized the forming of this commission on July 8, 1973.

The second reaction I have already mentioned briefly a number of times in this volume. It took the form of a discourse by Paul VI to the judges of the Roman Rota on February 9, 1976. As we shall see when examining it presently, Paul could not have spoken more clearly and emphatically to our paradigmatic woman's first question.

The Signatura commission's first move in overturning the Dutch courts' decisions was to undermine the premise from which they had drawn. These decisions were conclusions drawn from the understanding of marriage set forth by the bishops of Vatican II in *Gaudium et spes*. The commission rejoined that no conclusion valid for the Church's judicial regulation of marriage could be drawn from that constitution because, as the commission insisted, the bishops had not intended in it to define the juridical essence of marriage. The commission explained, "We must first recall that its intent was only to make some statements about marriage and family and to do this by throwing light on their importance and their existential value rather than on their properly juridical aspects." To reinforce this interpretation they quoted, from the *Acta* of the Council, excerpts from the dispositions of certain amendments to *Gaudium et spes'* statement on marriage proposed on December 3, 1965, just before the bishops' final vote that accepted the entire constitution.[3]

> In a pastoral text, which is intended to establish a dialogue with the world, these juridical elements are not needed [the amendment had urged that *Gaudium et spes'* declaration on the nature of marriage include long-enshrined subordinated ends of marriage—procreation and nurture as primary end; mutual help and the allaying of concupiscence as secondary ends]. . . . Moreover, in a text which speaks to the world in a direct and pastoral style, it seems that one should avoid terms which are too technical.

Then the Signatura commission took exact aim at the Dutch courts' interpretation that because the creating of a marriage is a continuing, processual activity by the spouses, a marriage can pass out of existence if this activity fails or comes to an end. The commission's retort to this was its own implicit definition of marriage, as well as of the act that creates a marriage. This definition said that a marriage is a juridical relationship, a bond, by which a man and a woman are constituted husband and wife. This bond continues to subsist independently of any subsequent change of will by the contracting parties, so that once their marital consent has been expressed, not even their later explicit withdrawal of consent can affect the marriage's validity.

But it was clearly about the nature of the act by which spouses create a marriage that the commission was the most seriously concerned. It was so because of the new and startling interpretation of this act coming from the Dutch courts—that it is a gradual, processual forming of the marital union, a forming that is never complete, a forming that can halt and even come to an end. In criticizing this the commission searched into not only the kind of act that creates a marriage, but into the object that this act bears upon.

> It is a bilateral and free act of the will, in the nature of a contract, albeit unique, of its own kind. It is also (in the words of *Gaudium et spes*) "a marital covenant of irrevocable personal consent." The object of this consent is the spouses themselves: "The human act by which the partners mutually surrender themselves to one another." To say this another way, the persons of the spouses, under the specific marital aspect, constitute the object of consent. It is the nature of this consent that once it has been legitimately posited it produces its effect once for all, the juridical effect of giving and surrendering. This effect continues throughout the entire life together of the spouses, independently

of and impervious to any subsequent revocation on the part of the spouses. This effect, understandable also as a bond, does not cease to exist if later love between the spouses ceases, or if the intimate communion of life and marital love, with its so-called existential nature, ceases.[4]

Since the commission drew all this from its interpretation of *Gaudium et spes,* it suggested this preliminary summation:

> It is clear from the above that it is false to say that the Council changed the doctrine about marital consent, as if it had substituted for the traditional notion a certain so-called existential consent, so that when this ceases the matrimonial bond automatically ceases to exist.[5]

The reader may have noticed two unexamined assumptions in this, the Signatura commission's criticism of the Dutch courts' decisions. One has to do with the interpretation of the mind of the approximately twenty-five hundred bishops offered by Cardinal Pericle Felici, Secretary General of the Second Vatican Council, in his *expensiones modorum,* his disposition of the amendments to this chapter of *Gaudium et spes.* The commission assumes that his interpretation is accurate, that the bishops did not intend to declare formally and authoritatively on the nature of marriage, and that they stopped short of this intent because *Gaudium et spes* is not a dogmatic but a pastoral constitution.

The second assumption by the commission is one that traditional-minded prelates and ecclesiastical judges have made commonly since the publication of *Gaudium et spes*—have made both as an implicit interpretation of its teaching on marriage and as a continuation of the post-conciliar definition of marriage. This assumption is that a marriage is a juridical entity, that its substantial essence is juridical, and therefore that any non-juridical traits in it—traits such as the community of love, the sharing in marital life and love named by *Gaudium et spes*—are no more than accessory to this essence, and are in fact reducible themselves to the juridical category of "mutual help." And, what is most significant for the question of a marriage's ending by disintegration, the exactly named juridical entity that a marriage is, is a bond that binds spouses to one another.

Once they assumed that this is the accurate definition of marriage, as well as the definition established in Catholic doctrine, it was easy for the prelates on the commission to add to it the trait that has been added ever since this definition was innovated in the twelfth and thirteenth centuries. The addition is that this juridical bond is indissoluble except by the death of one or of both the spouses. The commission's insistence that a marriage is this indissoluble juridical bond re-enacted a curious moment in the history of the Christian dialectic concerning divorce and remarriage. This was the tactic of blocking dissolution of marriage by natural or secular agency—or at least the possibility of dissolving it by these agencies—by simply defining marriage to be indissoluble. (A kindred move was to block the possibility of polygamous marriage by simply defining marriage to be monogamous. Students of philosophy who note the difference between two kinds of defining—the descriptive and the prescriptive—will recognize prescriptive defining again at work in this case.)

Pope Paul VI's Discourse to the Roman Rota

By the end of 1975 and early in 1976 Pope Paul himself was sufficiently alarmed by interpretations made, in turn, of the bishops' interpretation of marriage in *Gaudium et spes,* that he thought it necessary to say some things that are themselves interpretations of the bishops' minds. These things he said in his annual discourse (this one on February 9, 1976) to the judges, the advocates and the *officiales* of the Roman Rota at the beginning of this court's judicial year. I offer here a précis of the discourse, with an ample quotation from it at an essential point.[6]

Paul pointed out that certain thinkers and writers at times exaggerate the place in marriage of those marital goods that are love and the personal perfection of the spouses. They go so far as to subordinate to these goals that fundamental good that is offspring—some even to the point of ignoring the latter. What he saw as crucial to the issue of marriage's indissolubility was that some writers make marital love such an essential element even in the law that the validity of marriages would depend on its presence. And, Paul charged, they thereby open the way to divorce, for they go on to say that once this marital love fails—or rather once this first and primitive amorous longing fails (*primigenia cupiditas amoris* is the Latin of his epithet)—the validity of the irrevocable covenant also fails, a covenant created by the full and free consent of love.[7]

Paul acknowledged that the bishops of Vatican II had attributed great importance to marital love. They called it the fulfilled condition and the desired goal of marriage. But what he, Paul, wished to make emphatically clear in this address was that no Christian teaching on marriage can propose a concept of marital love which leads to abandoning or even diminishing the force and meaning of the principle, *matrimonium facit partium consensus*—"It is the consent of the parties that creates the marriage."

This was aimed, although without naming names, squarely at the Dutch judges who had interpreted spouses' creation of their marriage as a developmental, processual growth in love and union. Paul contradicted them. He insisted that in virtue of the principle he had just repeated, a marriage exists from the moment the spouses make a juridically valid consent. This consent is a single act of will made by each of them. It has the character of a pact—or of a covenant, to use the expression preferred nowadays to the term "contract."

In the paragraph I shall quote now from his discourse we shall see Paul repeating in his way what Cardinal Staffa and the Signatura commission had done. He too prescribes a definition of marriage, and prescribes it in such a way as to simply design out of marriage the possibility of dissolving it short of death. Or, to phrase it positively, he establishes the indissolubility of marriage by writing it into his prescriptive definition of it.

> Even though it is a pastoral document, *Gaudium et spes* taught this doctrine clearly, as is evident in its words, "The intimate partnership of married life and love has been established by the Creator and qualified by his laws. It is created by the conjugal covenant of irrevocable personal consent. Hence by the human act whereby spouses mutually bestow and accept each other, a relationship arises which by divine will and in the eyes of society too is a lasting one. For the good of the spouses and their offspring as well as of society, the existence of this sacred bond no longer depends on human decisions alone" (n. 48).
>
> Hence we firmly deny that with the failure of some subjective element such as marital love the marriage itself no longer exists as a "juridical reality." For this reality has its origin in a consent once for all juridically efficacious. So far as the law is concerned this "reality" continues to exist, since it in no way depends on love for its existence. For when they give their free consent the spouses do nothing other than to enter and be fixed in [*inseruntur*] an objective order or institution, which is something greater than themselves and in no way depends on them for either its nature or the laws proper to it. Marriage did not take its origin in the free will of men, but was instituted by God, who willed it to be reinforced and enlightened by his laws.

At the risk of explaining the obvious let me try to isolate the more significant elements of Paul's statement, those at least that are significant for our purpose because he intended them to be decisive about the possibility of marriage's dissolution.

In the statement he defines marriage categorically. By this I mean that he names the generic kind of entity that it is: It is a juridical reality. Since this is so, only those traits of marriage commonly attributed to it that are juridically intelligible belong to its essence.

Few of the principal traits that the bishops of Vatican II predicated of marriage seem juridically intelligible as Paul understood them. Those that do not are the community of love, the sharing of marital life and love, the intimate union of persons and actions. The reason why they do not is suggested in the second of the paragraphs I have just quoted. These are traits of marriage that can diminish and disappear. By his logic that begins with the conclusion that a marriage cannot either disappear or be dissolved, and works backward to the premise that the essence of marriage contains only those traits that cannot diminish and disappear, these predicates from *Gaudium et spes* name nothing essential to marriage.

The essence of marriage, which is the juridical bond, the spouses bring into existence by the act of will that is their expressed marital consent. This act is indivisible in time; it produces its effect immediately, once-for-always. It is not a processual growing in union that can subsequently come to an end and so end the marriage.

The spouses' marriage, being the juridical bond, is a thing of the objective order. Their marriage is not something in them or of them. It is not a condition of their wills, of their intentions, of their minds or souls. Therefore it is not a real relationship of their persons to one another. Therefore too, once they have created this bond by their acts of will, it exists apart from their control. Their subsequent withdrawal of consent, their will to not be married, their intent to no longer be spouses to one another, cannot affect this bond. It is simply "there," carrying on an existence of its own apart from their minds and wills. In this the student of the history of the Catholic defining of marriage may recognize Paul's unlabeled return to a concept of marriage that the bishops of Vatican II, and he himself in his encyclical of 1968, *Humanae vitae*, had consciously abandoned. This is the concept of marriage the contract, a concept invented by canonists and theologians in the twelfth and thirteenth centuries. They had got indissolubility into marriage by prescribing that the contract be non-voidable even by the contracting parties themselves, and had thus invented the first non-voidable contract in the history of law. Paul repeats equivalently the same prescription; he gets indissolubility into marriage here by simply prescribing that the latter be an unassailable juridical bond. It seems curious that he did not try to draw this indissolubility from the usual scriptural sources, from Christ's declaration that in marrying a man and woman become two in one flesh, and that they are joined by God himself in this union.

Like Cardinal Staffa and the Signatura commission, Pope Paul was selective in rejecting and accepting the defining value of the bishops' clauses, phrases and terms in *Gaudium et spes.* As I have already pointed out, he denied that such terms as "community of love," etc. are predicates denoting the essence of marriage. But here, when dealing with marriage's indissolubility, he reverses his logic of interpretation easily. He insists that "even though it is [only] a pastoral document," *Gaudium et spes* teaches authoritatively when it says that the consent by which a man and woman create their marriage is irrevocable. (This too is recognizable as prescriptive defining. To prescribe that marital consent is irrevocable is to provide the correlate to the prescribed effect of this consent, which is the unassailable bond, the non-voidable contract. And this irrevocable consent, like the bond-contract, is a juridical invention.)

One need not examine very carefully in order to notice a begging of the question in the second of the paragraphs I have quoted from Paul's discourse. He argues there that the reason, or at least one reason, why spouses cannot dissolve their marriage by subsequently withdrawing their wills to be married is that once they create this juridical bond it exists objectively, independently of their wills, unassailable by them. But he loses the *consequentia* from his argumentation when he urges that a reason for the marital bond's unassailability is that marriage's nature and laws do not depend on the wills of men, that these are the work of God, and that, apparently, God has revealed and prescribed by law that marriage is an unassailable juridical bond. That is, he says clearly enough that God instituted marriage, and instituted it as this unassailable bond. He must mean here that the non-voidable contract, the indissoluble bond, that first made its appearance in Catholic thought in the twelfth century, is proposed somewhere in divine revelation. If he does, he missed a capital opportunity by not identifying its place in this revelation.

Here, then, is one facet of the answer to the question asked by the woman in our paradigm. The reason that she cannot marry again is that she is still married. And the meaning of her being still married to her husband despite the irreparable destruction of any love, of any communication, of any will to be married, by his abandoning her and going to another woman, is that when they expressed their marital consent thirty-one years earlier they created a juridical bond that still exists objectively. And the reason for affirming its continued existence is that since the twelfth century such a bond has been defined as indestructible.

The Sacrament as the Cause of Indissolubility

But we have already seen the qualified truth of this much of the answer to the woman's question. The one final and effective reason that she cannot marry again, as Roman Catholic doctrine has it, is not the indestructibility that Paul VI claimed for the juridical bond, and not the irrevocability that he claimed for marital consent. I have pointed out several times that papal authority dissolves the indestructible bond where it is either not consummated or is not a sacrament, or is neither. We have already seen that what makes the woman's marrying again impossible is that her mariage is considered a Christian sacrament, and consummated as such a sacrament.

When one examines Catholic teaching to find out why it deems consummated sacramental marriages indissoluble one must take care not to detour into two related but accessory questions. One of these we have already probed. It asks if Christ himself asserted the indissolubility of all marriages or of any kinds of marriages, such as those that are sacraments. The other asks about an element of the traditional Catholic theology of marriage. It asks where, when and by which words Christ made the marriages of his followers to be sacraments. The traditional answer to this question is that he did so when he asserted the invulnerability to divorce of these marriages and thus in effect made them images of his own unfailing love for his Church. (Note that there is no causative logic claimed here. It is not said that Christ's making his followers' marriages indissoluble is what makes them sacraments. It is not said that these marriages' indissolubility *causes* them to be sacraments. What is said rather is that their sacramentality is found somehow in their indissolubility, that they are sacraments somehow in being indissoluble.)

At the risk of further complicating this already complex issue I must make another preliminary point clear. This is that Christ unquestionably demanded of his followers that when they marry they intend faithfulness, a faithfulness that includes perseverance in marriage even to the point of death. As for how and when he demanded this, I would for now suggest only that his words remembered in the Johannine tradition imply this faithfulness: "This is my command, that you love one another as I have loved you." He loved his own to the point of dying for them. And if his followers as single persons are to love one another in this way, a fortiori his followers who are spouses must do so.

I agree with the Catholic theology that says that Christ's followers of every epoch, impelled by the Holy Spirit given to them in baptism and again in confirmation, administer and receive the sacrament of marriage by committing themselves to manifest to the world, by the way they love one another, that the God of the universe is unfailing in his love. It is impossible for them to intend to manifest this love if they do not intend to be unfailing in their love for one another. Failing to intend this blocks their entry into the sacrament. And it is well to add that only by the power of the Spirit acting through this sacrament can they in fact and effectively intend this unfailingness. Their will for unfailingness in their marriage is otherwise helpless, in a way akin to the way "No one can say 'Jesus is Lord,' except by the Holy Spirit." But this will, though helpless in itself, is the *sine qua non* disposition they must bring to the creating of the sacrament.

The Logic of Causation in Indissolubility

But that is not my question. My question here asks about a logic of causation. It asks what it is, exactly, that goes beyond Christ's will that spouses be faithful unto death, beyond the spouses' intent and will for such faithfulness, to in fact produce the claimed indissolubility of consummated sacramental marriages—the indissolubility that is said to continue even if the spouses' will for unfailing faithfulness is withdrawn. For this is what Catholic doctrine of indissolubility asserts, that *because* the marriages of Christian spouses are sacraments, and where they are consummated as such, these marriages are indissoluble. Their indissolubility seems to be an effect of their consummated sacramentality. So my question urges a search for a quite specific cause-effect relationship.

Formulating the question this way is intelligible at all only if one first accepts the traditional Catholic reading of Ephesians 5:21–33, that in this passage Paul said that every marriage of two Christians is an image of the love relationship of Christ and his Church. For reasons that I will explain presently I do not accept this interpretation. But let us suppose that Paul did say this. The traditional theological argument drawing from this supposition is this: *Because* the imaged sacred reality—the relationship of Christ and the Church—is indestructible, the human reality imaging it—the husband-wife relationship—is indissoluble. It is not that the latter, *because* it images the indestructible relationship, merely *ought* to be indestructible. It is not merely that the Christian spouses, because their marriage is said to be an image of Christ's unfailing love for his Church, ought to intend this unfailingness in their marriage and strive for it. That is, the logic of causation here is not said to be deontological, a logic of *what ought to be* as an effect. The logic is said rather to be ontological in a unique way, a logic of *what is* as an effect: because the Christian spouses' marriage is an image of the unfailing love relationship of Christ and the Church it already is indissoluble.

Here is the point in this theology at which I find a logical leap instead of a needed consequential link. It fails to explain how a quality in the imaged relationship, the quality that is the indestructibility of the love of Christ and his Church, causes ontologically this same quality in the imaging relationship—the quality which is the alleged indissolubility of the marriage of the Christian spouses.

To say this another way and by contrast, there is a verifiable cause-effect link in the following theology, albeit the link of a moral demand reaching from the will of Christ to the wills of the spouses. Thus, where Christian spouses know that in marrying they have committed themselves to image the unfailingness of Christ's love for his Church, they have the obligation to strive to live this unfailingness in their marriage, with the obligation produced in them by the will of Christ precisely as lover of the community of his followers, which is the Church. But to say that the marriage of the spouses is already unfailing because it is already an image of Christ's unfailingness is not intelligible. To put this in Scholastic language, it is not accurate to say that the presence of a quality in the *signatum* of itself and spontaneously produces this quality in the *signum*. What is accurate to say is that unless the quality that is in the signatum is found also in the supposed *signum,* the latter is not truly a *signum* of the former.

There is another weakness in the theology of automatically caused indissolubility of Christian marriages. It is a failure in correspondence between the imaging relationship and the imaged relationship. In the latter, Christ's relationship with the Church, the relationship is the product of two wills that both choose freely to accept each other in love, and while choosing this freely choose also to do this with perpetual and predestined unfailingness. Neither the freedom nor the perpetual and

predestined unfailingness contradicts one another. The perpetual and predestined unfailingness is itself produced by the freely committed love.

But this essential and necessary trait of the Christ-Church relationship is often not found in the relationship of two Christian spouses, and in
fact cannot be found in it in the way that the traditional theology of
indissolubility presumes. A Christian man and woman can freely commit
themselves to one another and can will this commitment to be unfailing.
But if their committing themselves is to remain free, they must also be able
to withdraw it. They must be able to will that their love fail. Many
Christian spouses do withdraw their commitment and will the failure of
their love. But the traditional theology says that their marriage remains
unfailing, indissoluble nonetheless.

Thus the discordance in the imaging: while the unfailingness of the
imaged Christ-Church relationship is caused by the wills of the two
persons in the relationship, it is not caused in the human relationship by
the wills of the two persons, the spouses. It is a quality of their relationship
that is kept there coercively. Or to say it somewhat differently, the
unfailingness of the Christ-Church relationship is a product of their willing
freely to sustain it, but the presumably imaging unfailingness in the
spouses' relationship can be there in contradiction of their freedom. But if
this is so, how can the latter unfree relationship truly image the former free
relationship?

Let me bring this examination to the paradigm that begins this
volume and begins this final chapter. Let me do so first by taking note of a
potential tautology in any explanation of the unfailingness of a Christian
sacramental marriage. It is accurate to say that as long as such a marriage
is lived sacramentally—as long as in intent and in conduct it images the
unfailingness of the love of Christ and his Church—it is in fact unfailing.
Except for death there is no cause in existence that can dissolve this
marriage.

But what if this marriage ceases to be either intended to function or in
fact to function sacramentally after having once done so, and ceases finally
and irrecoverably? What if one spouse rejects the other emotionally and
physically, withdraws his sacramental intent, attempts marriage with another partner, begins a new family? No one doubts that his obligation to
honor his sacramental commitment at least in some way stays with him for
the rest of his life. But this obligation is not the issue at hand. The issue, in
interrogative form, is this: After the abandoning how does the signing
function of the sacrament, which was once freely taken up as a vocation by
both spouses, and which bound them in the *obligation* to unfailingness,
now continue to co-work with Christ in causing the effect that is unfailingness—now that this signing function has ceased, and ceased irrecoverably?
In short, how does the effect continue to exist now that the activity of one
of its needed causes has ceased?

The traditional theology of indissolubility would, of course, deny the supposition underlying the question and making it possible, and its denial would include one of the following assertions. It would say that while the spouses' commitment to unfailingness is needed to co-cause with the imaged love relationship of Christ and the Church in order to initially produce the spouses' relationship and its unfailingness, this co-causing is not needed to keep the unfailingness in existence. That is, the human causing is needed to produce the effect, but it is not needed to hold it in existence. That which cannot come into existence without the activity of the human instrumental cause can, however, continue to exist without the activity of this cause.[8]

Or if this theology recalled Augustine's reasoning in the fourth and fifth centuries it would deny that the sacramental marriage's role in co-causing its own unfailingness consists exclusively or even mainly in its imaging function. It would deny this if it were to say, with Augustine, that its causing rather consists of its forming an unbreakable bond between the spouses' relationship and the will of God. (What this would conclude to unwittingly would be that after one Christian spouse abandons the other and thus ends their marriage's active imaging of Christ's relationship with his Church, what remains is not a relationship of this now vanished image to the Christ-Church relationship, nor a relationship of the spouses' wills to one another. What remains rather is a relationship of each spouse's will to God. If I am accurate here, the indissolubility of a Christian sacramental marriage is more like the binding force of solemn vows pronounced in a religious order. And the Church dispenses from this binding force where sufficient reason for doing so is verified.)

Theologizing by Juridical Categories

I think too that the reasoning in this traditional Catholic theology of indissoluble sacramentality is the same kind of reasoning that Pope Paul used in his discourse of February 1976 to the Roman Rota. The piecing together of juridical categories in logical coherence has taken the place of theological analysis of marriage in its real life. Only such a substitution as this could make welcome the discordance noted just above, that which insists the marital bond surviving in coercion against the will of the parties can image the freely willed relationship of Christ and the Church.

The substituting of juridical categories for the real human relationship of marriage shows itself in another and kindred way. An essential element in each of the Christian sacraments is its human matrix, its anthropological substructure. The matrix in baptism is a washing with water. In confirmation it is a laying on of hands and an anointing with oil. In the Eucharist it is an offering, blessing, breaking, sharing and eating of bread, and the same offering, pouring out and drinking of wine.

In each sacrament the matrix is taken up by the action of God's Spirit. Working together these two causes, the human and the divine, produce their effect that is the strengthened union of the sacramental participants with God.

And working thus in union the action of the human matrix and that of God modify one another. In baptism the washing becomes the participant's rebirth into a new Spirit-filled existence. In confirmation the laying on of hands and the anointing become an infusion of strength to carry on God's work in the world. In the Eucharist the catena of action in the human matrix becomes a nourishing participation in Christ's death and resurrection. Reciprocally, in each of these sacraments the action of the Spirit is focused to a sensate bringing to birth, to a sensate infusing of strength, to a sensate nourishing.

But there must be a semantic correlation, a concordance of meaning between the matrix and the intent of God's Spirit in each sacrament. The Spirit could not produce birth into a new life through a sacramental use of water if the proffered water remained in a reflecting pool. He could not nourish by participation in Christ's death and resurrection if the matrix of the Eucharist were bread and wine proffered as an exhibition at a food fair. In the two cases the water must bathe and cleanse; the bread and wine must be shared, eaten and drunk, and nourish.

In marriage the matrix of the sacrament is a love relationship of the man and woman and its typical conduct. The intent of Christ in this sacrament is that the spouses grow in union with one another and with him by their love's imaging his relationship with his Church.

It is at this point that the anomalous effect of substituting juridical categories in this theology begins to appear. Pope Paul insisted, in his discourse to the Roman Rota, that a marriage is in essence a juridical reality, that it is something of the objective order, existing apart from and independently of the wills of the spouses. It is not some condition of their minds or wills. It is the independently surviving bond that has the juridical effect not of binding them to one another, but—to equivocate in this crucial term—only of binding them not to marry other partners.

How marriage thus understood could be the matrix of the sacrament is beyond understanding—unless one reduces the sacrament itself to a juridical category. This, I think, is precisely what many Catholic authorities have done, What else can they have done when they legislate that an indissoluble bond that is not really indissoluble, since it can be dissolved by papal authority, finally gains indissoluble indissolubility when it is a sacrament—although what becomes the sacrament is not a human image of Christ's love, but is still the detached, objective, juridical entity existing "out there," independently of the wills of the spouses? They make up for the juridical insufficiency of one category—the dissolubility of an indissoluble bond—by superimposing on it another category, that of the indissoluble sacrament. If I may describe briefly again the logic of this method, it seems a combining of abstract concepts of the juridical domain in order to produce an internally consistent legislation. For the purposes of this method the sacrament is no more than one abstract concept among others.

A Question About Automatic Sacramentality

Just underneath this questioning examination of the claim that its sacramental nature once consummated takes the marriage of two Christians beyond the possibility of disintegration is the more fundamental question at which I have already hinted more than once. This question asks if it is accurate to say that any and every marriage of two baptized persons is a Christian sacrament, if it is realistic to conclude that solely because the man and woman have received the sacrament of baptism, their marriage images the love relationship of Christ and his Church, and, as a consequence, once it is consummated as a sacrament, gains radical indissolubility.

The paradigmatic case against this assumption is familiar to any reader of the recent Catholic literature on marriage. I have proposed elements of it in critical asides earlier in this volume. It is this, that although a marriage of two Christians is said repeatedly in Church documents to be a sacrament in that it is an earthly sign, a sensate image, of the relationship of Christ and Church, Catholic law and the theology it uses in its support insist that there need be nothing Christian in either the attitude or the conduct of the spouses whose marriage is said to be such a sacramental image. Both spouses can have become non-religious and even agnostic since their baptism. They need believe nothing, hope in nothing promised by Christ, love neither him nor anyone else with a love that is energized by his Spirit. All that is needed is the fact of their having been baptized and the baptismal character abiding in their souls, whether they are aware of its abiding there or not.

What explanation do theologians offer for the possibility of the Christian sacramentality of the marriage of a man and woman who have become agnostically non-religious after having been earlier baptized as Christians? Let me cite as an example of an answer the reasoning of Matthias Joseph Scheeben in his *Mysterien Des Christentums,* whose original draft he completed in 1865.[9]

Scheeben took up this question obliquely and implicitly when explicating the sacramental nature of a Christian marriage. Here his theology of the sacrament of marriage is a component and a derivative of his theology of the mystical body of Christ. I offer here a précis of his theological reasoning whose intent is apparently to demonstrate that once they have been baptized as Christians, a man and a woman can marry only as members of the body of Christ.

Thus he explains that in the marriage of two baptized persons both are, by their baptism, already members of the body of Christ, are "members of his flesh and bone." They have already been received in and live in the indestructible union of Christ and his Church. As members of the bride of Christ they are already wedded to Christ. Consequently the mystery of the union between Christ and the Church is found in them also. From this there come necessary effects.

They can rightfully unite with each other in matrimony only for the end which Christ pursues in His union with the Church, that is, the further extension of the mystical body of Christ. Since their attitude must be regulated by the spirit of Christ's union with the Church, they can act only in the name of Christ and the Church; for their bodies belong to Christ and His Church, and consequently the right of disposing of them pertains in the first instance not to the earthly bridal couple, but to the heavenly nuptials. Therefore their union presupposes the union of Christ with His Church, and joins with it to cooperate with it for a single supernatural purpose. They must cooperate precisely as members of the body of Christ in His Church, and hence as organs of the whole. Hence they must unite with each other as organs of Christ's body, as organs of the whole that was brought into being by the union of Christ with the Church. Thus their union, their alliance, becomes an organic member in the grand and richly varied alliance between Christ and His Church, a member encompassed, pervaded, and sustained by this mystical alliance, and participating in the lofty, supernatural, and sacred character of the whole. The member represents and reflects the whole.[10]

Stated succinctly Scheeben's argument seems to be this: By their baptism the spouses are incorporated, grafted into the head-body relationship of Christ and Church. Their marriage becomes a component of this relationship, an extension of it. Therefore their marriage participates in the characteristics of it. Scheeben does not at this critical point say that one of these characteristics is the indestructibility of the head-body relationship of Christ and the Church. Writing in 1865 his concern was to show that there can be no separation of the human contract from the sacrament. But by his logic he could have said it, since this conclusion is in his premises virtually.

But this is far too easy a theological argument. To begin with, it makes a metaphoric marriage of a real Christ with a metaphoric bride-Church do the work of a middle term in a theological *demonstratio* about the nature of the real-life marriages of flesh-and-blood men and women. It also uses as one of the terms of its demonstration the metaphoric "insertion" of the spouses into a metaphoric body of Christ to become added "organs" of this body. Before doing this kind of thing a theologian ought to examine the biblical metaphors for the accuracy with which they manifest the reality of that for which they are metaphors. Being biblical does not guarantee this accuracy. Scheeben's failure to do this leaves his conclusion unverified.

In the thirteenth century Thomas Aquinas was more careful. He pointed out that the Church is in reality not the body of Christ, while conceding that calling it such helps to understand the relationship of

Christ with the Christian faithful.[11] In reality the Church is not a wife who, having been purified by her divine husband (as Paul pictures this metaphoric marriage in Ephesians 5), is unfailingly faithful to him. In reality it is a society of men and women, some of whom are faithful, some of whom are not, but none of whom is unfailingly so in the way that the metaphor demands. The only conclusion about real-life marriage that can be drawn from a theological demonstration using a metaphor of the Church as its middle term is that just as the men and women making up the real-life Church ought to strive to be as faithful to Christ as his ideal, metaphoric bride-Church is, so real-life spouses ought to strive to be as faithful to one another. In short, the demonstration can produce not knowledge of an ontological fact that is the nature of Christian marriages, but knowledge of a deontological urgency bearing upon these marriages.

There is another flaw in the theologizing about marriage the sacrament typified here in Scheeben's essay. The flaw emerges when a critic asks the following question: "How can the marriages of baptized but non-religious and even agnostic spouses image the sanctifying, religious union of Christ and the Church when these spouses are either ignorant of such a union or reject it?"

When I put this question recently to a Roman authority, he replied with the following distinction. If such spouses positively reject Christ and the Christian meaning of marriage, they reject the sacrament. And since, as the traditional theology presumes, Christians cannot create the contract without also creating the sacrament, such spouses do not marry at all—and the theological difficulty vanishes. But if these spouses do not positively reject but are only ignorant of the Christian sacramental meaning of their marriage, there takes place in it something akin to what takes place in baptism. An infant can be taken into union with God in the Christian community ("into the mystical body of Christ," Scheeben would explain) without being aware of this. Christ acts in the Church to use the sacrament as his instrument. Through it he can work the effect of incorporation in the unwitting but unresisting soul of the infant. So too in marriage, because the spouses have already been incorporated in the Church and have become instruments of Christ's saving action, their union can be made an image of the union of Christ and the Church without their knowing this, but provided they do not positively reject it, as atheistic spouses may do.

Surely a Christian must admit that God acts in supra-sensate causality to work effects in creation, and in human beings themselves, in which they need not co-work and of which they may be unaware. To deny this would be to indulge an empiricism that simply excludes the knowledge of any being or activity that cannot be measured sensately.

But this is not the point at issue in the sacrament of marriage. The source of the flaw in this reasoning is its failure to take into account that each of the sacraments functions in a way analogically related to the others. A component found in each is the human contribution to the sacrament's matrix that I have explained above. In each sacrament this is some human experience, as in baptism it is the passive experience of being bathed, or at least washed. It can be passive, it can take place without the knowledge or consent of the person being baptized, because baptism's meaning is the passing from an old life to birth in a new life—an experience in which the person may be passive and unaware.

But the meaning, the reality, of marriage is not passive. It is an active committing and giving of two persons to one another in belief, trust and love. Therefore the human element in the sacrament's matrix must be an active self-giving in belief, trust and love. A man and a woman cannot do this unwittingly. Therefore too their imaging of the love of Christ and the Church cannot be passive and unwitting, and their marriage cannot become automatically and unwittingly a sacrament.

One may object realistically that even many faithful and active Christians understand the sacramentality of their marriages only faintly. My reply to this is a distinction. What is necessary for a marriage's sacramentality is not that the spouses understand the theology of this sacramentality, but that they believe, trust and love as Christians. But if these go on only faintly in their lives despite their still identifying themselves as Christians, it follows that their marriages are only faintly sacramental, or are sacramental not at all while still marriages. I do not accept that among Christians the human covenant in marriage and the sacrament are inseparable. I hold that two Christians can be joined in a non-sacramental—or, better, a pre-sacramental—marriage. I hold also that where their marriage is a sacrament, it is the covenant that becomes sacramental, that becomes an image of the love of Christ and his Church.

The Consummated Sacrament and Indissolubility

For the sake of discussion let us accept the claim that it is its comsummation as a Christian sacrament that brings about a marriage's indissolubility. This claim is not as arbitrary as Alexander III's declaration, in the twelfth century, that when Christ commanded that man must not separate what God has joined, Christ had in mind only consummated marriages. Locating indissolubility in marriage's consummated sacramentality and only there is the end product of a medieval dispute in the Catholic regulation of marriage. We reviewed this dispute in an earlier chapter. It was not itself about where to locate indissolubility, but its resolution helped persuasively to set consummated sacramentality as the point of indissolubility.

The dispute arose gradually in western Europe, having begun at a time impossible for us to verify exactly. Certainly it had gained momentum by the eleventh century. It was a consequence of the collision of two societies, the Roman and the central European, and their traditions concerning marriage. The exact point of the dispute concerned the act or acts needed to create a marriage.

Roman tradition held that nothing more is needed for this than a man's and a woman's publicly verifiable expression of consent. This tradition was consecrated in the legal epigram, *Matrimonium facit partium consensus*—"It is the consent of the parties that creates the marriage."

Central European tradition—the Frankish, the Lombard, the German—demanded a multi-step act, or a sequence of acts. The sequential combination varied according to territory, but it was in any case some combination of betrothal promise, exchange of dowry and dotal gifts, the parties' consent to give and to take one another as spouses, the bride's father's or guardian's handing her over to the groom, the groom's leading her to their home, and their first sexual intercourse.

Three samples of the questions woven through the dispute are these: "Is the betrothal promise to marry in the future, followed by sexual intercourse, but with marital consent by-passed, sufficient to create the marriage?" "Can the betrothal promise followed by marital consent create the marriage short of the first intercourse?" "If a man has exchanged marital consent with one woman, but before having intercourse with her has it with a different woman and promises to marry her, to which of the two is he married? or is he married to either?"

This is not the place to detail again the long and tangled history of the dispute between the champions of the two traditions—the canonists of the University of Bologna, principal champions of the European tradition, and the theologians and canonists of the University of Paris, champions of the Roman. What is pertinent to the history of the problem of locating indissolubility is that the resolution of the dispute at the end of the twelfth century and the beginning of the thirteenth by Alexander III and Gregory IX was a mixture of inclusion and exclusion, a compromise. Betrothal promise, exchange of dowry and gifts, handing over of and leading of the bride were all excluded from the acts needed to create a marriage. Exchange of marital consent was interpreted to truly create a marriage; it alone makes the man and woman to be spouses to one another. But by itself it leaves the marriage incomplete, unconsummated. This completion comes only with the first sexual intercourse following the exchange of consent.

Thus, in a manner not adverted to by either the Signatura commission or Pope Paul VI when they scolded and corrected the Dutch marriage courts in 1975 and 1976, the conduct creating a marriage according to Catholic law is developmental. It is literally so, because what this interpretation has consummation do to a merely inchoate marriage is to develop it. It moves it from incompleteness to completeness.

But there is an obvious essential difference claimed for this traditional developmental creating. Where the Dutch judges asserted a continuing process, this ancient Catholic tradition sets acts intended and assumed to be exactly defined, temporally indivisible, and once-for-always effective. These are the exchange of consent and sexual intercourse.

It will not escape the reader that the traditional interpretation here virtually takes for granted that a marriage is a contract. It is a matter of history that the interpretation helped to fix in later medieval philosophy and law that what a marriage is, is a contract. And as a matter of fact consummation of a marriage by a first and single act of intercourse is consummation fitted perfectly to the completing of a marriage presumed to be a contract. For it is of the nature of contracting that two persons, free to do so and capable of doing so, exchange their right to some good or goods. In making this exchange they commit themselves to the subsequent delivery of this good or goods. The exchange of the right is the contract inchoate; it is made but is not yet completed. The completion comes with the delivery of all that has been committed. With this contractual format it is easy to identify the contractual good-to-be-exchanged in marriage. It is the right to sexual intercourse.

Waiting on the sidelines of this dispute was the congenial derivative of a key clause from Genesis 2, and from Christ's quotation of it in the Markan and Matthean records of his Synoptic instruction about marriage. This is the Genesis author's comment on the union of the man and woman in the Garden parable:

That is why a man leaves his father and mother
and clings to his wife,
and the two of them become one body (2:24).

"One body" in the Septuagint translation of this verse, and therefore in the Greek of the Synoptic version, is *mía sárx*. Since this reads literally "one flesh" it was easy for early Christian teachers to interpret this as sexual union.

Christ quoted this verse against his Pharisee adversaries, to use it as a lever in his challenge to their assumption that a husband has authority to dismiss his wife and thereby dissolve his marriage: "So that they are no longer two, but one body. Therefore what God has joined man must not separate" (Mark 10:8–9). Thus he seemed to say that the reason internal to a marriage over-riding any human will to dissolve it—a reason distinct from but correlated with the external reason that is God's command forbidding dissolution—is the sexual unity of the spouses. What is one not only must not be made two, but cannot be. (As we have seen, Paul used this interpretation in Ephesians 5:29–31 to urge the husbands to treat their wives lovingly. Since in marrying they become one body, for a husband to mistreat his wife is to mistreat himself.)

Thus the logic seemed indisputable: A marriage becomes invulnerable to dissolution when the sexual union of the spouses is realized in inter- course. Or in legal language, the contract becomes non-voidable once the promised contractual good has been fully delivered.

We recall it yet again: this interpretation holds that where a marriage is indissoluble, this is caused by its being a consummated sacrament. This could go unchallenged as long as everyone simply assumes that a marriage is a contract, that the exchanged contractual good is the parties' right to their sexual acts, and assumes too that the sacrament is nothing more than the contract elevated to become a grace-giving sacred sign.

But what happens to this interpretation of indissolubility when marriages are no longer thought to be contracts, but covenants in the biblical model? when what is exchanged in the covenanting marital consent is no longer said to be the juridical entity that is the right to sexual acts, but the persons themselves of the spouses? The reader will recall that these are exactly what the bishops of Vatican II said of the act that creates a marriage and of the exchange that is made in marital consent. They and the revised marriage law that has been drawn in great part from their teaching have deliberately refused to speak any longer of marriage as a consensual contract.

This is the first and most obvious inconsistency in the current Catholic doctrine and law concerning consummated sacramentality as the locus and cause of indissolubility in marriage. This doctrine still holds that the kind of act that consummates the marital covenant in which the spouses make a gift of their persons to one another is an act that completes marriage the contract, namely a first and single act of sexual intercourse. Do the teachers of this doctrine and of the discipline drawn from it really think that the *consortium,* the intimate sharing of all of life, the gifting of one's person to a spouse, can be completed in a single act? If they do, they owe it to the people of the Church to explain how this is done, to explain what consummation of marriage understood as the bishops of Vatican II understood marriage may mean.

But a second and perhaps more painful inconsistency surfaces when one considers that it is not the consummation of marriage the natural covenant that is said to be the cause of marriage's indissolubility. It is the consummation of this marriage become a sacrament. The current doctrine and discipline merely assume that the kind of act that completes the contract completes the sacrament. And this they assume because they first assume, as we have already seen, that the sacrament is no more than the contract elevated to become a grace-giving sign. Thus while they say that it is consummated sacramentality that brings indissolubility to a marriage, the consummation thus honored is defined according to the properties of contractuality.

But this is impossible. It is impossible first of all for the reasons I have set forth in the pages immediately preceding this consideration of indissolubility from consummation. Briefly again, in its created matrix, in its human substratum, the sacrament cannot be a contract.

Beyond this, the consummating of marriage as the kind of sacramental image it is, is a far more serious enterprise than the current teaching seems to suspect. We have seen many times in this volume that Catholic doctrine deems the marriage of two Christians a sacrament in that it images the love relationship, by re-enacting the self-giving love, of Christ and the Christian people for one another. More than this, every sacrament is, each in its own way, an imaging and continuing of Christ's rescuing work among human beings. To consummate any sacrament, to complete it, involves a sensate, observable continuation and imaging of this work. So if the Catholic authorities insist on holding that a first, single act of sexual intercourse can consummate a sacramental marriage as a sacrament, they must show how this single act can image in some inclusive way Christ's rescuing work.

The thesis that marriage the sacrament can be consummated by a single act of intercourse is undermined further by the Catholic authorities' own hesitation in answering an unavoidable question about the nature of marital consummation. The question confronted them when the subcommission working at the first draft of the revised marriage law came to Canon 1015 in the incumbent Code. This was the canon that defined the consummating act under the assumption, fixed in that Code, that a marriage is a contract. It said that a marriage is consummated if that act takes place between the spouses to which the marital contract is oriented by nature. In the revised Code Canon 1061.1 reads as follows.

> A valid marriage between baptized persons is said to be . . . ratified and consummated, if the spouses have in a human manner engaged together in a conjugal act in itself apt for the generation of offspring. To this act marriage is by its nature ordered and by it the spouses become one flesh.[12]

The element of this new canon that catches the eye is its phrase, ". . . in a human manner. . . ." The presence of this phrase in the canon was explained by the subcommission that put it there: the modifier *humano modo* is used in *Gaudium et spes* to describe a trait of marital love. There, in Article 49, the bishops explain how this love is most effectively put into act. This is by sexual lovemaking including intercourse.

> This love is expressed and completed in a way unique to the conduct of marriage. Thus those acts by which the spouses are united intimately and chastely are good and worthy. When they are carried on in a truly human way [*modo vere humano exerciti*] they signify and intensify the mutual self-giving with which they joyfully and gratefully enrich one another.

One need not guess that the modifier *humano modo* is in new Canon 1061.1 because it is first in *Gaudium et spes.* In one of its in-progress reports of its work in *Communicationes,* the official journal reporting the work of the papal commission revising the Code of Canon Law, this is said explicitly.[13]

The report explained briefly a motive for including the modifier that was fresh in Catholic jurisprudential history, as well as a disagreement about the wisdom of including it.

A question was raised asking if a marriage is consummated even if the intercourse, though physically complete, is carried on unconsciously or is even coerced. It was noted that the answer to this question has, to date, at least according to the more common teaching, been affirmative. This is an answer that the Congregation of the Holy Office itself once confirmed. But according to some this teaching seems hardly to agree with the Second Vatican Council in its teaching on marriage and especially on the marital act. For in the constitution *Gaudium et spes* one reads in no. 48, "Thus those acts by which the spouses are united, etc. . . ."[14]

Then the report took note of the unavoidable difficulty that is my reason for examining this authoritative teaching concerning consummation. It recorded the objection by some in the subcommission that was formulating the new canon, that a trait that is essential to some point of fact legislated in the law (the completing or not of consummation is such a fact) ought to be subject to judicial verification. But it is hardly possible to prove judicially that a presumably consummating act of intercourse has not been completed *modo vere humano*—"in a truly human way." Consequently the report explains in the following way:

Although the majority of the consultors [the members of the subcommission] agree that the words *humano modo* are to be included in the definition of the consummation of marriage, all agreed unanimously that the term should be put in parentheses so that their uncertainty in the matter may be made evident.[15]

In new Canon 1061.1 quoted above the parentheses are gone. And this comes to the point at issue in this discussion of consummated sacramentality as the ultimate cause of a marriage's indissolubility. Nowhere does the literature of explanation attending the new canons on marriage say that the parentheses are gone because the authorities have in the meantime resolved the doubts that inspired the parentheses in the first place. Note too that the acknowledged doubt had behind it a doubt unacknowledged. The former bore upon the dubious ability of the Church's courts to verify in a real-life case whether the intercourse supposedly consummating the marriage had been completed in a human way. The unacknowledged doubt ought to have borne upon the authorities' tentative and even elusive understanding of sexual intercourse carried on "in a human way."

And behind those two lay two other doubts. The first, in interrogative form, asks whether intercourse completed in a truly human way suffices to consummate a marriage that is a Christian sacrament. And the final doubt passes from that reasonable consideration to the near-ridiculous. It asks by what methods, under what conditions, ecclesiastical judges, adjudicating on the assumption that a single act of intercourse can consummate a sacramental marriage, and asked ten years after a wedding to verify whether such an act had ever been completed in a truly human way, could make such an adjudication.

It seems impossible that the Catholic authorities can now keep the consummated sacrament as a judicial criterion for ruling on the dissolubility and indissolubility of marriages except at the cost of maintaining the inconsistency I have pointed out above. That is, while calling marriage a community, a sharing in all of life that is created by a covenant in which the spouses make a gift of their persons to one another, the authorities continue to treat marriages judicially as contracts in which the spouses exchange their right to sexual intercourse and consummate the contract by a single episode of intercourse.

Ephesians 5:21–33 and the Doctrine of Indissolubility

The Catholic claim that marriage is at some point invulnerable to dissolution is proposed as the will of God made known through Christ. The establishing of this point at the consummation of marriage where it is a sacrament is also proposed as the will of God. But while the claim to invulnerability has its obvious source in Christ's instruction remembered in the Synoptic Gospels and in Paul's First Letter to the Corinthians, there is no instruction in either of these that warrants putting the point of invulnerability where Catholic theology has put it. This warrant, we know by now, is claimed elsewhere in the New Testament—in verses 21 through 33 of the Letter to the Ephesians.

The way in which this passage has been used to argue for invulnerability to dissolution takes the following syllogistic form.

Writing under divine inspiration the apostle Paul taught that the marriage of two Christians is an image of the love relationship of Christ and the Church.

But this relationship is indestructible.

Therefore the marriage of the two Christian spouses is indestructible in the sense that it is invulnerable to dissolution as long as both spouses live.

Two refinements of the logic here are these. First, because the marriage of two Christians is an image of the indestructible union of Christ and the Church, not only must no one try to dissolve it, but it is invulnerable to any attempt to do so. That it pass out of existence short of death is not so much forbidden. It is simply impossible.

Second, this radical indissolubility, as it is called, is found even among Christians only in those of their marriages that have been consummated. And consummation, as we have seen, is secured by the first complete sexual intercourse following the creating of the marriage as a sacrament, which means its creating as an image of the love relationship of Christ and the Church. If one or both parties are unbaptized at the time of marital consent, the image and therefore the sacrament come into existence finally when both are baptized. If they consummated their marriage before both were baptized, when the marriage was only a natural union, not yet an image of the Christ-Church relationship, their marriage does not gain its radical indissolubility until they consummate it a second time, after both are baptized and have thus made their marriage into this sacramental image.

The versions of this explanation that I have studied seem to say that the first of these refinements is contained at least implicitly in the instruction in Ephesians 5. About the second refinement it is generally acknowledged that it is an exact specification of the immediate and proportioned cause of radical indissolubility that has been supplied by Catholic theology, but also a specification warranted biblically in this way, that Genesis 2:24 (and Christ himself quoting this passage according to the Synoptic tradition of his instruction) ground a marriage's indissolubility in the spouses' becoming "two in one flesh." But they do this only in having complete sexual intercourse.

My first question at this point asks whether the first of the above-named refinements is an accurate finding. Does Ephesians 5 at least imply that because a marriage of two Christians is an image of the indestructible relationship of Christ and the Church, this marriage is in fact invulnerable to dissolution short of death? And cutting inside that question to ask a more immediate one, does this passage say, or at least imply, that a marriage of two Christians—any marriage of two Christians, as the traditional Catholic teaching has it—is an image of the indestructible relationship of Christ and the Church?

It will help to divide the elements of the answers to these questions and work through them separately and progressively. To begin with, the location of the verses in question, 21 through 33, is significant. As in others of Paul's letters, Ephesians too is divided clearly into a prior instruction on points of substantial belief and a following exhortation, or set of exhortations, to conduct demanded of Christians, demanded of them perhaps as a consequence of their belief. (The Letter to the Romans does this, with the point of transition from instruction to exhortation at the end of Chapter 11. The same transition in Galatians is at the end of Chapter 5 of its six chapters. In Colossians it is at Chapter 3, verse 5. Here in Ephesians it is at the end of the third of its six chapters.)

Interpreting it broadly, we find that the matter of belief about which Ephesians instructs in its prior part is the mystery of God's plan for the human race, his plan to make Christ the head of a new brotherhood of all human beings, a brotherhood that will obliterate the old, hate-filled divisions and distinctions—especially the distinction between Jews and Gentiles. This plan will be brought to reality by the active presence of the Holy Spirit in the followers of Christ.

Beginning in Chapter 4 Paul exhorts his readers to live lives that properly derive from God's plan and from their being moved by the Spirit of Christ.

> So then I exhort you—I the prisoner in the Lord—to lead lives worthy of the calling in which you have been called, with all loving kindness, and selflessness and great-heartedness, being patient with one another in love; striving to preserve the unity of the Spirit in the peace that binds you together (verses 1–3).

That much is a general exhortation to all his readers, regardless of their station in life. Paul urges all to "the work of service, building up the body of Christ" (verse 13). From about 4:17 Paul comes down to particulars, first by urging his readers away from sins that destroy peace and loving care in a community, sins such as lying, lust, vindictive anger, theft, foul talk, spitefulness, feuding, refusal to forgive, drunkenness.

Then at verse 19 of Chapter 5 Paul's itemized exhortation turns to positive conduct, to conduct Christians should show because they are "filled with the Spirit," as he repeats here. His exhortation then bears in sequence upon three stations in life, and on the relationships comprehended in these stations, that are the most substantial in the society he knows. These are the relationships of spouses to one another, of children and parents, of slaves and their masters.

The exhortation to spouses is that they love one another, and that they do so with a unique love. This uniqueness is explained by, and is even derived from, Paul's use of a metaphor. This metaphor has the Church as Christ's bride. Paul's use of this is to set the metaphorical marriage of Christ and the Church as the model on which the husbands and wives among his readers may form their marriages. (It may be that beginning with the second clause of verse 25 Paul quotes from a Christus hymn: "Husbands should love their wives just as *Christ loved the Church and gave himself up for her. . . .*") He works out the modeling in such a way that the husband is "head" of the wife, just as and because Christ is head of the Church, and that the wife is to submit to her husband just as and because the Church submits to Christ. But withal, the reciprocal loves are self-giving, consumingly so for the husband, according to the metaphor-model, because Christ gave up his life for his bride, the Church.

At this point it is essential to find out exactly the way in which Paul employs this metaphor. But first notice the structure of the metaphor. Christ is said to have a bride, who is the Church. This bride status itself involves metaphoric predication, since it personifies a group of human beings who are, in reality, not a bride nor a person at all. This metaphor of the Church bride is inserted, in turn, as a kind of subset, into the metaphor of the Christ-Church marriage. And a third metaphor is woven into these two, that of Christ as head and the Church as his body—thus providing a vehicle for the exhortation that the bride-body be submissive to the husband-head.

Even before one examines how these interwoven metaphors are employed, one finds an obvious forcing of reality. There is an asymmetry in the components of the metaphor. Christ, a physically real person, is said to have a bride who is not. The physical reality of this "bride," the Church, is that of a society of men and women who commune by intellect, will, emotions and senses through a transempiric bond who is the Spirit, and by this communication constitute the Church. So, to provide a spouse for Christ, Paul metaphorizes these physical persons into a figurative person, the Church. This has consequences that I noted earlier in this chapter. For one thing it tends to abstract from the flawed human reality found in the real-life Church. Not all the men and women making up this Church let themselves be loved or purified or ruled by Christ, as the metaphoric Church-bride does. If Paul's use of these three intertwined metaphors did not abstract from the reality I have just mentioned, he would have to say that the Church is at times grievously unfaithful to her spouse because Christian men and women singly and in groups sometimes sin grievously.

Having established this web of metaphors, Paul uses it to work out an analogical predication. To put it in most general terms, he asserts a similarity of two relationships—of that of Christ to the Church with that of Christian husbands to their wives.

For the theology of the sacrament and for the claimed indestructibility of sacramental marriages it is crucial to see exactly how Paul uses this analogy, to isolate and verify his intent in predicating through it.

One use of analogical prediction is for mere illustration, for disclosing reality. Thus, to call David the Lion of Judah—to say, that is, that he relates to his enemies as a lion does to its prey—is to do no more than to disclose the quality of David's strength and courage. Asserting this similarity of his strength and courage to those of a lion does not obligate him to be courageous and strong. And it certainly does not make him to be courageous and strong.

But there is another use of analogical predication, one which may also use metaphors. We see this in the parable of the prodigal son in Luke 15:11–32. Let us assume that the father in the parable represents God the Creator. The two relationships set in analogy here are the explicit relationship of forgiving father to repentant son, and the implied relationship of forgiving Creator to sinful but repentant men and women.

Christ's intent in setting forth this analogy was not merely to have us know that the Creator forgives antecedently and totally, as does the fictional father in the parable. His intent went beyond this merely noetic causation to a further double causation. One of these I choose to call deontological. That is, Christ intended that the analogy establish in the minds of his hearers, and with obligating valence, the accurate understanding of God's will to forgive. This intent was, by implication, "You *must* think of his forgiveness in this way."

The second of these further intents—and a variant of this second use of analogical predication—involves a kind of ontological causation. Christ intended that men's and women's understanding of this analogy in fact bring forgiveness to them. It is as if he had said, "If you understand and accept that God forgives you antecedently and totally as the father in the parable forgives his son (and I bid you understand it this way!), this forgiveness is already brought to you. My disclosure in this parable is itself the bringing of forgiveness to you. Now it is for you to accept it."

The Mode and Content of Paul's Instruction

Granted what is obvious in the passage, that Paul constructs a metaphoric marriage of Christ and the Church and uses it in analogic predication to instruct Christian spouses, what is his intent? In what way does he use this analogy and what effect does he intend to produce by the way he uses it?

First of all, the entire passage about marriage—verses 21 through 33—is parenetic in intent. It is an instruction and an exhortation concerning right conduct. It is one point of instruction in a series of parenetic instructions. It is not a declaration nor an exposition of doctrine, such as this same Letter to the Ephesians has in the hymn making up verses 3 through 14 of its first chapter. Thus Paul does not say what the marriage of any two baptized Christians is. He does not say what has been claimed for centuries about this passage, namely that in it he asserts that the marriages of baptized Christians are images of the metaphoric marriage of Christ and the Church. He does not here teach this religious ontology.

What he does in his parenesis is to urge Christian spouses to love and trust one another in a way that imitates the model of conduct that is the metaphoric marriage of Christ and the Church. (It is worth noting that among the qualities of the latter model marriage he does not list its objective indestructibility. He tells rather of the unreserved self-giving love of the metaphoric husband, Christ.)

Among the three ways of using the metaphoric marriage analogically he clearly goes beyond mere illustration, mere disclosing. He intends for his readers to find out from his analogy more than that Christ loves the Christian community with a self-giving love, and more than that a Christian marriage is lived rightly when it images the relationship of Christ to this community.

One is tempted to say that Paul's intent in using the analogy is deontological, that he uses it to lay an obligation upon the Christian spouses. But this is doubtful. There is a difference between exhorting persons to right conduct, which he clearly does, and obligating them to it. There is a difference between urging persons to what they ought to do as the best of which they are capable, and declaring to them what they are bound in conscience to do in order to avoid sin. The most that is deontological about Paul's use of the analogy is his implication that to think rightly about their marriages his Christian readers must acknowledge their capacity for imaging the love relationship of Christ and the Church.

But it is beyond questioning that Paul did not intend for his analogy the use that the traditional Catholic theology has made of it. This has been to force it to a unique causative function that is ontological. It has been used to assert this cause-effect relationship: *because* the metaphoric marriage of Christ and the Church is indestructible, the physically real marriages of any and all pairs of Christian spouses *are* indissoluble; not only *ought* they never be abandoned, but they *are incapable* of dissolution by any cause other than death.

Start with the fact that Paul himself does not say this. At most he implies only "the ought to be." Beyond this, there is serious difficulty in validating the claimed causal nexus between the two relationships: Why and how is it that the indestructibility of the Christ-Church relationship *makes* every marriage of two Christians to be indissoluble, *makes impossible* the ending of their marriage by any cause other than death? What could bring us to know that the indestructibility of the one relationship produces the indestructibility of the other?

As I have already said, Paul does not claim this. Neither did Augustine in his essay, *On the Good of Marriage.* There he said that the marriage of two Christians is imperishable because, already sealed with the sacrament of baptism, they make a commitment in their marital consent that produces in their souls a certain conjugal something—*quiddam coniugale*—that is imperishable. By this "certain conjugal something" he did not mean the image of the Christ-Church relationship but the spouses' obligation to keep their promise to God, an obligation apparently created by their promise to one another.

To point out exactly the flaw that voids the logical *consequentia* of the traditional theology of indissolubility purportedly drawn from this passage in Ephesians, there is an unexplained and unvalidated *saltus,* a logical leap, from what ought to be to what is. The reasoning of this theology fails to show how the causative capacity of one facet of the analogy, the metaphoric Christ-Church relationship and its indestructibility, produces the effect in the other facet of the analogy that is the alleged indissolubility of the real-life marriage of the Christian spouses. Since the reasoning fails to show *how* this causation produces this alleged effect, it fails to show that it does so at all.

One ought to be careful another way in using Paul's analogy to find out about the marriages of Christians and their alleged indissolubility. The major premise of the traditional argument for indissolubility asserts that the Christ-Church relationship, the metaphoric marriage, is indestructible. As I have already said, this is true in only a restricted way. For it is also true that some members of the Church do unilaterally end the union. No doubt Christ through his Spirit will always indefectibly call and draw them to himself. But there is no such thing as unilateral union. At least two persons and their will for union are needed. And the union in question here is a union of love, of will and of affectivity. If a person changes his will, turns it away, closes it, chooses against Christ, his personal union with him has been dissolved. This happens in the Church; the Church has this as its own internal experience. In this sense, then, the union of Christ and the Church is not indestructible. It experiences destructibility and destruction within itself.

What is true is that by a miracle of grace Christ will always have some men and women in union with himself. There will always be a Church. The metaphor of Christ-husband loving his bride-Church will always have a referent in reality. But in this qualified sense only is it accurate to say that the union of Christ and his Church is indestructible.

This qualified accuracy in the referability of the metaphor has an effect on the analogy's function as a cause of the alleged indissolubility of real-life Christian marriages. What kind of causality does one assert if he says: "Because Christ will always have a bride-Church, the marriages of Christians cannot go out of existence except by death?" Is one saying: "Because Christ will always through his Spirit impel and call the spouses into marital union—will always be acting to cause their union—they cannot not be in this union which is their marriage?" If this is what Paul were saying, he would imply that the spouses' freedom to choose against their union, even to the point of destroying it, has been taken from them. How then could theirs be a union of love, a union of wills in the sense of a union of free choice? How could it, since love in it has been destroyed, be an image of the love-union of Christ and the Church?

A careful examination of Paul's analogy finds rather that he does the following. He says that what the relationship of Christian husband and wife, as an image in real life of a transcendent reality, actually signifies is the effort of Christ to cause indestructibility in the Church as a whole by working to cause it in its members. The Christian husband and wife image forth not a finished reality, but one still contingent, still incomplete, still struggling for its own completion—and still vulnerable to failure in particular instances. Therefore one cannot reason that a sacramental marriage is in fact indissoluble *because* it images an indestructible relationship. Rather, because it images a relationship that struggles for an indestructibility really possible because the Spirit of Christ is in it making it possible, the marriage ought in itself to be a sincere struggle for an indestructibility really possible because the Spirit of Christ is in it too bringing this possibility.

To say all this succinctly: in this classic passage in his Letter to the Ephesians Paul exhorts the Christian spouses among his readers to live married lives containing a self-giving love for which they have a model in Christ's love for the Christian people as a whole, a self-giving love of which they are capable because the Spirit of this same Christ is active within them. The indestructibility of their love—the indissolubility of their marriages—Paul does not claim to be simply given, not even in virtue of this Spirit. He implies that this indestructibility is a goal that they can attain as a quality of their love provided they work with the Spirit of Christ and guide their marital conduct by the model that is Christ's love relationship with them as a community, a Church.

The Gospel Instruction Re-Examined

Near the end of this long and detailed examination of the Catholic doctrine and discipline of divorce and remarriage it will help to return to the Gospel instruction on this subject. A major element of the Catholic claim is that the doctrine was born in the words of Christ and is therefore the will of God, and so too is the discipline.

To be understood Christ's instruction must be examined by two inter-related uses of the mind. One is a comprehending of what is explicit in the instruction. The other is a drawing out by inference of what is there only implicitly and virtually.

At least as early as the Church's second generation its teachers understood Christ's instruction to not forbid dissolution of marriages unexceptionably. Evidence that this understanding took hold that early is in the exceptive clause of Matthew's version of the Synoptic tradition. It is also in Paul's permitting in the Corinthian community the dissolution of religiously mixed marriages, and in his apparently accepting that even where a Christian woman is abandoned by her Christian husband her marriage is at an end.

What the Church's teachers have apparently understood Christ to say is that only marriages of a special kind are invulnerable to dissolution. Having decided this they laid on themselves the task of verifying what must be done to marriages to give them this specialness and its consequent invulnerability. We have seen their judgment on this point worked out slowly down through the centuries. The apparent terminus of this working out is the judgment that only the sacramental marriages of baptized Christians are thus invulnerable, and of these only those that have been consummated as sacraments.

We must infer two things immediately about this gradually appropri-ated doctrine. Since Christ did not teach this explicitly, yet the teachers hold that this embodies his mind about the dissolution of marriages, they must assume also that he did not express his mind in a legal mandate. For at least the first meaning of such a mandate is understandable immediately in its explicit formulation. This meaning does not need to be inferred. This is an important point, and we shall return to it in a moment.

A second point here is that the Catholic teachers' understanding of Christ's mind on divorce and remarriage has been the product of their own inference and adaptation. And in their use of this hermeneutic method they have introduced a complication that has not always been noticed. The complication comes from the two levels of enunciation in Christ's instruc-tion. At one level he commands something clearly and simply. At another he repeats a principle of judgment and conduct, and implies that the principle must rule in conduct. The Catholic teachers' inferring and adapting have drawn from both these kinds of enunciation, but unevenly.

For an example of this second level of enunciation we return to Christ's instruction in the Synoptic passages. We recall that there his counter-challenge to the Pharisees who first challenged him included a denial of their assumptions regarding women and marriage. It also included a second denial. This gainsaid their assumption that the proper form of discourse for resolving their doubts about women, marriage and divorce is argument about juridical precedents and logic. He did not say that they had interpreted their own law incorrectly. He said that they had forgotten God's word on the subject, that they profoundly misunderstood the husband-wife relationship. So his reply to the Pharisees' challenge was not an imposition of new but correct legislation. It was in form a prophetic utterance.

How well Mark understood this is evident from the context, in his version of Christ's instruction, into which he inserted that instruction. The latter is preceded by Christ's second prophecy that his life will end in death by crucifixion but will be restored in resurrection (9:30–32). Then he sets out a series of Christ's declarations about the demands that will be laid on those who choose to be his followers. These are radical and cannot be confined to rules of conduct. His followers must not seek to be great by position and prestige but must be the servants of all (9:33–37). They must be willing to tear out an eye or cut off a hand if this is necessary in order to avoid lethal sin (9:43–49). Those who choose to be his must have the simplicity of children (10:13–16). They must give away their wealth and follow him in poverty (10:17–22). If they would be truly and completely his, they must be willing to give up father and mother, wives, children, home and homeland (10:28–32). And these utterances are all capped by the third prophecy of his death and resurrection (10:32–34).

The point here is that none of these demands is customary or statutory law. They are not, taken ensemble, a declaration of the nature of Christian holiness. They are a declaration of how a man or woman must be willing to live in order to be a true follower and intimate of Christ. They are a challenge, a demand, an invitation. Does one sin if one refuses them? The question is off the point. The point is that if one refuses them, one cannot be an intimate of Christ.[16]

In this light we can better understand Christ's enunciation at first level, his explicit command within this prophetic discourse. This command is most exact. It is not that his followers not procure or allow the dissolution of their marriages. It is that the husbands among them not continue the rabbinically sponsored practice of unilateral dismissal of wives. This negative command is directed immediately at his fellow male Jews and then by ready inference at the males among his followers in every century.

Christ adds the reason for his command, and in it we see again the second level of his enunciation, that which underlies it as a source of its own valence as well as of our understanding of it. This principle is that marriage is the most precious of all human relationships, and that in it a man and a woman become as one person, which means that a wife is not her husband's property to be disposed of at his will, but is his equal. And all this is God's design.

It is not only that this kind of husband-wife union is God's design but that when a man and woman unite in real life, it is God who unites them. Beyond this, a kind of encompassing principle of conduct gives marriage a special meaning for Christ's followers. A husband and wife are to be a sign of God's fidelity to all peoples and a carrier of this fidelity. A first sign within this communitarian sign is the private fidelity within a marriage. Thus a principle that Christ recalls in this enunciation is that the covenant of fidelity in marriage must be kept exactly as God has willed it from the beginning.

All this is what gives the lie to the Pharisees' interlocked assumptions, first that a husband may dismiss his wife, and second their assumption that the question is how to understand Deuteronomy's *erwat dabar,* the cause that justifies the husband's dismissing his wife.

Inference from and Adaptation of the Gospel Instruction

I said above that the Catholic teachers' understanding, down through the centuries, of Christ's mind on divorce and remarriage has been the product of their inference from the adaptations of his instruction. It is clear enough that they have taken their inferential conclusions not from his first-level enunciations, his commands, but from the deeper level, his prophetic declaration of principles. They have used their inferences to adapt his first-level commands to the varying situations of married life.

To say that the Church's teachers have produced their doctrine by inference and adaptation is not to accuse them of hedging, of attenuating Christ's demands. When I say "the Church's teachers" I refer not only to the bishops of later years who took the written Gospel traditions and applied them to married life in their lands. I refer also to those who first taught the Gospel that was subsequently put into written form. How could they have applied this teaching in any other way? As it stood Christ's command was applicable only to a society in which men dissolved their marriages by dismissing their wives. If the Church's teachers were to adapt, and to instruct by adapting, they had to draw on what Christ said at the deeper level, from the principles of judgment and conduct he took from God's design for marriage.

Let us look again at Paul's instruction in 1 Corinthians 7 as an example of this. If he was ever inclined to think that Christ had forbidden dissolution unexceptionably, he soon corrected this inclination. He was sure that Christ had forbidden a husband to dismiss his wife, even though when he passed this instruction on to his Corinthian readers Paul referred it only to Christian husbands and wives. He was also sure that it was Christ's will that wives not leave their husbands, although this appears to be his inference, since in the Synoptic tradition Christ said nothing about this. But his choice of words in relaying this second part of his instruction leaves us unsure of the consequences of Christian spouses' disobeying these commands of Christ. Unlike the shorter Matthean and Lukan versions of the Synoptic instruction, he did not say that the spouses commit adultery if they disobey Christ's commands. The options he held out to a Christian wife who left her husband, to either be reconciled with him or to remain unmarried (*ágamos*), suggest that her departure could end the marriage.

He countenanced and even advised that a Christian spouse not try to hold in marriage a non-Christian spouse who wished to leave it via divorce according to Roman law. The reasons he offered to justify this clearly draw not from any of Christ's commands but from a principle underlying his entire Gospel. This is not that the other spouse is non-Christian, and that such religiously mixed marriages threaten the faith of the Christian spouse. It is a different reason, one that could be verified in any marriage, including the marriage of two Christians. The Christian's attempt to hold the unwilling non-Christian spouse would reduce the former to a kind of slave. It would destroy the peace that Christ meant should be his or hers. About these reasons John Donahue offers the following explanation.

> The second major reason for permission of divorce is "in peace God has called you." One should not understand this "peace" simply as domestic harmony which would be shattered by bitter disputes over matters of religion. It is primarily a theological and eschatological concept. Paul begins his letters most often by wishing his communities "grace and peace" which are the *bona messianica,* the presence of God's graciousness and right order and harmony which is to characterize the new creation. In Romans Paul says that peace is the result of Christ's redemptive work (5:1). In his picture of the life in the Spirit consequent on baptism, Paul says that "the mind controlled by the Spirit is life and peace" (8:6). In Romans he also says that the kingdom of God is a matter of "righteousness, peace and joy" in the Holy Spirit, and counsels his community "to make every effort to do what leads to peace" (14:17, 19). In 1 Corinthians Paul allows divorce because the presumed unharmonious marriage creates a situation where that peace or *shalom* which is characteristic of the new age and the fruit of Christ's saving work cannot exist. In terms taken from later theology we might say that for Paul this marriage has ceased to be a sign and source of grace.[17]

That was Paul's interpretation and adaptation of Christ's instruction. We have already seen the interpretations and adaptations recorded in the

Synoptic Gospels. Mark has Christ forbid Palestinian Jewish wives to do what they could not have done in any case under their law, namely to dismiss their husbands. Luke has Christ say what none of the other New Testament authors record, that a man who dismisses his wife makes her an adulteress. Both Matthew and Luke have Christ say that a man commits adultery if he marries a dismissed woman, while Mark and Paul do not. In both the passages in which he records Christ's instruction Matthew has him make an exception to his warning that a husband who attempts marriage with a second woman after dismissing his wife commits adultery. In the case of the wife's *pornéia,* of her *erwat dabar,* the second marriage would not result in adultery. Neither of the other two Synoptic authors makes this adaptation by inventing this exception.

We would miss something crucial about the mentality as well as the method of this early interpretation and adaptation if we did not recall that they were done with full awareness of what Christ had said at his deeper level of enunciation—that he had said of marriages universally, for all times and in all places, that in them the spouses are joined by God, that men are not to separate them, that the spouses become as one person, that they owe one another unfailing covenantal fidelity, that theirs is the most precious of all human relationships. Consequently when the Church's teachers in later centuries interpreted and adapted, they continued what was begun by the first and second generation of teachers who gave to the Church the Gospel as we now have it.

Because these first teachers interpreted and adapted while holding inviolably to the values we have seen Christ assert, the goal of Catholic teachers through the centuries ought not to be first of all to legislate ethical demands on the conduct of divorcing and remarrying. Their goal ought to be first to complete a search, a search for which kinds of unions men call marriages have been joined by God, and joined by God in such a way that men cannot separate them. The search ought to be also for what it is in such marriages that makes of the partners one person, two in one flesh, what it is that sets the demand on the partners for unfailing covenantal fidelity.

Few of the Catholic teachers have ever thought that the mere fact of exchanging marital consent makes the spouses two in one flesh, or that the commitment itself to lifelong fidelity causes their marriages to be indissoluble. Augustine notwithstanding few have even thought that these qualities are brought into a union by its being the marriage of two Christians. This is evident in the practice, already established in patristic times, of Christian spouses' dissolving their marriages by entering into monastic life.

In the twelfth century Pope Alexander III interpreted and adapted Christ's words in the most flexible way imaginable to justify this practice, asserting that the kinds of marriages whose dissolving Christ forbade are only consummated marriages. Yet not he, nor the medieval Popes who installed the use of the Pauline privilege, nor the three sixteenth-century Popes who authorized the dissolution of consummated marriages, even of those that after consummation became sacraments, thought they were doing other than being faithful to Christ's instruction.

Since in each of these instances the Church's teachers interpreted Christ's words and adapted them in order to free men and women caught in a trap of human making, to free them for a chance at happiness and holiness, it is fair for the modern student to ask how the contemporary teachers may interpret and adapt these words for men and women trapped in ways that the world of the late twentieth century has devised, or at least come to recognize.

Take, for example, the woman in our thematic paradigm. By her husband's abandoning her she is trapped in a loneliness that, by her reckoning, threatens to destroy her emotionally and therefore morally. Or suppose a woman much like her who has taken the next step and, to escape her loneliness, has found another mate, has committed herself to him in a civil wedding ceremony, and has with him brought two children into the world. She is trapped in a moral ambivalence. Where is her ruling obligation? To the man she first married and their children, even though he abandoned her and the children are now adult and independent? Or to the man who is now father of her younger children, and to the children themselves?

We have already seen the authoritative answers to these questions, or, if not the answers themselves, at least the ingredients of the answers. Both women are still bound in their first marriages. Therefore their first responsibility is to those marriages, to not violate them by attempting adulterous second unions. The pastoral advice that would be given to the second woman is that in order to discharge her responsibility to her more recently born children she may continue to cohabit with her second consort but may not be sexually active with him.

Method and Motive in the Traditional Teaching

If this tracking of the long history of the Catholic regulation of divorce and remarriage has been reasonably accurate, I think it has detected the following strategy in the regulation. Or if the successive steps in the development of the regulation have been too much more the product of worthy expediency than of logical development from an earlier principled stand to be called a strategy, then it is more accurate to speak only of a consistent pattern. I think the pattern has been the following.

On examining marriage in its nature the Catholic teachers have not found that this nature is invulnerable to dissolution. They have not found that the needs of anyone involved in a marriage—the husband, the wife, the children, the legally related families, larger society—set an unexceptionable demand for the permanence of a marriage.

In their examination of the Scriptures they have not found that these teach that marriages are invulnerable to dissolution by God's command,

and then in obedience to this command have devised a doctrine and discipline fitted to obey this command.

What these teachers have done methodologically, it seems to me, are three things. First, with two doctrines and disciplines functioning in the Church by the end of the fourth century—mainly in the Eastern empire a permissive doctrine and discipline drawing from what is implicit in the Matthean exceptive clause to dissolve marriages damaged by adultery or equivalent crimes; a growing rigorous discipline in the Western empire that denied the use of this clause—the authorities in the Western Church gradually installed the latter discipline and its supporting interpretation of the New Testament divorce passages. This was a discipline that drew from the Markan version of the Synoptic instruction, excluded the permissive use of the Matthean version, but kept the Pauline instruction with its mixture of both rigor and openness to dissolution on the ground of disparity of religious belief.

Second, in the twelfth and thirteenth centuries the Western Catholic authorities invented a prescriptive definition of marriage that had indissolubility as one of its parts. They did not intend by this to say that marriages are really indissoluble, since they continued the dissolving of unconsummated marriages. What they apparently intended was only to strengthen marriages' resistance to dissolution by writing this invented indissolubility into marriage's abstract definition, and thereby to deny civil authorities' power to dissolve, and reserve this power to ecclesiastical authority.

Finally, since there were already in the Western Catholic tradition compelling reasons for making this a qualified indissolubility, the authorities moved the barrier of invulnerability inward toward marriage's religious center. That is, they reserved really indissoluble indissolubility for a special kind of marriages, for only those that are Christian sacraments, and, among these, for only those that are consummated as Christian sacraments.

As I have suggested above, it seems clear that the motive impelling this development was not fidelity to Christ's first level of enunciation, not simple obedience to his commands. Few authorities in the Church have escaped the painful necessity of adapting Christ's teaching to situations that these teachings did not address or even envision.

Interpretations, extensions, applications, adaptations of scriptual passages are necessary and inevitable. They belong to the substance of teaching and of government in the Church. In a way hardly noticed and certainly not acknowledged this teaching and governance have used 1 Corinthians 7:15 as a norm for interpretation and adaptation through the centuries: "The brother or the sister is not to play the slave in such matters, for God has called us in peace." Alexander III used it in the twelfth century to free spouses to enter religious life when he asserted that only consummated marriages make the spouses two in one flesh and thus invulnerable to dissolution. The three Popes of the sixteenth century used

it to free from their marriages converted polygamous natives and converted slaves torn from their slave spouses so that the converts could enter
second and sacramental marriages. With this on record as a rule of
pastoral governance, the question remains alive and pertinent: What forms
should this freeing interpretation of the New Testament teaching take in
the last quarter of the twentieth century?

An Alternative Pastoral Motivation

If it is true that the Catholic authorities have used 1 Corinthians 7:15
to free men and women from marital traps not of their own making, it is
also true that they have worked to protect persons from the exaggerations
of freedom. In this regard it is literally impossible to over-estimate the
seriousness of the need to save marriages in Western society from its
twentieth-century black plague of divorce. As I said in the Foreword to
this volume, I think that where a divorce really marks the end of a
marriage, this is a tragedy. It is the death of the most precious of human
experiences, an intimate sexual love. The ability to trust has been damaged, certainly in the spouses and probably in their children. Now it will
be much more difficult for them to believe that caring intimacy, and
therefore the richest happiness, will ever be within their reach.

But I think that even more than the desire to free men and women to
seek for happiness in a second marriage or in another vocation, the
Catholic doctrine and discipline of divorce have been motivated to save
marriage from ruin. Formulating the concern in this way suggests that it
has been concern for safeguarding an abstraction. Perhaps in some cases it
has been. But more probably it has been concern to save marriage taken as
a concrete universal, in the same sense that a political action group may
seek to save freedom of speech in a nation. Certainly within the inclusive,
societally measured motivation there has been the more particular concern
to protect the victims of divorce, those least able to protect themselves—
the children, and so often the women. But woven through this concern for
the concrete and real life has been the more ideally felt motive to save
traditional and treasured institutions taken globally and almost abstractly—the family, the state, the Church.

If I am accurate in seeing the motivation in these two domains, we
have the elements with which to explain a conflict within the Catholic
effort to save marriages and to save marriage. The way I formulate this
double effort suggests where I think the conflict lies. Let me put it in the
form of a question: Has it happened that in their effort to save marriage
the Catholic authorities have damaged the partners in marriage, have
damaged men and women who have no vocation for celibacy and who
could create and live sacramental marriages if given a second chance?

To explain what I mean let me turn again to the paradigm with which
this volume began. The woman there is an intelligent and informed
Catholic. She married because she believed that only by living a sexually

intimate life in a family would she be happy. The happiness she has in mind is not only the happiness reasonably within reach of men and women on earth within the span of this life. She means also eternal happiness in the life she believes continues beyond death. She knows that when St. Paul wrote to the Corinthian Christians about married life, widowed life and celibate single life, he acknowledged that each of these forms of life is a gift from God, and that he implied it is seriously unwise to try to live a life that is not one's own particular gift from God.

From all the evidence available to her she is convinced that it is her gift to be married—as honestly convinced as anyone who has ever decided that her gift is the consecrated celibate life. She knows that she needs a lasting, sexually expressed intimacy, that she is deeply unhappy without it. And she thought in the early years of her marriage that this is what her life would contain.

But after their twenty-nine years of marriage her husband has abandoned her, and has done so completely and finally by taking up life with another woman. She and another man, also an intelligent and informed Catholic, have come to know and love one another, and would marry if they could. But they cannot. There are no grounds for finding that her marriage was null, that it was only a supposed marriage. A retrospective examination of its early years has turned up no flaw in character of either herself or her husband, no impediment that could constitute grounds for finding nullity. She cannot marry the man she now loves, she is told, because she is still married. And a polygamous second marriage is not only forbidden but is impossible.

She has educated herself in the long and winding history of the Catholic doctrine concerning divorce and remarriage, in the centuries-long search to prove indissolubility and to find the place in the complex structure of a Christian sacramental marriage at which to locate it. She has been told that in the final analysis she cannot remarry because she is still a partner in a sacramental marriage that is consummated, that in effect she still participates in a full and integral imaging of Christ's love relationship with his Church.

Her question at this point does not, as earlier, ask how this can be when the man who is presumably her partner in this participation abandoned her two years ago. She asks now why such a theory of marriage's indissolubility has been designed, installed and kept, since there is no internal logic demanding its keeping, and the keeping of it cannot have fidelity to Christ's command as its reason. If the motive for keeping it is to protect something or someone, whom or what does it protect? And at what cost does it protect?

Does one say that it protects and saves marriage? If so, in what sense? Certainly not as lived, flesh-and-blood relationships. It is the shattering and disappearance of these relationships that raises the question to began with. Then marriage as a kind of concrete universal, as an institution conceived of globally? And by saving marriage in this sense are the Church and civil society saved too? If this is the motive, the saving has succeeded only dubiously, since the record shows that at least in recent decades the marriages of Roman Catholics in Western society have broken up at about the same rate as those in the rest of the population.

Or if the Church and civil society are somehow saved as reified institutions, are they not saved at the cost of the persons who make them up, and therefore at the cost of these institutions themselves as real-life communities of men and women? Is it thought better in principle for the stability not of these communities, but of the institutions taken in abstraction, to sacrifice the happiness of the persons who make them up?

But to preserve the communities in this abstract sense is not to save the common good in preference to the private good. This misunderstands the nature of the common good. It is not what remains in one's understanding of a society's needs after one has abstracted from the needs of the persons making it up. The common good consists of the needs, the fulfilling of the needs that these persons have because of the nature found commonly in all of them. Since this is so, a woman's happiness in sexual intimacy is an element of her common good. And the Catholic Church acknowledges this in declaring all men's and women's fundamental right to marry, fundamental since it is a right that grows out of a human need that is fundamental.

To return in more detail to a point made earlier, the Catholic authorities have been strangely inconsistent in their history of qualifying Christ's command concerning divorce in order to procure this common good of persons. He said, quoting the author of the garden parable in Genesis, that a husband and wife are two in one flesh, are one person before the law, and that they are not to be divided. But in the Pauline privilege the authorities have sanctioned the dividing of spouses for the personal exercise of the common good of the Christian spouse who has been abandoned by the non-Christian, or whose practice of the Catholic religion is hindered by the non-Christian.

In the sixteenth century three Popes sanctioned this dividing for the good of new Christian converts after physical separation from their pagan spouses. The Church has countenanced the separating of spouses since patristic times for the good of partners in unconsummated marriages who wish to enter religious life. And all this has been done with no evident anxiety about saving "marriage" in the Church or civil society.

But the authorities will not qualify Christ's command in order to save from unhappiness a Christian spouse abandoned by a Christian spouse. Here the line is drawn, and the reason it is drawn here is that their marriage, having been consummated as a sacrament, images unfailingly and for the rest of their lives Christ's love relationship with the Church— despite the abandonment.

But if this theological reason purportedly drawn from the New Testament is not in fact drawn from it, and if the logic in the reasoning itself is flawed, where is the compelling reason for denying her common good to a Christian woman trapped in this other way in an unforeseen and coerced celibacy?

It seems evident that the pastoral charity of the Church demands that these questions be now reopened and the evidence re-examined.

NOTES

1. A report of this case, both the proceedings in the marriage court of first instance at Utrecht as well as the approval of this court's decision by the appellate court of Haarlem, and then the reversal of these two decisions by the Sacred Signatura in Rome, was distributed in 1976 by the regional court of Vancouver, B.C., after its translation by Rev. Bernard Rossi of this court.

2. The principal function of the Signatura is to examine and to rule in procedural questions in diocesan courts as well as in the other Roman congregation, the Rota. The latter congregation is the ordinary final appellate court for marriage cases in the Catholic Church. But such cases can also go to the Signatura via an expediting or, as in this case, a review of precedure.

3. These amendments were called *modi,* the disposition of them the *expensio modorum.* The quotation here is from *expensio 15e.* (This is in *Acta Synodalia, Vol. IV, Periodus 4, Pars 7: Congregationes Generales CLXV-CLXVIII, Sessiones Publicae IX-X.*) It is worth noting that this denial of the doctrinal value of *Gaudium et spes'* informal definition of marriage has not kept this definition from being included, with but few key changes, in the revised Catholic marriage law's defining canons, 1055 and 1056.

4. From the author's *Marriage in the Catholic Church: What Is Marriage?* p. 316.

5. *Ibid.*

6. In detailing and examining this discourse I am taking with only minimal changes from my examination of it in Chapter 11 of my first volume mentioned above in note 4. The discourse itself is published in *Acta Apostolicae Sedis,* Vol. 68 (1976), pp. 204–208.

7. Paul was not quite accurate in saying that to give the presence and absence of love in marriage this function would open the way to divorce. A divorce has the effect of putting an existing marriage out of existence. But love functioning in the way Paul feared would by its failure end a marriage this side of divorce. He is also less than accurate in applying the epithet "first and primitive amorous longing" to the marital love whose death some say can end a marriage. In no explanation of marital love that I have ever read can this predicate be included accurately.

8. One catches here a theological echo of Pope Paul's juridical reasoning in refutation of the Dutch marriage court's decision. He acknowledged that the spouses' consent is needed absolutely to create their marriage. But he insisted that once their marriage is created, their consent is not only no longer needed to hold it in existence, but it cannot affect it in any way.

9. The explanation whose précis I offer here is in the English translation, *The Mysteries of Christianity,* St. Louis, 1941, Chapter 21, "Christian Matrimony."

10. *Op. cit.,* pp. 602–603.

11. In his *Summa Theologiae, Pars 3, Quaest. 8, ad 1m* he remarks, ". . . in

metaphoric predication there need not be total and inclusive similarity. Otherwise there would not be similarity but the reality itself."

12. Matrimonium inter baptizatos validum dicitur ... ratum et consummatum si coniuges inter se humano modo posuerunt coniugalem actum per se aptum ad prolis generationem, ad quem natura sua ordinatur matrimonium, et quo coniuges fiunt una caro.

13. In Vol. 5 (1973), p. 79.

14. This is a mistaken citation, since the passage quoted here is from Article 49 of *Gaudium et spes,* not from Article 48.

15. *Communicationes,* Vol. 5, *ibid.*

16. A contemporary scholar of the New Testament, John R. Donahue, has the following to say, in his essay, "Divorce—New Testament Perspectives," about Christ's instruction: "The teaching of Jesus must be evaluated always according to its context. In his ministry Jesus was the proclaimer of the kingdom who confronted people with the presence of God in his ministry and teaching. The proclamation of Jesus presents a radical ethic in major areas of life such as non-resistance to evil, renunciation of wealth, the breaking of family ties, and the giving of one's life for another. One cannot relativize some of the teaching of Jesus while absolutizing other aspects of it, without doing injustice to the New Testament and its interpretation. The teaching of Jesus is also in the context of a prophetic defense of marriage in the face of easy divorce laws which prevented marriage from being that kind of life between man and woman in mutual interdependence and harmony intended by the creator. It is also a protest against the innocent victims of such divorce laws, the woman spouse in the marriage." (In *Marriage Studies II,* edited by Thomas P. Doyle, Washington, D.C., 1982, p. 15)

17. *Op. cit.,* pp. 13–14.

Index of Proper Names

Index of Titles

Cols. 218–219, John Chrysostom, Homily 26 on Marriage, Ch. 7. note 22

Cols. 225–242, John Chrysostom, Homily 29 on Marriage Ch. 7 note 23

Vol. 57, Col. 259, John Chrysostom, Homily 17, on Matthew 5:31–32, Ch. 7, note 17

Vol. 58, Cols. 595–564, John Chrysostom, Homily 62, on Matthew 19:3–12, Ch. 7, note 18

Vol. 61, Cols. 155–156, John Chrysostom, Homily 19 on I Cor. 7, Ch. 7, note 19

Migne, J.-P., *Patrologia Latina*

Vol. 3, Col. 299, Minucius Felix, *Octavius,* Ch. 6, note 26

Vol. 6, Cols. 719–730, Lactantius, *De Divinis Institutionibus,* Ch. 6, note 36

Vol. 9, Cols. 939–940, Hilary of Poitiers, *Commentarium in Matthaeum,* Ch. 7, note 25

Vol. 11, Col. 299, Zeno of Verona, *Homilia 4,* Ch. 7, note 26

Vol. 14, Cols. 431–442, Ambrose of Milan, *De Abraham,* Ch. 7, note 34

Vol. 15, Cols. 1765–1768, Ambrose of Milan, *Expositio Evangelii Secundum Lucam, Lib. 8,* Ch. 7, notes 28–33

Vol. 16, Col. 273, Ambrose of Milan, *De Virginitate,* Ch. 6, Ch. 7, note 27

Vol. 20, Cols. 478–479, Innocent I, *Epistola ad Victricium,* Ch. 7 note 37

Cols. 499–501, Innocent I, *Epistola ad Exsuperium,* Ch. 7 note 38

Cols. 602–603, Innocent I, *Epistola ad Probum,* Ch. 7, note 39

Vol. 22, Cols. 562–563, Jerome, *Epistola ad Amandum*, Ch. 9, notes 11–12

Cols. 690–698, Jerome, *Epistola ad Oceanum de Morte Fabiolae,* Ch. 9. note 13

Vol. 23, Cols. 219–220, Jerome, *Adversus Jovinianum,* Lib. I, Ch. 9, notes 14, 15.

Vol. 42, Col. 133, Augustine, *Contra Adimantum,* Ch. 9. notes 24, 25

Vol. 43, Cols. 11–100, *De Diversis Quaestionibus 83,* Ch. 9, note 26

THE NEW TESTAMENT AND RABBINIC JUDAISM, David Daube, Ch. 3, note 10; Ch. 4, note 1.

Novellae of Justinian, 101–108

De Officio Hominis et Civis, Samuel von Pufendorf, 410–413

PAPAL TEACHINGS: MATRIMONY, edited by Michael J. Byrnes, Ch. 15, notes 24, 26; Ch. 16, notes 13, 26–44; Ch. 17, notes 7–9

Paraphrasis Novi Testamenti, Desiderius Erasmus, 371

A Prelude of Martin Luther on the Babylonian Captivity of the Church, 378–379

Populis ac nationibus (Constitution of Gregory XIII), 398–400

Quod apostolici, encyclical letter of Leo XIII, 423

Scripture Index